OXFORD CLASSICAL MONOGRAPHS

Published under the supervision of a Committee of the
Faculty of Classics in the University of Oxford

The aim of the Oxford Classical Monographs series (which replaces the Oxford Classical and Philosophical Monographs) is to publish books based on the best theses on Greek and Latin literature, ancient history, and ancient philosophy examined by the Faculty Board of Classics

Cicero's *Brutus*

Edition, Textual Commentary, and Study of the Transmission

DOUGLAS R. THOMAS

Great Clarendon Street, Oxford, OX2 6DP,
United Kingdom

Oxford University Press is a department of the University of Oxford.
It furthers the University's objective of excellence in research, scholarship,
and education by publishing worldwide. Oxford is a registered trade mark of
Oxford University Press in the UK and in certain other countries

© Douglas R. Thomas 2024

The moral rights of the author have been asserted

All rights reserved. No part of this publication may be reproduced, stored in
a retrieval system, or transmitted, in any form or by any means, without the
prior permission in writing of Oxford University Press, or as expressly permitted
by law, by licence or under terms agreed with the appropriate reprographics
rights organization. Enquiries concerning reproduction outside the scope of the
above should be sent to the Rights Department, Oxford University Press, at the
address above

You must not circulate this work in any other form
and you must impose this same condition on any acquirer

Published in the United States of America by Oxford University Press
198 Madison Avenue, New York, NY 10016, United States of America

British Library Cataloguing in Publication Data
Data available

Library of Congress Control Number: 2024931351

ISBN 978-0-19-888394-4

The manufacturer's authorised representative in the EU for product safety is
Oxford University Press España S.A., Parque Empresarial San Fernando de Henares,
Avenida de Castilla, 2 – 28830 Madrid (www.oup.es/en).

Links to third party websites are provided by Oxford in good faith and
for information only. Oxford disclaims any responsibility for the materials
contained in any third party website referenced in this work.

Acknowledgements

My research has been funded principally by the Oxford-Pearson Graduate Scholarship, and I thank Stephen Pearson and the University of Oxford for their financial support. Funding for manuscript reproductions and visits to libraries has been generously provided by the Faculty of Classics, Trinity College, and St Hugh's College. I am grateful to the staff of many libraries for responding to my enquiries, for supplying reproductions, and for various other kinds of help; particular thanks go to the staff of the Archivio di Stato di Cremona, the Biblioteca Ambrosiana, the Biblioteca Apostolica Vaticana, the Biblioteca Medicea Laurenziana, the Bodleian Libraries, and the Kungliga Bibliotek in Stockholm. I also thank the staff of Oxford University Press for their assistance throughout the publishing process.

I incurred many academic debts over the three years of my doctoral research. The following are only some of those who helped me in my studies: Giancarlo Abbamonte, James Adams, Gregory Hutchinson, Neil Martin, Marco Petoletti, Matthew Robinson, Gabriele Rota, Barnaby Taylor, Gail Trimble, Michael Winterbottom, and Massimo Zaggia. I would also like to thank Mrs Winch, Mrs Allen, and Mr Spooner, who taught me Latin at earlier stages of my education.

This book has been improved significantly, in matters both large and small, by the suggestions made by my two examiners, Stephen Heyworth and Michael Reeve, and by the two anonymous readers of Oxford University Press. Wolfgang de Melo assisted me greatly in revising the thesis for publication.

I am especially grateful to two men. Stephen Oakley taught me most of what I know about textual criticism and the transmission of the Latin classics. He suggested *Brutus* as a topic of study and supervised my undergraduate work on the manuscripts of the text. He also supplied photographs of several manuscripts and made detailed comments on the whole dissertation. My doctoral supervisor, Tobias Reinhardt, gave of his time very freely and provided guidance at every stage of the project. I would like to express my gratitude to him for his help in giving shape to my thesis, in directing me to numerous items of bibliography, in refining my arguments and correcting many errors, and in much else besides.

vi ACKNOWLEDGEMENTS

My parents have been very generous in supporting my studies financially, and I also thank them for their advice and their prayers. My children Arthur, Philip, and Reuben have been a joyful distraction over the last few years of my work on this book. I owe a uniquely significant debt to my wife, Tabitha: she has been unfailingly patient in listening to my monologues on Latin texts and manuscripts, faithful amid disappointments, loving in all things, even when I have not loved her well in return. I dedicate this book to her.

But it is to our God, who was on the throne before Cicero was born, and who will be on the throne after every manuscript of *Brutus* has disappeared into oblivion, that all the glory should go.

For from him and through him and to him are all things. (Rom. 11: 36)

Contents

List of Figures	ix
List of Abbreviations	xi

Introduction	1
1. Review of Scholarship	2
1.1 Textual Criticism	2
1.2 The Transmission of *Brutus*	4
2. The Stemmatic Method	6
3. Text and Apparatus: A Guide	8

PART ONE: THE TRANSMISSION OF *BRUTUS*

1. The Cremona Fragment	15
1.1 C and the Humanist Descriptions of L	16
1.2 Malcovati's Argument: C ≠ L	19
1.3 C = L	21
1.4 Concluding Remarks	24
1.5 Collation of C	25
2. A New Stemma	29
2.1 Coda: A Contaminated Descendant of β	44
2.2 Readings of O^v	45
3. A Textual History of Cicero's *Brutus*	48
3.1 *Brutus* Before 1421	48
3.2 The Discovery of the *Laudensis*	51
3.3 The *Laudensis* after Its Rediscovery	54
3.4 Raimondi's Transcription and Barzizza's Manuscript	62
3.5 The Descendants of ρ	64
3.6 The Descendants of B	65
3.7 The Descendants of F	67
3.8 The Descendants of λ	71

viii CONTENTS

PART TWO: TEXT AND COMMENTARY

Sigla   75

BRUTUS   77

Commentary   157

Appendix 1: The Manuscripts and Fifteenth-Century Editions of *Brutus*   231
Appendix 2: The Descendants of ρ and B   264
Appendix 3: The Descendants of F   291
Appendix 4: Alphabetical List of Sigla   331

Bibliography   335
Index   353

List of Figures

1. Cremona, Fragm. Com. 81 (ex 295), f.1^r. Archivio Stato di Cremona. Reproduced with permission.   20

2. Cremona, Fragm. Com. 81 (ex 295), f.2^r. Archivio Stato di Cremona. Reproduced with permission.   21

3. Cremona, Fragm. Com. 81 (ex 295), f.1^v. Archivio Stato di Cremona. Reproduced with permission.   22

4. Cremona, Fragm. Com. 81 (ex 295), f.2^r. Archivio Stato di Cremona. Reproduced with permission.   24

5. The Independent Descendants of L   29

6. Reis' Stemma   35

7. The Descendants of B, O, γ, and X   265

8. The Descendants of G   269

9. The Descendants of F   291

10. The Descendants of κ 300

11. The Descendants of π 313

List of Abbreviations

Classical texts and authors are abbreviated according to the norms of the *Oxford Classical Dictionary*, 4th edn.

AE	*L'Année épigraphique* (1889–).
CIL	*Corpus inscriptionum Latinarum* (Berlin: Reimer, 1862–).
DMLBS	R. K. Ashdowne, D. R. Howlett, and R. E. Latham (eds). *Dictionary of Medieval Latin from British Sources*, 3 vols (Oxford: British Academy, 2018).
FRHist	T. J. Cornell (ed.). *The Fragments of the Roman Historians*, 3 vols (Oxford: Oxford University Press, 2013).
Keil, *Gramm. Lat.*	H. Keil (ed.). *Grammatici Latini*, 8 vols (Leipzig: Teubner, 1855–1880).
K-S	Raphael Kühner and Carl Stegmann. *Ausführliche Grammatik der lateinischen Sprache: Satzlehre*, 3rd edn, rev. by Andreas Thierfelder, 2 vols (Leverkusen: Gottschalk, 1955).
LSJ	Henry George Liddell and Robert Scott. *A Greek-English Lexicon*, rev. by Henry Stuart Jones, 9th edn (Oxford: Clarendon Press, 1940).
Migne, *PL*	J.-P. Migne (ed.). *Patrologiae cursus completus: Series latina*, 217 vols (Paris: Migne, 1841–1855).
MRR	T. Robert. S. Broughton. *The Magistrates of the Roman Republic*, American Philological Association Philological Monographs 15, 3 vols (New York and Atlanta: American Philological Association, 1951–1986).
OLD	P. G. W. Glare (ed.). *Oxford Latin Dictionary*, 2nd edn, 2 vols (Oxford: Clarendon Press, 2012).
ORF[4]	H. Malcovati (ed.). *Oratorum Romanorum fragmenta*, 4th edn, vol. 1 (Turin: Paravia, 1976).
RE	A. Pauly et al. *Real-Encyclopädie der classischen Altertumswissenschaft*, 83 vols (Stuttgart: Metzler; Munich: Druckenmüller, 1894–1980).
RRC	Michael H. Crawford. *Roman Republican Coinage*, 2 vols (London: Cambridge University Press, 1974).
TLL	*Thesaurus linguae Latinae* (Leipzig: Teubner; Berlin: De Gruyter, 1900–).
TLRR	Michael C. Alexander. *Trials in the Late Roman Republic, 149 bc to 50 bc*, Phoenix Supplementary Volume 26 (Toronto: University of Toronto Press, 1990).

Introduction

Two dates stand out in the history of *Brutus*: 46 BC, when Cicero composed the work, and AD 1421, when it was rediscovered after having fallen into obscurity for centuries. The first of these dates marked, for Cicero, the beginning of a period of intense study and fruitful writing on rhetoric and philosophy which would continue until November 44, just over 12 months before his death. The second, when a manuscript was discovered which contained *Brut.* as well as complete texts of two other major rhetorical works by Cicero, *De oratore* and *Orator*, was a significant moment in the rekindling of interest in Cicero, Roman rhetoric, and the Latin classics in the Renaissance. Because the *Codex Laudensis* (L), the manuscript discovered in 1421, has since been lost, my goal in this book has been twofold: to trace back the text of *Brut.* to that contained in the archetype, and then to bridge the centuries of scribal copying between 1421 and 46 BC by reconstructing the original text as accurately as the evidence allows.

Brut. is a detailed history of Roman oratory, written in dialogue form. After a brief survey of Greek orators, Cicero describes and evaluates the qualities of more than 200 Roman orators, almost all from the previous 150 years. The work culminates in a brief autobiography in which Cicero sketches out the contours of his own oratorical education and career. Scholars have differed greatly in their evaluation of the literary merits of *Brut.* For some, it is 'a remarkable *tour de force*';[1] for others, 'its *urbanitas* is feeble, its composition too careless... to remove the *longueurs* of what is little more than a catalogue of Roman orators.'[2] But whatever its defects, it remains a highly innovative example of the flexibility of the dialogue form, and its value as a historical source for the development of rhetoric in the Roman Republic is immense.

This book falls into two parts. In Part One I provide the first comprehensive study of the transmission of *Brut.* I begin by discussing the significance of the ninth-century Cremona fragment, arguing that it is part of L, the archetype of the entire manuscript tradition. Next, I establish the stemmatic

---

[1] Douglas (1966: xxiii).   [2] Winterbottom (1967: 301).

2 INTRODUCTION

relationships between the independent descendants of L, placing the reconstructed text of the archetype on a firmer footing than has hitherto been possible. In the final chapter of this part, I present a textual history of *Brut.*, in which I synthesize the work of previous scholars (especially Remigio Sabbadini and Enrica Malcovati) with my own findings. My analysis in Part One is supported by material in the appendices: the first appendix is a catalogue of the extant manuscripts and fifteenth-century editions of *Brut.*, and in subsequent ones I examine the *codices descripti*, demonstrating their descent from other extant manuscripts and determining the relationships between them. In Part Two I offer a new text of *Brut.* with an *apparatus criticus*, and I explain many of my editorial decisions in a textual commentary.[3]

1. Review of Scholarship

1.1 Textual Criticism

Scholarly study of *Brut.* recommenced almost as soon as the text was rediscovered. The Renaissance humanists soon saw that L was corrupt in numerous places, and they were successful in correcting many of its most obvious errors. Chief among them in this regard was Poggio Bracciolini, whose manuscript, Ff, features frequently in my apparatus;[4] but good conjectures can be found in many manuscripts. In the sixteenth century, the works of Manutius (1514), Corradus (1552), and Lambinus (1566) are prominent, each of these scholars contributing many successful emendations to the text. The next major editions are Ernesti (1783) and Wetzel (1795), and these were followed, as one would expect, by a host of nineteenth-century editions. Most nineteenth-century editors of *Brut.* were bold in diverging from the paradosis. Although they were often too quick to doubt the transmitted reading, many editors proposed at least a few attractive emendations, Schütz (1815), Jahn (1849), and Stangl (1886) being especially fruitful. In the face of this trend, Peter (1839) stands out for his resolute conservatism: very often he defends convincingly a text which has been unfairly doubted,

---

[3] I do not discuss every textual crux: I have tried to comment upon the problems which are most important, i.e. those most significant for the understanding of *Brut.* and those which bear directly upon historical issues, as well as various others where I felt that I could add something new and useful to what has already been written.

[4] Ff is a *codex descriptus*, but it is often the first extant MS to correct an error of L.

INTRODUCTION 3

but almost as often he attempts to defend the indefensible. In the second half of the century, the deletion of suspected interpolations was in vogue; Jahn-Eberhard (1877) and Stangl (1886) are the extreme examples of this tendency, but it is also evident in the textual discussions of Campe (1860) and Simon (1887).

The final major editions of the nineteenth century are Piderit-Friedrich (1889) and Martha (1892), both with helpful notes. Wilkins (1903) has been much used in the Anglophone world, but it is lacking in originality and accuracy. Kroll and Kytzler, in their successive revisions of Jahn's edition,[5] both add useful entries and amendments in the commentary, but neither diverges significantly from Jahn's text. Jahn-Kroll-Kytzler is particularly valuable as a repository of twentieth-century emendations, and for its comprehensive bibliography. Reis (1934) is at times erratic in his choice of readings, but his text is generally good and would have been better known if it had not been superseded in the Teubner series by Malcovati (1965). Malcovati is markedly more conservative than her predecessors; as an editor she is judicious and reliable, although in my view she is occasionally satisfied too easily with the paradosis, sometimes accepting it even when she sees that a conjecture is superior.[6] Malcovati's second edition (1970) is an improvement on the first: she was persuaded to reject L's reading at §162 *defensione iuncta*, §213 *inluminatam*, and §273 *quam eius actionem*.[7] Douglas, whose commentary (1966) is still the best available on *Brut.*, frequently offers helpful remarks on textual matters; like Malcovati, he is of a conservative bent. Finally, Badian's detailed review (1967) of Malcovati (1965) and Douglas (1966) serves as a useful starting point for consideration of many of the most vexed textual problems.

Little work has been done on the text of *Brut.* since Malcovati (1970), which remains the standard edition. Sumner's prosopographical study (1973) occasionally has relevance to the constitution of the text. A few scholars have ventured to suggest fresh emendations (e.g. Willcock (1982), Watt (1983, 1996), and Kovacs (1989)), and very recently Kaster (2020) has produced an excellent annotated translation, with a few brief comments on textual matters. Essentially, however, the state of scholarship on the text of *Brut.* has not changed in half a century. The advances that have been made

---

[5] Jahn-Kroll (1908); Jahn-Kroll-Kytzler (1962).
[6] See, e.g., her comments on §167 *exemplorum] leporum* in Malcovati (1960: 335–336).
[7] She makes few other changes. For her comments on her second edition, see Malcovati (1968, 1971, 1975).

4 INTRODUCTION

in that period in history, linguistics, and many other fields, together with
the online databases, search tools, and other resources that have been made
available, have created opportunities for further advance in the editing of
this important work of Cicero.

1.2 The Transmission of *Brutus*

The disappearance of L in or after 1428 has made its reconstruction the
ultimate goal of all work on the manuscript tradition. All previous editions
have been based on the study of a mere fraction of the extant tradition.
Most nineteenth-century editors of *Brut.* worked from a small number of
manuscripts then located in France and Germany (DQWPaPbPcWf).[8] As
I will demonstrate later, almost all these manuscripts derive from β, a
manuscript which added many errors to those already present in L. Ellendt
(1844) gave preference to Italian manuscripts: this decision allowed him to
make use of the descendants of F, which lacks the errors of β. Ellendt also
seems to have been the first to report the readings of O, a manuscript independent of both β and F. But the first major step forward with regard to
the manuscript tradition was made by Stangl, before whom no scholar had
devoted any significant attention to the relationships between the manuscripts. Stangl's edition was based on six manuscripts, BFGOMhNp; the first
four are independent descendants of L and have been used in all subsequent
editions. Editors from Stangl onwards have judged F to be the *codex optimus* among those extant.[9]

Building on the foundational work on the transmission of Cicero's rhetorical works conducted by Heerdegen (1884), Sabbadini,[10] and Stroux
(1921), Reis advanced several correct conclusions concerning the relationships between the early manuscripts, and in this respect his edition was a
substantial improvement on Stangl's. However, Reis' stemma is imperfect.[11]
In particular, he failed to realize that B derives directly from L for most of
Brut., and he was apparently wholly unaware of the value of J and U. Stangl

---

[8] For the sigla used here, see Appendix 4.

[9] F is a MS of the first importance, but the primacy given to it has led editors astray at
points: see, for example, §197 *consecutis* B$\lambda\rho$ (three branches of my stemma)] *consecutus* F (the
fourth branch), §215 *erant* B$\lambda\rho$] *erantque* F, and §216 *instruendo* B$\lambda\rho$] *struendo* F (discussed
further below), where the designation of F as *optimus* has caused some scholars to accept its
reading as the paradosis.

[10] Most of Sabbadini's findings are summarized in Sabbadini (1971).

[11] Reis (1934: viii); for further discussion, see below, p. 35.

INTRODUCTION 5

had drawn attention to U in 1913, and both Kytzler and Malcovati regularly cite it, but neither seems to have had a clear idea of its relationship to the other principal witnesses. Malcovati (1958: 39 n. 24) perceived some of the weaknesses of Reis' stemma, but she chose not to print her own stemma, instead expressing her agreement with an anti-stemmatic view communicated to her by the German philologist Günther Jachmann.[12] I cannot follow Malcovati in despairing of the possibility of producing a reliable stemma of the early copies of L. However, even on her own terms she is inconsistent. If an editor cannot determine the relationships between the manuscripts, (s)he should cite the testimony of all manuscripts which cannot be proved to derive from other extant witnesses, since all such manuscripts could have authority in the reconstruction of the archetype. But Malcovati does not do this. Instead, she consistently cites five witnesses (BFGOU), presumably believing that L's reading can always be deduced from these manuscripts.

As it turns out, L's text can be reconstructed from BFGOU in almost every place, but only if the relationship between them is known. In *Brut.* 216, for example, BGOU read *instruendo*, whereas F has *struendo*. Malcovati prints *struendo* in her text, and we must assume that she believed this to be the reading of L. Yet B, GO, and U represent three independent branches of the stemma at this point in the text, and their agreement in the reading *instruendo* proves that it was in the archetype. Very probably F, the fourth branch of the stemma, has erred.[13] Similarly, in §322 Malcovati prints G^c's *ad* without angle brackets, thus apparently indicating that she believed that G^c alone had preserved the text of L. However, once the relationships between the witnesses are more clearly understood, this can be shown to be impossible. An accurate recension of the manuscripts can eliminate many similar errors. If Malcovati can be shown to be wrong and a stemma of the manuscripts of *Brut.* can be drawn, then certainty can replace doubt at many points in the reconstruction of L.

Isabella Pettenazzi's discovery of the Cremona fragment (C), two leaves of parchment from the ninth century containing several paragraphs of *Brut.*, was a key moment in the history of the text's transmission. Pettenazzi (1955–1957) argued that the fragment was part of the *Codex Laudensis*, but

---

[12] Malcovati (1959: 180–181).
[13] *Struendo* and *instruendo* could have been variants in the exemplar, but it is more likely that the prefix *in-* has dropped out in F after the preceding *in*. See further below, p. 204.

6   INTRODUCTION

this conclusion was opposed by Malcovati in an influential article.[14] Malcovati cited the testimony of C in her editions, but she could not establish the relationship between it and L. Further study of C can elucidate the history of the transmission of *Brut.* as well as the reconstructed text of the archetype.

As with the textual criticism of *Brut.*, knowledge of its transmission has not advanced much in the last half-century.[15] Malcovati's series of articles (1958, 1959, 1960) resolve several issues and illuminate the history of various manuscripts, but much is still unclear. Scarcia Piacentini (1983) sheds further light on the early dispersion of Cicero's rhetorical works from L, and a number of scholars, most notably Albinia de la Mare, have increased our knowledge of the date and provenance of individual manuscripts. Many manuscripts of *Brut.*, however, remain largely unstudied.

2. The Stemmatic Method

The stemmatic method has been fundamental to my investigations into the manuscript tradition of *Brut.* This method has been used, misused, defended, and critiqued by more scholars than I could list here.[16] The basic procedure can be stated briefly.[17] A text is collated, in part or in full, from all extant manuscripts, with every significant error of each manuscript being noted.[18] Families deriving from a common exemplar are identified by the presence of a set of shared significant errors. If manuscript X shares all the significant errors of manuscript Y and adds some of its own, X is deemed to derive from Y. Conversely, if X lacks some or all of the significant errors present in Y, X is deemed to be independent of Y (i.e. X does not derive from Y). By following these principles, one should be able to place the extant manuscripts of a text into a stemma, or family tree. This stemma will allow an editor to identify all manuscripts which have authority in the

---

[14] Malcovati (1958).
[15] For a summary of the *status quo*, see Winterbottom et al. in Reynolds (1983: 107–109).
[16] For an introduction to the various views, see Timpanaro (2005), Reeve (2011), and Trovato (2017).
[17] For a fuller account, see Maas (1958).
[18] A 'significant error' is an error which could not easily be corrected by a scribe or reader without knowledge of other MSS (or printed editions). The clearest example of a significant error is the omission of a substantial portion of text, but shorter omissions, transpositions, additions, and other corruptions can also be impossible, or virtually impossible, to correct.

INTRODUCTION 7

reconstruction of the archetype ('the latest copy from which all extant manuscripts derive')[19] and then to establish the text of that archetype.[20]

Two principal difficulties may hinder the reconstruction of the archetype. Firstly, if the stemma is bipartite rather than pluripartite, then in the places where the two branches differ, either may preserve the reading of the archetype. (These alternative readings are 'variants'.) Secondly, if contamination (where a manuscript inherits readings from multiple sources)[21] has taken place, it may not be possible to isolate sets of errors which are characteristic of particular manuscripts, families, or branches, and consequently it may be impossible to draw a stemma. However, the mere presence of contamination in a tradition does not make the reconstruction of a lost archetype impossible. If, for example, it can be proved that three manuscripts derive independently from the archetype and that no two of the three share an intermediate exemplar, it should be possible to determine the text of the archetype from these three branches in almost every place. The existence of contamination among their descendants, or in other parts of the tradition, would not hinder this reconstruction.

I have sought to establish the relationships between the extant manuscripts of *Brut*. After collating four sections of text (§§1–35, 215–228, 265–280, 309–333)[22] in all the available manuscripts,[23] I analysed the significant errors of each one. I have identified 11 manuscripts which are independent descendants of L for the whole of *Brut.*, or for as much of it as they still preserve, as well as a further four which derive independently from L for part of the text. The remaining 91 fifteenth-century manuscripts derive, either certainly or very probably, from other extant manuscripts. There is

---

[19] Oakley (2020: 2).

[20] Sometimes the archetype is extant for a part or the whole of a text; where this is the case, there will naturally be no need to reconstruct it from its offspring.

[21] Contamination can occur when a scribe has two exemplars open at the same time and copies from both, or when readings are imported into a MS after it has been transcribed. Copying from two exemplars is a slow and tedious process, and so the latter process was probably much more common. In my analysis in this book, I usually do not address the question whether contamination has occurred in an extant MS or in an ancestor, both because such discussions tend to be laboured and hard to follow and because it is often impossible to settle the matter. I also do not distinguish between these scenarios in my stemmata.

[22] I sometimes refer to these as sections I, II, III, and IV. The collated portions together make up around a quarter of the text. Choosing sections from throughout the text enabled me to identify MSS whose exemplars had been changed during the copying of *Brut*. I chose sections from the beginning and end, as well as sections containing the two portions of text for which C was extant.

[23] I have not been able to determine the current location of two MSS. (Another is probably no longer extant.) See pp. 260–261 for details.

8   INTRODUCTION

some contamination among the *codices descripti*, but in most cases the stemmatic relationships are clear.

In Chapter 2 I defend my stemma of the independent manuscripts. In §§1–130 the stemma has three branches, and in §§130–333 it has four. Except in orthographical matters, this stemma should permit a virtually certain reconstruction of L's text in almost every place.[24] Whereas Reis' bifid stemma meant that he often had to choose between variant readings of equal authority, my pluripartite stemma has allowed me to eliminate the errors of each branch. As has already been stated, Malcovati did not print a stemma and so was frequently unable to say with confidence which of her manuscripts had preserved the reading of L. I have been able to restore L's reading to the text in nine places where Malcovati, in company with many earlier editors, printed another reading as the probable text of L.[25]

3. Text and Apparatus: A Guide

In editing *Brut.*, I have sought to avoid the extremes of radicalism and conservatism. Sometimes I believe most editors have been too hasty in abandoning L's reading; in those instances I have returned to the paradosis. However, not all corruptions result in nonsense, and so in some places where L's reading has been plausibly defended, I have still decided to diverge from the transmitted text, having judged that an alternative reading was preferable, even if not strictly necessary. Across the whole text, I have adopted more emendations than Malcovati, but considerably fewer than many nineteenth-century editors.

---

[24] For my approach to spelling, see below. Where the archetype is lost, there will be always be some residual uncertainty as to its reading. This uncertainty has two main causes: the same error will occasionally arise independently in multiple branches, and the archetype will sometimes contain multiple readings (variants or corrections). I do not consider either to be a significant problem. Coincidence in error is rare and often relatively harmless, involving, for example, the transposition of a noun and an adjective or the omission of a preposition. Where a MS has two readings, scribes will frequently copy both variants or note the presence of alternative readings (e.g. in the margin). Variants are especially likely to leave traces when, as with the offspring of L, multiple MSS derive independently from the same exemplar. Additionally, only tiny corrections have been made in the Cremona fragment (which I will argue is part of L), and this gives us further reason not to worry excessively about the possibility of variants in the archetype of *Brut.*

[25] *Brut.* 70 *pulchriora etiam*, 111 *tecti*, 197 *consecutis*, 215 *erant*, 216 *instruendo*, 254 *Graecis*, 266 *nec*, 271 *Attium*, 331 *cura*. Other places where the conclusions from my recension were a factor in my decision to diverge from Malcovati's text include 15 *quae*, 62 *hae*, 86 *adornatior*, 88 *disquisitione*, 203 *vel maxime <omnium>*, 258 *Philum*, and 290 *<de> Aeschine*.

INTRODUCTION 9

A comparison with *De oratore* and *Orator* is salutary for editors of *Brut.*
Whereas *Brut.* survived to the fifteenth century only by a single thread of
transmission, much of *De or.* and *Orat.* is preserved in a mutilated tradition
as well as in the descendants of L. There are many variants between L and
the *mutili* in *De or.* and *Orat.*, and the text of the *mutili* is often to be preferred.[26] Most disturbingly, the superior readings of the *mutili* are frequently
of such a kind that they could not easily be restored by an editor only cogni-
zant of the readings of L;[27] in some of these places, L's reading might never
have been doubted. We can reasonably assume that the quality of L's text of
Brut. was similar to its text of the other two works. Hence, in the absence of
an alternative tradition to set against L, the editor of *Brut.* should be particularly alert to the possibility of corruption in the archetype.[28]

Nevertheless, my overall impression is that *Brut.* has not reached us in a
significantly worse condition than many other works of Cicero.[29] There are
a few lacunae, but nowhere does the text omitted seem to extend beyond a
clause or two.[30] Where I have been uncertain about the original reading,
I have often printed a text which I judged that Cicero might at least have
written, and I have registered my doubts in the apparatus or the commentary; I have only resorted to the obelus four times. I am aware that there is a
danger of giving readers false confidence in the reliability of the text,[31] but
I have sought to weigh this consideration against the desire to present a
readable text.

Decisions with regard to punctuation and paragraphing are mine.[32]
Unlike Malcovati,[33] I have adopted a uniform approach to orthography. I do

[26] For comment on the character of the two traditions, see, e.g., Sandys (1885: lxxxviii–
lxxxix, xci–xcii); Malcovati (1959: 183); Kumaniecki (1969: xx–xxii).
[27] e.g. *De or.* 1.17 *animorum* M (= *mutili*)] om. L; 1.22 *iam* M] om. L; 1.69 *opus erit* M] *volet*
L; 1.69 *si modo* M] *cum* L; 1.120 *dignum re* M] om. L.
[28] Cf. Parker (1904: 248).
[29] I sympathize more with Hendrickson's judgement ('The text on the whole is well preserved and scarcely merits the complaints of corruption which editors have bestowed on it.'
(1962: 18)) than with Badian's ('The text is perhaps in a worse state than any other work of
Cicero's (if we exclude the more difficult *Letters*).' (1967: 223)); cf. also Malcovati's description
of the text as 'tramandatoci in così tristi condizioni' (1975: 163).
[30] A few sentences may have been lost at the end of *Brut.*
[31] It is partly because of this consideration that I have not dispensed with the obelus entirely.
I have of course found it useful in its own right to highlight the few places where I am funda-
mentally unsatisfied with all the proposed solutions.
[32] Malcovati sometimes reports the punctuation of BFGOU in the apparatus, but I generally
do not do so. I have also largely neglected to report whether upper-case or lower-case letters
are used in the MSS; I have normalized capitalization in both text and apparatus.
[33] Malcovati followed L's orthography, so far as she could determine it. For her spelling policy, see Malcovati (1970: xiv–xv).

10   INTRODUCTION

not do so because I believe that Cicero, or his amanuensis, was always consistent in his spelling, but because I do not trust the transmitted orthography. The manuscript tradition is usually a poor guide to an author's practice in spelling, and this is especially the case with *Brut*. Not only is there a gap of nearly a millennium between the writing of the autograph and the copying of L, but also a corrector has revised many of L's spellings.[34] I have aimed at an approximation of Cicero's usual spelling practice, so far as it can be known. I have avoided archaisms, writing, for example, *-imus*, not *-umus*, and *vulgus*, not *volgus*. I use the ending *-is* for the accusative plural of i-stem nouns and adjectives. For the dative and ablative plural of *is*, I write *iis*, and for the nominative masculine plural, *ii*. I have also endeavoured to be consistent with assimilated prefixes, writing regularly, for example, *adm-*, *adn-*, and *ads-*, but *aff-*, *agg-*, and *all-*. I have generally excluded orthographical matters from the apparatus unless there is a substantive issue at stake (e.g. if there is genuine doubt over whether one should print an adjective ending in *-ae* or an adverb ending in *-e*).

I have adhered to my policy of uniform spelling even when an alternative spelling would more readily explain a corruption in the manuscripts. For instance, in §169 L had the corrupt *quo orationi*.[35] Malcovati follows Poggio in emending *quo* to *quoi*, but I have written *cui*. L's corruption may well be due to an earlier *quoi*, but even if that were the case, the presence of *quoi* in an earlier manuscript would not prove that the word was spelled thus in the autograph.

Before preparing my edition, I collated in full all independent manuscripts. I cite most non-trivial errors shared by a whole branch of the stemma, but otherwise I have been selective in citing the errors of individual manuscripts and families. The descendants of β have little weight in the reconstruction of the archetype, and I cite very few of their singular readings. I cite conjectures if I consider them to be plausible alternatives to the paradosis, or if they highlight a genuine difficulty in the text.[36] (These criteria are necessarily somewhat subjective.) If a conjecture is found in an independent descendant of L, I cite that manuscript; otherwise, I attribute conjectures to the earliest source, whether that be a manuscript or a printed edition. If I do not feel confident in identifying the earliest source, I write

---

[34] See p. 18.
[35] Where a more specific text reference is required, I refer to the section number in *Brut.* and then to the line number of Malcovati's 1970 Teubner edition (e.g. 169.11).
[36] Emendations are ordered (roughly) according to how likely I judge them to be.

INTRODUCTION   11

vulg. (= *vulgo*) instead. This is usually either because I cannot find the reading in an early edition—I have not seen every edition—or because I think it probable that the conjecture could be found in an extant manuscript, but I have not had time to search through every manuscript to locate the earliest instance.

I have assigned sigla to all manuscripts and all hypothetical lost exemplars. I have assigned a single capital letter to each independent manuscript,[37] and to all other extant manuscripts the combination of a capital and a lower-case letter. I have retained the sigla used by previous editors for all major manuscripts, but not for all *codices descripti*. I use Greek letters to indicate lost exemplars (except that I retain the traditional siglum L for the *Laudensis*). I have also assigned sigla to the six printed editions (Rom, VenA, VenB, VenC, Nur, Mil).

---

[37] Q and W are 'independent' only in that they can be used to reconstruct D where it is illegible.

PART ONE
THE TRANSMISSION OF *BRUTUS*

1

The Cremona Fragment

The text of *Brutus* was lost for several centuries before the discovery of the famous *Codex Laudensis* (L) in 1421.[1] L, discovered in Lodi, in northern Italy, apparently contained, in addition to an almost complete text of *Brut.*, four other rhetorical works then attributed to Cicero (*Rhet. Her.*, *Inv. rhet.*, *De or.*, and *Orat.*). L disappeared in or after 1428, but its *Brut.* was transcribed at least four times, and all extant manuscripts derive from it. Consequently, editors of the text have focused their efforts on the reconstruction of L from its earliest and most faithful descendants.

In 1954, a ninth-century fragment of *Brut.* was discovered in the Archivio di Stato in Cremona (C, Fragm. Cod. Comune 81 (ex 295)).[2] Since all other extant manuscripts can be dated to after 1421, C is by far the earliest surviving witness to the text. However, only two leaves of C survive (containing *Brut.* 218–227 and 265–274), and so it has been difficult for scholars to determine its relationship to L. Isabella Pettenazzi (1955–1957), who discovered the fragment, contended that C was part of L, but this view was opposed by Enrica Malcovati (1958: 40–47; 1970: vi–vii, xiii), whose arguments led to a scholarly consensus that C should not be identified with L, but is rather a copy or twin.[3] More recently, Bernhard Bischoff (1998: 209) and Emilio Giazzi (2005: 496) have expressed doubts about the validity of Malcovati's conclusion,[4] but neither has attempted to put forward a reasoned case for the identification of C with L.

In this chapter I intend to challenge the prevailing view and to suggest that Pettenazzi was correct in proposing that C is a fragment of the archetype L. I begin by comparing C with humanist descriptions of L, before

---

[1] For discussion of L's contents, see pp. 53–54.
[2] For a detailed description of C, see Pettenazzi (1955–1957) and Giazzi (2005: 495–496). Bischoff (1998: 209) dated the fragment to the second third of the ninth century.
[3] Jahn-Kroll-Kytzler (1962: xxiii); Douglas (1966: lv); Winterbottom et al. in Reynolds (1983: 108).
[4] Bischoff: 'Gegen die vermutete Zugehörigkeit des Fragments zu dem 1421 in Lodi aufgefundenen Cicero-Codex (Pettenazzi) gibt es kein schlüssiges Argument'; Giazzi: 'non sono stati addotti a tutt'oggi argomenti validi contro questa identificazione, che rimane quindi sostanzialmente accettabile'.

16   1. THE CREMONA FRAGMENT

responding to Malcovati's arguments against the identification of C with
L. I then suggest reasons why C should be considered part of L, before
finishing with a discussion of the impact that the conclusion, if accepted,
might have on our knowledge of the transmission of *Brut.*

1.1 C and the Humanist Descriptions of L

We are largely dependent upon three humanists, Gasparino Barzizza, Flavio
Biondo, and Giovanni Lamola, for an account of L's condition. Barzizza and
Biondo both stress two particular points concerning the codex: its great age
and its illegibility.[5] Barzizza, in a letter to Gerardo Landriani, praises him
for bringing to light complete copies of Cicero's major rhetorical works after
so many centuries (*omnes oratoriae institutionis partes illas, quibus careba-
mus, ex his tenebris, quibus tot saeculis delituerunt, in lucem eduxisti*), and
then goes on to describe the manuscript as 'very ancient and almost unusa-
ble' (*vetustissimo ac pene ad nullum usum apto*).[6] Biondo, in the subscription to his copy of *Brut.*, also describes L as *vetustissimus*, and in 1450/1451,
in his *Italia Illustrata*, Biondo recounts the discovery of L and says that the
codex was very old and there were very few who were able to read it (*perve-
tustus et cuius litteras vetustiores paucissimi scirent legere*).[7] Lamola, in a letter to Guarino Veronese written in 1428, also emphasizes the age of the
manuscript (*hic autem ipse codex, summae quidem venerationis et antiquitatis non vulgaris effigies*).[8] A final testimony to the age and illegibility of L can
be found in the second colophon to O, in which Francesco degli Ardizzi,
one of the three scribes who corrected the manuscript from L in 1425,
records that the old codex was *non sat a plerisque legibilem ob antiquarum
litterarum effigiem stilumque incognitum.*[9]

Four further details can be gleaned from the evidence of the Renaissance
writers. Firstly, the *Laudensis* lacked the chapter divisions that are present in

---

[5] Barzizza oversaw the first transcription of L: the discoverer of the codex, Gerardo
Landriani, bishop of Lodi, was unable to read it himself and sent it to Barzizza, a scholar highly
regarded for his work on Cicero's rhetorical works, in the hope that he might be able to transcribe it. Biondo produced a copy of *Brut.* (B) in 1422; the second part of his transcription was
made directly from L. Lamola made a copy of L in 1428; Lamola's MS (λ) is lost, but two
descendants (JU) survive.

[6] Furiettus (1723: 215–216).   [7] Biondo, *Italia Illustrata* (2011–2017: iii.151).

[8] Sabbadini (1915–1919: i.640–641).

[9] For a transcription of both colophons in full, see below, p. 254.

1. THE CREMONA FRAGMENT   17

many of the later manuscripts.[10] The absence of chapter divisions in L is stated explicitly by Biondo in B, his copy of *Brut.* (f.19^r: *in veteri continuat testus ubique sine capitulo vel testiculo*), and supporting evidence can be found in the absence of chapter divisions from FJU, three manuscripts which derive from L independently of Barzizza's codex, and from the second part of B, copied by Biondo directly from L. Secondly, an excerpt from Biondo's subscription (*Non erat amplius in exemplari: a quo abscisse sunt charte due*) indicates that the final two pages of L's *Brut.* had been removed before he completed his transcription in 1422. The scribe of Mn corroborates Biondo's testimony by quoting the following words, as he claims, from the writings of Gasparino Barzizza:

> Deficiunt pauca, non ultra folia duo ad plus, et ut ego coniecturam facio non ultra columnam. Plura enim in codice vetustissimo non comperi: ex quo in fine carte recise iniquitate fortune erant.[11]

Thirdly, it would appear from the same quotation in Mn that the pages of L were written in multiple columns. Finally, the following quotation from Lamola's letter to Guarino suggests that the text of L was subjected to many erasures, alterations, and additions by its fifteenth-century copyists:

> Hic autem ipse codex . . . ab istis in quorum manibus <fuit> quique ex eo accurato exemplari exemplum, quod vulgatum ubique est, traduxerunt, summis ignominiis adfectus est, quippe qui multa non intellexerunt, multa abraserunt, multa mutarunt, multa addiderunt . . .[12]

Thus, if the humanist descriptions of L are to be believed, we should expect a surviving fragment of L to date from several centuries before the 1420s, to be very difficult to read, to contain no chapter divisions, to be written in columns, and to be heavily corrected. Does C meet these criteria? On the

---

[10] Gasparino Barzizza was probably responsible for introducing these chapter divisions. See below, p. 63.

[11] After leaving a few lines empty, the same scribe adds: *Hec ex praeceptore doctissimo Gasparino de Barzizis Pergamensi scripta relicta habentur.* Cf. also Francesco degli Ardizzi's comment in O's colophon: *Non inveni plura in perveteri codice. fortunę quidem iniquitas id totum, si tamen quiddam erat, recidit.* The language used in Mn and O is so similar that their testimony probably derives from a common source. (Note especially the shared use of the phrase *iniquitas fortunae.*) For further discussion of the two MSS and their subscriptions, see below, p. 275.

[12] Sabbadini (1915–1919: i.640–641).

18   1. THE CREMONA FRAGMENT

basis of its script, a neat Caroline minuscule, the manuscript can be dated with confidence to the ninth century and so certainly meets the age requirement. There are no chapter divisions; each side contains two columns of text; and there are frequent corrections. Some corrections are by the initial scribe, but the majority are in a different, although roughly contemporary, hand (C^2). C^2's corrections predominantly involve the replacement of 'archaic' spellings (e.g. *quom, conlega*) with more standard medieval ones (*cum, collega*).[13] C^2 usually attempted to erase the original ink, sometimes even damaging the parchment in so doing, before writing an emended version on top. This practice could well have prompted Lamola to complain of the *summae ignominiae* with which L had been treated. However, if this were so, Lamola would have been wrong to attribute the corrections to his contemporaries, since C^2 is a ninth-century hand. Alternatively, it may be that Lamola was exaggerating the extent of the erasures and changes made in the fifteenth century, or that there simply were none on the pages which survived as C.

The criterion of illegibility, however, is harder to satisfy. Indeed, for Douglas, the neatness and clarity of the writing in C 'suffice to show that it cannot be a part of the Laudensis' (1966: lv). This conclusion is understandable, because it does seem hard to reconcile the condition of C with Barzizza's description of L as *pene ad nullum usum aptus* or with Biondo's comment that *litteras vetustiores paucissimi scirent legere*. Nevertheless, Douglas is too quick to exclude the possibility of C's having been part of L. Only two folios of C are extant, and other parts of the manuscript might have been much more difficult to read, perhaps because of damage to the pages or because another, less careful scribe, was responsible for other sections of text. We cannot assume from two folios that C was uniformly neat and easy to read. Additionally, the early copies of L do not differ wildly from one another in their texts of *Brut.*, as one might expect if L had been virtually illegible. The accuracy of the principal witnesses to the text of L is hard to quantify, and depends on the care taken by the scribes as well as the clarity of the exemplar, but F, for example, in 90 paragraphs of *Brut.*, contains around 25 non-trivial errors absent from the other branches of the stemma, while Lamola's copy of L (λ), which can be reconstructed from JU, apparently contained only a handful of errors in the entire work.[14]

---

[13] For a full collation of C, see below, pp. 25–28.
[14] For lists of the errors of F and λ, see below, pp. 29–30. Douglas (1966: lv–lvi) admits that the fifteenth-century copyists were generally accurate. On Lamola's *De or.*, see below, p. 72 n. 92.

1. THE CREMONA FRAGMENT   19

That L's copyists managed to produce relatively accurate transcriptions does not prove that the whole of its text was as legible as C, but it does allow room for doubt about the humanists' claims concerning L's condition. As Pettenazzi points out (1955–1957: 96), it would have been in the interest of the humanists to exaggerate the difficulty of transcribing L in order to accrue more glory for themselves. Gasparino Barzizza, in particular, having decided to keep L and return only a copy to its finder, Gerardo Landriani, had a further motive for describing L as *pene ad nullum usum aptus* in his letter to Landriani: to justify his appropriation of the *vetus codex*.

Both because other leaves of C may not have been easy to read, and because L may not have been as illegible as the humanists suggest, C's neat and legible script does not suffice to show that it cannot be a fragment of L.

1.2 Malcovati's Argument: C ≠ L

There are four main strands to Malcovati's argument that the Cremona fragment cannot be a part of the *Laudensis*. The first of these, which I have discussed already, is that C is clear and legible, whereas L, according to the humanists, was very difficult to read.[15] Malcovati infers from the humanists' testimony that L could not have been written in a script as simple as Caroline minuscule, but must rather have been in a pre-Carolingian script full of ligatures and abbreviations. She therefore suggests that L must have been at least a century older than C. However, in the absence of any detailed description of L's script or any reference to its containing ligatures and abbreviations, these conclusions are unwarranted. As pointed out earlier, other parts of C may have been much more obscure, and consequently this argument against the identification of C with L is weak.

The second component of Malcovati's argument is that L was written in *scriptio continua*, whereas C has word division.[16] To prove that L was in *scriptio continua*, Malcovati cites a few examples from *Brut.* where some of L's descendants have divided words incorrectly: 63.11 *lege repetit* FΛGᶜ] *legere petit* ρ; 72.5 *docuisse et* λρ] *docuisset* F; 97.19 *legi tabellariae* λρ] *legit abellariae* F; 101.25 *durior is* Gᶜ] *durioris* FΛρ; 119.32 *more se exercuit* λρ] *mores exercuit* F; 192.1 *in eis* BΛρ] *meis* F. None of these examples are from the sections of text where C is extant. As Malcovati demonstrates earlier in

---

[15] Malcovati (1958: 43–45).   [16] Malcovati (1958: 44).

20   1. THE CREMONA FRAGMENT

her article,[17] C sometimes divides words incorrectly, and so the examples she cites of incorrect word division in $F\lambda\rho$ are of no value; they may derive from incorrect word division in the archetype. Had Malcovati cited readings where C divides words correctly and L's descendants incorrectly, this argument would have some weight, but as it stands, it is invalid (see Figure 1).[18]

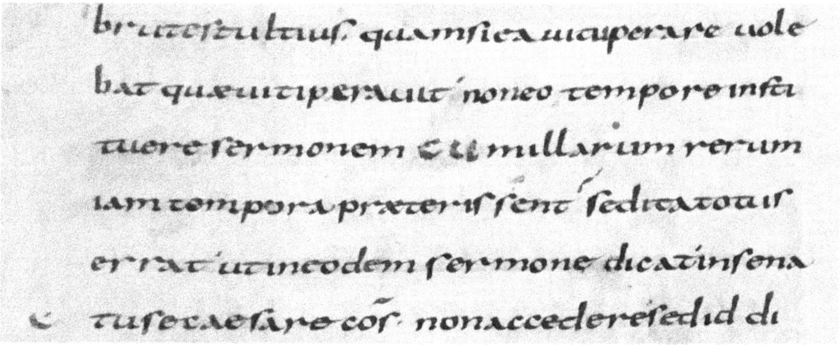

Figure 1: Cremona, Fragm. Com. 81 (ex 295), f.1ʳ

For her third argument, Malcovati compares the texts of C and F and seeks to prove that F cannot derive from C.[19] She suggests that F sometimes has modernized spellings where C has 'archaic' spellings. However, in all three cases which she cites (218.6 *paulo* C²F] *paullo* C; 218.7 *cum* C²F] *quom* C;[20] 222.29 *cui* C²F] *qui* C),[21] C² has updated the original 'archaic' spelling, and F's readings can derive without difficulty from C². Malcovati then points out that at 220.2 F has the 'archaic' *optumis*, while C has the standard medieval spelling *optimis*. Again, though, this does not prove that F is independent of C, because Niccolò Niccoli, the scribe of F, could have introduced the 'archaic' spelling here, either because of a desire for consistency with the immediately preceding *proxumus* (spelled thus in C and in F),

[17]   Malcovati (1958: 42).
[18]   The word division in C is ill defined, with words frequently running together with little or no gap (Figure 1). Malcovati's bald statement that 'C presenta le parole divise' (1958: 44) is therefore misleading; it is easy to understand how scribes copying from C might sometimes have divided words incorrectly.
[19]   Malcovati (1958: 45).
[20]   Malcovati does not provide a text reference for *cum*] *quom*, but C² frequently updates the 'archaic' form, and C²'s spelling is always shared with F; I provide here only the first instance.
[21]   Malcovati claims that F has *cui* in place of C's *quoi*, but *qui* appears to have been the spelling in Cᵃᶜ.

or as part of a more general attempt to restore the authentic Ciceronian orthography. Finally, Malcovati quotes readings where she believes that F has the truth and C a corruption: 266.19 *ne* BF] *nec* Cλρ; 269.10 *postumius* F] *postumus* CBλρ; 271.26 *spoletinum* BFJ^cU] *spolentinum* CJρ; 271.29 *accium* F] *attium* CBλρ; 271.4 *amentatae* CBFU^cX] *āmentatae* C^c (ut vid.) JODEGM. Of these instances, only at 271.26 *spoletinum*] *spolentinum* is C's text definitely corrupt. More significantly, however, in all these cases C's reading is found in some of the other independent descendants of L, and so one could not easily argue that L shared F's reading. It is far more likely that F's readings are due to conjecture. Malcovati has found nothing in the text of F which demonstrates its independence from C.

The last of Malcovati's arguments is significantly weakened by the fact that, at the time of writing her article on the Cremona fragment, she incorrectly believed that F was a direct copy of L.[22] Malcovati lists errors of F not found in BCλρ which, in her opinion, demonstrate that F was copied from an exemplar which was hard to read: 219.20 *stultius*] *sulpicius*; 220.2 *bonitatem*] *vanitatem*; 222.26 *cn.*] *m.*; 269.13 *acer nimis*] *acerrimus*. Since F is probably at best a copy of a copy of L,[23] these errors may be due to illegibility in F's exemplar. In any case, errors of this sort are very commonly found in manuscripts and may be due to scribal carelessness, rather than an illegible exemplar. The final error of F mentioned by Malcovati is actually a small piece of evidence in favour of C's being a part of L, because C's *acer nimis* (Figure 2) could easily be confused with *acerrimus*.

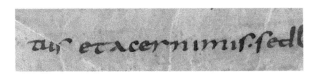

Figure 2: Cremona, Fragm. Com. 81 (ex 295), f.2^r

1.3 C = L

In this section, I hope to demonstrate that C not only might be part of L, but that it almost certainly is. As well as its compatibility with the humanist

---

[22] By 1960, Malcovati had changed her view (1960: 328–329), persuaded by Ullman's identification (1960: 60) of F as the work of Niccolò Niccoli.
[23] See further pp. 57–58.

22   1. THE CREMONA FRAGMENT

testimony concerning L, C has a text which (with two trivial exceptions)[24] matches exactly the reconstructed text of L. L, as reconstructed from its apographs, shares all the errors present in C: 219.24 *senatu*; 222.19 *m. aquili*; 223.2 *cognitionibus*; 226.27 *tacuisset*; 227.7 *quidem*; 227.9 *his*; 268.8 *ut... oratio*; 269.10 *postumus*; 271.26 *sunt* (with main verb omitted); 271.26 *spoletinum* BFJ^{c}U] *spolentinum* CJρ; 273.26 *quam*.[25] Each of L's descendants adds more errors of its own.[26]

Several details of C's text also correspond with what one would expect to find in L. C's *acernimis* (mentioned above) well explains F's *acerrimus*, and similarly at 226.29 *iuli illam* CBFλ] *iulullam* GO: *vilullam* M: *iululam* X^{vl}: *vilulam* DEX: *iullam* T, C's text, in which the two words *iuli* and *illam* are not properly separated (Figure 3), can explain the various corruptions in the descendants of ρ.[27] At 225.22 *cavendum est* Fλρ] *cavendum·st* C (*-um st* B), B shares the elided form with C, and the scribe, Flavio Biondo, has added a marginal note, *pro est*, to clarify the meaning of the archaism. These three readings are suggestive, but none can act as decisive proof that C is part of L: if C had instead been a copy of L, its scribe could have produced a faithful representation of the *Laudensis* in each of these places.

Figure 3: Cremona, Fragm. Com. 81 (ex 295), f.1^v

More important is 270.20 *quom* CBFλ] *cum* ρ: *quam* X^{vl}. There are fifteen other places in C where the initial scribe has written *quom*,[28] but in each one C^2 has erased the initial reading and replaced it with *cum*; this reading is the only uncorrected *quom*. In all the other places, BFλρ unanimously share C^2's spelling *cum*, but here, BFλ share the uncorrected *quom*. Flavio

---

[24] At 219.20 *vituperavit* BFλρ] *vitiperavit* C and at 220.4 *orationes* BFλρ] *oratones* C^2: C^{ac} incert., fort. *oratores*, the readings of C and C^2 could have been corrected by the scribes of BFλρ.
[25] Scribal emendation is a satisfactory explanation for the few places where C has an error and some of BFλρ have the truth: cf. above, p. 21.
[26] See the lists in Chapter 2.
[27] For the relationships between ρ's offspring, see Appendix 2.
[28] e.g. 218.8 *cum senatum*; 218.11 *cum inveheretur*; 219.22 *cum illarum* (Figure 1).

1. THE CREMONA FRAGMENT   23

Biondo has added in the margin of B a sign indicating that *quom* was the spelling found in L. There are only two plausible explanations for these data: either the humanists were copying from C, or they were copying from a descendant of C. In either of those scenarios, one could readily understand how the spelling *quom* came to be present in BFλ only (in the sections where C is extant) at 270.20. On Malcovati's view that L is over a century earlier than C, the presence of *quom* only at 270.20 is very difficult to explain.

In defence of Malcovati, one might argue that C²'s corrections derive from L. However, C²'s corrections are not of the sort which a scribe would typically copy from another manuscript. Almost all involve the modernization of spelling (*conlocemus*] *collocemus, conlega*] *collega, unquam*] *umquam*, etc.), and it would be odd for a scribe to be so careful in importing spellings from another manuscript that he would even, on its authority, leave one particular *quom* uncorrected, while altering all the others. It is much more probable that the corrector of C was making his own decisions as regards orthography, and that, in reading through the text of *Brut.*, he overlooked one instance of *quom*.[29]

The decisive proof that C is a part of L is 267.26 *app.* COλ] *appius* BFβ: *ap.p.* Oᵛ. At first sight, this reading might appear to be evidence against the identification of C with L, since the *vetus*-corrector in O has indicated that L read *ap.p.*,[30] whereas C has *app.* However, there is a mark on the parchment between the two 'p's in C (Figure 4). The mark resembles the dot which follows the second 'p', but the colour is different from that of the ink used to write the text; it seems instead to be a blemish, like the other lightly-coloured dots scattered over the page. The *vetus*-corrector has mistakenly identified it as a punctuation mark and consequently has added *ap.p.* in the margin of O. The possibility of there having been a similar mark on the parchment of C's exemplar is exceedingly remote, and so, for Oᵛ's reading to be explicable without C being identified with L, L would have to be a descendant of C. Yet L's scribe could not merely have copied *ap.p.* from C, because that reading would then have appeared in at least some of BFλρ. Oᵛ's correction puts the identification of C as part of L beyond all reasonable doubt.

---

[29] Bernard Bischoff and Mirella Ferrari have expressed the view that the scribe who corrected C was also responsible for the modernization of spellings in Biblioteca Ambrosiana, E 153 sup., an important MS of Quintilian (Bischoff (1998: 209); Ferrari (1998: 183–184)). For further information on the corrections in the Quintilian MS, see Ferrari (1984: 267–270).

[30] On these '*vetus*-corrections', see further below, pp. 33, 36.

1. THE CREMONA FRAGMENT

Figure 4: Cremona, Fragm. Com. 81 (ex 295), f.2ʳ

As well as these textual arguments, there is one further positive reason why C should be considered part of the archetype of *Brut.* C was discovered in Cremona, the home town of Cosimo Raimondi, the humanist who first transcribed the *Laudensis*. Although Gasparino Barzizza guarded L carefully and seems to have taken it with him when he left Milan for Pavia in or before 1425,[31] he may subsequently have given it to Raimondi.[32] Certainly, this hypothesis is intrinsically more likely than the main alternative, that there happened to be a second copy of *Brut.* from the early Middle Ages lying hidden and undetected in Cremona throughout the Renaissance.[33]

1.4 Concluding Remarks

The Cremona fragment is part of the *Laudensis*. Not only does C have a text which matches exactly the reconstructed text of L, but it was found in the home town of the man who produced the first fifteenth-century transcription of L. The age of the fragment and the presence of corrections cohere with the humanists' descriptions of the *Laudensis*; and even minor features of C, such as an uncorrected *quom* and a discolouring of the parchment, can account for details present in the descendants of L.

Should this conclusion have an effect on the editing of *Brut.* and Cicero's other rhetorical works? C's text cannot provide much help in solving textual

---

[31] Malcovati (1958: 32–34). See further below, p. 59.
[32] Pettenazzi (1955–1957: 85–87) summarizes what we know of the movements of Barzizza and Raimondi, and suggests that Raimondi might have left L, together with the rest of his library, in Cremona when he moved to Avignon in 1428. The paucity of evidence makes it hard to move beyond speculation.
[33] Cf. Pettenazzi (1955–1957: 94).

1. THE CREMONA FRAGMENT   25

problems, even where it is extant. The knowledge that C is part of L should, however, cause us to reassess Malcovati's approach to orthography. It is wrong to write *cum* at 218.8 and *quom* at 270.20, because the only reason that BFλ have the 'archaic' spelling in the second instance is due to an oversight by C[2]. More generally, the knowledge that the spellings in L, or at least in part of it, were altered by a second hand, should reduce our confidence in the authority of L's descendants with regard to orthography. A return to a more uniform approach to spelling is in order.

Perhaps it is the textual history of Cicero's rhetorical works that will be affected most. If Bischoff and Ferrari are right to identify the correctors of C and Biblioteca Ambrosiana, E 153 sup. as the same scribe, further comparison of the two manuscripts and further investigation of the Quintilian codex may shed fresh light on the date and provenance of L. The two manuscripts may well have been located in the same place during the ninth century, presumably, on the basis of the Quintilian's history, in Pavia, and they may even have been copied in the same scriptorium.[34] Closer analysis of the corrections in the two manuscripts may enable us to learn more about the habits of the corrector and hence about how he may have altered the rest of L's text.[35]

1.5 Collation of C

I list here all differences, including the purely orthographical, between C and the text of Malcovati (1970). I exclude differences in word division, because C is often unclear in this regard. Where the text of the first hand is no longer visible, I supply in brackets either a possible reconstruction or dots to indicate the approximate number of letters missing.

218.6   *paulo* C[c]] *paullo* C
218.7   *e* C[2]] *e*[*x*] C
218.8   *conloquentem* C] *colloquentem* C[c]
218.8   *cum* C[2]] [*quo*]*m* C
218.9   *est a*] *e* C
218.11   *cum* C[2]] [*quo*]*m* C
218.11   *disputatioque* C[2]] *disputati*[*oquae*] C

---

[34] Ferrari (1998: 184).
[35] I thank Stephen Oakley for suggesting some of the arguments presented in this chapter.

26   1. THE CREMONA FRAGMENT

218.12 *est* C^2] *e*[..] C
219.17 *tantamne* C^2] *ta*[*m*]*tamne* C
219.19 *flagiti*] *flagici* C: *flagicii* C^c
219.21 *vituperavit*] *vitiperavit* C
219.22 *cum* C^2] [*quo*]*m* C
219.24 *senatum*] *senatu* C
219.28 *est* C^2] [.] C
219.28 *dicenti* C^c] *dicendi* C
220.29 *cum* C^2] [*quom*] C
220.2 *optumis*] *optimis* C
220.4 *orationes*] *oratones* C^c: *orato*[*re*]*s* C
220.7 *mediocriter* C^2] *mediocrite*[.] C
220.8 *in* C^c] [*s*]*in* C
221.15 *fortis* C^1] *forti* C
222.19 *accusatione* C^c] *acusatione* C
222.19 *m'.*] *m̄* C
222.20 *m.*] *m̄.* C
222.22 *lucullum* C^c] *locullum* C
222.23 *publici* C^c] *public*[*um*] C
222.24 *lucullum* C^2] *l*[*o*]*cullum* C
222.24 *f.*] *filios* C
222.24 *auctoritate* C^c] *autoritate* C
222.28 *ab*] *a* C
222.29 *cui* C^2] [*q*]*ui* C
222.29 *co*[*n*]*locemus* C] *collocemus* C^c
223.2 *contionibus*] *cognitionibus* C
224.5 *est* C^1] *s*[*t*] C
224.11 *sed* C^c] *set* C
224.17 *simillimus* C^c] *simillumus* C
225.21 *cui* C^2] [*quoi*] C
226.29 *petitionem* C^2] [..]*titionem* C
226.31 *cum*] [*quom*] C, del. C^c
226.31 *ageret* C^c] *ager*[..] C
226.1 *co*[*n*]*lega* C] *collega* C^2
226.3 *maxumae*] *maxumę* C
227.7 *quidam*] *quidem* C
227.8 *cum* C^2] [*quo*]*m* C
227.8 *vi*[*t*]*io* C] *vicio* C^2
227.9 *iis quibus*] [.........] C: *his quibus* C^c

227.10 *sullae*] *syllae* C
266.16 *cum* C^2] [*quo*]*m* C
266.18 *civis* C] *cives* C^c
266.19 *ne*] *nec* C
266.20 *acerba* C^c] *acerda* C
266.21 *exspectatio*] *expectatio* C
266.21 *et* C^c] [. . .] C
266.22 *quaerimus*] *quęrimus* C
267.25 *cum* C^2] [*quom*] C
267.27 *conlega* C] *collega* C^2
267.28 *cum* C^2] [*quo*]*m* C
267.29 *cum* C^c] [*quo*]*m* C
267.29 *antiquitatisque*] *antiquitatis qu*[*ae*] C: *antiquitatis que* C^c
267.31 *cum* C^2] [*quom*] C
268.2 *quantumcumque* C^2] [*quam*]*tum*[*quo*]*mque* C
268.5 *asciscere*] *adsciscere* C
268.6 *obtineret*] *optineret* C
269.10 *postumius*] *postumus* C
269.12 *effrenatus* C^c] *e*[*x*]*frenatus* C
269.16 *ii* C^c] *ii*[*s*] C
269.16 *co*[*n*]*ligis* C] *colligis* C^c
270.22 *adsequor*] *assequor* C
271.26 *spoletinum*] *spolentinum* C
271.29 *accium*] *attium* C
271.29 *cuius* C^2] [*quo*]*ius* C
271.1 *cluentio* C^1] *cluenti* C
271.1 *eratque* C^2] *eratqu*[*ae*] C
271.2 *praeterea*] *pręterea* C
271.3 *hastae* C^c] [*ast*]*ae* C
271.4 *amentatae* C, ut vid.] *ammentatae* C^c, ut vid.
272.8 *umquam* C^2] [. . .]*quam* C
272.13 *cumque* C^2] [*quo*]*mque* C
272.14 *concinnae*] *concinnę* C
272.14 *acutaeque* C^2] *acutaequ*[*ae*] C
272.16 *quae*] *quę* C
272.16 *videretur* C^2] *vide*[*tur*] C
272.17 *plura quam* C^2] [. . . . .] C
272.18 *quod non* C^2] *qu*[..] C
272.18 *dici* C^2] [..]*ici* C

28   1. THE CREMONA FRAGMENT

272.20 *cum* C²] [*quom*] C
273.24 *civium* C²] *civi*[...] C
273.2 *quae*] *quę* C
273.3 *cum* Cᶜ] [...] C
273.5 *ceciditque* C²] *ceciditq*[*uae*] C
274.7 *m.*] *m̄.* C
274.10 *comprensio*] *conprensio* C.

2
A New Stemma

In *Brut*. 1–130, there are three lines of descent from the archetype L: F, λ, and ρ. From *Brut*. 130 onwards, B derives directly from L and represents a fourth line of descent (see Figure 5).

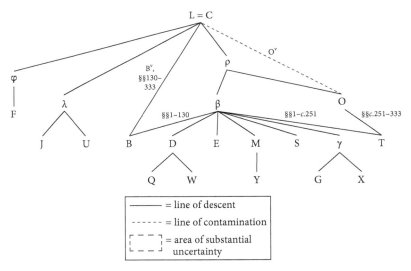

Figure 5: The Independent Descendants of L

That JU, O, and BDEGMSTX(QWY) are independent of F is proved by the presence of significant errors of F not found in these manuscripts, including:

59.23 *est*] *etiam* F: *et* S
131.11 *de plebe*] om.
149.11 *se tamen sic*] *sed tamen sic se*
156.11 *multo*] *nullo*
161.20 *quidem*] om.
185.5 *horum*] om.

30   2. A NEW STEMMA

200.24 *quod] cum* F: om. D
201.3 *hos] quos*
219.20 *stultius] sulpicius*
220.2 *bonitatem] vanitatem*
222.26 *cn.] m.*

JU share errors, which demonstrates that they derive from a common ances-tor λ and that F, O, and BDEGMSTX are independent of J, U, and λ.[1] Although λ appears to have been a very accurate copy of L, the agreement of JU in the following errors is sufficient to prove their derivation from a common source:[2]

5.11 *angimur* J²OBDEGM] *augimur* SX: *angitur* FOᵛBᵛEᵛˡ: *augitur* TXᵛˡ: *an igitur* JU
45.15 *in²*] om. JUB
65.26 *edisserendoque] disserendoque*
89.5 *rutili] rutilia* FJ²OBDGMTX: *rutila* JU
102.5 *t.] ti.*
127.6 *qui in* Jᶜ] *qu. in* J: *qum* U: *cum* Uᶜ
198.19 *neglegerentur] neglerentur*
233.31 *fimbria* J²] *fimbriam* JU
279.28 *dubitamus] dubitabamus* JUG
289.26 *relinquuntur] reliquuntur* U: *reliquntur* J
333.19 *est] ista.*

J cannot derive from U, because U has its own significant errors:

78.20 *enim]* om.
79.24 *isdem] ipse*
91.27 *est causae] cause est*
98.1 *constat summam] summam constat*
130.1 *fuit]* om.
163.19 *omnibus]* om.
299.4 *fuit]* om.
307.19 *me]* om.

---

[1] I discuss λ, the MS copied by Giovanni Lamola, in greater detail in Chapter 3.
[2] Corrections have been added to J by the initial scribe and by a later corrector. Corrections by the initial scribe I denote as J¹, corrections by the later corrector J², and those of uncertain origin Jᶜ. Most corrections *a prima manu* have been made from λ, but those of J² appear to derive predominantly, and perhaps entirely, from the contaminated and worthless MS ψ, the source of Vp and part of LcVa. There is no indication that any of J²'s readings has weight in the reconstruction of λ or L.

2. A NEW STEMMA 31

Similarly, J's significant errors prove that U is independent of it:

57.26 *etiam*] *enim*
105.27 *quoi*] *quo* FUOBDEGMTX: *quo ad* J (an emendation by the scribe of J)
170.19 *idem*] om.
215.6 *ei*] *enim*
227.11 *etiam*] *esse.*

O and (B)DEGMSTX(QWY) share errors absent from FJU.[3] These manuscripts therefore derive from a common ancestor ρ, of which FJU are independent. Further support for this derivation can be found in the set of chapter divisions shared by O(B)DEGMSTX(QWY), but absent from FJU and from §§130–333 of B (see Table 1). The errors of ρ include:

22.1 *ecquodnam* JUO] *et quodnam* F: *quodnam* O^{c}BDE^{c}GSTX: *quoddnam* EM
65.21 *nostrorum*] *nostrum* OBDEGMX: *nostram* T
75.26 *bellum punicum*] *bello punicum* FJU: *bello punico* U^c: *bello punico eum* J^{2}OBDEGMTX
104.20 *dicimus* FJUOBDEGMX] *didicimus* O^{vl}B^{c}E^{vl}G^{vl}TX^{vl} (variant reading evidently present in ρ)
109.2 *vir* FJUO^v] *iure* OBDEGMTX
133.9 *mediocris*] *mediocriter* ODEGMTX
146.25 *admirandus* (*amm-* BO^v)] *ammirabilis* ODEMTX^c: *amirabilis* GX
153.22 *et loquendi*] *et eloquendi* O: *eloquendi* DGMTX: *elloquendi* E
168.34 *m.*^{1}] om. ODEGMTX
209.14 *loco* O^2] om. ODEGMTX
225.23 *revecti* O^v] *reiecti* ODEGMTX
233.34 *tam*] *etiam* ODEGMTX
244.8 *ita*] *tam* ODEGMTX
261.20 *emendat*] *emendabat* ODEGMTX
305.31 *excesserat* O^{v}E^{c}T] om. ODEGMX
328.14 *afuisti*] *affuisses* ODEGTXY: *afuisses* O^c
331.24 *eloquentiae laude iunxisses*] *eloquentia deiunxisses* ODEGTXY.

---

[3] S now only preserves the text of *Brut.* from the beginning to 60.6 *secundo quaestor-*. M is extant until 317.19 *solute et*, from which point M's apograph Y is an independent descendant of β. D is damaged, but two descendants, Q and W, can be used to reconstruct its readings when it is illegible.

32 2. A NEW STEMMA

Table 1 Chapter divisions in ρ

Text Ref.	Chapter Division	Manuscripts
10.10	*Nam cum inambularem*	BDEGMOQSTWXYHo
25.23	*Hic ego laudare*	BDEGMOQSTWXYHo
39.17	*Videsne igitur vel*	BGOTX
44.5	*Sed tum fere*	EGMOTXYHo
49.17	*Et Graeciae quidem*	BEGMOSTXYHo
52.14	*Sed de Graecis*	EGOSX; 52.16 *Tum Brutus ista* M(T)YHo
74.13	*Haec si minus*	EGOTX
91.26	*Cum haec dixissem*	EGOTXHo
106.8	*Isque et orationes*	T, apparently accidentally (f.192ᵛ)
118.19	*Tum Brutus quam*	BDEGMOQTWXYHo
122.19	*Nunc reliquorum oratorum*	BDEGMOQTWXYHo
147.27	*Tum Brutus etsi*	DEGMOQTWXY
150.16	*Tum Brutus cum*	DEGMOQTWXY
157.23	*Hic Atticus dixeram*	EGOTX
163.16	*Hoc loco Brutus*	EGOTX
170.17	*Tum Brutus quid*	EGOTX
173.12	*Duobus igitur summis*	DEGMOQTWXY
176.16	*Iam ad oratores*	GOTX
183.18	*Hic Atticus quo*	EGOTX
201.29	*Cum haec disseruissem*	GOTX
201.2	*Quoniam ergo oratorum*	DEGMOQTWXY
210.25	*Sed magni interest*	EGOTX
219.17	*Tum Brutus admirans*	EGMOTXY
220.9	*Sed ad instituta*	DEGMOQTWXY
225.23	*Sed ad paulo*	EGMOTXY
248.4	*Hoc loco Brutus*	EGMOTXY
254.8	*Tum Brutus amice*	EGMOTXY
262.10	*Sed ad eos*	GOTX; 262.4 *Valde quidem inquam* E
266.10	*Tum Brutus Torquati*	EGMOTXY
269.15	*Hoc loco Atticus*	EGMOTXY
279.28	*Tum Brutus atque*	GMOTXY
291.14	*Sed redeamus rursus*	EGOTX
297.18	*Haec cum ille*	EGMOTXY
300.12	*Sed iam ad*	EGOTX
303.7	*Hoc igitur florescente*	DEGMOQTWXY
328.11	*Tum Brutus ego*	EGOTXY

O is an independent descendant of ρ. That none of BDEGMSX derives from O is demonstrated by a list of some of O's significant errors:

14.24 *posset esse*] *esse posset*
68.16 *id muta*] om.
83.13 *priscis*] om.
90.23 *scriptum reliquit*] *reliquit scriptum*

2. A NEW STEMMA   33

112.1 *habebat hoc*] *hoc habebat*
115.27 *consulares*] om.
170.14 *habitum ex latio*] *ex latio habitum*
291.11 *proprium esse*] *esse proprium*
328.19 *fato suo*] *suo fato.*

O, copied in 1422, was corrected from the archetype in 1425. Generally, the correctors added the reading from L in the margin, together with the word *vetus*, to indicate that the correction came from the *vetus codex*, but sometimes they seem to have made corrections without adding the note *vetus*.[4] A probable example is 209.14 *loco* O^2] om. ODEGMTX: *loco* has been added by the same hand which made *vetus*-corrections on the same page. Some readings of O^v have been cited above, but there are more than 80 in *Brut.*; I provide a full list at the end of this chapter.

(B)DEGMS(T)X(QWY) share many errors and must derive from a common ancestor, *β*. O is independent of *β*, since it does not contain these errors, which include:

16.14 *quom*] *quam* FJUOB^v: *saepe* BEGMQSTWX
34.14 *et*] om. BEGMQSTWX
35.20 *quoi*] *cui* J^{2}X^{vl}: *quo* FJUOE: *in quo* BDE^{c}G^{vl}MSTX: *cui quo* G
48.12 *aliis*] om. BDEGMSTX
56.21 *laena*] *veste* B^{1gl}E^{1gl}M^{1gl}X^{1gl} (gloss evidently present in *β*)
72.1 *conditam autem*] *autem conditam* BDEGMTX
73.10 *xl*] *xxxx* FJUO: *xxx* BDEGMTX
88.26 *exisse*] om. BDEGMTX
97.23 *clientes*] *dicentes* BDEGMTX
109.3 *frater*] om. BDEGMTX
111.26 *cum...diceret*] om. BDEGMTX
112.3 *huius...sunt*] om. BDEGMTX
150.23 *civile facile*] *facile civile* DEGMTX
163.21 *ex iis*] om. DEGMTX
170.17 *inquit*] om. DEGMTX
227.8 *cum vitio*] *cui convitio* DGMTX: *cui convicio* E
228.18 *non*] om. DEGMTX
246.21 *esset*] om. DEGMTX

---

[4] O^v denotes corrections with *vetus* added in the margin, O^1 corrections probably made by the original scribe, and O^2 those not by the initial copyist but without an accompanying *vetus*-note.

34 2. A NEW STEMMA

274.8 *prope*] om. DEGMX
281.27 *suis*] om. DEGMX
284.26 *ille*] om. DEGMX
322.18 *iudicum animos*] animos iudicum DGXY: animos iudicium E.

Before going on to work out the relationships between the offspring of β, I must admit that there is another possible explanation for these shared errors of (B)DEGMS(T)X(QWY): that ρ and β were in fact the same manuscript, and that the errors I have assigned to β were eliminated from O by comparison with L. This alternative hypothesis merits consideration, because Francesco degli Ardizzi, one of O's correctors, claimed that Francesco Bossi, the owner of O, was the first person to 'renew the old codex' (*idem Cumanus...primum veterem et superiorem codicem... in latinas et explicatas bene litteras, studioseque interpunctas, summa diligentia renovavit*), that is, to produce a legible transcription of it. Francesco degli Ardizzi's assertion is demonstrably false, because O shares an exemplar with (B)DEGMS(T)X(QWY) and cannot be the first transcription of L.[5] But if the initial scribe of O had been checking L as he was copying from ρ, there would be at least an element of truth in the corrector's claim. Yet even that possibility seems unlikely. To check one manuscript while copying from another is a difficult process.[6] It is even more difficult to be consistent in checking both exemplars throughout a text as long as *Brut.* Yet the errors of ρ and β are distributed evenly throughout *Brut.*, and so consistency would have been necessary. Francesco degli Ardizzi, writing three years after O was copied and from a desire to honour his patron, Francesco Bossi,[7] should not be expected to provide reliable testimony as to which exemplar was used by the initial scribe of O.

Two of the independent descendants of β, B and T, derive only the first part of their text from β, both changing their exemplar while copying *Brut.* As can be seen from an examination of the errors of ρ and β, B switches exemplar between 112.3 and 133.9. In fact, the change of exemplar can be

---

[5] It has been known for a long time that O is not a direct copy of L: see, e.g., Stangl (1886: x). In *De or.*, O apparently shares an exemplar with Pal. lat. 1469 (Stroux (1921: 123); Kumaniecki (1969: x), with the bibliography cited in n. 5).

[6] It would have been easier for the scribe of O to add corrections to his exemplar before copying from it, or to correct the text of O from L after it had been copied, but he can have done neither, because corrections in ρ would have appeared in at least some of BDEGMQSTWXY.

[7] Malcovati (1958: 35) suggests that Francesco degli Ardizzi's assertion betrays 'la preoccupazione del collazionatore di voler associare il vescovo di Como alla gloria del vescovo di Lodi scopritore del codice'.

located more precisely, because the scribe, Flavio Biondo, added the following note at the top of f.29ʳ of B: *Hic habui exemplar vetus*. Part-way down the page, he wrote a further note in the left margin: *hic vetus incepi habere exemplar*. This note is placed next to 130.4 *magnum fuit Brute*, and it is highly likely that Biondo began copying from L at this point.

Reis (1934: v–vi) argued that B and G were twins throughout the text, and that their exemplar shared an ancestor with O (Figure 6).[8] Reis believed that Biondo did not actually copy from L, but rather made use of the *vetus codex* in checking the readings of his exemplar. However, the evidence points decisively to the conclusion that Biondo copied directly from L from §130 onwards. B contains none of the 25 or so errors of ρ after this point, and only two of around 70 errors of β: 263.18 *patientes] patentes* and 294.16 *formam quandam] quandam formam*.[9] The first of these errors is quite trivial and could have been made independently in B and β. The second case is more striking, but the transposition of a noun and an adjective is a common error in the copying of Latin texts and this shared error is almost certainly due to coincidence. For B to have inherited these two errors from β but eliminated all the other errors of β and ρ, Biondo would have had to check his exemplar against L so thoroughly that it would almost amount to copying directly from L. Confirmation of the change of exemplar can be found in the fact that B shares the chapter divisions present in ODEGMSTX up to §130, but lacks them thereafter.[10]

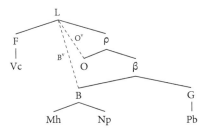

Figure 6: Reis' Stemma

---

[8] The mock-up of Reis' stemma in Figure 6 is with my sigla instead of his. Kytzler, in his revision of Jahn-Kroll (1908), agrees with Reis that none of B's text of *Brut.* is copied directly from L, but Kytzler provides no reason for this view (Jahn-Kroll-Kytzler (1962: xxii)).

[9] This second reading is the only one cited by Reis (1934: vi) from §§130–333 as evidence that Biondo continued to copy from G's exemplar after gaining access to L.

[10] Malcovati (1958: 39 n. 24), (1959: 180), starting from her collations of BG in the places where C is extant (i.e. after §130), and then extending these collations to other parts of the text, unsurprisingly found herself in disagreement with Reis' view that BG were twins, and instead

36 2. A NEW STEMMA

Upon gaining access to L, Biondo not only started copying from this manuscript instead, but he also corrected his copy of *Brut.* 1–130 from L, marking these with the note *in testu* (or *in t.*) to indicate that these corrections were from the archetype. Biondo was less thorough than the correctors of O, however, making only a handful of corrections from the *vetus codex*:[11]

1.8 *inauguratum* B^v] *mihi auguratum* B
5.11 *angimur* B] *angitur* B^v
9.5 *maxume* B^v] *maxime* B
11.27 *amicissume* B^v] *amicissime* B
12.3 *gravissumos* B^v] *gravissimos* B
15.3 *qua* B] *quo* B^v
16.14 *quom*] *quam* B^v, *sepe* B
21.26 *optumi* B^v] *optimi* B.

None of FJUODEGMSTX derives from B, since B has its own significant errors, including:

8.27 *ipsis*] om.
25.2 *unam*] om.
33.6 *aut...erat*] om.
37.15 *aculeos etiam*] *etiam aculeos*
44.12 *eiusdem*] om.
62.26 *ac monumenta*] om.
110.20 *fit...dicitur*] om.
147.27 *inquit*] om.
197.30 *conservando*] om.
225.24 *sumus locuti*] *locuti sumus*
232.13 *immo...hortensium*] om.
291.13 *sed...bene*] om.
333.12 *illis*] om.

---

she seems to have believed, correctly, that the scribe of B changed his exemplar and began to copy from L from §130. However, Malcovati did not discuss the convincing evidence Reis provides of the close relationship between B and G in §§1–130, and instead despaired of the possibility of establishing a stemma.

[11] Malcovati described Biondo's corrections in §§1–130 thus: 'cum vetere exemplari diligenter contulit et quaedam correxit addita in margine' (1960: x). However, the adverb 'diligenter' is unwarranted, since Biondo's corrections end at §21, and even before this several significant errors are left untouched.

The change of exemplar occurs considerably later in T than in B.[12] Until *c.*§251 T derives independently from β, but after this point it is free from β's errors, and instead shares errors with O. In fact, T shares all the non-trivial errors of O in §§251–333, including:

265.9 *gravitas* O^v] *dignitas* OT
276.28 *totumque*] *totidemque*
310.12 *loquuntur*] *eloquuntur*
311.24 *fecerunt*] *faciunt*
324.17 *idem*] *idemque*
325.25 *dictionis* O^v] *orationis* OT
328.19 *fato suo*] *suo fato*
328.21 *ominare*] *o mire* O^v: *omitte* OT
333.10 *binos*] *bonos*
333.15 *dicendi*] *loquendi.*

T's own significant errors prove that it is not the source of any of ODEGMSX:

7.25 *profecto*] om.
8.28 *essent*] om.
11.26 *est*] om.
14.19 *perdiligenter... inquam*] per
35.20 *perfectum et*] om.
111.26 *putares*] om.
226.30 *agens... causam*] om.
228.16 *erat*] om.
309.6 *et*] *ac*
329.24 *impendentis*] *impudentes.*

Given that T has all the significant errors of O in §§251–333, and adds some of its own, T almost certainly derives from O in this portion of *Brut.* Further support for this conclusion can be found in the fact that O and T were owned by the brothers Francesco and Luigi Bossi. If the scribes of T, commissioned by Luigi Bossi, had been deprived of access to β before they had finished copying *Brut.*, it is understandable that they might have had recourse to the manuscript owned by Francesco in order to complete the text.

---

[12] Malcovati studied the text of T, but discarded it on the grounds that, compared with BGO, it was 'un discendente deteriore dell'apografo barzizziano' (1958: 40).

38   2. A NEW STEMMA

Since T shares some of O^v's corrections in §§251–333, T must have been copied after the *vetus*-corrections were added to O, that is, after 1425. Readings shared by O^{v}T include:[13]

259.26 *q.* O^{v}T] om. Oβ
305.31 *excesserat* O^{v}T] om. Oβ
317.22 *mihi* O^{v}T] *nichil* O.

T's change of exemplar must have occurred between the errors of β at 247.32 (*memmius*] *meminius* DGMTX) and 255.15 (*non* OT] *non solum* DGMX). However, the change can be located more precisely. As well as the chapter divisions apparently inherited from ρ, five of the descendants of β, GMSTX, include a set of sub-divisions marking the changes of speaker;[14] these sub-divisions are not present in FJUO or their descendants.[15] Not all changes of speaker are marked in all of GMST, but the sets of sub-divisions are sufficiently similar that one can deduce that they derive from a common source, and therefore that they were present in β. T's sub-divisions cease after 251.10 *et ille praeclare*. GMX share this sub-division and then include another at the next change of speaker, 252.19 *sed tamen brute*. Hence, T's change of exemplar probably took place between these two points, perhaps at the end of f.217^v, before 251.13 *quare sive*.

Another independent descendant of β is S. S now contains only §§1–60 of *Brut.*, although it may previously have had a full text. S is very corrupt, with many of its own errors, such as:

10.12 *cum inter se*] *inter se cum*
11.26 *ex asia*] *ad alia*
17.21 *debes*] om.
31.14 *sermonibus*] om.
49.22 *commune*] *ratione*
51.13 *et nimis*] om.

---

[13] Some places where T follows O^{ac} rather than O^v are cited in the above list of the shared errors of OT; others include: 260.12 *accusante* O^v] *accusatore* OT, 295.28 *de*^{2} O^v] *et* OT, 317.17 *tum* O^v] *tamen* OT.
[14] For more general discussion of chapter divisions and speaker changes in MSS, see Schröder (1999); Jażdżewska (2018).
[15] The sub-divisions are absent from BDE, either because the scribes of these MSS chose not to include them or because BDE derive from β before the sub-divisions were added.

2. A NEW STEMMA 39

52.19 *veniamus . . . intellegere*] *vere*
57.8 *ennius*] *fluvius.*

A fourth independent descendant of β is M. M is incomplete, having lost the final part of Brut. (§§317–333). M is the most accurate of the extant descendants of β, but it nevertheless has several significant errors not present in BDEGSTX, including:

16.14 *ager qui*] *qui ager*
177.24 *eius aliquot*] *aliquot eius*
185.11 *doctis . . . dissensio*] om.
203.23 *malebat*] om.
216.18 *e luntre*] *elucubre*
232.15 *vero inquit*] *inquit vero*
243.27 *enim*] om.

M has one surviving copy, Y. As stated earlier, Y has a complete text of Brut. and can therefore be used in the reconstruction of β in §§317–333. Y has all the non-trivial errors of M, including all those listed above, as well as several of M's minor errors (e.g. 219.29 *effluere*] *affluere*, 228.16 *proximus*] *proximius*, 310.11 *commentabar*] *comentabat*), and adds some mistakes of its own:

4.5 *viro*] om.
21.21 *vero inquam*] *inquam vero*
28.26 *illum quidem*] *illud quod*
278.25 *tenebamus*] om.

The best proof of the derivation of Y from M that I have found is the dittography of *videor . . . esse* at 18.30, present in both manuscripts. In M, the phrase is first written at the very end of one page, and then it is written again at the start of the next page. Since there is nothing in the Latin words themselves that would make the dittography likely, the scribe of M probably introduced the error, having lost the point he had reached in his exemplar as he moved on to a new page.

A fifth independent descendant of β is D. D is perhaps the most corrupt of BDEGMSTX, and has many of its own significant errors, including:

26.14 *et litteris*] om.
35.22 *dicam . . . non*] om.

40   2. A NEW STEMMA

46.24 *plerosque...paratas*] om.
95.33 *victu excultus*] *excultus victu*
122.24 *aliae et*] om.
153.23 *nulla sunt*] om.
187.25 *ego...efficiatur*] om.
231.4 *quid...poteritis*] om.
268.5 *asciscere...obtineret*] om.
276.8 *opus...memini*] om.

Two extant manuscripts derive from D: Q and W. The close relationship of these three manuscripts is evident in their chapter divisions. Whereas ρ and β seem to have had 36 chapter divisions, DQW display only seven of these, and the trio is unique in preserving this combination of chapter divisions (see Table 1).

In all the portions of QW I collated, and in all the readings listed above, the two manuscripts share all the significant errors of D. The only possible exception is 324.16 *tu es* QW] *es tu* D. However, D is very damaged here, and I suspect that, as elsewhere in the manuscript, the scribe of D corrected the word order by writing the letters *b* and *a* above the words, but that the subsequent damage to the page has made it impossible to see this correction. In any case, there is decisive proof that W derives from D. At 226.26, the word *coniunctus* is split across two lines in D (*coniunc/tus*), and this has prompted W's corruption *comune ius*. Also, at 273.27 *splendida et*] *splendida oratio et* W, the scribe of W has initially jumped to the line below to copy *oratio*, which is directly beneath *et* in D, before returning to the line above.[16]

The following singular errors of W prove that it is neither the source of D nor of Q:

217.3 *totam*] *datam*
224.13 *factus esset*] *esset factus*
226.26 *coniunctus*] *comune ius*
227.5 *utebatur*] *videbatur*
323.6 *idem...coniunxerat*] om.
331.15 *transversa*] om.

---

[16] W also jumps to the line below in D at 323.6, omitting *idem...coniunxerat*, although homoioteleuton renders this example less cogent.

2. A NEW STEMMA   41

Decisive proof that Q derives from D is lacking, but there is little room for doubt, since Q has all of D's significant errors and adds the following of its own:

1.6 *cogitatione*] *cognitione*
8.32 *ipsa*] om.
8.2 *ipsi*] om.
21.21 *ego*] *ecce*
323.6 *mearum*] om.
324.20 *orationes utriusque*] om.
329.29 *sunt*] om.

A sixth independent descendant of β is E, which also has significant errors of its own:

82.2 *orationes*] *errores*
99.4 *fuerunt*] om.
118.22 *paene...traducti*] om.
121.11 *loquatur*] om.
131.11 *de...fecissem*] om.
177.21 *et aequalibus*] om.
180.20 *rustici etiam*] *etiam rustici*
194.17 *coponio*] *co. m. currium pomo*
234.9 *nullo...locum*] om.
263.16 *rationes*] om.

The two remaining independent descendants of β, G and X, apparently share an exemplar. Each has many errors of its own.

G: 9.9 *quodam*] om.
12.4 *mihi accidit*] *accidit mihi*
20.14 *mihi nuper*] *nuper mihi*
46.19 *tyrannis*] *nostra vis*
82.29 *rem*] om.
107.18 *scipionem*] om.
142.22 *quod*] om.
157.22 *devenerint*] om.
227.9 *quibus*] om.
265.7 *quaedam*] om.

42   2. A NEW STEMMA

275.25 *agitur autem*] *autem agitur*
287.29 *consequitur*] om.
289.22 *proditum esse*] om.

X: 5.11 *grato*] om.
22.31 *saepe*] om.
219.27 *quidem*] om.
226.2 *multae ad eum*] *ad eum multae*
270.22 *sed... dicere*] om.
274.18 *rerum*] om.
322.12 *continetur*] om.
328.18 *dictatore*] om.
331.13 *brute*] om.
332.29 *iam*] om.

GX share the following errors:

57.1 *tarsumennum*] *tarsumentium* GX
70.9 *usi*] *nisi* GX
105.33 *fuisse* X^c] *esse* G, X^{ac} (ut vid.)
129.23 *paulo* FOBEM] *pavilo* λO^{v}G^{c}T: *pavilio* GX
143.30 *utro*] *vero*
179.14 *t.* G^c] *et* G: *ut* X
212.6 *vero*] *non*
217.1 *peroravissem*] *procuravissem*
228.16 *doctus... deditus*] om.
230.14 *vigebat* X] *iungebat* G: *iungebatur* G^{vl}X^{vl}
273.22 *eius in*] *in eius*
276.7 *habebat*] *habebat quid inter abesse et deesse referat* G: *habebat*
        (*quid... referat* in marg.) X.[17]

Individually, each of these shared errors could be explained by appeal to coincidence or to corrections, glosses, and variants in β, but together they constitute a compelling case for a close relationship between G and X.[18] The likeliest and most economical explanation of this set of shared errors is that

---

[17] Note also 71.20 *ait*] *aut* GX, 201.29 *disseruissem*] *desseruissem* G: *deseruissem* X, 226.30 *agens*] *agensi* GX, 301.22 *et*^{1}] om. GX, and 305.28 *tenebar* G^{c}X^c] *tenebat* GX.
[18] The fact that GX were probably copied by the same scribe points to the same conclusion.

GX share an exemplar, γ, which derived from β. In order to have produced only the errors listed above in the copying of *Brut.*, the scribe of γ must have been a careful copyist, but this degree of accuracy is not impossible.[19]

There are two alternative explanations: that G is a contaminated copy of X, and that X is a contaminated copy of G. This contamination could provide a mechanism for the elimination of the majority of X's errors from G, or of G's errors from X. However, both G and X contain all the significant errors of β, and neither shows any evidence of influence from a manuscript independent of β, or from another extant descendant of β. This fact would necessitate the conclusion that the supposed contamination in G or X was from β, or from a lost copy of β, because otherwise errors of β would have been removed.

I cannot disprove these two alternatives, but it is simpler to hypothesize a common ancestor of GX. The only slight argument against this theory is the provenance of G. G was at one time in the possession of Guiniforte Barzizza, son of Gasparino. If, as I shall suggest later, β was a manuscript owned by Gasparino Barzizza, then one might expect Guiniforte's copy of the text to have been copied directly from his father's; to interpose an intermediate manuscript is inconvenient. Nevertheless, this consideration is certainly not fatal to the hypothesis of a shared exemplar of GX, especially since β is not extant and I cannot prove that it was indeed a manuscript owned by Barzizza. The relationship between G and X is the most doubtful part of my stemma, but since there is no need to postulate contamination, it is best to assume that GX derive from a common exemplar, γ.

A few errors shared by some of DEGMSTWX can be attributed to coincidence (e.g. 90.19 *tum*] *tamen* DM and 277.11 *rem*] om. DG), and others probably reveal places where β had corrections and minor errors (3.23 *ab*] *ab ab* MT, 163.19 *crasso*] *crasso quoque* DEM, and 225.23 *ad* G^c] *ad ad* GMT). A small set of errors shared by GT merits more attention:

143.4 *mira explicatio*] *explicatio mira*
160.17 *cenavisset*] *cenavisset lucilius tribunum plebis*
197.3 *delicato*] *dedicato*
239.24 *natura*] *vero.*

---

[19] The scribes of GX may, of course, also have corrected some additional minor errors present in γ. As comparanda, Lamola's transcription of L, λ, seems to have been even more accurate, and the scribe of M also made only a handful of errors in his copy of *Brut.*

44   2. A NEW STEMMA

With the exception of the second error, these shared innovations could all have arisen independently; such coincidences are to be expected in the copying of a text of a moderate length, like *Brut*. The second error, in which homoioteleuton is involved (*cenavisset... narravisset*), is also quite a straightforward problem to resolve: if the scribe of β had jumped from *cenavisset* to *lucilius*, before realizing his error and adding dots of expunction underneath *lucilius tribunum plebis*, some of the copyists could easily have failed to notice the correction. There is no need to postulate a shared exemplar of GT, or contamination from one into the other, to explain these readings.

2.1 Coda: A Contaminated Descendant of β

As I demonstrate in appendices 2–3, all the surviving manuscripts of *Brut*. not mentioned above are either certainly or probably *codices descripti* of other extant manuscripts. The only exception is Ho,[20] which shares some of the errors of β and ρ, but which is independent of BDEMSTγ, since it lacks the distinctive errors of each. Ho's *Brut*. has been copied by two scribes. The section copied by the second scribe, §§126–333, derives primarily not from β but from F, and will be discussed among the descendants of τ. In §§1–126, the section copied by the first scribe, Ho derives primarily from β, because it shares almost all the errors of β (e.g. 16.14 *quom*] *sępe*, 48.12 *aliis*] om., and 72.19 *conditam autem*] *autem conditam*). However, Ho lacks the following significant errors of β in §§1–126:

34.14 *et*] om.
88.26 *exisse*] om.
109.3 *frater*] om.
111.26 *cum... diceret*] om.
112.3 *huius... sunt*] om.

Therefore, Ho cannot derive exclusively from β. Since Ho also lacks a few of the errors of ρ (e.g. 65.21 *nostrorum*] *nostrum*), the first part of Ho's text probably derives from β, but with some of the errors of β and ρ corrected from another manuscript. Ho's independence from BDEMSTγ means that it

---

[20] I exclude here the contaminated and corrupt descendants of ψ, which may have been an independent descendant of γ.

2. A NEW STEMMA   45

could be used in the reconstruction of L in §§1–126. However, the contamination apparently present in Ho complicates any attempt to use it to determine the readings of β and ρ, since particular readings of Ho may not actually derive from β. For this reason, and also because Ho's text is very corrupt,[21] I have chosen to exclude it from the stemma in Figure 5, which is intended as a guide for editors of *Brut.* on how to reconstruct the text of the archetype.

2.2 Readings of O^v

1.6 *dolebam* O^v] *videbam* O
2.17 *gloriosi* O^v] *generosi* O
4.5 *clarissumo et beatissumo* O^v] *clarissimo et beatissimo* O
5.11 *angimur* O] *angitur* O^v
7.21 *cum* O^v] *tum* O
10.12 *cum* O^v] *tum* O
11.25 *epistulam* O^v] *epistolam* O
13.14 *ulla* O^v] *illa* O
21.28 *tractum* O^v] *tractatum* O
25.26 *confirmaverim* O] *comferam veri* O^v
30.6 *multi* O^v] *multo* O
35.17 *versatus* O] *versatur* O^v
41.6 *saeculo*] *sacculo* O: *seculo* O^v
47.4 *antiphontem* O] *antiphoontem* O^v
53.22 *qui*] *quem* O: *que* O^v
55.14 *interrege appio*] *inter* [spat. vac. v litt.] *a. p.* O: *interrege a. p.* O^v, ut vid.: *interregea p.* O^{2vl}
56.24 *ullum* O^v] *illum* O
58.11 *nono* O^v] *novo* O
59.5 *dixerit…quaestor-*] *vetus*-note added next to this line, but it is unclear to what it refers
61.24 *nonnullae*] *nonnullorum* O: *nonulle* O^v
62.3 *cum* O^v] *tum* O
64.14 *certos* O] *certo* O^v
66.1 *ut* O^v] *et* O

---

[21] For a list of some of Ho's errors, see p. 285.

46   2. A NEW STEMMA

70.2 *imitentur* O^v] *imiterentur* O
73.9 *senensi* O] *senesi* O^v
73.13 *naevius*] *ennius* O: *nevius* O^v
79.24 *qui bis* O^v] *quibus* O
79.29 *aiunt* O^{mg}] *al* [spat. vac. vi litt.] O: *aliunt* O^v
81.15 *numerius*] *miaserius* O: *nuaserius* O^v
81.16 *quinctusque* O^v] *quintusque* O
82.3 *catonis* O] *caπonis* O^v
84.16 *ipsa* O^v] *ipse* O
84.16 *viriathi bello*] *viri adhibet* [spat. vac. v litt.] O: *viri adhibet to* O^v: *viriaci bello* O^{mg}
85.28 *societatis…redemisset de-*] *vetus*-note added next to this line, but it is unclear to what it refers
89.11 *cognitast* O^v] *cognita* [spat. vac. iv litt.] O
93.16 *motusque…quod*] *vetus*-note added next to this line, perhaps referring to *flaccesciebat*
95.32 *gaiusque* O^v] *gravisque* O
95.4 *m.*² O^v] *l.* O
109.2 *vir* O^v] *iure* O
109.3 *etiam* O^v] *et* O
129.23 *paulo* O] *pavilo* O^v
130.3 *patrocinio* O] *patricinio* O^v
134.16 *qui…18 audires* O^v] om. O
146.25 *admirandus*] *ammirabilis* O: *ammirandus* O^v
150.24 *vostrae*] *vestre* O: *vostre* O^v
154.24 *cumque* O] *quunque* O^v
155.2 *sapientissume* O^v] *apsentissume* O
167.29 *afranius* O^v] *africanus* O
169.9 *asculanus* O^v] *esculanus* O
175.9 *itam in iure* O^{c}O^v] [spat. vac. v litt.] *in iure* O
178.2 *consularium* O^v] *consulatum* O
178.8 *t.*] *ti.* O: *t. i.* O^v
182.14 *p. antistius*] *pasticius* O: *patistius* O^v
191.33 *movere*] *mereri* O: *moveri* O^v
204.33 *et lenissimo* O^v] *edenissimo* O
205.7 *eam* O^v] *etiam* O
207.19 *scriptis* O^v] om. O
211.31 *c.* O^v] om. O
216.15 *cacinnos* O^v] *cachinos* O

216.18 *e luntre*] *cluntre* OOᵛ: *eluntre* O²ᵛˡ
225.23 *revecti* Oᵛ] *reiecti* O
231.3 *ii* Oᵛ] *ut* O
243.33 *anni* Oᵛ] *animi* O
252.21 *fere* Oᵛ] *fore* O
256.30 *duo* O] *duos* Oᵛ
258.19 *barbaries* Oᵛ] *barbari* O
259.26 *q.* Oᵛ] om. O
260.12 *accusante* Oᵛ] *accusatore* O
265.9 *gravitas* Oᵛ] *dignitas* O
267.26 *appius*] *app.* O: *ap.p.* Oᵛ
268.8 *plena* Oᵛ] *plane* O
295.28 *de*² Oᵛ] *et* O
305.31 *excesserat* Oᵛ] om. O
307.21 *et* O] *ei* Oᵛ
309.3 *me mecumque*] *me cum .q.* O: *me cumque* Oᵛ
312.27 *sulla* Oᵛ] *silla* O
313.3 *quoniam…vide-*] *vetus*-note added next to this line, perhaps referring to *crepundis*
313.11 *vi* Oᵛ] *in* O
316.3 *cnidius* Oᵛ] *enidius* O
317.17 *tum* Oᵛ] *tamen* O
317.22 *mihi* Oᵛ] *nichil* O
317.25 *canuleio* Oᵛ] *camuleio* O
325.25 *dictionis* Oᵛ] *orationis* O
328.18 *sulla* Oᵛ] *sylla* O
328.21 *ominare*] *omitte* O: *o mire* Oᵛ
330.6 *rei publicae*] *rei pu.* O: *re in. p.* Oᵛ

3

A Textual History of Cicero's *Brutus*

3.1 *Brutus* Before 1421

It seems that Cicero had largely completed *Brut.* by April 46 BC,[1] just a few months before he composed *Orat.*, another of his major rhetorical works.[2] *Brut.* enjoyed a wide readership in the subsequent centuries: the text is cited or paraphrased by Valerius Maximus, Quintilian, Tacitus, Suetonius, Aulus Gellius, Ammianus Marcellinus, Diomedes, Servius, Jerome, Macrobius, and Rufinus.[3] Indeed, in the late fourth or early fifth century, Jerome, in his *Praefatio in Librum Paralipomenon*, reports that, apparently on account of its length, several people (*nonnulli*) had split the dialogue up into three parts.[4] No trace of this ancient division of the work has survived, but it further attests the wide circulation of *Brut.* in late antiquity. After Rufinus' citation of two paragraphs of *Brut.* in the fifth century, however, the evidence for an active readership dries up, and there is a long period of silence.

In the ninth century, the silence, from our perspective, was punctured by the copying of a manuscript of Cicero's rhetorical works, including *De or.*, *Orat.*, and *Brut.* as well as *Rhet. Her.* and *Inv. rhet.* This manuscript, probably copied in northern Italy in the second third of the century, and now known as the *Codex Laudensis* (L), indicates that there was at least some demand for copies of *Brut.* during the Carolingian period.[5] The text of *Brut.* in L was

---

[1] On the date of composition, see Robinson (1951), Marinone (1997: 191), and Gowing (2000: 62–64).

[2] The history presented in this chapter owes much to the work of Remigio Sabbadini, whose findings are summarized in Sabbadini (1971), and Enrica Malcovati (1958, 1959, 1960, and 1970).

[3] Val. Max. 8.1.2; Quint. *Inst.* 3.1.8–12, 7.9.12, et al.; Tac. *Dial.* 30.3; Suet. *Iul.* 55–56; Gell. *NA* 11.2.4; Amm. Marc. 30.4.5; Diom. in Keil, *Gramm. Lat.*, i.313.9–10; Serv. *Aen.* 1.505; Jer. *Ep.* 7.1.2 (with Hagendahl (1958: 103)); Macrob. *Sat.* 6.2.34; Rufinus in D'Alessandro (2004: p. 30, l.6–19). Cassiodorus apparently alludes to *Brut.* 46 in *Var.* 1 *Ep.* 3 (see below, p. 166 n. 45). On Horace's interaction with *Brut.*, see, e.g., Feeney (2002), Goh (2018).

[4] Jerome in Migne, *PL*, xxix, col. 425: *qui* [i.e. *liber Paralipomenon*] *propter magnitudinem apud nos divisus est, quod nonnulli etiam in Bruto, Ciceronis dialogo, faciunt, ut eum in tres partes secent, cum unus a suo auctore sit editus.*

[5] For further discussion of L, particularly with regard to its relationship to other parts of the MS tradition of Cicero's rhetorical works, see Taylor-Briggs (2006: 102–107). The date of L depends on my identification of it with the Cremona fragment (see 'The Cremona Fragment'),

3. A TEXTUAL HISTORY OF CICERO'S *BRUTUS*   49

corrupt in many places, but it probably did originally contain the now-lost ending of the work.

After being copied, L was corrected by a second hand. In the two leaves which survive as the Cremona fragment (C), the corrections are exclusively orthographical, 'archaic' spellings (e.g. *paullo, quom*) being replaced with ones current in the ninth century (*paulo, cum*). The corrections in this small portion of the manuscript may or may not be representative of the rest of its text. The spellings found elsewhere in *Brut.* in the descendants of L follow the same pattern as in the portions of text where C is extant: in general spellings such as *paulo* and *cum* prevail, but archaisms (e.g. 89.11 *cognita st* O^{v}U, 172.8 *quom* BF) are occasionally found. In C, the corrector seldom leaves 'archaic' spellings untouched: he may have corrected the whole manuscript in the same way, carefully and thoroughly updating the orthography, but from time to time overlooking individual words. Nowhere, though, do the texts of C or of L's descendants suggest that L's *Brut.* contained variant readings or significant (i.e. not simply orthographical) corrections, whether introduced by the initial scribe or by the corrector.

If Bischoff (1998: 209) is right that the corrector of C is the same as the corrector of a ninth-century Quintilian (Biblioteca Ambrosiana, E 153 sup.), then L may have been corrected, and perhaps also copied, in Pavia, where the Quintilian manuscript was produced. However, since the Cremona fragment contains only a small sample of the corrector's hand, Bischoff's suggestion must remain only a possibility. Even if it can be established with confidence that the corrector of the Quintilian was the same scribe who emended the text of C, this scribe may not have remained in Pavia throughout his life, and so L may still have been copied and corrected elsewhere.

Apart from these details concerning L, little can be said about the textual history of *Brut.* in the Middle Ages. If any copies of *Brut.* were made between the ninth and fifteenth centuries, they have been lost. Nor has evidence that anyone read the text in this period survived. Nevertheless, there is one hint that the text of *Brut.* might not have fallen into total oblivion during these intervening centuries: Richard de Fournival's mention of the work in his *Biblionomia*.[6] Richard, the Chancellor of the Cathedral of Amiens, composed the *Biblionomia* c.1240–1250, at least notionally as a catalogue of the

---

which Bischoff (1998: 209) dates to the second third of the ninth century. On the basis of the humanist descriptions of L, Taylor-Briggs preferred a date before the ninth century.

[6] The *Biblionomia* was transcribed by Delisle (1874: 518–535). Nearly a century later, De Vleeschauwer (1965) reprinted Delisle's transcription, together with a facsimile of the MS in which it was preserved.

50   3. A TEXTUAL HISTORY OF CICERO'S *BRUTUS*

contents of his library, and if he did own a copy of *Brut.*, this would prove that the text was known in northern France in the thirteenth century. The 28th entry in the *Biblionomia* is as follows: *Eiusdem de oratore libri tres, et quartus Brutus, et quintus Orator, in uno volumine cuius signum est littera C.*[7]

However, whether the *Biblionomia* constituted a list of the books actually possessed by Richard de Fournival, or was rather an idealized library, has been the subject of debate. Léopold Delisle (1874: 520) raised doubts about the reality of Richard's collection, but Aleksander Birkenmajer (1922)[8] identified 17 manuscripts from the BnF with items mentioned in the *Biblionomia*, thus demonstrating that Richard did possess at least some of the works he had listed. Birkenmajer's researches revealed that after Richard's death, his library had passed via Gérard d'Abbeville to the Collège de Sorbonne.[9] R. H. Rouse (1974; 1979: 138 n. 31) identified many more manuscripts from Richard's library, and around a third of the 132 entries from the first section of the *Biblionomia* have now been located.

Nevertheless, there are several reasons to be cautious about whether Richard owned a copy of *Brut.* Firstly, the catalogue of the Sorbonne Library contains no record of a manuscript containing *De or., Brut.*, and *Orat.* Of course, there are various possible reasons why the manuscript might not have been transferred to the Sorbonne with the rest of Richard's library, and even if it had reached the Sorbonne, it might somehow have evaded the compilers of the catalogue. More serious doubts concerning the existence of this manuscript of *Brut.* arise from the similarity between Richard's entry in the *Biblionomia* and Cicero's own words in *Div.* 2.4: *Ita tres erunt de oratore, quartus Brutus, quintus Orator.* Winterbottom et al. (in Reynolds (1983: 109)) point out that Richard often appears to have been guided by *Div.* when composing the titles of his copies of Ciceronian works, and they conclude that Richard probably possessed only a *mutilus* of *De or.* and *Orat.*

More recently, Thomas Haye (2010) has examined further the question of whether Richard de Fournival's *Biblionomia* describes a real or an idealized library. Haye draws our attention to a metaphor employed by Richard in the introduction to the catalogue, in which he pictures his library as a garden whose fruits might help to introduce students *in secretum phylosophie cubiculum.*[10] These two images, of the library as a garden and of the goal of

---

[7] Delisle (1874: 525).   [8] Translated into French as Birkenmajer (1970).
[9] On the formation of the library of the Sorbonne, see Rouse (1967).
[10] Delisle (1874: 520–521); Haye (2010: 215). For a broader discussion of the garden-library metaphor with reference to medieval book collections, see Hinton (2016).

3. A TEXTUAL HISTORY OF CICERO'S *BRUTUS*   51

entering the *phylosophie cubiculum*, suggest that Richard may have aimed at least in part at describing an idealized library. This metaphor, together with the title (*Biblionomia*, rather than the more common *Catalogus*) and the careful structuring of the first section of philosophical texts into eleven shelves (*tabulae*), each with exactly 12 volumes, led Haye to conclude that, although Richard's library is not exclusively virtual, 'l'organisation et la présentation des manuscrits et des textes dans la *Biblionomia* relèvent probablement très largement de l'idéalisation' (2010: 224). Hence, I suspect that Richard, being in possession of a *mutilus* of *De or.* and *Orat.*, used Cicero's words from *Div.* 2.4 in the description of his manuscript, and that, for the sake of completeness, he mentioned *Brut.* together with the other two texts.[11] The *Biblionomia* does not prove that copies of *Brut.* were available in thirteenth-century France, and therefore, apart from L, there is no definite evidence that copies of *Brut.* existed between the fifth and fifteenth centuries.[12]

3.2 The Discovery of the *Laudensis*

One of the key sources for the discovery of L is *Italia Illustrata*, a history composed by Flavio Biondo between 1447 and 1453. In it Biondo writes:

> ...Philippus, Mediolanensis dux tertius, Gasparinum a Bergomo subditum hominem invitum Mediolanensibus edocendis Padua et Venetia evocavit, ubi id maxime adiumenti studiis eloquentiae attulit quod, repertus Laudae a summo viro Gerardo Landriano, tunc ibi episcopo, multis maximisque in ruderibus codex Ciceronis pervetustus et cuius litteras vetustiores paucissimi scirent legere, ad eius perveniens manus interitum evasit. Continebat is codex, praeter *Rhetoricorum novos* et *veteres* qui habebantur, tres quoque *De oratore* integerrimos, *Brutum de oratoribus claris* et *Oratorem ad Brutum* M. Tullii Ciceronis...et cum nullus Mediolani esset repertus qui eius vetusti codicis litteram sciret legere, Cosmus quidam egregii ingenii Cremonensis tres *De oratore* libros primus transcripsit multiplicataque inde

---

[11] Given their absence from the Sorbonne catalogue, Richard may not even have owned a copy of *De or.* and *Orat.*, and he may have included them on his 'shelf' of 12 books on rhetoric after having judged all three to be canonical texts of classical rhetorical theory.

[12] On the basis of Haenel's catalogue (1830: 919) of the Biblioteca de los Carmelitos Delcalzos, Scarcia Piacentini (1983: 124 n. 1) suggested that the text might also have existed in Spain before the fifteenth century. However, Haenel dated one of the two MSS of *Brut.* in the library of the Carmelites (Bc) incorrectly, and it is much more likely that he also erred in dating the other MS than that he discovered a copy of the text from before 1421.

52   3. A TEXTUAL HISTORY OF CICERO'S *BRUTUS*

exempla omnem Italiam desideratissimo codice repleverunt. Nos vero, cum publicis patriae tractandis negotiis, adolescentes Mediolanum adiissemus, *Brutum de claris oratoribus* primi omnium mirabili ardore ac celeritate transcripsimus, ex quo, primum Veronam Guarino, post Leonardo Iustiniano Venetias misso, omnis Italia exemplis pariter est repleta.[13]

This passage of *Italia Illustrata* supplies the basic facts of the discovery of L. A very old codex was discovered in Lodi by the bishop Gerardo Landriani 'amid a mass of ruins'.[14] This manuscript, which contained *Rhet. Her.*, *Inv. rhet.*, *De or.*, *Brut.*, and *Orat.*, subsequently ended up in the hands of Gasparino Barzizza, then in Milan. Biondo claims that Cosimo of Cremona, identified by Sabbadini as Cosimo Raimondi,[15] was the first to transcribe *De or.*, and that he himself executed the first transcription of *Brut.* from L. Biondo's account can be supplemented from several other sources.

The rediscovery of L must have taken place in 1421, and probably in the second half of the year. In a letter dated 9 January 1422, Guarino Veronese reveals that he knew by this point both that L had been discovered and that it was in the possession of Gasparino Barzizza in Milan.[16] Hence, when one allows time for the manuscript to be brought to Barzizza and for news to reach Guarino, the final months of 1421 provide a *terminus post quem non* for the discovery of L. Barzizza was in Padua between 1407 and 1421, and was still there on 19 June 1421, but he had returned to Milan by 27 October 1421.[17] Since Biondo's narrative makes clear that L was brought to Barzizza while he was in Milan, we can conclude that Barzizza obtained the codex after 19 June 1421, and before the end of the year. We do not know how much time passed between Landriani's discovery of the codex and its arrival in Milan, but, given the magnitude of the discovery and the degree of scholarly excitement that it occasioned, it is unlikely that Landriani, on finding no one in Lodi who could read the manuscript, would have delayed long before sending it on to someone with the requisite skills to be able to read it. For these reasons, the codex was probably discovered in the second half of 1421.[18]

As regards the location of the discovery, Vespasiano da Bisticci contradicts Biondo's claim that L was found in Lodi. Vespasiano, in his life of

---

[13] Biondo, *Italia Illustrata* (2011–2017: iii.150–152).   [14] Tr. White (Biondo (2005)).
[15] Sabbadini (1971: 86–91).   [16] Sabbadini (1915–1919: i.332–333;1971: 99–101).
[17] Mercer (1979: 128), with the bibliography he cites at 128 n. 39. See also Martellotti (1983: 468–478).
[18] As Scarcia Piacentini argues (1983: 138–139), the subscription to *Orat.* in Vat. lat. 3237 indicates that it was copied on 25 December 1422, not 25 December 1421. But even if Vat. lat. 3237 was copied in December 1421, the date of the discovery of L would not need to be moved to earlier than the likely period of June–December 1421.

3. A TEXTUAL HISTORY OF CICERO'S *BRUTUS*   53

Niccolò Niccoli, writes that the ancient codex was found 'a Pavia in una chiesa antichissima, in uno cassone, ch'era stato infinito tempo non s'era mai aperto'.[19] Francesco degli Ardizzi, in his subscription to O, corroborates Vespasiano's claim that L was found in a church (*quem Gerardus Landrianus Episcopus Laudensis et Comes in archivio ecclesie sue repperit*), and the additional detail that the manuscript was found in a chest which had not been opened for a very long time is credible. However, Vespasiano must have been mistaken when he suggested that L was found in Pavia. Gerardo Landriani was Bishop of Lodi, not Pavia, and Francesco degli Ardizzi and Flavio Biondo, two men who saw the codex and who must have had contact with Barzizza, both assert that it was discovered in Lodi.[20] L was almost certainly found in the archives of Lodi Cathedral.

I turn now to consider what we know of the contents and condition of L at its rediscovery. Flavio Biondo is the only eyewitness of L who lists the works it contained in full. In his subscription to B, which he wrote with L in front of him on 15 October 1422, Biondo gives the contents as follows: *Rhetoricarum: ad herennium rhetorica: De oratore: Orator ad brutum: et brutus de oratoribus claris.*[21] In *Italia Illustrata*, as we have already seen, he describes the contents thus: *Rhetoricorum novos et veteres...tres quoque De oratore integerrimos, Brutum de oratoribus claris et Oratorem ad Brutum.* On the basis of Biondo's later account, the confusing opening words of the description in B (*Rhetoricarum: ad herennium rhetorica*) probably indicate the presence of both *Rhet. Her.* (known in many manuscripts as *Rhetorica nova*) and *Inv. rhet.* (also known as *Rhetorica vetus*).[22] Biondo's two lists differ as to the

---

[19] Vespasiano, *Le Vite*, p. 229.

[20] Biondo states this not only in *Italia Illustrata*, but also in his subscription to B (*scripsi hunc* Brutum...*ad exemplar uetustissimum repertum nuper Laude...*). The same conclusion can be inferred from Gasparino Barzizza's letter to Landriani, part of which is quoted below; and cf. Poggio, *Lettere* (1984: 56).

[21] A facsimile of the subscription can be seen in Chatelain (1884–1892: pl. XXa).

[22] Because no humanist except Biondo mentions the presence of *Rhet. Her.* and *Inv. rhet.* in L, while several refer to *De or.*, *Orat.*, and *Brut.* (in particular, Gasparino Barzizza in *De orthographia* (Sabbadini (1971: 92)) and Giovanni Lamola in a letter to Guarino Veronese (Sabbadini (1915–1919: i.636–643))), and because no copy of *Rhet. Her.* or *Inv. rhet.* ever seems to have been made from L, some scholars have doubted whether L ever contained these works (Stroux (1921: 10 n. 2); Malcovati (1958: 33 n. 13)). However, as Taylor (1993: 132 n. 63) points out, Biondo would have had little reason to lie about L's contents, and since he apparently composed the subscription to B immediately after copying directly from L, he could hardly have been mistaken about its contents. Additionally, *Rhet. Her.* and *Inv. rhet.* were so widely available in the fifteenth century that another MS, even a very old one, would not have been considered valuable. (Biondo's lack of interest is evident from the way he phrases his account in *Italia Illustrata*: *Continebat is codex, praeter* Rhetoricorum novos *et* veteres *qui habebantur...*) *Rhet. Her.* and *Inv. rhet.* may, however, have been removed and disposed of after October 1422, because Barzizza (in *De orthographia*, cited by Sabbadini (1971: 92) and quoted below), in

54   3. A TEXTUAL HISTORY OF CICERO'S *BRUTUS*

order of the three later works in L. Biondo's subscription, however, is surely correct, not only because it was written with L immediately in front of him, while *Italia Illustrata* was composed around thirty years later, but also because *Orat.* precedes *Brut.* in all the extant manuscripts which derive independently from L and which contain both works (DFJMOSTUX).[23] Hence, L seems, on its rediscovery, to have contained *Rhet. Her.* and *Inv.* (perhaps in that order), followed by *De or.*, *Orat.*, and *Brut.*

L included complete copies of *De or.* and *Orat.*, but the ending of *Brut.* was lost before 1421. This is clear from a reconstruction of L's text, because the final sentence of *Brut.*, as transmitted in L's descendants, is obviously incomplete. The humanists' testimony suggests that L originally contained a complete text of *Brut.*, but that the final two pages of the manuscript were lost before it was rediscovered in Lodi. In the subscription to B, Flavio Biondo wrote: *Non erat amplius in exemplari: a quo abscisse sunt charte due: quamquam ut mihi videtur nedum charte sed pauca admodum verba deficiunt.* Biondo's words agree with the testimony of Francesco degli Ardizzi, who wrote in the colophon of O: *Non inveni plura in perveteri codice. fortunę quidem iniquitas id totum, si tamen quiddam erat, recidit.* Finally, the copyist of Mn's *Brut.* ascribes the following quotation to Gasparino Barzizza: *Deficiunt pauca, non ultra folia duo ad plus et ut ego coniecturam facio non ultra columnam. Plura enim in codice vetustissimo non comperi, ex quo in fine carte recise iniquitate fortune erant.*

I have already discussed the testimony of the humanists concerning the condition of L in 'The Cremona Fragment.' I will therefore merely summarize here what we know. L was several centuries old, and its script apparently rendered it difficult to read (although the humanists may have exaggerated its illegibility). It was written in columns, and it was not divided into chapters. The final two pages had apparently been cut off.

3.3 The *Laudensis* after Its Rediscovery

After discovering L, Gerardo Landriani found that he was unable to read it, and so he sent the codex to Gasparino Barzizza, then living in Milan, to be

---

describing the MS, mentions only *De or.*, *Orat.*, and *Brut.* See further Taylor-Briggs (2006: 105–107).

[23] See also Barzizza in *De orthographia*, quoted below.

3. A TEXTUAL HISTORY OF CICERO'S *BRUTUS*   55

transcribed.[24] The actual work of transcribing the manuscript was carried out by Cosimo Raimondi of Cremona. This can be seen from the excerpt from *Italia Illustrata* quoted above, and it coheres with the details given by Barzizza in a letter written to Landriani. I cite part of the letter here:[25]

> Gasparinus Barzizius Gerardo Landriano Laudensi episcopo s. p. d.
>
> Etsi voluptate maxima affectus sim, Pater Reverendissime, quod ad me *Oratorem* a te compertum misisses; multo tamen maiore gaudio cumulari me sensi, cum a Iohanne Homodeo, homine, ut nosti, tuae dignitatis observantissimo, me amari a te plurimum intellexi ... summasque tibi gratias habeo, quod huiusce inventionis tuae socium me, ac participem primum omnium esse voluisti. feci autem, ut pro illo vetustissimo, ac pene ad nullum usum apto, novum manu hominis doctissimi scriptum, ad illud exemplar correctum alium codicem haberes; quem ad te pro tuo is defert, qui primus munus hoc a tua in eum singulari benevolentia pro me impetravit. nunc ad te librum nudum ac inornatum mitto. neque mihi enim aliter per occupationes meas licuit; nec prius exemplari [Biblioteca Ambrosiana, P 4 sup.: expediri Furiettus, fort. recte] a librario meo, qui hoc exemplo usus fuit, tametsi instarem, potuit. ignosces itaque, Pater praestantissime; et quod a me omissum est, tu illud pro tuo arbitrio expolies, atque exornabis ... Vale Mediolani.

Barzizza's letter reveals that Giovanni Omodei was responsible for bringing L from Lodi to Milan. It also corroborates Biondo's claim that Barzizza did not copy *Brut.* himself, but rather delegated the work to another (*novum manu hominis doctissimi scriptum*). Scarcia Piacentini outlines two possible interpretations of Barzizza's rather unclear account of the copies made from L. The *homo doctissimus* may be different from *librarius meus*, and *illud exemplar* and *hoc exemplum* may refer to different manuscripts. Alternatively,

---

[24] Malcovati (1958: 31) refers to 'laboriose trattative' which took place before the MS was sent to Milan. I am not sure on what basis she postulates these laborious negotiations, unless it is an undated letter, probably written by Barzizza to Landriani, in which Barzizza informs Landriani that Giovanni Omodei, an associate of Landriani's, has explained to him *mandata tua super libro* De oratore. The letter is cited by Sabbadini (1971: 85). Gasparino Barzizza was an obvious person to whom to entrust the transcription of the precious codex. Barzizza's expertise on Cicero, and on the rhetorical works in particular, was well known (Sabbadini (1971: 79–84); Mercer (1979: 72–75); Pigman III (1981)), and the proximity of Lodi to Milan, where Barzizza had just arrived, would, of course, have helped Landriani's decision.

[25] The text is taken primarily from Sabbadini (1971: 84–85), who cites only part of the letter. Where Sabbadini's text is absent, I follow Furiettus (1723). Sabbadini improved upon Furiettus's edition by comparing it to Biblioteca Ambrosiana, P 4 sup.

56   3. A TEXTUAL HISTORY OF CICERO'S *BRUTUS*

homo doctissimus and *librarius meus* are one and the same, and *exemplum* is used as a synonym for *exemplar*, with the ablative *exemplo* preferred to avoid confusion with the verb *exemplari* which precedes it. In the first scenario, the *homo doctissimus* would denote Cosimo Raimondi, who produced a direct transcription of L, and the *librarius meus* could then be a different scribe who copied Raimondi's transcription. In the second, Barzizza is describing one single transcription of L, and the reason he seeks pardon for the delay is not that he took a copy of the transcription before sending it on to Landriani, but simply that the transcription took a long time to complete. Scarcia Piacentini prefers the first interpretation, and this does seem the more natural reading of the letter. *Illud exemplar* looks back to *illo vetustissimo* (i.e. L), and *hoc exemplo*, by contrast, indicates the manuscript sent with the letter (i.e. Raimondi's transcription).[26]

In any case, on the strength of Biondo's testimony, the *homo doctissimus* who, according to Barzizza, executed the initial transcription of L, should be identified as Cosimo Raimondi. Whether Raimondi transcribed the whole of L, or only a part, remains unclear. Biondo claimed that he himself was the first to transcribe L's *Brut.* (Brutum de claris oratoribus *primi omnium mirabili ardore ac celeritate transcripsimus*), but this is patently false. The first part of B, the manuscript written by Biondo, was undoubtedly copied from a descendant of L, not from L itself, and so the text must already have been transcribed by the time that Biondo began his copy in October 1422. Biondo's memory may have been to blame for this error, but equally he might have believed, three decades after the events and with both Cosimo Raimondi and Gasparino Barzizza long dead, that he could get away with exaggerating the importance of his role in the recovery of the text of *Brut.*

In view of this inaccuracy, Biondo's suggestion that Raimondi transcribed only *De or.* becomes suspicious. It would have been strange for Raimondi to have left *Orat.* and *Brut.* uncopied, given the great excitement their discovery had provoked. Additionally, Barzizza must surely have returned at least a copy of *De or.*, *Orat.*, and *Brut.* to Gerardo Landriani, and since it seems that Raimondi's transcription was the manuscript sent to the bishop, we can deduce that Raimondi transcribed all three works. (He may not have bothered to copy *Rhet. Her.* and *Inv. rhet.*) Raimondi must have finished his transcription before the copying of B in October 1422, perhaps several months before.[27]

---

[26] Later, I will suggest that Raimondi's transcription is probably ρ, and that the transcription made from it for Barzizza is probably β.

[27] Sabbadini (1888: 109–114) argued that Raimondi's sojourn in Milan lasted from the beginning of 1422 until the middle of 1423, but he subsequently admitted (1971: 89–91) that some of the evidence he had cited related instead to Raimondi's second stay in Milan, between

3. A TEXTUAL HISTORY OF CICERO'S *BRUTUS*   57

After Raimondi's transcription was finished, Barzizza kept hold of L.[28] In his second edition of *De orthographia*, produced at some point between 1421 and 1430, Barzizza discusses the 'archaic' use of *u* for *i* in old manuscripts:[29]

> Similiter *u* pro *i* in plerisque scribi non solum codices antiqui sed quorundam etiam modernorum usus testatur... Et pene omnia superlativa, velut in antiquissimo codice meo legi, ubi tres expleti *De oratore* libri ad Q. f., item *Orator ad Brutum* et alius qui *Brutus* dicitur continetur.

By the time of his revision of *De orthographia*, Barzizza evidently considered that L belonged to him. Barzizza seems to have been willing to allow others to study his ancient codex, since it was seen by Flavio Biondo in 1422, by the correctors of O in 1425, and by Giovanni Lamola in 1428.

After Raimondi finished his transcription, the next known use made of L's *Brut.* was by Flavio Biondo in his copy of the text (B), executed between 7 and 15 October 1422.[30] Biondo was only given access to L after he had started copying *Brut.*, perhaps because L was being used by another scholar. Biondo then used L as his exemplar for the remainder of *Brut.*, and he corrected the first part of his text from it.

F, copied between April and September 1423, derives from L independently of Raimondi's transcription. Therefore, another copy of L's *Brut.* must have been completed before the end of September 1423, and this copy must either be F or a lost intermediary between F and L. Neither textual nor historical evidence settles the matter, but a few details lead me to prefer the latter alternative.

First, F contains only *Orat.* and *Brut.*, while L also contained a full version of *De or.*[31] The discovery of the complete text of *De or.* was no less exciting than the discovery of the other two rhetorical works, and if F had

---

1427 and 1428. Raimondi's first stay lasted nine months, and must have included some portion of the time between June 1421 and October 1422, but to locate it more precisely is not possible at present.

[28] Cf. Malcovati (1958: 32–35).

[29] Cited by Sabbadini (1971: 92) from Pavia, Biblioteca Universitaria, Aldini 253.

[30] Because I have not studied the MSS of *De or.* and *Orat.*, I discuss here only the history of the descendants of L which contain *Brut.* Of the early descendants of L in which *Brut.* is absent, Giovanni Arzignano's lost MS of *Orat.*, written in the second half of 1422 for Guarino Veronese, may have been copied directly from L. Vat. lat. 3237 (probably 25 Dec 1422) and Vat. lat. 2901 may also derive from L independently of other transcriptions, either directly or via lost intermediaries. See further Scarcia Piacentini (1983), and below, p. 72 n. 92.

[31] It is clear from a letter of Giovanni Lamola that the three rhetorical works were still bound together in L in 1428: *tribus Ciceronis De oratore libris, Oratori quoque ipsi et Bruto, quos ex vetusto illo... traduximus* (Sabbadini (1915–1919: i.636–643). See further below.

58   3. A TEXTUAL HISTORY OF CICERO'S *BRUTUS*

been copied directly from L, one would have expected Niccolò Niccoli, the scribe of F, to have transcribed all three texts. Doubtless, there are various circumstances that might have prevented Niccoli from copying *De or.*, but its absence from F is suggestive. We should also note the testimony of Vespasiano da Bisticci, who states specifically that a manuscript of *Orat.* and *Brut.* was sent to Niccoli.[32] Vespasiano's testimony is from some decades later and not wholly reliable, but it fits better with the postulation of an intermediary between F and L, a manuscript containing only *Orat.* and *Brut.*, than with the direct transcription of F from L.

Other historical evidence points to the same conclusion. According to Vespasiano, the manuscript sent to Niccoli was brought from Milan by the envoys of Duke Filippo Maria Visconti. Giovanni Corvini, the Duke's secretary and a friend of both Gasparino Barzizza and Cosimo Raimondi,[33] was among the envoys who came to Florence in April 1423,[34] and it was probably he who brought the codex to Niccoli in Florence.[35] Corvini is known to have acquired a manuscript containing the unmutilated text of *De or.* before the end of 1422,[36] and he may well have obtained a copy of *Orat.* and *Brut.* at around the same time. The manuscript of *De or.* seems to have been bound separately from the other two works, and if it was unavailable when Corvini set out for Florence, this could explain why only *Orat.* and *Brut.* were brought to Niccoli.

Finally, if Corvini had brought L to Florence, before later taking it back to Milan, he would have had to persuade first Barzizza and then Niccoli to give up the ancient codex. Barzizza appears to have guarded the *Laudensis* jealously,[37] not even returning it to its discoverer, Gerardo Landriani, and it is doubtful if even the Duke's ambassadors could have prised the precious manuscript out of his hands and then out of Niccoli's.

None of these considerations is decisive, but it is probable that a lost codex, φ, was copied from L before the end of 1422 and then brought to Florence in 1423. In any case, by 1423 at least two full transcriptions of L's

---

[32] Vespasiano, *Le Vite*, pp. 228–229: '*Orator* et *Bruto* fu mandato a Nicolaio di Lombardia, et arrecorollo gli oratori del duca Filippo, quando vennono a domandare la pace, nel tempo di papa Martino'.

[33] Sabbadini (1971: 316–320).

[34] Malcovati (1960: 328); cf. Sabbadini (1971: 102), Scarcia Piacentini (1983: 132).

[35] Giovanni Corvini had an impressive library, and several of his MSS were requested by some of the most influential humanists of the period (Sabbadini (1971: 102–104, 313–329)).

[36] In a letter written on 9 December 1422, Guarino Veronese reports that Corvini has a MS of Macrobius and asks Ugo Mazzolato to send him a copy of it: *hunc transcribendum esse cuperem ita ut eius copiam haberemus, sicut intercessione domini Marchionis* [i.e. Niccolò III, Marquis of Ferrara] *habuimus Ciceronem* De oratore (Sabbadini (1915–1919: i.356–358)). Sabbadini (1971: 102) mistakenly believed that F was a twin of Corvini's *De or.*

[37] Malcovati (1958: 34).

3. A TEXTUAL HISTORY OF CICERO'S *BRUTUS*   59

Brut. had been completed, as well as Biondo's partial copy.[38] From 1423 until the beginning of 1425, nothing is known either of L or of its owner, Gasparino Barzizza. In February 1425, a letter of Barzizza reveals that he was then in Pavia.[39] He must have brought L with him to Pavia, because O was corrected from L in Pavia on 26 April 1425. The work of correcting the manuscript was carried out by Antonio and Simone Bossi, as well as by the author of O's subscription, Francesco degli Ardizzi.

Between 1426 and 1428, Gasparino Barzizza seems to have been lecturing in Bologna, although he was back in Milan in September 1427.[40] We do not know whether Barzizza took L with him on these journeys, but the codex was certainly in Milan in May 1428, because Giovanni Lamola, in a lengthy letter to Guarino Veronese written on 31 May 1428, makes clear that he has produced a new transcription of L in Milan. I quote the relevant parts here:[41]

...nunc porro ad Latinum textum [i.e. of Macrob. *Sat.*] corrigendum accedam. Sed prius tamen ultimam manum et septimam addam correctionem tribus Ciceronis *De oratore* libris, *Oratori* quoque ipsi et *Bruto*, quos ex vetusto illo, fautore Cambio [i.e. Cambio Zambeccari], traduximus; velimque hos ipsos non tibi minus caros fore Macrobio ipso, quos quippe nondum vidisti proprios; et si te vidisse putas, falleris. Nec credas inconstantiam illam et volubilitatem Arzignariam [i.e. of Giovanni Arzignano] illos proprios ad nos detulisse, quoniam ille nos egregie fraudavit. Hic autem ipse codex, summae quidem venerationis et antiquitatis non vulgaris effigies, ab istis in quorum manibus <fuit> quique ex eo accurato exemplari exemplum, quod vulgatum ubique est, traduxerunt, summis ignominiis adfectus est, quippe qui multa non intellexerunt, multa abraserunt, multa mutarunt, multa addiderunt...Ego tamen quantum diligentiae ac ingenii peritiaeque in me fuit et in nonnullo antiquitatis callentissimo viro mecum idem sentiente adhibui, ut omnia secundum priorem textum restituerem, notarem etiam marginibus ubique <al>legationes istorum logodaedalorum et sane barbaricarum belluarum. Curavi etiam ut usque ad punctum minimum omnia ad veteris speciem exprimerem, etiam ubi essent nonnullae vetustatis delirationes; nam velim

---

[38] See 'A New Stemma' for discussion of Francesco degli Ardizzi's false claim that O was copied directly from L.
[39] Sabbadini (1971: 96).   [40] Mercer (1979: 135).
[41] Sabbadini (1915–1919: i.636–643).

60   3. A TEXTUAL HISTORY OF CICERO'S *BRUTUS*

potius cum veteri illo delirare quam cum istis diligentibus sapere...Ex Mediolano pridie kal. iunias[42]...

Lamola's letter not only proves that L was still in existence in 1428 and that it was then located in Milan, but also reveals that Lamola had taken it upon himself, with the support of Cambio Zambeccari, to make a fresh transcription of the manuscript. That Lamola completed his transcription of L is confirmed both by a letter written in response by Guarino Veronese,[43] acknowledging receipt of the manuscript and praising Lamola's diligence in copying L, and by the subscription to U, in which the scribe writes that he has copied his text *ex emendatissimo codice Iohannis Lamole*. As I demonstrated in 'A New Stemma', U and its brother J are free from the errors introduced by φ, ρ, and B, and they derive from another transcription of L, λ. In view of the subscription to U, there is no difficulty in identifying λ as Giovanni Lamola's copy of L.[44] λ, when reconstructed from JU, seems to have been a very accurate transcription, containing markedly fewer errors than either ρ or B: this is certainly coherent with the level of care Lamola claimed to have taken.[45]

The quality of Giovanni Lamola's transcription can be verified through the comparison of its descendants' texts, but the accuracy of his description of the state of L in 1428 cannot be tested so easily. Lamola complains of the ignominious treatment L had suffered at the hands of its previous owners: *multa abraserunt, multa mutarunt, multa addiderunt*. This phrase, frequently quoted in the scholarship on L,[46] is probably an exaggeration. Even if one leaves aside the possibility that Lamola might have erroneously attributed to

---

[42] Lamola gives only the day and the month; the dating of the letter to 1428 was secured beyond doubt by Sabbadini (1915–1919: iii.235–237; 1971: 107) on the grounds of the mention of a plague in Verona, a reference to a speech delivered by Guarino, and the arrival of Lamola in Milan 18 months earlier.

[43] Sabbadini (1915–1919: i.643–644).

[44] Malcovati did not accept that U derived from Lamola's codex, instead suggesting that 'l'unica supposizione lecita è che U sia la copia pulita di un esemplare corretto secondo la collazione del Lamola' (1959: 180). But although Guarino, in the letter to Lamola cited above, says only that he has begun to emend his MSS from those which he has just received from Lamola (*Meos igitur emendare horum adiumento coepi, ut eos meliores faciam*), there is no reason why Guarino, or an associate such as Martino Rizzoni, should not subsequently have wanted a complete copy of Lamola's codex (Scarcia Piacentini (1983: 129)). Brightbill (1932), followed by Kumaniecki (1969: xv–xvi), believed that U's *De or.* had been contaminated from the *mutili*. This may well be the case, but U's *Brut.* is a pure copy of λ and shows no signs of contamination from elsewhere.

[45] λ has considerably fewer errors than F as well, but this does not prove that λ was a better transcription than φ.

[46] e.g. Stroux (1921: 14–19), Malcovati (1958: 36).

3. A TEXTUAL HISTORY OF CICERO'S *BRUTUS* 61

his fellow humanists the emendations carried out by the ninth-century corrector of L, the alterations he claims were made to L between 1421 and 1428 do not seem to have made his reconstruction of the earlier text difficult. In fact, if one were to reconstruct L from BFρ and λ from JU, their texts of *Brut.* would differ in only a handful of places. Therefore, if Barzizza, Raimondi, Biondo, or any other fifteenth-century reader did alter L's text in any way, the changes did not obscure completely what was originally written. For this reason, and also because C shows no sign of the shameful treatment to which Lamola claims L had been subjected (*summis ignominiis adfectus est*), I suspect that if the humanists did meddle with L in any way, it was only by the addition of a few marginal annotations, interlinear glosses, emendations, and the like, and that Lamola has exaggerated the extent of their interventions. The tone of the letter, with its lengthy invective against the *depravatores* of the *Laudensis*, only part of which I cite, lends itself to this conclusion. Even in his criticism of Giovanni Arzignano, who copied *Orat.* for Guarino in 1422, Lamola is excessive. Arzignano's only crime seems to have been that he produced a rather inaccurate copy of L,[47] but Lamola accuses him of inconstancy (*inconstantiam*) and fraud (*ille nos egregie fraudavit*).[48]

After 1428, the history of L becomes very obscure. Since Lamola refers nowhere in his letter to Gasparino Barzizza, we do not know whether the codex was still in his possession at this time. Barzizza visited Padua and Pavia before his death in Milan in 1430,[49] but there is no evidence that he took L with him on those occasions. Barzizza apparently did not leave the codex to his son Guiniforte in his will. Pettenazzi (1955–1957: 86) speculates that he might have given the manuscript to Cosimo Raimondi, who was in Milan from 1427 to 1428,[50] but there is no proof. After being transcribed three times in 1421–1422 and once in 1428, the *Laudensis* was again lost to history.

It is only with the rediscovery of the Cremona fragment that anything further can be said of L. If I am right to identify C with L, then two folios from L were used in the sixteenth century as a cover for documents relating to a census taken of two villages near Cremona, Scandolara Ravara and Castelponzone.[51] The rest of the manuscript may have been dismembered and used for similar purposes at this time; in any case, only those two leaves

---

[47] Sabbadini (1915–1919: iii.236).
[48] Thomson (1969: 133–134) takes rather more seriously the accusation of fraud and suggests that Arzignano might have bought a copy of inferior quality in the hope of making profit for himself from the fee which Guarino would pay to him. It is more likely that Arzignano's copy of *Orat.* simply proved less accurate than Lamola had believed it to be.
[49] Mercer (1979: 135–136).   [50] Sabbadini (1971: 89–91).   [51] Giazzi (2005: 495).

62   3. A TEXTUAL HISTORY OF CICERO'S *BRUTUS*

of *Brut.* survive. They found their way to the Archivio di Stato in Cremona, where they were eventually identified by Isabella Pettenazzi in 1954.

3.4 Raimondi's Transcription and Barzizza's Manuscript

As has already been established, Cosimo Raimondi transcribed L in late 1421 or in 1422. If Scarcia Piacentini's interpretation of Gasparino Barzizza's letter to Gerardo Landriani is correct,[52] a copy of Raimondi's manuscript was made for Barzizza before it was sent to Landriani. Apart from this, the only detail concerning Raimondi's manuscript that can be known with confidence is that it was *nudus ac inornatus* (i.e. that it lacked illuminations) when Barzizza sent it to the bishop.[53] Barzizza suggested that Landriani might arrange for the manuscript to be decorated (*quod a me omissum est, tu illud pro tuo arbitrio expolies, atque exornabis*), but we do not know whether Landriani acted on this suggestion.

How then do Raimondi's transcription of *Brut.* and Barzizza's copy of it fit into my stemma of the manuscripts of *Brut.*? Neither can be identified with any extant manuscript of the text.[54] I suspect that Raimondi's manuscript may be ρ, the lost exemplar of O and β, and that Barzizza's manuscript may be β. I cannot prove that this reconstruction is correct, but certain details point in this direction. Firstly, the presence of multiple copies deriving independently from β coheres well with what we know of Barzizza's manuscript. In a letter perhaps written in 1428 to Bartolomeo della Capra, the Archbishop of Milan, Barzizza says that he wanted to send his copy of *Brut.* to Bartolomeo after it had been returned to him by someone else, but that he has been unable to do so.[55] The letter implies that, by 1428, Barzizza's

---

[52] See above, pp. 55–56.

[53] Since Raimondi's transcription was apparently plain and unadorned, O might have been the first decorated parchment codex to derive from L. There might therefore be at least a modicum of truth in Francesco degli Ardizzi's claim that Francesco Bossi *primum veterem et superiorem codicem... in latinas et explicatas bene litteras, studioseque interpunctas, summa diligentia renovavit.*

[54] The same may not be true of Barzizza's copy of *De or.* and *Orat.*: although doubt remains, the colophon and some marginalia in Pal. lat. 1469 seem to be in Gasparino Barzizza's hand (Scarcia Piacentini (1983: 126–127), Barbero (2016: 156–158)), and this MS may therefore be a companion of Barzizza's *Brut.* Pal. lat. 1469 and O apparently derive from a common exemplar in *De or.* and *Orat.* (Stroux (1921: 123), Kumaniecki (1969: x)), just as β and O do in *Brut.*: this fact lends credence to the theory that Pal. lat. 1469 and β constituted the two parts of Barzizza's MS of *De or., Orat.,* and *Brut.*

[55] *Postquam* Brutus *noster ad me rediit, pater reverendissime, sepe illum, ut pollicitus eram, mittere ad te volui* (Sabbadini (1971: 93–94)). Sabbadini believed that Barzizza was referring to G, but G, although owned by Barzizza's son, does not seem to have been the MS copied from Raimondi's transcription (see above, pp. 41–43).

3. A TEXTUAL HISTORY OF CICERO'S *BRUTUS*   63

Brut. had been separated from the other texts copied from Raimondi's transcription, and it also reveals that Barzizza was willing to lend his manuscript to those who wished to obtain a copy of *Brut.* Hence, we can deduce that Barzizza's manuscript, just like β, was copied several times. Because several of β's independent descendants are known to be of Milanese origin (BGMTX, and probably also D), β was almost certainly located in Milan, and the presence of G, owned by Guiniforte Barzizza, among β's offspring is especially suggestive.

Further evidence that ρ and β should be identified respectively as Raimondi's transcription and Barzizza's copy can be found in the chapter divisions present in ρ's progeny.[56] Gasparino Barzizza introduced chapter divisions into the *mutili* of *De or.* and *Orat.* before the discovery of L,[57] and scholars have assumed,[58] quite reasonably although without explicit proof, that Barzizza was also responsible for the transfer of these chapter divisions to the early apographs of L and for the addition of chapter divisions to *Brut.* One might expect the chapter divisions to have originated in Barzizza's manuscript, but their presence in O, which derives from ρ rather than from β, is not necessarily a problem: Barzizza, or his student Cosimo Raimondi, could have added the chapter divisions directly to Raimondi's initial transcription.[59]

The final indication is the disappearance of ρ after the copying of O in 1422. If, on the basis of its chapter divisions, one were to prefer to assign ρ to Barzizza (or, more precisely, to his *librarius*) rather than to Raimondi, one would need to explain why β, rather than ρ, was used as the exemplar of BDEMSTγ (or their ancestors). If ρ was the manuscript sent to Gerardo Landriani in Lodi, this would provide a ready explanation for the absence of extant direct copies of it from after 1422.[60]

If, as I have argued, Raimondi's transcription is ρ, then the transcription was copied not only by Barzizza's *librarius* but also by the scribe of O, and it

---

[56] Not all the descendants of ρ contain every chapter division (although only Vv lacks them entirely), but there is sufficient similarity between the various MSS for one to be sure that the divisions have a common origin.

[57] Sabbadini (1971: 81–82).   [58] e.g. Scarcia Piacentini (1983: 127).

[59] The supposition that chapter divisions were present in Raimondi's transcription in no way conflicts with Barzizza's description of the MS as *nudus ac inornatus*: the divisions could have been marked and space left for the decorated initials to be added subsequently.

[60] The copying of O from ρ in November 1422 would necessitate a gap of perhaps a year or more between Barzizza's receipt of L and his sending of Raimondi's transcription to Landriani. This lengthy delay would explain why Barzizza felt the need to apologize to Landriani, but was by no means unheard of. Guarino, for example, received B from Biondo in late 1422 and only returned the codex in April 1425. Cf. also Niccoli's delays in sending copies of Cicero's rhetorical works to Aurispa and Poggio (Ullman (1960: 35–36, 61–62)).

64   3. A TEXTUAL HISTORY OF CICERO'S *BRUTUS*

was only in late 1422, at the earliest, that Raimondi's manuscript was dispatched to Lodi. Barzizza's manuscript, probably β, remained in Milan and was loaned out several times to be copied. Flavio Biondo copied the first part of B's *Brut.* from β in early October 1422. γ, the exemplar of GX, was copied at some point between 1421 and 1428, and probably between 1421 and 1423. In *c.*1428 β seems to have been sent to Bartolomeo della Capra, then based in Genoa, and, perhaps around the year 1430, β acted as the exemplar for most of T's *Brut.*[61] M was copied in Milan in the 1430s, perhaps directly from β, and from M derives Y, copied in northern Italy in the middle or third quarter of the century. Other descendants of β of less certain date are D (and its apographs QW) and S.

3.5 The Descendants of ρ

O was written in Milan in November 1422. Lb,[62] a contaminated descendant of O, was in the possession of Lorenzo Benvenuti in Florence by October 1423. Since Lb shares errors with δ, it may derive from O via an intermediate manuscript, onto which corrections from δ had been imposed. Further work is needed to establish whether Lb was copied in Milan or Florence. In either case, it may be the earliest surviving copy of *Brut.* to have been in Florence.

O was corrected from L in Pavia in 1425, but it seems to have been brought back to Milan after 1425, where the final part of T's *Brut.* was copied from it *c.*1430 (if Cipriani's date (1968: 18) is to be believed). O was also used by the scribe of θ, from which three further manuscripts derive: Bo, copied in Emilia-Romagna between 1430 and 1450, Fl, and Lu.

More significant in the dispersion of *Brut.* was the role played by G. G, which derives from β via the lost exemplar γ, was copied by 1428, and probably between 1421 and 1423. It was owned at one time by Guiniforte Barzizza (1406–1463) and therefore may have been in the library of Guiniforte's father Gasparino. G was copied several times, since at least four independent manuscript families derive from it. The largest of these, whose parent is δ, may also be the earliest: Vn, copied in Parma, is dated to

---

[61] It is evident from Barzizza's letter to Bartolomeo della Capra that β was in high demand, and this fact may explain T's change of exemplar.

[62] For evidence to support the place in the stemma that I have assigned to Lb and to the other *codices descripti* mentioned in the following pages, see Appendices 2 and 3.

3. A TEXTUAL HISTORY OF CICERO'S *BRUTUS*   65

February 1428, and Lb, which shares errors with δ, was copied by October 1423. Another descendant of δ, Pb, was probably copied in Milan before 1430, and another, Mg, was copied in Parma in 1438. The location of origin of its other offspring, Bc and Wf, has not been established. ζ, another descendant of G, was the source of Vk, copied in northern Italy, and Me, owned by Nicolò Arcimboldi (1404–1459), a jurist and friend of Cosimo Raimondi.[63] The third family, α, is made up of FkPaVv, with Pa copied in Milan in 1461. The fourth, deriving from ε, includes Mn and MiMb, two manuscripts of Lombard origin. Hence, the descendants of G seem to have spread throughout at least Lombardy and Emilia-Romagna.

In the second half of the fifteenth century, a contaminated family of manuscripts provides evidence that ρ had a wider impact on the transmission of *Brut.* ψ, which appears to derive in part from γ, was the source not only of Va (in sections I–II of my collations), but also of two Florentine manuscripts: Vp, copied between 1450 and 1473, and Lc, copied partially from ψ in the 1470s. However, ρ's text was dispersed even further from Milan, since the *editio princeps* (Rom), printed in Rome in 1469, shows influence from Lb, a descendant of O contaminated from δ. Therefore, although the descendants of ρ seem to have been limited largely to northern Italy, copies deriving from Raimondi's transcription must have travelled at least as far as Florence and Rome. Rome and Florence were such dominant centres of manuscript production in this period that they drew in strands of the tradition from all over Italy.

3.6 The Descendants of B

Flavio Biondo copied *Brut.* in Milan between 7 and 15 October 1422, partly from β and partly from L. In *Italia Illustrata*, Biondo wrote the following concerning the subsequent history of B, his copy of *Brut.*: *ex quo* [sc. *codice*] *primum Veronam Guarino, post Leonardo Iustiniano Venetias misso omnis Italia exemplis pariter est repleta.* A letter written by Guarino Veronese to Ugo Mazzolato,[64] dated to 9 December 1422, reveals that Guarino had received Biondo's copy by this point (*deinde accepi libellum quem Biondus meus... dedit*), and so Biondo must have sent the manuscript to Guarino in

---

[63] Meyenberg (1990: 77–78). On Arcimboldi, see Raponi in *Dizionario biografico degli italiani*, iii.79–81, and the bibliography cited there.

[64] Sabbadini (1915–1919: i.356–357).

66   3. A TEXTUAL HISTORY OF CICERO'S *BRUTUS*

Verona quite soon after he finished copying it. In the letter to Mazzolato, Guarino writes initially that he is sending B with the letter, and asks Mazzolato to arrange for a copy of *Brut.* to be made for him (*sed unum oro ut, si quis apud vos non imperitus sit qui eum transcribat, et mihi exarari librum ipsum facias*). In a postscript, however, Guarino, worried about possible damage to the manuscript from the rain, changes his mind and promises to send it later with Giovanni Coado.[65] Guarino sent B to Mazzolato soon afterwards, as is evident from his next letter, written on 22 December 1422 (*aliquot iam dies misi ad te libellum illum Ciceronis, quem a Biondo susceperam*).[66] In this letter, Guarino again asks Mazzolato to make a copy of *Brut.*, and, since he has already received two requests from Biondo for B to be returned (*hunc autem Biondus ipse geminatis ad me litteris repetit*), Guarino gives permission for Mazzolato to send it back to Biondo when he has finished copying it. Mazzolato's copy of *Brut.* survives as Np; it derives, as one would expect, entirely from B.

Guarino, however, delayed for a long time before sending B back to Biondo. Probably in 1423, Guarino wrote to Biondo that he would send the manuscript when he had finished with it,[67] and two further letters to Biondo show that Guarino finally returned it between 13 and 18 April 1425.[68] Mh's *Brut.* may have been copied in the period between the production of Np and the eventual return of B to Biondo in April 1425, and may help to explain why Guarino delayed for so long before sending B back to Biondo. Mh was written by Francesco Calcagnini in Mantua, and it could be a direct copy of B. Although Mh's *Orat.* is dated to September 1425, the text of *Brut.* may have been copied some months earlier, Guarino perhaps having supplied the manuscript to Calcagnini.[69]

After B was returned to him, Biondo lent the manuscript to Leonardo Giustiniani in Venice; Giustiniani's codex is now lost. Whether B was copied again after this is unclear: the only other independent descendant to survive is Vr, and its early provenance is unknown. Vr is now located in Verona, though, and it may have been copied there, perhaps also in the period when B was in the possession of Guarino Veronese. It is clear from

---

[65] Guarino adds that he is writing a letter of thanks to Biondo: the autograph of this letter survives, for it is written in B, directly after Biondo's subscription (Sabbadini (1915–1919: i.355)).

[66] Sabbadini (1915–1919: i.361).

[67] Sabbadini (1915–1919: i.373–375).   [68] Ibid., i.467–469.

[69] In *Italia Illustrata*, Biondo records only that he sent his copy of *Brut.* to Guarino and to Leonardo Giustiniani, and so it may have been Guarino, rather than Biondo, who sent B to Calcagnini in Mantua.

3. A TEXTUAL HISTORY OF CICERO'S *BRUTUS* 67

Italia Illustrata that Biondo believed that his manuscript contributed significantly to the diffusion of *Brut.* throughout Italy (*ex quo...omnis Italia exemplis pariter est repleta*). However, if one can judge from the extant manuscripts, B was dwarfed by both ρ and F in the number of offspring produced and in their geographical spread. When Biondo wrote *Italia Illustrata* in the middle of the fifteenth century, the copies of B may have been limited to Verona, Mantua, and Venice.[70] After Biondo's death in 1463, however, his claim gained more credibility, as the second printed edition of *Brut.*, VenA, was based largely on the text of Mh. Each of the next four printed editions, VenB, VenC, Nur, and Mil, derives ultimately from VenA, and hence they all include many of the distinctive readings of B and Mh. Therefore, although Biondo exaggerated the significance of the role of B in the dispersion of the manuscripts of *Brut.*, his transcription of L did have an important part to play in shaping the text of the early printed editions.

3.7 The Descendants of F

φ, containing *Orat.* and *Brut.*, was brought from Milan to Florence by Giovanni Corvini in April 1423. φ acted as the exemplar for Niccolò Niccoli's manuscript of *Brut.*, F, copied between April and September 1423. Corvini may have taken φ back to Milan with him after this, since F seems to have been the only manuscript copied from it. F remained in Niccoli's possession, and it was lent out as an exemplar several times in the following years. In his life of Niccoli, Vespasiano da Bisticci records that Niccoli was generous with his books, lending them out to anyone who asked,[71] and the arrival of *Brut.* and the complete text of *Orat.* in Florence would certainly have led to demand for copies.

Perhaps the first copy of F to be made was Fb, completed on 1 October 1423 by the scribe Giacomo Curlo for Cosimo de' Medici. In 1424, Niccoli arranged for a copy of *Orat.* and *Brut.* to be made for Giovanni Aurispa; Aurispa, then based in Bologna, acknowledged receipt of the copy in a letter to Ambrogio Traversari, written on 1 December 1424 (*accepi Oratorem et Brutum, librum tanta diligentia, tanta cura ornatum*).[72]

---

[70] Admittedly, we do not know the place of origin of Vr or of BlOd, the descendants of Mh.

[71] 'Era Nicolaio liberalissimo et prestava libri a chi gliene domandava, in modo che alla sua morte n'aveva prestati a più persone volumi dugento...' (Vespasiano, *Le Vite*, p. 231); cf. Ullman (1960: 62).

[72] Sabbadini (1931: 8, 15–20). See also Ullman (1960: 61).

68   3. A TEXTUAL HISTORY OF CICERO'S *BRUTUS*

Aurispa's manuscript has not been identified, but it must have been copied from F. On the basis of the dates of their offspring, several more independent copies of F can be dated to the period 1423–1428: π was copied by 1425, κ by *c*.1425, and Vm by 1428. ξ had probably also been copied by *c*.1425. From these four manuscripts, copies of *Brut.* were multiplied not just in Florence, but throughout Italy and even in France. On his death in 1437, Niccolò Niccoli bequeathed F, along with the rest of his library, to the Biblioteca di San Marco.[73] F was still used as an exemplar after this point, though: Fn, copied in Florence in 1464, is probably a direct copy, and Fd may also have been copied directly from F in 1461.[74]

Of the descendants of F, π produced the most offspring. The first of these may have been Ff, copied by the prominent humanist Poggio Bracciolini.[75] Poggio's letters to Niccoli allowed Ullman (1960: 35–36) to date the copying of Ff to the second half of 1425.[76] In one of these letters, Poggio asked Niccoli to send him either his copy or that of Nicola de' Medici (*Itaque quam primum mitte mihi vel volumen tuum, si habes, vel dicas Nicole nostro, ut mittat ad me eundemmet librum, quem alias habui*).[77] Since Ff does not appear to derive directly from F, it may have been the manuscript of Nicola de' Medici that was eventually sent to Poggio. However, Poggio never acknowledges receipt of an exemplar of *Orat.* and *Brut.* in his letters, and so he may have obtained the manuscript from an entirely different source. Poggio's letters do not provide any certain information on the provenance of π.

Ff, which Poggio copied while he was in Rome, was the source of another Roman manuscript, Bn, written by Johannes Swabenheym in 1429. Vj, the other independent copy of Ff, also has a Roman provenance and it too may have been copied there.[78] Bn is an ancestor of three manuscripts, FjPdVe, and it is also one of two sources of the text of Rom. For this latter reason, Bn may well have remained in Rome until at least 1469.

Another early copy of π was σ, produced between 1423 and *c*.1425. σ was the ancestor of various Florentine manuscripts in the first half of the fifteenth century. These include Fi, copied by the 'Puccini' scribe, and its

---

[73] Ullman and Stadter (1972: 226).   [74] Na, an undated MS, may also be a direct copy.
[75] Poggio was absent from Italy when L was discovered, but he had heard of the discovery by June 1422 (*Lettere* (1984: 56)), and his letters to Niccoli reveal his eagerness to obtain a copy of L: *Libros Tullii De oratore perfectos itemque Oratorem et Brutum integros esse repertos summe gaudeo neque mihi quicquam est molestius quam quod nequeo fieri quamprimum huius particeps voluptatis (Lettere* (1984: 59)).
[76] See also Malcovati (1960: 330–331).   [77] Poggio, *Lettere* (1984: 142–143).
[78] Vj derives purely from Ff only in the first part of *Brut.* In the remainder of the text, it is more closely related to χ and its descendants (CjCmMd). These MSS, of uncertain date and localization, may be contaminated descendants of Ff.

3. A TEXTUAL HISTORY OF CICERO'S *BRUTUS* 69

offspring Vd (c.1442–1450),[79] as well as the lost manuscript τ. From τ derived Vl, copied in Florence between 1425 and 1430 and later owned by Federico da Montefeltro, and its offspring Ob, copied by Antonio di Mario for William Gray in 1445, as well as Lf, copied in Florence in the same period as Vl. Two Florentine manuscripts, Gw (copied c.1425) and Pc (*s*. $xv^{2/4}$), which derive partially from τ (via Ec and μ), may both have been written by Giovanni Aretino.[80] Another Florentine codex, Vi, derives from τ via Sg. Other manuscripts which derive wholly or in part from τ, but whose places of origin are unknown, include BeFeHo.

Perhaps the most interesting of the sub-families deriving from π is the group of six Florentine manuscripts which descend from the lost ancestor v: the five independent copies of v, FcFgFhGeLa, were all copied between 1450 and 1470, and the hand of the scribe Leonardo di Giovanni Tolosani da Colle is found in three of them (FcFhLa). Leonardo was closely associated with the book-seller Vespasiano da Bisticci, as were several others who worked on these manuscripts (Hubertus W, Gherardo del Ciriagio, the Master of the Trivulziana Pharsalia, the 'Master of the Pear-Shaped Putti');[81] the buyers of two of these manuscripts were known clients of Vespasiano (Giovanni and Piero de' Medici).[82] Since Vespasiano da Bisticci's bookshop was in its prime in the 1450s and 1460s,[83] it seems very likely that v was a stock exemplar owned by Vespasiano and kept ready to be lent to his scribes when a copy of Cicero's rhetorical works was ordered.

The subscription to *Orat.* in La, written by Leonardo di Giovanni Tolosani, indicates that the manuscript was copied *ex emendatissimo codice Leonardo Arretini*. Apparently, then, the exemplar for La's *Orat.* was a codex previously owned by Leonardo Bruni. Bruni died in 1444, before the copying of any of the descendants of v, but his manuscript might subsequently have come into the possession of Vespasiano da Bisticci, and, in my view, it should be identified with v. One might object to this identification in two ways. Firstly, Bruni's manuscript could have been a copy of v, and secondly, La might derive from Bruni's manuscript in *Orat.* but not in *Brut.* I address the first of these objections in Appendix 3.[84] The second could only be dealt

---

[79] Es, of unknown provenance, also derives from Fi. It is unsurprising that Fi produced multiple copies: the 'Puccini' scribe's MSS seem often to have been used by Vespasiano da Bisticci as exemplars to be lent to his scribes (Oakley (2016: 346)).

[80] The derivation of GwPc from the same MS supports de la Mare's hypothesis (1985: 425) that the scribe of the Barcelona Eusebius (who copied Pc) was Giovanni Aretino.

[81] De la Mare (1985: 428, 435, 459).   [82] Ibid., 428.

[83] Ibid., 401–406.   [84] p. 324.

70   3. A TEXTUAL HISTORY OF CICERO'S *BRUTUS*

with fully by a demonstration that the offspring of v form a family in *Orat.* as well as in *Brut.* However, all six of v's descendants contain both *Orat.* and *Brut.*, and it is not far-fetched to infer that v contained *Orat.* and that La probably derives from v in both texts.

With the exception of the Roman family deriving from Ff, the dispersion of π's descendants was limited largely to Florence. Vm's descendants, by contrast, spread considerably further. The earliest copy of Vm may have been Re, produced for the cardinal Guillaume Fillastre, who died in Rome in 1428. The relatives of this manuscript are Sd, copied in Friuli in 1439, and Mf, perhaps copied in Bologna. Vm also produced copies in Florence, with Vh copied for the Florentine humanist Giannozzo Manetti sometime before his death in 1459. From Vh derived another codex owned by Manetti, Vg, as well as Lc, copied in Florence between 1470 and 1480, and Mu. Most striking among the descendants of Vm is the family of manuscripts deriving from ι. GlStVfVb were all copied in France in the second half of the fifteenth century. This French family provides the only certain evidence for the copying of manuscripts of *Brut.* beyond the borders of Italy in the fifteenth century. ι must have been brought from Italy to France, perhaps because of a request from a French bibliophile for a copy of Cicero's rhetorical works.

Like Vm, ξ was the source of manuscripts copied both inside and outside Florence. Ma is probably Florentine, and Fa, copied *c.*1425, is also of Tuscan origin; Br (*s.* $\text{XV}^{2/4}$), however, is Milanese, and the illuminations in Mc (1430–1460) also suggest production in Lombardy.

The last of F's independent descendants to be discussed is κ. Notable among κ's offspring is the manuscript owned by Leon Battista Alberti, Vc, which was copied between 1423 and *c.*1425.[85] κ must have been copied at least five times, since Ox, copied in Florence in the middle of the fifteenth century, Ec, Mo, and ν also derive from κ independently of other extant manuscripts. Ec was the source, via a lost manuscript μ, of two Florentine copies, Gw and Pc. From ν, however, arose many more descendants. In addition to Ld, copied in Florence between 1430 and 1440, there are Vq, another Florentine manuscript copied only partially from ν, and Vw. Vq produced a further five offspring: Vu (copied in Florence and owned at one time by Giulio Pomponio Leto)[86] and its apograph Fo (perhaps copied in Venice by Giovanni Aretino), as well as Fm, copied in Bologna in 1437, Fm's

---

[85] For Alberti's interaction with *Brut.*, see McLaughlin (2009).
[86] Vq and Vu were both illuminated by Bartolomeo Varnucci.

3. A TEXTUAL HISTORY OF CICERO'S *BRUTUS* 71

parent Ro, and El. Vw was the source of LePeVaVoVsVt and was also one of the major influences upon Bc, copied between 1450 and 1470. Of these manuscripts, Le may have been copied in Rome, and Vo perhaps in Naples. This survey of the descendants of F reveals a few interesting details. Firstly, there are several instances of the pattern of multiple copies deriving from the same exemplar, which is a feature of the transmission of texts in fifteenth-century Italy, and which is particularly noticeable with newly discovered texts.[87] Demand for new texts like *Brut.* was very high, especially in Florence, and this seems to have resulted in some manuscripts, like that of Niccolò Niccoli, being requested for use as exemplars again and again. Secondly, the transmission of *Brut.* bears witness to the primacy of Florence in the dispersion of classical texts in the first half of the fifteenth century. Even though *Brut.* was rediscovered in Lodi, the number of copies of the text produced in Lombardy and northern Italy seems soon to have been swamped by those produced in Florence. Because Niccolò Niccoli succeeded in obtaining early access to the text of *Brut.*, and because of his position of eminence among the humanists of fifteenth-century Florence, his manuscript played a central role in the dispersion of the work, descendants of it being copied in Florence, Rome, Bologna, and Friuli. F's progeny spread back to Lombardy, where L was discovered, and even, in the second half of the century, to France. Thirdly, and finally, *v*, which may have been the codex owned by Leonardo Bruni, was probably the manuscript lent out by Vespasiano da Bisticci to his scribes; further investigation of this lost manuscript and its descendants may enable scholars to develop further our knowledge of the workings of Vespasiano's bookshop, which exercised great influence on the later transmission of many classical texts.

3.8 The Descendants of λ

λ, containing *De or.*, *Orat.*, and *Brut.*, was copied by Giovanni Lamola in Milan directly from L in 1428. Lamola sent λ to Guarino Veronese, together with a letter written on 31 May 1428.[88] Guarino wrote back to notify Lamola that he had received the codex, to praise Lamola for his diligence in transcribing it, and to inform him that he had begun to correct his own manuscripts of Cicero's rhetorical works from Lamola's copy:[89]

---

[87] Rizzo (1995: 395–398), Oakley (2016: 345).
[88] Sabbadini (1915–1919: i.636–643).   [89] Ibid., i.643–644.

72   3. A TEXTUAL HISTORY OF CICERO'S *BRUTUS*

Accepi postremo Macrobium et *Oratorem* Ciceronis,[90] quos illis probe litteris depingebas...quantum abs te servatum diligentiae; ut cum sis miri-
fice antiquitatis amator, illam in transcribendo effingeres et exprimeres, ut
vel minima omnia ab exemplari excerpseris. Meos igitur emendare horum
adiumento coepi, ut eos meliores faciam.

Afterwards, perhaps around 1433, U was copied from λ by Alessio Tedesco,
an associate of Guarino. Somewhat later, a second copy, J, was made from λ.
The resemblance between J's watermarks and Briquet 8441, found in documents from Bologna dated to 1455, suggests that J might have been copied
in Bologna. Giovanni Lamola, who probably died in Bologna *c.*1449–1450,[91]
might have taken λ back to Bologna at some point after 1433. Because of the
existence of these two independent copies, the text of λ can be reconstructed
with some confidence, even though λ's *Brut.* is now lost.[92]

---

[90] *Orator* is used here as a general title for the three rhetorical works (Sabbadini (1971: 107
n. 2), and cf. Barzizza's letter to Landriani, quoted above (p. 55)).
[91] Arbizzoni in *Dizionario biografico degli italiani*, lxiii.236; cf. Sabbadini (1890: 435).
[92] Lamola's transcription of *De or.* may be less shrouded in mystery than some scholars have
believed: de la Mare (unpublished) has attributed Vat. lat. 2901 (known as V to editors of *De
or.*) to the hand of Lamola. V is a direct copy of L's *De or.* (Stroux (1921: 116–118)); it contains
no other works. As noted long ago by Pasquali (1932: 71), 'le "note vetus" di...Vat. 2901, V,
corrispondono al metodo del Lamola così esattamente da far pensare che esse risalgano alla
sua cerchia'. Additionally, according to Pellegrin et al. (1975–2010: iii/2.17), the watermarks of
V resemble Briquet 2185 (Milan, 1429–1432), which fits well with V's having been copied by
Lamola in Milan in 1428. A brief examination of Kumaniecki's apparatus leads me to suspect
that U's *De or.* derives from V. Not only do UV share various corrections (many of these readings taken from the *mutili*), but they also share the following errors (not all significant): *De or.*
1.16 *erunt*] *erint* U^{ac}V; 1.161 *ea*] om. UV^{ac}: *tanta* V^2; 1.210 *propriae*] *propria*; 2.43 *minus est
tamen* M] *tamen minus est* UV: *tamen est minus* OCmCj; 2.77 *ita*] *tam*; 2.262 *Corinthiis*]
Corinthis. The matter awaits further investigation.

PART TWO
TEXT AND COMMENTARY

Sigla

B	Ottobonianus lat. 1592
C	fragmentum Cremonense, Fragm. Com. 81 (ex 295)
D	Dresdenensis Dc. 108
E	Escorialensis T. III. 23
F	Florentinus Conv. Soppr. J. I. 14
G	Neapolitanus IV A 44
J	Vaticanus lat. 1709
L	archetypus Laudensis deperditus, i.e. consensus BDEFGJMOSTXY vel omnium vel plurimorum
M	Montepessulanus H 214
O	Ottobonianus lat. 2057
Q	Parisinus lat. 7705
S	Vindobonensis 3090
T	Ambrosianus C 75 sup.
W	Guelferbytanus 12. 13. Aug. 4°
X	Ambrosianus H 22 inf.
Y	Yalensis Marston. 6
β	consensus codicum BDEGMSTX (§§1–60 *secundo quaestor-*) vel omnium vel plurimorum, BDEGMTX (§§60 *-que his* – 130 *in quo*), DEGMTX (§§130 *magnum fuit* – 251 *Staienos incurreres*), DEGMX (§§251 *quare sive* – 317 *solute et*), DEGXY (§§317 *facile sententiam* – 333)
γ	consensus codicum GX
λ	consensus codicum JU
ρ	consensus codicum BDEGMOSTX (§§1–60 *secundo quaestor-*) vel omnium vel plurimorum, BDEGMOTX (§§60 *-que his* – 130 *in quo*), DEGMOTX (§§130 *magnum fuit* – 251 *Staienos incurreres*), DEGMOX (§§251 *quare sive* – 317 *solute et*), DEGOXY (§§317 *facile sententiam* – 333)

B, Bᵃᶜ	lectio in B ante correctionem
B¹	correctio in B a prima manu facta

76 SIGLA

B^2, B^3 correctio in B a manu recentiore facta

B^c correctio in B vel a prima manu vel a recentiore facta (incertum utrum)

B^{gl} glossema in B

B^{mg} B in margine

B^v, O^v correctio in B, vel in O, e vetere archetypo facta

B^{vl} varia lectio in B

M. Tulli Ciceronis

Brutus

(1) Cum e Cilicia decedens Rhodum venissem et eo mihi de Q. Hortensi morte esset allatum, opinione omnium maiorem animo cepi dolorem. Nam et amico amisso cum consuetudine iucunda tum multorum officiorum 5 coniunctione me privatum videbam et interitu talis auguris dignitatem nostri collegi deminutam dolebam; qua in cogitatione et cooptatum me ab eo in collegium recordabar, in quo iuratus iudicium dignitatis meae fecerat, et inauguratum ab eodem, ex quo augurum institutis in parentis eum loco colere debebam. (2) Augebat etiam molestiam quod magna sapientium civ- 10 ium bonorumque penuria vir egregius coniunctissimusque mecum consiliorum omnium societate alienissimo rei publicae tempore exstinctus et auctoritatis et prudentiae suae triste nobis desiderium reliquerat; dolebamque quod non, ut plerique putabant, adversarium aut obtrectatorem laudum mearum sed socium potius et consortem gloriosi laboris amiseram. 15 (3) Etenim si in leviorum artium studio memoriae proditum est poetas nobilis poetarum aequalium morte doluisse, quo tandem animo eius interitum ferre debui cum quo certare erat gloriosius quam omnino adversarium non habere? Cum praesertim non modo numquam sit aut illius a me cursus impeditus aut ab illo meus, sed contra semper alter ab altero adiutus et 20 communicando et monendo et favendo.

(4) Sed quoniam perpetua quadam felicitate usus ille cessit e vita suo magis quam suorum civium tempore et tum occidit cum lugere facilius rem publicam posset, si viveret, quam iuvare, vixitque tam diu quam licuit in civitate bene beateque vivere, nostro incommodo detrimentoque, si est ita 25 necesse, doleamus, illius vero mortis opportunitatem benevolentia potius quam misericordia prosequamur, ut, quotienscumque de clarissimo et

---

Codd. citt.: FJUOBDEGMSTX

2 M. TULLI. CICERONIS. BRUTUS. INCIPIT. LEGE. FELICITER *inscr.* F: INCIPIT BRUTUS. LEGE FELICITER. U: incipit brutus J: BRUTUS SIVE DE CLARIS ORATORIBUS D: M. Tullii Ciceronis Brutus *in primo folio* G: Cicero de claris oratoribus *in primo folio* E 10 augebat G^c] augebam L   <in> magna *Fuchs*   16 poetas $F^1J^2\rho$] poetae $F\lambda$

78 BRUTUS

beatissimo viro cogitemus, illum potius quam nosmet ipsos diligere videamur. (5) Nam si id dolemus, quod eo iam frui nobis non licet, nostrum est
id malum; quod modice feramus ne id non ad amicitiam sed ad domesti-
cam utilitatem referre videamur. Sin tamquam illi ipsi acerbitatis aliquid
5 acciderit angimur, summam eius felicitatem non satis grato animo interpre-
tamur. (6) Etenim si viveret Q. Hortensius, cetera fortasse desideraret una
cum reliquis bonis et fortibus civibus, hunc autem aut praeter ceteros aut
cum paucis sustineret dolorem, cum forum populi Romani, quod fuisset
quasi theatrum illius ingeni, voce erudita et Romanis Graecisque auribus
10 digna spoliatum atque orbatum videret.

(7) Equidem angor animo non consili, non ingeni, non auctoritatis armis
egere rem publicam, quae didiceram tractare quibusque me adsuefeceram
quaeque erant propria cum praestantis in re publica viri tum bene moratae
et bene constitutae civitatis. Quod si fuit in re publica tempus ullum cum
15 extorquere arma posset e manibus iratorum civium boni civis auctoritas et
oratio, tum profecto fuit cum patrocinium pacis exclusum est aut errore
hominum aut timore. (8) Ita nobismet ipsis accidit ut, quamquam essent
multo magis alia lugenda, tamen hoc doleremus quod, quo tempore aetas
nostra perfuncta rebus amplissimis tamquam in portum confugere deberet
20 non inertiae neque desidiae, sed oti moderati atque honesti, cumque ipsa
oratio iam nostra canesceret haberetque suam quandam maturitatem et
quasi senectutem, tum arma sunt ea sumpta, quibus illi ipsi, qui didicerant
iis uti gloriose, quem ad modum salutariter uterentur non reperiebant. (9)
Itaque ii mihi videntur fortunate beateque vixisse cum in ceteris civitatibus
25 tum maxime in nostra, quibus cum auctoritate rerumque gestarum gloria
tum etiam sapientiae laude perfrui licuit. Quorum memoria et recordatio in
maximis nostris gravissimisque curis iucunda sane fuit, cum in eam nuper
ex sermone quodam incidissemus.

(10) Nam cum inambularem in xysto et essem otiosus domi, M. ad me
30 Brutus, ut consueverat, cum T. Pomponio venit, homines cum inter se
coniuncti tum mihi ita cari itaque iucundi ut eorum aspectu omnis quae me
angebat de re publica cura consederit. Quos postquam salutavi:

Quid vos, inquam, Brute et Attice? Numquid tandem novi?

Nihil sane, inquit Brutus, quod quidem aut tu audire velis aut ego pro
35 certo dicere audeam.

Codd. citt.: FJUOBDEGMSTX

5 angimur *J²OBDEGM*] angitur *FO^vB^vE^vl*: augitur *TX^vl*: augimur *SX*: an igitur *λ*
7 autem aut *Ff*] autem et *L*: autem *Ernesti*: aut *Lambinus*   16 errore *La²*] terrore *L*
30 venit *ζ*] venerat *L*   31 itaque] atque *O*   33 numquid *π*] nunc quid *L*

BRUTUS   79

(11) Tum Atticus: Eo, inquit, ad te animo venimus, ut de re publica esset silentium et aliquid audiremus potius ex te quam te afficeremus ulla molestia. Vos vero, inquam, Attice, et praesentem me cura levatis et absenti magna solacia dedistis. Nam vestris primum litteris recreatus me ad pristina studia revocavi.   5

Tum ille: Legi, inquit, perlibenter epistulam quam ad te Brutus misit ex Asia, qua mihi visus est et monere te prudenter et consolari amicissime.

(12) Recte, inquam, est visus; nam me istis scito litteris ex diuturna perturbatione totius valetudinis tamquam ad aspiciendam lucem esse revocatum. Atque ut post Cannensem illam calamitatem primum Marcelli ad   10 Nolam proelio populus se Romanus erexit posteaque prosperae res deinceps multae consecutae sunt, sic post rerum nostrarum et communium gravissimos casus nihil ante epistulam Bruti mihi accidit quod vellem aut quod aliqua ex parte sollicitudines allevaret meas.

(13) Tum Brutus: Volui id quidem efficere certe et capio magnum fruc-   15 tum, si quidem quod volui tanta in re consecutus sum. Sed scire cupio quae te Attici litterae delectaverint.

Istae vero, inquam, Brute, non modo delectationem mihi, sed etiam, ut spero, salutem attulerunt.

Salutem? inquit ille. Quodnam tandem genus istuc tam praeclarum lit-   20 terarum fuit?

An mihi potuit, inquam, esse aut gratior ulla salutatio aut ad hoc tempus aptior quam illius libri quo me hic affatus quasi iacentem excitavit?

(14) Tum ille: Nempe eum dicis, inquit, quo iste omnem rerum memoriam breviter et, ut mihi quidem visum est, perdiligenter   25 complexus est?

Istum ipsum, inquam, Brute, dico librum mihi saluti fuisse.

Tum Atticus: Optatissimum mihi quidem est quod dicis; sed quid tandem habuit liber iste quod tibi aut novum aut tanto usui posset esse?

(15) Ille vero et nova, inquam, mihi quidem multa et eam utilitatem   30 quam requirebam, ut explicatis ordinibus temporum uno in conspectu omnia viderem. Quae cum studiose tractare coepissem, ipsa mihi tractatio litterarum salutaris fuit admonuitque, Pomponi, ut a te ipso sumerem aliquid ad me reficiendum teque remunerandum si non pari, at grato tamen

---

Codd. citt.: FJUOBDEGMSTX

3 praesentem *FΛDEM*] praesente *BOSTγ*   17 attice λ, *corr. J^c*   24 dicis *Ff*] dices *L*   omnium *Fa^{ac}*   rerum <gestarum> *vel* <veterum> *Douglas*: rerum <nostrarum> *Jahn*: rerum <Romanarum> *Bake*   29 esse posset *OE^{ac}*

80   BRUTUS

munere; quamquam illud Hesiodium laudatur a doctis, quod eadem mensura reddere iubet quae acceperis aut etiam cumulatiore, si possis. (16)
Ego autem voluntatem tibi profecto emetiar, sed rem ipsam nondum
posse videor; idque ut ignoscas a te peto. Nec enim ex novis, ut agricolae
5 solent, fructibus est unde tibi reddam quod accepi — sic omnis fetus repressus exustusque flos siti [veteris ubertatis] exaruit — nec ex conditis, qui
iacent in tenebris et ad quos omnis nobis aditus, qui paene solis patuit,
obstructus est. Seremus igitur aliquid tamquam in inculto et derelicto solo;
quod ita diligenter colemus ut impendiis etiam augere possimus largitatem
10 tui muneris, modo idem noster animus efficere possit quod ager, qui cum
multos annos quievit, uberiores efferre fruges solet.

(17) Tum ille: Ego vero et exspectabo ea quae polliceris, nec exigam nisi
tuo commodo et erunt mihi pergrata, si solveris.

Mihi quoque, inquit Brutus, [et] exspectanda sunt ea quae Attico pollic-
15 eris, etsi fortasse ego a te huius voluntarius procurator petam quod ipse, cui
debes, incommodo <tuo> exacturum negat.

(18) At vero, inquam, tibi ego, Brute, non solvam nisi prius a te cavero
amplius eo nomine neminem, cuius petitio sit, petiturum.

Non mehercule, inquit, tibi repromittere istuc quidem ausim. Nam hunc,
20 qui negat, video flagitatorem non illum quidem tibi molestum, sed adsid-
uum tamen et acrem fore.

Tum Pomponius: Ego vero, inquit, Brutum nihil mentiri puto. Videor
enim iam te ausurus esse appellare, quoniam longo intervallo modo primum animadverti paulo te hilariorem. (19) Itaque quoniam hic quod mihi
25 deberetur se exacturum professus est, quod huic debes ego a te peto.

Quidnam id? inquam.

Ut scribas, inquit, aliquid; iam pridem enim conticuerunt tuae litterae.
Nam ut illos de re publica libros edidisti, nihil a te sane postea accepimus,
iisque nosmet ipsi ad rerum nostrarum memoriam comprehendendam
30 impulsi atque incensi sumus. Sed illa cum poteris; atque ut possis rogo. (20)
Nunc vero, inquit, si es animo vacuo, expone nobis quod quaerimus.

Codd. citt.: FJUOBDEGMSTX

2 quae *VaVr*] quo *FλBᵛ*: qua *F¹ρ*: quod *J²*   3 remetiar *Rivius*   5–6 repressus
<est> *Bake*   6 flos siti] siti flos *Lambinus*: flos *Orelli*: flos, sic vis *Ammon*   veteris ubertatis
del. A. Eberhard   10 cum *Mil*] quam *FλOBᵛ*: saepe *β*   14 exspectanda *Od*] et
exspectanda *L*: pergrata et exspectanda *Reis*   16 tuo *add. Vv*] se tuo *add.*
A. Eberhard   19 ausim *Gᶜ*] ausus sim *FλOBDEMSTX*: ausum *G*   29 rerum nostrarum *Lambinus*] rerum naturalium *L*: veterum annalium *Pisanus*: rerum et magistratuum
Reis coll. Nep. Att. 18.2

BRUTUS 81

Quidnam est id? inquam.

Quod mihi nuper in Tusculano inchoavisti de oratoribus: quando esse coepissent, qui etiam et quales fuissent. Quem ego sermonem cum ad Brutum tuum, vel nostrum potius, detulissem, magnopere hic audire se velle dixit. Itaque hunc elegimus diem, cum te sciremus esse vacuum. 5 Quare, si tibi est commodum, ede illa quae coeperas et Bruto et mihi.

(21) Ego vero, inquam, si potuero, faciam vobis satis.

Poteris, inquit: relaxa modo paulum animum aut sane, si potes, libera.

Nempe igitur hinc tum, Pomponi, ductus est sermo, quod erat a me mentio facta causam Deiotari fidelissimi atque optimi regis ornatissime et copi- 10 osissime a Bruto me audisse defensam.

Scio, inquit, ab isto initio tractum esse sermonem teque Bruti dolentem vicem quasi deflevisse iudiciorum vastitatem et fori.

Feci, inquam, istuc quidem et saepe facio. (22) Nam mihi, Brute, in te intuenti crebro in mentem venit vereri ecquodnam curriculum aliquando 15 sit habitura tua et natura admirabilis et exquisita doctrina et singularis industria. Cum enim in maximis causis versatus esses et cum tibi aetas nostra iam cederet fascisque submitteret, subito in civitate cum alia ceciderunt tum etiam ea ipsa, de qua disputare ordimur, eloquentia obmutuit.

(23) Tum ille: Ceterarum rerum causa, inquit, istuc et doleo et dolendum 20 puto; dicendi autem me non tam fructus et gloria quam studium ipsum exercitatioque delectat, quod mihi nulla res eripiet te praesertim tam studiosum et < ... >. Dicere enim bene nemo potest nisi qui prudenter intellegit; quare qui eloquentiae verae dat operam, dat prudentiae, qua ne maximis quidem in bellis aequo animo carere quisquam potest. 25

(24) Praeclare, inquam, Brute, dicis eoque magis ista dicendi laude delector, quod cetera, quae sunt quondam habita in civitate pulcherrima, nemo est tam humilis qui se non aut posse adipisci aut adeptum putet; eloquentem neminem video factum esse victoria. Sed quo facilius sermo explicetur, sedentes, si videtur, agamus. 30

Codd. citt.: FJUOBDEGMSTX

7 potero *S*   8 plane *Wetzel*   12 tractum *FλOᵛB*] tractatum *EMOSTγ*
15 ecquodnam λO] et quodnam *F*: quodnam *OᶜB*   22 res] vis *Müller*   22–23 studiosum. Et *L*: studioso. Et *O²ᵛⁱ*: studioso mei *Orelli*: studioso et <dicendi et intellegendi magistro> *Hoffmann*: studiosum et <optumarum artium cupidum intuenti> *Kroll*: studiosum et <exercitatum audienti> *Friedrich*: studiosum et <doctum et exercitatum intuenti> *vel* <prudenter intuenti> *Amundsen*: studiosum et <dicendi et intellegendi intuenti> *ego*   24 verae *T*] verę *BGM*: vere *FλODES*   27 pulcherrima *J¹BE¹GᶜM*] pulcherrime *FλODESTγ*
29 quod *F*

82 BRUTUS

Cum idem placuisset illis, tum in pratulo propter Platonis statuam consedimus.

(25) Hic ego: Laudare igitur eloquentiam et quanta vis sit eius expromere quantamque iis qui sint eam consecuti dignitatem afferat, neque proposi-
5 tum nobis est hoc loco neque necessarium. Hoc vero sine ulla dubitatione confirmaverim, sive illa arte pariatur aliqua sive exercitatione quadam sive natura, rem unam esse omnium difficillimam. Quibus enim ex quinque rebus constare dicitur, earum una quaeque est ars ipsa magna per sese. Quare quinque artium concursus maximarum quantam vim quantamque
10 difficultatem habeat existimari potest.

(26) Testis est Graecia, quae cum eloquentiae studio sit incensa iamdiuque excellat in ea praestetque ceteris, tamen omnis artis vetustiores habet et multo ante non inventas solum sed etiam perfectas quam haec est a Graecis elaborata dicendi vis atque copia. In quam cum intueor, maxime
15 mihi occurrunt, Attice, et quasi lucent Athenae tuae, qua in urbe primum se orator extulit primumque etiam monumentis et litteris oratio est coepta mandari. (27) Tamen ante Periclem, cuius scripta quaedam feruntur, et Thucydidem, qui non nascentibus Athenis sed iam adultis fuerunt, littera nulla est, quae quidem ornatum aliquem habeat et oratoris esse videatur.
20 Quamquam opinio est et eum, qui multis annis ante hos fuerit, Pisistratum et paulo seniorem etiam Solonem posteaque Clisthenem multum, ut temporibus illis, valuisse dicendo. (28) Post hanc aetatem aliquot annis, ut ex Attici monumentis potest perspici, Themistocles fuit, quem constat cum prudentia tum etiam eloquentia praestitisse; post Pericles, qui cum floreret
25 omni genere virtutis, hac tamen fuit laude clarissimus. Cleonem etiam temporibus illis turbulentum illum quidem civem, sed tamen eloquentem constat fuisse. (29) Huic aetati suppares Alcibiades Critias Theramenes; quibus temporibus quod dicendi genus viguerit ex Thucydidi scriptis, qui ipse tum fuit, intellegi maxime potest. Grandes erant verbis, crebri sententiis,
30 compressione rerum breves et ob eam ipsam causam interdum subobscuri.

(30) Sed ut intellectum est quantam vim haberet accurata et facta quodam modo oratio, tum etiam magistri dicendi multi subito exstiterunt. Tum Leontinus Gorgias, Thrasymachus Calchedonius, Protagoras Abderites,

---

Codd. citt.: FJUOBDEGMSTX

3 laudare *Ff*] laudari *L*   exprimere *D*   4 iis *Ff*] his *L*   6 confirmaverim *J¹ρ*]
conferam veri *FλOᵛ*   illa *λOGᶜ*] ulla *FOᵛᶦβ*   10 habeat *GᶜM*] habeant *FλOBEGMᶜST*
existimare *F*   12 excellat...praestetque *J²BG*] -et...-atque *FλOS*: -at...-atque *DE¹M*:
-et...-etque *ETX*   13–14 a Graecis] *del. Meyer*: ab eis *Piderit*   23 Atticis *θ*
27 Critias *Jᶜ*] Critas *L*   29 crebri *FˣBᶜ*] crebris *L*   33 Abderites *F¹Eᶜ*] Abderitas
Fλβ: Abderita *O*

BRUTUS 83

Prodicus Cius, Hippias Elius in honore magno fuit; aliique multi temporibus isdem docere se profitebantur, arrogantibus sane verbis, quem ad modum causa inferior — ita enim loquebantur — dicendo fieri superior posset. (31) His opposuit sese Socrates, qui subtilitate quadam disputandi refellere eorum instituta solebat †verbis†. Huius ex uberrimis sermonibus 5 exstiterunt doctissimi viri; primumque tum philosophia non illa de natura, quae fuerat antiquior, sed haec, in qua de bonis rebus et malis deque hominum vita et moribus disputatur, inventa dicitur. Quod quoniam genus ab hoc quod proposuimus abhorret, philosophos aliud in tempus reiciamus; ad oratores, a quibus digressi sumus, revertamur.   10

(32) Exstitit igitur iam senibus illis quos paulo ante diximus Isocrates, cuius domus cunctae Graeciae quasi ludus quidam patuit atque officina dicendi, magnus orator et perfectus magister, quamquam forensi luce caruit intraque parietes aluit eam gloriam quam nemo meo quidem iudicio est postea consecutus. Is et ipse scripsit multa praeclare et docuit alios; et cum 15 cetera melius quam superiores, tum primus intellexit etiam in soluta oratione, dum versum effugeres, modum tamen et numerum quendam oportere servari. (33) Ante hunc enim verborum quasi structura et quaedam ad numerum conclusio nulla erat, aut, si quando erat, non apparebat eam dedita opera esse quaesitam — quae forsitan laus sit — verum tamen 20 natura magis tum casuque non numquam, <quam> aut ratione aliqua aut ulla observatione fiebat. (34) Ipsa enim natura circumscriptione quadam verborum comprehendit concluditque sententiam, quae cum aptis constricta verbis est, cadit etiam plerumque numerose. Nam et aures ipsae quid plenum, quid inane sit iudicant et spiritu quasi necessitate aliqua 25 verborum comprehensio terminatur, in quo non modo defici, sed etiam laborare turpe est.

(35) Tum fuit Lysias, ipse quidem in causis forensibus non versatus, sed egregie subtilis scriptor atque elegans, quem iam prope audeas oratorem

---

Codd. citt.: FJUOBDEGMSTX

1 Prodicus *FEMT*] Prodigus λOBG: Prodicgus S   5 verbis] urbanius *Vitelli*: urbanissime *Orelli*: verbis inversis *Ronconi*: acerbius *Marggraff*: versute *Sydow*: usitatis verbis *Simchen*: verbis suis *Ammon*: verba *Pinkster, qui etiam* instituta *ante* refellere *transp.*: del. *Wetzel* 14 quidem meo *UB*   quidem *om. Rufin.* (*D'Alessandro 30.6-19*)   15 postea] poeta *Rufin. codd. pler.*   16 melius] melius est *Rufin.* superiores] superior *Rufin.*   17 effugeret G^c *Rufin.*   21 non numquam quam aut *Ff*^c] non numquam aut *L, Rufin. codd. quidam*: non numquam haud *Rufin. codd. pler.*: non unquam aut τ: nonne quam aut *et tum* fiebat? *Reis*   22 ulla *Rufin.*] *om.* L   23 verborum *del. Schütz* 23–24 constricta *FJO*] constructa *U*: conscripta *DEMST*: circumscripta *Bγ*   25 et *om.* β 28 versatus *FJ²ρ*] versatur λO^v

84 BRUTUS

perfectum dicere. Nam plane quidem perfectum et cui nihil admodum desit
Demosthenem facile dixeris. Nihil acute inveniri potuit in iis causis quas
scripsit, nihil, ut ita dicam, subdole, nihil versute, quod ille non viderit;
nihil subtiliter dici, nihil presse, nihil enucleate, quo fieri possit aliquid
5 limatius; nihil contra grande, nihil incitatum, nihil ornatum vel verborum
gravitate vel sententiarum, quo quicquam esset elatius. (36) Huic
Hyperides proximus et Aeschines fuit et Lycurgus et Dinarchus et is, cuius
nulla exstant scripta, Demades aliique plures. Haec enim aetas effudit hanc
copiam; et, ut opinio mea fert, sucus ille et sanguis incorruptus usque ad
10 hanc aetatem oratorum fuit, in qua naturalis inesset, non fucatus nitor.
(37) Phalereus enim successit iis senibus adulescens eruditissimus ille quidem horum omnium, sed non tam armis institutus quam palaestra. Itaque
delectabat magis Atheniensis quam inflammabat. Processerat enim in solem
et pulverem non ut e militari tabernaculo, sed ut e Theophrasti doctissimi
15 hominis umbraculis. (38) Hic primus inflexit orationem et eam mollem
teneramque reddidit et suavis, sicut fuit, videri maluit quam gravis, sed
suavitate ea qua perfunderet animos, non qua perfringeret, et tantum ut
memoriam concinnitatis suae, non, quem ad modum de Pericle scripsit
Eupolis, cum delectatione aculeos etiam relinqueret in animis eorum a qui-
20 bus esset auditus.
(39) Videsne igitur ut in ea ipsa urbe, in qua et nata et alta sit eloquentia, quam ea sero prodierit in lucem? Si quidem ante Solonis aetatem et
Pisistrati de nullo ut diserto memoriae proditum est. At hi quidem, ut populi Romani aetas est, senes, ut Atheniensium saecula numerantur, adules-
25 centes debent videri. Nam etsi Servio Tullio regnante viguerunt, tamen
multo diutius Athenae iam erant quam est Roma ad hodiernum diem. Nec
tamen dubito quin habuerit vim magnam semper oratio. (40) Neque enim
iam Troicis temporibus tantum laudis in dicendo Ulixi tribuisset Homerus
et Nestori, quorum alterum vim habere voluit, alterum suavitatem, nisi iam
30 tum esset honos eloquentiae; neque ipse poeta hic tam [idem] ornatus in
dicendo ac plane orator fuisset. Cuius etsi incerta sunt tempora, tamen
annis multis fuit ante Romulum, si quidem non infra superiorem Lycurgum
fuit, a quo est disciplina Lacedaemoniorum astricta legibus. (41) Sed

---

Codd. citt.: FJUOBDEGMSTX

1 cui J^2X^{vl}] quo FλOE: in quo $BE^cG^{vl}MSTX$: cui quo *G*   6 esset *L Char. (Gramm. 259.3
Barwick)*] exstet *Stangl*: sit *Ellendt*   10 quo *Reiz*   12 palaestrae *Lambinus*
17 et *del. Manutius*   21 ut] *del. 'alii' (teste Corrado)*: vel *Heusinger*: Brute *Martha*
30 eloquentiae J^2EG^cMS] eloquentia FλOBTγ idem *del. Koch*] valde *Koch*: gravis aut idem
Friedrich

BRUTUS   85

studium eius generis maiorque vis agnoscitur in Pisistrato. Denique hunc
proximo saeculo Themistocles insecutus est, ut apud nos, perantiquus, ut
apud Atheniensis, non ita sane vetus. Fuit enim regnante iam Graeca, nostra autem civitate non ita pridem dominatu regio liberata. Nam bellum
Volscorum illud gravissimum, cui Coriolanus exsul interfuit, eodem fere   5
tempore quo Persarum bellum fuit, similisque fortuna clarorum virorum;
(42) si quidem uterque, cum civis egregius fuisset, populi ingrati pulsus iniuria se ad hostis contulit conatumque iracundiae suae morte sedavit. Nam
etsi aliter apud te est, Attice, de Coriolano, concede tamen ut huic generi
mortis potius adsentiar.   10
    At ille ridens: Tuo vero, inquit, arbitratu, quoniam quidem concessum est
rhetoribus ementiri in historiis ut aliquid dicere possint argutius. Ut enim
tu nunc de Coriolano, sic Clitarchus, sic Stratocles de Themistocle finxit.
(43) Nam quem Thucydides, qui et Atheniensis erat et summo loco natus
summusque vir et paulo aetate posterior, tantum <morbo> mortuum scrip- 15
sit et in Attica clam humatum, addidit fuisse suspicionem veneno sibi cons-
civisse mortem, hunc isti aiunt, cum taurum immolavisset, excepisse
sanguinem patera et eo poto mortuum concidisse. Hanc enim mortem
rhetorice et tragice ornare potuerunt; illa mors vulgaris nullam praebebat
materiem ad ornatum. Quare quoniam tibi ita quadrat omnia fuisse   20
Themistocli paria et Coriolano, pateram quoque a me sumas licet, praebebo
etiam hostiam ut Coriolanus sit plane alter Themistocles.
    (44) Sit sane, inquam, ut libet, de isto; et ego cautius posthac historiam
attingam te audiente, quem rerum Romanarum auctorem laudare possum
religiosissimum. Sed tum fere Pericles Xanthippi filius, de quo ante dixi, 25
primus adhibuit doctrinam; quae quamquam tum nulla erat dicendi, tamen
ab Anaxagora physico eruditus exercitationem mentis a reconditis abstru-
sisque rebus ad causas forensis popularisque facile traduxerat. Huius suavitate maxime hilaratae Athenae sunt, huius ubertatem et copiam admiratae,
eiusdem vim dicendi terroremque timuerunt.   30
    (45) Haec igitur aetas prima Athenis oratorem prope perfectum tulit.
Nec enim in constituentibus rem publicam nec in bella gerentibus nec in
impeditis ac regum dominatione devinctis nasci cupiditas dicendi solet.

Codd. citt.: FJUOBDEGMSTX

3 Graeca *Jahn*] Graecia *L*   15 tantum morbo *Teuffel e Thuc. 1.138.4 (Νοσήσας δὲ*
τελευτᾷ τὸν βίου)] tantum *L*: aegrotantem *Simon*   16 addidit<que> *Kayser*
20 ornandum *Lambinus*   21 Themistocli *E^cM*] Themistocle *FλOBESTγ*: in Themistocle *Ff*
32 in² *FO²*] *om.* λρ   in³ *FODEMSTγ*] *om.* λB

86 BRUTUS

Pacis est comes otique socia et iam bene constitutae civitatis quasi alumna quaedam eloquentia. (46) Itaque ait Aristoteles, cum sublatis in Sicilia tyrannis res privatae longo intervallo iudiciis repeterentur, tum primum, quod esset acuta illa gens et controversiae nata, artem et praecepta Siculos
5 Coracem et Tisiam conscripsisse — nam antea neminem solitum via nec arte, sed accurate tamen et de scripto plerosque dicere —; scriptasque fuisse et paratas a Protagora rerum illustrium disputationes, quae nunc communes appellantur loci. (47) Quod idem fecisse Gorgiam cum singularum rerum laudes vituperationesque conscripsisset, quod iudicaret hoc oratoris
10 esse maxime proprium, rem augere posse laudando vituperandoque rursus affligere. Huic Antiphontem Rhamnusium similia quaedam habuisse conscripta; quo neminem umquam melius ullam oravisse capitis causam, cum se ipse defenderet se audiente, locuples auctor scripsit Thucydides. (48) Nam Lysiam primo profiteri solitum artem esse dicendi; deinde, quod Theodorus
15 esset in arte subtilior, in orationibus autem ieiunior, orationes eum scribere aliis coepisse, artem removisse. Similiter Isocratem primo artem dicendi esse negavisse, scribere autem aliis solitum orationes, quibus in iudiciis uterentur; sed cum ex eo, quia quasi committeret contra legem 'quo quis iudicio circumveniretur', saepe ipse in iudicium vocaretur, orationes aliis destitisse
20 scribere totumque se ad artis componendas transtulisse.

(49) Et Graeciae quidem oratorum partus atque fontis vides, ad nostrorum annalium rationem veteres, ad ipsorum sane recentis. Nam ante quam delectata est Atheniensium civitas hac laude dicendi, multa iam memorabilia et in domesticis et in bellicis rebus effecerat. Hoc autem studium non
25 erat commune Graeciae sed proprium Athenarum. (50) Quis enim aut Argivum oratorem aut Corinthium aut Thebanum scit fuisse temporibus illis? Nisi quid de Epaminonda docto homine suspicari libet. Lacedaemonium vero usque ad hoc tempus audivi fuisse neminem. Menelaum ipsum dulcem illum quidem tradit Homerus, sed pauca dicentem. Brevitas
30 autem laus est interdum in aliqua parte dicendi, in universa eloquentia

---

Codd. citt.: FJUOBDEGMSTX

1 et iam F^c] etiam *L*   2 Sicilia G^c] Siciliam *L*   4 controversiae nata *Marggraff*] controversia natura *L*: controversia nata G^c: controversiae nara *vel* controversiae nara natura *Parker*: controversa natura *Ascensius*: controversiae cupida natura *Harnecker*   6 de scripto $JDE^cMT\gamma$ (descripto *FUOBES*)] descripte *Ho*: discripte *A. Eberhard*   7 quae] qui *Marggraff* (*sed cf. K-S i.38*)   11 Antiphontem *OB*] Antiphoontem $F\Lambda O^vDEMS$ $T\gamma$ 13 se audiente *del. Campe*   16 Isocratem *JOBS* (-en $F^{lmg}EMT$)] Socratem $FU\gamma$ (-en F^l)   18 quo] ne *Reis coll. Clu. 151*: a quo *Jahn*   21 partus atque fetus *Ernesti*: ortus atque fontes *Jahn*   27 licet F^{ac}

BRUTUS 87

laudem non habet. (51) At vero extra Graeciam magna dicendi studia fuerunt maximique huic laudi habiti honores illustre oratorum nomen reddiderunt. Nam ut semel e Piraeo eloquentia evecta est, omnis peragravit insulas atque ita peregrinata tota Asia est ut se externis oblineret moribus omnemque illam salubritatem Atticae dictionis et quasi sanitatem perderet 5 ac loqui paene dedisceret. Hinc Asiatici oratores non contemnendi <illi> quidem nec celeritate nec copia, sed parum pressi et nimis redundantes; Rhodii saniores et Atticorum similiores. (52) Sed de Graecis hactenus; etenim haec ipsa forsitan fuerint non necessaria.

Tum Brutus: Ista vero, inquit, quam necessaria fuerint non facile dixerim; 10 iucunda certe mihi fuerunt neque solum non longa, sed etiam breviora quam vellem.

Optime, inquam; sed veniamus ad nostros, de quibus difficile est plus intellegere quam quantum ex monumentis suspicari licet. (53) Quis enim putet aut celeritatem ingeni L. Bruto illi nobilitatis vestrae principi defuisse? 15 Qui de matre savianda ex oraculo Apollinis tam acute arguteque coniecerit; qui summam prudentiam simulatione stultitiae texerit; qui potentissimum regem clarissimi regis filium expulerit civitatemque perpetuo dominatu liberatam magistratibus annuis legibus iudiciisque devinxerit; qui collegae suo imperium abrogaverit ut e civitate regalis nominis memoriam 20 tolleret; quod certe effici non potuisset nisi esset oratione persuasum. (54) Videmus item paucis annis post reges exactos, cum plebes prope ripam Anienis ad tertium miliarium consedisset eumque montem qui Sacer appellatus est occupavisset, M'. Valerium dictatorem dicendo sedavisse discordias, eique ob eam rem honores amplissimos habitos et eum primum 25 ob eam ipsam causam Maximum esse appellatum. Ne L. Valerium quidem Potitum arbitror non aliquid potuisse dicendo, qui post decemviralem invidiam plebem in patres incitatam legibus et contionibus suis mitigaverit. (55) Possumus Appium Claudium suspicari disertum, quia senatum iamiam inclinatum a Pyrrhi pace revocaverit; possumus C. Fabricium, quia sit ad 30 Pyrrhum de captivis recuperandis missus orator; Ti. Coruncanium, quod ex pontificum commentariis longe plurimum ingenio valuisse videatur; M'.

Codd. citt.: FJUOBDEGMSTX

4 oblineret *vulg.*] optineret *FλBEMTγ* (obt- *ODS*)   6 *add. Lambinus*   9 fuerunt *BD^{ac}G*   15 aut *del. Piderit*   ingeni <aut eloquentiam> *Lambinus*   16 qui *DE^cG^cMS*] quae *FλO^v*: quem *OBETγ*   23 Anienis *O^cE^2*] Aneonis *L*: Anionis *G^c* 24 M'. *scripsi (cf. RE s.v. 'Valerius 243', MRR i.14)*] M. *FλOBX*: M̄. *DEGMT*   32 M'. *Lambinus*] M. *FλOBDEMTX*: M̄. *G*

88 BRUTUS

Curium, quod is tribunus plebis interrege Appio Caeco diserto homine comitia contra leges habente, cum de plebe consulem non accipiebat, patres ante auctores fieri coegerit; quod fuit permagnum nondum lege Maenia lata. (56) Licet aliquid etiam de M. Popilli ingenio suspicari, qui cum consul
5 esset eodemque tempore sacrificium publicum cum laena faceret, quod erat flamen Carmentalis, plebei contra patres concitatione et seditione nuntiata, ut erat laena amictus, ita venit in contionem seditionemque cum auctoritate tum oratione sedavit. Sed eos oratores habitos esse aut omnino tum ullum eloquentiae praemium fuisse nihil sane mihi legisse videor; tantummodo
10 coniectura ducor ad suspicandum. (57) Dicitur etiam C. Flaminius, is qui tribunus plebis legem de agro Gallico et Piceno viritim dividendo tulerit, qui consul apud Tarsumennum sit interfectus, ad populum valuisse dicendo. Q. etiam Maximus Verrucosus orator habitus est temporibus illis et Q. Metellus, is qui bello Punico secundo cum L. Veturio Philone consul fuit.
15 Quem vero exstet et de quo sit memoriae proditum eloquentem fuisse et ita esse habitum, primus est M. Cornelius Cethegus; cuius eloquentiae est auctor et idoneus quidem mea sententia Q. Ennius, praesertim cum et ipse eum audiverit et scribat de mortuo, ex quo nulla suspicio est amicitiae causa esse mentitum. (58) Est igitur sic apud illum in nono, ut opinor, annali:
20 'Additur orator Cornelius suaviloquenti
ore Cethegus Marcus Tuditano collega
Marci filius.'
Et oratorem appellat et suaviloquentiam tribuit, quae nunc quidem non tam est in plerisque — latrant enim iam quidam oratores, non loquuntur —;
25 sed est ea laus eloquentiae certe maxima:
'Is dictus popularibus ollis,
qui tum vivebant homines atque aevum agitabant,
flos delibatus populi' —
(59) probe vero; ut enim hominis decus ingenium, sic ingeni ipsius
30 lumen est eloquentia, qua virum excellentem praeclare tum illi homines florem populi esse dixerunt —

Codd. citt.: FJUOBDEGMSTX

1 appio E^2 (ap. *JB*)] a. P. *FUO (et O^v, ut vid.) DEMSTγ*; inter regea P. O^{2vl} 3 fuit *vulg.*] fuerit *L*   10 Flaminius J^2OE^c (Flamm- F^cUE^{mg})] Flamininus $B^{vl}DEMST\gamma$: Flamininius *J*: Flamineus *B*: Flamminium *F*   15 et^1 *om.* β 21–22 Tuditano collega Marci *Lambinus*] studio collegam *L*   26 dictus popularibus ollis *Merula*] dictus ollis popularibus olim *L*: dictus tollis popularibus olim *Gell. 12.2.3:* dictust ollis popularibus olim *Gronovius*   27 agitabant *Gell.*] agebant *L*   30 est] etiam *F:* et *S*

BRUTUS 89

'Suadai<que> medulla'.

Πειθώ quam vocant Graeci, cuius effector est orator, hanc Suadam appellavit Ennius. Eius autem Cethegum medullam fuisse vult, ut, quam deam in Pericli labris scripsit Eupolis sessitavisse, huius hic medullam nostrum oratorem fuisse dixerit. 5

(60) At hic Cethegus consul cum P. Tuditano fuit bello Punico secundo quaestorque his consulibus M. Cato, modo plane annis CXL ante me consulem; et id ipsum nisi unius esset Enni testimonio cognitum, hunc vetustas, ut alios fortasse multos, oblivione obruisset. Illius autem aetatis qui sermo fuerit ex Naevianis scriptis intellegi potest. His enim consulibus, ut 10 in veteribus commentariis scriptum est, Naevius est mortuus; quamquam Varro noster diligentissimus investigator antiquitatis putat in hoc erratum vitamque Naevi producit longius. Nam Plautus P. Claudio L. Porcio viginti annis post illos quos ante dixi consulibus mortuus est Catone censore.

(61) Hunc igitur Cethegum consecutus est aetate Cato, qui annis IX 15 post eum fuit consul. Eum nos ut perveterem habemus, qui L. Marcio M'. Manilio consulibus mortuus est, annis LXXXVI ipsis ante me consulem. Nec vero habeo quemquam antiquiorem, cuius quidem scripta proferenda putem, nisi quem Appi Caeci oratio haec ipsa de Pyrrho et nonnullae mortuorum laudationes forte delectant. (62) Et hercules hae quidem 20 exstant; ipsae enim familiae sua quasi ornamenta ac monumenta servabant et ad usum, si quis eiusdem generis occidisset, et ad memoriam laudum domesticarum et ad illustrandam nobilitatem suam. Quamquam his laudationibus historia rerum nostrarum est facta mendosior. Multa enim scripta sunt in iis quae facta non sunt: falsi triumphi, plures consulatus, genera 25 etiam falsa et ad plebem transitiones, cum homines humiliores in alienum eiusdem nominis infunderentur genus; ut si ego me a M'. Tullio esse dicerem, qui patricius cum Ser. Sulpicio consul anno x post exactos reges fuit.

(63) Catonis autem orationes non minus multae fere sunt quam Attici Lysiae, cuius arbitror plurimas esse — est enim Atticus, quoniam certe 30 Athenis est et natus et mortuus et functus omni civium munere, quamquam

---

1–7 quaestor- *codd. citt.* FJUOBDEGMSTX | 7 -que – 31 FJUOBDEGMTX

1 Suadaique *Mariotti*] suadat FΛBESTX (sua dat O): suadai F¹ (-ae FˣJˣE²M): suadeat DG: suada *Gell.* 2 Πειθώ *vulg.*] pitho L 4 labris Fˣ] libris L sessitavisse *vulg.*] se sitavisse Uρ: sessitavisse F: se scitavisse J 7 is L, *corr. vulg.* 14 cos. B: consules FΛODEMTγ 15 VIIII FGᶜ: IIIIII UOBEMTγ (VI JUᶜ, sex D) 16 M'. *vulg.*] M. FΛOBDEᶜM: M̄. GT: *om.* EX 17 LXXXVI F¹] LXXXIII L 19 nisi <si> *Manutius* nonnullorum O: non ulle Oᵛ 20 hae quidem *Lambinus*] aequidem JUᶜ (ǫqu- F, equ- β): eae quidem F¹ (eaequidem U, ee quidem O) 27 M'. *vulg.*] M. FΛOBDEX: M̄. GMT

90 BRUTUS

Timaeus eum quasi Licinia et Mucia lege repetit Syracusas — et quodam modo est nonnulla in iis etiam inter ipsos similitudo: acuti sunt, elegantes faceti breves; sed ille Graecus ab omni laude felicior. (64) Habet enim certos sui studiosos, qui non tam habitus corporis opimos quam gracilitates
5 consectentur; quos, valetudo modo bona sit, tenuitas ipsa delectat — quamquam in Lysia sunt saepe etiam lacerti, sic ut eo fieri nihil possit valentius; verum est certe genere toto strigosior — sed habet tamen suos laudatores, qui hac ipsa eius subtilitate admodum gaudeant.

(65) Catonem vero quis nostrorum oratorum, qui quidem nunc sunt,
10 legit? Aut quis novit omnino? At quem virum, di boni! Mitto civem aut senatorem aut imperatorem; oratorem enim hoc loco quaerimus. Quis illo gravior in laudando, acerbior in vituperando, in sententiis argutior, in docendo edisserendoque subtilior? Refertae sunt orationes amplius centum quinquaginta, quas quidem adhuc invenerim et legerim, et verbis et
15 rebus illustribus. Licet ex his eligant ea quae notatione et laude digna sint: omnes oratoriae virtutes in iis reperientur. (66) Iam vero Origines eius quem florem aut quod lumen eloquentiae non habent? Amatores huic desunt, sicuti multis iam ante saeculis et Philisto Syracusio et ipsi Thucydidi. Nam ut horum concisis sententiis, interdum etiam non satis apertis
20 [autem] cum brevitate tum nimio acumine, offecit Theopompus elatione atque altitudine orationis suae — quod idem Lysiae Demosthenes —, sic Catonis luminibus obstruxit haec posteriorum quasi exaggerata altius oratio. (67) Sed ea in nostris inscitia est, quod hi ipsi qui in Graecis antiquitate delectantur eaque subtilitate quam Atticam appellant hanc in
25 Catone ne noverunt quidem. Hyperidae volunt esse et Lysiae. Laudo; sed cur nolunt Catones? (68) Attico genere dicendi se gaudere dicunt: sapienter id quidem, atque utinam imitarentur nec ossa solum sed etiam sanguinem! Gratum est tamen quod volunt. Cur igitur Lysias et Hyperides amatur, cum penitus ignoretur Cato? Antiquior est huius sermo et quaedam
30 horridiora verba. Ita enim tum loquebantur. Id muta, quod tum ille non potuit, et adde numeros et, <ut> aptior sit oratio, ipsa verba compone et

---

Codd. citt.: FJUOBDEGMTX

2 his *U*   3–4 certos sui $F^1J^2\rho$] certo sui λO^v (certosui *F*)   5 delectet *Ernesti, fort. recte*   6 ut eo *Manutius*] ut et *L*: ut *Lambinus*: uti *Stangl*   9 nostrorum *Fλ*] nostrum *ρ*   10 at *ρ*] ad *Fλ*   13 disserendoque *λ*   16 omnes *Rom*] omnis *L*   19 etiam] autem *Martha*   20 autem *del. vulg.*   offecit *Wetzel*] officit *L*   21 quod…Demosthenes *del. Schütz*   22 posteriorum *vulg.*] posterorum *FJU^cρ*: posterum *U*   23 ea *Bake*] et *L*: etiam *Simon*: id *Heusinger*   25 ne *Camerarius*] non *L*   26 Catones *vulg.*] Catonis *L*   31 ut *Ve*] *om. L*

BRUTUS 91

quasi coagmenta, quod ne Graeci quidem veteres factitaverunt: iam neminem antepones Catoni. (69) Ornari orationem Graeci putant si verborum
immutationibus utantur, quos appellant τρόπους, et sententiarum
orationisque formis, quae vocant σχήματα; non veri simile est quam sit in
utroque genere et creber et distinctus Cato. Nec vero ignoro nondum esse 5
satis politum hunc oratorem et quaerendum esse aliquid perfectius, quippe
cum ita sit ad nostrorum temporum rationem vetus ut nullius scriptum
exstet dignum quidem lectione quod sit antiquius. Sed maiore honore in
omnibus artibus quam in hac una arte dicendi versatur antiquitas.

(70) Quis enim eorum qui haec minora animadvertunt non intellegit 10
Canachi signa rigidiora esse quam ut imitentur veritatem? Calamidis dura
illa quidem, sed tamen molliora quam Canachi; nondum Myronis satis ad
veritatem adducta, iam tamen quae non dubites pulchra dicere; pulchriora
etiam Polycliti et iam plane perfecta, ut mihi quidem videri solent.
Similis in pictura ratio est, in qua Zeuxim et Polygnotum et Timanthem 15
et eorum qui non sunt usi plus quam quattuor coloribus formas et linia-
menta laudamus; at in Aetione Nicomacho Protogene Apelle iam perfecta sunt omnia. (71) Et nescio an reliquis in rebus omnibus idem eveniat;
nihil est enim simul et inventum et perfectum; nec dubitari debet quin fuerint ante Homerum poetae, quod ex iis carminibus intellegi potest quae apud 20
illum et in Phaeacum et in procorum epulis canuntur. Quid, nostri veteres
versus ubi sunt,

          'quos olim Fauni vatesque canebant,'
    cum 'neque Musarum scopulos <...>
    nec dicti studiosus' quisquam erat 'ante hunc'?   25
Ait ipse de se nec mentitur in gloriando; sic enim sese res habet. Nam et
Odyssia Latina est [sic in] tamquam opus aliquod Daedali et Livianae
fabulae non satis dignae quae iterum legantur. (72) Atqui hic Livius
[qui] primus fabulam C. Claudio Caeci filio et M. Tuditano consulibus
docuit, anno ipso ante quam natus est Ennius, post Romam conditam 30
autem quarto decimo et quingentesimo, ut hic ait, quem nos sequimur.
Est enim inter scriptores de numero annorum controversia. Accius autem a

---

Codd. citt.: FJUOBDEGMTX

3 tropos *L*   4 schemata *L*   5 creber et *F¹J²*] crebere *FJBDEGT*: crebre
UOE^cMX   9 arte *del. vulg.*   14 etiam *FλO] om. β*: autem *Simon*   et iam *FO^{2vl}*]
etiam *λρ*   15 Zeuxim *FU*] Zeusim *JOEG^cM*: Zeusum *BTγ*   17 Apelle *E*] Appelle
FλOBDMTγ   24 scopulos <quisquam superarat> *Victorius*   24–25 cum *et*
quisquam erat *Ciceroni attrib. Skutsch (1968: 31–34, 119–121)*   25 <docti> dicti *Baehrens*
27 sic in *del. Ellendt*] sic [in] *vulg.*   28 atqui *Pb*] atque *L*   29 qui *del. Schütz*] <est>
qui *Orelli*   Claudio *Rom*] Clodio *L*   30–31 autem conditam *β*

92 BRUTUS

Q. Maximo quintum consule captum Tarento scripsit Livium, annis xxx post quam eum fabulam docuisse et Atticus scribit et nos in antiquis commentariis invenimus; (73) docuisse autem fabulam annis post xi C. Cornelio Q. Minucio consulibus ludis Iuventatis quos Salinator
5 Senensi proelio voverat. In quo tantus error Acci fuit ut his consulibus xl annos natus Ennius fuerit; cui aequalis fuerit Livius: minor fuit aliquanto is qui primus fabulam dedit quam ii qui multas docuerant ante hos consules, et Plautus et Naevius. (74) Haec si minus apta videntur huic sermoni, Brute, Attico adsigna, qui me inflammavit studio illustrium hom-
10 inum aetates et tempora persequendi.

Ego vero, inquit Brutus, et delector ista quasi notatione temporum et ad id quod instituisti, oratorum genera distinguere aetatibus, istam diligentiam esse accommodatam puto.

(75) Recte, inquam, Brute, intellegis. Atque utinam exstarent illa carmina
15 quae multis saeculis ante suam aetatem in epulis esse cantitata a singulis convivis de clarorum virorum laudibus in Originibus scriptum reliquit Cato. Tamen illius, quem in vatibus et Faunis adnumerat Ennius, bellum Punicum quasi Myronis opus delectat. (76) Sit Ennius sane, ut est certe, perfectior; qui si illum, ut simulat, contemneret, non omnia bella perse-
20 quens primum illud Punicum acerrimum bellum reliquisset. Sed ipse dicit cur id faciat. 'Scripsere', inquit, 'alii rem vorsibus' — et luculente quidem scripserunt, etiam si minus quam tu polite. Nec vero tibi aliter videri debet, qui a Naevio vel sumpsisti multa, si fateris, vel, si negas, surripuisti.

(77) Cum hoc Catone grandiores natu fuerunt C. Flaminius C. Varro Q.
25 Maximus Q. Metellus P. Lentulus P. Crassus, qui cum superiore Africano consul fuit. Ipsum Scipionem accepimus non infantem fuisse. Filius quidem eius, is qui hunc minorem Scipionem a Paullo adoptavit, si corpore valuisset, in primis habitus esset disertus; indicant cum oratiunculae tum historia quaedam Graeca scripta dulcissime. (78) <In> numeroque eodem fuit
30 Sex. Aelius, iuris quidem civilis omnium peritissimus, sed etiam ad dicendum paratus.

Codd. citt.: FJUOBDEGMTX

1 consule B^{c}DEG^c] consulem OBMγ: cos. FU (cons. J) captum] capto β: et capto J^2 Tarenti *Ernesti* 2 docuisse et] docuisset F 3 xii *Wetzel* 4 iuventatis Ho] luentatis FλOMTγ: luctantis BE 5 senensi J^{2}Uρ] senesi FJU^{c}O^v voverat FJ^{2}B^{c}E^c] noverat $\lambda\rho$ 6 xxxx FλO: xxx β cui *vulg.*] quod L: cui si *Rom*: quoi ut *Castiglioni:* quoius si *Baehrens* fuerit] fuit *Madvig* 7 ii *vulg.*] hi L 17 tamen] nam *Kroll*: ita me *Weidner* 17–18 bellum Punicum Ff] bello Punicum Fλ: bello Punico U^c: bello Punico eum J$^2\rho$ 28 <quod> indicant *Fuchs* 29 *add. Ammon*

BRUTUS 93

De minoribus autem C. Sulpicius Galus, qui maxime omnium nobilium Graecis litteris studuit; isque et oratorum in numero est habitus et fuit reliquis rebus ornatus atque elegans. Iam enim erat unctior quaedam splendidior<que> consuetudo loquendi. Nam hoc praetore ludos Apollini faciente cum Thyesten fabulam docuisset, Q. Marcio Cn. Servilio 5 consulibus mortem obit Ennius. (79) Erat isdem temporibus Ti. Gracchus P. f., qui bis consul et censor fuit, cuius est oratio Graeca apud Rhodios; quem civem cum gravem tum etiam eloquentem constat fuisse. P. etiam Scipionem Nasicam, qui est Corculum appellatus, qui item bis consul et censor fuit, habitum eloquentem aiunt, illius qui sacra acceperit 10 filium; dicunt etiam L. Lentulum, qui cum C. Figulo consul fuit. Q. Nobiliorem M. f. iam patrio instituto deditum studio litterarum — qui etiam Q. Ennium, qui cum patre eius in Aetolia militaverat, civitate donavit, cum triumvirum coloniam deduxisset — et T. Annium Luscum huius Q. Fulvi collegam non indisertum dicunt fuisse; (80) atque etiam L. Paullus 15 Africani pater personam principis civis facile dicendo tuebatur.

Et vero etiam tum Catone vivo, qui annos quinque et octoginta natus excessit e vita, cum quidem eo ipso anno contra Ser. Galbam ad populum summa contentione dixisset, quam etiam orationem scriptam reliquit — sed vivo Catone minores natu multi uno tempore oratores floruerunt. (81) 20 Nam et A. Albinus, is qui Graece scripsit historiam, qui consul cum L. Lucullo fuit, et litteratus et disertus fuit; et tenuit cum hoc locum quendam etiam Ser. Fulvius et Numerius Fabius Pictor et iuris et litterarum et antiquitatis bene peritus; Quintusque Fabius Labeo fuit ornatus isdem fere laudibus. Nam Q. Metellus, is cuius quattuor filii consulares fuerunt, 25 in primis est habitus eloquens, qui pro L. Cotta dixit accusante Africano; cuius et aliae sunt orationes et contra Ti. Gracchum exposita est in C. Fanni annalibus. (82) Tum ipse L. Cotta est veterator habitus; sed C. Laelius et P. Africanus in primis eloquentes, quorum exstant orationes, ex quibus existimari de ingeniis oratorum potest. Sed inter hos aetate 30

Codd. citt.: FJUOBDEGMTX

1 Gallus *L*   qui *del. Ernesti*   3 unctior] vinctior *Peter.* lautior *Orelli*
4 splendidiorque *B*] splendidior *FλODEMTγ*: et splendidior *Rom*   6 mortem *O²β*]
morte *FλO*   7 qui bis *FˣλO'β*] quibus *FO*   10 eloquentem *vulg.*] eloquentem.
M. L   aiunt *O^{mg}M^c*] aliunt *FλO'β* (*cf. Quint. Inst. 1.4.11*): aũt *J^c*: al [*spat. vac.* VI *litt.*]
O^{ac}   <Idaea> sacra *Stangl*   12 patrio *vulg.*] patre *L*   14 triumvirum] triumvir
Ff   17 et¹ *Lambinus*] at *L*   23 Numerius *Martha*] Nuaserius *FλO'*: Miaserius *O*:
una serius *J²EMTγ*: una ser. *B*   24 Quintusque *ρ*] Quinctusque *FλO'*: Quinctiusque
F¹   Fabius *Ho*] Fabio *L*   25 laudibus *F¹Jρ*] laudidus *FU*   27 <quae> contra
Kayser   28 Cotta est *Fc*] Cottae *L*   30 existimari *J²ρ*] existimare *Fλ*

94 BRUTUS

paulum his antecedens sine controversia Ser. Galba eloquentia praestitit; et nimirum is princeps ex Latinis illa oratorum propria et quasi legitima opera tractavit, ut egrederetur a proposito ornandi causa, ut delectaret animos, ut permoveret, ut augeret rem, ut miserationibus, ut communi-
5 bus locis uteretur. Sed nescio quo modo huius, quem constat eloquentia praestitisse, exiliores orationes sunt et redolentes magis antiquitatem quam aut Laeli <aut> Scipionis aut etiam ipsius Catonis, itaque exaruerunt vix iam ut appareant.

(83) De ipsius Laeli et Scipionis ingenio quamquam ea est fama, ut
10 plurimum tribuatur ambobus, dicendi tamen laus est in Laelio illustrior. At oratio Laeli de collegiis non melior quam de multis quam voles Scipionis; non quo illa Laeli quicquam sit dulcius aut quo de religione dici possit augustius, sed multo tamen vetustior et horridior ille quam Scipio; et cum sint in dicendo variae voluntates, delectari mihi magis antiquitate
15 videtur et libenter verbis etiam uti paulo magis priscis Laelius. (84) Sed est mos hominum ut nolint eundem pluribus rebus excellere. Nam ut ex bellica laude aspirare ad Africanum nemo potest, in qua ipsa egregium Viriathi bello reperimus fuisse Laelium, sic ingeni litterarum eloquentiae sapientiae denique, etsi utrique primas, priores tamen libenter deferunt Laelio.
20 Nec mihi ceterorum iudicio solum videtur, sed etiam ipsorum inter ipsos concessu ita tributum fuisse. (85) Erat omnino tum mos, ut in reliquis rebus melior, sic in hoc ipso humanior, ut faciles essent in suum cuique tribuendo.

Memoria teneo Smyrnae me ex P. Rutilio Rufo audisse, cum diceret adulescentulo se accidisse ut ex senatus consulto P. Scipio et D. Brutus, ut
25 opinor, consules de re atroci magnaque quaererent. Nam cum in silva Sila facta caedes esset notique homines interfecti insimulareturque familia, partim etiam liberi societatis eius quae picarias de P. Cornelio L. Mummio censoribus redemisset, decrevisse senatum ut de ea re cognoscerent et statuerent consules. (86) Causam pro publicanis accurate, ut semper solitus
30 esset, eleganterque dixisse Laelium. Cum consules re audita 'amplius' de consili sententia pronuntiavissent, paucis interpositis diebus iterum

---

Codd. citt.: FJUOBDEGMTX

1 his] iis *Jahn*   4 ut¹ G^c] aut L   ut² FΛBG^c] aut DEMTγ   7 *add. vulg.*   Catonis FJ^cρ] Caπonis O^v: Cationis J: cat–onis U   9 fama *Baiter*] iam L: iam opinio *Rom*   11 collegis L, *corr. vulg.*   12 quo de ΛG^c] quode F: quod e O: quo e β
13 vetustior O²] venustior L   17–18 viriathi bello *Ho* (viriaci bello O^mg)] viri athibet to FUγ (viri athibetto J): viri ahibet to MTX^c: viri adhibet [*spat. vac.* VI *litt.*] O, *add.* to O^v: virum athibet J²: viri habet te E: a hibet to B   19 priores Ff] prioris L   23 smyrnae F¹] myrnae L   25 in silva Sila *Turnebus*] in stivas ita FΛO: istivas ita β: intra stivas ita J²: estivas ita E^c   26 insimularenturque F

BRUTUS 95

Laelium multo diligentius meliusque dixisse iterumque eodem modo a consulibus rem esse prolatam. Tum Laelium, cum eum socii domum reduxis-
sent egissentque gratias et ne defatigaretur oravissent, locutum esse ita: se
quae fecisset honoris eorum causa studiose accurateque fecisse, sed se arbit-
rari causam illam a Ser. Galba, quod is in dicendo adornatior acriorque 5
esset, gravius et vehementius posse defendi. Itaque auctoritate C. Laeli
publicanos causam detulisse ad Galbam; (87) illum autem, quod ei viro
succedendum esset, verecunde et dubitanter recepisse. Unum quasi
comperendinatus medium diem fuisse, quem totum Galbam in consid-
eranda causa componendaque posuisse; et cum cognitionis dies esset et ipse 10
Rutilius rogatu sociorum domum ad Galbam mane venisset ut eum admo-
neret et ad dicendi tempus adduceret, usque illum, quoad ei nuntiatum
esset consules descendisse, omnibus exclusis commentatum in quadam
testudine cum servis litteratis fuisse, quorum <alii> aliud dictare eodem
[a] tempore solitus esset. Interim cum esset ei nuntiatum tempus esse, 15
exisse in aedis eo colore et iis oculis ut egisse causam, non commentatum putares. (88) Addebat etiam, idque ad rem pertinere putabat, scriptores illos male mulcatos exisse cum Galba; ex quo significabat illum non
in agendo solum, sed etiam in meditando vehementem atque incensum
fuisse. Quid multa? Magna exspectatione, plurimis audientibus, coram ipso 20
Laelio sic illam causam tanta vi tantaque gravitate dixisse Galbam ut nulla
fere pars orationis silentio praeteriretur. Itaque multis querelis multaque
miseratione adhibita socios omnibus approbantibus illa disquisitione
liberatos esse.

(89) Ex hac Rutilia<na> narratione suspicari licet, cum duae summae 25
sint in oratore laudes, una subtiliter disputandi ad docendum, altera graviter agendi ad animos audientium permovendos, multoque plus proficiat
is qui inflammet iudicem quam ille qui doceat, elegantiam in Laelio, vim
in Galba fuisse. Quae quidem vis tum maxime cognita est, cum Lusitanis
a Ser. Galba praetore contra interpositam, ut existimabatur, fidem 30

Codd. citt.: FJUOBDEGMTX

5 adornatior *Vc^c, ut vid.*] adortor *F\E*: adhortor *OBE²MTγ*: adhortator *O²*: ornatior *J²*:
ardentior *Corradus*: uberior *Marggraff*: atrocior *Triller*: asperior *Moser*: acerbior *Orelli*: incitatior *Busche*   14 <alii> aliud *Manutius, qui etiam coni.* aliud <alii>   15 a *del. vulg.*]
alii *Reis*   16 colore *J²ρ*] color *F*   his *L, corr. vulg.*   18 mulcatos *F*] mulctatos *β*:
multatos *B^cJ^c*   23 illa disquisitione *scripsi*] illa dis quaestione *F\β*: illa die quaestione *O^c*:
O^{ac} incert., fort. illa die quaestione: illo die quaestione *Lambinus*: illa quaestione *vel* illa de
caede quaestione *Orelli*: illa tandem quaestione *Weidner*   25 Rutiliana *Fp*] Rutilia *FJ²ρ*:
Rutila *λ*: Rutili *Orelli*   29 vis tum *J²*] ut istum *L*   cognita est *F*] cognita st *UO^v*: cognita
sit *J²β*: cognita sunt *J*: cognita [*spat. vac.* IV *litt.*] *O^{ac}*

96 BRUTUS

interfectis L. Libone tribuno plebis populum incitante et rogationem in Galbam privilegi similem ferente, summa senectute, ut ante dixi, M. Cato legem suadens in Galbam multa dixit; quam orationem in Origines suas rettulit, paucis ante quam mortuus est an diebus an mensibus. (90) Tum
5 igitur <nihil> recusans Galba pro sese et populi Romani fidem implorans cum suos pueros tum C. Gali etiam filium flens commendabat, cuius orbitas et fletus mire miserabilis fuit propter recentem memoriam clarissimi patris; isque se tum eripuit flamma, propter pueros misericordia populi commota, sicut idem scriptum reliquit Cato. Atque etiam ipsum Libonem
10 non infantem video fuisse, ut ex orationibus eius intellegi potest.

(91) Cum haec dixissem et paulum interquievissem: Quid igitur, inquit, est causae, Brutus, si tanta virtus in oratore Galba fuit, cur ea nulla in orationibus eius appareat? Quod mirari non possum in iis qui nihil omnino scripti reliquerunt.
15 Nec enim est eadem, inquam, Brute, causa non scribendi et non tam bene scribendi quam dixerint. Nam videmus alios oratores inertia nihil scripsisse, ne domesticus etiam labor accederet ad forensem — pleraeque enim scribuntur orationes habitae iam, non ut habeantur —; (92) alios non laborare ut meliores fiant — nulla enim res tantum ad dicendum proficit
20 quantum scriptio; memoriam autem in posterum ingeni sui non desiderant, cum se putant satis magnam adeptos esse dicendi gloriam eamque etiam maiorem visum iri, si in existimantium arbitrium sua scripta non venerint —; alios, quod melius putent dicere se posse quam scribere, quod peringeniosis hominibus neque satis doctis plerumque contingit, ut ipsi Galbae.
25 (93) Quem fortasse vis non ingeni solum sed etiam animi et naturalis quidam dolor dicentem incendebat efficiebatque ut et incitata et gravis et vehemens esset oratio; dein cum otiosus stilum prehenderat motusque omnis animi tamquam ventus hominem defecerat, flaccescebat oratio. Quod iis qui limatius dicendi consectantur genus accidere non solet,
30 propterea quod prudentia numquam deficit oratorem, qua ille utens eodem modo possit et dicere et scribere; ardor animi non semper adest, isque cum consedit, omnis illa vis et quasi flamma oratoris exstinguitur. (94) Hanc

---

Codd. citt.: FJUOBDEGMTX

1 L. *Corradus*] T. *L*   rogationem ρ] rogatione *F*λ   4 an[1] *del. Pareus, fort. recte*   5 nihil *add. Corradus ex Val. Max. 8.1.absol.2* (reus pro se iam nihil recusans)   6 Galli *L*   13 apparet *L, corr. Lambinus*   23 *lac. post* scribere *fort. statuenda est*   23–24 quod peringeniosis] peringeniosis quidem *Cavarzere*   24 ut] quod *Cavarzere*   28 flaccescebat *G*[c]] flaccesciebat *L*   29 iis *OBDEMTX*] his *F*λ: is *G*

BRUTUS 97

igitur ob causam videtur Laeli mens spirare etiam in scriptis, Galbae autem
vis occidisse.

Fuerunt etiam in oratorum numero mediocrium L. et Sp. Mummii
fratres, quorum exstant amborum orationes; simplex quidem Lucius et
antiquus, Spurius autem nihilo ille quidem ornatior, sed tamen astrictior; 5
fuit enim doctus ex disciplina Stoicorum. Multae sunt Sp. Albini orationes. Sunt etiam L. et C. Aureliorum Orestarum, quos aliquo video in
numero oratorum fuisse. (95) P. etiam Popillius cum civis egregius tum non
indisertus fuit; Gaius vero filius eius disertus. Gaiusque Tuditanus cum
omni vita atque victu excultus atque expolitus, tum eius elegans est habitum 10
etiam orationis genus. Eodemque in genere est habitus is qui iniuria accepta
fregit Ti. Gracchum patientia, civis in rebus optimis constantissimus
M. Octavius.

At vero M. Aemilius Lepidus, qui est Porcina dictus, isdem temporibus
fere quibus Galba sed paulo minor natu, et summus orator est habitus et 15
fuit, ut apparet ex orationibus, scriptor sane bonus. (96) Hoc in oratore
Latino primum mihi videtur et levitas apparuisse illa Graecorum et verborum comprehensio et iam artifex, ut ita dicam, stilus. Hunc studiose duo
adulescentes ingeniosissimi et prope aequales C. Carbo et Ti. Gracchus
audire soliti sunt; de quibus iam dicendi locus erit cum de senioribus pauca 20
dixero. Q. enim Pompeius non contemptus orator temporibus illis fuit, qui
summos honores homo per se cognitus sine ulla commendatione maiorum
est adeptus. (97) Tum L. Cassius multum potuit non eloquentia, sed
dicendo tamen; homo non liberalitate, ut alii, sed ipsa tristitia et severitate
popularis, cuius quidem legi tabellariae M. Antius Briso tribunus plebis diu 25
restitit M. Lepido consule adiuvante; eaque res P. Africano vituperationi
fuit, quod eius auctoritate de sententia deductus Briso putabatur. Tum duo
Caepiones multum clientis consilio et lingua, plus auctoritate tamen et
gratia sublevabant. Sex. Pompei sunt scripta nec nimis extenuata, quamquam veterum est similis, et plena prudentiae. (98) P. Crassum valde proba- 30
tum oratorem isdem fere temporibus accepimus, qui et ingenio valuit et
studio et habuit quasdam etiam domesticas disciplinas. Nam et cum summo

---

Codd. citt.: FJUOBDEGMTX

3 Mummii G^cO^c] Mummi *L* 5 illo λ 6 ex *vulg.*] et *L*: e G^c 7 c. aureliorum *F*] caureliorum λOBD: cauteliorum *EMT*γ 9 Gaiusque FλO^vBE^c] gravisque
J²ODEMγ: griusque *T* 12 civis $FE^{2vl}G^cM$] cuius λOBDETγ 15 minor $J^2E^{2vl}M$]
minus FλOBDETγ 17 levitas *Fλβ*] lenitas *J²O* 18 etiam *L, corr. Faber*
24 liberalitate] hilaritate Ff^1 tristitia $F^1ρ$] tristia Fλ 28 clientes FλO: dicentes β
29 Sex. *Madvig*] sed *L*

98 BRUTUS

illo oratore Ser. Galba, cuius Gaio filio filiam suam collocaverat, affinitate
sese devinxerat et, cum esset P. Muci filius fratremque haberet P. Scaevolam,
domi ius civile cognoverat. In eo industriam constat summam fuisse maxi-
mamque gratiam, cum et consuleretur plurimum et diceret. (99) Horum
5 aetatibus adiuncti duo C. Fannii C. M. filii fuerunt, quorum Gai filius, qui
consul cum Domitio fuit, unam orationem de sociis et nomine Latino contra Gracchum reliquit sane et bonam et nobilem.

Tum Atticus: Quid ergo? Estne ista Fanni? Nam varia opinio pueris nobis
erat: alii a C. Persio litterato homine scriptam esse aiebant, illo quem signifi-
10 cat valde doctum esse Lucilius; alii multos nobilis quod quisque potuisset in
illam orationem contulisse.

(100) Tum ego: Audivi equidem ista, inquam, de maioribus natu, sed
numquam sum adductus ut crederem; eamque suspicionem propter hanc
causam credo fuisse, quod Fannius in mediocribus oratoribus habitus esset,
15 oratio autem vel optima esset illo quidem tempore orationum omnium. Sed
nec eiusmodi est ut a pluribus confusa videatur — unus enim sonus est
totius orationis et idem stilus — nec de Persio reticuisset Gracchus, cum
ei Fannius de Menelao Maratheno et de ceteris obiecisset; praesertim
cum Fannius numquam sit habitus elinguis. Nam et causas defensitavit et
20 tribunatus eius arbitrio et auctoritate P. Africani gestus non obscurus fuit.
(101) Alter autem C. Fannius, M. filius, C. Laeli gener, et moribus et ipso
genere dicendi durior. Is soceri instituto, quem, quia cooptatus in augurum
collegium non erat, non admodum diligebat, praesertim cum ille
Q. Scaevolam sibi minorem natu generum praetulisset — cui tamen Laelius
25 se excusans non genero minori dixit se illud, sed maiori filiae detulisse — is
tamen instituto Laeli Panaetium audiverat. Eius omnis in dicendo facultas
historia ipsius non ineleganter scripta perspici potest, quae neque nimis
est infans neque perfecte diserta. (102) Mucius autem augur quod pro se
opus erat ipse dicebat, ut de pecuniis repetundis contra T. Albucium. Is
30 oratorum in numero non fuit, iuris civilis intellegentia atque omni prudentiae genere praestitit. L. Coelius Antipater scriptor, quem ad modum videtis,
fuit ut temporibus illis luculentus, iuris valde peritus, multorum etiam, ut
L. Crassi, magister.

(103) Utinam in Ti. Graccho Gaioque Carbone talis mens ad rem pub-
35 licam bene gerendam fuisset quale ingenium ad bene dicendum fuit;

Codd. citt.: FJUOBDEGMTX

5 Fannii *G^c*] Fanni *L*   7 <C.> Gracchum *Jahn*   18 ei *Gruter*] et *L*   Menelao
vulg.] Menelauo FΛOE^{c}M: Menelano BETX: Nicolao *J^2*   22 durior is *G^c*] durioris *L*
27 historia *L (cf. Fam. 2.19.1)*] ex historia *Ho*   29 Ti. λ

BRUTUS 99

profecto nemo his viris gloria praestitisset. Sed eorum alter propter turbulentissimum tribunatum, ad quem ex invidia foederis Numantini bonis iratus accesserat, ab ipsa re publica est interfectus; alter propter perpetuam in populari ratione levitatem morte voluntaria se a severitate iudicum vindicavit. Sed fuit uterque summus orator. (104) Atque hoc memoria patrum 5 teste dicimus; nam et Carbonis et Gracchi habemus orationes nondum satis splendidas verbis, sed acutas prudentiaeque plenissimas. Fuit Gracchus diligentia Corneliae matris a puero doctus et Graecis litteris eruditus. Nam semper habuit exquisitos e Graecia magistros, in iis iam adulescens Diophanem Mytilenaeum Graeciae temporibus illis disertissimum. Sed 10 ei breve tempus ingeni augendi et declarandi fuit. (105) Carbo, cui vita suppeditavit, est in multis iudiciis causisque cognitus. Hunc qui audierant prudentes homines, in quibus familiaris noster L. Gellius, qui se illi contubernalem in consulatu fuisse narrabat, canorum oratorem et volubilem et satis acrem atque eundem et vehementem et valde dulcem et perfacetum 15 fuisse dicebat; addebat industrium etiam et diligentem et in exercitationibus commentationibusque multum operae solitum esse ponere. (106) Hic optimus illis temporibus est patronus habitus eoque forum tenente plura fieri iudicia coeperunt. Nam et quaestiones perpetuae hoc adulescente constitutae sunt, quae antea nullae fuerunt; L. enim Piso tribunus plebis 20 legem primus de pecuniis repetundis Censorino et Manilio consulibus tulit — ipse etiam Piso et causas egit et multarum legum aut auctor aut dissuasor fuit, isque et orationes reliquit, quae iam evanuerunt, et annalis sane exiliter scriptos —; et iudicia populi, quibus aderat Carbo, iam magis patronum desiderabant tabella data; quam legem L. Cassius Lepido et Mancino consu- 25 libus tulit.

(107) Vester etiam D. Brutus M. filius, ut ex familiari eius L. Accio poeta sum audire solitus, et dicere non inculte solebat et erat cum litteris Latinis tum etiam Graecis, ut temporibus illis, eruditus. Quae tribuebat idem Accius etiam Q. Maximo L. Paulli nepoti; et vero ante Maximum illum 30 Scipionem, quo duce privato Ti. Gracchus occisus esset, cum omnibus in rebus vehementem tum acrem aiebat in dicendo fuisse. (108) Tum etiam

---

Codd. citt.: FJUOBDEGMTX

6 dicimus *FΛOBDEMγ*] didicimus *B*^x*E*^vl*G*^vl*O*^vl*TX*^vl   10 Diophanem *F*^x] Diaphanem *L* 11 ei *Lambinus*] et *L*   cui *Frotscher*] quo *FUρ*: quo ad *J*: quod *Manutius*   16 dicebant addebant *Lambinus*   17 commentationibusque *Fc*] commendationibusque *FJU*^c*ρ*: commendationibus *U*   29 tribuebat *Lallemand*] tribuerat *L*   31 esset] est *Ho*

100 BRUTUS

P. Lentulus ille princeps ad rem publicam dumtaxat quod opus esset satis habuisse eloquentiae dicitur; isdemque temporibus L. Furius Philus perbene Latine loqui putabatur litteratiusque quam ceteri; P. Scaevola valde prudenter et acute; paulo etiam copiosius nec multo minus prudenter M'.
5 Manilius. Appi Claudi volubilis sed paulo fervidior oratio. Erat in aliquo numero etiam M. Fulvius Flaccus et C. Cato Africani sororis filius, mediocres oratores; etsi Flacci scripta sunt, sed ut studiosi litterarum. Flacci autem aemulus P. Decius fuit non infans ille quidem, sed ut vita sic oratione etiam turbulentus. (109) M. Drusus C. f., qui in tribunatu C. Gracchum col-
10 legam iterum tribunum fregit, vir et oratione gravis et auctoritate; eique proxime adiunctus C. Drusus frater fuit. Tuus etiam gentilis, Brute, M. Pennus facete agitavit in tribunatu C. Gracchum, paulum aetate antecedens. Fuit enim M. Lepido et L. Oreste consulibus quaestor Gracchus, tribunus Pennus, illius Marci filius qui cum Q. Aelio consul fuit;
15 sed is omnia summa sperans aedilicius est mortuus. Nam de T. Flaminino, quem ipse vidi, nihil accepi nisi Latine diligenter locutum.

(110) His adiuncti sunt C. Curio M. Scaurus P. Rutilius C. Gracchus. De Scauro et Rutilio breviter licet dicere, quorum neuter summi oratoris habuit laudem et uterque in multis causis versatus. Erat in quibusdam laudan-
20 dis viris, etiam si maximi ingeni non essent, probabilis tamen industria; quamquam his quidem non omnino ingenium, sed oratorium ingenium defuit. Neque enim refert videre quid dicendum sit, nisi id queas solute et suaviter dicere; ne id quidem satis est, nisi id quod dicitur fit voce vultu motuque conditius. (111) Quid dicam opus esse doctrina? Sine qua etiam si
25 quid bene dicitur adiuvante natura, tamen id, quia fortuito fit, semper paratum esse non potest. In Scauri oratione, sapientis hominis et tecti, gravitas summa et naturalis quaedam inerat auctoritas, non ut causam, sed ut testimonium dicere putares, cum pro reo diceret. (112) Hoc dicendi genus ad patrocinia mediocriter aptum videbatur, ad senatoriam vero sententiam,
30 cuius erat ille princeps, vel maxime; significabat enim non prudentiam

---

Codd. citt.: FJUOBDEGMTX

2 Pilus *L*   3 litteratiusque *FO*] litteratusque λβ   4 M'. *Baiter*] M. FλOBETγ: M̄. *M*   7 sunt <gratiora> *Fuchs*   10 fregit *Pisanus*] fecit FJUᶜOBᶜDEMTγ: febcit *B*: fecerat *U*   vir FλOᵛ] iure ρ   11 etiam FλOᵛ] et ρ   12 facete *Lambinus*] facile *L*: faecem *Carcopino*: facete peregrinos *Martha*   C. Gracchum paulum *vulg.*] paulum C. Gracchum *L*   <ei> aetate *Stangl*   13 M.] L. β   19 et *L* (*cf.* §204)] at *Ernesti*: etsi *Schneider*   versatus <est> *Madvig*   20 probabilis *vulg.*] probabiles FλOBDEMγ: probabille *T*   21 oratorium FλX] oratorum *OBDEGMT*   22 videre *Gᶜ*] videri *L*   26 tecti FλODEMTγ] recti FᶜB, *pler. edd.*

BRUTUS 101

solum, sed, quod maxime rem continebat, fidem. Habebat hoc a natura
ipsa, quod a doctrina non facile posset; quamquam huius quoque ipsius rei,
quem ad modum scis, praecepta sunt. Huius et orationes sunt et tres ad
L. Fufidium libri scripti de vita ipsius acta sane utiles, quos nemo legit; at
Cyri vitam et disciplinam legunt, praeclaram illam quidem, sed neque tam 5
nostris rebus aptam nec [tamen] Scauri laudibus anteponendam. (113)
Ipse etiam Fufidius in aliquo patronorum numero fuit.

Rutilius autem in quodam tristi et severo genere dicendi versatus est. Erat
uterque natura vehemens et acer, itaque cum una consulatum petivis-
sent, non ille solum qui repulsam tulerat accusavit ambitus designatum 10
competitorem, sed Scaurus etiam absolutus Rutilium in iudicium vocavit.
Multaque opera multaque industria Rutilius fuit, quae erat propterea gratior
quod idem magnum munus de iure respondendi sustinebat. (114) Sunt eius
orationes ieiunae; multa praeclara de iure; doctus vir et Graecis litteris
eruditus, Panaeti auditor, prope perfectus in Stoicis; quorum peracutum et 15
artis plenum orationis genus scis tamen esse exile nec satis populari adsen-
sioni accommodatum. Itaque illa, quae propria est huius disciplinae, philosophorum de se ipsorum opinio firma in hoc viro et stabilis inventa est.
(115) Qui cum innocentissimus in iudicium vocatus esset, quo iudicio
convulsam penitus scimus esse rem publicam, cum essent eo tempore elo- 20
quentissimi viri L. Crassus et M. Antonius consulares, eorum adhibere
neutrum voluit. Dixit ipse pro sese et pauca C. Cotta, quod sororis erat filius — et is quidem tamen ut orator, quamquam erat admodum adulescens —
sed Q. Mucius enucleate ille quidem et polite, ut solebat, nequaquam
autem ea vi atque copia quam genus illud iudici et magnitudo causae 25
postulabat.

(116) Habemus igitur in Stoicis oratoribus Rutilium, Scaurum in antiquis; utrumque tamen laudemus, quoniam per illos ne haec quidem in civitate genera hac oratoria laude caruerunt. Volo enim ut in scaena sic etiam in
foro non eos modo laudari qui celeri motu et difficili utantur, sed eos etiam 30
quos statarios appellant, quorum sit illa simplex in agendo veritas, non
molesta. (117) Et quoniam Stoicorum est facta mentio, Q. Aelius Tubero
fuit illo tempore, L. Paulli nepos; nullo in oratorum numero, sed vita severus

---

Codd. citt.: FJUOBDEGMTX

1 continet *Campe*   3 et[1]] etiam *U*   4 acta] lectu *Geel*   6 tamen *om. D*
8 erat *Jahn*] et *L*   9 consolatum *E^{ac}F^{ac}U^{ac}*   14 praeclare *Ernesti*: <et> praeclara
Orelli   15 eruditus *J^c*] eruditi *L*   19 qui cum *vulg.*] qui quam *FJp*: quamquam *U*
24 sed *L*] et *Bake*   27 habeamus *Madvig, fort. recte*: locemus *Friedrich*

102 BRUTUS

et congruens cum ea disciplina quam colebat, paulo etiam durior; qui quidem in triumviratu iudicaverit contra P. Africani avunculi sui testimonium
vacationem augures, quo minus iudiciis operam darent, non habere; sed ut
vita sic oratione durus incultus horridus; itaque honoribus maiorum
5 respondere non potuit. Fuit autem constans civis et fortis et in primis
Graccho molestus, quod indicat Gracchi in eum oratio; sunt etiam in
Gracchum Tuberonis. Is fuit mediocris in dicendo, doctissimus in
disputando.

(118) Tum Brutus: Quam hoc idem in nostris contingere intellego quod
10 in Graecis, ut omnes fere Stoici prudentissimi in disserendo sint et id arte
faciant sintque architecti paene verborum, idem traducti a disputando ad
dicendum inopes reperiantur. Unum excipio Catonem, in quo perfectis-
simo Stoico summam eloquentiam non desiderem; quam exiguam in
Fannio, ne in Rutilio quidem magnam, in Tuberone nullam video fuisse.
15 (119) Et ego: Non, inquam, Brute, sine causa, propterea quod istorum in
dialecticis omnis cura consumitur; vagum illud orationis et fusum et multiplex non adhibetur genus. Tuus autem avunculus, quem ad modum scis,
habet a Stoicis id quod ab illis petendum fuit, sed dicere didicit a dicendi
magistris eorumque more se exercuit. Quod si omnia a philosophis
20 essent petenda, Peripateticorum institutis commodius fingeretur oratio.
(120) Quo magis tuum, Brute, iudicium probo, qui eorum [id est ex vetere
Academia] philosophorum sectam secutus es quorum in doctrina atque
praeceptis disserendi ratio coniungitur cum suavitate dicendi et copia; quamquam ea ipsa Peripateticorum Academicorumque consuetudo in ratione
25 dicendi talis est ut nec perficere oratorem possit ipsa per sese nec sine ea
orator esse perfectus. Nam ut Stoicorum astrictior est oratio aliquantoque
contractior quam aures populi requirunt, sic illorum liberior et latior quam
patitur consuetudo iudiciorum et fori. (121) Quis enim uberior in dicendo
Platone? Iovem sic [ut] aiunt philosophi, si Graece loquatur, loqui. Quis
30 Aristotele nervosior, Theophrasto dulcior? Lectitavisse Platonem studiose,
audivisse etiam Demosthenes dicitur — idque apparet ex genere et grandi-
tate verborum; dicit etiam in quadam epistula hoc ipse de sese — sed et
huius oratio in philosophiam translata pugnacior, ut ita dicam, videatur
et illorum in iudicia pacatior.

Codd. citt.: FJUOBDEGMTX

2 iudicaverit *FUO*] iudicaverat *Jβ*   6 <C.> Graccho *Jahn*   19 more se] mores *F*
20 Peripateticorum   <atque   Academicorum>   *Martha*   21–22 *del.*   *Lambinus*
25 docendi *Martha*   29 sic *Jᶜ*] sicut *FJᵃᶜJ²* *(ut vid.) Uρ*: sic ut illum *Reis*   31 ex] et
FT   33 videatur *Ernesti*] videtur *L*

BRUTUS 103

(122) Nunc reliquorum oratorum aetates, si placet, et gradus persequamur.

Nobis vero, <inquit> Atticus, et vehementer quidem, ut pro Bruto etiam respondeam.

Curio fuit igitur eiusdem aetatis fere sane illustris orator, cuius de inge- 5 nio ex orationibus eius existimari potest; sunt enim et aliae et pro Ser. Fulvio de incestu nobilis oratio. Nobis quidem pueris haec omnium optima putabatur, quae vix iam comparet in hac turba novorum voluminum.

(123) Praeclare, inquit Brutus, teneo qui istam turbam voluminum effecerit. 10

Et ego, inquam, intellego, Brute, quem dicas; certe enim et boni aliquid attulimus iuventuti, magnificentius quam fuerat genus dicendi et ornatius; et nocuimus fortasse, quod veteres orationes post nostras non a me quidem — meis enim illas antepono — sed a plerisque legi sunt desitae.

Me numera, inquit, in plerisque; quamquam video mihi multa legenda 15 iam te auctore quae antea contemnebam.

(124) Atqui haec, inquam, de incestu laudata oratio puerilis est locis multis: de amore, de tormentis, de rumore loci sane inanes, verum tamen nondum tritis nostrorum hominum auribus nec erudita civitate tolerabiles. Scripsit etiam alia nonnulla et multa dixit et illustria et in numero patrono- 20 rum fuit, ut eum mirer, cum et vita suppeditavisset et splendor ei non defuisset, consulem non fuisse.

(125) Sed ecce in manibus vir et praestantissimo ingenio et flagranti studio et doctus a puero C. Gracchus. Noli enim putare quemquam, Brute, pleniorem aut uberiorem ad dicendum fuisse. 25

Et ille: Sic prorsus, inquit, existimo atque istum de superioribus paene solum lego.

Immo plane, inquam, Brute, legas censeo. Damnum enim illius immaturo interitu res Romanae Latinaeque litterae fecerunt. (126) Utinam non tam fratri pietatem quam patriae praestare voluisset! Quam ille facile tali 30 ingenio, diutius si vixisset, vel paternam esset vel avitam gloriam consecutus! Eloquentia quidem nescio an habuisset parem neminem. Grandis est verbis, sapiens sententiis, genere toto gravis. Manus extrema non accessit operibus eius: praeclare inchoata multa, perfecta non plane. Legendus,

Codd. citt.: FJUOBDEGMTX

3 *add. vulg.*   7–8 putabatur *FλOᶜ*] putabantur *ρ*   11 intellego inquam *Schütz:* [inquam] intellego *Friedrich*   15 me numera inquit *Weidner*] enumera inquit *L:* numera inquit me *Ernesti*   20 illustria *Ho*] illustri *L*   28 immo *del. Weidner*

104 BRUTUS

inquam, est hic orator, Brute, si quisquam alius, iuventuti; non enim solum
acuere, sed etiam alere ingenium potest.

(127) Huic successit aetati C. Galba, Servi illius eloquentissimi viri filius, P. Crassi eloquentis et iuris periti gener. Laudabant hunc patres nostri,
5 favebant etiam propter patris memoriam, sed cecidit in cursu. Nam rogatione Mamilia Iugurthinae coniurationis invidia, cum pro sese ipse dixisset, oppressus est. Exstat eius peroratio, qui epilogus dicitur; qui tanto in
honore pueris nobis erat ut eum etiam edisceremus. Hic, qui in collegio
sacerdotum esset, primus post Romam conditam iudicio publico est con-
10 demnatus. (128) P. Scipio, qui est in consulatu mortuus, non multum ille
quidem nec saepe dicebat, sed et Latine loquendo cuivis erat par et omnis
sale facetiisque superabat. Eius collega L. Bestia <a> bonis initiis orsus
tribunatus — nam P. Popillium vi C. Gracchi expulsum sua rogatione resti-
tuit — vir et acer et non indisertus, tristis exitus habuit consulatus. Nam
15 invidiosa lege [Manilia quaestio] C. Galbam sacerdotem et quattuor consu-
laris, L. Bestiam C. Catonem Sp. Albinum civemque praestantissimum
L. Opimium, Gracchi interfectorem, a populo absolutum, cum is contra
populi studium stetisset, Gracchani iudices sustulerunt.

(129) Huius dissimilis in tribunatu reliquaque omni vita civis improbus
20 C. Licinius Nerva non indisertus fuit. C. Fimbria temporibus isdem fere,
sed longius aetate provectus, habitus est sane, ut ita dicam, luculentus
patronus; asper maledicus, genere toto paulo fervidior atque commotior,
diligentia tamen et virtute animi atque vita bonus auctor in senatu; idem
tolerabilis patronus nec rudis in iure civili et cum virtute tum etiam ipso
25 orationis genere liber; cuius orationes pueri legebamus, quas iam reperire
vix possumus. (130) Atque etiam <acri> ingenio et sermone eleganti,
valetudine incommoda C. Sextius Calvinus fuit; qui etsi, cum remiserant
dolores pedum, non deerat in causis, tamen id non saepe faciebat. Itaque
consilio eius cum volebant homines utebantur, patrocinio cum licebat.
30 Isdem temporibus M. Brutus, in quo magnum fuit, Brute,

Codd. citt.: FJUOBDEGMTX

3 C. *vulg.*] P. *L*   Servi   illius   *vulg.*] Servilius *L*   6 Mamilia *Fλ*] Manilia
F²ρ   8 qui in *FJ°ρ*] qu. in *J*: qum *U*: cum *U°*   11 cuivis *FUBEMTγ*] cuius *JOD*
12 *add. Müller*   15 lege *Peter*] lege Manilia quaestio *L*: illa quaestione *Piderit*: lege
Mamilia *Ernesti*: lege Mamilia quaestorium *Kroll*: lege Mamilia quaestio cum esset *Lichtenfeld*
20 C.¹] P. *Martha*   21 luculentus] lutulentus *Jahn*: truculentus *Ernesti*: turbulentus
Ammon   22 patronus *del. Ernesti*   paulo *FOBEM*] pavilo λO′G°T: pavilio γ
24 virtute] veritate *Martha*   26 atque etiam acri *Hendrickson*] atque etiam *FλOBDE*:
atque etam *MTX* (atque e tam *G*): acuto etiam *Kayser*   30 *lac. ante* isdem *stat. Douglas*
in quo] *del. Jahn*: isque non *Reis*

BRUTUS 105

dedecus generi vestro, qui, cum tanto nomine esset patremque optimum virum habuisset et iuris peritissimum, accusationem factitaverit, ut Athenis Lycurgus. Is magistratus non petivit, sed fuit accusator vehemens et molestus, ut facile cerneres naturale quoddam stirpis bonum degeneravisse vitio depravatae voluntatis. (131) Atque eodem tempore accusator de plebe 5 L. Caesulenus fuit, quem ego audivi iam senem, cum ab L. Salevio multam lege Aquilia de <damno> iniuria petivisset. Non fecissem hominis paene infimi mentionem nisi iudicarem qui suspiciosius aut criminosius diceret audivisse me neminem. Doctus etiam Graecis T. Albucius vel potius paene Graecus. Loquor ut opinor; sed licet ex orationibus iudicare. 10 Fuit autem Athenis adulescens, perfectus Epicureus evaserat, minime aptum ad dicendum genus.

(132) Iam Q. Catulus non antiquo illo more, sed hoc nostro, nisi quid fieri potest perfectius, eruditus: multae litterae, summa non vitae solum atque naturae sed orationis etiam comitas, incorrupta quaedam 15 Latini sermonis integritas. Quae perspici cum ex orationibus eius potest tum facillime ex eo libro quem de consulatu et de rebus gestis suis conscriptum molli et Xenophonteo genere sermonis misit ad A. Furium poetam, familiarem suum; qui liber nihilo notior est quam illi tres, de quibus ante dixi, Scauri libri. 20

(133) Tum Brutus: Mihi quidem, inquit, nec iste notus est nec illi; sed haec mea culpa est, numquam enim in manus inciderunt. Nunc autem et a te sumam et conquiram ista posthac curiosius.

Fuit igitur in Catulo sermo Latinus, quae laus dicendi non mediocris ab oratoribus plerisque neglecta est. Nam de sono vocis et suavitate appel- 25 landarum litterarum, quoniam filium cognovisti, noli exspectare quid dicam. Quamquam filius quidem non fuit in oratorum numero, sed non deerat ei tamen in sententia dicenda cum prudentia tum elegans quoddam et eruditum orationis genus. (134) Nec habitus est tamen pater ipse Catulus princeps in numero patronorum; sed erat talis ut, cum quosdam audires qui 30

Codd. citt.: BFJUODEGMTX

1 dedecus *Pa^c*] genus *L*: decus *Pa, Reis*: vulnus *Rom*: caenum *Stangl*   5 de plebe *om. F*
6 ab Lucio *FOγ*] ab lutio *BJ^cU^cEM* (ablutio λ*T*)   Salevio *Badian*] Savelio *L*: Sabellio *vulg.*:
Saufeio *Martha*   7 de damno iniuria *Peter*] de iustitia *L*: de iniuria *Pisanus*: damni iniuria *Hotman*: DC sestertia *Martha*: *del. Friedrich*   9 Albucius *vulg.* (-tius *B*)] Albicius
FJODE (-tius *B^cUD^cMTγ*)   10 paene *L*] plane *Vogel coll. Fin. 1.8, fort. recte*)] loquor
vulg.] loquar *L*   13 nisi] vel si *A. Eberhard*   14 eruditus *ET*] eruditius
BFλOMT^cγ   summa *B^c*] summae *L*   22 <non> mea *Fuchs*   23 ista] ita *B*
24 mediocriter *ρ*

106 BRUTUS

tum erant praestantes, videretur esse inferior, cum autem ipsum audires sine comparatione, non modo contentus esses sed melius non quaereres. (135) Q. Metellus Numidicus et eius collega M. Silanus dicebant de re publica quod esset illis viris et consulari dignitati satis. M. Aurelius
5 Scaurus non saepe dicebat, sed polite; Latine vero in primis est eleganter locutus. Quae laus eadem in A. Albino bene loquendi fuit; nam flamen Albinus etiam in numero est habitus disertorum; Q. etiam Caepio, vir acer et fortis, cui fortuna belli crimini, invidia populi calamitati fuit. (136) Tum etiam C. L. Memmii fuerunt oratores mediocres, accusatores acres
10 atque acerbi; itaque in iudicium capitis multos vocaverunt, pro reis non saepe dixerunt. Sp. Thorius satis valuit in populari genere dicendi, is qui agrum publicum vitiosa et inutili lege vectigali levavit. M. Marcellus Aesernini pater non ille quidem in patronis, sed et in promptis tamen et non inexercitatis ad dicendum fuit, ut filius eius P. Lentulus. (137)
15 L. etiam Cotta praetorius in mediocrium oratorum numero; dicendi non ita multum laude processerat, sed de industria cum verbis tum etiam ipso sono quasi subrustico persequebatur atque imitabatur antiquitatem.

Atque ego et in hoc ipso Cotta et in aliis pluribus intellego me non ita disertos homines et rettulisse in oratorum numerum et relaturum. Est enim
20 propositum colligere eos qui hoc munere in civitate functi sint, ut tenerent oratorum locum; quorum quidem quae fuerit ascensio et quam in omnibus rebus difficilis optimi perfectio atque absolutio ex eo quod dicam existimari potest. (138) Quam multi enim iam oratores commemorati sunt et quam diu in eorum enumeratione versamur, cum tamen spisse atque vix, ut
25 dudum ad Demosthenem et Hyperidem, sic nunc ad Antonium Crassumque pervenimus! Nam ego sic existimo, hos oratores fuisse maximos et in his primum cum Graecorum gloria Latine dicendi copiam aequatam.

(139) Omnia veniebant Antonio in mentem eaque suo quaeque loco, ubi plurimum proficere et valere possent, ut ab imperatore equites pedites levis
30 armatura, sic ab illo in maxime opportunis orationis partibus collocabantur. Erat memoria summa, nulla meditationis suspicio: imparatus semper aggredi ad dicendum videbatur, sed ita erat paratus ut iudices illo dicente non numquam viderentur non satis parati ad cavendum fuisse. (140) Verba

---

Codd. citt.: BFJUODEGMTX

4 esset *B*ρ] essent *F*λ   6 bene loquendi *del. Kayser*   8 cui *B*ᶜ*O*ᵛˡ*M*] qui *BF*λ*ODET*γ   11 Torius *L*   12 vectigali levavit *J*] vectigale levavit *BFJ*ᶜ*U*ρ: vectigali locavit *Willcock*: vectigali vexavit *Seager*: vectigalem levavit *Douglas*: vectigalem liberavit *Lintott*   13 Aesernini *BF*] Aefernini λρ   et *om. VenC*   14 inexercitatus *O*: exercitatis *B*   17 prosequebatur *B*   24 tamen] tandem *Scheving*   27 Gracchorum *F*

BRUTUS 107

ipsa non illa quidem elegantissimo sermone, itaque diligenter loquendi
laude caruit — neque tamen est admodum inquinate locutus — sed illa,
quae propria laus oratoris est in verbis. Nam ipsum Latine loqui est
illud quidem [est], ut paulo ante dixi, in magna laude ponendum, sed
non tam sua sponte quam quod est a plerisque neglectum; non enim tam 5
praeclarum est scire Latine quam turpe nescire, neque tam id mihi oratoris
boni quam civis Romani proprium videtur. Sed tamen Antonius in verbis et
eligendis, neque id ipsum tam leporis causa quam ponderis, et collocandis
et comprehensione devinciendis nihil non ad rationem et tamquam ad
artem dirigebat; verum multo magis hoc idem in sententiarum ornamentis 10
et conformationibus. (141) Quo genere quia praestat omnibus Demosthenes, idcirco a doctis oratorum est princeps iudicatus. Σχήματα enim
quae vocant Graeci, ea maxime ornant oratorem eaque non tam in verbis
pingendis habent pondus quam in illuminandis sententiis. Sed cum haec
magna in Antonio tum actio singularis; quae si partienda est in gestum 15
atque vocem, gestus erat non verba exprimens sed cum sententiis congruens: manus umeri latera supplosio pedis status incessus omnisque motus
cum rebus sententiisque consentiens; vox permanens, verum subrauca
natura. Sed hoc vitium huic uni in bonum convertebat. (142) Habebat
enim flebile quiddam in questionibus aptumque cum ad fidem faciendam 20
tum ad misericordiam commovendam, ut verum videretur in hoc illud
quod Demosthenem ferunt ei qui quaesivisset quid primum esset in
dicendo, actionem, quid secundum, idem, et idem tertium respondisse.
Nulla res magis penetrat in animos eosque fingit format flectit talisque oratores videri facit qualis ipsi se videri volunt. 25

(143) Huic alii parem esse dicebant, alii anteponebant L. Crassum. Illud
quidem certe omnes ita iudicabant, neminem esse qui horum altero utro
patrono cuiusquam ingenium requireret. Equidem quamquam Antonio
tantum tribuo quantum supra dixi, tamen Crasso nihil statuo fieri potuisse
perfectius. Erat summa gravitas, erat cum gravitate iunctus facetiarum et 30
urbanitatis oratorius, non scurrilis lepos; Latine loquendi accurata et sine
molestia diligens elegantia; in disserendo mira explicatio; cum de iure civili,
cum de aequo et bono disputaretur, argumentorum et similitudinum copia.

Codd. citt.: BFJUODEGMTX

2 <non> illa *Kayser*   3 propria *Lambinus*] proprie *L*   est[2] *om. M*[c]   4 *del.*
vulg.   9 comprensione   *La:*   compressione   *L*   13 orationem   *Lambinus*
18 cum...consentiens *del. Bernhardy* rebus *Schütz*] verbis *L*   19 convertebatur *J*[2]
20 in questionibus *BOEG*] in quaestionibus *FJ* (in quę- *UMTX*): *del. Weidner:* in conquestionibus
Lambinus

108 BRUTUS

(144) Nam ut Antonius coniectura movenda aut sedanda suspicione aut excitanda incredibilem vim habebat, sic in interpretando in definiendo in explicanda aequitate nihil erat Crasso copiosius; idque cum saepe alias tum apud centumviros in M. Curi causa cognitum est. (145) Ita enim multa
5 tum contra scriptum pro aequo et bono dixit ut hominem acutissimum Q. Scaevolam et in iure, in quo illa causa vertebatur, paratissimum obrueret argumentorum exemplorumque copia; atque ita tum ab his patronis aequalibus et iam consularibus causa illa dicta est, cum uterque ex contraria parte ius civile defenderet, ut eloquentium iuris peritissimus Crassus,
10 iuris peritorum eloquentissimus Scaevola putaretur.

Qui quidem cum peracutus esset ad excogitandum quid in iure aut in aequo verum aut esset aut non esset, tum verbis erat ad rem cum summa brevitate mirabiliter aptus. (146) Quare sit nobis orator in hoc interpretandi explanandi edisserendi genere mirabilis sic ut simile nihil
15 viderim; in augendo in ornando in refellendo magis existimator metuendus quam admirandus orator. Verum ad Crassum revertamur.

(147) Tum Brutus: Etsi satis, inquit, mihi videbar habere cognitum Scaevolam ex iis rebus quas audiebam saepe ex C. Rutilio, quo utebar propter familiaritatem Scaevolae nostri, tamen ista mihi eius dicendi
20 tanta laus nota non erat; itaque cepi voluptatem tam ornatum virum tamque excellens ingenium fuisse in nostra re publica.

(148) Hic ego: Noli, inquam, Brute, existimare his duobus quicquam fuisse in nostra civitate praestantius. Nam ut paulo ante dixi consultorum alterum disertissimum, disertorum alterum consultissimum fuisse, sic in
25 reliquis rebus ita dissimiles erant inter sese, statuere ut tamen non posses utrius te malles similiorem. Crassus erat elegantium parcissimus, Scaevola parcorum elegantissimus; Crassus in summa comitate habebat etiam severitatis satis, Scaevolae multa in severitate non deerat tamen comitas. (149) Licet omnia hoc modo; sed vereor ne fingi videantur haec ut
30 dicantur a me quodam modo; res se tamen sic habet. Cum omnis virtus sit, ut vestra, Brute, vetus Academia dixit, mediocritas, uterque horum medium

---

Codd. citt.: BFJUODEGMTX

1 aut[1]] et *Ernesti*   2 in[1] *om.* F   4 centum viros in *F[1]M*] c. viros in. *O[2] (O[ac] incert.)*: c. u. in. *ETγ*: c. u. i. n. *Fλ*: c. u. i. ti. *B*   M. *vulg.*] M. *FDEGT*: M̄. BλOMX   8 etiam *L, corr.* *vulg.*   8–9 ius civile ex contraria parte *B*   12 cum *om.* B   13 sit] hic *Kroll*: fuit *Schütz*   14 sic ut λρ] sicut *BF*   16 admirandus *BFλO[v]*] admirabilis ρ   17 inquit *om.* BX   habere *J[2]G[c]*] haberi *L*   18 iis *Ff*] his *L*   utebar *Ff[1]*] utebatur *L*: utebamur *Gebhardt*   18–19 utebatur perfamiliariter Scaevola ut nosti *Bezzenberger*   19 eius *F[x]λρ*] eiusdem *F*: *om.* B   26 elegantium parcissimus *L*] parcissimus elegantium *Gell.* 11.2.4   30 se tamen sic] sed tamen sic se *F*

BRUTUS 109

quiddam volebat sequi; sed ita cadebat ut alter ex alterius laude partem, uterque autem suam totam haberet.

(150) Tum Brutus: Cum ex tua oratione mihi videor, inquit, bene Crassum et Scaevolam cognovisse, tum de te et de Ser. Sulpicio cogitans esse quandam vobis cum illis similitudinem iudico.

Quonam, inquam, istuc modo?

Quia mihi et tu videris, inquit, tantum iuris civilis scire voluisse quantum satis esset oratori, et Servius eloquentiae tantum adsumpsisse ut ius civile facile posset tueri; aetatesque vestrae, ut illorum, nihil aut non fere multum differunt.

(151) Et ego: De me, inquam, dicere nihil est necesse; de Servio autem et tu probe dicis et ego dicam quod sentio. Non enim facile quem dixerim plus studi quam illum et ad dicendum et ad omnis bonarum rerum disciplinas adhibuisse. Nam et in isdem exercitationibus ineunte aetate fuimus et postea una Rhodum ille etiam profectus est quo melior esset et doctior; at inde ut rediit, videtur mihi in secunda arte primus esse maluisse quam in prima secundus. Atque haud scio an par principibus esse potuisset; sed fortasse maluit, id quod est adeptus, longe omnium non eiusdem modo aetatis sed eorum etiam qui fuissent in iure civili esse princeps.

(152) Hic Brutus: Ain tu? inquit. Etiamne Q. Scaevolae Servium nostrum anteponis?

Sic enim, inquam, Brute, existimo, iuris civilis magnum usum et apud Scaevolam et apud multos fuisse, artem in hoc uno; quod numquam effecisset ipsius iuris scientia nisi eam praeterea didicisset artem quae doceret rem universam tribuere in partis, latentem explicare definiendo, obscuram explanare interpretando, ambigua primum videre, deinde distinguere, postremo habere regulam qua vera et falsa iudicarentur et quae quibus propositis essent quaeque non essent consequentia. (153) Hic enim attulit hanc artem omnium artium maximam quasi lucem ad ea quae confuse ab aliis aut respondebantur aut agebantur.

Dialecticam mihi videris dicere, inquit.

Recte, inquam, intellegis; sed adiunxit etiam et litterarum scientiam et loquendi elegantiam, quae ex scriptis eius, quorum similia nulla sunt, facillime perspici potest. (154) Cumque discendi causa duobus peritissimis

---

Codd. citt.: BFJUODEGMTX

4 de[2] *om.* B   9 posset δ] possit *L*   14 in *om.* B   15 una *del. Jahn*
Rhodum ille] Rhodi; nam illo *Madvig*   at *Martha*] et *L*   20 ain] an *B*
26 ambigua *Lambinus*] ambiguam *L*   31 dicere inquit] inquit dicere *EMTX*: dicere *G*
32–33 et eloquendi *O*: eloquendi β   34 discendi BλO²β] dicendi *FO*

110 BRUTUS

operam dedisset, L. Lucilio Balbo C. Aquilio Gallo, Galli hominis acuti et
exercitati promptam et paratam in agendo et in respondendo celeritatem
subtilitate diligentiaque superavit; Balbi docti et eruditi hominis in utraque
re consideratam tarditatem vicit expediendis conficiendisque rebus. Sic et
5 habet quod uterque eorum habuit, et explevit quod utrique defuit. (155)
Itaque ut Crassus mihi videtur sapientius fecisse quam Scaevola — hic enim
causas studiose recipiebat in quibus a Crasso superabatur; ille se consuli
nolebat ne qua in re inferior esset quam Scaevola — sic Servius sapientissime, cum duae civiles artes ac forenses plurimum et laudis haberent et
10 gratiae, perfecit ut altera praestaret omnibus, ex altera tantum adsumeret
quantum esset et ad tuendum ius civile et ad obtinendam consularem dignitatem satis.

(156) Tum Brutus: Ita prorsus, inquit, et antea putabam — audivi enim
nuper eum studiose et frequenter Sami, cum ex eo ius nostrum pontificium,
15 qua ex parte cum iure civili coniunctum esset, vellem cognoscere — et nunc
meum iudicium multo magis confirmo testimonio et iudicio tuo; simul
illud gaudeo, quod et aequalitas vestra et pares honorum gradus et artium
studiorumque quasi finitima vicinitas tantum abest ab obtrectatione
invidia<que>, quae solet lacerare plerosque, uti ea non modo non
20 exulcerare vestram gratiam, sed etiam conciliare videatur. Quali enim te
erga illum perspicio, tali illum in te voluntate iudicioque cognovi. (157)
Itaque doleo et illius consilio et tua voce populum Romanum carere tam
diu; quod cum per se dolendum est tum multo magis consideranti ad quos
ista non translata sint, sed nescio quo pacto devenerint.
25   Hic Atticus: Dixeram, inquit, a principio, de re publica ut sileremus;
itaque faciamus. Nam si isto modo volumus singulas res desiderare, non
modo querendi sed ne lugendi quidem finem reperiemus.

(158) Pergamus ergo, inquam, ad reliqua et institutum ordinem persequamur. Paratus igitur veniebat Crassus, exspectabatur, audiebatur; a prin-
30 cipio statim, quod erat apud eum semper accuratum, exspectatione dignus
videbatur. Non multa iactatio corporis, non inclinatio vocis, nulla inambu-
latio, non crebra supplosio pedis; vehemens et interdum irata et plena
iusti doloris oratio, multae et cum gravitate facetiae; quodque difficile est,

---

Codd. citt.: BFJUODEGMTX

8 nolebat *vulg.*] solebat *L*: sinebat *J*[2]   8–9 sapientissime *J*[2]*O*[2]] apsentissime *BF*[1]λODMT*γ*:
absentissime *FE*   9 <qui> cum *A. Eberhard*: <nam> cum *Weidner*   due *DEM*: duo
*BF*λOT*γ*   16 multo] nullo *F*   19 invidiaque *B*[c]] invidia *B*[1]*F*λ*ρ*: invidie *B*: et invidia
Manutius   macerare *Madvig*   uti *Manutius*] ut in *L*   32 crebro *F*   et interdum]
interdum et *Campe*

BRUTUS 111

idem et perornatus et perbrevis; iam in altercando invenit parem neminem. (159) Versatus est in omni fere genere causarum; mature in locum principum oratorum venit. Accusavit C. Carbonem eloquentissimum hominem admodum adulescens; summam ingeni non laudem modo sed etiam admirationem est consecutus. (160) Defendit postea Liciniam virginem, 5 cum annos XXVII natus esset. In ea ipsa causa fuit eloquentissimus, orationisque eius scriptas quasdam partis reliquit. Voluit adulescens in colonia Narbonensi causae popularis aliquid attingere eamque coloniam, ut fecit, ipse deducere; exstat in eam legem senior, ut ita dicam, quam aetas illa ferebat oratio. Multae deinde causae; sed ita tacitus tribunatus ut, nisi in eo 10 magistratu cenavisset apud praeconem Granium idque nobis bis narravisset Lucilius, tribunum plebis nesciremus fuisse.

(161) Ita prorsus, inquit Brutus; sed ne de Scaevolae quidem tribunatu quicquam audivisse videor et eum collegam Crassi credo fuisse.

Omnibus quidem aliis, inquam, in magistratibus, sed tribunus anno 15 post fuit eoque in rostris sedente suasit Serviliam legem Crassus; nam censuram sine Scaevola gessit; eum enim magistratum nemo umquam Scaevolarum petivit. Sed haec Crassi cum edita oratio est, quam te saepe legisse certo scio, quattuor et triginta tum habebat annos totidemque annis mihi aetate praestabat. Iis enim consulibus eam legem suasit quibus 20 nati sumus, cum ipse esset Q. Caepione consule natus et C. Laelio, triennio ipso minor quam Antonius. Quod idcirco posui, ut dicendi Latine prima maturitas in qua aetate exstitisset posset notari et intellegeretur iam ad summum paene esse perductam, ut eo nihil ferme quisquam addere posset nisi qui a philosophia a iure civili ab historia fuisset instructior. 25

(162) Erit, inquit [M.] Brutus, aut iam est iste quem exspectas?

Nescio, inquam. Sed est etiam L. Crassi in consulatu pro Q. Caepione defensiuncula, non brevis ut laudatio, ut oratio autem brevis; postrema censoris oratio, qua anno duodequinquagesimo usus est. In his omnibus inest quidam sine ullo fuco veritatis color; quin etiam comprehensio et 30 ambitus ille verborum, si sic περίοδον appellari placet, erat apud illum

---

Codd. citt.: BFJUODEGMTX

3 C. *om.* B   6 ipsa *om.* B   9 extat in eam B^cJρ: extat ineam U: exta tineam B: statineam F: extatineam F^1   11 bis *om.* O   13 quidem *om.* F   15 in *om.* B   19 tum] dum F   20 iis *Corradus*] his BFλODMTγ: hiis E   21 consule *om.* B   26 *del. Heusinger*   28 defensiuncula *Lange*] defensione iuncta L: laudatio cum defensione iuncta *Petersen*: defensione senatus iuncta *Sydow*: oratiuncula *Murgia*: defensio *Piderit*   29 his BFλOE] iis DMTγ   31 perhiodorum L, *corr. vulg.*

112 BRUTUS

contractus et brevis, et in membra quaedam, quae κῶλα Graeci vocant, dispertiebat orationem libentius.

(163) Hoc loco Brutus: Quando quidem tu istos oratores, inquit, tanto opere laudas, vellem aliquid Antonio praeter illum de ratione dicendi
5 sane exilem libellum, plura Crasso libuisset scribere; cum enim omnibus memoriam sui tum etiam disciplinam dicendi nobis reliquissent. Nam Scaevolae dicendi elegantiam satis ex iis orationibus quas reliquit habemus cognitam.

(164) Et ego: Mihi quidem a pueritia quasi magistra fuit, inquam, illa in
10 legem Caepionis oratio; in qua et auctoritas ornatur senatus, quo pro ordine illa dicuntur, et invidia concitatur in iudicum et in accusatorum factionem, contra quorum potentiam populariter tum dicendum fuit. Multa in illa oratione graviter, multa leniter, multa aspere, multa facete dicta sunt; plura etiam dicta quam scripta, quod ex quibusdam capitibus expositis nec
15 explicatis intellegi potest. Ipsa illa censoria contra Cn. Domitium collegam non est oratio, sed quasi capita rerum et orationis commentarium paulo plenius; nulla est enim altercatio clamoribus umquam habita maioribus. (165) Et vero fuit in hoc etiam popularis dictio excellens; Antoni genus dicendi multo aptius iudiciis quam contionibus.
20 Hoc loco ipsum Domitium non relinquo. Nam etsi non fuit in oratorum numero, tamen pone satis in eo fuisse orationis atque ingeni quo et magistratus personam et consularem dignitatem tueretur. Quod idem de C. Coelio dixerim, industriam in eo summam fuisse summasque virtutes, eloquentiae tantum quod esset in rebus privatis amicis eius, in re publica
25 ipsius dignitati satis. (166) Eodem tempore M. Herennius in mediocribus oratoribus Latine et diligenter loquentibus numeratus est; qui tamen summa nobilitate hominem, cognatione sodalitate collegio, summa etiam eloquentia, L. Philippum in consulatus petitione superavit. Eodem tempore C. Claudius, etsi propter summam nobilitatem et singularem
30 potentiam magnus erat, tamen etiam eloquentiae quandam mediocritatem afferebat. (167) Eiusdem fere temporis fuit eques Romanus C. Titius, qui

---

Codd. citt.: BFJUODEGMTX

1 cola BFλβ: colla O   2 dispertiebat M] dispertibat BFλODETγ   orationem F] oratione Bλρ   4 ratione Bλρ] oratione F   5 Crasso] Crasso quoque DEM   7 ex iis Ff] ex his BFλO: om. β   11 iudicum BF°JU°OE°MTX] iudicium FUEG   in² BFλO²] om. ρ   13 leviter EGTᶜ   15 Cn.] G. B   21 pono BM   23 Coelio FU] Caelio J: Cęlio BMTγ: Celio ODE   25 dignitati BᶜUᶜOᶜDMTγ] dignitatis BFλOE   26 Latine<que> Stangl   29 Claudius Meyer] Clodius L   29–30 potentiam] prudentiam Campe

BRUTUS 113

meo iudicio eo pervenisse videtur quo potuit fere Latinus orator sine
Graecis litteris et sine multo usu pervenire. Huius orationes tantum argutiarum, tantum leporum, tantum urbanitatis habent ut paene Attico stilo
scriptae esse videantur. Easdem argutias in tragoedias satis ille quidem
acute, sed parum tragice transtulit. Quem studebat imitari L. Afranius 5
poeta, homo perargutus, in fabulis quidem etiam, ut scitis, disertus. (168)
Fuit etiam Q. Rubrius Varro, qui a senatu hostis cum C. Mario iudicatus est,
acer et vehemens accusator, in eo genere sane probabilis. Doctus autem
Graecis litteris propinquus noster, factus ad dicendum, M. Gratidius
M. Antoni perfamiliaris, cuius praefectus cum esset in Cilicia est interfec- 10
tus, qui accusavit C. Fimbriam, M. Mari Gratidiani pater.

(169) Atque etiam apud socios et Latinos oratores habiti sunt Q. Vettius
Vettianus e Marsis, quem ipse cognovi, prudens vir et in dicendo brevis;
Q. D. Valerii Sorani, vicini et familiares mei, non tam in dicendo admira-
biles quam docti et Graecis litteris et Latinis; C. Rusticelius Bononiensis, 15
is quidem et exercitatus et natura volubilis; omnium autem eloquentissimus extra hanc urbem T. Betutius Barrus Asculanus, cuius sunt aliquot
orationes Asculi habitae, illa Romae contra Caepionem nobilis sane,
cui orationi Caepionis ore respondit Aelius, qui scriptitavit orationes multis, orator ipse numquam fuit. (170) Apud maiores autem nostros video 20
disertissimum habitum ex Latio L. Papirium Fregellanum Ti. Gracchi P.
f. fere aetate; eius etiam oratio est pro Fregellanis colonisque Latinis habita
in senatu.

Tum Brutus: Quid tu igitur, inquit, tribuis istis externis quasi oratoribus?

Quid censes, inquam, nisi idem quod urbanis? Praeter unum, quod non 25
est eorum urbanitate quadam quasi colorata oratio.

(171) Et Brutus: Qui est, inquit, iste tandem urbanitatis color?

Nescio, inquam; tantum esse quendam scio. Id tu, Brute, iam intelleges,
cum in Galliam veneris. Audies tu quidem etiam verba quaedam non trita
Romae, sed haec mutari dediscique possunt; illud est maius, quod in voci- 30
bus nostrorum oratorum retinnit quiddam et resonat urbanius. Nec hoc in

---

Codd. citt.: BFJUODEGMTX

3 leporum *Simon*] exemplorum *L*   9 M *om. ρ*   11 pater *vulg.*] patrem *BF¹λρ*:
patem *F*   14 Valerii *om. B*   15 Rusticellus *L, corr. vulg.*   16 et¹ *Bρ*] *om. F*λ
18 illa] et illa *Bake*: una *Madvig*   19 cui *vulg.*] quo *L*   orationi *del. Martha*   <L.>
Aelius *Stangl*   21 Ti. *vulg.*] T. *L*   P.] Ti. *Ellendt*   22 etiam] autem *B*
coloniisque *Corradus*   24 inquit *om. β*   29 tu (*cf. Tusc. 3.82*)] tum *Weidner, pler.*
edd. post eum: ibi *Koch*   31 retinnit *Ff*] retinuit *F*λρ: recinuit *B*: recinit *Fd^c*

114 BRUTUS

oratoribus modo apparet, sed etiam in ceteris. (172) Ego memini
T. Tincam Placentinum hominem facetissimum cum familiari nostro
Q. Granio praecone dicacitate certare.
Eon', inquit Brutus, de quo multa Lucilius?
5   Isto ipso. Sed Tincam non minus multa ridicule dicentem Granius
obruebat nescio quo sapore vernaculo; ut ego iam non mirer illud
Theophrasto accidisse, quod dicitur, cum percontaretur ex anicula quadam
quanti aliquid venderet et respondisset illa atque addidisset, 'hospes, non
pote minoris', tulisse eum moleste se non effugere hospitis speciem, cum
10   aetatem ageret Athenis optimeque loqueretur omnium. Sic, ut opinor, in
nostris est quidam urbanorum, sicut illic Atticorum sonus. Sed domum
redeamus, id est ad nostros revertamur.
     (173) Duobus igitur summis Crasso et Antonio L. Philippus proximus
accedebat, sed longo intervallo tamen proximus. Itaque eum, etsi nemo
15   intercedebat qui se illi anteferret, neque secundum tamen neque tertium
dixerim. Nec enim in quadrigis eum secundum numeraverim aut tertium
qui vix e carceribus exierit cum palmam iam primus acceperit, nec in oratoribus qui tantum absit a primo vix ut in eodem curriculo esse videatur.
Sed tamen erant ea in Philippo quae, qui sine comparatione illorum spec-
20   taret, satis magna diceret: summa libertas in oratione, multae facetiae; satis
creber in reperiendis, solutus in explicandis sententiis; erat etiam in primis,
ut temporibus illis, Graecis doctrinis institutus; in altercando cum aliquo
aculeo et maledicto facetus.
     (174) Horum aetati prope coniunctus L. Gellius, non tam vendibilis ora-
25   tor quam ut nescires quid ei deesset. Nec enim erat indoctus nec tardus
ad excogitandum nec Romanarum rerum immemor et verbis solutus
satis; sed in magnos oratores inciderat eius aetas. Multam tamen operam
amicis et utilem praebuit, atque ita diu vixit ut multarum aetatum oratoribus implicaretur. (175) Multum etiam in causis versabatur isdem fere
30   temporibus D. Brutus, is qui consul cum Mamerco fuit, homo et Graecis
doctus litteris et Latinis. Dicebat etiam L. Scipio non imperite, Gnaeusque
Pompeius Sex. f. aliquem numerum obtinebat. Nam Sex. frater eius

---

Codd. citt.: BFJUODEGMTX

2 Tincam] Tingam *Badian ex Quint. Inst. 1.5.12*   5 multa *om. D*   9 cum *Fdᶜ*]
quom *BF*: quō *BˡᵐᵍJDEM*: quo modo *UOT*γ   10 loqueretur. Omnino *Rivius*   ut
del. Orelli   11 illic] ille *F*: illis *G*   12 id…revertamur *del. Lambinus*   17–18 ora-
toribus] cursoribus *Klotz*   25 quam ut] quamvis *Jeep, pler. edd.*   26 Romanarum
del. Douglas   29 implicaretur, multum…versaretur. Isdem *L, corr. Kayser*
32 aliquem *vulg.*] at quem *BFJ*ρ: et quem *U*

BRUTUS 115

praestantissimum ingenium contulerat ad summam iuris civilis et ad perfectam geometriae rerum<que> Stoicarum scientiam. Item in iure
<eminuer>at ante hos M. Brutus, et paulo post eum C. Billienus, homo
per se magnus, simili ratione prope summus evaserat; qui consul factus
esset nisi in Marianos consulatus et in eas petitionis angustias incidisset. 5
(176) Cn. autem Octavi eloquentia, quae fuerat ante consulatum ignorata,
in consulatu multis contionibus est vehementer probata. Sed ab iis, qui tantum in dicentium numero, non in oratorum fuerunt, iam ad oratores
revertamur.

Censeo, inquit Atticus; eloquentis enim videbare, non sedulos velle 10
conquirere.

(177) Festivitate igitur et facetiis, inquam, C. Iulius L. f. et superioribus et
aequalibus suis omnibus praestitit oratorque fuit minime ille quidem vehemens, sed nemo umquam urbanitate, nemo lepore, nemo suavitate conditior.
Sunt eius aliquot orationes, ex quibus, sicut ex eiusdem tragoediis, lenitas 15
eius sine nervis perspici potest. (178) Eius aequalis P. Cethegus, cui de re
publica satis suppeditabat oratio — totam enim tenebat eam penitusque
cognoverat; itaque in senatu consularium auctoritatem adsequebatur —
sed in causis publicis nihil, privatis satis veterator videbatur. Erat
in privatis causis Q. Lucretius Vispillo et acutus et iuris peritus; nam 20
Afella contionibus aptior quam iudiciis. Prudens etiam T. Annius Velina et
in eius generis causis orator sane tolerabilis. In eodem genere causarum
multum erat T. Iuventius, nimis ille quidem lentus in dicendo et paene
frigidus, sed et callidus et in capiendo adversario versutus et praeterea nec
indoctus et magna cum iuris civilis intellegentia. (179) Cuius auditor 25
P. Orbius meus fere aequalis in dicendo non nimis exercitatus, in iure autem
civili non inferior quam magister fuit. Nam T. Aufidius, qui vixit ad summam senectutem, volebat esse similis horum eratque et bonus vir et inno-
cens, sed dicebat parum; nec sane plus frater eius M. Verginius, qui
tribunus plebis L. Sullae imperatori diem dixit. Eius collega P. Magius in 30

Codd. citt.: BFJUODEGMTX

1–2 perfectam *EM*] perfectum BFλODTγ   2 rerumque *Fc*] rerum *L*: et rerum *vulg.*   item
in iure *UE^c*] itam in iure *BJU^{c}O^{c}O^{v}γ*: [*spat. vac.* v *litt.*] in iure *O^{ac}*: ita m iniure *F*: sitam in iure
DEM   3 eminuerat *Prohasel*] et *L*; pro itam in iure et *(L) Reis coniec.* ita eminuerat inter
aequalis in iure ut   4 simili ratione prope *Schütz*] prope simili ratione *L*: prope sine ulla
oratione *Bake*   15 levitas *E*   19 <in> privatis *Rom*   erat *Fc*] erant *L*
20 Vespillo *Manutius*   21 Afella *Heraeus*] a filia *L*: Ofella *Pisanus*   23 multum (*cf.
Caes. BGall. 4.1.8)*] multus *vulg.*: multarum *Jahn*   T. D] T. i. FλO^v: Ti. BOEMTγ:
C. Douglas   25 cum (*cf. Att. 8.11B.1)*] cum antiquitatis memoria tum *Stangl (alii alia
suppl.)*: comprobatus *Reis*   29 plus *om.* B   Verginius *Corradus ex Plut. Sull. 10.4*]
Vergilius *Bλρ, fort. recte*: Virgilius *F*

116 BRUTUS

dicendo paulo tamen copiosior. (180) Sed omnium oratorum sive rabularum, qui et plane indocti et inurbani aut rustici etiam fuerunt, quos quidem ego cognoverim, solutissimum in dicendo et acutissimum iudico nostri ordinis Q. Sertorium, equestris C. Gargonium. Fuit etiam facilis et
5 expeditus ad dicendum et vitae splendore multo et ingenio sane probabili T. Iunius L. f. tribunicius, quo accusante P. Sextius praetor designatus damnatus est ambitus; is processisset honoribus longius nisi semper infirma atque etiam aegra valetudine fuisset.

(181) Atque ego praeclare intellego me in eorum commemoratione ver-
10 sari qui nec habiti sint oratores neque fuerint, praeteririque a me aliquot ex veteribus commemoratione aut laude dignos. Sed hoc quidem ignoratione: quid enim est [superioris aetatis] quod scribi possit de iis, de quibus nulla monumenta loquuntur nec aliorum nec ipsorum? De his autem quos ipsi vidimus neminem fere praetermittimus eorum quos aliquando dicentis
15 audivimus. (182) Volo enim sciri in tanta et tam vetere re publica maximis praemiis eloquentiae propositis omnis cupisse dicere, non plurimos ausos esse, potuisse paucos. Ego tamen ita de uno quoque dicam ut intellegi possit quem existimem clamatorem, quem oratorem fuisse.

Isdem fere temporibus aetate inferiores paulo quam Iulius, sed aequales
20 propemodum fuerunt C. Cotta P. Sulpicius Q. Varius Cn. Pomponius C. Curio L. Fufius M. Drusus P. Antistius; nec ulla aetate uberior oratorum fetus fuit. (183) Ex his Cotta et Sulpicius cum meo iudicio tum omnium facile primas tulerunt.

Hic Atticus: Quo modo istuc dicis, inquit, cum tuo iudicio tum omnium?
25 Semperne in oratore probando aut improbando vulgi iudicium cum intellegentium iudicio congruit, an alii probantur multitudini, alii autem ab iis qui intellegunt?

Recte requiris, inquam, Attice; sed audies ex me fortasse quod non omnes probent.
30 (184) An tu, inquit, id laboras, si huic modo Bruto probaturus es?

Codd. citt.: BFJUODEGMTX

1 dicendo <par> *Watt*   2 et...et   *PbWf*]   et...aut   *L:*   aut...et   *Heusinger*
6 Sextius *BFOEγ*] Sestius *λDM:* Sesertius *T*   12 superioris aetatis *del. Kayser] post* ignoratione *transp. Mommsen*   scribi *L*] sciri *A. Eberhard*   iis *BJρ*] his *FU*   15 audivimus
Ruhnken] vidimus *L*   sciri *vulg.*] scire *L*   15–16 vetere. p. haec *L*   20 Pomponius]
Pompeius *UD*   21 P. Antistius *Gᶜ*] Patistius *BFλOᵛβ:* Pasticius *O*   26 multitudini
Ströbel coll. §184] multitudine *L:* a multitudine *Ff*   iis *Ff*] his *BFλODMTγ:* hiis *E*
27 qui] qui me *F*   30 laboras si *Manutius*] laborasse *L*

BRUTUS 117

Plane, inquam, Attice, disputationem hanc de oratore probando aut improbando multo malim tibi et Bruto placere, eloquentiam autem meam populo probari velim. Etenim necesse est, qui ita dicat ut a multitudine probetur, eundem doctis probari. Nam quid in dicendo rectum sit aut pravum ego iudicabo, si modo is sum qui id possim aut sciam iudicare; 5 qualis vero sit orator ex eo quod is dicendo efficiet poterit intellegi. (185) Tria sunt enim, ut quidem ego sentio, quae sint efficienda dicendo: ut doceatur is apud quem dicetur, ut delectetur, ut moveatur vehementius. Quibus virtutibus oratoris horum quidque efficiatur aut quibus vitiis orator aut non adsequatur haec aut etiam in his labatur et cadat, artifex aliquis 10 iudicabit. Efficiatur autem ab oratore necne ut ii qui audiunt ita afficiantur ut orator velit, vulgi adsensu et populari approbatione iudicari solet. Itaque numquam de bono oratore aut non bono doctis hominibus cum populo dissensio fuit.

(186) An censes, dum illi viguerunt quos ante dixi, non eosdem gradus 15 oratorum vulgi iudicio et doctorum fuisse? De populo si quem ita rogavisses, 'Quis est in hac civitate eloquentissimus?', in Antonio et Crasso aut dubitaret aut hunc alius, illum alius diceret. Nemone Philippum, tam suavem oratorem tam gravem tam facetum, his anteferret, quem nosmet ipsi, qui haec arte aliqua volumus expendere, proximum illis fuisse diximus? Nemo profecto; id enim ipsum est summi oratoris, summum oratorem populo videri. (187) Quare tibicen Antigenidas dixerit sane discipulo frigenti ad populum, 'Mihi cane et Musis'; ego huic Bruto dicenti, ut solet, apud multitudinem, 'Mihi cane et populo, mi Brute', dixerim, ut qui audient quid efficiatur, ego etiam cur id efficiatur intellegam. 25 Credit iis quae dicuntur qui audit oratorem, vera putat, adsentitur, probat; fidem facit oratio: (188) tu artifex, quid quaeris amplius? Delectatur audiens multitudo et ducitur oratione et quasi voluptate quadam perfunditur: quid habes quod disputes? Gaudet dolet, ridet plorat, favet odit, contemnit invidet, ad misericordiam inducitur ad pudendum ad pigendum, 30 irascitur mitigatur, sperat timet; haec perinde accidunt ut eorum qui adsunt mentes verbis et sententiis et actione tractantur: quid est quod exspectetur

---

Codd. citt.: BFJUODEGMTX

5 parvum $U^{ac}\beta$ 6 is] ipse *Weidner*   8 dicetur] dicatur *A. Eberhard*
9 oratoriis *Stangl*   horum *om. F*   11 ii *Ff*] hi *L*   ita *om. B*   22 tibi cenanti
genidas *ρ*: tibicen altigenidas *O^c*   22–23 sane discipulo *Madvig*] discipulo sane *L*   23 frigenti]
strigenti *B*: fugienti *U^{ac}*   25 id *om. B*   26 iis *vulg.*] his *L*   30 pudendum]
puniendum *Vassis*   31 mitigatur *Schütz coll. Orat. 131*] miratur *L*

118 BRUTUS

docti alicuius sententia? Quod enim probat multitudo, hoc idem doctis probandum est. Denique hoc specimen est popularis iudici, in quo numquam fuit populo cum doctis intellegentibusque dissensio: (189) cum multi essent oratores in vario genere dicendi, quis umquam ex his excellere
5 iudicatus est vulgi iudicio, qui non idem a doctis probaretur? Quando autem dubium fuisset apud patres nostros eligendi cui patroni daretur optio, quin aut Antonium optaret aut Crassum? Aderant multi alii; tamen utrum de his potius dubitasset aliquis, quin alterum nemo. Quid? Adulescentibus nobis cum esset Cotta et Hortensius, num quis, cui quidem
10 eligendi potestas esset, quemquam his anteponebat?

(190) Tum Brutus: Quid tu, inquit, quaeris alios? De te ipso nonne quid optarent rei, quid ipse Hortensius iudicaret videbamus? Qui cum partiretur tecum causas — saepe enim interfui —, perorandi locum, ubi plurimum pollet oratio, semper tibi relinquebat.
15 Faciebat ille quidem, inquam, et mihi benevolentia, credo, ductus tribuebat omnia. Sed ego quae de me populi sit opinio nescio; de reliquis hoc affirmo, qui vulgi opinione disertissimi habiti sint, eosdem intellegentium quoque iudicio fuisse probatissimos. (191) Nec enim posset idem Demosthenes dicere quod dixisse Antimachum clarum poetam ferunt; qui
20 cum convocatis auditoribus legeret iis magnum illud, quod novistis, volumen suum et eum legentem omnes praeter Platonem reliquissent, 'Legam', inquit, 'nihilo minus. Plato enim mihi unus instar est omnium milium.' Et recte; poema enim reconditum paucorum approbationem, oratio popularis adsensum vulgi debet movere. At si eundem hunc Platonem unum
25 auditorem haberet Demosthenes, cum esset relictus a ceteris, verbum facere non posset. (192) Quid tu, Brute? Possesne, si te ut Curionem quondam contio reliquisset?

Ego vero, inquit ille, ut me tibi indicem, in iis etiam causis in quibus omnis res nobis cum iudicibus est, non cum populo, tamen si a corona rel-
30 ictus sim, non queam dicere.

Ita se, inquam, res habet. Ut, si tibiae inflatae non referant sonum, abiciendas eas sibi tibicen putet, sic oratori populi aures tamquam tibiae

---

Codd. citt.: BFJUODEGMTX

2–3 in...dissensio *del.* A. *Eberhard*   4 his] is F^{ac} 7 aderant] at erant *Ernesti*   9 cui *vulg.*] quo L   12 optarent] opinarentur *Watt*   22 omnium millium *'alii' (teste Corrado)*: omnium me illum L: omnium ne illum J²: omnium. *Merito Rom*: centum milium *Orelli coll. Att. 2.5.1, pler. edd.*: omnium illorum *Turnebus*: milium *Jahn*: hominum milium *Lennep*   24 movere B^c] moveri BFλO^vβ: mereri O   26 possesne si *vulg.*] posses nisi L: posses si B^cO^c 28 in iis] meis F

BRUTUS 119

sunt; eae si inflatum non recipiunt, aut si auditor omnino tamquam equus non facit, agitandi finis faciendus est. (193) Hoc tamen interest, quod vulgus interdum non probandum oratorem probat, sed probat sine comparatione: cum a mediocri aut etiam malo delectatur, eo est contentus; esse melius non sentit; illud quod est, qualecumque est, probat. Tenet enim 5 auris vel mediocris orator, sit modo aliquid in eo; nec res ulla plus apud animos hominum quam ordo et ornatus orationis valet.

(194) Quare quis ex populo, cum Q. Scaevolam pro M. Coponio dicentem audiret in ea causa de qua ante dixi, quicquam politius aut elegantius aut omnino melius aut exspectaret aut posse fieri putaret? (195) Cum is hoc 10 probare vellet, M'. Curium, cum ita heres institutus esset, 'si pupillus ante mortuus esset quam in suam tutelam venisset', pupillo non nato heredem esse non posse, quid ille non dixit de testamentorum iure, de antiquis formulis? Quem ad modum scribi oportuisset, si etiam filio non nato heres institueretur; (196) quam captiosum esse populo quod scriptum esset neg- 15 legi et opinione quaeri voluntates et interpretatione disertorum scripta simplicium hominum pervertere. (197) Quam ille multa de auctoritate patris sui, qui semper ius illud esse defenderat? Quam omnino multa de conservando iure civili? Quae quidem omnia cum perite et scienter, cum item breviter et presse et satis ornate et pereleganter diceret, quis esset in 20 populo qui aut exspectaret aut fieri posse quicquam melius putaret?

At vero, ut contra Crassus ab adulescente delicato, qui in litore ambulans scalmum repperisset ob eamque rem aedificare navem concupivisset, exorsus est, similiter Scaevolam ex uno scalmo captionis centumvirale iudicium hereditatis effecisse; hoc [in illo] initio, consecutis multis eiusdem 25 generis sententiis delectavit animos[que] omnium qui aderant <et> in hilaritatem a severitate traduxit; quod est unum ex tribus quae dixi ab oratore effici debere. Deinde hoc voluisse eum qui testamentum fecisset, hoc sensisse, quoquo modo filius non esset qui in suam tutelam veniret, sive non natus sive ante mortuus, Curius heres ut esset; ita scribere plerosque et 30 id valere et valuisse semper. Haec et multa eius modi dicens fidem faciebat;

Codd. citt.: BFJUODEGMTX

2 <ad obsequium> non *Reis:* non <ad iussa> *Fuchs*   4 malo] a malo *Fm*   delectetur ρ   9 audisset B^{ac} 10 fieri posse *GO*   11 M'. *vulg.*] M. FλOETγ: M̄. *BM* 17 simplicium $B^1U^cβ$] simplicum FλO: simplicu B^{ac}, *ut vid.*   19 conservando *om.* B   19–20 cum item *Reis*] tum ita *L, def. Ellendt:* tum *Friedrich:* item *Haupt:* sumpta *Martha:* inventa *Douglas*   21 aut exspectaret aut *del. Jahn*   25 in illo *del. Douglas*] ille *Rom*   initium *Douglas*   consecutis Bλρ] consecutus FJ^2: constituto *Jahn*   26 delectavit <iudices> *Fuchs*   animos...aderant <et> *Madvig*   29 venisset B

120 BRUTUS

quod est ex tribus oratoris officiis alterum. (198) Deinde aequum bonum, testamentorum sententias voluntatesque tutatus est: quanta esset in verbis captio cum in ceteris rebus tum in testamentis, si neglegerentur voluntates; quantam sibi potentiam Scaevola adsumeret, si nemo auderet testamentum
5 facere postea nisi de illius sententia. Haec cum graviter tum ab exemplis copiose, tum varie, tum etiam ridicule et facete explicans eam admirationem adsensionemque commovit, dixisse ut contra nemo videretur; hoc erat oratoris officium partitione tertium, genere maximum. Hic ille de populo iudex, qui separatim alterum admiratus esset, idem audito altero iudicium
10 suum contemneret; at vero intellegens et doctus audiens Scaevolam sentiret esse quoddam uberius dicendi genus et ornatius. Ab utroque autem causa perorata si quaereretur uter praestaret orator, numquam profecto sapientis iudicium a iudicio vulgi discreparet.

(199) Qui praestat igitur intellegens imperito? Magna re et difficili; si
15 quidem magnum est scire quibus rebus efficiatur amittaturve dicendo illud, quicquid est, quod aut effici dicendo oportet aut amitti non oportet. Praestat etiam illo doctus auditor indocto, quod saepe, cum oratores duo aut plures populi iudicio probantur, quod dicendi genus optimum sit intellegit. Nam illud quod populo non probatur, ne intellegenti quidem auditori
20 probari potest. Ut enim ex nervorum sono in fidibus quam scienter ii pulsi sint intellegi solet, sic ex animorum motu cernitur quid tractandis his perficiat orator. (200) Itaque intellegens dicendi existimator non adsidens et attente audiens, sed uno aspectu et praeteriens de oratore saepe iudicat. Videt oscitantem iudicem, loquentem cum altero, non numquam etiam cir-
25 culantem, mittentem ad horas, quaesitorem ut dimittat rogantem: intellegit [oratorem] in ea causa non adesse qui possit animis iudicum admovere orationem tamquam fidibus manum. Idem si praeteriens aspexerit erectos intuentis iudices, ut aut doceri de re idque etiam vultu probare videantur, aut ut avem cantu aliquo sic illos viderit oratione quasi suspensos teneri,
30 aut, id quod maxime opus est, misericordia odio motu animi aliquo perturbatos esse vehementius — ea si praeteriens, ut dixi, aspexerit, si nihil audiverit, tamen oratorem versari in illo iudicio et opus oratorium fieri aut perfectum iam esse profecto intelleget.

Codd. citt.: BFJUODEGMTX

1 ex Bλβ] *om. FO*   5 tum *vulg.*] cum *L*   6 facete *vulg. (cf. De or. 1.243)]* facile
L   11 sentires *F*   15 dicendo] in dicendo *Friedrich: del. Kraffert*   16 dicendo
del. Meyer   26 *del. Weidner*   28 aut *del. Martha*   30 quod] cum *F: om. D*
31 si²] etiamsi *Fuchs*

BRUTUS 121

(201) Cum haec disseruissem, uterque adsensus est, et ego tamquam de integro ordiens: Quando igitur, inquam, a Cotta et Sulpicio haec omnis fluxit oratio, cum hos maxime iudicio illorum hominum et illius aetatis dixissem probatos, revertar ad eos ipsos; tum reliquos, ut institui, deinceps persequar. Quoniam ergo oratorum bonorum — hos enim quaerimus — 5 duo genera sunt, unum attenuate presseque, alterum sublate ampleque dicentium, etsi id melius est quod splendidius et magnificentius, tamen in bonis omnia quae summa sunt iure laudantur. (202) Sed cavenda est presso illi oratori inopia et ieiunitas, amplo autem inflatum et corruptum orationis genus. Inveniebat igitur acute Cotta, dicebat pure ac solute; et ut ad infirmi- 10 tatem laterum perscienter contentionem omnem remiserat, sic ad virium imbecillitatem dicendi accommodabat genus. Nihil erat in eius oratione nisi sincerum, nihil nisi siccum atque sanum; illudque maximum, quod, cum contentione orationis flectere animos iudicum vix posset nec omnino eo genere diceret, tractando tamen impellebat ut idem facerent a se commoti 15 quod a Sulpicio concitati. (203) Fuit enim Sulpicius vel maxime <omnium>, quos quidem ego audiverim, grandis et, ut ita dicam, tragicus orator: vox cum magna tum suavis et splendida; gestus et motus corporis ita venustus ut tamen ad forum, non ad scaenam institutus videretur; incitata et volubi- lis nec ea redundans tamen nec circumfluens oratio. Crassum hic volebat 20 imitari, Cotta malebat Antonium; sed ab hoc vis aberat Antoni, Crassi ab illo lepos.

(204) O magnam, inquit, artem, Brutus, si quidem istis, cum summi essent oratores, duae res maximae altera alteri defuit.

Atque in his oratoribus illud animadvertendum est, posse esse sum- 25 mos qui inter se sint dissimiles. Nihil enim tam dissimile quam Cotta Sulpicio, et uterque aequalibus suis plurimum praestitit. Quare hoc docto- ris intellegentis est videre, quo ferat natura sua quemque, et ea duce utentem sic instituere, ut Isocratem in acerrimo ingenio Theopompi et lenissimo Ephori dixisse traditum est, alteri se calcaria adhibere, alteri 30 frenos. (205) Sulpici orationes quae feruntur, eas post mortem eius scrip- sisse P. Cannutius putatur aequalis meus, homo extra nostrum ordinem

---

Codd. citt.: BFJUODEGMTX

3 iudicio…aetatis] cum meo iudicio tum omnium illius aetatis *A. Eberhard coll. §183*: et meo iudicio et omnium ex illius aetatis oratoribus *Jahn*: iudicio omnium hominum illius aeta- tis *Piderit*   5 hos] quos *F*   16 omnium *Ff*] *om. L (recte, ut cens. Martha)*: *ante* vel *add.* B^2 21 malebat *om. M*   25 illud <inquam> *Weidner*   est *om. B*   27 et] at *Lambinus*   29–30 et lenissimo $BF\lambda O^vDMT\gamma$] Edenissimo *O*: et levissimo *E*: et lentis- simo *Vogel ex Quint. Inst. 2.8.11*

122 BRUTUS

meo iudicio disertissimus. Ipsius Sulpici nulla oratio est, saepeque ex eo audivi, cum se scribere neque consuesse neque posse diceret. Cottae pro se lege Varia quae inscribitur, eam L. Aelius scripsit Cottae rogatu. Fuit is omnino vir egregius et eques Romanus cum primis honestus idemque eru-
5 ditissimus et Graecis litteris et Latinis, antiquitatisque nostrae et in inventis rebus et in actis scriptorumque veterum litterate peritus. Quam scientiam Varro noster acceptam ab illo auctamque per sese, vir ingenio praestans omnique doctrina, pluribus et illustrioribus litteris explicavit. (206) Sed idem Aelius Stoicus <esse> voluit, orator autem nec studuit umquam nec
10 fuit. Scribebat tamen orationes quas alii dicerent, ut Q. Metello <...> f., ut Q. Caepioni, ut Q. Pompeio Rufo; quamquam is etiam ipse scripsit eas quibus pro se est usus, sed non sine Aelio. (207) His enim scribendis etiam ipse interfui, cum essem apud Aelium adulescens eumque audire perstudi-ose solerem. Cottam autem miror summum ipsum oratorem minimeque
15 ineptum Aelianas levis oratiunculas voluisse existimari suas.

His duobus eiusdem aetatis adnumerabatur nemo tertius, sed mihi place-bat Pomponius maxime, vel dicam, minime displicebat. Locus erat omnino in maximis causis praeter eos de quibus supra dixi nemini, propterea quod Antonius, qui maxime expetebatur, facilis in causis recipiendis erat; fastidi-
20 osior Crassus, sed tamen recipiebat. Horum qui neutrum habebat, confu-giebat ad Philippum fere aut ad Caesarem; Cotta Sulpicius<que rarius> expetebantur. Ita ab his sex patronis causae illustres agebantur; neque tam multa quam nostra aetate iudicia fiebant, neque hoc quod nunc fit, ut causae singulae defenderentur a pluribus, quo nihil est vitiosius. (208)
25 Respondemus iis quos non audivimus: in quo primum saepe aliter est dic-tum, aliter ad nos relatum; deinde magni interest coram videre me quem ad modum adversarius de quaque re adseveret, maxime autem quem ad modum quaeque res audiatur. Sed nihil vitiosius quam, cum unum corpus debeat esse defensionis, nasci de integro causam cum sit ab altero perorata.
30 (209) Omnium enim causarum unum est naturale principium, una perora-tio; reliquae partes quasi membra suo quaeque loco locata suam et vim et

Codd. citt.: BFJUODEGMTX

9 Stoicus esse *vulg.*] Stoicus *L:* Stoicum se *Stangl*   10 alii *Fρ*] ali *Bλ*   *lac. stat. Jahn*] <Q.> *Badian:* <Balearici> *Lambinus:* <L.> *Martha:* <Pio> *Douglas*   11 Cepioni *DEM:* Caepione *BFJU^cOγ:* Scipione *U*   12 scribendis *'alii' (teste Corrado)]* scriptis *BFJO^vβ:* scripsitis *U^1:* scripsit eas quibus pro se est usus *U, ut vid.: om. O:* scribentibus *Kraffert* 18 praeter] propter *O^ac*   21 Cotta Sulpiciusque rarius *Reis*] Cotta Sulpicius *L:* Cotta et Sulpicius *Ff:* Cotta tum et Sulpicius *Malcovati:* dein Cotta et Sulpicius *ego:* rarius Cotta et Sulpicius *A. Eberhard:* parum Cotta et Sulpicius *Sauppe*   25 iis *B*] his *FλODMTγ:* hiis *E* 31 loco *BFλO^2*] *om. ρ*

BRUTUS 123

dignitatem tenent. Cum autem difficile sit in longa oratione non aliquando aliquid ita dicere ut sibi ipse non conveniat, quanto difficilius cavere ne quid dicas quod non conveniat eius orationi qui ante te dixerit? Sed quia et labor multo maior est totam causam quam partem dicere, et quia plures ineuntur gratiae si uno tempore dicas pro pluribus, idcirco hanc consue- 5 tudinem libenter adscivimus.

(210) Erant tamen quibus videretur illius aetatis tertius Curio, quia splendidioribus fortasse verbis utebatur et quia Latine non pessime loquebatur usu, credo, aliquo domestico; nam litterarum admodum nihil sciebat. Sed magni interest quos quisque audiat cotidie domi, quibuscum loquatur a 10 puero, quem ad modum patres paedagogi matres etiam loquantur. (211) Legimus epistulas Corneliae matris Gracchorum: apparet filios non tam in gremio educatos quam in sermone matris. Auditus est nobis Laeliae C. f. saepe sermo; ergo illam patris elegantia tinctam vidimus et filias eius Mucias ambas, quarum sermo mihi fuit notus, et neptis Licinias, quas nos 15 quidem ambas, hanc vero Scipionis etiam tu, Brute, credo, aliquando audisti loquentem.

Ego vero ac libenter quidem, inquit Brutus; et eo libentius, quod L. Crassi erat filia.

(212) Quid Crassum, inquam, illum censes istius Liciniae filium, Crassi 20 testamento qui fuit adoptatus?

Summo iste quidem dicitur ingenio fuisse, inquit, et vero hic Scipio collega meus mihi sane bene et loqui videtur et dicere.

Recte, inquam, iudicas, Brute. Etenim istius genus est ex ipsius sapientiae stirpe generatum. Nam et de duobus avis iam diximus, Scipione et Crasso, et 25 de tribus proavis, Q. Metello, cuius quattuor <illi> filii, P. Scipione, qui ex dominatu Ti. Gracchi privatus in libertatem rem publicam vindicavit, Q. Scaevola augure, qui peritissimus iuris idemque percomis est habitus. (213) Iam duorum abavorum quam est illustre nomen P. Scipionis, qui bis consul fuit, qui est Corculum dictus, alterius omnium sapientissimi, C. Laeli! 30

O generosam, inquit, stirpem et, tamquam in unam arborem plura genera, sic in istam domum multorum insitam atque †inluminatam† sapientiam!

Codd. citt.: BFJUODEGMTX

2 sibi ipsum non conveniat *Lambinus*: tibi ipse non convenias *Ernesti*   13 in¹ *om. F*
C. BλO'β] *om. FO*   18 quidem *om. B*   23 bene et *BFJ'U*] et bene *Jρ*
26 illi filii *Jahn*] filii *L*: filii consulares *Orelli*   27 Ti. *om. F*   32 atque inluminatam
del. Kayser   inluminatam *FU* (ill- *BJOEMTWγ*)] illuminatum *D (ut vid.)* Q: inseminatam
Koch, fort. recte: illigatam *Ernesti*: inoculatam *Schütz*: innatam *Cuiaccius*

124 BRUTUS

Similiter igitur suspicor, ut conferamus parva magnis, Curionis, etsi pupillus relictus est, patrio fuisse instituto puro sermone adsuefactam domum; et eo magis hoc iudico, quod neminem, ex iis quidem qui aliquo in numero fuerunt, cognovi in omni genere honestarum artium tam indoc-
5 tum tam rudem. (214) Nullum ille poetam noverat, nullum legerat oratorem, nullam memoriam antiquitatis collegerat, non publicum ius, non privatum et civile cognoverat. Quamquam id quidem fuit etiam in aliis et magnis quidem oratoribus, quos parum his instructos artibus vidimus, ut Sulpicium, ut Antonium. Sed ii tamen unum illud habebant dicendi opus
10 elaboratum; idque cum constaret ex quinque notissimis partibus, nemo in aliqua parte earum omnino nihil poterat; in quacumque enim una plane clauderet, orator esse non posset; sed tamen alius in alia excellebat magis. (215) Reperiebat quid dici opus esset et quo modo praeparari et quo loco locari, memoriaque ea comprehendebat Antonius; excellebat autem actione.
15 Erant ei quaedam ex his paria cum Crasso, quaedam etiam superiora; at Crassi magis nitebat oratio. Nec vero Sulpicio neque Cottae dicere possumus neque cuiquam bono oratori rem ullam ex illis quinque partibus plane atque omnino defuisse.

(216) Itaque in Curione hoc verissime iudicari potest, nulla re una magis
20 oratorem commendari quam verborum splendore et copia. Nam cum tardus in cogitando tum in instruendo dissipatus fuit. Reliqua duo sunt, agere et meminisse: in utroque cachinnos irri<sionemque au>dientium commovebat. Motus erat is quem et C. Iulius in perpetuum notavit, cum ex eo in utramque partem toto corpore vacillante quaesivit quis loqueretur
25 e luntre, et Cn. Sicinius, homo impurus sed admodum ridiculus — neque aliud in eo oratoris simile quicquam. (217) Is cum tribunus plebis Curionem et Octavium consules produxisset Curioque multa dixisset sedente Cn. Octavio collega, qui devinctus erat fasciis et multis medicamentis propter dolorem artuum delibutus, 'numquam', inquit, 'Octavi, collegae tuo
30 gratiam referes; qui nisi se suo more iactavisset, hodie te istic muscae comedissent.' Memoria autem ita fuit nulla ut aliquotiens, tria cum proposuisset,

---

Codd. citt.: BFJUODEGMTX

1 igitur <inquam> *Stangl*   3 iis *Ff*] his BFλODMTγ: hiis *E*   7 id] hic *F*
9 tamen] tantum *U*   12 claudicaret *F^{mg}J²*: claudicet *O²*   13 praeparari *vulg.*]
praeparare *L*: apparari *Campe*   15 erant] erantque *F*   his] is *F*   17 rem *del.*
Lambinus   21 instruendo] struendo *F*   22 irrisionemque audientium *scripsi*] irridentium *L*   24–25 quis in luntre loqueretur *Quint. Inst. 11.3.129*   24 loqueretur
Quint.] loquetur *L*   25 eluntre *B (ut vid.)* FO^{2vl}GQTW: cluntre λO^{ac}O^vEX *(ut vid.)*: cliviter *J²*:
elucubre *M*: in luntre *Quint.*   26 oratori *F*   30 gratias *B*

BRUTUS   125

aut quartum adderet aut tertium quaereret; qui in iudicio privato vel
maximo, cum ego pro Titinia Cottae peroravissem, ille contra me pro
Ser. Naevio diceret, subito totam causam oblitus est idque veneficiis et
cantionibus Titiniae factum esse dicebat. (218) Magna haec immemoris
ingeni signa; sed nihil turpius quam quod etiam in scriptis obliviscebatur   5
quid paulo ante posuisset; ut in eo libro, ubi se exeuntem ex senatu et cum
Pansa nostro et cum Curione filio colloquentem facit, cum senatum Caesar
consul habuisset, omnisque ille sermo ductus e percontatione fili quid in
senatu esset actum. In quo multis verbis cum inveheretur in Caesarem
Curio disputatioque esset inter eos, ut est consuetudo dialogorum, cum   10
sermo esset institutus senatu misso, quem senatum Caesar consul habuisset, reprehendit eas res quas idem Caesar anno post et deinceps reliquis
annis administravisset in Gallia.

(219) Tum Brutus admirans: Tantamne fuisse oblivionem, inquit, in
scripto praesertim, ut ne legens quidem umquam senserit quantum flagiti   15
commisisset?

Quid autem, inquam, Brute, stultius quam, si ea vituperare volebat quae
vituperavit, non eo tempore instituere sermonem, cum illarum rerum iam
tempora praeterissent? Sed ita totus errat ut in eodem sermone dicat in
senatum se Caesare consule non accedere, sed id dicat ipso consule exiens   20
e senatu. Iam qui hac parte animi, quae custos est ceterarum ingeni par-
tium, tam debilis esset ut ne in scripto quidem meminisset quid paulo ante
posuisset, huic minime mirum est ex tempore dicenti solitam effluere
mentem. (220) Itaque cum ei nec officium deesset et flagraret studio
dicendi, perpaucae ad eum causae deferebantur. Orator autem, vivis eius   25
aequalibus, proximus optimis numerabatur propter verborum bonitatem,
ut ante dixi, et expeditam ac profluentem quodam modo celeritatem. Itaque
eius orationes aspiciendas tamen censeo. Sunt illae quidem languidiores,
verum tamen possunt augere et quasi alere id bonum quod in illo mediocriter fuisse concedimus, quod habet tantam vim ut solum sine aliis in   30
Curione speciem oratoris alicuius effecerit. Sed ad instituta redeamus.

(221) In eodem igitur numero eiusdem aetatis C. Carbo fuit, illius eloquentissimi viri filius, non satis acutus orator; sed tamen orator numeratus est.

1–5 ingeni *codd. citt.* BFJUODEGMTX | 5 signa – 33 *exstat* C

3 Sex. *Corradus*   6 ex U] e C^2 *(in ras.* II *litt.),* BFJρ   7–8 cum²...habuisset *del.*
Ernesti   8 ductus C] ductus est M*i*: ductus esset *Lambinus*: ducitur *vulg.*   13 adminis-
travit *Stangl*   18 vituperavit BFλρ] vitiperavit C   20 senatum F*f*] senatu C   sed
C] et Mo^vl   28 orationes BFλρ] oratones C*c*: C^{ac} *incert., fort.* oratores   33 <is>
non *Jahn*

126 BRUTUS

Erat in verbis gravitas et facile dicebat et auctoritatem naturalem quandam habebat oratio. Acutior Q. Varius rebus inveniendis nec minus verbis expeditus. Fortis vero actor et vehemens et verbis nec inops nec abiectus et quem plane oratorem dicere auderes Cn. Pomponius, lateribus pugnans,
5 incitans animos, acer acerbus criminosus. (222) Multum ab his aberat L. Fufius, tamen ex accusatione M'. Aquili diligentiae fructum ceperat. Nam M. Drusum tuum magnum avunculum, gravem oratorem ita dumtaxat cum de re publica diceret, L. autem Lucullum etiam acutum, patremque tuum, Brute, iuris quoque et publici et privati sane peritum, M. Lucullum,
10 M. Octavium Cn. f., qui tantum auctoritate dicendoque valuit ut legem Semproniam frumentariam populi frequentis suffragiis abrogaverit, Cn. Octavium M. f., M. Catonem patrem, Q. etiam Catulum filium abducamus ex acie, id est a iudiciis, et in praesidiis rei publicae, cui facile satis facere possint, collocemus. (223) Eodem Q. Caepionem referrem, nisi nimis
15 equestri ordini deditus a senatu dissedisset.

Cn. Carbonem M. Marium et ex eodem genere compluris minime dignos elegantis conventus auribus, aptissimos cognovi turbulentis contionibus. Quo in genere, ut in his perturbem aetatum ordinem, nuper L. Quinctius fuit; aptior etiam Palicanus auribus imperitorum. (224) Et quoniam
20 huius generis facta mentio est, seditiosorum omnium post Gracchos L. Appuleius Saturninus eloquentissimus visus est; magis specie tamen et motu atque ipso amictu capiebat homines quam aut dicendi copia aut mediocritate prudentiae. Longe autem post natos homines improbissimus C. Servilius Glaucia, sed peracutus et callidus cum primisque ridiculus. Is
25 ex summis et fortunae et vitae sordibus in praetura consul factus esset, si rationem eius haberi licere iudicatum esset. Nam et plebem tenebat et equestrem ordinem beneficio legis devinxerat. Is praetor eodem die quo Saturninus tribunus plebis Mario et Flacco consulibus publice est interfectus; homo simillimus Atheniensis Hyperboli, cuius improbitatem veteres
30 Atticorum comoediae notaverunt. (225) Quos Sex. Titius consecutus, homo loquax sane et satis acutus, sed tam solutus et mollis in gestu ut saltatio quaedam nasceretur, cui saltationi Titius nomen esset. Ita cavendum est ne quid in agendo dicendove facias cuius imitatio rideatur. Sed ad paulo

exstat C

3 forti *C, corr. C¹*   6 M'. *vulg.*] M⁻ C   cepit *Stangl*   13 id...iudiciis *del. Manutius*   17 contionibus *DE*] cognitionibus *C*   19 <M.> Palicanus *Stangl* 27 <at> is *ego*: igitur *Stangl*   30 consecutus est *Fm*   31 dissolutus *Bᵃᶜ* 32–33 cavendum est *FλΡ*] cavendum·st *C* (-um st *B*)

BRUTUS   127

superiorem aetatem revecti sumus; nunc ad eam de qua aliquantum sumus locuti revertamur.

(226) Coniunctus igitur Sulpici aetati P. Antistius fuit, rabula sane probabilis, qui multos cum iacuisset annos neque contemni solum sed irrideri etiam solitus esset, in tribunatu primum contra C. Iuli illam consulatus 5 petitionem extraordinariam veram causam agens est probatus; et eo magis quod eandem causam cum ageret eius collega ille ipse Sulpicius, hic plura et acutiora dicebat. Itaque post tribunatum primo multae ad eum causae, deinde omnes maximae quaecumque erant deferebantur. (227) Rem videbat acute, componebat diligenter, memoria valebat; verbis non ille qui- 10 dem ornatis utebatur, sed tamen non abiectis; expedita autem erat et perfacile currens oratio, et erat eius quidam tamquam habitus non inurbanus; actio paulum cum vitio vocis tum etiam ineptiis claudicabat. Hic temporibus floruit iis quibus inter profectionem reditumque L. Sullae sine iure fuit et sine ulla dignitate res publica; hoc etiam magis probabatur, 15 quod erat ab oratoribus quaedam in foro solitudo. Sulpicius occiderat, Cotta aberat et Curio, vivebat e reliquis patronis eius aetatis nemo praeter Carbonem et Pomponium, quorum utrumque facile superabat.

(228) Inferioris autem aetatis erat proximus L. Sisenna, doctus vir et studiis optimis deditus, bene Latine loquens, gnarus rei publicae, non sine 20 facetiis, sed neque laboris multi nec satis versatus in causis; interiectusque inter duas aetates Hortensi et Sulpici nec maiorem consequi poterat et minori necesse erat cedere. Huius omnis facultas ex historia ipsius perspici potest, quae cum facile omnis vincat superiores, tum indicat tamen quantum absit a summo quamque genus hoc scriptionis nondum sit satis Latinis 25 litteris illustratum.

Nam Q. Hortensi admodum adulescentis ingenium ut Phidiae signum simul aspectum et probatum est. (229) Is L. Crasso Q. Scaevola consulibus primum in foro dixit et apud hos ipsos quidem consules, et cum eorum qui adfuerunt tum ipsorum consulum, qui omnibus intellegentia anteibant, 30 iudicio discessit probatus. Undeviginti annos natus erat eo tempore, est autem L. Paullo C. Marcello consulibus mortuus; ex quo videmus eum in patronorum numero annos quattuor et quadraginta fuisse. Hoc de oratore

---

1–15 ulla² *exstat C* | 15 dignitate – *codd. citt.* BFJUODEGMTX

4 iacuisset *Baehrens*] tacuisset *C, pler. edd.*   10 dividebat *Fuchs coll.* §303
12 quidam *Manutius*] quidem *C*   14 iis *Ff*] his *C*: *C^{ac} incert., fort.* hiis   15 ulla
del. Jahn   etiam *BUβ*] etiam autem *FO*: esse *J*   20 non *om. β*   22 maiorem *Ff²*]
maioris *L*   23 percipi *F*   27 nam Q. *Ff*] namque *L*   30 omnibus *Diom.*
(Keil, Gramm. Lat. i.313.10)] omnis *L*   anteibant *L*] anteibat *Diom.*

128 BRUTUS

paulo post plura dicemus; hoc autem loco voluimus <eius> aetatem in disparem oratorum aetatem includere. Quamquam id quidem omnibus usu venire necesse fuit quibus paulo longior vita contigit, ut et cum multo maioribus natu quam essent ipsi et cum aliquanto minoribus compararen-
5 tur. Ut Accius isdem aedilibus ait se et Pacuvium docuisse fabulam, cum ille octoginta, ipse triginta annos natus esset, (230) sic Hortensius non cum suis aequalibus solum, sed et mea cum aetate et cum tua, Brute, et cum aliquanto superiore coniungitur, si quidem et Crasso vivo dicere solebat, et magis iam etiam vigebat Antonio, et cum Philippo iam sene pro
10 Cn. Pompei bonis dicens in illa causa, adulescens cum esset, princeps fuit, et in eorum quos in Sulpici aetate posui numerum facile pervenerat, et suos inter aequalis M. Pisonem M. Crassum Cn. Lentulum P. Lentulum Suram longe praestitit, et me adulescentem nactus octo annis minorem quam erat ipse multos annos in studio eiusdem laudis <se> exercuit, et
15 tecum simul, sicut ego pro multis, sic ille pro Appio Claudio dixit paulo ante mortem.

(231) Vides igitur ut ad te oratorem, Brute, pervenerimus tam multis inter nostrum tuumque initium dicendi interpositis oratoribus; ex quibus, quoniam in hoc sermone nostro statui neminem eorum qui viverent nom-
20 inare, ne vos curiosius eliceretis ex me quid de quoque iudicarem, eos qui iam sunt mortui nominabo.

Tum Brutus: Non est, inquit, ista causa quam dicis, quam ob rem de iis qui vivunt nihil velis dicere.

Quaenam igitur, inquam, est?
25 Vereri te, inquit, arbitror ne per nos hic sermo tuus emanet et ii tibi suscenseant quos praeterieris.

Quid? Vos, inquam, tacere non poteritis?

Nos quidem, inquit, facillime; sed tamen te arbitror malle ipsum tacere quam taciturnitatem nostram experiri.
30 (232) Tum ego: Vere tibi, inquam, Brute, dicam. Non me existimavi in hoc sermone usque ad hanc aetatem esse venturum; sed ita traxit ordo aetatum orationem ut iam ad minores etiam pervenerim.

Codd. citt.: BFJUODEGMTX

1 eius aetatem *Marggraff*] aetatem *L*: aetatem eius *Stephanus*: eum *Ernesti*: aetatem *del. Schütz* 2 aetatem *om. O* 3 cum] tum *F* 5 aedilibus *JU^cODEMTy*] aedibus *BU*: et idibus *F* cum *vulg.*] qua *L* 9 <vivo> vigebat *Tittler*: vig<ente flor>ebat *Kayser* cum *ante* Antonio *transp. Madvig* 10 dicens *Schütz*] dicente *L* 14 *add. Douglas* 20 eliceretis *Fc*] eligeretis *L* 22 iis *Ff*] his *L* 28 ipsum] id ipsum *B* 30 inquam tibi *BD* 32 minores *vulg.*] minoris *L* perveneris *F*

BRUTUS 129

Interpone igitur, inquit, si quos videtur; deinde redeamus ad te et ad Hortensium.

Immo vero, inquam, ad Hortensium; de me alii dicent, si qui volent.

Minime vero, inquit. Nam etsi me facile omni tuo sermone tenuisti, tamen is mihi longior videtur quod propero audire de te; nec vero tam de 5 virtutibus dicendi tuis, quae cum omnibus tum certe mihi notissimae sunt, quam quod gradus tuos et quasi processus dicendi studeo cognoscere.

(233) Geretur, inquam, tibi mos, quoniam me non ingeni praedicatorem esse vis sed laboris mei. Verum interponam, ut placet, alios, et a M. Crasso, qui fuit aequalis Hortensi, exordiar. 10

Is igitur mediocriter a doctrina instructus, angustius etiam a natura, labore et industria et quod adhibebat ad obtinendas causas curam etiam et gratiam, in principibus patronis aliquot annos fuit. In huius oratione sermo Latinus erat, verba non abiecta, res compositae diligenter, nullus flos tamen neque lumen ullum, animi magna, vocis parva contentio, omnia fere ut 15 similiter atque uno modo dicerentur. Nam huius aequalis et inimicus C. Fimbria non ita diu iactare se potuit, qui omnia magna voce dicens verborum sane bonorum cursu quodam incitato ita furebat tamen, ut mirarere tam alias res agere populum ut esset insano inter disertos locus. (234) Cn. autem Lentulus multo maiorem opinionem dicendi actione facie- 20 bat quam quanta in eo facultas erat; qui cum esset nec peracutus, quam-quam et ex facie et ex vultu videbatur, nec abundans verbis, etsi fallebat in eo ipso, sic intervallis, exclamationibus, voce suavi et canora, †admirando inridebat calebat† in agendo, ut ea quae deerant non desiderarentur. Ita tamquam Curio copia nonnulla verborum, nullo alio bono, tenuit oratorum 25 locum, (235) sic Lentulus ceterarum virtutum dicendi mediocritatem actione occultavit, in qua excellens fuit. Nec multo secus P. Lentulus, cuius et excogitandi et loquendi tarditatem tegebat formae dignitas, corporis motus plenus et artis et venustatis, vocis et suavitas et magnitudo. Sic in hoc nihil praeter actionem fuit, cetera etiam minora quam in superi- 30 ore. (236) M. Piso quicquid habuit, habuit ex disciplina maximeque ex

---

Codd. citt.: BFJUODEGMTX

1 ad² *FJρ*] *om. BU*   3 immo…Hortensium *om. B*   7 quod *del. Ernesti* 11 instructus] instructus et *β*   17 Fimbriam *λ, corr. J²*   19 tam] etiam *ρ* 23–24 admirando inridebat calebat *BFλ* (a. irr- c. *β*; a. irr- callebat *O*)] admiranda dignitate valebat *Kayser* (valebat *Ernesti*): admirando ore dicebat, calebat *Friedrich*: admirantes irretiebat et sic calebat *Schütz*: admirando irridendo latebat *Lambinus*: [admirando inridebat] valebat *Douglas*: admirando ardore calebat *vel* admirando ardebat calore *ego*   27 in…fuit *del. Weidner*   neque *F*   28 et¹ *om. B*   30 sic] sed *Orelli*: scilicet *Stangl*

130 BRUTUS

omnibus qui ante fuerunt Graecis doctrinis eruditus fuit. Habuit a natura
genus quoddam acuminis, quod etiam arte limaverat, quod erat in repre-
hendendis verbis versutum et sollers, sed saepe stomachosum, non numquam frigidum, interdum etiam facetum. Is laborem quasi cursum
5 forensem diutius non tulit quod et corpore erat infirmo et hominum
ineptias ac stultitias, quae devorandae nobis sunt, non ferebat iracundi-
usque respuebat sive morose, ut putabatur, sive ingenuo liberoque fastidio.
Is cum satis floruisset adulescens, minor haberi est coeptus postea; deinde
ex virginum iudicio magnam laudem est adeptus et ex eo tempore quasi
10 revocatus in cursum tenuit locum tam diu quam ferre potuit laborem;
postea quantum detraxit ex studio, tantum amisit ex gloria.

(237) P. Murena mediocri ingenio sed magno studio rerum veterum, litterarum et studiosus et non imperitus, multae industriae et magni laboris
fuit. C. Censorinus Graecis litteris satis doctus, quod proposuerat explicans
15 expedite, non invenustus actor, sed iners et inimicus fori. L. Turius
parvo ingenio sed multo labore, quoquo modo poterat, saepe dicebat;
itaque ei paucae centuriae ad consulatum defuerunt. (238) C. Macer auctoritate semper eguit, sed fuit patronus propemodum diligentissimus. Huius
si vita, si mores, si vultus denique non omnem commendationem ingeni
20 everteret, maius nomen in patronis fuisset. Non erat abundans, non inops
tamen; non valde nitens, non plane horrida oratio; vox gestus et omnis
actio sine lepore; at in inveniendis componendisque rebus mira
accuratio, ut non facile in ullo diligentiorem maioremque cognoverim, sed
eam ut citius veteratoriam quam oratoriam diceres. Hic etsi etiam in
25 publicis causis probabatur, tamen in privatis illustriorem obtinebat locum.

(239) C. deinde Piso statarius et sermonis plenus orator, minime ille quidem tardus in excogitando, verum tamen vultu et simulatione multo etiam
acutior quam erat videbatur. Nam eius aequalem M'. Glabrionem bene
institutum avi Scaevolae diligentia socors ipsius natura neglegensque
30 tardaverat. Etiam L. Torquatus elegans in dicendo, in existimando admodum prudens, toto genere perurbanus. Meus autem aequalis Cn. Pompeius,
vir ad omnia summa natus, maiorem dicendi gloriam habuisset, nisi eum

Codd. citt.: BFJUODEGMTX

4 quasi cursum] *del. Jahn:* et quasi cursum *Castiglioni*   7 ingenuo *Bλ*] ingenio *Fρ*
8 is] itaque *Kayser:* igitur *Stangl*   9 et ex *FJ¹ρ*] et *BU:* ex *J*   16 <ac> saepe *Weidner:*
<et> saepe *Bake*   17 ei *vulg.*] et *L*   C. Macer *vulg.*] cancer *L*   21 vox] mox
MTγ   22 in *om. FD*   23 accuratio] cura ac ratio *Madvig*   ullo] nullo *F*
24 etsi] si *F*   28 M'. *vulg.*] M. *FλODETγ:* M̄. *BM*   29 avi *vulg.*] aut *L*   diligentia]
industria *B, corr. B¹*   32 eum *om. β*

BRUTUS 131

maioris gloriae cupiditas ad bellicas laudes abstraxisset. Erat oratione satis
amplus, rem prudenter videbat; actio vero eius habebat et in voce magnum
splendorem et in motu summam dignitatem. (**240**) Noster item aequalis
D. Silanus, vitricus tuus, studi ille quidem habuit non multum, sed acuminis
et orationis satis.   5

Q. Pompeius A. f., qui Bithynicus dictus est, biennio quam nos fortasse
maior, summo studio dicendi multaque doctrina, incredibili labore atque
industria; quod scire possum, fuit enim mecum et cum M. Pisone cum
amicitia tum studiis exercitationibusque coniunctus. Huius actio non satis
commendabat orationem; in hac enim satis erat copiae, in illa autem leporis 10
parum. (**241**) Erat eius aequalis P. Autronius, voce peracuta atque magna
nec alia re ulla probabilis, et L. Octavius Reatinus, qui cum multas iam
causas diceret, adulescens est mortuus — is tamen ad dicendum veniebat
magis audacter quam parate —, et C. Staienus, qui se ipse adoptaverat et de
Staieno Aelium fecerat, fervido quodam et petulanti et furioso genere 15
dicendi; quod quia multis gratum erat et probabatur, ascendisset ad honores, nisi in facinore manifesto deprehensus poenas legibus et iudicio dedisset. (**242**) Eodem tempore C. L. Caepasii fratres fuerunt, qui multa opera,
ignoti homines et repentini, quaestores celeriter facti sunt, oppidano
quodam et incondito genere dicendi. Addamus huc etiam, ne quem vocalem 20
praeterisse videamur, C. Cosconium Calidianum, qui nullo acumine eam
tamen verborum copiam, si quam habebat, praebebat populo cum multa
concursatione magnoque clamore. Quod idem faciebat Q. Arrius, qui fuit
M. Crassi quasi secundarum. Is omnibus exemplo debet esse quantum in
hac urbe polleat multorum oboedire tempori multorumque vel honori vel 25
periculo servire. (**243**) His enim rebus infimo loco natus et honores et pecu-
niam et gratiam consecutus etiam in patronorum — sine doctrina, sine
ingenio — aliquem numerum pervenerat. Sed ut pugiles inexercitati, etiam
si pugnos et plagas Olympiorum cupidi ferre possunt, solem tamen saepe
ferre non possunt, sic ille, cum omni iam fortuna prospere functus labores 30
etiam magnos excepisset, illius iudicialis anni severitatem quasi solem
non tulit.

(**244**) Tum Atticus: Tu quidem de faece, inquit, hauris idque iam dudum,
sed tacebam; hoc vero non putabam, te usque ad Staienos et Autronios
esse venturum.   35

Codd. citt.: BFJUODEGMTX
   8 et *om.* F   19 homines] honores *F*   30 ferre *del. Weidner*   34 puta-
ram *Weidner*

132 BRUTUS

Non puto, inquam, existimare te ambitione me labi, quippe de mortuis; sed ordinem sequens in memoriam notam et aequalem necessario incurro. Volo autem hoc perspici, omnibus conquisitis qui in multitudine dicere ausi sint, memoria quidem dignos perpaucos, verum qui omnino nomen
5 habuerint, non ita multos fuisse. Sed ad sermonem institutum revertamur.
(245) T. Torquatus T. f., et doctus vir ex Rhodia disciplina Molonis et a natura ad dicendum satis solutus atque expeditus — cui si vita suppeditavisset, sublato ambitu consul factus esset —, plus facultatis habuit ad dicendum quam voluntatis. Itaque studio huic non satis fecit, officio vero
10 nec in suorum necessariorum causis nec in sententia senatoria defuit. (246) Etiam M. Pontidius municeps noster multas privatas causas actitavit, celeriter sane verba volvens nec hebes in causis, vel dicam plus etiam quam non hebes, sed effervescens in dicendo stomacho saepe iracundiaque vehementius, ut non cum adversario solum sed etiam, quod mirabile esset,
15 cum iudice ipso, cuius delenitor esse debet orator, iurgio saepe contenderet. M. Messalla minor natu quam nos, nullo modo inops sed non nimis ornatus genere verborum, prudens acutus, minime incautus patronus, in causis cognoscendis componendisque diligens, magni laboris, multae operae multarumque causarum. (247) Duo etiam Metelli, Celer et Nepos,
20 nihil in causis versati nec sine ingenio nec indocti hoc erant populare dicendi genus adsecuti. Cn. autem Lentulus Marcellinus nec umquam indisertus et in consulatu pereloquens visus est, non tardus sententiis, non inops verbis, voce canora, facetus satis. C. Memmius L. f. perfectus litteris, sed Graecis, fastidiosus sane Latinarum, argutus orator verbisque dulcis,
25 sed fugiens non modo dicendi verum etiam cogitandi laborem, tantum sibi de facultate detraxit quantum imminuit industriae.
(248) Hoc loco Brutus: Quam vellem, inquit, de his etiam oratoribus qui hodie sunt tibi dicere liberet; et si de aliis minus, de duobus tamen quos a te scio laudari solere, Caesare et Marcello, audirem non minus libenter
30 quam audivi de iis qui fuerunt.
Cur tandem? inquam. An exspectas quid ego iudicem de istis qui tibi sunt aeque noti ac mihi?
Mihi mehercule, inquit, Marcellus satis est notus, Caesar autem parum; illum enim saepe audivi, hic, cum ego iudicare iam aliquid possem, afuit.

Codd. citt.: BFJUODEGMTX

4 indignos *B*   verum] eorum *Weidner:* videri *Stangl*   5 ita] tam *p*   7 cui] qui
Kayser   13 exfervescens *L*   14 esset] est *Meyer*   15 delinitor *OE^c:* delinitior
BFλβ   21 Cn. *Manutius*] Gaius *Bλρ:* G. *F:* C. *F^c*   27 his] is *E:* iis *Rom*   30 his
UG   34 iam *om. B*

BRUTUS   133

(249) Quid igitur de illo iudicas quem saepe audivisti? Quid censes, inquit, nisi id quod habiturus es similem tui? Ne ego, inquam, si ita est, velim tibi eum placere quam maxime. Atqui et ita est, inquit, et vehementer placet; nec vero sine causa. Nam et didicit et, omissis ceteris studiis, unum id egit seseque cotidianis com- 5 mentationibus acerrime exercuit. (250) Itaque et lectis utitur verbis et frequentibus <sententiis>, et splendore vocis dignitate motus fit specio-sum et illustre quod dicitur, omniaque sic suppetunt ut ei nullam deesse virtutem oratoris putem; maximeque laudandus est, qui hoc tempore ipso, cum liceat in hoc communi nostro et quasi fatali malo, consoletur se 10 cum conscientia optimae mentis tum etiam usurpatione et renovatione doctrinae. Vidi enim Mytilenis nuper virum atque, ut dixi, vidi plane virum. Itaque cum eum antea tui similem in dicendo viderim, tum vero nunc a doctissimo viro tibique, ut intellexi, amicissimo Cratippo instructum omni copia multo videbam similiorem.   15

(251) Hic ego: Etsi, inquam, de optimi viri nobisque amicissimi laudibus libenter audio, tamen incurro in memoriam communium miseriarum, quarum oblivionem quaerens hunc ipsum sermonem produxi longius. Sed de Caesare cupio audire quid tandem Atticus iudicet.

Et ille: Praeclare, inquit, tibi constas, ut de iis qui nunc sint nihil velis ipse 20 dicere; et hercule si sic ageres ut de iis egisti qui iam mortui sunt, neminem ut praetermitteres, ne tu in multos Autronios et Staienos incurreres. Quare sive hanc turbam effugere voluisti sive veritus ne quis se aut praeteritum aut non satis laudatum queri posset, de Caesare tamen potuisti dicere, praesertim cum et tuum de illius ingenio notissimum iudicium esset nec 25 illius de tuo obscurum.

(252) Sed tamen, Brute, inquit Atticus, de Caesare et ipse ita iudico et de hoc huius generis acerrimo existimatore saepissime audio, illum omnium fere oratorum Latine loqui elegantissime; nec id solum domestica consuetu-dine, ut dudum de Laeliorum et Muciorum familiis audiebamus, sed quam- 30 quam id quoque credo fuisse, tamen, ut esset perfecta illa bene loquendi laus, multis litteris et iis quidem reconditis et exquisitis summoque studio et diligentia est consecutus: (253) qui[n] etiam in maximis occupationibus

---

1–22 incurreres *codd. citt. BFJUODEGMTX* | 22 quare – 33 *BFJUODEGMX*

1 iudicas <inquam> *Jahn*   3 ita est] ita st *B*   4 atqui *vulg.*] atque *L*
7 *add. Jahn*   et *del. Martha*   vocis <et> *vulg.*   8 dicitur] dicit *Orelli*   10 cum
L, def. Douglas] quod *Peter*   14 Cratippo *FJ²E^cG^c*] Gratippo Bλρ   23 veritus <es>
vulg., edd.   24 possit *B*   25 nec *F^xJ²*] ne *L*   33 qui *Schneider*] quin *L*

134 BRUTUS

ad te ipsum, inquit in me intuens, de ratione Latine loquendi accuratissime
scripserit, primoque in libro dixerit verborum dilectum originem esse
eloquentiae, tribueritque, mi Brute, huic nostro, qui me de illo maluit
quam se dicere, laudem singularem. Nam scripsit his verbis, cum hunc
5 nomine esset affatus: 'Ac si, <ut> cogitata praeclare eloqui possent, nonnulli
studio et usu elaboraverunt, cuius te paene principem copiae atque inventorem bene de nomine ac dignitate populi Romani meritum esse existimare
debemus, hunc facilem et cotidianum novisse sermonem nunc pro relicto
est habendum.'
10 (254) Tum Brutus: Amice hercule, inquit, et magnifice te laudatum puto,
quem non solum principem atque inventorem copiae dixerit, quae
erat magna laus, sed etiam bene meritum de populi Romani nomine et dignitate. Quo enim uno vincebamur a victa Graecia, id aut ereptum illis est
aut certe nobis cum Graecis communicatum. (255) Hanc autem, inquit,
15 gloriam testimoniumque Caesaris tuae quidem supplicationi non, sed
triumphis multorum antepono.
Et recte quidem, inquam, Brute, modo sit hoc Caesaris iudici, non benev-
olentiae testimonium. Plus enim certe attulit huic populo dignitatis, quis-
quis est ille, si modo est aliquis, qui non illustravit modo, sed etiam genuit
20 in hac urbe dicendi copiam, quam illi qui Ligurum castella expugnaverunt;
ex quibus multi sunt, ut scitis, triumphi. (256) Verum quidem si audire
volumus, omissis illis divinis consiliis, quibus saepe constituta est [impera-
torum sapientia] salus civitatis aut belli aut domi, multo magnus orator
praestat minutis imperatoribus. 'At prodest plus imperator.' Quis negat? Sed
25 tamen — non metuo ne mihi acclametis; est autem quod sentias dicendi
liber locus — malim mihi L. Crassi unam pro M'. Curio dictionem quam
castellanos triumphos duo. 'At plus interfuit rei publicae castellum capi
Ligurum quam bene defendi causam M'. Curi.' (257) Credo; sed
Atheniensium quoque plus interfuit firma tecta in domiciliis habere quam
30 Minervae signum ex ebore pulcherrimum; tamen ego me Phidiam esse mallem quam vel optimum fabrum tignuarium. Quare non quantum quisque

---

Codd. citt.: BFJUODEGMX

2 scripserit $B^1\lambda\rho$] scripsit BF   dixerit] disserit F^{2mg}: dixit *A. Eberhard*   3 tribuitque
A. Eberhard   5 si ut *Fc*] si *L*; ut *add. post* eloqui *Ernesti*   8 facilem *Fc*] facile
L   nunc] num *Lallemand*   delicto *Schütz*   13 <per te> ereptum *Piderit ex*
Plut. Cic. 4.7   14 nobis cum graecis $F\lambda\rho$] nobis cum illis *B*: nobiscum *Simon*
15 non] non solum β; non *ante* tuae *transp. Ernesti*   22–23 *del. Lambinus*   26 libere
Jahn   *L. om. F*   M'. *vulg.*] M. FΛOETγ: M̄. BM   27–28 capiligurum λ   28 M'.
vulg.] M. FΛOETγ: M̄. BG^c (*ut vid.*) M

BRUTUS 135

prosit, sed quanti quisque sit ponderandum est; praesertim cum pauci pingere egregie possint aut fingere, operarii autem aut baiuli deesse non possint. (258) Sed perge, Pomponi, de Caesare et redde quae restant.

Solum quidem, inquit ille, et quasi fundamentum oratoris vides locutionem emendatam et Latinam, cuius penes quos laus adhuc fuit, non fuit 5
rationis aut scientiae sed quasi bonae consuetudinis. Mitto C. Laelium
Philum Scipionem: aetatis illius ista fuit laus tamquam innocentiae sic
Latine loquendi — nec omnium tamen, nam illorum aequalis Caecilium et
Pacuvium male locutos videmus — sed omnes tum fere qui nec extra urbem
hanc vixerant neque eos aliqua barbaria domestica infuscaverat recte loque- 10
bantur. Sed hanc certe rem deteriorem vetustas fecit et Romae et in Graecia.
Confluxerunt enim et Athenas et in hanc urbem multi inquinate loquentes
ex diversis locis. Quo magis expurgandus est sermo et adhibenda tamquam
obrussa ratio, quae mutari non potest, nec utendum pravissima consuetudinis regula. (259) T. Flamininum, qui cum Q. Metello consul fuit, pueri vidi- 15
mus; existimabatur bene Latine, sed litteras nesciebat. Catulus erat ille
quidem minime indoctus, ut a te paulo est ante dictum, sed tamen suavitas
vocis et levis appellatio litterarum bene loquendi famam confecerat. Cotta,
qui se valde dilatandis litteris a similitudine Graecae locutionis abstraxerat
sonabatque contrarium Catulo subagreste quiddam planeque subrusticum, 20
alia quidem quasi inculta et silvestri via ad eandem laudem pervenerat.
Sisenna autem quasi emendator sermonis usitati cum esse vellet, ne a
C. Rusio quidem accusatore deterreri potuit quo minus inusitatis verbis
uteretur.

(260) Quidnam istuc est, inquit Brutus, aut quis est iste C. Rusius?   25

Et ille: Fuit accusator, inquit, vetus, quo accusante C. Hirtilium Sisenna
defendens dixit quaedam eius sputatilica esse crimina. Tum C. Rusius:
'Circumvenior', inquit, 'iudices, nisi subvenitis. Sisenna quid dicat nescio;

Codd. citt.: BFJUODEGMX

2 baiuli deesse *F* (baioli d. *B*)] baioli de esse λ*G*^{c}: baiolide esse *ρ*   4–5 elocutionem *β*
6 bono *F*   7 Philum *Heraeus*] pilum *BF*λ*O*: publium *E*^{c}*G*^{vl}*MX* (p. *F*^{c}): publium *post*
Scipionem *E*: *om. DG*: L. Philum P. *Reis*   10 aliqua *O*^{c}*E*^{c}*G*^{vl}] aliquae *L*   barbaria *Ff*]
barbari *BFUODM*γ: barbaries *JO*^{c}*G*^{vl}: barbarie *E*   domestica *G*^{vl}] indomestica λ*OO*^{v}: in
domestica *BF*β   12 et^1 *om. B*   13 tamquam *Manutius*] quantum λ*ρ*: quamtum *F*:
quam *B*: *om. E*^{c} 15 Flamininum *F*^{c}] Flamminium *F*λ*O*: Flaminium *B*β   Q. *om. ρ, add.*
O^v 16 Latine <loqui> *Kayser*   Catulus *F*λ*D*γ] Catullus *BOEM*   18 levis
*BF*λ*EQW*γ] lenis *J*^{2}*OMX*^{c} 19 qui *Ernesti*] quia *F*λ*ρ*: qui a *B*   Graecae] rectae
Simon   21 silvestri via] silvestria *F*   23 accusatore *del. Kayser*   usitatis *B*
26 C. Hirtilium *Müller*] Chirtilium *L*: C. Hirtuleium *Ellendt*   27 criminatum. C. Rusium
L, corr. Ff   28 dicat *Ff*] dicas *L*

136　BRUTUS

metuo insidias. "Sputatilica": quid est hoc? Sputa quid sit scio, tilica nescio.' Maximi risus; sed ille tamen familiaris meus recte loqui putabat esse inusitate loqui. (261) Caesar autem rationem adhibens consuetudinem vitiosam et corruptam pura et incorrupta consuetudine emendat. Itaque cum ad
5 hanc elegantiam verborum Latinorum — quae, etiam si orator non sis et sis ingenuus civis Romanus, tamen necessaria est — adiungit illa oratoria ornamenta dicendi, tum videtur tamquam tabulas bene pictas collocare in bono lumine. Hanc cum habeat praecipuam laudem, in communibus non video cui debeat cedere. Splendidam quandam minimeque veteratoriam
10 rationem dicendi tenet, voce motu forma etiam magnificam et generosam quodam modo.

(262) Tum Brutus: Orationes quidem eius mihi vehementer probantur. Compluris autem legi; atque etiam commentarios quosdam scripsit rerum suarum.
15 Valde quidem, inquam, probandos; nudi enim sunt, recti et venusti, omni ornatu orationis tamquam veste detracta. Sed dum voluit alios habere parata, unde sumerent qui vellent scribere historiam, ineptis gratum fortasse fecit, qui illa volent calamistris inurere: sanos quidem homines a scribendo deterruit; nihil est enim in historia pura et illustri brevitate dul-
20 cius. Sed ad eos, si placet, qui vita excesserunt, revertamur.

(263) C. Sicinius igitur, Q. Pompei illius qui censor fuit ex filia nepos, quaestorius mortuus est; probabilis orator, iam vero etiam probatus, ex hac inopi ad ornandum, sed ad inveniendum expedita Hermagorae disciplina. Ea dat rationes certas et praecepta dicendi; quae si minorem habent
25 apparatum — sunt enim exilia — tamen habent ordinem et quasdam errare in dicendo non patientis vias. Has ille tenens et paratus ad causas veniens, verborum non egens, ipsa illa comparatione disciplinaque dicendi iam in patronorum numerum pervenerat. (264) Erat etiam vir doctus in primis C. Visellius Varro, consobrinus meus, qui fuit cum Sicinio aetate coniunc-
30 tus. Is cum post curulem aedilitatem iudex quaestionis esset, est mortuus; in quo fateor vulgi iudicium a iudicio meo dissensisse. Nam populo non erat satis vendibilis; praeceps quaedam et cum idcirco obscura quia

Codd. citt.: BFJUODEGMX

4 emendabat ρ　　9 veteratoriam $B^cFJ^2\rho$] vetetoriam $B\lambda$　　10 etiam] et F magnificam et generosam *Corradus ex Suet. Iul. 55.1*] magnifica et generosa L 13 quosdam] quos idem *Stangl*　　15 enim *om. Suet. (Iul. 56.2)*　　16 detracta L *Suet.*] detracto *Lambinus*　　17 <si> qui *Kovacs*　　18 illa volent J^2 *Suet.*] volunt illa $F\lambda\rho$: nolunt illa B　　19 enim est B　　21 Sicinius Ff] Sinicius $F\lambda O$: Sinitius β: Sinucius B　　23 inopi BF] inopia $\lambda\rho$　　26 patientes $F\lambda OG^{vl}X^{vl}$: patentes $B\beta$　　30 aedilitatem] dignitatem B

BRUTUS 137

peracuta, tum rapida et celeritate caecata oratio; sed neque verbis aptiorem
cito alium dixerim neque sententiis crebriorem; praeterea perfectus in litteris, iurisque civilis iam a patre Aculeone traditam tenuit disciplinam.

(265) Reliqui sunt, qui mortui sint, L. Torquatus, quem tu non tam cito
rhetorem dixisses, etsi non deerat oratio, quam, ut Graeci dicunt, πολιτικόν. 5
Erant in eo plurimae litterae nec eae vulgares, sed interiores quaedam et
reconditae, divina memoria, summa verborum et gravitas et elegantia;
atque haec omnia vitae decorabat gravitas et integritas. Me quidem admodum delectabat etiam Triari in illa aetate plena litteratae senectutis oratio.
Quanta severitas in vultu! Quantum pondus in verbis! Quam nihil non con- 10
sideratum exibat ex ore!

(266) Tum Brutus Torquati et Triari mentione commotus — utrumque
enim eorum admodum dilexerat —: Ne ego, inquit, ut omittam cetera, quae
sunt innumerabilia, de istis duobus cum cogito, doleo nihil tuam perpetuam
auctoritatem de pace valuisse. Nam nec istos excellentis viros nec multos 15
alios praestantis civis res publica perdidisset.

Sileamus, inquam, Brute, de istis nec augeamus dolorem. Nam et praet-
eritorum recordatio est acerba et acerbior exspectatio reliquorum. Itaque
omittamus lugere et tantum quid quisque dicendo potuerit, quoniam id
quaerimus, praedicemus. 20

(267) Sunt etiam ex iis qui eodem bello occiderunt M. Bibulus, qui et
scriptitavit accurate, cum praesertim non esset orator, et egit multa constan-
ter; App. Claudius socer tuus, collega et familiaris meus: hic iam et satis
studiosus et valde cum doctus tum etiam exercitatus orator et cum
auguralis tum omnis publici iuris antiquitatisque nostrae bene peritus fuit. 25
L. Domitius nulla ille quidem arte, sed Latine tamen et multa cum libertate
dicebat. (268) Duo praeterea Lentuli consulares, quorum Publius ille nostrarum iniuriarum ultor, auctor salutis, quicquid habuit, quantumcumque
fuit, illud totum habuit e disciplina; instrumenta naturae deerant; sed tantus
animi splendor et tanta magnitudo ut sibi omnia quae clarorum virorum 30
essent non dubitaret adsciscere eaque omni dignitate obtineret. L. autem
Lentulus satis erat fortis orator, si modo orator, sed cogitandi non ferebat
laborem; vox canora, verba non horrida sane < . . . > ut plena esset animi

---

1–9 oratio *codd. citt.* BFJUODEGMX | 10 quanta – 33 *exstat* C

1 rapida] rapiditate *Dederich*   et *del. Schütz*   5 politicon *L*   8 gravitas
BFΛO^vβ] dignitas *O*: castitas *Stangl*   17 nec C] ne BF   23 App. CΛO] Appius BFβ:
Ap.p. O^v   33 non *del. Barwick*   *lac. aliquot verborum stat. Hendrickson*   at plena et
Weidner: plena *Schütz*

138 BRUTUS

et terroris oratio; quaereres in iudiciis fortasse melius, in re publica quod erat esse iudicares satis. (269) Ne T. quidem Postumius contemnendus in dicendo; de re publica vero non minus vehemens orator quam bellator fuit, effrenatus et acer nimis, sed bene iuris publici leges atque instituta
5 cognoverat.

Hoc loco Atticus: Putarem te, inquit, ambitiosum esse, si, ut dixisti, ii quos iam diu colligis viverent. Omnis enim commemoras qui ausi aliquando sunt stantes loqui, ut mihi imprudens M. Servilium praeterisse videare.

10 (270) Non, inquam, ego istuc ignoro, Pomponi, multos fuisse qui verbum
· numquam in publico fecissent, cum melius aliquanto possent quam isti oratores quos colligo dicere; sed his commemorandis etiam illud adsequor, ut intellegatis primum ex omni numero quam non multi ausi sint dicere, deinde ex iis ipsis quam pauci fuerint laude digni. (271) Itaque ne hos
15 quidem equites Romanos amicos nostros, qui nuper mortui sunt, <praeteribo>, P. Cominium Spoletinum, quo accusante defendi C. Cornelium, in quo et compositum dicendi genus et acre et expeditum fuit; T. Attium Pisaurensem, cuius accusationi respondi pro A. Cluentio, qui et accurate dicebat et satis copiose, eratque praeterea doctus Hermagorae praeceptis,
20 quibus etsi ornamenta non satis opima dicendi, tamen, ut hastae velitibus ammentatae, sic apta quaedam et parata singulis causarum generibus argumenta traduntur.

(272) Studio autem neminem nec industria maiore cognovi, quamquam ne ingenio quidem qui praestiterit facile dixerim C. Pisoni genero meo.
25 Nullum tempus illi umquam vacabat aut a forensi dictione aut a commentatione domestica aut a scribendo aut a cogitando. Itaque tantos processus efficiebat ut evolare, non excurrere videretur; eratque verborum et dilectus elegans et apta et quasi rotunda constructio; cumque argumenta excogitabantur ab eo multa et firma ad probandum tum concinnae acutaeque
30 sententiae; gestusque natura ita venustus ut ars etiam, quae non erat, et e disciplina motus quidam videretur accedere. Vereor ne amore videar plura quam fuerint in illo dicere, quod non ita est; alia enim de illo maiora dici

---

exstat C

1 terroris (cf. Caes. BCiv. 1.1-2)] fervoris Purgold   2 T.] L. Corradus: C. Sumner Postumius F] Postumus C   4 acer nimis] acerrimus FJ[2]   15–16 praeteribo addidi] omittam hic add. Kayser, post Romanos Hertz   16 Spoletinum BFJ[c]UE[c]] Spolentinum C   17 Attium C] Accium F   21 āmentatae C[c](ut vid.) JODEGM] ament- C (ut vid.) BFU[c]X: arment- U

BRUTUS 139

possunt. Nam nec continentia nec pietate nec ullo genere virtutis quemquam eiusdem aetatis cum illo conferendum puto.

(273) Nec vero M. Caelium praetereundum arbitror, quaecumque eius in exitu vel fortuna vel mens fuit; qui quamdiu auctoritati meae paruit, talis tribunus plebis fuit ut nemo contra civium perditorum popularem turbulentamque dementiam a senatu et a bonorum causa steterit constantius. 5
†Quam† eius actionem multum tamen et splendida et grandis et eadem in primis faceta et perurbana commendabat oratio. Graves eius contiones aliquot fuerunt, acres accusationes tres eaeque omnes ex rei publicae contentione susceptae; defensiones, etsi illa erant in eo meliora quae dixi, 10 non contemnendae tamen saneque tolerabiles. Hic cum summa voluntate bonorum aedilis curulis factus esset, nescio quo modo discessu meo discessit a sese ceciditque, posteaquam eos imitari coepit quos ipse perverterat.

(274) Sed de M. Calidio dicamus aliquid, qui non fuit orator unus e multis, potius inter multos prope singularis fuit: ita reconditas exquisitasque 15 sententias mollis et pellucens vestiebat oratio. Nihil tam tenerum quam illius comprehensio verborum, nihil tam flexibile, nihil quod magis ipsius arbitrio fingeretur, ut nullius oratoris aeque in potestate fuerit; quae primum ita pura erat ut nihil liquidius, ita libere fluebat ut nusquam adhaeresceret; nullum nisi loco positum et tamquam in vermiculato emblemate, ut 20 ait Lucilius, structum verbum videres; nec vero ullum aut durum aut insolens aut humile aut [in] longius ductum; ac non propria verba rerum sed pleraque translata, sic tamen ut ea non irruisse in alienum locum sed immigrasse in suum diceres; nec vero haec soluta nec diffluentia sed astricta numeris, non aperte nec eodem modo semper sed varie dissimulanterque 25 conclusis. (275) Erant autem et verborum et sententiarum illa lumina quae vocant Graeci σχήματα, quibus tamquam insignibus in ornatu distinguebatur omnis oratio. 'Qua de re agitur' autem illud, quod multis locis in iuris consultorum includitur formulis, id ubi esset videbat. (276) Accedebat ordo rerum plenus artis, actio liberalis totumque dicendi placidum et sanum 30 genus. Quod si est optimum suaviter dicere, nihil est quod melius hoc quaerendum putes. Sed cum a nobis paulo ante dictum sit tria videri esse quae orator efficere deberet, ut doceret ut delectaret ut moveret, duo summe

---

1–21 Lucilius *extat C* | 21 structum – 34 *codd. citt. BFJUODEGMX*

7 quam eius] cuius *Fiᶜυ*   quam] iniquam *Hendrickson*: scaenicam *Weidner*: quamvis molestam *Barwick*: quamvis miram *Busche*: antiquam *Hertz*: nimiam A. *Eberhard*: nequam *Della Corte*   actionem] dictionem *Martha*   21 ullum *H*] nullum *L*   22 in *L, om. Faᵃᶜ*   29 id *Corradus*] et *L*   31 est[1] *om. B*

140 BRUTUS

tenuit, ut et rem illustraret disserendo et animos eorum qui audirent
devinciret voluptate; aberat tertia illa laus, qua permoveret atque incitaret
animos, quam plurimum pollere diximus; nec erat ulla vis atque contentio,
sive consilio, quod eos quorum altior oratio actioque esset ardentior furere
5 et bacchari arbitraretur, sive quod natura non esset ita factus, sive quod non
consuesset, sive quod non nosset. Hoc unum illi si nihil utilitatis habebat,
afuit; si opus erat, defuit.

(277) Quin etiam memini, cum in accusatione sua Q. Gallio crimini
dedisset sibi eum venenum paravisse, idque a se esse deprehensum seseque
10 chirographa testificationes indicia quaestiones manifestam rem deferre
diceret, deque eo crimine accurate et exquisite disputavisset, me in
respondendo, cum essem argumentatus quantum res ferebat, hoc ipsum
etiam posuisse pro argumento, quod ille, cum pestem capitis sui, cum indicia mortis se comperisse manifesto et manu tenere diceret, tam solute egis-
15 set, tam leniter, tam oscitanter. (278) 'Tu istuc, M. Calidi, nisi fingeres, sic
ageres? Praesertim cum ista eloquentia alienorum hominum pericula
defendere acerrime soleas, tuum neglegeres? Ubi dolor, ubi ardor animi,
qui etiam ex infantium ingeniis elicere voces et querelas solet? Nulla perturbatio animi, nulla corporis; frons non percussa, non femur; pedis, quod
20 minimum est, nulla supplosio. Itaque tantum afuit ut inflammares nostros
animos, somnum isto loco vix tenebamus.' Sic nos summi oratoris vel sanitate vel vitio pro argumento ad diluendum crimen usi sumus.

(279) Tum Brutus: Atque dubitamus, inquit, utrum ista sanitas fuerit an
vitium? Quis enim non fateatur, cum ex omnibus oratoris laudibus longe
25 ista sit maxima, inflammare animos audientium et quocumque res postulet
modo flectere, qui hac virtute caruerit, id ei quod maximum fuerit defuisse?

Sit sane ita, inquam; sed redeamus ad eum qui iam unus restat,
Hortensium; tum de nobismet ipsis, quoniam id etiam, Brute, postulas,
pauca dicemus. Quamquam facienda mentio est, ut quidem mihi videtur,
30 duorum adulescentium qui, si diutius vixissent, magnam essent eloquentiae
laudem consecuti.

Codd. citt.: BFJUODEGMX

2 devinciret G^c] devinceret BFλOEGM: devincerent D   6 nosset *Friedrich*] posset
L   8 crimini J^2] crimine BFJU^{c}ρ: criminet U   10 deferre *La*] differre L
11 crimine BF^{ac}F^{c}J^{2}ρ] crimen F^1λ   15 leviter X   16 cum ista eloquentia] ista eloquentia? Cum *Lambinus*: ista eloquentia? *Martha*   17 soleas *Ff*] soles L   19 frons
non] non frons *Quint. Inst. 11.3.123*   20 afuit BFλO^c (abf- J^2β)] affuit O: abest *Quint.
Inst. 11.3.155*   23 dubitamus λG   27 redeamus] respondeamus F

BRUTUS 141

(280) C. Curionem te, inquit Brutus, et C. Licinium Calvum arbitror dicere.

Recte, inquam, arbitraris; quorum quidem alter [quod verisimile dixisset] ita facile soluteque verbis volvebat satis interdum acutas, crebras quidem certe sententias, ut nihil posset ornatius esse, nihil expeditius. 5 Atque hic parum a magistris institutus naturam habuit admirabilem ad dicendum; industriam non sum expertus, studium certe fuit. Qui si me audire voluisset, ut coeperat, honores quam opes consequi maluisset.

Quidnam est, inquit, istuc, et quem ad modum distinguis?

(281) Hoc modo, inquam: cum honos sit praemium virtutis iudicio 10 studioque civium delatum ad aliquem qui eum sententiis, qui suffragiis adeptus est, is mihi et honestus et honoratus videtur. Qui autem occasione aliqua etiam invitis suis civibus nactus est imperium, ut ille cupiebat, hunc nomen honoris adeptum, non honorem puto. Quae si ille audire voluisset, maxima cum gratia et gloria ad summam amplitudinem pervenisset, ascen- 15 dens gradibus magistratuum, ut pater eius fecerat, ut reliqui clariores viri. Quae quidem etiam cum P. Crasso M. f., <cum> initio aetatis ad amicitiam se meam contulisset, saepe egisse me arbitror, cum eum vehementer hortarer ut eam laudis viam rectissimam esse duceret quam maiores eius ei tritam reliquissent. (282) Erat enim cum institutus optime tum etiam perfecte 20 planeque eruditus, ineratque et ingenium satis acre et orationis non inelegans copia, praetereaque sine arrogantia gravis esse videbatur et sine segnitia verecundus. Sed hunc quoque absorbuit aestus quidam insolitae adulescentibus gloriae; qui quia navarat miles operam imperatori, imperatorem se statim esse cupiebat, cui muneri mos maiorum aetatem certam, 25 sortem incertam reliquit. Ita gravissimo suo casu, dum Cyri et Alexandri similis esse voluit, qui suum cursum transcurrerant, et L. Crassi et multorum Crassorum inventus est dissimillimus.

(283) Sed ad Calvum — is enim nobis erat propositus — revertamur; qui orator fuit cum litteris eruditior quam Curio, tum etiam accuratius 30 quoddam dicendi et exquisitius afferebat genus; quod quamquam scienter eleganterque tractabat, nimium tamen inquirens in se atque ipse sese observans metuensque ne vitiosum colligeret, etiam verum sanguinem deperdebat.

Codd. citt.: BFJUODEGMX

3-4 *del. Lambinus*   6 a magistris parum *B*   9 quinam *F*   16 clariores] maiores clari omnes *Jahn*: clari omnes *Castiglioni*   17 *add. vulg.*   20 perfecte <litteratus> *Stangl*   25 muneri *F^{c}J^2*] munere *L*   maiorum *U*] malorum *BFJρ*   30 fuit cum *Corradus*] fuisset cum *L*: cum esset *Piderit*   <erat> eruditior *Marggraff*   33 deperdebat *F^{c}J^{c}O^{2vl}E^c*] dependebat *L*: perdidisse *Quint. Inst. 10.1.115 (in or. obl.)*

142 BRUTUS

Itaque eius oratio nimia religione attenuata doctis et attente audientibus erat illustris, <a> multitudine autem et a foro, cui nata eloquentia est, <non> devorabatur. (284) Tum Brutus: Atticum se, inquit, Calvus noster dici oratorem
5 volebat; inde erat ista exilitas quam ille de industria consequebatur.

Dicebat, inquam, ita; sed et ipse errabat et alios etiam errare cogebat. Nam si quis eos qui nec inepte dicunt nec odiose nec putide Attice putat dicere, is recte nisi Atticum probat neminem. Insulsitatem enim et insolentiam tamquam insaniam quandam orationis odit, sanitatem autem et integ-
10 ritatem quasi religionem et verecundiam oratoris probat. Haec omnium debet oratorum eadem esse sententia. (285) Sin autem ieiunitatem et siccitatem et inopiam, dummodo sit polita, dum urbana, dum elegans, in Attico genere ponit, hoc recte dumtaxat; sed quia sunt in Atticis alia <aliis> meliora, videat ne ignoret et gradus et dissimilitudines et vim et varietatem
15 Atticorum. 'Atticos', inquit, 'volo imitari.' Quos? Nec enim est unum genus. Nam quid est tam dissimile quam Demosthenes et Lysias? Quam idem et Hyperides? Quam horum omnium Aeschines? Quem igitur imitaris? Si aliquem, ceteri ergo Attice non dicebant? Si omnis, qui potes, cum sint ipsi dissimillimi inter se? In quo illud etiam quaero, Phalereus ille Demetrius
20 Atticene dixerit. Mihi quidem ex illius orationibus redolere ipsae Athenae videntur. At est floridior, ut ita dicam, quam Hyperides, quam Lysias: natura quaedam aut voluntas ita dicendi fuit. (286) Et quidem duo fuerunt per idem tempus dissimiles inter se, sed Attici tamen; quorum Charisius multarum orationum, quas scribebat aliis, cum cupere videretur imitari Lysiam;
25 Demochares autem, qui fuit Demostheni sororis filius, et orationes scripsit aliquot et earum rerum historiam quae erant Athenis ipsius aetate gestae non tam historico quam oratorio genere perscripsit. At Charisi vult Hegesias esse similis, isque se ita putat Atticum ut veros illos prae se paene agrestis putet. (287) At quid est tam fractum, tam minutum, tam in
30 ipsa, quam tamen consequitur, concinnitate puerile? 'Atticorum similes esse volumus.' Optime; suntne igitur hi Attici oratores? 'Quis negare potest? Hos imitamur.' Quo modo, qui sunt et inter se dissimiles et aliorum?

Codd. citt.: BFJUODEGMX

2 a *add. Ff*   non *add. Leeman*   3 deserebatur *Purgold*   6 et[1] *om. B*   13 *add. hic Bake, ante* alia *Piderit*   17 si *F^cE²*] sed *L*   23 dissimilis *L, corr. vulg.*
25 Demosthenis *ρ*   27 at] atque *Stangl:* ac *Jahn*   28 Egesias *J²E²*: Hegestas *BF¹λOMγ*: egestas *DE*: egesta *F*   32 imitamur *β*] imitantur *BFλO*   quo quo modo *B*

BRUTUS 143

'Thucydidem', inquit, 'imitamur.' Optime, si historiam scribere, non si causas dicere cogitatis. Thucydides enim rerum gestarum pronuntiator sincerus et grandis etiam fuit; hoc forense concertatorium iudiciale non tractavit genus. Orationes autem quas interposuit — multae enim sunt — eas ego laudare soleo; imitari neque possim, si velim, nec velim fortasse, si pos- 5 sim. Ut si quis Falerno vino delectetur, sed eo nec ita novo ut proximis consulibus natum velit, nec rursus ita vetere ut Opimium aut Anicium consulem quaerat. 'Atqui hae notae sunt optimae.' Credo; sed nimia vetustas nec habet eam quam quaerimus suavitatem nec est iam sane tolerabilis. (288) Num igitur qui hoc sentiat, si is potare velit, de dolio sibi hauriendum 10 putet? Minime; sed quandam sequatur aetatem. Sic ego istis censuerim et novam istam quasi de musto ac lacu fervidam orationem fugiendam nec illam praeclaram Thucydidi nimis veterem tamquam Anicianam notam persequendam. Ipse enim Thucydides, si posterius fuisset, multo maturior fuisset et mitior. 15

(289) 'Demosthenem igitur imitemur.' O di boni! Quid, quaeso, nos aliud agimus aut quid aliud optamus? At non adsequimur; isti enim videlicet Attici nostri quod volunt adsequuntur. Ne illud quidem intellegunt, non modo ita memoriae proditum esse sed ita necesse fuisse, cum Demosthenes dicturus esset, ut concursus audiendi causa ex tota Graecia 20 fierent. At cum isti Attici dicunt, non modo a corona, quod est ipsum miserabile, sed etiam ab advocatis relinquuntur. Quare si anguste et exiliter dicere est Atticorum, sint sane Attici; sed in comitium veniant, ad stantem iudicem dicant: subsellia grandiorem et pleniorem vocem desiderant. (290) Volo hoc oratori contingat, ut, cum auditum sit eum esse dicturum, locus in 25 subselliis occupetur, compleatur tribunal, gratiosi scribae sint in dando et cedendo loco, corona multiplex, iudex erectus; cum surgat is qui dicturus sit, significetur a corona silentium, deinde crebrae adsensiones, multae admirationes; risus, cum velit, cum velit, fletus: ut qui haec procul videat, etiam si quid agatur nesciat, at placere tamen et in scaena esse Roscium 30 intellegat. Haec cui contingant, eum scito Attice dicere, ut de Pericle audimus, ut de Hyperide, <de> Aeschine, de ipso quidem Demosthene maxime. (291) Sin autem acutum prudens et idem sincerum et solidum et exsiccatum genus orationis probant nec illo graviore ornatu oratorio utuntur et hoc proprium esse Atticorum volunt, recte laudant. Est enim in arte 35

Codd. citt.: BFJUODEGMX

12 musto ac] musti *Baehrens*: del. *Ellendt*   16 quaeso *vulg.*] quasi *L*   19 ita¹ *om. B*
32 de² *Rom*] *om.* FΛρ: ut de *B*

144 BRUTUS

tanta tamque varia etiam huic minutae subtilitati locus. Ita fiet ut non
omnes qui Attice, idem bene, sed ut omnes qui bene, idem etiam Attice
dicant. Sed redeamus rursus ad Hortensium.

(292) Sane quidem, inquit Brutus; quamquam ista mihi tua fuit periu-
5 cunda a proposita ratione digressio.

Tum Atticus: Aliquotiens sum, inquit, conatus, sed interpellare nolui.
Nunc quoniam iam ad perorandum spectare videtur sermo tuus, dicam,
opinor, quod sentio.

Tu vero, inquam, Tite.

10 Tum ille: Ego, inquit, ironiam illam quam in Socrate dicunt fuisse, qua
ille in Platonis et Xenophontis et Aeschini libris utitur, facetam et elegantem
puto. Est enim et minime inepti hominis et eiusdem etiam faceti, cum de
sapientia disceptetur, hanc sibi ipsum detrahere, iis tribuere illudentem
qui eam sibi arrogant, ut apud Platonem Socrates in caelum effert laudi-
15 bus Protagoram Hippiam Prodicum Gorgiam ceteros, se autem omnium
rerum inscium fingit et rudem. Decet hoc nescio quo modo illum, nec
Epicuro, qui id reprehendit, adsentior. Sed in historia, qua tu es usus in
omni sermone, cum qualis quisque orator fuisset exponeres, vide, quaeso,
inquit, ne tam reprehendenda sit ironia quam in testimonio.

20 (293) Quorsus, inquam, istuc? Non enim intellego.

Quia primum, inquit, ita laudavisti quosdam oratores ut imperitos posses
in errorem inducere. Equidem in quibusdam risum vix tenebam, cum
Attico Lysiae Catonem nostrum comparabas, magnum mehercule hominem vel potius summum et singularem virum — nemo dicet secus — sed
25 oratorem? Sed etiam Lysiae similem, quo nihil potest esse politius? Bella
ironia, si iocaremur; sin adseveramus, vide ne religio nobis tam adhibenda
sit quam si testimonium diceremus. (294) Ego enim Catonem tuum ut
civem, ut senatorem, ut imperatorem, ut virum denique cum prudentia
et diligentia tum omni virtute excellentem probo; orationes autem eius ut
30 illis temporibus valde laudo; significant enim formam quandam ingeni, sed
admodum impolitam et plane rudem. Origines vero cum omnibus
oratoris laudibus refertas diceres et Catonem cum Philisto et Thucydide

---

Codd. citt.: BFJUODEGMX

2 sed…bene *om. B*   5 ratione *scripsi (cf. §307)*] oratione *L*   6 conatus] commotus *E. Eberhard*: concitatus *A. Eberhard*: paene conatus *Friedrich*   9 Tite] Attice *B*
13 disceptur *G*: disceptatur *G^c*   14 arrogant] adrogent *Ernesti*   22 <ut> cum
Ernesti   24–25 sed…sed] sin…sin *F^c*   25 politius *Beier*] pictius *L*: perfectius
Sarpe   30 formam quandam *FλO*] quandam formam *Bβ*   32 oratoriis *Manutius*

BRUTUS 145

comparares, Brutone te id censebas an mihi probaturum? Quos enim ne e
Graecis quidem quisquam imitari potest, his tu comparas hominem
Tusculanum nondum suspicantem quale esset copiose et ornate dicere.
(295) Galbam laudas. Si ut illius aetatis principem, adsentior — sic enim
accepimus — sin ut oratorem, cedo, quaeso, orationes — sunt enim — et dic 5
hunc, quem tu plus quam te amas, Brutum velle te illo modo dicere. Probas
Lepidi orationes. Paulum hic tibi adsentior, modo ita laudes ut antiquas.
Quod item de Africano, de Laelio, cuius tu oratione negas fieri quicquam
posse dulcius, addis etiam nescio quid augustius; nomine nos capis
summi viri vitaeque elegantissimae verissimis laudibus. Remove haec: ne 10
ista dulcis oratio ita sit abiecta ut eam aspicere nemo velit. (296) Carbonem
in summis oratoribus habitum scio; sed cum in ceteris rebus tum in dicendo
semper, quo iam nihil est melius, id laudari, qualecumque est, solet. Dico
idem de Gracchis, etsi de iis ea sunt a te dicta quibus ego adsentior. Omitto
ceteros; venio ad eos in quibus iam perfectam putas esse eloquentiam, quos 15
ego audivi, sine controversia magnos oratores, Crassum et Antonium. De
horum laudibus tibi prorsus adsentior, sed tamen non isto modo: ut Polycliti
Doryphorum sibi Lysippus aiebat, sic tu suasionem legis Serviliae tibi magistram fuisse. Haec germana ironia est. Cur ita sentiam non dicam, ne me
tibi adsentari putes. (297) Omitto igitur quae de his ipsis, quae de Cotta, 20
quae de Sulpicio, quae modo de Caelio dixeris. Hi enim fuerunt certe oratores; quanti autem et quales tu videris. Nam illud minus curo, quod con-
gessisti operarios omnis, ut mihi videantur mori voluisse nonnulli ut a te in
oratorum numerum referrentur.

Haec cum ille dixisset: Longi sermonis initium attulisti, inquam, Attice, 25
remque commovisti nova disputatione dignam, quam in aliud tempus dif-
feramus. (298) Volvendi enim sunt libri cum aliorum tum in primis Catonis.
Intelleges nihil illius liniamentis nisi eorum pigmentorum quae inventa
nondum erant florem et colorem defuisse. Nam de Crassi oratione sic existimo, ipsum fortasse melius potuisse scribere, alium, ut arbitror, neminem. 30
Nec in hoc εἴρωνα me duxeris esse, quod eam orationem mihi magistram
fuisse dixerim. Nam etsi tute melius existimare videris de ea, si quam nunc

---

Codd. citt.: BFJUODEGMX

1 te *om.* B   8 de²] et *O, corr. O^v*   9 augustius *F¹J²G*] angustius *BFλODMX*
11 ita *λO^{2vl}DE^cMγ*] ista *BFJ^{1mg}U^cOE*   sit] erit *Weidner*   ut eam *E²*] autem *L*: ut *O^{2vl}*
13 quo iam *Jahn*] quoniam *L*: quo *E^c*   laudare *L, corr. vulg.*   15 venis *L, corr.*
vulg.   21 dixeris] dixisti *Schütz*   24 referrentur *BFG^c (ut vid.)*] referentur
λρ   25 attulisti *Lambinus*] depulisti *L*: intulisti *Schütz*: protulisti *Watt*: detulisti *Manutius*:
pepulisti *vulg., pler. edd.*   31 εἴρωνα me duxeris *Baehrens*] ironiam eduxeris *L*: ironiam
duxeris *J^c*: me yrona edixeris *E^c*   32 tute *Stangl*] ut tu *BFJU¹ρ*: tu *U*

146 BRUTUS

habemus, facultate, tamen adulescentes quid in Latinis potius imitare-
mur non habebamus. (299) Quod autem plures a nobis nominati sunt, eo
pertinuit, ut paulo ante dixi, quod intellegi volui, [in] eo, cuius omnes
cupidissimi essent, quam pauci digni nomine evaderent. Quare εἴρωνα
5 me, ne si Africanus quidem fuit, ut ait in historia sua C. Fannius, existimari velim.

Ut voles, inquit Atticus. Ego enim non alienum a te putabam quod et in
Africano fuisset et in Socrate.

(300) Tum Brutus: De isto postea; sed tu, inquit me intuens, orationes
10 nobis veteres explicabis?

Vero, inquam, Brute; sed in Cumano aut in Tusculano aliquando, si
modo licebit, quoniam utroque in loco vicini sumus. Sed iam ad id unde
digressi sumus revertamur.

(301) Hortensius igitur, cum admodum adulescens orsus esset in foro
15 dicere, celeriter ad maiores causas adhiberi coeptus est; <et> quamquam
inciderat in Cottae et Sulpici aetatem, qui annis decem maiores <erant>,
excellente tum Crasso et Antonio, dein Philippo, post Iulio, cum his ipsis
dicendi gloria comparabatur. Primum memoria tanta quantam in
nullo cognovisse me arbitror, ut quae secum commentatus esset, ea sine
20 scripto verbis isdem redderet quibus cogitavisset. Hoc adiumento ille tanto
sic utebatur ut sua et commentata et scripta et nullo referente omnia adver-
sariorum dicta meminisset. (302) Ardebat autem cupiditate sic ut in nullo
umquam flagrantius studium viderim. Nullum enim patiebatur esse diem
quin aut in foro diceret aut meditaretur extra forum; saepissime autem
25 eodem die utrumque faciebat. Attuleratque minime vulgare genus dicendi;
duas quidem res quas nemo alius: partitiones quibus de rebus dicturus
esset et collectiones eorum quae essent dicta contra quaeque ipse dixisset. (303) Erat in verborum splendore elegans, compositione aptus, facultate copiosus; eaque erat cum summo ingenio tum exercitationibus
30 maximis consecutus. Rem complectebatur memoriter, dividebat acute,
nec praetermittebat fere quicquam quod esset in causa aut ad

Codd. citt.: BFJUODEGMX

1 facultatem F^c quid] quod *fort. legendum est*   3 *del. Barwick*   4 εἴρωνα
vulg.] ironia L: yrona E^c 5 menesi $F\lambda\rho$: mene si B: nesi E^c 13 digressi sumus $F^c\lambda\rho$]
disgressimus B: digressimus B^c: digessimus F   15 *add. Ellendt*   16 *add. hic Rau,*
post decem A. *Eberhard*   18 quantam $B^cE^cG^c$] quanta L   18–19 in nullo Fc] in vito
FJD (invito BO): in viro $B^cJ^2UEM\gamma$: in nullo viro O^{2vl} 21 omnia ρ] omnia. omnia BFλ:
omnia omnium *Stangl*   25 <ad> minime *Fuchs*   27 coniectiones L, *corr.* E^c
eorum *Jahn*] memor et $B\lambda\rho$ (memoret F)   30 videbat *Douglas coll.* §227

BRUTUS 147

confirmandum aut ad refellendum. Vox canora et suavis; motus et gestus etiam plus artis habebat quam erat oratori satis. Hoc igitur florescente Crassus est mortuus, Cotta pulsus, iudicia intermissa bello, nos in forum venimus.

(304) Erat Hortensius in bello primo anno miles, altero tribunus mili- 5 tum, Sulpicius legatus; aberat etiam M. Antonius; exercebatur una lege iudicium Varia, ceteris propter bellum intermissis; cui frequens aderam, quamquam pro se ipsi dicebant oratores non illi quidem principes, L. Memmius et Q. Pompeius, sed oratores tamen, teste diserto utique Philippo, cuius in testimonio contentio et vim accusatoris habebat et 10 copiam. (305) Reliqui qui tum principes numerabantur in magistratibus erant cotidieque fere a nobis in contionibus audiebantur. Erat enim tribunus plebis tum C. Curio, quamquam is quidem silebat, ut erat semel a contione universa relictus; Q. Metellus Celer non ille quidem orator, sed tamen non infans; diserti autem Q. Varius C. Carbo Cn. Pomponius, et hi quidem 15 habitabant in rostris; C. etiam Iulius aedilis curulis cotidie fere accuratas contiones habebat. Sed me cupidissimum audiendi primus dolor percussit, Cotta cum est expulsus. Reliquos frequenter audiens acerrimo studio tenebar cotidieque et scribens et legens et commentans oratoriis tantum exercitationibus contentus non eram. Iam consequente anno 20 Q. Varius sua lege damnatus excesserat. (306) Ego autem iuris civilis studio multum operae dabam Q. Scaevolae P. f., qui quamquam nemini <se> ad docendum dabat, tamen consulentibus respondendo studiosos audiendi docebat. Atque huic anno proximus Sulla consule et Pompeio fuit. Tum P. Sulpici in tribunatu cotidie contionantis totum genus dicendi peni- 25 tus cognovimus; eodemque tempore, cum princeps Academiae Philo cum Atheniensium optimatibus Mithridatico bello domo profugisset Romamque venisset, totum ei me tradidi admirabili quodam ad philosophiam studio concitatus; in quo hoc etiam commorabar attentius — etsi rerum ipsarum varietas et magnitudo summa me delectatione retinebat — sed 30 tamen sublata iam esse in perpetuum ratio iudiciorum videbatur. (307) Occiderat Sulpicius illo anno tresque proximo trium aetatum oratores erant

---

Codd. citt.: BFJUODEGMX

6 legatus aberat, <aberat> *Wex*   7 cui *vulg.*] qui *L*   9 utique *Jahn*] uterque *L*
16–17 accuratas contiones] accusationes *B*: contiones *B¹*   19 oratoriis *Ff*] oratoris *L*
20 tantum] tamen *Corradus*   21 excesserat *om.* ρ, *add.* E^cO^v <in> iuris
Müller   22 P.] Q. *Fabricius*   se *add. hic vulg., ante* dabat *E²G^c, ante* nemini
Reis   29 hoc *om. BX*   etsi] quod etsi *Ff*   30 sed] *om. Ff.* quod *Madvig*

148 BRUTUS

crudelissime interfecti, Q. Catulus M. Antonius C. Iulius. Eodem anno etiam
Moloni Rhodio Romae dedimus operam, et actori summo causarum et
magistro. Haec etsi videntur esse a proposita ratione diversa, tamen
idcirco a me proferuntur ut nostrum cursum perspicere, quoniam
5 voluisti, Brute, possis — nam Attico haec nota sunt — et videre quem ad
modum simus in spatio Q. Hortensium ipsius vestigiis persecuti.

(308) Triennium fere fuit urbs sine armis; sed oratorum aut interitu aut
discessu aut fuga — nam aberant etiam adulescentes M. Crassus et Lentuli
duo — primas in causis agebat Hortensius, magis magisque cotidie proba-
10 batur Antistius, Piso saepe dicebat, minus saepe Pomponius, raro Carbo,
semel aut iterum Philippus. At vero ego hoc tempore omni noctis et dies in
omnium doctrinarum meditatione versabar. (309) Eram cum Stoico
Diodoto, qui cum habitavisset apud me <me>cumque vixisset, nuper
est domi meae mortuus. A quo cum in aliis rebus tum studiosissime in
15 dialectica exercebar, quae quasi contracta et astricta eloquentia putanda est;
sine qua etiam tu, Brute, iudicavisti te illam iustam eloquentiam, quam
dialecticam esse dilatatam putant, consequi non posse. Huic ego doctori et
eius artibus variis atque multis ita eram tamen deditus ut ab exercitationibus oratoriis nullus dies vacuus esset. (310) Commentabar declamitans —
20 sic enim nunc loquuntur — saepe cum M. Pisone et cum Q. Pompeio aut
cum aliquo cotidie, idque faciebam multum etiam Latine, sed Graece
saepius, vel quod Graeca oratio plura ornamenta suppeditans consuetudinem similiter Latine dicendi afferebat, vel quod a Graecis summis doctori-
bus, nisi Graece dicerem, neque corrigi possem neque doceri. (311)
25 Tumultus interim recuperanda re publica et crudelis interitus oratorum
trium, Scaevolae Carbonis Antisti, reditus Cottae Curionis Crassi
Lentulorum Pompei, leges et iudicia constituta, recuperata res publica; ex
numero autem oratorum Pomponius Censorinus Murena sublati. Tum primum nos ad causas et privatas et publicas adire coepimus, non ut in foro
30 disceremus, quod plerique fecerunt, sed ut, quantum nos efficere potuissemus, docti in forum veniremus. (312) Eodem tempore Moloni dedimus

---

Codd. citt.: BFJUODEGMX

1–3 eodem…magistro *del. Wetzel (v. comm.)*   3 proposita *JG^c*] proposito *BFJ^{c}Uρ*   ora-
tione *Ascensius*   5 et *F^{1}OG^c*] ei *BλO^{v}β*: eive *F*: licuit ei *J^2*   13 Diodoto *FJ^2*] Dioto
Bλρ: Diodoro *B^{mg}*   mecumque *Es^{2}Vs^2*] cumque *B (ut vid.) FλO^v*: cum Q. *ρ*   15 quae
B^{c}J^{2}UG^{vl}X^{vl}] qua *BFJU^{c}ODMγ*: quam *E*   17 dilatatam *G^c*] dilatam *L*   24 possem
O] possim *BFλO^{c}β*   25 recuperanda re publica] in r. r. p. *Mf: del. Kayser*   27 re *Dγ*
30 faciunt *O*   31 Moloni *BFJU^{c}OE^{c}G^c*] Miloni *Uβ*

BRUTUS 149

operam; dictatore enim Sulla legatus ad senatum de Rhodiorum praemiis
venerat. Itaque prima causa publica pro Sex. Roscio dicta tantum commen-
dationis habuit ut non ulla esset quae non digna nostro patrocinio
videretur. Deinceps inde multae, quas nos diligenter elaboratas et
tamquam elucubratas afferebamus.   5

(313) Nunc quoniam totum me non naevo aliquo aut crepundiis sed corpore omni videris velle cognoscere, complectar nonnulla etiam quae fortasse videantur minus necessaria. Erat eo tempore in nobis summa gracilitas
et infirmitas corporis, procerum et tenue collum; qui habitus et quae figura
non procul abesse putatur a vitae periculo, si accedit labor et laterum magna 10
contentio. Eoque magis hoc eos quibus eram carus commovebat, quod
omnia sine remissione, sine varietate, vi summa vocis et totius corporis
contentione dicebam. (314) Itaque cum me et amici et medici hortarentur
ut causas agere desisterem, quodvis potius periculum mihi adeundum
quam a sperata dicendi gloria discedendum putavi. Sed cum censerem   15
remissione et moderatione vocis et commutato genere dicendi me et
periculum vitare posse et temperatius dicere, ut consuetudinem dicendi
mutarem, ea causa mihi in Asiam proficiscendi fuit. Itaque cum essem
biennium versatus in causis et iam in foro celebratum meum nomen
esset, Roma sum profectus.   20

(315) Cum venissem Athenas, sex mensis cum Antiocho veteris
Academiae nobilissimo et prudentissimo philosopho fui studiumque
philosophiae numquam intermissum a primaque adulescentia cultum et
semper auctum hoc rursus summo auctore et doctore renovavi. Eodem
tamen tempore Athenis apud Demetrium Syrum veterem et non ignobilem   25
dicendi magistrum studiose exerceri solebam. Post a me Asia tota peragrata
est cum summis quidem oratoribus, quibuscum exercebar ipsis libentibus;
quorum erat princeps Menippus Stratonicensis meo iudicio tota Asia
illis temporibus disertissimus; et si nihil habere molestiarum nec inept-
iarum Atticorum est, hic orator in illis numerari recte potest. (316)   30
Adsiduissime autem mecum fuit Dionysius Magnes; erat etiam Aeschylus
Cnidius, Adramyttenus Xenocles. Hi tum in Asia rhetorum principes
numerabantur. Quibus non contentus Rhodum veni meque ad eundem

---

Codd. citt.: BFJUODEGMX

3 habuit *TVf*] habui *L*   nostro digna *B*   4–5 et tamquam *Ff*] etiam quam *BFJU¹ρ*: *om. U*
10 putantur *OX*   accedit *F¹*] accidit *L*   18 mutarem *ρ*] mutarim *BFλ*   19 et iam *F*]
etiam *Bλρ*   27 cum] fuique cum *Kayser*: referta tum *Friedrich*   29 nec] et *B*
32 Cnidius *BλOᵛ*] Gnidius *FJ²*: Cuidius *W*: Enidius *O*: Evidius *Q*: Ovidius *EG*

150 BRUTUS

quem Romae audiveram Molonem applicavi, cum actorem in veris causis
scriptoremque praestantem tum in notandis animadvertendisque vitiis et
instituendo docendoque prudentissimum. Is dedit operam, si modo id consequi potuit, ut nimis redundantis nos et supra fluentis iuvenili quadam
5 dicendi impunitate et licentia reprimeret et quasi extra ripas diffluentis
coerceret. Ita recepi me biennio post non modo exercitatior sed prope
mutatus. Nam et contentio nimia vocis resederat et quasi deferverat oratio
lateribusque vires et corpori mediocris habitus accesserat.

(317) Duo tum excellebant oratores qui me imitandi cupiditate incitar-
10 ent, Cotta et Hortensius; quorum alter remissus et lenis et propriis verbis
comprehendens solute et facile sententiam, alter ornatus, acer et non talis
qualem tu eum, Brute, iam deflorescentem cognovisti, sed verborum et
actionis genere commotior. Itaque cum Hortensio mihi magis arbitrabar
rem esse, quod et dicendi ardore eram propior et aetate coniunctior.
15 Etenim videram in isdem causis, ut pro M. Canuleio, pro Cn. Dolabella
consulari, cum Cotta princeps adhibitus esset, priores tamen agere partis
Hortensium. Acrem enim oratorem, incensum et agentem et canorum,
concursus hominum forique strepitus desiderat. (318) Unum igitur annum,
cum redissemus ex Asia, causas nobilis egimus, cum quaesturam nos, con-
20 sulatum Cotta, aedilitatem peteret Hortensius. Interim me quaestorem
Siciliensis excepit annus, Cotta ex consulatu est profectus in Galliam, princeps et erat et habebatur Hortensius. Cum autem anno post ex Sicilia me
recepissem, iam videbatur illud in me, quicquid esset, esse perfectum et
habere maturitatem quandam suam. Nimis multa videor de me, ipse prae-
25 sertim; sed omni huic sermoni propositum est non ut ingenium et eloquentiam meam perspicias, unde longe absum, sed ut laborem et industriam.
(319) Cum igitur essem in plurimis causis et in principibus patronis quinquennium fere versatus, tum in patrocinio Siciliensi maxime in certamen
veni designatus aedilis cum designato consule Hortensio.
30 Sed quoniam omnis hic sermo noster non solum enumerationem oratorum verum etiam praecepta quaedam desiderat, quid tamquam notandum
et animadvertendum sit in Hortensio breviter licet dicere. (320) Nam is

---

1–11 et[1] *codd. citt. BFJUODEGMX* | 11 facile – 32 *BFJUODEGXY*

2 tum <magistrum> *Fuchs*   3 <in> instituendo *Ld*   5 diffluentis *Ff*] difflu-
entem *Bλρ*: diffluenti *F*   7 resederat *Lambinus*] reciderat *L*   deferverat *H*] referverat
L   8 corpori *Be*] corporis *L*   9 tum *BFJO[v]β*] tamen *UO*   10 levis
EX   11 et[2]] *del. Bake:* certe *Weidner:* id est *Stangl*   14 quod] cui *Jahn:* quod ei
ego   15 dolabella *F*] dolobella *BF[1]λρ*   17 <et> incensum *FkBe*   22 e *B*
23 esset] erat *Stangl*   28 tum] tamen *U:* cum *X*   maximum *Ho*   30–31 oratorum
Mo[2vl]] oratoriam *L*

BRUTUS 151

post consulatum — credo quod videret ex consularibus neminem esse secum comparandum, neglegeret autem eos qui consules non fuissent — summum illud suum studium remisit quo a puero fuerat incensus, atque in omnium rerum abundantia voluit beatius, ut ipse putabat, remissius certe vivere. Primus et secundus annus et tertius tantum quasi de picturae veteris 5 colore detraxerat, quantum non quivis unus ex populo sed existimator doctus et intellegens posset cognoscere. Longius autem procedens, ut in ceteris eloquentiae partibus, tum maxime in celeritate et continuatione verborum adhaerescens, sui dissimilior videbatur fieri cotidie.

(321) Nos autem non desistebamus cum omni genere exercitationis 10 tum maxime stilo nostrum illud quod erat augere, quantumcumque erat. Atque ut multa omittam in hoc spatio et in his post aedilitatem annis, et praetor primus et incredibili populari voluntate sum factus. Nam cum propter adsiduitatem in causis et industriam tum propter exquisitius et minime vulgare orationis genus animos hominum ad me dicendi novitate 15 converteram. (322) Nihil de me dicam: dicam de ceteris, quorum nemo erat qui videretur exquisitius quam vulgus hominum studuisse litteris, quibus fons perfectae eloquentiae continetur; nemo qui philosophiam complexus esset, matrem omnium bene factorum beneque dictorum; nemo qui ius civile didicisset, rem ad privatas causas et ad oratoris prudentiam maxime 20 necessariam; nemo qui memoriam rerum Romanarum teneret, ex qua, si quando opus esset, ab inferis locupletissimos testis excitaret; nemo qui breviter arguteque incluso adversario laxaret iudicum animos atque a severitate paulisper ad hilaritatem risumque traduceret; nemo qui dilatare posset atque a propria ac definita disputatione hominis ac temporis <ad> 25 communem quaestionem universi generis orationem traducere; nemo qui delectandi gratia digredi parumper a causa; nemo qui ad iracundiam magno opere iudicem, nemo qui ad fletum posset adducere; nemo qui animum eius, quod unum est oratoris maxime proprium, quocumque res postularet impellere. 30

Codd. citt.: BFJUODEGXY

1 videret G^c] viderit L 3 suum *om. B*   6 exstumator G^c (extum- *BO*, extim- *Y*): aestumator $B^cF\lambda$: etstumator *EG* (et stum- *D*): et senator J^2 7 cognoscere *vulg.*] magnum scelus *L*: cognoscere magnum scelus F^1: agnoscere *Orelli*   ut] cum *Lambinus*, *fort. recte*   11 quod erat *om. B*   12 et...annis *del. Ellendt*   his Ff] iis *L* 12–13 et praetor] praetor et *Lambinus*: praetor *Kroll*   13 <consul> sum *Friedrich* 23 incluso] illuso *Schütz*   25 *add.* G^c 26 traduceret *L, corr. v*   30 impelleret *L, corr. W*

152 BRUTUS

(323) Itaque cum iam paene evanuisset Hortensius et ego anno meo, sexto autem post illum consulem, consul factus essem, revocare se ad industriam coepit, ne, cum pares honore essemus, aliqua re superior videret. Sic duodecim post meum consulatum annos in maximis causis, cum ego
5 mihi illum, sibi me ille anteferret, coniunctissime versati sumus, consulatusque meus, qui illum primo leviter perstrinxerat, idem nos rerum mearum gestarum, quas ille admirabatur, laude coniunxerat. (324) Maxime vero perspecta est utriusque nostrum exercitatio paulo ante quam perterritum armis hoc studium, Brute, nostrum conticuit subito et obmutuit, cum
10 lege Pompeia ternis horis ad dicendum datis ad causas simillimas inter se vel potius easdem novi veniebamus cotidie. Quibus quidem causis tu etiam, Brute, praesto fuisti complurisque et nobiscum et solus egisti, ut qui non satis diu vixerit Hortensius tamen hunc cursum confecerit: annis ante decem causas agere coepit quam tu es natus; idem quarto <et> sexa-
15 gesimo anno, perpaucis ante mortem diebus, una tecum socerum tuum defendit Appium. Dicendi autem genus quod fuerit in utroque, orationes utriusque etiam posteris nostris indicabunt.

(325) Sed si quaerimus cur adulescens magis floruerit dicendo quam senior Hortensius, causas reperiemus verissimas duas. Primum, quod genus
20 erat orationis Asiaticum adulescentiae magis concessum quam senectuti. Genera autem Asiaticae dictionis duo sunt: unum sententiosum et argutum, sententiis non tam gravibus et severis quam concinnis et venustis, qualis in historia Timaeus, in dicendo autem pueris nobis Hierocles Alabandeus, magis etiam Menecles frater eius fuit, quorum utriusque orationes sunt in
25 primis ut Asiatico in genere laudabiles. Aliud autem genus est non tam sententiis frequentatum quam verbis volucre atque incitatum, quali est nunc Asia tota, nec flumine solum orationis sed etiam exornato et faceto genere verborum, in quo fuit Aeschylus Cnidius et meus aequalis Milesius Aeschines. In his erat admirabilis orationis cursus, ornata sententiarum
30 concinnitas non erat. (326) Haec autem, ut dixi, genera dicendi aptiora sunt adulescentibus, in senibus gravitatem non habent. Itaque Hortensius utroque genere florens clamores faciebat adulescens. Habebat enim et Meneclium illud studium crebrarum venustarumque sententiarum, in quibus, ut in illo Graeco, sic in hoc erant quaedam magis venustae dulcesque

---

Codd. citt.: BFJUODEGXY

3 superior videret *Lambinus*] superiores videremur *L*: superior esse videret *Jahn* 6 leniter *F* 14 decem] sedecim *Nipperdey* idem] idemque *O* *add. Fm* 22 et severis quam *Vl²*] et si veris numquam *L* 25 aliud] alterum *E. Eberhard* 26 quali *Fλρ*] quale *B*: qualis *Ob* 27 facto *Bo* 33 in...153,1 utiles *del. Friedrich*

BRUTUS 153

sententiae quam aut necessariae aut interdum utiles; et erat oratio cum incitata et vibrans tum etiam accurata et polita. Non probabantur haec senibus — saepe videbam cum irridentem tum etiam irascentem et stomachantem Philippum — sed mirabantur adulescentes, multitudo movebatur. (327) Erat excellens iudicio vulgi et facile primas tenebat adulescens. 5 Etsi enim genus illud dicendi auctoritatis habebat parum, tamen aptum esse aetati videbatur. Et certe, quod et ingeni quaedam forma lucebat et exercitatione perfecta erat verborumque erat astricta comprehensio, summam hominum admirationem excitabat. Sed cum iam honores et illa senior auctoritas gravius quiddam requireret, remanebat idem nec decebat idem; 10 quodque exercitationem studiumque dimiserat, quod in eo fuerat acerrimum, concinnitas illa crebritasque sententiarum pristina manebat, sed ea vestitu illo orationis quo consuerat ornata non erat. Hoc tibi ille, Brute, minus fortasse placuit quam placuisset, si illum flagrantem studio et florentem facultate audire potuisses. 15

(328) Tum Brutus: Ego vero, inquit, et ista quae dicis video qualia sint et Hortensium magnum oratorem semper putavi maximeque probavi pro Messalla dicentem, cum tu afuisti.

Sic ferunt, inquam, idque declarat totidem quot dixit, ut aiunt, scripta verbis oratio. Ergo ille a Crasso consule et Scaevola usque ad Paulum et 20 Marcellum consules floruit; nos in eodem cursu fuimus a Sulla dictatore ad eosdem fere consules. Sic Q. Hortensi vox exstincta fato suo est, nostra publico.

Melius, quaeso, ominare, inquit Brutus.

(329) Sit sane ut vis, inquam, et id non tam mea causa quam tua; sed fortunatus illius exitus, qui ea non vidit cum fierent quae providit futura. 25 Saepe enim inter nos impendentis casus deflevimus, cum belli civilis causas in privatorum cupiditatibus inclusas, pacis spem a publico consilio esse exclusam videremus. Sed illum videtur felicitas ipsius, qua semper est usus, ab iis miseriis quae consecutae sunt morte vindicavisse.

Codd. citt.: BFJUODEGXY

1 *post* sententiae *iterata* sunt verba in quibus ut in (in *om.* O) illo graeco sic in hoc erant quaedam magis, *expuncta* F^{c}G^c 2 probabantur J] probantur BFUρ 7 et^2 BFO] *om.* λβ   elucebat *Lambinus*   7–8 et exercitatione BFλODEγ] ex exercitatione Y: et exercitatio *Rom*: exercitatione *Schütz*: usu et exercitatione *Malcovati*: et studio et exercitatione *Barwick*   8 erat verborumque erat *Mg*] erat verborum eratque L: eratque verborum *vulg.*: verborum erat atque *Sydow*: verborumque erat arte *Hendrickson*: erat verborum *Kaster*: verborum erat *Douglas*   comprehensio] comprensa B: comprehensione *Martha*   9 excitabat F^{c}J^cρ] exercitabat BFλ   11 remiserat *Bake*   16 et^1 *om.* B   18 afuisti Fλ (aff- B)] affuisses ρ (af- O^c)   19 idque] idemque B   23 ominare G^c] o mire FλO^{v}β: omitte BO: o marce X^{vl}

154 BRUTUS

(330) Nos autem, Brute, quoniam post Hortensi clarissimi oratoris mortem orbae eloquentiae quasi tutores relicti sumus, domi teneamus eam saeptam liberali custodia et hos ignotos atque impudentis procos repudiemus tueamurque ut adultam virginem caste et ab amatorum impetu, 5 quantum possumus, prohibeamus. Equidem etsi doleo me in vitam paulo serius tamquam in viam ingressum, priusquam confectum iter sit, in hanc rei publicae noctem incidisse, tamen ea consolatione sustentor quam tu mihi, Brute, adhibuisti tuis suavissimis litteris, quibus me forti animo esse oportere censebas, quod ea gessissem quae de me etiam me tacente ipsa 10 loquerentur mortuoque viverent; quae, si recte esset, salute rei publicae, sin secus, interitu ipso testimonium meorum de re publica consiliorum darent.

(331) Sed in te intuens, Brute, doleo, cuius in adulescentiam per medias laudes quasi quadrigis vehentem transversa incurrit misera fortuna rei pub 15 licae. Hic me dolor angit, haec cura sollicitat et hunc mecum socium eiusdem et amoris et iudici. Tibi favemus, te tua frui virtute cupimus, tibi optamus eam rem publicam in qua duorum generum amplissimorum renovare memoriam atque augere possis. Tuum enim forum, tuum erat illud curriculum, tu illuc veneras unus qui non linguam modo acuisses exercita 20 tione dicendi, sed et ipsam eloquentiam locupletavisses graviorum artium instrumento et isdem artibus decus omne virtutis cum summa eloquentiae laude iunxisses. (332) Ex te duplex nos afficit sollicitudo, quod et ipse re publica careas et illa te. Tu tamen, etsi cursum ingeni tui, Brute, premit haec importuna clades civitatis, contine te in tuis perennibus studiis et effice id 25 quod iam propemodum vel plane potius effeceras, ut te eripias ex ea quam ego congessi in hunc sermonem turba patronorum. Nec enim decet te ornatum uberrimis artibus, quas cum domo haurire non posses, accessivisti ex urbe ea quae domus est semper habita doctrinae, numerari in vulgo patronorum. Nam quid te exercuit Pammenes vir longe eloquentissimus 30 Graeciae, quid illa vetus Academia atque eius heres Aristus hospes et familiaris meus, si quidem similes maioris partis oratorum futuri sumus? (333) Nonne cernimus vix singulis aetatibus binos oratores laudabilis constitisse? Galba

---

Codd. citt.: BFJUODEGXY

4 amatorum *Fm*] armatorum BFJU$^1\rho$: armentorum *U*   9 me^2 *om. Sd*   10 mortuoque viverent *vulg.*] mortuo viverentque *L*: mortuo viverent *Ho*: viverentque mortuo *Stangl*: mortuoque me viverent *Ernesti*   essent U^{ac}Y   saluti *L, corr. vulg.*   15 angit *Mb*] tangit *L*   cura] me cura *B*: cura et me *Fuchs*   16 moris *F*   21–22 eloquentia deiunxisses ρ 27 domi *Rom*   29 quid G^c] qui *L*   32 constitisse] extitisse *Be*

BRUTUS 155

fuit inter tot aequalis unus excellens, cui, quem ad modum accepimus, et
Cato cedebat senior et qui temporibus illis aetate inferiores fuerunt; Lepidus
postea, deinde Carbo — nam Gracchi in contionibus multo faciliore et liberiore genere dicendi, quorum tamen ipsorum ad aetatem laus eloquentiae
perfecta nondum fuit — Antonius Crassus, post Cotta Sulpicius, Hortensius. 5
Nihil dico amplius, tantum dico: si mihi accidisset ut numerarer in multis
< ... > si operosa est concursatio magis opportunorum < ... >

Codd. citt.: BFJUODEGXY

1 tot aequalis] cottę quales *B*   2 illis *om. B*   3 contionibus <usi sunt> *Piderit*
4 dicendi <utebantur> *Be*   5 post] p. et *F*   7 est] ista λ   concursatio] a concursatio *FY* (aconcursatio *DE*)   optumorum *Ld*   *in subscr. B add. Flavius Blondus* Non
erat amplius in exemplari: a quo abscisse sunt charte due: quamquam ut mihi videtur nedum
charte: sed pauca admodum verba deficiunt., *et in subscr. O Viglevius de Ardiciis* Non inveni
plura in perveteri codice: fortunę quidem iniquitas id totum, si tamen quiddam erat, recidit.

Commentary

6. *autem aut* Ff] *autem et* L: *autem* Ernesti: *aut* Lambinus. Some editors adopt Lambinus' *aut*, but *autem* should be retained, since it serves a useful function in signalling the contrast between the griefs which Hortensius would share with many people and the one which he would feel more keenly than most. L's *et*, however, is evidently corrupt. It could be deleted, but emending to *aut* is more economical.[1] This conjecture, often attributed to Piderit, was first made by Poggio.

10. *venit* ζ] *venerat* L. Douglas and Jahn-Kroll-Kytzler defend the pluperfect on the ground that Brutus and Atticus arrived before the conversation mentioned in §9.[2] However, *venerat* is more naturally taken after *inambularem*,[3] which would then produce the unwanted idea that Brutus and Atticus arrived before Cicero began his stroll in the garden. The difficulty is well illustrated by Hendrickson's translation, in which he was compelled to translate *venerat* as if it were a perfect: 'For one day when I was at home..., Marcus Brutus dropped in on me'. *Venit*, present in the descendants of ζ and later proposed by Alfred Fleckeisen (1883: 208), is a simple solution. *Venerat* is a Perseverationsfehler after *consueverat*; W. S. Watt (1983: 229–230) has pointed out the frequency of this type of error in the *Laudensis*.

14. *omnem*] *omnium* Fa[ac] | *rerum <gestarum>* vel *<veterum>* Douglas: *rerum <nostrarum>* Jahn: *rerum <Romanarum>* Bake. The lack of an adjective with *rerum* has troubled some scholars, and I can find no close parallels for this use of *rerum memoria* ('history') on its own before Ammianus (Amm. Marc. 31.5.10 *cum explicandae rerum memoriae ubique*

---

[1] There are 22 instances of *autem aut...aut* in Cicero.

[2] If a date and page number do not accompany the name of a scholar, the reference is to the edition or commentary cited in the bibliography, *ad loc.*

[3] *Nam cum* is a standard formula used by Cicero in setting the scene of a dialogue (cf. *Fin.* 1.14, *Nat. D.* 1.15, *Div.* 1.8), and so the primary function of *nam* is to mark the start of a new section, not to tie the sentence to the preceding clause (*cum...incidissemus*).

158   COMMENTARY

debeatur integritas fida).[4] Cicero does, however, use *memoria* without a
defining genitive to give the same sense (e.g. *Vat.* 33 *in omni memoria est
omnino inauditum, Har. resp.* 37; *OLD s.v. memoria* 7), and the phrase here
is a natural extension of this usage.

Were emendation necessary, Douglas' *rerum <gestarum>* would be the
best option. The frequent coupling of *omnis* and *memoria* tells against Fa[ac]'s
omnium,[5] and, because of *Orat.* 120 (*Cognoscat etiam rerum gestarum et
memoriae veteris ordinem, maxime scilicet nostrae civitatis, sed etiam impe-
riosorum populorum et regum illustrium. Quem laborem nobis Attici nostri
levavit labor, qui conservatis notatisque temporibus, nihil cum illustre
praetermitteret, annorum septingentorum memoriam uno libro colligavit*),
any adjective supplied should not exclude non-Roman history (as do the
emendations of Bake and Jahn)[6] or recent history (as does Douglas'
<veterum>) from the content of Atticus' *Liber annalis*. The hyperbole voiced
here by Brutus (*omnem rerum memoriam… complexus est*) is subsequently
picked up by Cicero's own character in §15 *omnia viderem*.

15. *quae* VaVr] *quo* FλB[v]: *qua* F[1]ρ: *quod* J[2]. Cf. Hes. *Op.* 349–350 εὖ μὲν
μετρεῖσθαι παρὰ γείτονος, εὖ δ' ἀποδοῦναι, / αὐτῷ τῷ μέτρῳ, καὶ λώιον, αἴ κε
δύνηαι; *Off.* 1.48 *ea, quae utenda acceperis, maiore mensura, si modo possis,
iubet reddere Hesiodus*; *Att.* 13.12.3. From the agreement of F[1]OB[ac]G, editors have deduced that L's reading was *qua*. However, the agreement of
F[ac]λB[v] demonstrates that L actually read *quo*. Since *quo* is manifestly corrupt, we are left with a choice between three emendations, all found in the
manuscript tradition: *quod, qua,* and *quae*. Douglas defends *qua* on the
ground that it is closer to Hesiod's syntax, but Cicero is paraphrasing, not
translating. It is better for *acceperis* to have an expressed object, and so *quod*
and *quae* are superior. Of these two, *quae* is preferable: the movement from
the plural *quae* in the Hesiodic maxim to the singular *quod* (§16 *tibi reddam
quod accepi*) in the particular case of Cicero's debt to Atticus is effective, and
the repetition of *quod* in *quod eadem mensura reddere iubet quod acceperis*
would be somewhat awkward. The parallel from *Off.* 1.48 provides further
support for *quae*.

---

[4] Cf., however, Cic. *Phil.* 12.12 *num etiam memoriam rerum delere possumus?*; Gell. *NA*
15.28.1 *Cornelius Nepos et rerum memoriae non indiligens*. Münzer (1905: 78) saw in *Brut.* 14 a
possible allusion to Catull. 1.5–7 *ausus es unus Italorum / omne aevum tribus explicare chartis /
doctis, Iuppiter, et laboriosis*, in which Catullus praises Cornelius Nepos' *Chronica*.

[5] e.g. at *Vat.* 33 (cited above), *Caec.* 80, *Flac.* 3.

[6] In *Orat.* 120, Cicero merely implies that Atticus included non-Roman history in the *Liber
annalis*, but cf. below on §28 *Attici*; Drummond in *FRHist* i.348–349.

COMMENTARY   159

16. *repressus* <*est*> Bake | *flos siti*] *siti flos* Lambinus: *flos* Orelli: *flos, sic vis* Ammon | *veteris ubertatis* del. A. Eberhard. Hendrickson translates the transmitted text thus: 'all new growth has been checked within me, and drought has burned and withered all that flowering which once promised abundance'. However, the word order requires that *veteris ubertatis* depend not upon *flos*, but upon *siti* ('the flower withered through thirst for its old fruitfulness'). The image of a flower withering with longing for its old fruitfulness is rather odd, and in context, *sitis* should mean 'lack of rain', 'drought', not 'longing', 'thirst'.[7] *Sitis* = 'drought' is not otherwise found in prose before the Imperial period,[8] but the semantic field of aridity is already present in *exustus...exaruit*, and so it is not much of a stretch for Cicero to give *sitis* the meaning 'drought' in a metaphorical context such as this.

Lambinus transposed *siti* and *flos*, allowing *flos* to govern *veteris ubertatis*.[9] Nevertheless, as Watt (1996: 373–374) has pointed out, *flos veteris ubertatis* is no easier to understand than *sitis veteris ubertatis*. Eberhard's deletion of *veteris ubertatis* is preferable. The genitival phrase could have intruded as an explanatory gloss on *siti*. It adds little to the sense, and deleting it yields a more satisfactory balance between *flos* and *fetus*, which has no defining genitive.[10]

Even with Eberhard's deletion, however, the clause is difficult: the initial *sic* is used in a peculiar way; the placing of the attributive participle *exustusque* after *repressus* is awkward; and *exustusque...exaruit* is, if not strictly tautological, at least unattractive.[11] Sticking-plaster solutions such as Bake's *repressus* <*est*> and Friedrich's *exortusque* (for *exustusque*) are to be avoided.[12] One might contemplate excising the whole of *sic...exaruit*. However,

---

[7] Some commentators compare *sitis* + gen. here with *Rep.* 1.66 *inexplebiles populi fauces exaruerunt libertatis siti*, but *libertatis siti* is much easier to understand than *siti veteris ubertatis*.

[8] But cf. *Orat.* 81, where Cicero admits that the metaphor *sitire agros* (probably the correct reading) is common in rustic Latin.

[9] Orelli achieved a similar result by deleting *siti*. However, the coupling of *sitis* and *exurere* in other passages tells in favour of retaining *siti* here. Cf., e.g., Lucr. 3.917 *quod sitis exurat miseros atque arida torrat*, Colum. *Rust.* 10.144 *ne sitis exurat concepto semine partum*, Sen. *Agam.* 19 *fervida exustus siti*. Watt (1996: 374) instead supplies *oblitus* after *veteris*, but this strains the metaphor and complicates the already difficult syntax.

[10] Stephen Oakley suggests transposing *veteris ubertatis* to after *fetus*, and compares §182 *nec ulla aetate uberior oratorum fetus fuit*.

[11] For further analysis of some of these problems, see Friedrich (1873: 845–846).

[12] On the omission of *est* after *repressus*, see below on §218 *ductus*. Ammon replaced *siti* with *sic vis*, thus enabling *exustus* to be taken predicatively with *flos* and eliminating the awkwardness of *repressus exustusque*, but *vis* is out of place here. While *vires* can mean 'vigour, full strength', I doubt whether the singular was used thus.

160 COMMENTARY

without the clause the reader is left with no explanation of why Cicero cannot repay Atticus from the new crop. The stylistic infelicities may be due to hasty composition.[13] In my judgement, Eberhard's deletion is the best available option and leaves us with something which Cicero at least might have written.

18. *ausim* G^c] *ausus sim* FΛOBDEMSTX: *ausum* G. If G^c's emendation is accepted, this would be the only instance of *ausim* in Cicero;[14] the only other archaic sigmatic subjunctive forms employed by Cicero are *faxit* and *faxint* (e.g. *Verr.* 2.3.81 *di immortales faxint*, *Leg.* 2.19). However, *ausim* is usually combined with verbs of speaking and would fit well here with *repromittere*.[15] *Ausim* and forms of *fax-* persisted long after other sigmatic subjunctives had disappeared,[16] and so it would not be surprising to find only these forms in Cicero.

An additional reason to suspect corruption here is that there are no instances of the deponent perfect subjunctive of *audeo* in independent clauses in classical Latin. Indeed, potential perfect subjunctives of all deponent verbs are rare,[17] and in Cicero the only example is *Tusc.* 1.55 *Ego vero facile sim passus ne in mentem quidem mihi aliquid contra venire.*[18] The corruption of an unfamiliar *ausim* would have been easy, especially if it had been spelled *aussim*.[19]

19. *rerum nostrarum* Lambinus] *rerum naturalium* L: *veterum annalium* Pisanus: *rerum et magistratuum* Reis coll. Nep. *Att.* 18.2. In defence of the transmitted reading, Van den Bruwaene (1967: 821) cites *Fin.* 1.16 as evidence for Atticus' expertise and interest in Epicurean philosophy. However, it is unlikely that Cicero's *De re publica* would have aroused Atticus' zeal for natural philosophy. Rather, *rerum naturalium memoriam* must conceal a reference to Atticus' historical investigations, which culminated in the *Liber annalis*.

---

[13] Cf. Winterbottom (1967: 302): 'the sentence is in any case irremediably inelegant'.

[14] Cicero usually uses the present subjunctive to give this sense (e.g. *Brut.* 10 *aut ego pro certo dicere audeam*). For a list of the instances of *ausim* in Latin prose, see De Melo (2007: 344 n. 14).

[15] De Melo (2007: 345).

[16] De Melo (2007: 338–353); Pinkster (2015: 491–492). Even in Terence the sigmatic subjunctive is limited almost exclusively to *facere* and *audere*: see De Melo (2007: 194–195).

[17] K-S i.176–177. Admittedly, this could be an accident of survival, given that deponent verbs are relatively uncommon.

[18] The subjunctive *sim passus* has been contested, but it is accepted by recent editors. See Kennedy (2010: *ad loc.*).

[19] I owe this observation to Wolfgang de Melo.

COMMENTARY 161

Of the proposed emendations, Lambinus' *rerum nostrarum* is by far the best.[20] Although the *Liber annalis* almost certainly contained some non-Roman history, Nepos' description shows that the work dealt largely with Roman affairs.[21] Additionally, in *Rep.* 2.1–63, the part of that text most similar in subject matter to the *Liber annalis*, Cicero's focus is on Roman history, and so it would make sense for Atticus to say that he has been inspired by it to compile a record of Roman history. In *Brut.* 14, Brutus made the exaggerated claim that Atticus had encompassed all of history (*omnem rerum memoriam*) in the *Liber annalis*, and here Atticus, in keeping with Cicero's characterization of him, is more modest in his summary of its contents.

Pisanus and Reis are much less economical in their emendations. Reis introduces *et magistratuum* in order to achieve greater coherence with Nepos' account, but in so doing he sacrifices coherence with *Rep.*, in which the record of magistrates is not a major preoccupation. Pisanus' removal of *rerum* is infelicitous, in view of §14 *omnem rerum memoriam* and §322 *memoriam rerum Romanarum* (cf. §§44, 62), and it unduly confines the scope of Atticus' work to ancient history.[22]

23. *studiosum. Et* L] *studioso. Et* O^{2vl}: *studioso mei* Orelli: *studioso et <dicendi et intellegendi magistro>* Hoffmann: *studiosum et <optumarum artium cupidum intuenti>* Kroll: *studiosum et <exercitatum audienti>* Friedrich: *studiosum et <doctum et exercitatum intuenti>* vel *<prudentem intuenti>* Amundsen: *studiosum et <dicendi et intellegendi intuenti>* ego. The sense is incomplete in the transmitted text. Orelli proposed *studioso mei* for *studiosum et*, but this emendation meets with two difficulties. Firstly, the following *enim* needs a purpose, and Orelli's conjecture does not provide an obvious causal link between the two sentences. Secondly, *studiosus* is usually used of the devotion of a disciple (cf. §64 *certos sui studiosos*) or a

---

[20] Cf. §62 *historia rerum nostrarum*, §44 *te audiente, quem rerum Romanarum auctorem laudare possum religiosissimum*. For a more general statement of the value placed by Cicero on the investigation of Roman history, see *Acad.* 1.9.

[21] Nep. *Att.* 18.1–2 *Moris etiam maiorum summus imitator fuit antiquitatisque amator, quam adeo diligenter habuit cognitam, ut eam totam in eo volumine exposuerit quo magistratus ordinavit* (*ornavit* MSS). *Nulla enim lex neque pax neque bellum neque res illustris est populi Romani, quae non in eo suo tempore sit notata, et, quod difficillimum fuit, sic familiarum originem subtexuit, ut ex eo clarorum virorum propagines possimus cognoscere.*

[22] Cf. *Orat.* 120 *annorum septingentorum memoriam uno libro colligavit*. Douglas (1966: *ad loc.*) points out that ancient history was also the subject of *Rep.* 2, but *rerum nostrarum memoria* remains a more suitable description of the subject of the *Liber annalis*.

162 COMMENTARY

political supporter,[23] rather than that of an experienced role model and mentor towards a protégé.

Most editors postulate a lacuna after *et*. Friedrich's addition of a dative participle to agree with *mihi* and to govern *studiosum* has some plausibility, but Kroll's *intuenti* seems preferable to Friedrich's *audienti*, in view of §22 *mihi, Brute, in te intuenti* (and cf. §§253, 300, 331).[24] In some respects, though, Hoffmann's conjecture (1876) is the most appealing. *Studiosus* is often used with a genitive of something eagerly pursued or studied,[25] and the two gerunds *dicendi* and *intellegendi* allow for a natural movement of thought to the next sentence.[26] *Saut du même au même*, which is frequently involved in scribal omissions, would easily explain the loss of *dicendi...magistro*. However, there is no reason to suspect *studiosum* of corruption. One might instead synthesize Hoffmann's supplement with Kroll's: *studiosum et <dicendi et intellegendi intuenti>*. Together, the words added are about as long as one line of text in the Cremona fragment, and if the lines in L's exemplar had been of similar length, this could have made a leap from *dicendi* to *dicere* even easier.

28. *Attici* L] *Atticis* θ. *Atticis*, proposed by Lambinus but found already in the descendants of θ, is accepted by Kaster on the ground that the plural *monumenta* has the sense 'documentary record' throughout *Brut*. Yet, while the noun can denote generally 'the records which survive' (e.g. *Brut*. 52), it can also be applied more specifically to records written by particular authors (e.g. *Fam*. 5.12.1 *ut cuperem quam celerrime res nostras monumentis commendari tuis, Brut*. 181, Plin. *HN* 13.21).[27] There is therefore no linguistic difficulty with *Attici monumentis*. The context strongly favours the transmitted reading: chronological enquiry was central to the *Liber annalis*, and it is the topic on which Cicero appeals to Atticus' authority here. While Atticus was principally concerned with Roman history, *Orat*. 120 (quoted above at §14 *omnem rerum*) implies that he also referred to the history of other peoples.[28] The dates of major figures from Greek history such as Solon

---

[23] *OLD s.v. studiosus* 2, 3.
[24] Cf. Amundsen (1939: 127).   [25] *OLD s.v. studiosus* 1a.
[26] For *studiosus dicendi*, cf. *De or*. 1.251, *Orat*. 141. The gerunds *dicendum* and *intellegendum* are found together several times in Cicero: *De or*. 3.73 *veteres dicendi et intellegendi mirificam societatem esse voluissent, Orat*. 10, 17 (and cf. *De or*. 1.90).
[27] See further Drummond in *FRHist* iii.459; *OLD s.v. monumentum* 4, 5; *TLL* 8.1464.28–8.1465.23.
[28] For further discussion, see Münzer (1905), especially 80–85; Drummond in *FRHist* i.347–350.

COMMENTARY   163

and Themistocles are just the kind of details which Atticus might have included in his work.

31. *verbis*] *urbanius* Vitelli: *urbanissime* Orelli: *verbis inversis* Ronconi: *acerbius* Marggraff: *versute* Sydow: *usitatis verbis* Simchen: *verbis suis* Ammon: *verba* Pinkster, qui etiam *instituta* ante *refellere* transp.: del. Wetzel. This textual problem has attracted a wide range of conjectures. Either the redundant *verbis* must be emended, or an adjective must be supplied with it. The deletion of *verbis*, favoured by some nineteenth-century editors, is now rightly considered unsatisfactory, since it causes the sentence to end with the heroic clausula *instituta solebat*. Alessandro Ronconi (1958), in a perceptive discussion of the problem, pointed out that any emendation cannot simply repeat the sense of *subtilitate quadam disputandi*, but must add some further detail to the manner of Socrates' refutation of the sophists. Sydow's *versute* and Reis' *sagacibus verbis* are good examples of conjectures which fail to meet this test.[29] Ronconi's suggestion, *verbis inversis* ('with ironic words'),[30] is supported by §§292 and 299, the only other places where Socrates is mentioned in *Brut*. In §292, Atticus describes how Socrates makes use of irony in his arguments with the sophists; four of the five sophists mentioned in §30 are also listed in §292. Further Ciceronian references to Socrates' irony include *De or*. 2.270 *Socratem opinor in hac ironia dissimulantiaque longe lepore et humanitate omnibus praestitisse* and *Acad*. 2.15 *Socrates autem de se ipse detrahens in disputatione plus tribuebat iis quos volebat refellere; ita cum aliud diceret atque sentiret, libenter uti solitus est ea dissimulatione quam Graeci εἰρωνείαν vocant.*

However, Ronconi's emendation raises the thorny question of Cicero's philosophical position in 46 BC. Socrates' 'irony' was a live issue in the debate between Philo's New Academy and Antiochus' Old Academy: the sceptical New Academy took Socrates' professions of ignorance seriously, while the Old Academy, who believed instead in a dogmatic Socrates, interpreted his disavowals of knowledge as ironic.[31] Glucker (1997: 67)

---

[29] Sydow (1932: 240) compares *Orat*. 22 *versute et subtiliter*, where the adverbs are virtually synonymous; but in *Brut*. 31 the pairing of a phrase and an adverb is less satisfactory on stylistic grounds, and the mere reiteration of *subtilitate quadam disputandi* is pointless.

[30] For *inversus* ≈ 'ironic', cf. Ter. *Haut*. 372 *inversa verba*; Cic. *De or*. 2.261–262; *OLD s.v. inverto* 2c.

[31] This may be an oversimplification: in *Acad*. 1.15–17, Varro, a follower of Antiochus, apparently takes Socrates' professions of ignorance at face value. Glucker (1997: 73) comments, ' "Varro" does seem to be prepared to "give up the possession of Socrates", as long as he can keep Plato.'

164   COMMENTARY

finds that, in *Orat.* 237–238, 'Cicero already expresses himself in terms as typical of the sceptical Academy as we find in his later philosophical works', and he suggests that it may be significant that it is 'Atticus', not 'Cicero', who discusses Socrates' irony in *Brut.* 292. If Cicero was already sympathetic to the scepticism of the New Academy when writing *Brut.*, he may have used the character Atticus to distance himself from the assertion of Socrates' irony.[32] In view of this consideration, it is hazardous to assign to Cicero's own character the same claim in our passage.[33]

Instead, we might consider Vitelli's *urbanius*,[34] which produces a double cretic, one of Cicero's favourite clausulae. To remove *verbis* is to remove the contrast with the sophists' *arrogantia verba* (§30), but it is also to eliminate a cumbersome second ablative from the clause. Indeed, the earlier *verbis* might easily explain the corruption of *urbanius*. It is less philosophically controversial to attribute to Socrates wit than irony. Cf., in addition to the passages cited above, *Fin.* 2.2 *illum quem nominavi et ceteros sophistas... lusos videmus a Socrate, Rep.* 1.16 *leporem Socraticum subtilitatemque sermonis, De or.* 3.67. Nevertheless, while I deem Vitelli's conjecture the best option available, significant uncertainty remains, and I prefer to obelize.[35]

39. *ut*] del. 'alii' (teste Corrado): *vel* Heusinger: *Brute* Martha. Douglas defends the paradosis by citing several Plautine examples of the construction *ut...quam*. However, all the parallels he adduces are in colloquial exclamations, and this construction is rather different from *videsne igitur ut...quam*, which we find here.[36] In the absence of more exact parallels, it is doubtful whether Cicero would have used a colloquialism such as this. Corradus more plausibly defends the transmitted text by appealing to epanalepsis, with *quam* resuming the indirect question introduced by *ut*. If Cicero had started the sentence with the common *videsne (igitur) ut*,[37] the slight change of direction with *quam...sero* would have been quite natural.

---

[32] Cf. *Acad.* 2.15, cited above, where Lucullus, the proponent of Antiochus' dogmatism, voices a similar statement to Atticus' in *Brut.* 292.

[33] The statements of the character Cicero need not always represent Cicero's own views, but it is methodologically questionable to introduce here a potential conflict between the two by means of an emendation, especially when the passage does not demand a reference to Socratic irony.

[34] I see no reason to diverge further from the paradosis with Orelli's *urbanissime.*

[35] Marggraff's *acerbius* (1855: 4) and Philippson's *verissumis verbis* (1936: 1342) do not seem to me to fit well with Cicero's description of Socrates' *subtilitas disputandi.* For further discussion of the textual problem, see Simchen (1953: 167), Pinkster (1970), Malcovati (1971: 400).

[36] Cf. Malcovati (1968: 125).

[37] Cf. §231 *Vides igitur ut ad te oratorem, Brute, pervenerimus.*

COMMENTARY 165

Of the alternatives, Heusinger's *vel* ('even') is superficially attractive, especially given the frequent confusion of *ut* and *vel* in the manuscript tradition. However, *vel* clashes with *ipsa*, which already serves to draw attention to the surprising conclusion that even in Athens, eloquence came to prominence only late in the city's history. Martha adds a vocative to allow *videsne* to address a named character (cf. §§231, 307). However, unlike in §231, there is no particular reason for Cicero to address Brutus directly here, and the second person singular verb is employed merely to maintain the dialogic character of the work (cf. §49 *Et Graeciae quidem oratorum partus atque fontis vides*, §112 *quem ad modum scis*). The corruption of *Brute* into *ut* is very unlikely. The simplest solution would be to delete *ut*. I find this solution first reported by Corradus, who attributes to some unnamed scholars ('alii potius illam tollunt...') the suggestion that it might have arisen from the final syllable of *igitur*. But the anacoluthon is defensible in a conversational context like this.[38]

40. *idem* del. Koch] *valde* Koch: *gravis aut idem* Friedrich. The paradosis is hard to defend. Not only is the combination *ipse...hic...idem* cumbersome and without parallel,[39] but also, as Watt observed (1983: 230), the order *ipse idem* is not found before Christian Latin.[40] Despite Watt's defence,[41] the corruption of Koch's *valde* into *idem* is unlikely, and we do not want the intensifying adverb here.[42] No other emendations merit serious consideration,[43] and so the editor must either delete *idem* or follow Friedrich (1880: 138–139) in introducing another adjective.[44] *Idem* is sometimes used to join two contrasting adjectives (cf. §105 *eundem et vehementem et valde dulcem et perfacetum*, §158 *idem et perornatus et perbrevis*; *OLD s.v. idem* 8), and while it cannot join *ornatus in dicendo* and *plane orator* in this way, since there is no opposition between them, it could have linked *ornatus* with some lost adjective. One might consider, for example,

---

[38] For some striking anacolutha in Cicero and other authors, see Mayer (2005).
[39] Cf. Malcovati (1968: 125).   [40] *TLL* 7.1.203.25–31.
[41] '[The conjecture] assumes little more than the disappearance of *va* after *tā*' (Watt (1983: 230)). Cf. Koch (1861: 485).
[42] The adverb's purpose is much easier to understand in *Div.* 2.81 (*Quasi vero quicquam sit tam valde quam nihil sapere vulgare*), the only other instance of *tam valde* + adjective in Cicero.
[43] Stangl's *interdum* and Baehrens' *identidem*, cited by Malcovati, are quite inappropriate and do not deserve a place in the apparatus.
[44] Friedrich's addition of *gravis aut* before *idem* is not itself very inviting. Surely <*gravis et*> *idem* or <*gravis, tam*> *idem* would be preferable? *Gravitas* and *ornatus* are both stylistic features which would have made Homer the complete orator (*plane orator*). For examples of *gravis* and *ornatus* used in conjunction, see below on §86 *adornatior*.

166 COMMENTARY

ornatus <et limatus> or, perhaps better, *ornatus <et politus>*. Cf. *Cael.* 8 *quod ornate politeque dixisti, De or.* 1.31, and for the contrast between *ornatus* and *politus, De optimo genere oratorum* 12 *dicant se quiddam subtile et politum velle, grande ornatumque contemnere.* Nevertheless, on balance I think it more probable that *idem* was a gloss on *ipse poeta hic. Tam ornatus in dicendo* and *plane orator* complement each other well without any other description of Homer's style.

41. *Graeca* Jahn] *Graecia* L. If L's *Graecia* is correct, *regnante* would presumably have to be roughly equivalent to *florente*, given that Greece was not in any meaningful sense 'ruling' in Themistocles' time. The desire for an antithesis with *dominatu regio liberata* could perhaps justify the unusual usage, but Jahn's *Graeca* (sc. *civitate*) eliminates the difficulty with great economy. In the previous sentence, Cicero has contrasted *nos* and *Atheniensis*, and Jahn's emendation allows him to retain this contrast. Themistocles' Athens did hold a dominant position in Greece, and so *regnante* can take on its ordinary meaning.

46. *controversiae nata* Marggraff] *controversia natura* L: *controversia nata* G[c]: *controversiae nara* vel *controversiae nara natura* Parker: *controversa natura* Ascensius: *controversiae cupida natura* Harnecker. Cicero, quoting Aristotle, provides reasons why it was in Sicily that the first works on rhetoric were written. The Sicilians are described as an *acuta gens*, and the corrupt *controversia natura* must conceal a second characteristic which made their society a natural place for rhetorical theory to be developed. The original text presumably had the meaning 'naturally given to controversy' (*vel sim.*).[45] The most economical way to produce this sense is Ascensius' *controversa natura*, but the adjective *controversus* usually means 'disputed', not 'quarrelsome'.[46] Wilhelm Heraeus (1934: 56 n. 1), developing an earlier argument by Moritz Haupt (1876: 380), suggested that Ammianus was alluding to *Brut.* 46 in his description of the Egyptians as a *genus hominum controversum* (Amm. Marc. 22.6.1; cf. Amm. Marc. 22.16.23 *Aegyptii...*

---

[45] Cf. Cassiod. *Var.* 1 *Ep.* 3 *novimus enim, testante Tullio, Siculorum natura quam sit facilis ad querelas, ut solita consuetudine possint iudices etiam de suspicionibus accusare* (with Haupt (1876: 380)). Although Cicero refers several times to the Sicilians' characteristic sharpness of tongue (see Jahn-Kroll-Kytzler (1962: *ad loc.*)), he does not specifically mention their litigiousness outside of *Brut.* Hence, Cassiodorus may well have been alluding to *Brut.* 46 in particular. However, Cassiodorus diverges too much from Cicero's phrasing for this allusion to be of much use in resolving the textual crux.
[46] *TLL* 4.788.28–75.

COMMENTARY   167

controversi). While Ammianus was familiar with *Brut.*,[47] the parallels between these passages and *Brut.* 46 are too slim to justify the claim made by Haupt and Heraeus that they constitute an allusion to our text.

Much more attractive, and only slightly further from the paradosis, is Marggraff's *controversiae nata* ('born for controversy').[48] Also possible is Parker's *controversiae nara natura*,[49] perhaps a slight improvement on his alternative suggestion *controversiae nara*;[50] however, the simpler idea of a natural inclination towards controversy is preferable to that of an innate expertise in controversy. Harnecker's *controversiae cupida natura* produces satisfactory sense, but there is no need to depart so far from the transmitted text.

46. *de scripto* JDE^cMTγ (*descripto* FUOBES)] *descripte* Ho: *discripte* A. Eberhard. All recent editors print either *descripte* or *discripte*, but, while one might expect a second adverb after *accurate*, the transmitted *de scripto* may well be correct.[51] The phrase *dicere de scripto* ('to speak from a script') is well attested in Cicero: *Planc.* 74 *Recitetur oratio, quae propter rei magnitudinem dicta de scripto est*, *Phil.* 10.5, *Fam.* 10.13.1, *Att.* 4.3.3.[52] In all these examples, the phrase indicates that the orator brought the script with him and consulted it during his delivery, and it may signify the same here. However, because Cicero is translating from Aristotle, there is a possibility that he is using the phrase differently in our passage.[53] Cicero might conceivably mean only that the orators before Corax and Tisias memorized

---

[47] See, e.g., Amm. Marc. 29.1.42 *Maximus ille philosophus, vir ingenti nomine doctrinarum, cuius ex uberrimis sermonibus ad scientiam copiosus Iulianus exstitit imperator* (with *Brut.* 31; cf. Den Boeft 2015: 230); 30.4.5 (with *Brut.* 289). On Ammianus' familiarity with Cicero, see, e.g., Michael (1874), Kelly (2008).

[48] *Natus* + dat., 'born for…', is well attested: see *TLL* 9.1.87.54–9.1.88.3. Malcovati claimed this emendation as her own, but she was anticipated by Marggraff (1855: 6) and Castiglioni (1935: 350).

[49] On the spelling of *narus*, see *Orat.* 158.

[50] Parker (1904: 248); cf. Simchen (1953: 168).

[51] *Descripte* ('in an orderly manner') is unattested elsewhere in classical Latin, while *discripte* ('in an orderly arrangement') occurs only at *Inv. rhet.* 1.49 (*TLL* 5.664.21–25; the MSS cannot, of course, be trusted to transmit accurately the distinction between forms of *describ-* and *discrib-*). One would expect the adverbial forms to be rare, but their rarity should still be a concern to those who wish to introduce either word here.

[52] Cf. *Brut.* 301 *ea sine scripto verbis eisdem redderet quibus cogitavisset*; OLD *s.v. scriptum* 3.

[53] Schöpsdau (1994: 193–198) considers the relationship between *Brut.* 46–48 and Aristotle's *Technon synagoge*, its probable source. The Thucydidean interruption (§47 *quo neminem…scripsit Thucydides*) and the use of Roman legal terminology (§48 *quo quis iudicio circumveniretur*) amply demonstrate that our passage is not simply a translation of Aristotle, but Cicero may nevertheless have rendered some phrases and clauses more literally, and so may have used a phrase such as *de scripto dicere* atypically.

168   COMMENTARY

written drafts, but did not bring the scripts before their audiences.[54] Regardless of which of these two meanings is intended (I suspect the former), *de scripto* would fit with *accurate* and with *sed... tamen*: before Corax and Tisias, orators lacked theoretical training, but most still spoke from a script prepared carefully beforehand.

Several Greek writers discuss the use of written drafts. Alcidamas (*Soph.*) criticizes the use of scripts in an orator's preparation, but does not discuss their use in the delivery of speeches. From the *Rhetorica ad Alexandrum*, perhaps the oldest extant rhetorical textbook, we know that at the time of its composition (probably *c.*340–330 BC) the law did not forbid the delivery of prepared speeches in court;[55] we can also infer from the same passage that some orators did in fact use scripts at that time:[56]

ἐὰν δὲ διαβάλλωσιν ἡμᾶς ὡς γεγραμμένους λόγους λέγομεν ἢ λέγειν μελετῶμεν ἢ ὡς ἐπὶ μισθῷ τινι συνηγοροῦμεν, χρὴ πρὸς τὰ τοιαῦτα ὁμόσε βαδίζοντας εἰρωνεύεσθαι, καὶ περὶ μὲν τῆς γραφῆς, λέγειν μὴ κωλύειν τὸν νόμον ἢ αὐτὸν γεγραμμένα λέγειν ἢ ἐκεῖνον ἄγραφα· τὸν γὰρ νόμον οὐκ ἐᾶν τοιαῦτα πράττειν, λέγειν δὲ ὅπως ἄν τις βούληται συγχωρεῖν (*Rh. Al.* 1444a18–25).

For the fifth century BC, we have evidence from the *Suda*, which gives the following entry concerning Pericles: ῥήτωρ καὶ δημαγωγός· ὅστις πρῶτος γραπτὸν λόγον ἐν δικαστηρίῳ εἶπε, τῶν πρὸ αὐτοῦ σχεδιαζόντων (*Sud.* π 1180). If the *Suda* is to be trusted,[57] the practice of speaking from a written draft did not pre-date Pericles.[58] This is initially hard to harmonize with *Brut.* 46, where we are told that most speakers before Corax and Tisias used a script. Corax and Tisias wrote their textbooks after the expulsion of the tyrants from Sicily (*Brut.* 46 *sublatis in Sicilia tyrannis*), and so very probably after 466 BC, when Thrasybulus was overthrown in Syracuse. This would make Corax and Tisias contemporaries of Pericles, and so would

---

[54] Cf. *QFr.* 3.8.5 *laudavit pater scripto meo*, where *scriptum* might denote a written draft memorized by the father.

[55] At least, that is, in the place where the author of *Rh. Al.* lived.

[56] The phrases γεγραμμένους λόγους λέγειν and λέγειν μελετᾶν apparently represent two different possibilities: i) reading from a script, and ii) practising the speech beforehand. The former is probably a reference to the reading of a script prepared by a logographer: see Chiron (2002: *ad loc.*).

[57] On the statement's reliability, see Gonzalez (2011: 596 n. 55).

[58] Again, we cannot be certain whether the script was used in delivery or only in preparation.

COMMENTARY 169

allow little time for the practice of using a script to become widespread before the publication of the first rhetorical textbooks. However, Cicero has already claimed that there was no theory of rhetoric in Pericles' day (*Brut.* 44), and so he must have believed that Pericles preceded Corax and Tisias. Cicero, quoting from Aristotle, is probably writing from an Athenian perspective: the manuals of Corax and Tisias may not have reached Athens for several decades, and the delay would have left ample time for other orators to imitate Pericles' practice of using a script in the delivery of forensic speeches. Hence, the transmitted text of *Brut.* does seem compatible with the testimony of the *Suda*.

Another relevant text is Sopater's commentary on Hermogenes. In a passage which appears to derive from the same Aristotelian source as *Brut.* 46–48, Sopater writes:[59]

μετὰ δὲ ταῦτα Κόραξ πρῶτον ἁπάντων συνεστήσατο διδασκαλίαν περὶ ῥητορικῆς. οἱ γὰρ πρὸ αὐτοῦ ἐπιτηδεύοντες τὴν τέχνην ὡς ἐμπειρίᾳ τινὶ καὶ ἐπιμελείᾳ χρώμενοι ἐπετήδευον, καὶ οὕτως [οὗτος MSS] μὲν οὐ μετὰ λόγου καὶ αἰτίας οὐδὲ τέχνης τινός (Walz (1832–1836: 5.6.20–24)).

Cicero's *via nec arte* corresponds quite well with οὐ μετὰ λόγου καὶ αἰτίας οὐδὲ τέχνης τινός, and *accurate* fits with ἐπιμελείᾳ, but none of *de scripto*, *descripte*, and *discripte* matches Sopater's ἐμπειρίᾳ. Ἐμπειρία can denote 'practice, without knowledge of principles',[60] and Sopater is not the only author to place it in opposition to τέχνη.[61] The noun ἐμπειρία is appropriate here, and one might suspect that *de scripto* conceals some adverb or phrase conveying the same idea in Latin. However, the versions given by Sopater and Cicero are sufficiently different in other respects, and so the variation here is not a cause for concern.[62] Sopater does not help the editor of *Brut.* in choosing between *de scripto*, *descripte*, and *discripte*.

W. Rhys Roberts (1904) sought to draw parallels between P.Oxy.III 410, a fragment of a rhetorical treatise in the Doric dialect, and the accounts of Corax and Tisias. The fragment begins thus:[63]

---

[59] For comparison of the two passages, see Cole (1991: 69), Schöpsdau (1994: 210). No other account of Corax and Tisias seems to derive from this source. See further Hinks (1940), Radermacher (1951: 28–35), Kennedy (1963: 52–61).

[60] *LSJ s.v.* ἐμπειρία A.II. For discussion of the contrast and its history, see Schiefsky (2005: App. I).

[61] Cf., e.g., Pl. *Grg.* 463b.

[62] Μετὰ λόγου καὶ αἰτίας, for example, is rather different from Cicero's *via*.

[63] Grenfell and Hunt (1903: 26–31).

170 COMMENTARY

...καὶ ἄλλοι τινὲς τὲ ἀξιώσοντι. καὶ αἴ κ᾽ ἐν τᾶι λέξει τᾶι <κατ᾽> ἀρχὰς τᾶν ἐφόδων καὶ μὴ γεγραμμέναις δοκῆι χρῆσθαι [τις] ἀλλὰ ἰδιωτικαῖς [κα]ὶ μηδὲν ὡς ἀκρι<βέως εἰ>[δ]ὼς ἀλλ᾽ ὡς οἰόμε[ν]ος καὶ ἀκακοὼς λέγηι ἢ τῶν δικαστή[ρ]ων ἢ ἄλλων τινῶν.

'...And others will esteem you; and also if in speaking at the commencement of the address of ingratiation one appears to use common phrases and not written ones, and speaks of nothing as a matter of certain knowledge, but of opinion and hearsay, whether from the jury or others.' (tr. Grenfell and Hunt)

Roberts compares the fragment's ἀκριβέως and γεγραμμέναις with the words *accurate* and *de scripto* from *Brut.* 46.[64] The parallel would support the reading *de scripto*, but Roberts fails to convince. The distinctions between 'common phrases' (ἰδιωτικαῖς) and 'written ones' (γεγραμμέναις), and between 'certain knowledge' (ἀκριβέως εἰδὼς) and 'opinion and hearsay' (οἰόμενος καὶ ἀκακοὼς), refer not to the absence of theoretical knowledge or the careful preparation of a speech, but to a particular strategy for winning favour from the audience. Additionally, Grenfell and Hunt date the composition of the text to the beginning of the fourth century BC, that is, before Aristotle wrote the *Technon synagoge*, from which Cicero's account probably derives. Nevertheless, although P.Oxy.III 410 cannot serve to confirm the reading *de scripto*, public speakers in Athens apparently did make use of written drafts between the start of Pericles' public career and the arrival of Corax and Tisias' textbooks in the city.

51. illi quidem Lambinus] quidem L. The idiom *ille quidem... sed* (*tamen*), 'admittedly X, but nevertheless Y', is frequent in *Brut.*,[65] and the absence of *illi* in the paradosis is surprising. I can find only one instance where Cicero uses this idiom without placing *ille* or another pronoun before *quidem*.[66] This exception, *Phil.* 2.6 (*querela misera quidem et luctuosa, sed mihi... necessaria*), is due to an earlier *illa*, which was required to connect the sentence to the previous one. I suspect that Lambinus, Orelli, and Meyer are right to add the pronoun here.

---

[64] Roberts (1904: 18).

[65] It occurs at least sixteen times: see Hamilton (1968: 412 n. 5), and for examples from other texts and authors, Solodow (1978: 38–40). Cf. below on §112 *tamen*; *OLD s.vv. quidem* 4, *ille* 17a.

[66] I have checked all instances of *quidem... sed tamen*, but only some of *quidem... sed*.

COMMENTARY   171

66. *offecit* Wetzel] *officit* L. In the previous sentence, Cicero has said that Cato lacks admirers, just as, many centuries before (*multis iam ante saeculis*), Philistus and even Thucydides lacked them. In this sentence, Cicero gives the reason why (*nam*): 'Just as their terse aphorisms, which were sometimes even made obscure by their brevity and excessive subtlety, were overshadowed by Theopompus' elevated and exalted style (Demosthenes did the same to Lysias), so the style of later writers, built up rather higher, has blocked out Cato's light.' The past tense *offecit* is necessary or the point is lost. In the first century BC, Philistus, Thucydides, and Lysias do not lack admirers: cf. §68 *cur igitur Lysias et Hyperides amatur, cum penitus ignoretur Cato?*, §294, *Orat.* 31 [*Thucydides*] *laudatus est ab omnibus*. They did, however, lack admirers for a while after their successors (Theopompus and Demosthenes) had come onto the scene.

70. *etiam* FλO] om. β: *autem* Simon | *et iam* FO²ᵛˡ] *etiam* λρ. Malcovati and a few other editors opt for the reading of BG, presumably believing it to have been the text of L, but there can be no doubt that the archetype had *etiam Polycliti etiam. Etiam* is often found with comparatives: cf. *Brut.* 92; *Off.* 1.107 *Ut enim in corporibus magnae dissimilitudines sunt...*, *sic in animis exsistunt maiores etiam varietates; Fin.* 5.55 *sunt autem etiam clariora vel plane perspicua...indicia naturae; TLL* 5.948.69–5.949.39. For the use of *etiam* and *et iam* in close proximity, cf. *Att.* 7.1.8, Plin. *Ep.* 4.17.6.

71. *sic in* del. Ellendt] *sic* [*in*] vulg. Most editors resolve the problem of L's impossible *sic in tamquam* by deleting *in*. However, Douglas rightly describes *sic tamquam* as 'an unusual collocation, especially where *tamquam* has no verb'. From *Fam.* 13.69.1 (*Apud eum ego sic Ephesi fui, quotienscumque fui, tamquam domi meae*) and *De or.* 2.180 (*Ac res quidem ista, quam ego, quia non noram, sic tamquam ignotum hominem praeteribam*) one can form a reasonable case that Cicero might have juxtaposed *sic* and *tamquam* in this way.[67] However, the transmitted *in* is a complicating factor. There is no ready explanation for its addition; the hypothesis that *sic in* was a progressive corruption of an initial error, *sicut*, is convoluted and unconvincing. More probably, *sic enim*, which is on the line immediately above in many manuscripts, prompted the accidental insertion of *sic in*. Had a scribe started to copy *sic enim*, before realizing his mistake and returning to the

---

[67] Leeman et al. (1981–2008: *ad De or.* 2.180) compare *QFr.* 2.14.1 and *Tusc.* 1.88.

172   COMMENTARY

correct line of his exemplar, he could easily have produced L's reading.[68] The
redundant *sic* should be deleted as well as *in*.

72. *captum* FλO] *capto* β: *et capto* J[2]. This is one of several places in *Brut.*
where the application of stemmatic principles permits the elimination of a
reading once defended as the paradosis.

73. *cui* vulg.] *quod* L: *cui si* Rom: *quoi ut* Castiglioni: *quoius si* Baehrens |
fuerit] *fuit* Madvig.[69] L's *quod* does not fit into the sentence and must be
corrupt. The emendation *cui*, which provides the necessary connection
between *aequalis fuerit Livius* and the preceding clause, is probably correct.[70] Even with the adoption of *cui*, however, the relative clause *cui aequalis fuerit Livius* remains somewhat obscure. It would have to function as a
hypothetical concession ('suppose that Livius was a contemporary of
Ennius'), introducing the following indicatives. The subjunctive is certainly
used in this way in both independent and relative clauses, but usually the
concessive sense is clearer from the immediate context than it is here (e.g.
Verr. 2.1.37 *'Malus civis, improbus consul, seditiosus homo Cn. Carbo fuit.'*
Fuerit aliis: tibi quando esse coepit?; *Phil.* 1.13), or some word such as *sane*
or *esto* is added to clarify the meaning (e.g. *Brut.* 76, *Fin.* 2.61; cf. K-S
i.189–190). In addition to the apparent obscurity, another ground for suspicion is the presence of *fuerit* immediately before the relative clause. Watt
(1983: 229), following Madvig (1884: 101), suggested that the second *fuerit*
might be a Perseverationsfehler. However, Madvig emended *fuerit* to *fuit*
because he wrongly believed that *cui si aequalis fuerit* was the paradosis. If
cui si had been L's reading, *fuit* would be a simple and satisfactory correction, but since L read *quod*, Madvig's solution is uneconomical. Castiglioni's
quoi <ut> is closer to the transmitted text, but I am not convinced that it
does much to clarify the meaning. The slight obscurity is probably due to a
desire to be succinct: Cicero wants to avoid labouring his point, and so he
makes the final element of his argument against Accius' chronology as brief
as possible, tacking it on with a connecting relative.

---

[68] Much less likely are the ingenious explanations put forward by Simon (1887: 19), who
proposed that *sic in* was a corruption of *signum*, a gloss on *opus*, and Martha, who suggested
that *sicin* might originally have been a gloss added by a scribe exasperated by Cicero's assess-
ment of Livius Andronicus.

[69] Confusion over L's reading has persisted from some nineteenth-century editions into
Wilkins (1903) and Jahn-Kroll-Kytzler (1962).

[70] On the question of orthography, and in particular why I prefer the spelling *cui* even when
quoi allows the corruption to be explained more easily, see Introduction.

COMMENTARY   173

77. *indicant*] *quod indicant* Fuchs. Harald Fuchs (1956) proposed many supplements to the text of *Brut*. The addition of *quod* here is one of the most reasonable:[71] the absence of an object for *indicant* or of any word connecting the clause with the preceding one makes the transition rather awkward. In support of his conjecture, Fuchs cited *Brut.* 117 *quod indicat Gracchi in eum oratio*.[72] However, the absolute use of *indico* is attested,[73] and there are close Ciceronian parallels: *Off.* 1.37 *Hostis enim apud maiores nostros is dicebatur, quem nunc peregrinum dicimus. Indicant duodecim tabulae: 'aut status dies cum hoste'*; *Orat.* 152. L's text should be accepted here.

78. *in* add. Ammon. *In numero* appears 17 times in *Brut.*, while the bare ablative is transmitted only here.[74] The structure *in numero* + gen. pl. ('in the class of...') is a favourite of Cicero's, and variations (with other prepositions, or with *eodem* or another demonstrative adjective in place of the gen. pl.) are also common. The only example without a preposition that I can find in Cicero's dialogues is *Tusc.* 1.98 *ab iis, qui se iudicum numero haberi volunt*. The omission of *in* would have been made particularly easy in our passage by the slightly unusual (although unproblematic: cf., e.g., §315 *a primaque adulescentia*) joining of *-que* to the second word in the phrase.

78. *unctior*] *vinctior* Peter: *lautior* Orelli | *splendidiorque* B] *splendidior* FΛODEMTγ: *et splendidior* Rom. Although *unctus* is not used elsewhere of oratorical style, there is no reason to doubt it here. Both Hendrickson and Kaster translate *unctior* as 'richer' (≈ *opimior, pinguior*), but in view of the accompanying *splendidiorque*, I suspect the intended sense is rather 'more radiant', 'more lustrous' (≈ *lautior, nitidior*).[75] As Jahn pointed out (1865: *ad loc.*), 'die Wirkung der Salben ist *splendor* und *nitor*', and cf., for example, *Att.* 12.6.2, Sen. *Ep.* 51.10 *in primo deficit pulvere ille unctus et nitidus*. Cicero uses the adjective *lautus* in rhetorical contexts (*De optimo genere oratorum* 4), and there is no difficulty with *unctus* being used metaphorically in a similar way.

Peter's *vinctior* involves only a tiny change, but it introduces a reference to prose rhythm which is wholly out of place. Orelli's *lautior* gives the right sense,[76] but there is no need to emend. Indeed, Cicero uses *lautus*

---

[71] One might also consider <*ut*> *indicant*: cf., e.g., *Acad.* 2.131, 2.137 *ut indicat ipsius historia, Verr.* 2.2.185, *De or.* 3.197. For further examples of *quod* and *ut* with *indico*, see *TLL* 7.1.1151.60–7.1.1152.42.
[72] Cf. also *Pis.* 36.   [73] *TLL* 7.1.1151.47–60.
[74] I am grateful to Michael Reeve for drawing this to my attention.
[75] Cf. *Brut.* 238 *non valde nitens... oratio*.
[76] Cf. *Off* 2.52 *illa* [sc. *opera*] *lautior ac splendidior*.

174   COMMENTARY

metaphorically several times,[77] and nowhere else does he add an apologetic *quidam* or *quasi* (*vel sim.*). The following *quaedam*, which indicates the use of an unfamiliar metaphor, fits better with *unctior*.

Many editors were not aware that L's reading was *splendidior*, not *splendidiorque*. The absence of a conjunction might invite one to delete *splendidior* as a gloss on *unctior*, but the adjective helps the reader to understand *unctior quaedam* and should be retained. A conjunction is, of course, required, and B's *splendidiorque* is the best option.

79. *triumvirum*] *triumvir* Ff. Neue and Wagener (1902: 659–660) offer many instances of this idiom, in which a partitive genitive such as *triumvirum* or *decemvirum* is applied to a particular member of a college.[78] Cf., for example, *Att.* 2.6.1 *Anti...ubi quidem ego mallem duumuirum quam Romae fuisse*; *Rep.* 2.61 *Gai Iuli...quod decemvirum sine provocatione esset*;[79] Livy 9.34.1; Augustus, *Res gestae* 1.4, 7.1, 7.3.[80] For examples without *esse* or *creari*, cf. Varro *ap.* Gell. *NA* 13.12.6 *Ego triumvirum vocatus a Porcio tribuno plebis non ivi*, Livy 3.40.12, Tac. *Ann.* 6.12.1. Our passage, where *triumvirum* is not in apposition to a stated noun or pronoun, is particularly difficult, but in view of the frequency of the idiom, the paradosis is probably sound.[81]

86. *adornatior* Vc^c, ut vid.] *adortor* FλE: *adhortor* OBE²MTγ: *adhortator* O²: *ornatior* J²: *ardentior* Corradus: *uberior* Marggraff: *atrocior* Triller: *asperior* Moser: *acerbior* Orelli: *incitatior* Busche. Previous editors believed that ρ's *adhortor* was the text of L, but the agreement of Fλ proves that L's reading was actually *adortor*. *Adortor* must be a corruption of a comparative adjective, and the most economical emendation is Vc^c's *adornatior*.[82] The adjective *adornatus* is rare (although cf. *Verr.* 2.1.58 *forum comitiumque adornatum ad speciem magnifico ornatu*), and the comparative unattested. However, the adverb *adornate* may have been used in a rhetorical context (Suet. *Gram. et rhet.* 30.2 *declamabat autem genere vario, modo splendide atque adornate* [λ: *adoranter* ω: *ornate* Kaster]), and the verb *adorno*

---

[77]   *OLD s.v. lautus* 2.

[78]   See also Oakley (2005: 429–430).

[79]   The transmitted reading: see Oakley (2005: 430 n. 1), Powell (2006: *ad loc.*).

[80]   There is no need to rely upon the Greek version of *Res gestae* 7.1 (as does Oakley (2005: 430)); the Latin text is sufficiently preserved: see Scheid (2007: *ad loc.*).

[81]   *Pace* Malcovati (1968: 126), Watt (1983: 229).

[82]   The letters *rna* have been added above an original *adortor*; the scribe's intention was presumably to suggest *adornatior*, not *adornator*. The conjecture may have been made by Leon Battista Alberti, who owned Vc.

COMMENTARY   175

certainly was.[83] The desire for alliteration with *acrior* could have motivated Cicero to employ *adornatus* instead of the common *ornatus*.

Adornatior ('more elaborate', 'more embellished') is a very suitable epithet for describing Galba's oratorical style.[84] Additionally, the pair *adornatior acriorque* corresponds well with *gravius et vehementius* in the following clause (and cf. §88 *tanta vi tantaque gravitate*).[85] Cicero often uses forms of *gravitas* and *ornatus* in conjunction (e.g. *Brut.* 35 *nihil ornatum vel verborum gravitate vel sententiarum*), and in some places the terms are virtually synonymous (e.g. *Inv. rhet.* 2.50, *Leg. Man.* 52, *De or.* 1.54). For the combination of *ornatus* and *acer*, cf. *Brut.* 317 *alter ornatus, acer et non talis qualem tu eum, Brute, iam deflorescentem cognovisti, sed verborum et actionis genere commotior*.

Of the numerous other emendations which have been proposed, the best is Corradus' *ardentior*. The metaphor of heat is picked up in §§88 *incensum*, 89 *inflammet*, 93 *incendebat*, and 93 *flamma oratoris exstinguitur*. Yet Corradus' conjecture, like most of the others, is inferior to *adornatior* in three respects. Most obviously, it is further from the paradosis. Secondly, the contrast with *gravius et vehementius* is less exact. Finally, as Orelli observed, *ardentior* is arguably stronger than *acrior*, and so the combination would be more effective if the adjectives were transposed. While the passionate intensity of Galba's delivery is emphasized throughout §§86–90, it is only one element of a broader stylistic contrast between Laelius and Galba, between the two oratorical *laudes: una subtiliter disputandi ad docendum, altera graviter agendi ad animos audientium permovendos* (§89). In §86, the references to Galba's richer supply of rhetorical embellishments (*adornatior*) and his greater ferocity (*acrior*) are both apposite as Laelius initiates this contrast.

87. *alii aliud* Manutius] *aliud* L: *aliud alii* Manutius | *a* del. vulg.] *alii* Reis. The phrase *eodem tempore* should not be interrupted by *alii*, which belongs either before or after *aliud*. The Brepols *Library of Latin Texts* offers 21 instances of *aliud alii* in classical Latin (nine in Cicero), but only one relevant example of *alii aliud* from before the twelfth century.[86] Nevertheless, in spite of this significant fact, I prefer to add *alii* before *aliud* in our

---

[83] *OLD s.v. adorno* 6.
[84] Compare the description of Galba's style in §82 (especially *ut egrederetur a proposito ornandi causa*).
[85] Marggraff (1855: 10–11) made the same point. His conjecture, *uberior*, is plausible, but the corruption to *adortor* is more easily explained with *adornatior*.
[86] Ambrose, *Expositio Evangelii secundum Lucam* 10.115 *alii aliud sorte defertur*.

176   COMMENTARY

passage. In none of the instances of *aliud alii* is *alii* dependent on a genitive, whereas here *alii* belongs with *quorum*. Additionally, if the transmitted order is correct, then Cicero did write *aliis aliud* at *Rep.* 1.49.[87]

88. illa disquisitione scripsi] *illa dis quaestione* FΛβ: *illa die quaestione* O[c]: O[ac] incert., fort. *illa dies quaestione*: *illo die quaestione* Lambinus: *illa quaestione* vel *illa de caede quaestione* Orelli: *illa tandem quaestione* Weidner. O[c]'s *die* is a good example of a conjecture which has gained a far wider acceptance than it deserved. Printed by almost all modern editors, *die* is merely a plausible, but not very probable, emendation of the nonsensical *dis*. *Illa die* produces an apt contrast between the single day which Galba needed to persuade the court to acquit the defendants and the multiple adjournments which had followed Laelius' defence speeches. However, the feminine *illa* poses a major problem, because Cicero overwhelmingly favours the masculine gender of *dies*. *Illa die* is unattested in Cicero, whereas *illo die* is found 44 times. When variations and expansions are included (*eo die, illo ipso die*, etc.), there are well over 100 examples of a masculine *die* with the meaning 'on that day', but just one of a feminine *die* (*Div.* 1.103 *ea ipsa die*).[88]

This clear preference for *illo die* would give one pause for thought even if *illa die* were the transmitted reading, but when it is a conjecture, it renders it highly unattractive. One could, with Lambinus, emend *illa* to *illo*, but the feminine *illa* is surely an indication that it belongs with *quaestione*. We might follow Orelli's suggestion and delete *dis*, but it is not easy to explain how *dis* would have entered the text. Weidner's *illa tandem quaestione* (1879: 66–67) and Orelli's *illa de caede quaestione* are even more difficult to explain palaeographically, and it can hardly be said that the sense produced by either is sufficient to merit its acceptance in spite of this objection. A much more economical solution is *illa disquisitione* ('from that investigation').[89] This relatively rare word, attested twice in Cicero and only a few times elsewhere in classical Latin,[90] could easily have been corrupted.

---

[87] Cf. *Rhet. Her.* 3.38 *alii videtur aliud*, and below on §285 *alia <aliis>*. *Aliis aliud* is found several times in Latin poetry (*metri causa*).

[88] The four instances of *ex ea die* and *ex hac die* (*Pis.* 61, *Verr.* 2.1.34, *Att.* 5.14.1, 9.6.3) involve a quite distinct use of the word: the final two, for example, refer to particular days which have just been named. In the single instance where *ipsa die* is found on its own (*Fam.* 1.6.1), *dies* is used instrumentally ('will be worn down... by time itself').

[89] Gregory Hutchinson suggests that *disquisitione* and *quaestione* might once have been variant readings, and that *dis-* might be the remnant of *disquisitione*. He further points out that *illa quaestione* would take up §85 *quaererent*.

[90] *TLL* 5.1450.79–5.1451.7; Heumann and Seckel (1907: 152). The word is admittedly more common in medieval Latin.

COMMENTARY 177

In *Sull.* 79 (*in magnis disquisitionibus*), *disquisitio* apparently denotes simply a trial, and in *Har. resp.* 13 (*ad facinoris disquisitionem interest adesse quam plurimos*), it refers to an inquiry conducted by the *collegium pontificum*. Cf. Livy 26.31.2 *in disquisitionem venit* (of an inquiry in the senate), Suet. *Iul.* 15 *disquisitionem populi*, Suet. *Nero* 2.2 *disquisitionem senatus*, Tac. *Ann.* 3.60.1 *disquisitionem patrum*, 5.11.1.

89. *an*] del. Pareus. The use of *an* to introduce an alternative ('or perhaps') is widely attested,[91] but the repetition of *an* ('perhaps X, perhaps Y') is properly paralleled only at *Att.* 11.6.7 *Is dicitur vidisse Quintum an euntem an iam in Asia.* Many scholars would delete the first *an* in both places.[92] Yet in neither sentence is there an obvious explanation for the addition of *an*, and the structure *an... an* is employed in a very similar way in the two passages. Examples of the use of *an... an* after verbs of doubting and uncertainty would provide a helpful comparandum for this use. However, while *an* is used after such verbs throughout all periods, structures such as *nescio an... an, quaero an... an* are hard to find in Republican Latin. Nevertheless, it is more probable that Cicero used a repeated *an* in *Brut.* 89 and *Att.* 11.6.7 than that the word was accidentally introduced in both places. The doubling of conjunctions (*et... et, aut... aut*, etc.) is more frequent in classical Latin than in many modern languages; here, the doubling of *an* would serve to emphasize Cicero's uncertainty about the period of time between the addition of Cato's speech to the *Origines* and his death.

92. *quod peringeniosis*] *peringeniosis quidem* Cavarzere | *ut*] *quod* Cavarzere. In §§91–93, Cicero is examining why some orators do not write and why others do not write as well as they speak. The first two groups described by Cicero do not write down their speeches, and the third group seems also to be made up of orators who do not write. Syntactically, this group is placed in parallel with the two previous ones (*alios oratores...; alios...; alios...*), and the absence of an infinitive with the third *alios* suggests that we should supply either *nihil scripsisse* or *non laborare ut meliores fiant* from earlier in the sentence. Furthermore, these orators are aware that they cannot write as well as they can speak (*melius putent dicere se posse quam scribere*), which would be an understandable reason for reluctance to write. In the transmitted text, Cicero apparently goes on to comment that

---

[91] *OLD s.v. an* 9; *TLL* 2.6.61–2.7.33.
[92] So K-S ii.527. There is a slightly fuller discussion in an earlier edition (Kühner (1877–1878: 2.2.1024)). Cf. Hand (1829: 307–309).

178   COMMENTARY

this awareness of the inferiority of one's writing is characteristic of those of great talent but insufficient training (*quod peringeniosis hominibus neque satis doctis plerumque contingit*), and he cites Servius Galba as an example of this type of orator. However, as Cavarzere (2012) has pointed out, Galba certainly did write down his speeches (§§91, 93). Even without this difficulty, the similarity between the second and third groups of orators would be problematic: the second group's belief that its glory will be greater if its written speeches are not read by the critics implies an awareness that its written output would be less impressive than the speeches as delivered.

We might instead take the third *alios* as a reference to orators, like Galba, who did write down their speeches, but whose written works did not live up to their oratorical reputations. Cavarzere rejects this option on the ground that orators possessed of great ability in public speaking and the knowledge that their writing, by comparison, is unimpressive are very unlikely to publish written versions of their speeches, especially since there was no expectation that they should do so. Cavarzere's solution is to transfer *peringeniosis... Galbae* to the following sentence by replacing *quod peringeniosis* with *peringeniosis quidem* and *ut* with *quod*. Even with these interventions, though, the text is not smooth: the final group which chooses not to write (*alios... scribere*) is dealt with in a very cursory fashion, and the transition between *scribere* and *peringeniosis* is abrupt.

If the text is corrupt, I would prefer to postulate a lacuna before *quod peringeniosis*. This lacuna might have included further discussion of the third group which chooses not to write, as well as an explicit transition to the second question, why some orators do not write as well as they speak. But if *quod peringeniosis... refers* only to a greater ability in speaking than in writing, rather than to the awareness of that difference in abilities, the paradosis is defensible. On this interpretation, the transition to *quod peringeniosis* would conceal a shift in focus from the *causa non scribendi* to the *causa non tam bene scribendi quam dixerint* (cf. §91).[93] Such imprecise composition seems possible, and I accept the transmitted text.

97. Sex. Madvig] *sed* L. The transmitted text is unsatisfactory: the Pompeius mentioned here would have to be the Quintus Pompeius of §96, and the return to this minor orator is abrupt and uncharacteristic of Cicero's practice in *Brut*. Gnaeus and Quintus Caepio, who have just been discussed, bore witness against Quintus Pompeius in a trial of *c*.138;[94] this fact might

---

[93] Jahn-Kroll-Kytzler (1962): 'Der Übergang zu diesem zweiten Gedanken (*quod peringeniosis...*) ist verschleiert'.
[94] *Font.* 23; *TLRR* no. 8.

COMMENTARY 179

have brought Pompeius back into Cicero's mind, but the connection between the two sentences (*Tum... sublevabant* and *Sed... prudentiae*) is still obscure. Sumner (1973: 52) suggests that Cicero intended to contrast Pompeius' extant works with the speeches of the Caepiones, which did not survive. If Cicero had merely stated that Pompeius' writings were extant, this interpretation would be plausible, but he then goes on to assess the quality of Pompeius' works (*nec nimis extenuata, quamquam veterum est similis, et plena prudentiae*). These evaluative comments do not fit so easily with Sumner's reading and seem rather to indicate that we have here the introduction of a new orator, not the reappearance of Quintus Pompeius. Madvig's emendation yields a much smoother text.

In defending the paradosis, Sumner was motivated by the difficulty of identifying Madvig's Sextus Pompeius. Commentators have assumed that he was the father of Gnaeus Pompeius Strabo and his brother Sextus Pompeius, both mentioned in §175. However, Sumner (1973: 51) argues that this Sextus Pompeius was a promagistrate in Macedonia in 119 and that his probable birth-date in or before 160 puts him out of place among the orators older than Gaius Carbo and Tiberius Gracchus.[95] Neither the identification with the promagistrate in Macedonia nor the promagistrate's date of birth is certain, but Sumner nevertheless raises a real issue for the view that this man is the father of the Pompeii of §175. One could emend the text in some other way, but the economy of Madvig's emendation makes it appealing. Perhaps another Sextus Pompeius, otherwise unknown, is in view: we cannot expect to have heard of this figure, given that many other people mentioned in *Brut.* are not known from elsewhere. One candidate is the grandfather of the Pompeii of §175. If their father had been born in 160 or shortly before, their grandfather could have been born between 180 and 190, which would make him similar in age to the other orators in this section.

99. Gracchum] *C. Gracchum* Jahn. Tiberius Gracchus was mentioned in §96 and will return in §104, while Gaius Gracchus, against whom Fannius' speech was directed, makes his first appearance in this passage. Consequently, many editors have followed Jahn in adding the *praenomen*. However, it is evident from §§99–100 that Fannius' speech was a famous one,[96] and Cicero would have expected his audience to know that it was

---

[95] Cf. §96 *C. Carbo et Ti. Gracchus... de quibus iam dicendi locus erit, cum de senioribus pauca dixero.*
[96] Cicero apparently quotes from the same speech at *De or.* 3.183; cf. *ORF*[4] 142–145.

180 COMMENTARY

Gaius Gracchus, not Tiberius, who proposed the extension of citizenship to the *socii* and the *nomen Latinum*.[97]

109. *facete* Lambinus] *facile* L: *faecem* Carcopino: *facete peregrinos* Martha | *C. Gracchum paulum* vulg.] *paulum C. Gracchum* L | *aetate*] *ei aetate* Stangl. Those who defend the absolute use of *agitare* cite as parallels Ter. *Ad.* 501 (*quam vos facillume agitis*) and Porcius Licinus fr. 3 (Courtney) 10 (*tres per idem tempus qui agitabant nobiles facillime*).[98] However, it is an overstatement to call *facile agitare* ('to be prosperous') a 'well-attested idiom',[99] especially given that Porcius is probably imitating Terence's phrase.[100] Additionally, Terence and Porcius use the phrase with the sense of material prosperity ('to live easily'), a meaning quite different from the political context of *Brut.* 109. Lastly, we should expect a more explicit comment on Pennus' oratorical abilities than that offered by the paradosis. We must resort to emendation.

The transposition of *paulum* and *C. Gracchum* allows *agitare* to govern an eminently suitable object. In 126 BC, while he was tribune, Pennus enacted a law expelling all non-Romans from Rome,[101] and Gaius Gracchus is known to have delivered a speech on this law.[102] Hence, although we know little else about Pennus' tribunate, the supposition that it was characterized by fierce hostility to Gaius is reasonable.[103] As well as its historical plausibility, this emendation gives point to *tuus etiam gentilis*: *etiam* highlights the similarities between Marcus Drusus and Marcus Pennus, both of whom opposed Gaius during their tribunates. Finally, the transposition, by supplying an object for *agitare*, provides the needed reference to Pennus' oratory.[104] The transposition leaves *aetate antecedens* without an object, but

---

[97] Malcovati suggests that 'Gracchus κατ᾽ ἐξοχήν Gaius fuit', but whether Cicero chooses to omit the *praenomen* apparently depends more on the context: at *Caec.* 87 (*Unde qui cum Graccho* [sc. *deiecti*] *fuerunt? Ex Capitolio.*) Tiberius Gracchus is in view, while in *De or.* 3.214 the subsequent quotation makes it clear that the reference is to Gaius.

[98] Outside of *Brut.* 109, Cicero never uses *agitare* without a direct object. Douglas questioned the use of a personal subject with the verb *agitare*. But see, e.g., *Att.* 14.18.1 *saepius me iam agitas quod*...; *Rosc. Am.* 66; *Leg.* 1.40.

[99] Hendrickson (1962: 98).   [100] Courtney (1993: 90).

[101] *Off.* 3.47; Stockton (1979: 94–95).   [102] *ORF*⁴ 179–180; Stockton (1979: 218).

[103] Carcopino (1929: 8–9) objected that Gaius Gracchus spent the year 126 in Sardinia, and that as a result he could not have taken part in an oratorical duel with Pennus in that year. But, as Stockton points out (1979: 95), such a duel could have taken place early in 126, before Gaius set out for Sardinia. Alternatively, Pennus could have spoken against Gaius during his absence in Sardinia, with Gaius eventually responding upon his return in 125/124.

[104] Carcopino's conjecture *faecem* is more economical (cf. *OLD* s.v. *faex* 4a '(of persons) dregs, scum'), but *faecem agitavit* is an unappealing combination of words. I do not find Martha's *facete <peregrinos> agitavit* attractive either: Pennus' attempt to expel the *peregrini* from Rome was rather more than mere witty provocation or harassment.

COMMENTARY   181

the slight awkwardness can be tolerated, especially in view of parallels such as *Rep.* 1.18 *domi vicissim Laelium, quod aetate antecedebat, observaret in parentis loco Scipio.*[105] *L's facile* has also been doubted. Reis compared §180 *facilis et expeditus ad dicendum*, but, like Malcovati (1960: 337; 1968: 129), I find this parallel unsatisfactory: the context in §109 suggests *facile* should mean 'easily', not 'fluently', and Gaius Gracchus was not an easy opponent to overcome. Lambinus' *facete* is persuasive, particularly since the same corruption occurs in §198.

111. *tecti* FλODEMTγ] *recti* F^cB. At this point in *Brut.*, B derives from β, and so the agreement of F^cB is not sufficient to put L's reading in doubt: the archetype read *tecti*. All recent editors print *recti*, but the transmitted text poses no difficulty. *Tectus* = 'guarded', 'cautious' is well attested in Cicero (e.g. *De or.* 2.296 *unum te in dicendo mihi videri tectissimum, Orat.* 146; *OLD s.v. tectus* 2b), and is sometimes associated, as here, with wisdom (*Deiot.* 16 *Quis consideratior illo? Quis tectior?*[106] *Quis prudentior?; Phil.* 13.6 *quid sapientia? Cautioribus utitur consiliis, in posterum providet, est omni ratione tectior.*). Scaurus' guarded manner fits well with his *gravitas summa et naturalis quaedam...auctoritas*, and would help to explain why he seemed more like a witness than a defence speaker (*non ut causam, sed ut testimonium dicere putares, cum pro reo diceret*). Scaurus' terse and careful style of speaking can also be deduced from Antonius' words in *De or.* 1.214: *iam, credo,* [sc. *Scaurus*] *huc veniat, et hanc loquacitatem nostram vultu ipso aspectuque conterreat: qui, quamquam est in dicendo minime contemnendus, prudentia tamen rerum magnarum magis quam dicendi arte nititur.* Cicero intimates that Scaurus epitomized the opposite of the *loquacitas* of Antonius and Crassus.[107]

In support of *recti*, one might observe that *sapientis hominis et recti* anticipates more precisely the observation in §112 that Scaurus' style conveyed not only practical wisdom, but also trustworthiness (*significabat enim non prudentiam solum, sed, quod maxime rem continebat, fidem*). However, this argument is not sufficient to motivate the emendation: Scaurus' *gravitas* and *auctoritas* would themselves have served to engender *fides*, and the

---

[105] Alternatively, Stangl's *ei* might easily have been lost after the transposition of C. *Gracchum paulum.*
[106] *Tectior* has been corrupted into *rectior* in some MSS.
[107] The same point may be implicit in *Font.* 24 *M. Aemilio Scauro...cuius iniurati nutu prope terrarum orbis regebatur*, and perhaps even in Sall. *Iug.* 15.4 *Aemilius Scaurus, homo nobilis inpiger factiosus, avidus potentiae honoris divitiarum, ceterum vitia sua callide occultans.*

182   COMMENTARY

reference to moral rectitude is not necessary.[108] In fact, emending to *recti* would create a more substantial problem than that which it would solve. Cicero only applies the adjective *rectus* to a person in *Fam.* 12.5.2 (*unus L. Caesar firmus est et rectus*), where it denotes 'faithful', 'committed to our cause', not 'morally upright'.[109] *Rectus* appears not to be used of people in this latter sense until Imperial Latin. On several counts, then, *tecti* is superior to *recti*.

112. *acta*] *lectu* Geel. The second supine *lectu*, not attested before the fourth-century grammarians, has been adopted by many editors.[110] The rare form would certainly have been liable to corruption, and *lectu* would have point: 'Scaurus' books were worth reading, but no-one reads them'. Additionally, *acta*, while often coupled with *vita* in Cicero, even without modifying adverbs (e.g. *Tusc.* 1.109 *vita acta perficiat ut satis superque vixisse videamur; Fam.* 4.13.4 *quid gravitas, quid altitudo animi, quid acta tua vita...a te flagitent, tu videbis; Sen.* 38), typically has a clearer purpose.[111] Finally, Scaurus' autobiography is usually given the title *De vita sua*,[112] and the elimination of *acta* would draw Cicero's title closer to the normal designation.

However, other considerations make *lectu* less appealing. (1) The sequence *lectu...legit...legunt* is rather laboured. (2) Elsewhere, Cicero uses the noun *lectio*, not the supine (e.g. *Brut.* 69 *ut nullius scriptum exstet dignum quidem lectione*).[113] (3) Cicero never uses a supine with *utilis*.[114] (4) The second supine is usually placed immediately after its adjective in prose (70% of the time), and 'most exceptions to this tendency are due to (contrastive) focus on the supine' (e.g. Plin. *HN* 17.78 *non perflatu modo utilis*

---

[108] According to Sallust, Scaurus accepted bribes from Jugurtha (e.g. *Iug.* 29.2 *Scaurus...magnitudine pecuniae a bono honestoque in pravom abstractus est*), and it is perhaps because of these allegations that Cicero, who often praises Scaurus, emphasizes his *gravitas*, *consilium*, and *constantia* (e.g. *Pro Rabirio perduellionis reo* 26, *Mur.* 36, *Fam.* 1.9.16) rather than his *integritas* and *virtus*.

[109] *OLD s.v. rectus* 7, 10c.

[110] The supine was already becoming fossilized in Terence; *lectu* in later Latin is artificial. See further Adams (2016).

[111] Badian (1967: 226) suggested that *de vita ipsius acta* would imply 'written after his death', but one can reflect on one's life before reaching the very end (cf. *Sen.* 9 *conscientia bene actae vitae...iucundissima est*). The question of whether Scaurus wrote the work near the end of his life or some years earlier has not been settled (Smith in *FRHist* i.268–269).

[112] e.g. Val. Max. 4.4.11, Plin. *HN* 33.21; for further examples, see Smith in *FRHist* i.268. *De vita sua* was apparently a standard title for an autobiographical work: cf. the autobiographies of Rutilius (Smith in *FRHist* i.279) and Augustus (e.g. Suet. *Aug.* 85.1, Ulp. *Dig.* 48.24.1).

[113] But cf. *cognitu*, *cognitione*, both used by Cicero.

[114] But cf., e.g., Ps.-Sall. *Ad Caes. sen.* 2.4.5 *vera atque utilia factu*, 2.13.8.

COMMENTARY 183

verum et aspectu grata).[115] Such a contrastive focus is obviously inappropriate here.[116] In view of these factors, I retain the superfluous, but otherwise unobjectionable, *acta.*

112. *tamen* **om. D.** *Tamen* is accepted by Wilkins, Reis, and Malcovati, but the strong adversative is inappropriate here; we want simply, 'neither is it so suited to our affairs, nor ought it to be preferred to the praises of Scaurus'. *Tamen* has probably arisen through a dittography of *neque tam*, and we should follow A. Eberhard in excising it.

115. *sed*] *et* **Bake.** Marggraff (1855: 12), defending L's *sed*, maintains that the conjunction establishes an antithesis between Cotta, who spoke like a real orator (*ut orator*), and Scaevola, who lacked the force and abundance which the case required (*nequaquam autem ea vi atque copia quam genus illud iudici et magnitudo causae postulabat*). Marggraff may be correct, but *sed* may be merely resumptive, as it is at §117 *sed ut vita* (cf. §§64, 80, 140).[117] *Sed* is frequently used to indicate the conclusion of a parenthetical remark and the resumption of the main subject.[118] In any case, there is no need to follow the majority of recent editors in adopting Bake's emendation. An additional hint that the text is sound can be found in the *ille quidem...nequaquam autem* construction. Cicero typically uses the structure *ille quidem...sed (tamen),*[119] and in fact this is the only place in the Ciceronian corpus where *autem* replaces *sed* in this idiom. Cicero has probably diverged from his usual practice in order to avoid repeating *sed.*

128. *lege* **Peter**] *lege Manilia quaestio* **L:** *illa quaestione* **Piderit:** *lege Mamilia* **Ernesti:** *lege Mamilia quaestorium* **Kroll:** *lege Mamilia quaestio cum esset* **Lichtenfeld.** L's *Manilia* is obviously a corruption of *Mamilia*, and *Mamilia quaestio* has every appearance of being a gloss on *invidiosa lege*. Ernesti deleted only *quaestio*, but *Mamilia quaestio* is the more likely gloss.[120] Kroll emends *quaestio* to *quaestorium*, but Galba's status as a *quaestorius* is irrelevant here. Cicero's point is that five men of great distinction were convicted under the *lex Mamilia*: Galba, a priest, and four ex-consuls.

---

[115] Kroon (1989: 217 n. 42).
[116] Malcovati asks (1968: 127), 'Come altrimenti un libro potrebbe essere utile?'.
[117] Bake wishes to emend *sed* to *et* in §117 as well.
[118] e.g. *De or.* 1.82 *sed cum*, and see further *OLD s.v. sed* 2b, K-S ii.76.
[119] Cf. above on §51 *illi quidem*.
[120] For an account of the *quaestio Mamilia* of 109 BC, see Gruen (1968: 136–156); cf. Sall. *Iug.* 40.

184 COMMENTARY

It is Galba's membership of a priestly college, not his quaestorian rank, that made his conviction remarkable.[121]

130. atque etiam acri Hendrickson] *atque etiam* FλOBDE: *atque etam* MTX (*atque e tam* G): *acuto etiam* Kayser. Two objections have been made to the transmitted text. Firstly, there seem to be few similarities between Gaius Fimbria and Gaius Sextius Calvinus to make sense of *atque etiam*. However, *atque etiam* can be understood as indicating simply that these men were contemporaries, rather than that they both possessed *ingenium* and *sermo elegans*. Cf. §131 *doctus etiam Graecis*, where *etiam* evidently does not mean that Lucius Caesulenus was learned in Greek literature. The second, and more substantial, problem is that *ingenio* lacks a qualifying adjective. When he uses *ingenio* as an ablative of description, Cicero usually qualifies it in some way (e.g. §55 *longe plurimum ingenio valuisse*, §125 *praestantissimo ingenio*, §205 *ingenio praestans*), and one would especially expect an adjective here for the sake of balance with *sermone eleganti*.

To solve this stylistic difficulty, Martha takes *eleganti* with both *ingenio* and *sermone*, and he cites Quint. *Inst.* 5.13.48 (*Vibius Crispus, vir ingenii iucundi et elegantis*) as evidence for the phrase *ingenium elegans*. But, although a person may be described as having a pleasant and elegant character, in *Brut.* 130 *ingenium* clearly denotes 'talent', 'natural aptitude', and in this sense it does not fit comfortably with *elegans*. We need another adjective to go with *ingenio*. Kayser's emendation is plausible, but it is best not to meddle with the combination *atque etiam*, which also marks transitions between orators in §§80, 90, and 169. The loss of an adjective is at least as easy as the corruptions postulated by Kayser. The phrase *acre ingenium* is found several times in Cicero, and Hendrickson's supplement is attractive. Cf. §204, §282 *ineratque et ingenium satis acre et orationis non inelegans copia*.[122]

131 *de damno iniuria* Peter] *de iustitia* L: *de iniuria* Pisanus: *damni iniuria* Hotman: *DC sestertia* Martha: del. Friedrich. L's *de iustitia* is undoubtedly corrupt. Only one *lex Aquilia* is known from the historical record, a law providing compensation to the victims of wrongful damage (the killing of slaves and quadrupeds, and the vandalism of property).[123] Mommsen

---

[121] Cf. §127 *Hic, qui in collegio sacerdotum esset, primus post Romam conditam iudicio publico est condemnatus.*

[122] Other options are, of course, possible. For a list of adjectives used with *ingenium*, see *TLL* 7.1.1527.79–7.1.1529.21.

[123] For bibliography on the *lex*, see Crook (1984), Rodger (2006).

COMMENTARY 185

(1899: 826 n. 4) suggested that Cicero might have been referring to another *lex Aquilia*. However, the punishment under the attested *lex Aquilia* was the payment of compensation (goods or money) to the wronged party, and the reference to the seeking of a fine (*multam... petivisset*) fits well with this.[124] The similarity between *iustitia* and *iniuria*, a noun which features frequently in connection with the *lex Aquilia*, also tells in favour of the identification of the two laws.

There remains the question of how Cicero would have described the law.[125] Elsewhere, he mentions it explicitly only in *Tull*. He twice defines the law as *de damno* (*Tull. 9 cum sciret de damno legem esse Aquiliam*; *Tull.* 42 *lege Aquilia... quae de damno est*), but his argument in *Tull*. 10–12, 41–43 makes it clear that the key phrase in the law was *damnum iniuria* (e.g. *Tull.* 10–11 [*M. Lucullus*] *necesse putavit esse... illam latebram tollere: 'damnum iniuria'*; cf. *QRosc.* 32, 54). This phrase, found also in the jurists' discussions of the *lex Aquilia*,[126] has been construed in two ways: (1) with *iniuria* as an adverbial ablative ('wrongfully'), the full phrase being *damnum iniuria datum*;[127] or (2) as an asyndeton bimembre ('loss and unlawful harm').[128] The first interpretation has received almost universal support from scholars, but more recently Alan Rodger (2006) has argued for the latter. In view of Gaius' use of the phrase *damni iniuriae actio* (*Inst.* 3.210; cf. *Inst.* 4.9, 4.37, Justinian *Dig.* 2.12.3.pr),[129] Rodger may well be correct with regard to the classical jurists, but he neglects the testimony of Cicero.[130] Yet throughout *Tull*. Cicero unambiguously uses *iniuria* as an adverbial ablative.[131] Moreover, in *Tull*. 38–43, Cicero is contrasting the *actio* of the praetor Lucullus with the *lex Aquilia*, and he stresses that the absence of *iniuria* from Lucullus' *actio* marks a key difference from the *lex*.[132] Since the word *iniuria* in the *lex Aquilia* is integral to Cicero's argument, *Tull*. provides

---

[124] *Multa* can denote a fine paid to the state or to an individual (*TLL* 8.1580.69–8.1581.37).

[125] Friedrich deletes *de iustitia*, and it is true that Cicero does not always specify the contents of a law, especially when there is only one law sponsored by members of a particular *gens*. But we know of only one *lex Cincia* and one *lex Varia*, and yet see *Sen.* 10 *legis Cinciae de donis et muneribus*, *Corn.* 1 fr. 54 Crawford *lege Varia de maiestate*.

[126] See the passages collected in Crawford (1996: ii.724–725) and Rodger (2006).

[127] *OLD s.v. iniuria* 1b.

[128] On asyndeton bimembre in legal Latin, see De Meo (2005: 116–120); on the meaning of *iniuria*, Paschalidis (2008).

[129] Mommsen (1899: 826 n. 1) viewed Gaius' *damni iniuriae* as 'eigentlich wohl eine Missform'.

[130] Rodger (2006: 422).

[131] e.g. *Tull.* 39 *recuperatoribus persuaderes non esse iniuria M. Tullio damnum datum*.

[132] *Tull.* 41; cf. Lintott (2008: 69–73).

186 COMMENTARY

secure evidence as to his interpretation of the phrase *damnum iniuria* in the law.

What title would Cicero have used for the *lex*? Hotman proposed *damni iniuria*, but Martha and Douglas rightly find his explanation of the corruption unconvincing.[133] Additionally, the construction *de* + abl. is much more frequent with *lex* than the genitive, and there is no reason to suspect the transmitted *de*. Pisanus' *de iniuria* is economical,[134] but the absence of *damnum*, a key identifying word for the law, leaves it unusually vague. If, as I think, Cicero interpreted *iniuria* in the *lex Aquilia* as an adverbial ablative, *de iniuria* becomes even less tempting. Instead, I prefer Peter's *de <damno> iniuria*.[135] The difficulty of construing the two successive ablatives probably led to the omission of *damno*, with *iniuria* being corrupted independently to *iustitia*.

136. *vectigali levavit* J] *vectigale levavit* BFJᶜUρ: *vectigali locavit* Willcock: *vectigali vexavit* Seager: *vectigalem levavit* Douglas: *vectigalem liberavit* Lintott. Because of the historical complexities of the post-Gracchan agrarian legislation, this single sentence on Spurius Thorius has received much critical attention. I do not intend to summarize or evaluate the numerous theories on the relationship between Appian's three agrarian laws (*B Civ.* 1.121–124), Cicero's *lex Thoria* (mentioned in *Brut.* 136 and *De or.* 2.284), and the epigraphic *lex agraria*.[136] The sentence itself (*Sp. Thorius satis ualuit in populari genere dicendi, is qui agrum publicum uitiosa et inutili lege uectigale levavit*) is grammatically ambiguous: after accepting the simple emendation of *vectigale* to *vectigali*, one has to decide whether to take *vectigali* as ablative of separation and *lege* as ablative of means ('he relieved public land from a rent by means of a defective and useless law'), or vice versa ('he relieved public land from a defective and useless law by means of a rent').[137] The first interpretation is illogical: a defective and useless law cannot provide relief.[138] The second,

---

[133] Hotman suggested that *damni iniuriae* was abbreviated to *d. i.*, and that the contracted form was then incorrectly expanded to *de iustitia*.

[134] This emendation, favoured by Badian (1967: 226) and Kaster (2020), is often attributed to Lambinus, but was first proposed by Victor Pisanus.

[135] This emendation occurred to me before I found it in Peter (1839). For the full phrase, see Ulp. *Dig.* 9.2.1.pr.

[136] Noteworthy recent studies are Lintott (1992: 34–58), Crawford (1996: i.57–60, 113–180), De Ligt (2001), Roselaar (2010: 261–271), and Sisani (2015: 230–243).

[137] The fullest examination of the syntactical possibilities remains Badian (1964: 235–242). Badian rightly dismisses the possibility of taking *vectigali* as an adjective; cf. Lintott (1992: 283). Scholars have also taken different views on the meaning of *levavit*: see Sacchi (2006: 21–23).

[138] Badian (1964: 238–239).

COMMENTARY   187

however, remains plausible, and, in my view, no scholar has put forward a persuasive reason why it should not be accepted.[139]

Seager (1967) objected that only the introduction of a new law, not the imposition of a rent, can provide relief from a bad law,[140] but *vectigali* can easily stand as shorthand for 'rent introduced by a law'. Willcock (1982: 474) argued that Cicero's description of Thorius' oratory (*valuit in populari genere dicendi*) implies that Thorius was a popular tribune whose actions Cicero was unlikely to praise. Yet, as Morstein-Marx (2004: 204–240) has shown, ability in speaking before the people was an important tool for both *populares* and *optimates*, and we cannot conclude from *Brut.* 136 that Thorius was a *popularis* or that Cicero disapproved of his law.[141] Willcock further objected that 'there is no parallel instance... of *ager* (or any word like it) being used as an object of *levare*' (1982: 474–475). However, the meaning of *levare* ('relieve') makes it unsurprising that it was used predominantly with a personal object, or with a burden as the direct object and a person in the ablative; this does not preclude Roman writers from using the verb, in special circumstances, with a noun such as *ager* as its object.[142] The liberation of public land from a bad law provides a suitable context for the sense given by *levare. Att.* 1.19.4 *liberabam agrum*, where *liberare* is almost synonymous with *levare*, forms an additional reason for confidence in *levare* here.

Hence, there are no compelling linguistic or semantic grounds for emending *levavit*. Nor do the historical data prove that the transmitted description of the *lex Thoria* is inaccurate. Among others, Badian (1964), Johannsen (1971), De Ligt (2001), and Sisani (2015) have found ways of reconciling our text with the other sources without adopting any emendation except *vectigali*. Some, perhaps all, of these accounts can be challenged,[143] but the lack of agreement among historians on the aims and effects of the *lex Thoria* is itself an argument against emendation.

---

[139] For the construction with the two ablatives, Crawford (1996: i.59) compares *De or.* 1.166 *ne is... turpi tutelae iudicio atque omni molestia stultitia adversarii liberaretur*; he further adds, 'Cicero surely could not have imagined the notion that anything could be achieved with a *vitiosa... lex* as an instrument'.

[140] With Seager's emendation *vectigali vexavit*, the two instrumental ablatives are awkward. Willcock (1982: 475 n. 8) also objected to the clausula.

[141] Cf. *Brut.* 164–165, 191, 247; *TLL* 10.1.2702.11–29.

[142] Other examples of the use of *levare* with a non-personal object include: Plin. *HN* 17.210 *arbor... adsiduo levata onere*; Tac. *Ann.* 2.23.4 *equi, iumenta... praecipitantur quo levarentur alvei*; Julian Dig. 14.2.8 *levandae navis gratia res aliquas proiciunt.*

[143] I find De Ligt's interpretation most persuasive. The grounds for the identification of Appian's second law, introduced by a certain Sp. Borius (who must, of course, be Sp. Thorius), with Cicero's Thorian law are strong; the law's purpose may well have been to make the

188   COMMENTARY

Although change to the vulgate text is unnecessary, two emendations still deserve consideration. Douglas' *vectigalem levavit* is only a little further from the paradosis and removes the ambiguity of the two ablatives. This emendation, however, forces *vectigalem* ('made to bear rent by...') to do too much work.[144] Willcock's *locavit*, with *vectigali* as an ablative of price, is an attractive solution, clarifying the sense without straining the syntax.[145] Nevertheless, Willcock's case against the paradosis is weak, and the historical details of the Thorian law are uncertain.[146] I prefer to retain *levavit*.

141. *cum...consentiens*] del. Bernhardy | *rebus* Schütz] *verbis* L. There are two principal difficulties with the paradosis. Firstly, *cum verbis sententiisque consentiens* repeats what Cicero has already said in *cum sententiis congruens*. Secondly, the assertion that all of Antonius' movements were in harmony with his words as well as his thoughts apparently contradicts the earlier claim that his gestures did not depict his words (*gestus erat non verba exprimens*). These are substantial problems, and it is not surprising that many editors have followed Bernhardy in deleting *cum...consentiens*. Yet, as Douglas writes (1966: *ad loc.*), 'Deletion of the phrase, leaving *manus umeri*, etc. in loose opposition to *gestus* does not greatly help matters.' The redundancy of the repetition, while unattractive, does not make the text impossible.

The abruptness of the movement from the opposition between *verba* and *sententiae* to their use in tandem is a greater concern. As is clear from the more detailed treatment of the subject in *De or.* 3.220 and Quint. *Inst.* 11.3.88–91,[147] the phrase *verba exprimens* refers to a style of gesticulation in

---

holdings of the *veteres possessores* their private property, with the damage to the poor mitigated by a rent. De Ligt's explanation of Appian's '15 years' and the consequent dating of the *lex Thoria* to 118 BC are more questionable. However, unless fresh evidence comes to light, the triple forces of the unreliability of Appian, the fragmentary state of the epigraphic *lex agraria*, and the ambiguity of Cic. *Brut.* 136 will continue to make certainty unattainable.

[144] It also compels us to conclude that Appian erred in assigning the second, rather than the third, of the agrarian laws to Sp. Thorius (Douglas (1966: 247–250)). Lintott (1992: 283) criticizes the use of *levare* = 'relieve' without a separative ablative, and instead suggests *liberavit*. He thus diverges further from the MSS while not addressing the other problems with Douglas' emendation.

[145] *Pace* Willcock (1982), L's corrupt *vectigale* does not significantly increase the probability of *levavit* also being corrupt: the corruption of the ablative singular of i-stem nouns to -*e* is exceedingly common.

[146] Roselaar (2010: 270 n. 152) further objects that *locavit* is a verb ill suited to a law which prescribed the privatization of public land.

[147] *De or.* 3.220 *Omnis autem hos motus subsequi debet gestus, non hic verba exprimens scaenicus sed universam rem et sententiam non demonstratione sed significatione declarans, laterum inflexione hac forti ac virili, non ab scaena et histrionibus, sed ab armis aut etiam a palaestra; manus autem minus arguta, digitis subsequens verba, non exprimens.* Quint. *Inst.* 11.3.88–89 *Et*

COMMENTARY 189

which the speaker mimics the meaning of individual words and phrases through his gestures. The speaker might, for example, imitate a lyre-player by pretending to strike the strings with his hands (*citharoedum formatis ad modum percutientis nervos manibus ostendas* (Quint. *Inst.* 11.3.88)). Cicero regarded this type of gesture as suited to the actor, not the orator. The orator should rather reproduce in his gestures the whole thought which he is trying to express. By saying that Antonius' gestures were in harmony with his words (*cum verbis... consentiens*), Cicero cannot be referring to the theatrical type of gesture, since he has just said that Antonius did not practise that style. If the text is sound, the pair *verbis sententiisque* must refer together to the thought, not the individual words. Cf. *De or.* 3.220 *manus autem minus arguta, digitis subsequens verba, non exprimens* ('but the movements of the hand must be less rapid, following the words and not eliciting them with the fingers' (tr. Rackham)). But it is hard to see why Cicero would write *verbis sententiisque* rather than simply *sententiis*. *Non verba exprimens* and *cum verbis sententiisque consentiens* are not totally contradictory, but Schütz's *cum rebus sententiisque consentiens* is an improvement. Cicero often uses *res* ('the subject matter') and *sententiae* ('the ideas') to represent two different aspects of the same concept, the topic of the speech. See, for example, *De or.* 2.56, 2.58 *Timaeus... longe eruditissimus et rerum copia et sententiarum varietate abundantissimus*, 2.145, 3.220 (cited above at n. 147), *Inv. rhet.* 2.49, *Leg.* 2.17. The remembrance of *verba* could have caused the corruption.

142. *in questionibus* BOEG] *in quaestionibus* FJ (*in quę-* UMTX): del. Weidner: *in conquestionibus* Lambinus. *Conquestio* is considerably more common than *questio* both in Cicero and in classical Latin as a whole, but the use of *questio* at *Orat.* 135 is sufficient to confirm the paradosis here. In both passages, the proximity of other words with the prefix *con-* (*Brut.* 141–142 *consentiens... convertebat... commovendam*, *Orat.* 135 *corrigimus... commutantur*) may have motivated Cicero's avoidance of *conquestio*. Alternatively, Cicero may have viewed *conquestio* as the more technical term and may have avoided it in his later rhetorical works for that reason.[148]

---

hi quidem de quibus sum locutus cum ipsis vocibus naturaliter exeunt gestus: alii sunt qui res imitatione significant, ut si aegrum temptantis venas medici similitudine aut citharoedum formatis ad modum percutientis nervos manibus ostendas, quod est genus quam longissime in actione fugiendum. Abesse enim plurimum a saltatore debet orator, ut sit gestus ad sensus magis quam ad verba accommodatus.

[148] Most of the occurrences of *conquestio* in Cicero are from *Inv. rhet.* On the use of *conquestio* in rhetoric, see further Lausberg (1998: 207–208); *TLL* 4.352.56–71.

190 COMMENTARY

151. *una*] del. Jahn | *Rhodum ille*] *Rhodi; nam illo* Madvig. ʻ*una* without either *cum* or a plural verb is hard to parallel except in the doubtful passage 81.23.'[149] But cf. *Quinct.* 24 *L. Albius... una profectus est*, 58, *Flac.* 43 *Pari felicitate legatus una venit Nicomedes, Att.* 9.13A.2 *quod si una essem.* There is no need for either Jahn's deletion or Madvig's conjecture. The ellipsis of *mecum* is well suited to the informality of the dialogic context. (Compare the colloquial *ain tu?* in §152.)

151. *at* Martha] *et* L. Martha's emendation produces much better sense. Both Cicero and Sulpicius had energetically pursued rhetorical training, and Sulpicius' return from Rhodes marked an apparent change in his career goals, as he turned to pursue legal expertise rather than oratorical renown; *at* draws attention to this change of direction.[150] The corruption is very easy, especially after *et doctior.*

162. *defensiuncula* Lange] *defensione iuncta* L: *laudatio cum defensione iuncta* Petersen: *defensione senatus iuncta* Sydow: *oratiuncula* Murgia: *defensio* Piderit. Douglas succinctly summarizes the two major problems present in the transmitted text: the absence of a subject for the sentence and the poor sense given by the phrase ʻ[a speech] combined with a defence'. Sydow (1932: 240–241) supplied *senatus* as an objective genitive with *defensione*, thus partially resolving the second of these difficulties, but the first remained unaddressed. Petersen's emendation,[151] by contrast, deals with the first issue, but not the second. Rather than attempting to fill a lacuna, however, we could instead consider the possibility that *defensione iuncta* is corrupt. Lange's *defensiuncula* is an excellent emendation. The diminutive fits well with the comment which follows on the speech's brevity, and the corruption of so rare a word would have been easy.

Of course, the rarity of *defensiuncula* is the reason some editors have found it hard to accept (it is unattested elsewhere), but many such diminutives occur only once.[152] Murgia objected that ʻone says not *defensio pro*, but *defensio of* (with objective genitive)' (2002: 69), and he proposed instead *oratiuncula*. However, *oratiuncula* is not only markedly further from the

---

[149] Douglas (1966: *ad loc.*).

[150] The adversative force in the examples cited at *OLD s.v. et* 14 is less significant than that present here.

[151] Fuchs (1956: 141), following a similar line of reasoning to Petersen, proposed *defensione iuncta <oratio>*.

[152] See further Douglas (1966: *ad loc.*). The editors of the *TLL* included *defensiuncula* as a separate lemma on the basis of Lange's emendation.

COMMENTARY   191

paradosis and less prone to corruption (given the presence of the word in §§77 and 207), but it is also inept before *ut oratio autem brevis*.

One would indeed expect a genitive with *defensio* (although compare Val. Max. 8.7.1 *defensionem suam pro Hispania opposuit*),[153] but in our passage, as in Valerius, there is a reason for the exception. Cicero has just mentioned Crassus' speech in support of a law proposed by the elder Quintus Servilius Caepio, the consul of 106 BC (§161 *suasit Serviliam legem Crassus*),[154] and he will return to this speech in §164 (*illa in legem Caepionis oratio*). In §162, however, Crassus' speech *in consulatu pro Q. Caepione* is a defence of the younger Quintus Servilius Caepio.[155] The desire to avoid confusion with the more famous speech on the *lex Servilia* may well have motivated Cicero's use of the unusual construction *pro Q. Caepione defensiuncula*. Alternatively, Cicero may merely have wanted to avoid the need to rewrite the first part of the sentence, since he could hardly have written *L. Crassi in consulatu Q. Caepionis defensiuncula*.

166. *potentiam* L] *prudentiam* Campe. The transmitted *potentiam* is confirmed by *Planc.* 51 *potentissimo et clarissimo civi C. Claudio*.

167. *leporum* Simon] *exemplorum* L. Reis adopted Simon's *leporum* (1887: 40), but subsequent editors have preferred to keep the paradosis.[156] Although Cicero, like the author of *Rhet. Her.*, seems to have viewed the *exemplum* as a *figura sententiae* without any argumentative function,[157] the noun is still clearly out of place in a tricolon with *argutiae* and *urbanitas*. Nor are *exempla*/παραδείγματα distinctively Attic, as the following consecutive clause requires.[158] Additionally, the following sentences refer only to the sharpness of Titius' wit, and *easdem argutias*, which picks up the first member of the tricolon, seems to imply that all three members are from the

---

[153] Gertz' emendation, adopted by Shackleton Bailey (2000), would make this parallel irrelevant, but Briscoe (1998, 2019) accepts the transmitted reading.

[154] *RE s.v.* 'Servilius 49'; R 96 in Sumner (1973).

[155] *RE s.v.* 'Servilius 50'; R 162 in Sumner (1973). See further Badian (1964: 34–70).

[156] Malcovati admitted that '[s]enza dubbio alla logica soddisfa più *leporum* che *exemplorum*' (1960: 335), but she argued that *exemplorum* was still possible in the context. However, if an emendation is superior, sometimes we should accept it even when sense can be found in the paradosis. The noun is much more at home in §145 *Q. Scaevolam ... [Crassus] obrueret argumentorum exemplorumque copia*.

[157] On the history of the exemplum in rhetorical theory, see Demoen (1997). Demoen contrasts Aristotle, for whom the exemplum (παράδειγμα) was 'the rhetorical counterpart of logical induction' (133), with Cicero and the *auctor ad Herennium*, for whom its purpose was the adornment of speeches.

[158] Cf. Douglas (1966: *ad loc.*).

192 COMMENTARY

same semantic field. Hence, instead of *exemplorum*, we should expect another noun denoting the shrewd or witty use of language, and *leporum* is an attractive suggestion: 'His speeches were so full of shrewd aphorisms,[159] witty remarks, and humour that they almost seem to have been written by an Attic pen.' Cf. §143 *facetiarum et urbanitatis oratorius, non scurrilis lepos*; §177 *nemo umquam urbanitate, nemo lepore, nemo suavitate conditior*; *De or.* 1.159; and for the plural, *Orat.* 96, *OLD s.v. lepos* 2b. The corruption would have been easy, especially if *leporum* had been mistaken for an abbreviated *exemplorum*.

169. *et exercitatus* Bρ] *exercitatus* Fλ. This is one of a handful of places where L's reading is in real doubt. The coincidental omission of *et* by Fλ is somewhat more likely than its addition in Bρ, but L may have contained variants or a scribal correction. *Et* should be retained. Cicero is juxtaposing practice (*exercitatus*) and natural ability (*natura volubilis*), two members of the traditional triad, and the *et... et* construction helps to clarify this.

171. *tu* L] *tum* Weidner: *ibi* Koch. Koch (1861: 485) objected to the word order *audies tu* after *tu... intelleges*, and proposed emending *tu* to *ibi*. Weidner (1879: 70) improved on Koch's emendation with his *tum*, which picks up from the preceding *iam... cum* and stays closer to the transmitted text; Weidner's conjecture has been adopted by most subsequent editors. However, Cicero often places an emphatic *tu quidem* after a second person verb: cf. *Tusc.* 3.82 *de quibus audies tu quidem*, *Att.* 1.20.2 *disputas tu quidem, Fin.* 2.80, *Off.* 1.2, *Fam.* 1.9.1, et al.[160] By contrast, the word order with a verb followed by *tum quidem* is unparalleled in Cicero. The structure *tu quidem... sed* is equivalent to *ille quidem... sed* (discussed above at §51 *illi quidem* and §115 *sed*), and has concessive force: 'Although you also will hear certain words not much used in Rome, these can be exchanged and unlearned.'[161] Finally, the purpose of *etiam* is clearer after *tu quidem*: Cicero

---

[159] For the association of *argutiae* with Greek writers, cf. *Leg.* 1.7 *Nam quid Macrum numerem? Cuius loquacitas habet aliquid argutiarum, nec id tamen ex illa erudita Graecorum copia, sed ex librariolis Latinis*; and for the meaning, see Krostenko (2001: 157 n. 6). In Imperial Latin, *argutiae* sometimes took on the meaning 'humour, wit', but there is no evidence that the noun was so used in the Republican period, and such a sense does not seem appropriate in *Brut.* 167. In saying that Titius was 'not very tragic' (*parum tragice*) in transferring *argutiae* to his tragedies, Cicero probably refers to excessive cleverness and refinement in the use of words, not to humour. (Cf. *Amic.* 45 *sed nihil est quod illi non persequantur argutiis*.)

[160] For discussion of the use of *quidem* with pronouns, see Solodow (1978: 36–42).

[161] Translation adapted from Adams (2007: 133). On the type of words Cicero is thinking of, see Adams (2003: 442–443).

COMMENTARY   193

has already heard speech which lacks the *color urbanitatis*, and in Gaul Brutus will *also* hear words not common in Rome.[162]

171. *retinnit* Ff] *retinuit* Fλρ: *recinuit* B: *recinit* Fd^c. The verb *retinnio* ('ring back') is found only here and in Varro *Rust.* 2.pr.2 (of a house 'ringing with many Greek names'), where some editors accept Gesner's *retinniat* in place of the manuscripts' *retineant*. Given the weak attestation of *retinnio*, *recinit* deserves consideration. *Recinit* is not much further from the transmitted *retinuit*: *recino* and *retineo* are easily confused in minuscule scripts.[163] In discussing the orator's voice at *Orat.* 57, Cicero comments: *Est autem etiam in dicendo quidam cantus obscurior...quem significat Demosthenes et Aeschines, cum alter alteri obicit vocis flexiones.*[164] However, in *Brut.* Cicero cannot be talking about the similarity between the orator's vocal modulation and that of a singer, since he goes on to say that the *color urbanitatis* is found not only in the voices of orators, but also in those of other people at Rome (*nec hoc in oratoribus modo apparet, sed etiam in ceteris*). *Recinit* would have to refer rather to pronunciation, and there is no evidence that *recino* was used in this sense. The verb *tinnio* is used to denote shrillness of voice (e.g. Plaut. *Poen.* 33; *OLD s.v. tinnio* 2),[165] and Quintilian employs it to describe the sound of the letter *v* at the end of Greek words (Quint. *Inst.* 12.10.31 *At illi ny iucundam et in fine praecipue quasi tinnientem illius loco ponunt*). The more specific use of *retinnio* here with reference to a Roman accent is a natural development, and *resonat* helps to clarify the word's sense.[166] Consequently, although the evidence for *retinnio* is slender, we can be confident that it was used by Cicero here.

172. *Tincam* L] *Tingam* Badian ex Quint. *Inst.* 1.5.12. In the only other extant reference to this man, Quintilian reports how Hortensius criticized *Tinga Placentinus* for saying *precula* instead of *pergula*.[167] Badian (1967: 227) suggested bringing the transmitted *Tinca* in *Brut.* into alignment with Quintilian's spelling.[168] However, even though in Quintilian the interchange

---

[162]   Marchese (2011): 'con le tue orecchie ascolterai parole non usuali a Roma'.
[163]   For some instances of the confusion, see *TLL* 11.2.326.16–18.
[164]   On the similarities between the orator's voice and music, see also Quint. *Inst.* 1.10.22–33, especially 24–25.
[165]   Cf. Tac. *Dial.* 26.1 *tinnitus Gallionis.*
[166]   For *resono* in the context of accents, cf. Quint. *Inst.* 11.3.30 *os...in quo nulla neque rusticitas neque peregrinitas resonet.*
[167]   On Tinga's provincial dialect, see further Adams (2007: 134–135).
[168]   Badian's proposal was accepted by Sumner (1973). Malcovati, who kept the spelling *Tinca*, suggested (1968: 125) that the name might derive from the fish (*tinca*, 'tench'), which is first mentioned in Auson. *Mos.* 125.

194 COMMENTARY

of the letters *g* and *c* is central to the anecdote, we cannot be certain that the name is spelled correctly there. But if Hortensius' jibe toward Tinga had been well known at the time, then perhaps Cicero was himself making fun of the man by deliberately misspelling his name. A joke of this kind would fit well within the account of Tinga's *sapor vernaculus*, which apparently cost him in his battle of wit with Granius. Therefore, whether or not *Tinca* was the correct spelling, it should be retained in this passage.

174. *Romanarum*] **del. Douglas.** Douglas suggests that the memory of Roman history is out of place among the 'traditional rhetorical categories' which structure Cicero's portrayal of Gellius' oratory. By expunging the word, Douglas simplifies the reference to *memoria* and clarifies the antithesis between *res* and *verba*. Nevertheless, in spite of these arguments, one should not be too hasty to delete *Romanarum*. Douglas argues that the emphatic positioning of the adjective before *rerum* implies 'a contrast, e.g. with Greek, here hard to explain'. However, of the 18 instances of the use of *immemor* in Cicero, this is the only one in which a dependent genitive precedes the adjective,[169] and so *rerum*, as well as *Romanarum*, is in an emphatic position; it is difficult to see a reason for this if *Romanarum* is deleted. If *nec...indoctus* looks back to §173 *Graecis doctrinis institutus*, then the word order of *Romanarum rerum immemor* may indeed set up an opposition with Greek: Gellius was both learned in Greek theory and well versed in Roman history.

But more significantly, Cicero alludes several times in *Brut.* to the value of the knowledge of Roman culture and history to the orator. His most explicit comment is found in his lament for the deficiencies of the other orators of his generation: §322 *nemo qui memoriam rerum Romanarum teneret, ex qua, si quando opus esset, ab inferis locupletissimos testis excitaret.*[170] Thus, if Gellius had possessed a deep knowledge of Roman history, we should not be surprised that Cicero chose to mention it.

175. *item in iure* UE[c]] *itam in iure* BJU[c]O[c]O[v]γ: [spat. vac. v litt.] *in iure* O[ac]: *ita m iniure* F: *sitam in iure* DEM | *eminuerat* Prohasel] *et* L; pro *itam in iure et* (L) Reis coniec. *ita eminuerat inter aequalis in iure ut.* Having praised Sextus Pompeius for his knowledge of civil law, Cicero extends his brief digression on jurists with a discussion of two other eminent figures from the field, Marcus Brutus and Gaius Billienus. The correction of L's

---

[169] On word order tendencies with regard to *immemor*, see further Devine and Stephens (2006: 391–393).

[170] Cf. (on Curio) *Brut.* 214 *Nullum ille poetam noverat, nullum legerat oratorem, nullam memoriam antiquitatis collegerat*, and *Brut.* 205, 267, *De or.* 1.201. See also Gowing (2000: 51).

COMMENTARY   195

nonsensical *itam* to *item* (of UE^c) is compelling, highlighting the continu-
ation of the legal excursus; the corruption was probably due to perseveration
from *scientiam*.

However, *pace* Badian (1967: 227) and Kaster (2020: 108, 278), this simple change is not sufficient to restore the text to a satisfactory condition.
Firstly, if *item* is to be construed with both Brutus and Billienus, then *simili
ratione* merely reiterates *item in iure* and has no purpose. Secondly, the
phrase *homo per se magnus* can apply only to Billienus, since Brutus was not
a *novus homo*, and likewise *prope ... evaserat* must apply exclusively to
Billienus, because the *qui*-clause which follows describes him alone. As a
result, the first half of the sentence (*item ... Brutus*) should be taken as a
separate main clause, and a comma should be placed before *et paulo*. The
first clause, though, still lacks a verb.

One might contemplate deleting the sentence's first *et*, or replacing *et*
with *fuerat*, but, even though this Marcus Brutus has already been mentioned as an expert in law in §130,[171] some further description of his legal
abilities is needed. Prohasel's *eminuerat* is an elegant solution. *Eminuerat*
corresponds well with *summus evaserat*, leaving *item in iure* in parallel with
simili ratione. Palaeographically, the similarity of the letter sequences

---

[171] Two men named Marcus Brutus are mentioned in §130: a son (*M. Brutus, in quo magnum fuit, Brute, dedecus* [Pa^c: *genus* L] *generi vestro...*) and a father (*patremque optimum
virum...et iuris peritissimum*). Douglas suggested that the jurist of §175 was probably the
father, but Sumner (1973: 77, 105) argued that chronology favoured identification with the son.
Two factors tell against Sumner's conclusion. Firstly, while Cicero calls the father *iuris peritissimum*, his portrayal of the son (*dedecus generi vestro... accusator vehemens et molestus*) is very
unflattering; although there is no necessary contradiction between the son's having been an
expert in law and his also having been, in other respects, a blot on the family name, one would
at least expect Cicero to have supplied an explanation of these conflicting descriptions.
Secondly, there is no indication that any of the three jurists of §175 was also an orator, whereas
the younger Brutus of §130 was a frequent prosecutor. And in fact there is no chronological
obstacle to Douglas' identification of the jurist Brutus with the father of §130. The son did not
hold any magistracies (§130 *is magistratus non petivit*), and his birth-date is consequently hard
to pin down: Sumner suggested the range 150–145 BC, but this depends on the son's having
been the legal expert mentioned in §175. He may have been born later. Gaius Billienus, who
was a little younger than the jurist of §175 (*paulo post eum C. Billienus*), was certainly born by
143, since Cicero states that he would have become consul at some point between 104 and 100,
had not the successive consulships of Gaius Marius limited his opportunities (§175 *nisi in
Marianos autem consulatus... incidisset*). On this basis, Sumner suggests a birth-date of
*c.*147/146 for Billienus, but, as a *novus homo* (*homo per se magnus*), he may have had a slower
career, and there is no reason why he cannot have been born some years earlier. (On the
retarded careers of *novi homines*, see Wiseman (1971: 166).) Finally, Brutus the father also has
uncertain dates: he may have been aedile in 146 and praetor *c.*140, but equally he may not
(*MRR* i.466, 480). Hence, I suggest that the following birth-dates are compatible with the available evidence: M. Brutus the father *c.*165, C. Billienus *c.*160–155, M. Brutus the son *c.*140. If
these dates are roughly correct, then Brutus senior was indeed a little older than Billienus and
can be identified as the jurist of §175.

196   COMMENTARY

[*it*]*eminiure* and *eminuer*[*at*] could easily have led to the loss of *eminuerat*. If *at* had been the only surviving remnant of *eminuerat*, it might have been corrupted into *L*'s *et*. Cf. *Orat*. 104 *Demosthenes, qui quamquam unus eminet inter omnis in omni genere dicendi, tamen non semper implet auris meas*.

175. simili ratione prope Schütz] *prope simili ratione* L: *prope sine ulla oratione* Bake. 'Prope simili ratione, c'est-à-dire *scientia juris*, mais sans la géométrie ni la philosophie.'[172] But even if the strange collocation *prope similis* can sometimes make sense,[173] here *prope* must modify *summus*, because Billienus failed to reach the consulship and did not become *summus*. We cannot emend, with Bake, to *prope sine ulla oratione*, both because *simili ratione* performs an important function in looking back to *item in iure*, and because this change does not solve the problem of the inconsistency between *summus evaserat* and *qui...incidisset*. The transmitted word order is needlessly unclear, and it is best to follow Schütz and Reis in transposing *prope* and *simili ratione*. For *prope* + superlative, cf. Bibaculus fr. 1 (Courtney) 6–8 *quem tres cauliculi...ad summam prope nutriant senectam*, *De or*. 1.6 *permultos excellentis in quoque genere videbis, non mediocrium artium, sed prope maximarum*, Caes. *BGall*. 2.32.4.

179. Verginius Corradus **ex Plut.** *Sull*. **10.4]** *Vergilius* Bλρ: *Virgilius* F. Theoretically, Cicero's greater proximity to the events of 87 BC would give his testimony more weight than Plutarch's. However, the difference between Cicero's *Vergilius* and Plutarch's Οὐεργίνιος is very slight and probably results from a copyist's slip rather than an author's error. Badian (1964: 100 n. 87) remarked that the influence of the poet's name makes corruption of *Verginius* to *Vergilius* more likely than the reverse. On the other hand, none of the many Republican Verginii is known to have had the *praenomen* Marcus, while the name M. Vergilius is found in first-century BC inscriptions.[174] This consideration has less weight than it might, though, since this man, as a tribune of the plebs, must have been a plebeian. Plebeian members of patrician *gentes* often show a wider range of *praenomina* than the noble branches.[175] On the balance of probabilities, Corradus' *Verginius* is to be preferred.

---

[172] Martha (1892: *ad loc.*).   [173] Cf. Livy 2.47.1 *prope similis fortuna est versata*.
[174] e.g. *CIL* 14, 03451; *AE* 1991, 00117. The tribune may be identical with the *monetalis* VER of 86 BC (*RRC* 350A/1a, et al.). The presence of the names VER and GAR on the same coins is interesting, in view of the mention of C. Gargonius in *Brut*. 180, but the coincidence does not prove the identification of either VER or GAR with the figures named by Cicero.
[175] Shackleton Bailey (1976: 59).

COMMENTARY   197

181. *superioris aetatis* del. Kayser] post *ignoratione* transp. Mommsen. Martha supposes that *superioris aetatis* is dependent upon *quid*, but it is hard to find much sense in the phrase as a partitive genitive. If the transmitted text is sound, *superioris aetatis* must belong with *de iis*: 'What can be written about those of an earlier age?' However, if Powell's principles concerning the limits of hyperbaton in Cicero's writings are to be trusted,[176] the word order is not just harsh, but in fact impossible. The rhetorical question makes sense without *superioris aetatis*: Cicero has already indicated that he is talking about people of an earlier age (*aliquot ex veteribus*), and the relative clause which follows *de iis* provides further clarity. Mommsen therefore transposed *superioris aetatis* to before *quid* and allowed it to depend on *ignoratione*. However, in so doing Mommsen reduces the pungency of the terse statement *sed hoc quidem ignoratione*.[177] Additionally, while inversions of two or three words are extremely common, larger-scale transpositions of this kind occur much less frequently. The phrase *superioris aetatis* does not improve the text in its transmitted position or in the preceding clause, and I prefer to follow Kayser in deleting the words as a facile gloss (either on *aliquot ex veteribus* or on *de iis*).[178]

187. *sane discipulo* Madvig] *discipulo sane* L. In its transmitted position, *sane* qualifies *frigenti* ('received very coldly'),[179] but Madvig (1884: 105) pointed out that the purpose of *sane*, as often, is to highlight the concessive sense of the subjunctive *dixerit* ('granted that Antigenidas said to his student...'). Yet, when it performs this function, *sane* is almost always placed next to the verb it modifies,[180] and when it is separated from the verb,[181] the word order does not allow for the kind of ambiguity present in this passage. Some editors have tried to circumvent the difficulty by placing a comma

---

[176] Powell (2010), especially 174–175. On hyperbaton in Latin prose, see further Devine and Stephens (2006: 524–610).

[177] The absolute use of *ignoratio* is unproblematic: cf. *Marcell.* 13 *a plerisque ignoratione... bellum esse susceptum*, TLL 7.1.309.38–62. The transmitted *sed hoc quidem ignoratione* is equivalent to the structure *hoc quidem* + adverb, used several times by Cicero without a verb in short sentences and parenthetical remarks: see, e.g., *Phil.* 13.22 *Satis hoc quidem scite*, 13.36, *Fin.* 2.5 *Praeclare hoc quidem*, *Tusc.* 1.40, 1.90.

[178] Kayser bracketed the phrase in his edition (Baiter and Kayser (1860)); the deletion was also proposed by Koch (1861: 485–486).

[179] The unusual construction *frigere ad*, paralleled only in Julius Valerius in the fourth century A D (*Res gestae Alexandri Macedonis* 1.9 *regibus... ad deos tamen potentia frixerit*), is presumably due to a desire for correspondence with *dicenti... apud multitudinem*.

[180] e.g. *Tusc.* 3.83 *Hanc dicant sane naturalem*; *Cat.* 2.15 *dicatur sane eiectus esse a me*. For further examples, see K-S i.189–190.

[181] e.g. *Tusc.* 5.34 *Quare demus hoc sane Bruto*.

198 COMMENTARY

after *sane*, but this step is merely an admission that the word order is confusing. It is better to transpose *sane* and *discipulo*.

188. *pudendum*] *puniendum* Vassis | *mitigatur* Schütz] *miratur* L. With the exception of the trio *misericordiam...pudendum...pigendum*, this list of emotions aroused by the orator is grouped into pairs of opposites (or virtual opposites).[182] In this context, the lack of a connection between *irascitur* and *miratur* is surprising. *Admiretur* is included in a similar list in *Orat.* 131, but *miratur* should not be retained here simply because it is not absurd. Schütz's emendation, *mitigatur*, introduces a precise antithesis with *irascitur*, and is confirmed by *Orat.* 131 *ut irascatur iudex mitigetur*.[183] The corruption to the more common *miratur* would have been easy.

Vassis' conjecture *puniendum* is also motivated by the desire to restore an antithesis, and finds support from *De or.* 2.185 *aut misereantur aut punire velint*. However, the relationship between *misericordiam*, *pudendum*, and *pigendum* is easier to understand than that between *irascitur* and *miratur*. Pity, shame, and regret are related sentiments, and two of the three are often found in close association.[184] More significantly, though, Vassis' emendation leaves *ad pigendum* awkwardly placed after the two opposites *misericordiam* and *puniendum*.

190. *optarent*] *opinarentur* Watt. Watt (1996: 374) wanted *de te ipso* to be construed in the same way with both indirect questions. An additional advantage of his emendation is that it produces an opposition between the lay person (*opinari*) and the expert (*iudicare*), anticipating the same contrast in Cicero's reply (*vulgi opinione...intellegentium quoque iudicio*). However, while this contrast is undoubtedly congenial to the wider context, in the immediately preceding paragraph Cicero has been discussing the choice of defence speakers as evidence for the people's opinion of orators. That this is still the theme of Brutus' reply can be seen from the choice of *rei* rather than *vulgus/populus*; *optarent*, picking up §189 *optio...optaret*, is therefore necessary.

---

[182] *Contemnit invidet* are almost antithetical: *contemptus* esteems something as worthless, *invidia* esteems it highly and holds a grudge against the possessor. More exact opposites are found in *Orat.* 131: *invideat faveat, contemnat admiretur.*

[183] For an example of the power of oratory to soothe and mollify, see *Brut.* 54 *qui* [i.e. L. Valerius Potitus] *post decemviralem invidiam plebem in patres incitatam legibus et contionibus suis mitigaverit.*

[184] e.g. Plaut. *Trin.* 431 *miseret te aliorum, tui nec miseret nec pudet*; Enn. ap. Cic. *Div.* 1.66; Ter. *Ad.* 392; Fronto *Ep. ad verum imperatorem* 2.1.10.

COMMENTARY   199

191. *omnium millium* 'alii' (teste Corrado): *omnium me illum* L: *omnium ne illum* J[2]: *omnium. Merito* Rom: *centum milium* Orelli:[185] *omnium illorum* Turnebus: *milium* Jahn: *hominum milium* Lennep. On the basis of *Att.* 2.5.1 *Cato ille noster, qui mihi unus est pro centum milibus*, recent editors have adopted Orelli's *centum milium*. Yet there is no evidence for the idiom 'worth a hundred thousand' outside of *Att.* 2.5.1, and variation in the choice of number is to be expected.[186] Cf. *Att.* 16.11.1 εἷς ἐμοὶ μύριοι, Catull. 9.1–2 *Verani, omnibus e meis amicis / antistans mihi milibus trecentis.* The argument from *Att.* 2.5.1 is further weakened by the fact that Cicero is quoting from Antimachus: even if 'worth a hundred thousand' were an established idiom in late Republican Rome, we could not assume that it was also in use in Colophon four centuries earlier. Finally, the corruption of *centum* to *omnium*, while made easier by the preceding *omnes*, is still not very probable.

Of the many other emendations suggested, most do not merit discussion. Lennep's *hominum milium* is palaeographically plausible, but *hominum* is superfluous and unattractive. Jahn instead deletes *omnium*, but it is hard to explain how the word might have entered the text. Turnebus proposed *omnium illorum*, but this turns a hyperbolic exclamation into a rather more mundane comment. Also, a number would contrast better with *unus*.

The most economical emendation, *omnium milium*, was approved by Peter, but has been dismissed as impossible Latin by most subsequent editors. Orelli, for example, comments, 'Hoc certum est: *omnium millium* omnium linguarum indoli repugnare'. In defence of its Latinity, Peter compared *Leg. Man.* 11 *tot milibus civium Romanorum... necatis*; *omnis* is combined with numerals at *B. Alex.* 35.2 *omnes tres legiones* and Gell. *NA* 3.7.16 *quadringenti omnes... cadunt.* None of these passages would sufficiently justify the unusual *omnium milium* here, even in the context of exclamatory hyperbole. However, Cicero is translating a quotation from Antimachus, and so evidence from Greek authors is also relevant. Μυρία πάντα is a widely attested Greek idiom meaning 'a vast number', 'a great abundance': cf., for example, Hdt. 3.74.2 ὑπισχνεύμενοι τὰ πάντα οἱ μυρία δώσειν; Pl. *Leg.* 4.711d3–4 ὅταν δὲ ξυμβῇ, μυρία καὶ πάντ' ἐν πόλει ἀγαθὰ ἀπεργάζεται, ἐν ᾗ

---

[185] Malcovati incorrectly cites Camerarius as the source of this conjecture: in fact, Camerarius suggested *multorum milium*, an emendation which yields acceptable sense, but at the cost of a significant departure from the paradosis.

[186] Cf. Otto (1890: 222).

200 COMMENTARY

ποτ' ἄν ἐγγένηται; Callim. *Hymn* 6.87–88 ἐνδόμυχος δῆπειτα πανάμερος εἰλαπιναστὰς / ἦσθιε μυρία πάντα; Aratus *Phaen.* 113.[187] *Instar... omnium milium* would be hard to defend in ordinary circumstances, but as a translation of ἄξιος μυρίων πάντων (*vel sim.*) it is acceptable here.

197. *cum item* Reis] *tum ita* L: *tum* Friedrich: *item* Haupt: *sumpta* Martha: *inventa* Douglas. Ellendt retained L's reading and explained *ita* as an abridgement of *ita ut nosti*. But it is unclear why Brutus should have been familiar with Scaevola's brief and compressed style any more than with his expertise and knowledge, or why Cicero should draw attention to this. *Ita* is surely corrupt, and *tum* is also awkward after a causal *cum*. Most editors rightly emend. Martha and Douglas suggest that a participle may have been corrupted, but what is needed is something to mark the division between the first two adverbs in the list, which refer to Scaevola's legal acumen, and the remaining four, which describe his eloquence. Haupt's *item* is perfectly acceptable, but Reis' *cum item* is closer to the paradosis. For *cum... cum item*, cf. *Clu.* 43, Caes. *BGall.* 3.25.1, Varro *Ling.* 9.67. In these examples, two *cum*-clauses with separate verbs are placed next to each other, but for a resumptive *cum*, cf. *Brut.* 277 *cum pestem capitis sui, cum indicia mortis se comperisse manifesto et manu tenere diceret, Fin.* 3.66, *Nat. D.* 1.100. *Cum etiam* would also be possible, but the corruption of *item* to *ita* is simpler to explain.

197. *in illo* del. Douglas] *ille* Rom | *initio*] *initium* Douglas | *consecutis* Bλρ] *consecutus* FJ[2]: *constituto* Jahn. Martha, followed by Laurand (1908: 448) and Malcovati,[188] translates *hoc... consecutus* as 'ayant poursuivi cette comparaison'. Yet the conjunction of *hoc* and *illo* in this interpretation is strange, as is the sense of *consecutus*. Some editors adopt Rom's *ille*, but there is no particular reason for the pronoun to be present. Douglas' suggestion that *in illo* might have arisen from a dittography of *initio* is attractive. Two considerations, though, tell against Douglas' *hoc initium consecutus*: the agreement of Bλρ confirms that *consecutis* was the reading of L, and the construction *consequor* + acc. + abl., 'to follow X with Y', is doubtful.[189] Badian (1967: 227) answers both of these objections with his proposal, *hoc initium consecutis*. However, I am not convinced that *consecutis* needs an object; the deletion of *in illo* seems to me to produce an acceptable text:

---

[187] See further *LSJ s.v.* πᾶς C.   [188] Cf. Peter (1839: *ad loc.*).
[189] In the structure *consequor* + acc. + *verbis* (*vel sim.*, 'to express in words'; *OLD s.v. consequor* 6b), the verb is used in a quite different sense.

COMMENTARY 201

'With this exordium, [and] with many arguments of the same type having been added, he delighted the hearts of all present.'[190] Another possibility is to combine the deletion of *in illo* with Jahn's *constituto*: 'With this exordium having been established, he delighted the hearts of all present with many arguments of the same type.' For *initium* + *constituo*, cf. *Fin.* 3.20 *Initiis igitur ita constitutis, Acad.* 2.24. But *consecutis* fits well in the sentence and should be retained. One might, of course, emend to *hoc initio* <*constituto*>, *consecutis* (cf. *Nat. D.* 2.75 *quo constituto sequitur*...), but it is simpler and more economical merely to delete *in illo*.

200. *oratorem* del. Weidner. *Oratorem*... *orationem* sounds inelegant to the modern ear, but this is not in itself sufficient reason to justify emendation. Weidner (1879: 72) puts a stronger argument for the deletion of *oratorem*: the clause *qui*... *manum* describes the central skill of an orator, without which he would not be an orator at all. Consequently, *oratorem*... *qui* cannot mean 'the sort of orator who...', and *oratorem* and *qui*... *manum* must simply be saying the same thing twice. While the redundancy is possible, the text is improved by Weidner's deletion. The omission of the antecedent would have made the interpolation of *oratorem* easy.

204. *et lenissimo* BFλOᵛDMTγ] *Edenissimo* O: *et levissimo* E: *et lentissimo* Vogel. Cf. Quint. *Inst.* 2.8.11 *cum de Ephoro atque Theopompo sic iudicaret ut alteri frenis, alteri calcaribus opus esse diceret, aut in illo lentiore tarditatem aut in illo paene praecipiti concitationem adiuvandam docendo existimavit.* But Isocrates' equestrian metaphor has influenced Quintilian's language more than Cicero's, and while *acer* and *lentus* are sometimes opposed (e.g. *Cat.* 2.21), *lenissimo* [sc. *ingenio*] provides a more suitable contrast for *acerrimo ingenio*. Cf. *Brut.* 317 *Cotta et Hortensius: quorum alter remissus et lenis*... *alter ornatus, acer; De or.* 2.212.

207. *scribendis* 'alii' (teste Corrado)] *scriptis* BFJOᵛβ: *scripsitis* U¹: *scripsit eas quibus pro se est usus* U, ut vid.: om. O: *scribentibus* Kraffert. Laughton (1964: 11–12, 94–95) argued persuasively that *his scriptis* cannot mean 'while they were being written'. Martha suggested that, whereas *scribendis* would indicate that Cicero was present while Pompeius was writing the

---

[190] I adopt Madvig's conjecture (1884: 106), *animos*[*que*]... *aderant* <*et*>. Although the absolute use of *delecto* is well attested (e.g. §75 *bellum Punicum quasi Myronis opus delectat*, §276, §322; cf. *TLL* 5.423.30–45, 5.425.52–84), in *Brut.* 197 *animos* clearly belongs with both *delectavit* and *traduxit*. *Et* was presumably omitted, with -*que* then being added to *animos* to rectify the syntax.

202 COMMENTARY

speeches, *scriptis* implies that Pompeius had sent his finished speeches to Aelius, and that Cicero was present when Aelius was correcting them.[191] However, the use of *interesse* with a past participle is unparalleled, and, if Martha's interpretation is what Cicero intended, one would expect a clearer explanation.[192] *Scribendis* is preferable.[193] Laughton thought it unlikely that Cicero was actually present when the speeches were being written, but the rest of the sentence shows why this was the case: not only was Cicero spending time with Aelius then, but he was paying keen attention to his teaching (*eumque audire perstudiose solerem*). We can infer that Cicero would have wanted to see Aelius at work as he helped Pompeius with his speech-writing.

207. Cotta Sulpiciusque rarius Reis] *Cotta Sulpicius* L: *Cotta et Sulpicius* Ff: *Cotta tum et Sulpicius* Malcovati: *dein Cotta et Sulpicius* ego: *rarius Cotta et Sulpicius* A. Eberhard: *parum Cotta et Sulpicius* Saupe. Cicero uses two main kinds of asyndeton bimembre with names: official totalities (e.g. the two consuls) and illustrative pairs.[194] In the latter type, the two names serve only as examples, and others could be added.[195] The transmitted *Cotta Sulpicius* fits into neither category: the two men constitute a totality, the last of the three pairs of principal orators (cf. §207 *Ita ab his sex patronis causae illustres agebantur*), but they are not named in any official capacity. This fact does not itself prove that a conjunction has been omitted: the asyndeton bimembre at §154 (*L. Lucilio Balbo C. Aquilio Gallo*), for example, seems also to fit into neither group. Yet in our passage the lack of an adverb, which leaves the clause without an explicit connection to the previous one, is an additional ground for suspicion.

Malcovati simply adds *tum et*, and in the same vein, one might consider *dein Cotta et Sulpicius*: *dein* could easily have dropped out after *-rem*, and cf. 301 *dein Philippo*. However, *tum* or *dein* would imply that defendants usually pursued the rather mechanical approach of first asking Antonius and Crassus, then Philippus or Caesar, and finally Cotta or Sulpicius. Cicero is probably referring primarily to the frequency with which these men

---

[191] Cf. Malcovati (1968: 127).

[192] Hendrickson translates, 'I had some knowledge of these compositions', but I can find no evidence that *interesse* was used thus. The rest of the sentence makes clear that *interfui* denotes physical presence; cf. also §190 *saepe enim interfui*.

[193] Douglas compares the phrase *scribendo adesse* ('to be present at drafting'; OLD *s.v. adsum* 7b).

[194] Adams (2021: 446–447).

[195] e.g. *Att.* 6.1.13 *Thermum Silium uere audis laudari*; *Att.* 6.3.5 *amicos habet meras nugas, Ma<ti>nium Scaptium*; *Off.* 2.59.

COMMENTARY   203

spoke *in maximis causis*. This is implied by *fere* ('generally'), and Eberhard's *rarius* gives a better contrast with *fere* than *tum* or *dein*. On transcriptional grounds, Reis' *Cotta Sulpiciusque rarius* is an improvement on Eberhard's emendation: -*que rarius* could have been omitted through *saut du même au même*.

213. *atque inluminatam*] del. Kayser | *inluminatam* FU (*ill-* BJOEMTWγ)] *illuminatum* D (ut vid.) Q: *inseminatam* Koch: *illigatam* Ernesti: *inoculatam* Schütz: *innatam* Cuiaccius. In her first edition, Malcovati was content to accept the transmitted *inluminatam*, and after obelizing the word in the second edition, she later reverted to her original view (1975: 160–161). The passages cited by Malcovati in which *illuminare* is used in rhetorical contexts ('to brighten with stylistic adornments') do not help here, though, where the sense would be more straightforwardly that of bringing glory to the house of Scipio.[196] A synonym for *insitam* ('grafted') is required. Because Cicero uses *insitus* in conjunction with *innatus* in six other places,[197] Cuiaccius' *innatam* has tempted many critics. Yet, as Douglas has pointed out, in none of those passages does *innatus* mean 'engrafted', and the meaning 'born into' would conflict with the context. Additionally, the corruption of *innatam* to *inluminatam* is unlikely. The popularity of *innatam* illustrates well the danger of a careless use of parallels.

Schütz was the first to suggest *inoculatam*:[198] *inoculare* is the only attested synonym of *inserere* = 'graft' in classical Latin (*TLL* 7.1.1734.28–41, and cf. especially Plin. *HN* 17.133 *inoculare et inserere*). *Illuminatam* could conceivably be a gloss on *inoculatam* that has intruded into the text. However, the verb is not found in Cicero, or in any author before Columella. Prompted by Verg. *G.* 2.76–77 *huc aliena ex arbore germen / includunt udoque docent inolescere libro*, I have considered *inolitam*.[199] Yet the past participle is not attested until Julius Valerius (although cf. *adolescere, adultus*; *exolescere, exoletus*), and this emendation also labours under the disadvantage of the word's absence from extant Republican Latin. In support of Ernesti's *illigatam*, Schütz compares Colum. *Rust.* 5.11, where forms of *ligare* and *alligare* are used to describe the action of binding a graft onto a tree.[200] I am not

---

[196] Gowers (2019: 14) accepts *inluminatam* and translates, 'on that house was grafted and shone out the wisdom of many ancestors'.

[197] *Verr.* 2.4.106, 2.5.139, *Top.* 69, *Fin.* 4.4, *Nat. D.* 1.44, *Tim.* 45.

[198] The emendation was proposed again by Della Corte (1971), who was apparently unaware of Schütz.

[199] Cf. Paulinus of Nola, *Ep.* 23.41 *in arborem vestrae stirpis inolevimus*.

[200] Cf. also Varro *Rust.* 1.40.5 *quem ad modum obligetur*.

204 COMMENTARY

convinced, however, that a reference to one particular aspect of grafting is desirable here.

Koch's *inseminatam* (1861: 486) is very close to the paradosis, and would seem a natural synonym for *insitam*, given that *inserere* = 'graft' is an extension of the basic meaning 'sow, plant'. Cf. Varro, *Rust.* 1.39.3 *semina quae inseruntur ex arboribus in arbores*. However, there is no evidence that *inseminare* ever meant 'graft'. Moreover, although Cicero did use the rare verbs *disseminare* and *proseminare* (as well as the more common *seminare*),[201] *inseminare* is not attested before the Imperial period. Consequently, while I judge *inseminatam* the most plausible of the proposed emendations, I prefer to obelize.

216. *instruendo* Bλρ] *struendo* F. This reading may be compared with §215 *erant* Bλρ] *erantque* F.[202] Malcovati, who believed that F sometimes preserves the reading of the archetype on its own, even against the agreement of BGOU,[203] accepted F's text in both places. However, the agreement of three of the four branches of the stemma (Bλρ) proves that L had *instruendo*.[204] Cicero uses *struere* and *instruere* to signify 'arrange' or 'construct', both in the field of rhetoric and in a range of other spheres. But when discussing speech-writing, he employs *struere* only in the specific sense of the rhythmical arrangement of words, not in describing *dispositio*, one of the five divisions of oratory.[205] He does use *instruere*, though, with reference to *dispositio*. Cf., for example, *De or.* 2.145 *eam materiem orationis...omnibus locis discriptam, instructam ornatamque*, 2.315, 2.318. Since he is evidently structuring his account of Curio's oratory under the five traditional headings, *in instruendo dissipatus fuit* must refer to *dispositio*. Therefore, *instruendo* is not only the transmitted reading, but also conforms better to Cicero's practice elsewhere.

216. *irrisionemque audientium* scripsi] *irridentium* L. The combination *cachinnos irridentium* is very awkward, and *cachinnos* already makes clear that the audience is laughing. I have considered simply emending

---

[201] *Leg.* 1.1 *nullius autem agricolae cultu stirps tam diuturna quam poetae versu seminari potest.*

[202] In §215 *erant* is the superior reading as well as the text of the archetype. Having assessed the strengths of Antonius' oratory, Cicero turns to compare Antonius with Crassus. Hence, *erant* marks a change of direction, and it should not be joined to the preceding clause with *-que*.

[203] Malcovati (1959: 179), (1968: 127).

[204] There is a small chance that L had variant readings, and so F's reading could also derive from the archetype. But *struendo* is much more likely to be an error in F (or an ancestor of F).

[205] e.g. *De or.* 3.171, *Brut.* 33, 274, and see Douglas' note on *Brut.* 216 *struendo*.

COMMENTARY 205

irridentium to *audientium*. But Quintilian's use of the verb *irridere* in *Inst.* 11.3.129 (*quam in Curione patre inrisit et Iulius*), a passage in which he is evidently drawing on *Brut.* 216, may be an indication that a related word was present. Consequently, I emend instead to *irrisionemque audientium*. Cf. *Off.* 1.137 *cum irrisione audientium*, and for the pairing of two words from the semantic field of amusement, *Brut.* 322 *hilaritatem risumque*, *De or.* 2.221 *hilaritate quadam et ioco*, *Orat.* 138. *Cachinnos* denotes 'guffaws, loud laughter', and *irrisionem* indicates that this laughter arose from a scornful attitude on the part of the audience. For the species of corruption, cf. *Brut.* 316 *supra fluentis*] *suprates* Be, 321 *exercitationis tum*] *exercitatum* Pb.

218. ***ductus*] *ductus est* Mi: *ductus esset* Lambinus: *ducitur* vulg.** According to Pinkster (2015: 198), the omission of finite forms of *esse* in periphrastic tenses is rare in Cicero; *est* could easily have dropped out here before *e percontatione*. But one can compare §16 *repressus*, §110 *versatus*, §174 *coniunctus*, and §225 *Quos Sex. Titius consecutus*, and also the following places where some editors have added an auxiliary *est*: *Mur.* 59 *nam traditum memoriae <est>*, *Font.* 44, *Dom.* 101, *Rab. Post.* 7, 38, *Sull.* 56, *Har. resp.* 49, *Balb.* 28, *Caec.* 22, *Tusc.* 4.75, *Att.* 16.11.4.[206] Of course, in many of these passages, the absence of *est* from the paradosis may be due to a scribal error, but on the other hand, the process of transmission tends to lead to the removal of oddities such as missing auxiliary verbs. I suspect that Cicero omitted auxiliary *est* more often than we realize.

220. ***vivis eius*] *vivis eius aetatis* Friedrich: *vivis etiam* Stangl: *a suis* Piderit: *visus est* Watt.** Many critics have judged L's reading corrupt,[207] but, in my view, unfairly so. At the end of a lengthy passage censuring many aspects of Curio's oratory, Cicero now admits that, as a public speaker, Curio was counted as next to the very best (*proximus optimis*) on account of his language and the fluency of his speech. The ablative absolute *vivis eius aequalibus* provides an important qualification: it was only while his contemporaries were alive that Curio was counted as *proximus optimis*.[208] Curio's generation had produced a rich crop of orators (§182 *nec ulla aetate uberior oratorum fetus fuit*), but many had died during the turbulence of the 80s (§227 *vivebat e reliquis patronis eius aetatis nemo praeter Carbonem et*

---

[206] For examples from other authors, see Pinkster (2015: 198–199).
[207] Most recently, Watt (1996: 374–375) and Kaster (2020: *ad loc.*).
[208] Cf. Martha (1892: *ad loc.*).

206 COMMENTARY

Pomponium). Cotta lived on until 74/73 BC, but Curio survived through most of the careers of Hortensius and Cicero, only dying in 53 BC; long before his death, though, Cicero implies, Curio had been outshone by the younger generations, and he certainly would not have been considered *proximus optimis* in Cicero's heyday.[209] For the use of an ablative absolute with *vivus* to designate a period of time, cf. §80 *Catone vivo*, §230 *Crasso vivo…et magis iam etiam vigebat Antonio*.

None of the emendations improves the text. Stangl replaces *eius* with *etiam* ('while his contemporaries were *still* alive'), but the pronoun is useful in clarifying the generation to which Cicero refers. Friedrich's *eius <aetatis>* merely duplicates the sense of *aequalibus*, which is already perspicuous. Watt replaces *vivis eius* with *visus est*, but this obscures the link between *orator* and *proximus optimis*, and the verb is unnecessary before *numerabatur*. Finally, Piderit misses the point with his *a suis* (another replacement for *vivis eius*): it was not that Curio was approved only by those of his generation, but that he was approved by everyone for a brief period of time. As Cicero has already set forth at length (§§184–200), the prestige of orators was the same among the whole people.

221. *fortis…auderes*. Some scholars, including Kaster (2020), take these words as further description of Quintus Varius, but they belong rather with Gnaeus Pomponius. Firstly, the repetition of *verbis* would be unattractive if both instances were part of the same account of Varius. Secondly, the characterization of Pomponius would be left abrupt and unconnected to its context. Thirdly, the description *fortis vero actor ac vehemens* agrees well with what we are told of Pomponius (*lateribus pugnans, incitans animos, acer acerbus criminosus*). The external evidence is less clear, but also leans in favour of taking these words with Pomponius. Cicero is not complimentary towards either man in *De or.* The significant qualification present in the description of Varius' oratorical abilities (*De or.* 1.117 *illa ipsa facultate, quamcumque habet*) does not cohere very well with the wholehearted praise given in *Brut.* in the clause *quem plane oratorem dicere auderes*. Neither, though, does *De or.* 3.50, in which Cicero characterizes the speech of Pomponius and Fufius as *confusa* and *perturbata*. However, Cicero goes on to say that Pomponius and Fufius use 'a flood of out-of-the-way words'

---

[209] Cicero may have been thinking especially of 90 BC as the date when Curio's reputation began to wane: while serving as tribune of the plebs, Curio was abandoned by the whole assembly during a speech, and he temporarily stopped speaking in public in that year (§305 *is quidem silebat, ut erat semel a contione universa relictus*; cf. §192, *MRR* ii.26).

COMMENTARY 207

(*tantaque insolentia ac turba verborum*, tr. Rackham), a description which readily accords with our passage's *verbis nec inops nec abiectus*. More significantly, we know from *Brut*. 207 (*His duobus eiusdem aetatis adnumerabatur nemo tertius, sed mihi placebat Pomponius maxime, vel dicam, minime displicebat*) that Cicero regarded Pomponius more highly than Varius,[210] and indeed more highly than any other orator of his generation except Cotta and Sulpicius.

224. *is*] *at is* ego: *igitur* Stangl. The absence of a connecting particle is a little abrupt. Stangl's *igitur* is unattractive in sense, but *at* would draw the reader's attention to the fact that it was Glaucia's death that prevented him from eventually translating his popularity into a successful bid for the consulship. The word could have been lost through haplography. However, the clause *si... esset* has already supplied the reason why Glaucia failed in his attempt to be elected consul during his praetorship, and Cicero may simply be completing the account of Glaucia's praetorship with the observation that he died at the same time as his ally Saturninus.

226. *iacuisset* Baehrens] *tacuisset* C, pler. edd. In the transmitted text, the first part of the *cum*-clause (*multos cum tacuisset annos*) tells us that Publius Antistius was silent for many years, and the second (*neque contemni solum sed irrideri etiam solitus esset*) that he was subjected to scorn and ridicule. Reconciling these two parts is not easy: they seem to refer to the same time period, and yet it is difficult to understand how Antistius' oratorical silence could have provoked scorn and ridicule. Baehrens' *iacuisset* is a good solution to this problem: 'After being at the bottom of the heap for many years, during which he was accustomed to scorn and even ridicule,...'. Cicero uses *iaceo* to refer to a poor reputation at *Att*. 2.17.3 *iacet enim ille sic ut 'Phocis' Curiana stare videatur*, *Att*. 6.1.18.[211] The corruption would have been easy in both majuscule and minuscule scripts.

227. *videbat*] *dividebat* Fuchs. The striking similarity between this passage and §303 (*rem complectebatur memoriter, dividebat acute*) makes Fuchs' emendation (1956: 141) tempting, but the paradosis should be retained. Cicero has arranged his analysis of Antistius' strengths and weaknesses according to the five 'parts' of oratory, and the description of his skill in *inventio* (*rem videbat acute*) should not be sacrificed for another allusion to

[210] Both men are included among the *diserti* in §305.
[211] See further *TLL* 7.1.29.25–36.

208 COMMENTARY

dispositio.[212] Forms of *acutus* often feature in references to *inventio* (e.g. §35 *nihil acute inveniri potuit...quod ille non viderit*, §202 *inveniebat igitur acute Cotta*, §221). Most importantly, though, *rem videre* = 'to see the points at issue' is paralleled at §239 *rem prudenter videbat.*[213]

230. se exercuit Douglas] *exercuit* L. Douglas rightly rejects attempts to take *me* as the object of *exercuit* ('he harassed me' or 'he trained me'), but he does not consider the possibility that *multos annos* might instead be its object ('he spent many years'). The first prose examples of this use of *exercere* are from Seneca the Elder (e.g. *Con. ex.* 8.5 *ille annos suos exercuit*; see further *TLL* 5.1377.50–60), but it is a natural extension of *OLD s.v. exerceo* 3 'to put (instruments, materials, resources, etc.) to use, employ, work', of which there are instances in Republican Latin, although not in Cicero. Nevertheless, because it remains doubtful whether Cicero would have used *exercere* in this way, and because the addition of *se* is only a small change, especially between *laudis* and *exercuit*, I accept Douglas' emendation.

234. admirando inridebat calebat BFλ (*a. irr- c. β; a. irr- callebat* O)] *admiranda dignitate valebat* Kayser (*valebat* Ernesti): *admirando ore dicebat, calebat* Friedrich: *admirantes irretiebat et sic calebat* Schütz: *admirando irridendo latebat* Lambinus: [*admirando inridebat*] *valebat* Douglas: *admirando ardore calebat* vel *admirando ardebat calore* ego. Cicero recounts how Gnaeus Lentulus' delivery secured for him a better reputation than his oratory deserved. He mentions Lentulus' use of pauses and exclamations (*intervallis, exclamationibus*), as well as the sweetness of his voice (*voce suavi et canora*). References to wonder (*admirando*) and mockery (*inridebat*) are out of place in this list. Santini (1979: 50–54), who prefers Lambinus' *admirando irridendo* (but with *calebat* rather than the inept *latebat*), argues that *irridendo* denotes irony, but the link he attempts to draw between irony and *actio* is unconvincing.

---

[212] Douglas suggested that the text of §303 might instead be brought into line with this passage, but there too the context tells against the emendation. At §303, a reference to *inventio* is already present in *nec praetermittebat fere quicquam, quod esset in causa aut ad confirmandum aut ad refellendum*, whereas the only remark about Hortensius' *dispositio* is *rem...dividebat acute.* (The *partitiones...et collectiones* ('divisions and summaries') mentioned in §302 were quite distinct from *dispositio*: they were not techniques used in an orator's preparation, but rather were employed for rhetorical effect in previewing material to be covered later in a speech, and in recapitulating what had already been said.) This sole reference to *dispositio* in §303 should not be removed.

[213] Douglas also compares Quint. *Inst.* 8.pr.17 *neque enim Asiani...res non viderunt.* *Prudens* and *acutus* are sometimes almost synonymous: cf. §104, §108 *valde prudenter et acute*, §246 *prudens acutus*, §291.

COMMENTARY 209

Of the three words which editors have suspected (*admirando inridebat calebat*), *inridebat* is indefensible and must be emended or obelized. However, both *admirando* and *calebat* may be sound. Rather than being a gerund, *admirando* could be a gerundive ('admirable') whose noun has been omitted or corrupted. (For this use of *admirandus*, cf. *Rep.* 3.44 *admiranda opera Phidiae, Deiot.* 26.) The use of *calere* is not paralleled in rhetorical contexts, but Douglas is wrong to claim that Cicero employs the verb only of situations and activities, and not of people: see *Att.* 7.20.2, 15.6.2.[214] Therefore, *calebat in agendo* is conceivably Ciceronian, although Ernesti's *valebat* remains attractive.

The series of ablatives *intervallis exclamationibus*... is introduced by *sic*, which signals that a consecutive clause (*ut...desiderarentur*) will follow. The syntax would be simpler if one of the two verbs *inridebat calebat* were removed.[215] One way to achieve this would be to follow Douglas and delete *admirando inridebat*. Douglas suggests that these words could be a gloss on *exclamationibus*, but it would be a strange gloss to add. More probably, one of *inridebat* and *calebat* conceals a noun referring to another feature of Lentulus' delivery. The influence of the other word would provide a ready explanation for the corruption. I find Kayser's *admiranda dignitate valebat* the most tempting of the proposed emendations, although one must admit that the corruption of *dignitate* to *inridebat*, even before *valebat/calebat*, is unlikely. I have considered instead *admirando ardore calebat* (or, alternatively, *admirando ardebat calore*). *Vox canora et suavis* does not conflict with a vigorous style of delivery: Cicero uses the same phrase to describe Hortensius (§303), who certainly did not lack ardour in his oratory (§317). For *ardor* in connection with *actio*, cf. *Brut.* 276 *actioque esset ardentior*, *QFr.* 3.9.3 *Hortensi calor multum valebit, De or.* 2.188. Nevertheless, *ardor/calor* would be more general in scope than the other elements of Lentulus' delivery mentioned by Cicero, and although I do not think this is a fatal objection to the emendation, it is best to obelize.

250. *sententiis et* Jahn] *et* L: *sententiis* Martha | *vocis*] *vocis et* vulg. The second Asiatic style of §325 exemplifies the type of oratory characterized by a flood of words (*non tam sententiis frequentatum quam verbis volucre atque incitatum*) but without the elegant structuring of thoughts and sentences

---

[214] Santini (1979: 52). Santini also compares the use of *frigidus*: e.g. *Rhet. Her.* 4.21 *in re frigidissima cales, in ferventissima friges* (cf. *OLD s.v. frigidus* 8b).

[215] For this reason, as well as because of the poor sense and deficient style of the Latin, the emendations of Friedrich and Schütz, together with other similar suggestions, should be rejected.

210   COMMENTARY

(*ornata sententiarum concinnitas non erat*). If *frequentibus* is to be taken with *verbis*, Brutus would be indicating something similar to this Asiatic style. Yet in other respects, the picture of Marcellus' oratory is markedly different from that described in §325: *lectis verbis...splendore vocis dignitate motus*. In particular, *lectis* suggests almost the opposite of *frequentibus*. Additionally, outside of *Brut.* 325 *frequentia verborum* is something to be avoided, not praised (e.g. *De or.* 1.149, *Rhet. Her.* 4.27): it implies a superfluity of words, verbiage. By contrast, *frequentia rerum* ('a wealth of ideas'; cf. *De or.* 2.56) is a positive quality in an orator. *Frequens* is almost synonymous with *creber*, which is often used in conjunction with *sententia*: e.g. *Brut.* 29, 173, 264 *verbis aptiorem...sententiis crebriorem*, 280, 326, 327.[216] *Frequentibus sententiis* combines well with *lectis verbis* to signify the concise expression of many ideas. Jahn's supplement is an excellent solution to the textual problem.[217]

Some editors delete the *et* before *splendore*, and others supply another *et* after *vocis*. However, there is no problem with the asyndeton between *splendore vocis* and *dignitate motus*, and the *et* before *splendore* helps the reader to divide the sentence correctly. There are three clauses, each with its own verb (*utitur...fit...suppetunt*). The first contains an *et...et* construction ('both...and') within it, and then two further conjunctions (*et splendore...omniaque*) serve to join the clauses together.

251. veritus] *veritus es* vulg., edd. As noted above (on §218 *ductus*), Pinkster (2015: 198) states that the omission of finite forms of auxiliary *sum* is rare in Cicero. While *est* is the form most easily omitted, Pinkster notes that, 'If the context is clear enough, other forms may be absent as well.' Here, the second person singular verb *voluisti* occurs almost immediately before *veritus*, and the reader can supply *es* after the participle. A similar example is *Scaur.* 49 *atque utinam, sicut mihi tota in hac causa versatus ante oculos* (*<es>* edd.), *sic nunc horum te offeras mentibus et in horum animis adhaerescas!*, although the distance between *versatus* and *offeras* provides greater justification for the editors' supplement in that passage.[218]

---

[216] Cf. *De or.* 2.93 *sententiisque magis quam verbis abundantes.*

[217] Piderit suggests that *sententiis* might have been abbreviated and then lost. However, although *sententia* certainly was often contracted, the lack of abbreviations in the Cremona fragment and the general rarity of such abbreviations in MSS from before the ninth century tell against this possibility (both here and elsewhere in texts transmitted by L). *Sententiis* was probably simply omitted.

[218] The addition seems necessary at *Flac.* 78 *reprehensurus <es>*; cf. also *Dom.* 47 and *Pro Rabirio perduellionis reo* 28, where the paradosis lacks a copulative *es*.

COMMENTARY   211

253. *facilem* Fc] *facile* L | *nunc*] *num* Lallemand | *relicto*] *delicto* Schütz. This passage is the longest extant quotation from Caesar's *De analogia*. Garcea (2012: 87), who adopts only the necessary emendation of *facile* to *facilem*, translates the clause *hunc... habendum* as a rhetorical question: 'Are we now to consider that the knowledge of this easy and everyday speech may be neglected?' Yet the translation 'may be neglected' is unwarranted. *Pro relicto habere* means 'to regard as neglected',[219] and so, if the clause is to be taken as a question, a more accurate translation would be: 'Is knowledge of this easy and everyday speech now to be regarded as neglected?' There is no indication, however, that the clause is a question.[220] Caesar is not suggesting that knowledge of everyday speech should be neglected (*relinquendum est*), or that it should not be neglected (*num relinquendum est?*); he is simply stating that the knowledge is now neglected (*pro relicto est habendum*). In the protasis of the conditional, Caesar granted that some people have mastered the art of *cogitata praeclare eloqui* ('expressing their thoughts with distinction', tr. Kaster), but now in the apodosis he indicates that everyone has stopped pursuing the knowledge of everyday speech. This sentiment makes sense at the start of a work in which Caesar will aim to enable his readers to gain mastery of the *sermo cotidianus*. Thus Willi (2010: 241) comments of *De analogia*, 'Its dedicatory sentence... presents Cicero as the inventor of a new Latin style, whereas Caesar himself acts as the advocate of an almost forgotten one.'

256. *imperatorum sapientia* del. Lambinus. The deletion of *imperatorum sapientia* as a gloss on *divinis consiliis* was first proposed by Lambinus (1584), and then suggested again, apparently independently, by Wetzel and Fuchs (1956: 143). It is motivated by two considerations: the awkwardness of the two ablatives *quibus* and *sapientia* in the same clause, and the difficulty of understanding how the wisdom of generals could bring about the safety of the city 'at home' (*domi*). Ellendt defends the two ablatives by comparing §213 *patrio fuisse instituto puro sermone adsuefactam domum*, but there the different uses of the ablatives are much more easily distinguished.

---

[219] *OLD s.v. habere* 24, *TLL* 6.2445.65–6.2446.8. Garcea reports Papke's suggestion that *pro relicto habere* is a military idiom (Papke (1988: 81): 'der Feldherr betrachtet einen Ort als verloren'). The only other instance of the phrase in classical Latin is *Att.* 8.1.1 *accepi haec oppida atque oram maritimam illum pro relicto habere*, which does support Papke's case. But one need not conclude that Caesar intended to signify that knowledge of the *sermo cotidianus* was irreversibly lost. (*Att.* 8.1.1 helps to show that Schütz's *delicto* is unnecessary.)

[220] Some editors print Lallemand's *num*, but *nunc* serves an important function and should not be emended away.

212 COMMENTARY

In order to deal with the second difficulty, Garcea (2012: 92) proposed that *imperatores* 'refers not only to the generals who crushed foreign aggressors or defended the vital interests of the state, but also to the magistrates who prevented Republican institutions from being overthrown'. If Garcea is correct, Cicero could be alluding to his self-characterization as *dux togatus* in the Catilinarian orations: *Cat.* 2.28, 3.23 *togati me uno togato duce et imperatore vicistis.*[221] But the broadened meaning of *imperator* is ruled out by the context. In the final clause of the sentence, *multo magnus orator praestat minutis imperatoribus*, *imperatores* is opposed to *orator* and must denote merely 'generals'. This opposition between the orator and the general is retained throughout §§255–256.

With *imperatorum sapientia* removed, the *divina consilia* can be applied without difficulty not only to major triumphs in battle (*belli*), but also to significant interventions in domestic political life (*domi*), such as Cicero's suppression of Catiline's conspiracy.[222] Orelli objected that the deletion of *imperatorum sapientia* obscures the meaning of *divinis consiliis*, but the phrase's very vagueness allows for the use of an appropriate range of talents (military, oratorical, etc.) in the protection of the city. At first sight, the following contrast between the great orator and the minor generals (*multo magnus orator praestat minutis imperatoribus*) creates a more substantial problem for those who would delete *imperatorum sapientia*, since the contrast seems to indicate that the best generals have been removed from the picture, but that the best orators have been left. However, Cicero's meaning becomes clear in the subsequent comparison of Crassus' speech in the *causa Curiana* (*L. Crassi unam pro M'. Curio dictionem*) with inconsequential military victories (*castellanos triumphos duo*). Cicero is claiming that forensic oratory, not political oratory, is more valuable to the city than the achievements of minor generals.[223]

258. Philum Heraeus] *pilum* BFλO: *publium* E^cG^vlMX (*p.* F^c): *publium* post *Scipionem* E: om. DG: *L. Philum P.* Reis. Even after Heraeus (1934) argued for the presence of Lucius Furius Philus in this passage,[224] most

---

[221] On the *dux togatus* motif, see further Nicolet (1960), Hall (2013: 217). For the importance of *sapientia* to the establishment of the state, cf. *Leg. agr.* 2.10 *Gracchos...quorum consiliis, sapientia, legibus multas esse video rei publicae partis constitutas; De or.* 2.154 *Pythagoras...illam sapientiam constituendae civitatis...cognovit.*

[222] Cf. Douglas (1966: *ad loc.*).

[223] On the weight given by Cicero to forensic oratory in *Brut.*, see Douglas (1966: xxix).

[224] Heraeus is usually cited as the source of the emendation *Philum*, although he actually argued for the transmitted spelling *Pilum*. For further details concerning the man, see Sumner (1973: 61), *RE s.v.* 'Furius 78'.

COMMENTARY 213

editors have continued to adopt the reading *C. Laelium P. Scipionem*. Yet the case for *Philum* is incontrovertible. (1) The agreement of BF^{ac}λO leaves no room for doubt that *pilum* was the reading of L. (2) In the only other place where *Philus* is mentioned in *Brut.* (§108), the paradosis gives his name as *pilus*, and hence the reading *Philum* here hardly even counts as an emendation. (3) In §108, it is Philus' Latinity that is stressed (*L. Furius Philus perbene Latine loqui putabatur*), and in §258 Cicero is again discussing the Latinity of Laelius, Scipio, and their contemporaries. (4) Philus was a close associate of Scipio and Laelius, and he is frequently mentioned in connection with them, both by Cicero and by other authors. See, for example, *Rep.* 3.5 *aut quid P. Scipione, quid C. Laelio, quid L. Philo perfectius cogitari potest?*; *De or.* 2.154 *P. Africano, C. Laelio, L. Furio*; Porcius Licinus fr. 3 (Courtney) 8–10.[225] Needless to say, the corruption of *publium* to *pilum* is highly unlikely.

Malcovati objected to Heraeus' suggestion on the ground that Cicero never places another name between Scipio and Laelius. But cf. *Att.* 4.16.2 *in Africani personam et Phili et Laeli*; *Fin.* 5.2 *Scipionem, Catonem, Laelium*. Reis found the absence of *praenomina* before *Philum* and *Scipionem* problematic, but his conjecture <*L.*> *Philum* <*P.*> is unnecessary. Cicero omits the *praenomen* more often with Scipio than with Laelius (e.g. *Sen.* 77 *tu Scipio tuque C. Laeli*; *Arch.* 16 *ex hoc…Africanum, ex hoc C. Laelium, L. Furium*; *Off.* 1.108), and once Laelius has been named, Philus and Scipio are readily identifiable whether or not their *praenomina* are stated.[226]

258. *barbaria* Ff] *barbari* BFUODM*y*: *barbaries* JO^{c}G^{vl}: *barbarie* E | *domestica* G^{vl}] *indomestica* λOO^v: *in domestica* BFβ. The reading *barbaries domestica* is printed by most editors, but L read *barbari indomestica*. *Barbaria* is the form always used by Cicero, and it is to be preferred here. *Barbaries* is a later form.[227]

259. *levis* BFλEQW*y*] *lenis* J^{2}OMX^c. Choosing between *lēvis* and *lēnis* is difficult, since both denote smoothness,[228] and each could easily be corrupted

---

[225] For a fuller list of examples, see Heraeus (1934: 55–56), and add *Att.* 2.19.5, Apul. *Apol.* 20.5.

[226] On naming conventions in Cicero, see further Adams (1978).

[227] *TLL* 2.1729.5–22.

[228] For *lenis*, see *TLL* 7.2.1144.25–48, and for *levis*, *TLL* 7.2.1222.80–7.2.1223.48. Note, though, that the readings of the MSS are not reported reliably in these entries. (The same is true of some passages cited in *OLD* s.vv. *lenis, levis*.) Cf. also Walldén (1943), a diachronic study of the uses of *lenis* and *levis*. Walldén, however, devotes his attention to the trends in later medical texts, and his findings do not shed much light on the question here.

214   COMMENTARY

into the other. In a similar situation at Quint. *Inst.* 10.1.44, Russell (2002: 274–275) translates the transmitted *lenis* as 'smooth', and comments, 'This would translate either *lēnis* or *lēvis*; but *lēnis* is a quality of movement, *lēvis* of surface. If the underlying Greek term is λεῖος, Meyer's *lēvis* is perhaps more probable'. In our passage, *levis* was the reading of the archetype (a fact of which previous editors were apparently unaware). *Levis* was largely replaced by *lenis* in late antiquity,[229] and so one might expect many instances of *levis* to be corrupted to *lenis* in the process of transmission. Nevertheless, if one excludes passages referring to smoothness of style and delivery, focusing only on those which refer to smoothness of voice and sound, *levis/levitas* is consistently the earliest recoverable reading in the texts of Cicero and Quintilian: *De or.* 3.43 *levitate* RᵛUV Non.] *lenitate* OPRⁿUᵐ;[230] 3.45 *leviter* RᵛV] *leniter* OPRⁿU; 3.171 *levis* MPRᵛUV] *lenis* OP²RⁿU²; 3.216 *leve* LM] *lene* U²; *Part. or.* 17 *leviora*; 21 *levium* pler. codd.] *lenium* W: *lenum* N;[231] *Nat. D.* 2.146 *leve*; Quint. *Inst.* 11.3.15 *levis*.[232] This pattern may be an accident of transmission, but it may alternatively reveal a preference of Cicero and Quintilian for *levis* in describing smoothness of sound. Further investigation would be necessary to show whether this preference was shared by other authors, but there is certainly no reason to diverge from the paradosis in *Brut.* 259.

259. Graecae] *rectae* **Simon.** There is no need to emend. Catulus' close links to Greek culture and literature were well known, and his imitation of Hellenistic epigram was an innovation in Rome.[233] His proficiency in the Greek language was also highly regarded (*De or.* 2.28 *Catulus...cui non solum nos Latini sermonis, sed etiam Graeci ipsi solent suae linguae subtilitatem elegantiamque concedere*), and we can infer that his *suavitas vocis et levis appellatio litterarum* were perceived as *similis Graecae locutionis*.[234] By contrast, Cotta's broad vowels (*dilatandis litteris*) sounded rustic and quite

---

[229] *Lēvis* did not become extinct in medieval Latin: see the passages cited in *DMLBS s.v. lēvis.*

[230] For these sigla, see Kumaniecki (1969); and for further discussion, Kumaniecki (1965: 202–203). Leeman et al. (1981–2008: *ad loc.*) report that the MSS of Nonius have *levitate*, not *lenitate*, printed by his editors.

[231] For these sigla, see Giomini (1996).

[232] At *De or.* 2.58 (*Xenophon leviore/leniore quodam sono est usus*) *leviore* (M) and *leniore* (L) are variants; but the reference there is to the tone of Xenophon's writing, not of his speech.

[233] *De or.* 2.28, 2.151, 2.154–156; Courtney (1993: 75). Cicero describes Catulus' autobiographical work as written *molli et Xenophonteo genere sermonis* (*Brut.* 132).

[234] Interestingly, though, this did not compromise his reputation as a speaker of pure Latin (*Brut.* 132 *incorrupta quaedam Latini sermonis integritas*).

COMMENTARY 215

different from Catulus' 'Greek' pronunciation. Cotta's accent may also have sounded harsh, as Douglas suggests, but it is the breadth of his vowels that Cicero emphasizes, both here and elsewhere (*De or.* 2.91 *verborum latitudinem*, 3.46).[235] For a similar description of the differences in vocal delivery between Catulus and his *sodalis* Cotta, see *De or.* 3.42.

260. C. Hirtilium Müller] *Chirtilium* L: *C. Hirtuleium* Ellendt. Friedrich Münzer, although aware of the transmitted spelling of this man's name, nevertheless includes him in a list of four men named Hirtuleius.[236] In defence of the name Hirtilius, Ellendt (1836: 261) tentatively suggested analogy with the names Sextilius and Quintilius, and in fact Hirtilii are found in the epigraphic record just as frequently as Hirtuleii.[237] The name Hirtuleius is more familiar to the modern world because there happened to be members of the *gens* among the supporters of Quintus Sertorius,[238] but *C. Hirtilium* should be accepted here.

269. T.] L. Corradus: C. Sumner | Postumius F] Postumus C. Emendation of the *cognomen* Postumus to the *nomen* Postumius seems advisable. Adams has demonstrated (1978: 154) that 'the formal method of naming by the two names *praenomen* + *cognomen*...was rarely accorded to those of low status in upper-class society', and consequently we should expect a man introduced simply as T. Postumus to be a figure of some eminence. However, the only notable T. Postumus we know of from this period, T. Furfanus Postumus, cannot be the man mentioned here, because the orator of *Brut.* 269 had died by the first half of 46 BC, whereas Furfanus was proconsul in Sicily in 45.[239]

But emending *Postumus* to *Postumius* creates a different problem, because, as Sumner observes (1973: 144), 'no T. Postumii occur in the whole era of the Republic'. For this reason, scholars have suggested that the *praenomen* should also be emended, and that this man might be identified with a Postumius mentioned elsewhere. Four men are relevant to the discussion:[240]

---

[235] For discussion of vowel lengths in Latin and Greek, and of the meaning of *similitudo Graecae locutionis*, see Büttner (1893: 161–164) and Adams (2003: 109–110); cf. Adams (2007: 139–140).
[236] *RE s.v.* 'Hirtuleius'.
[237] For Hirtilii from Rome and Tusculum, see *CIL* 14, 02711; *CIL* 06, 07780; *CIL* 06, 17688; and *AE* 1996, 00220. For other comparable names, see Schulze (1904: 457–459).
[238] e.g. Livy, *Per.* 90–91; Frontin. *Str.* 1.5.8.   [239] *MRR* ii.309.
[240] A Postumius mentioned in *Att.* 5.21.9 has also drawn some attention in this connection, but the reference is too fleeting to be of any use here.

216   COMMENTARY

Postumius (1): C. Postumius, a *monetalis* c.74 BC.[241]

Postumius (2): A candidate for the praetorship in 63, who joined Cato in the prosecution of Lucius Murena and is mentioned five times in *Mur.* (54, 56, 57 (twice), 69).[242] The transmitted text of *Mur.* nowhere supplies a *praenomen* for this Postumius. In *Mur.* 54, a *praenomen* has presumably been lost, because in the same sentence the other prosecutors, Ser. Sulpicius and M. Cato, are given their *praenomina*. At *Mur.* 56, the name *Postumus* is preceded by the word *tum*, which is very probably a corruption of the *praenomen*. The corrupt *tum* is the only evidence as to this Postumius' first name. Of the three *praenomina* suggested (C. Zumpt (accepted by Clark), P. Halm, T. Nohl), *tum* would be emended most economically to *T.*, although the corruption of *C.* would not have been much more difficult.

Postumius (3): A man to whom the senate entrusted the defence of Sicily against Caesar in 49 BC, and who refused to go without Cato (*Att.* 7.15.2).[243] No *praenomen* is given.[244]

Postumius (4): L. Postumius, mentioned by (the manuscripts of) Pseudo-Sallust (*Ad Caes. sen.* 2.9.4) as a member of the anti-Caesarian faction.[245]

Which of these men should be identified with each other? The connection with Cato ties together Postumii (2) and (3), and since Postumii (3) and (4)

---

[241]   *RRC* 394/1a, 394/1b. Because of similarities in typology between his coins and those of *monetales* from the Postumii Albini, Sumner initially suggested (1973: 144) that C. Postumius was a member of this family, and therefore a *nobilis*, but he later gave up this suggestion (1978: 161), persuaded by Shackleton Bailey (1976: 60).

[242]   With the exception of the ambiguous *Postumi* at *Mur.* 57, the transmitted name is Postumus, not Postumius. Clark (1905) retained the *cognomen*, but Sumner (1971: 254), Fantham (2013: 160), and others believe the man had a *nomen* Postumius, not a *cognomen* Postumus, and would emend the text accordingly. This person is certainly not to be identified with C. Rabirius Postumus, defended by Cicero in *Rab. Post.* (as suggested by Broughton in *MRR* ii.481), because Rabirius Postumus was only an *eques Romanus* in 54/53, whereas the prosecutor of Murena was candidate for praetor in 63 (Sumner (1971: 254 n. 26)).

[243]   Here too *Postumus* is the transmitted reading, but it must be emended to *Postumius*: T. Furfanus, whose authority in Sicily was being handed over to this man, is mentioned just a few words later, and consequently, since Furfanus' *cognomen* was Postumus, it would have been intolerably confusing for Cicero to have referred to him as Furfanus and to his proposed successor as Postumus.

[244]   Kaster's note (2020: *ad loc.*) incorrectly implies that we know that Postumius (3) had the *praenomen* Gaius.

[245]   Shackleton Bailey (1960: 256–257) infers from Ps.-Sall. that L. Postumius was not a *nobilis*, but Syme (1962: 177–179) rightly resists this conclusion. The author is claiming that Postumius was in fact a *nobilis*, but given the uncertainty surrounding the letter's date and authorship, and the fact that Ps.-Sall. was certainly wrong in thinking that M. Favonius, mentioned in conjunction with L. Postumius, was a *nobilis*, this counts for little. On the provenance of the letter, see Syme (1958, 1962), Santangelo (2012).

COMMENTARY 217

were both active opponents of Caesar, they too are probably the same person. The Postumius of *Brut.* 269 is included in a list of men who died fighting against Caesar, and so he should be identified with Postumii (2), (3), and (4). Since Postumius (1) is the only man whose *praenomen* is certain, Sumner proposed that Postumii (2–4) and our Postumius are all to be identified with him, and that the praenomen *C.* should be adopted in *Brut.* 269, *Mur.* 54, 56, and Ps.-Sall. *Ad Caes. sen.* 2.9.4.[246] Yet there is no evidence to connect the Postumius of *Brut.* 269 and Postumii (2–4) with C. Postumius the *monetalis*, and if Sumner's solution, which involves emending the *praenomen* in both Pseudo-Sallust and in *Brut.*, can be avoided, it should be. In my view, in spite of the fact that the *praenomen* Lucius is common among the Postumii, while Titus is unattested, the combined evidence of *Mur.* 56 *tum Postumius* and *Brut.* 269 *T. quidem Postumius* outweighs the testimony of Pseudo-Sallust's *L. Postumii*, and *T. quidem Postumius* should be accepted.[247]

271. *praeteribo* addidi] *omittam* hic add. Kayser, post *Romanos* Hertz. Hendrickson retained the paradosis, believing that readers could supply the verb from §269 *praeterisse*. The intervening sentence, however, is too lengthy to allow this; rather, a verb of omitting must have been lost. In view of §269 *praeterisse* and §273 *praetereundum*, I prefer *praeteribo* to the usual supplement *omittam*.

273. *quam*] *iniquam* Hendrickson: *scaenicam* Weidner: *quamvis molestam* Barwick: *quamvis miram* Busche: *antiquam* Hertz: *nimiam* A. Eberhard: *nequam* Della Corte | *quam eius*] *cuius* Fiᶜᵛ | *actionem*] *dictionem* Martha. The parallel §240 *huius actio non satis commendabat orationem* serves to show that *eius actionem* is not corrupt,[248] and confirms that the verb *commendo* is being used in the sense 'to make attractive'.[249] Malcovati at one time believed that the paradosis could be defended if *actio* was taken to mean 'political activity',[250] but the contrast with *oratio* and the

---

[246] Shackleton Bailey (1976: 58–60) argued for the identification of Postumii (1) and (2) as one man, and of Postumii (3) and (4), as well as our Postumius, as another; but he neglects to take into account the evidence of *Mur.* 56 *tum Postumius* or of the Catonian link between Postumii (2) and (3).

[247] The name Gaius Postumius is also rare: there are no patricians of the *gens Postumia* with this *praenomen*, and only two others are attested in the history of Republican Rome (Livy 45.6.9 (a military tribune), *Div.* 1.72 (Sulla's *haruspex*)).

[248] *Pace* Kaster (2020).

[249] Cf. §261 *nulla re una magis oratorem commendari quam verborum splendore et copia*, and for further examples see *OLD s.v. commendo* 6.

[250] Malcovati (1965: *ad loc.*); in her second edition, she obelizes *quam eius actionem*.

218 COMMENTARY

use of the word elsewhere in *Brut.* tell firmly in favour of its meaning
'delivery'.[251] Since no reference to Caelius' delivery precedes, *quam* cannot
be a connecting relative and must be corrupt. *Quam* could easily have been
added after the comparative *constantius*, but simply deleting it would leave
actionem under-defined.[252] Some adjective describing Caelius' *actio* has
either been omitted, or has been corrupted into *quam*.[253]

Because Cicero adds little of substance to our knowledge of Caelius' oratorical style outside this passage,[254] editors have looked to later testimony to
furnish a suitable adjective. Tacitus' description of Caelius' oratory as antiquated has tempted some to accept Hertz's *antiquam*,[255] but Douglas rightly
points out both that the speaker in Tacitus is referring to *elocutio*, not to
actio, and that there is no implication that Caelius was more antiquated
than his contemporaries.[256] The only substantial piece of evidence which is
concerned specifically with Caelius' delivery is an excerpt from a defence
speech quoted by Quintilian: *ne cui vestrum atque etiam omnium qui ad rem
agendam adsunt meus aut vultus molestior aut vox inmoderatior aliqua aut
denique, quod minimum est, iactantior gestus fuisse videatur* (Quint. *Inst.*
11.1.51). This quotation prompted several of the emendations which have
been proposed in our passage. However, Caelius' apology for his oratorical
foibles in a speech in his own defence is unreliable evidence for his actual
practice; one should be careful not to lean too heavily on this quotation.
Other passages which help to build up a picture of Caelius' oratory include:
Sen. *De ira* 3.8.6 *Caelium oratorem fuisse iracundissimum constat*; Tac. *Dial.*
25.4 *Astrictior Calvus, nervosior Asinius, splendidior Caesar, amarior
Caelius, gravior Brutus*; Quint. *Inst.* 10.1.115 *Multum ingenii in Caelio et
praecipue in accusando multa urbanitas*; 10.2.25 *vim Caesaris, asperitatem
Caeli, diligentiam Pollionis, iudicium Calvi.*

---

[251] Badian (1967: 226).

[252] *Cuius actionem*, which may have been conjectured independently by the 'Puccini' scribe
(in Fi) and by Leonardo Bruni (in *v*), would achieve the same effect as the deletion of *quam*.

[253] Less economically, one might postulate a lacuna of a clause or sentence, in which reference was made to Caelius' *actio*.

[254] Cicero's complimentary portrait of Caelius in *Cael.* 45 is largely conventional, and the
other references in *Cael.* (*ORF*⁴ 480–481) merely reinforce the account given here of an orator
known more as a prosecutor than as a defence speaker.

[255] *Sordes autem illae verborum et hians compositio et inconditi sensus redolent antiquitatem;
nec quemquam adeo antiquarium puto, ut Caelium ex ea parte laudet qua antiquus est* (Tac.
Dial. 21.4; cf. *Dial.* 18.1).

[256] To obviate the first of these difficulties, Martha also emended *actionem* to *dictionem*, but
the contrast between *actio* and *oratio* should be retained (cf. §§240, 276). *Dictio* is a synonym
for *oratio*: see §325 *genus erat orationis Asiaticum adulescentiae magis concessum quam senectuti. Genera autem Asiaticae dictionis duo sunt.*

COMMENTARY 219

The contrast implied by *tamen* indicates that Cicero's evaluation of Caelius' *actio* was not complimentary, but, as Busche (1919: 312) helpfully observes, *multum...commendabat oratio* tells against an excessively negative description. Thus, for example, Della Corte's *nequam* (1971) is excessive in its condemnation of Caelius. Of the other proposed emendations, Busche's *miram* is bizarre, and Eberhard's coupling of the adjective *nimius* with *actio* is questionable and unsatisfactory. Weidner's *scaenicam* is possible,[257] although it might be more suitable in describing an orator such as Hortensius, rather than the *iracundissimus* and *asper* Caelius. Better are Barwick's *molestam* (improved by the removal of *quamvis*, which is redundant before *tamen*) and Hendrickson's *iniquam*. One might also consider *ardentem* (cf. *Brut.* 276), *immoderatam*, or perhaps *invenustam* (*Brut.* 237). Since none of these is especially compelling, *quam* should be obelized.

283. *fuit cum* Corradus] *fuisset cum* L: *cum esset* Piderit | <*erat*> *eruditior* Marggraff. The pluperfect subjunctive *fuisset* is out of place in this *cum...tum* construction. Piderit emends *fuisset cum* to *cum esset*, but Corradus' *fuit cum* is simpler. Marggraff (1855: 24–25) would punctuate after *fuisset* and add *erat* before *eruditior*, thus producing the sense, 'he would have been an orator—he had certain very commendable qualities— but by excessive self-criticism he lost his true vitality'. However, although Cicero's portrayal of the Atticists is tendentious and polemical, he could hardly claim that Calvus was not an orator, given the man's reputation: Sen. *Controv.* 7.4.6 *Calvus, qui diu cum Cicerone iniquissimam litem de principatu eloquentiae habuit*, Quint. *Inst.* 10.1.115 *inveni qui Calvum praeferrent omnibus.*[258] For this use of *orator* ('as an orator,...'), cf. *Brut.* 220 *orator autem.*

283. *non devorabatur* Leeman] *devorabatur* L: *deserebatur* Purgold. Editors explain *devorabatur* as meaning 'gulped down without tasting'.[259] Yet, as Leeman (1969: 94) saw, this sense of *devoro* is unparalleled; in such contexts the verb can mean only 'swallow eagerly' or 'put up with'.[260] (It is used in the latter sense in §236.) Here, though, the first of these senses is obviously inappropriate, and the second is too weak: Cicero surely means that the crowd did not put up with the Atticists' style of speaking (cf. §289

---

[257] Or *tragicam*? Cf. *Orat.* 86 *actio non tragica nec scaenae.*
[258] Cf. Leeman (1969: 94–95).
[259] Thus, e.g., Piderit (1875), Martha (1892), Jahn-Kroll-Kytzler (1962), Douglas (1966).
[260] *OLD s.v. devoro* 1b, 4.

220   COMMENTARY

cum isti Attici dicunt, non modo a corona, quod est ipsum miserabile, sed etiam ab advocatis relinquuntur.).[261] That Kaster felt compelled to translate *devorabatur* as 'had no taste for' reveals the strangeness of the traditional interpretation. Purgold suggested emending to *deserebatur*, but while the crowd could desert Calvus, the image of the forum (*a foro*) deserting him is odd. In view of *Tusc.* 2.3 *Atticorum...qui iam conticuerunt paene ab ipso foro irrisi*, I have wondered about *deridebatur*, but this is probably too harsh for the tone of this passage. Leeman's addition of *non* is the best solution.

285. *alia aliis* Bake] *alia* L: *aliis alia* Piderit.[262] Malcovati shows intelligent critical judgement in resisting her conservative inclinations here. Hendrickson had retained the paradosis, translating the sentence thus: 'But because there are in the category of Attic other qualities better than these, one must beware not to overlook the gradations and dissimilarities, the force and variety of Attic orators.' In §285, however, Cicero is not trying to argue that a more forceful style of oratory is better than the plain style imitated by the Atticists, but only that there are different styles within the corpus of Attic oratory. The addition of *aliis* allows the clause to fit better into the flow of the passage: 'But because, in the category of Attic, some qualities are better than others, ...'[263]

The order *alia aliis* is preferred by prose authors: there are 29 instances of *alia aliis* in prose before the fourth century AD, and six of *aliis alia* (three in Livy, three in Quintilian).[264] Only 2 of the 29 are from Cicero (*Fin.* 4.67 *vitia alia* [*in*] *aliis esse maiora*, 4.68 *vitia alia aliis maiora non sunt*), but the presence of the comparative in both makes them a close parallel to *Brut.* 285. Malcovati objects that the order *alia aliis* results in a heroic clausula, but this consideration would only have significant weight at a sense-break.

292. *ratione* scripsi] *oratione* L. At §307 *haec etsi videntur esse a proposita* (*proposito* L) *ratione diversa*, Ascensius, motivated by the similarity with

---

[261] Cf. Catull. 53, which describes a rather more enthusiastic response to Calvus' oratory from the *corona*.

[262] Piderit (1860: 12); editors attribute the emendation to Friedrich, but I cannot find it in Friedrich's writings on *Brut.*

[263] Whether *aliis* is added before or after *alia*, it should be taken as an ablative of comparison. Kaster translates, 'But since some Attic orators are superior in some respects, others in others, ...', but the word order would seem to prohibit taking *aliis* with *Atticis*. (For this sense, we might expect instead, e.g., *alia aliis in Atticis*; cf. *Nat. D.* 2.130 *opportunitates...aliae aliis in locis reperiuntur*.) There is apparently a slight shift in focus from this sentence to the next: here Cicero is concentrating his attention on the different styles within the Attic corpus, and in the following sentence he will turn to the differences between individual Attic orators.

[264] Sen. *Ep.* 19.5 *ex aliis alia* is irrelevant. Cf. above on §87 *alii aliud*.

COMMENTARY 221

this passage, emended *ratione* to *oratione*. One of the two passages should be brought into line with the other, and L's *proposito* at §307 tells in favour of printing *oratione* in both places. However, while Cicero sometimes writes that his speech is wandering from its course, or that he is bringing it back to his stated topic (e.g. *Tusc.* 4.5 *Sed ut ad propositum redeat oratio*; *Tusc.* 5.66 *redeat unde aberravit oratio*; *TLL* 9.2.886.58–79), in *Brut.* 292 and 307 *oratio* would have to mean not simply 'speech, discussion', but rather 'plan' or 'topic of discussion'. *Ratio* is therefore more suitable. Cf. *Fin.* 3.74 *Sed iam sentio me esse longius provectum quam proposita ratio postularet*; *Fin.* 5.46 *Et adhuc quidem ita nobis progressa ratio est ut...*; *Orat.* 162 *longius autem quam instituta ratio postulabat.*[265] Additionally, the subject matter of *Brut.* makes corruption of *ratio* to *oratio* more likely than the reverse.[266] The corruption *proposito* in §307 may have arisen through familiarity with the common phrase *a proposito* (cf. §82).

293. *politius* **Beier]** *pictius* **L:** *perfectius* **Sarpe.** One might see in *pictius* a reference to the vivid narratives which were a feature of Lysias' speeches (cf. *QFr.* 2.13.2 *Britanniam quam pingam coloribus tuis, penicillo meo*).[267] However, elsewhere in rhetorical contexts, the metaphor of 'painting' or 'colouring' one's speech is used by Cicero to denote embellishment and ornamentation,[268] and *pictius* should have this sense here. Hence, since *quo...pictius* is manifestly inappropriate as a description of Lysias, the phrase must either be taken as a rhetorical question applied to Cato, or it must be considered corrupt. Martha and Douglas opt for the former solution and appeal to §69 *non veri simile quam sit in utroque genere et creber et distinctus Cato* (cf. also §66 *iam vero Origines eius quem florem aut quod lumen eloquentiae non habent?*). Yet this interpretation involves a distortion of Cicero's contentions concerning Cato. Cicero had not claimed that Cato had reached perfection in the adornment of his speeches. Rather, he made clear that something better still remained to be discovered: §69 *nec vero ignoro nondum esse satis politum hunc oratorem et quaerendum esse aliquid perfectius* (cf. §66).

Quo...*pictius* reads more naturally as a description of Lysias, and we should therefore emend *pictius* to some more suitable adjective. Sarpe

---

[265] Other instances of *rationem proponere* include *Verr.* 2.4.140, *Font.* 19, *Planc.* 5, and *Rab. Post.* 28.

[266] Cf. §163 *ratione* Bλρ] *oratione* F.

[267] So Kaster (2020): 'Lysias, whose vividness could not be bettered'.

[268] *OLD s.v. pingo* 5.

222 COMMENTARY

(1819: 48–49) and Reid (1905: 356) independently conjectured *perfectius*.[269] Sarpe cites Quint. *Inst.* 10.1.78 *Lysias…quo nihil, si oratori satis sit docere, quaeras perfectius*, and Reid compares *Brut.* 35 *Lysias…quem prope audeas oratorem perfectum*. In both places, though, Lysias' 'perfection' is subject to a significant caveat. Quintilian's *si oratori satis sit docere* effectively constitutes a denial that Lysias was the perfect orator, because the orator was expected to do much more than merely inform, and in *Brut.* 35 Cicero follows his comment that Lysias was *prope perfectus* by stating that Demosthenes, not Lysias, was in fact the perfect orator (*nam plane quidem perfectum et cui nihil admodum desit Demosthenem facile dixeris*). Cicero's caveat in §35 would not necessarily have prevented him from allotting to the character Atticus the view that Lysias was unsurpassed in his perfection (whether as a representation of Atticus' actual opinion or as hyperbole), but for this reason I nevertheless prefer Beier's *politius*.[270] Cicero often connects the adjective *politus* with the plain style (e.g. *Brut.* 115, 194, 285, *De optimo genere oratorum* 12 *dicant se quiddam subtile et politum velle, grande ornatumque contemnere*), and cf. *Orat.* 29 *venustissimus ille scriptor ac politissimus Lysias*.

297. *attulisti* Lambinus] *depulisti* L: *intulisti* Schütz: *protulisti* Watt: *detulisti* Manutius: *pepulisti* vulg., pler. edd. L's *depulisti* produces nonsense ('You have pushed down(?) the beginning of a long conversation'), but Watt (1983: 230–231) is justifiably suspicious of the commonly accepted correction *pepulisti*. It results in a heroic clausula,[271] and there is no parallel for the use of *pello* in this context. The most economical alternative, Manutius' *detulisti*, is also unsatisfactory: *defero* can be used of reporting information (*OLD s.v. defero* 8; even this sense is not close to that required here), but it is almost always *ad aliquem*, because it retains the core meaning of 'bringing something to somewhere'. Watt could not decide between *attulisti, intulisti*, and *protulisti*. However, Ciceronian practice favours *attulisti*, since only *affero* is used with *initium* + gen. to give the sense 'initiate': *Att.* 12.7.1 *cogitationis initium tu mihi attulisti, Acad.* 2.26 *quaerendi initium ratio attulit, Tusc.* 1.91, *Marcell.* 1. Confusion of *a* and *d*, and of *p* and *t*, is easy in some uncial scripts.

---

[269] This emendation is commended by Watt (1983: 230).
[270] Cf. §294 *significant enim formam quandam ingeni, sed admodum impolitam et plane rudem*.
[271] The unit may not end before *inquam*, however: Gregory Hutchinson suggests comparison with §292 *Tu vero, inquam, Tite*. On postpositive vocatives and the division of cola, see Murgia (1981: 306–307).

COMMENTARY   223

304. *utique* Jahn] *uterque* L. Kaster, prompted by Malcovati's punctuation, translates *sed... Philippo* as, 'yet they both deserved the name "orator", at least according to the eloquent Philippus'. This interpretation of *teste* is untenable: in the context of the trials of Memmius and Pompeius, and especially in view of the following *cuius in testimonio, teste... Philippo* must mean 'with Philippus as witness'. To make this clear, a comma should be placed after *tamen*.

However, altering the punctuation is not sufficient to resolve the historical problem raised by this sentence. The transmitted *teste diserto uterque Philippo* would seem to suggest that Philippus gave testimony in the defence of both Memmius and Pompeius. However, the following relative clause (*cuius... copiam*) reveals that Philippus, although only acting as a witness, had all the force and abundance of a prosecutor. This description of Philippus' testimony does not prove that he was a witness for the prosecution rather than the defence,[272] but it is suggestive. More significant is the historical evidence. The *lex Varia*, under which Memmius and Pompeius were tried, involved the prosecution of many of those who had supported M. Livius Drusus, the tribune of 91,[273] in his programme of reform. The identity of the L. Memmius mentioned here is uncertain,[274] but Q. Pompeius is Quintus Pompeius Rufus (praetor 91, consul 88).[275] Rufus was closely associated with the Metelli,[276] who had been among Drusus' principal supporters. L. Philippus, consul in 91, had been a vehement opponent of Drusus, and was even suspected of his murder.[277] Hence, Philippus, although known to history as a survivor rather than for his loyalty to a particular cause,[278] is unlikely to have acted as a defence witness for Pompeius in 90. We may legitimately conclude that Philippus was a witness for the prosecution.

One could still defend the paradosis by arguing that *teste diserto uterque Philippo* means only that Philippus was a witness in the trials of both Memmius and Pompeius, and does not imply that he testified in their defence.[279] This seems to me to resist the natural interpretation of the phrase, but there is an additional point in favour of Jahn's *utique*. Cicero has described Memmius and Pompeius as *non illi quidem principes... sed*

---

[272] *Pace* Gruen (1965: 65 n. 84), Badian (1967: 226).
[273] Badian (1964: 34–70), Gruen (1965: 61–62), *MRR* ii.21–22.
[274] Douglas (1966: *ad loc.*), Wiseman (1967), Sumner (1973: 85–90). Wiseman praises Biedl's transposition of *sed oratores tamen* to before *L. Memmius* (Biedl (1930: 100–101)), but Hamilton (1968) rightly rejects this idea. Biedl had misunderstood the Ciceronian idiom *non illi quidem... sed... tamen* (cf. above on §51 *illi quidem*).
[275] *MRR* ii.20.   [276] Gruen (1965: 65).   [277] *MRR* ii.20; *De vir. ill.* 66.13.
[278] For a brief biography, see *RE s.v.* 'Marcius 75'.   [279] So Badian (1967: 226).

224 COMMENTARY

oratores tamen ('not leading orators, but orators nonetheless'), and he contrasts them with the genuinely eloquent Philippus. *Utique* ('certainly') serves an important purpose in highlighting this contrast.[280]

307. eodem... magistro] del. Wetzel. Molo's two visits to Rome (cf. §312) are not in themselves problematic,[281] although only the second is attested elsewhere. Nevertheless, there are significant grounds for suspicion concerning this passage: (1) the similarity between §307 *eodem anno etiam Moloni Rhodio Romae dedimus operam* and §312 *eodem tempore Moloni dedimus operam*; (2) the absence, in §312, of an *iterum* or other acknowledgement that Cicero has already mentioned Molo;[282] (3) the fact that the reference to Molo in §312 interrupts the flow of the passage, especially the obvious connection between §311 *tum primum nos ad causas... adire coepimus* and §312 *itaque prima causa publica pro Sex. Roscio...*; (4) the repetition of §307 *actori summo causarum et magistro* in §316 *cum actorem... prudentissimum*.

Taken together, these problems are too substantial to be attributed merely to careless writing. However, Wetzel's deletion of §307 *eodem... magistro* is unconvincing. Throughout this account, Cicero has been juxtaposing the significant events in politics and in the careers of other orators in each year with details of his own life, and one would expect some such detail to follow the mention of the deaths of Catulus, Antonius, and Caesar Strabo in 87 BC.[283] Additionally, it is hard to see any motivation for an interpolator to add a sentence about Molo here, given the lack of any other surviving evidence that Molo visited Rome in 87.

There are two main possibilities.[284] Cicero may initially have erred in including the reference to Molo's visit to Rome in §307, and then he may subsequently have realized his mistake and transferred part of the sentence to §312 in order to restore the correct chronological order. He may also have expanded his description of Molo in §316 by transferring, and developing, *actori... magistro* from §307. This first hypothesis would explain the similarities between the three passages, and it would provide a reason why

---

[280] *Utique* is commonly used in this way: see *OLD s.v. utique* 4.
[281] Douglas plausibly suggests that Molo might have joined Posidonius' embassy to Rome, mentioned in Plut. *Mar.* 45.7.
[282] Cf. Norden (1913: 3).
[283] The remarks which follow (*haec etsi videntur...*) fit well immediately after some autobiographical detail.
[284] For further discussion, see Norden (1913: 2–6), Gudeman (1915), Fuchs (1956: 123–124), Douglas (1966: *ad loc.*).

COMMENTARY   225

the mention of Molo in §312 interrupts the flow of the text. One would have to assume, though, that Cicero forgot to remove, or was unsuccessful in removing, the reference to Molo from §307. Alternatively, a later reader, aware of Molo's visit to Rome in 81 BC, may have added the sentence in §312.[285] This reader may also have added *cum...prudentissimum* in §316, although Cicero could have included the words to remind his audience of Molo's credentials. I prefer the first explanation, because in my judgement §312 *eodem...venerat* is more likely to have been written by Cicero than by a later author.[286]

315. *cum*] *fuique cum* Kayser: *referta tum* Friedrich. Many editors have found unbelievable the idea of Cicero travelling through Asia with some of the foremost orators of the day, but Douglas is right to dismiss these suspicions: 'the itinerant public speaker...[was] a feature of Greek life from the fifth-century sophists onwards'. In any case, the text is secured by §316 *Adsiduissime autem mecum fuit Dionysius Magnes*.

319. *oratorum* Mo²ᵛˡ] *oratoriam* L. Orelli and Martha argue that *oratoriam* is sound, and that Cicero preferred it to *oratorum* because he intended the adjective also to be taken with *praecepta quaedam*. However, *praecepta* will obviously denote 'rhetorical precepts' whether or not *oratoriam* is retained. Apart from in its use as a technical term of rhetoric, *enumeratio* is always used, by Cicero and all other classical writers, with a defining genitive.[287] Corruption of *oratorum* to *oratoriam* would have been easy.

320. *cognoscere* vulg.] *magnum scelus* L: *cognoscere magnum scelus* F¹: *agnoscere* Orelli. *Cognoscere* is used of the acquisition of new knowledge, *agnoscere* of the recognition of something that was already familiar.[288] The experts had not already seen Hortensius' decline, and so *cognoscere* is more suitable here. The corruption of *cognoscere* to *magnum scelus* would have been made easier in some scripts by the similarity between *co* and open *a*.

322. *incluso*] *illuso* Schütz. The paradosis ('with the opponent briefly and cleverly shut in') is at first sight strange, and several editors have been tempted by Schütz's *illuso* (perhaps written in the unassimilated form *inluso*

---

[285] If this theory is correct, then Molo did come to Rome twice, but Cicero only chose to mention the first visit.
[286] In particular, compare the use of the phrase *dictatore enim Sulla* in giving the date for Molo's visit with §328 *a Sulla dictatore ad eosdem fere consules*.
[287] *TLL* 5.617.13–38. The absolute use by a few late writers (*TLL* 5.617.39–44) is irrelevant.
[288] *TLL* 1.1354.19–28, 3.1501.33–47.

226 COMMENTARY

at some point in the text's transmission). However, Martha compares §178 *callidus et in capiendo adversario versutus*, and also relevant is *De or.* 2.236, where Cicero, in listing the advantages afforded to the orator by humour, writes that it can 'obstruct the opponent' (*vel quod frangit adversarium, quod impedit, quod elevat, quod deterret, quod refutat*). The image is apparently military in origin: see *OLD s.v. includo* 2b ('*(of hostile forces)* to hem in, blockade, etc.'); *Phil.* 13.35 *militibus inclusis opem fertis. Incluso adversario* is a plausible description of the effect of humour on the opponent. Cicero may well be playing subtly with the spatial metaphor of *incluso adversario* by continuing the sentence with the verbs *laxaret...traduceret*. In particular, the opposition between the literal meaning of *laxo* ('spread out' or 'release') and *includo* ('confine', 'enclose') is unlikely to be coincidental.[289]

324. decem] sedecim Nipperdey. Most scholars now agree that L's text is sound and that Brutus was born *c.*85 BC. The primary piece of evidence to the contrary is Vell. Pat. 2.72.1, where the paradosis gives his age at death as 37: this would imply a date of birth of *c.*78. Brutus' praetorship in 44 is of little help in establishing his birth-date, since Caesar often bypassed the statutory age requirements during this period.[290] But Brutus' quaestorship in 54/53, securely attested by *De vir. ill.* 82.3–4,[291] cannot be so easily disregarded.

Douglas cites two further passages in support of Velleius' date: Plut. *Brut.* 3.1, where Brutus is described as a μειράκιον in 58, and Cic. *Brut.* 248, where Brutus claims that he was not old enough to form a judgement of Caesar's oratory before his departure for Gaul in 58. Neither does much to strengthen the case. μειράκιον is usually applied to those under 20, but Plutarch uses it of men significantly older in age.[292] *Brut.* 248, as Badian observes (1967: 229), 'has no real bearing on Brutus' age; it shows Cicero eager not to put a judgment on Caesar's oratory in Brutus' mouth'; in any case, Caesar had probably not delivered a forensic speech since 63. In summary, then, there are only three substantial pieces of evidence on Brutus' birth-date, and the *cursus* and *Brut.* 324 outweigh the testimony of Velleius.[293]

---

[289] Cf. Plin. Ep. 4.30.5 *Spiritusne aliquis occultior os fontis et fauces modo laxat modo includit...?*

[290] Sumner (1971), especially 364–366.

[291] See further Pina Polo and Díaz Fernández (2019: 268–269).

[292] Moles (2017: 77–78).

[293] Woodman (1983) and Watt (1998) both conclude that Velleius' *XXXVII* is corrupt.

COMMENTARY   227

325. *faceto*] *facto* Bo. Lucarini (2015: 11 n. 2) argued for Ruhnken's *facto* (found also in the manuscript Bo) on the basis of the correspondence between, on the one hand, §325 *genus... volucre atque incitatum* and §326 *cum incitata et vibrans*, and, on the other, §325 *exornato et fac[e]to genere verborum* and §326 *tum etiam accurata et polita*. However, *facetus* can act as a suitable parallel for *politus*. Cicero usually uses *facetus* to mean 'witty', 'humorous', but, in a looser sense, the adjective can signify 'clever' or 'adept'.[294] See, for example, *Orat.* 20 *concinniores, id est faceti, florentes etiam et leviter ornati*, 99, *Brut.* 63 *acuti sunt, elegantes faceti breves*.[295]

The use of *factus* suggested by Ruhnken is not well attested in Cicero. Cicero employs forms of *facere* in the sense 'mould' or 'craft' (e.g. *De or.* 1.63 *ignarusque sit faciundae ac poliendae orationis, Orat.* 172),[296] but in both places where the past participle is used thus (*Brut.* 30 *accurata et facta quodammodo oratio, De or.* 3.184 *orationem, quae quidem sit polita atque facta quodammodo*), the addition of *quodammodo* ('constructed in a certain way') is important. The unproblematic *faceto* is to be preferred.

327. *quod et* BFO] *quod* λβ | *lucebat*] *elucebat* Lambinus | *et exercitatione* BFλODEγ] *ex exercitatione* Y: *et exercitatio* Rom: *exercitatione* Schütz: *usu et exercitatione* Malcovati: *et studio et exercitatione* Barwick | *erat verborumque erat* Mg] *erat verborum eratque* L: *eratque verborum* vulg.: *verborum erat atque* Sydow: *verborumque erat arte* Hendrickson: *erat verborum* Kaster: *verborum erat* Douglas | *comprehensio*] *comprensa* B: *comprehensione* Martha | *excitabat* FᶜJᶜρ] *exercitabat* BFλ. This sentence has been the subject of many emendations, but most are of little value, being based on the incorrect citation of L's reading as *verborum eratque*, rather than *erat verborum eratque*.[297] Malcovati was aware of the transmitted text, but she still chose to adopt three emendations: her own addition of *usu* before *et exercitatione*, the vulgate *eratque verborum* (for *erat verborum eratque*), and *excitabat* (for L's *exercitabat*). This final emendation is necessary, but with the other alterations Malcovati diverges quite far from the paradosis.

---

[294] *OLD s.v. facetus* 1; Krostenko (2001: 90–94), and see also pp. 59–64 (on pre-Ciceronian usage).
[295] Jahn-Kroll-Kytzler (1962: *ad loc.*): '*faceto* müßte etwa = *eleganti* sein, gewählt'.
[296] Lucarini cites *Orat.* 68, but there *faciendorum... verborum* refers to the coining of new words (cf. Sandys (1885: *ad loc.*), *Part. or.* 72, *OLD s.v. factus* 4b).
[297] Friedrich did not independently conjecture the reading *erat verborum eratque*, as some have believed (e.g. Wilkins (1903), Jahn-Kroll-Kytzler (1962)); he was aware that this was L's reading (see Piderit-Friedrich (1889: 304–305), Friedrich (1902: *ad loc.*)). His own conjecture, *erat verborum exornatio atque*, interferes unhelpfully with the phrase *comprehensio verborum*.

228 COMMENTARY

The first two textual issues in the sentence can be dealt with briefly. *Quod et* was almost certainly the reading of L and should stand. (Just possibly, the agreement of λβ might indicate that L had variants (or a correction), but even then the reading of BFO would be superior.) The transmitted *lucebat* is sufficient to convey the sense 'was evident', 'was conspicuous' (cf. *Att.* 3.15.4 *meaque officia et studia, quae parum antea luxerunt*; *OLD s.v. luceo* 3); there is no need for Lambinus' *elucebat*.

The only other instance of *forma ingeni* in Cicero is *Brut.* 294 *orationes* [*Catonis*] ... *significant enim formam quandam ingeni, sed admodum impolitam et plane rudem*. In both passages the phrase apparently denotes a rough and uncultivated 'outline' of oratorical talent, unrefined by *ars* and *exercitatio*.[298] With this understood, the second element of the causal clause (*et exercitatione perfecta erat*) follows very naturally from the first (*et ingeni quaedam forma lucebat*): the undeveloped shape of Hortensius' talent was visible, and was brought to perfection through practice. In view of the frequent occurrence of the triad of *ingenium, exercitatio*, and *ars* in *Brut.*,[299] we should expect the third element (*verborum eratque astricta comprehensio*) to refer to the role of *ars* in the refinement of Hortensius' natural talent. A single change, the emendation of *verborum eratque* to *verborumque erat*, allows *verborum* to be taken with *comprehensio*, not with *exercitatione*,[300] and provides the suitable reference to *ars*: 'because the outline of his talent was conspicuous and had been brought to perfection through practice, and because his words were put compactly into periods'.[301] I have considered adopting Martha's *comprehensio<ne>* as well,[302] which would enable *forma* to remain the subject. However, one would expect Hortensius' *oratio*, rather than his *forma ingeni*, to be 'bound' (*astricta*) in a periodic structure. The desire to retain the same structure in all three elements of the tricolon might explain the incongruity, but there is no need to introduce the difficulty.

The solutions proposed by other editors, of which I list only a selection above, are much less economical. Additionally, many of them obscure the allusion to the traditional rhetorical triad. Attempts to make *perfecta* qualify *exercitatione*, whether as an ablative absolute or through emending

---

[298] Cf. §70, Douglas' note at §294, and *OLD s.v. forma* 3.

[299] For a list of passages, see Douglas (1966: xxviii).

[300] Peter, with some others, takes *verborum* with *exercitatione*; but *comprehensio verborum* is used several times by Cicero to denote a periodic sentence structure (*Brut.* 34, 96, 162, 274, *Orat.* 199), whereas *exercitatio verborum* is unattested and obscure.

[301] Translation partially adapted from Hendrickson (1962).

[302] Martha suggested this emendation as part of a different, and much more radical, intervention.

COMMENTARY 229

exercitatione to *exercitatio*,[303] are especially unappealing: practice makes perfect, but it is not itself in need of perfecting.

330. *mortuoque viverent* vulg.] *mortuo viverentque* L: *mortuo viverent* Ho: *viverentque mortuo* Stangl: *mortuoque me viverent* Ernesti. In cases such as this, the search for objective criteria on which to make a decision is not always successful. Douglas objected to *mortuoque viverent* and *viverentque mortuo* on the grounds of rhythm, but, as Hutchinson (1995: 485–486) has shown, trochee + cretic should be regarded as a rhythmical clausula, and in Cicero another trochee often precedes this pattern. The paradosis (cretic + double trochee), Hendrickson's deletion of *-que* (double cretic), and Ernesti's *mortuoque me viverent* (double cretic) also involve acceptable clausulae, and so prose rhythm cannot help with this question. Similarly, with the exception of Ernesti's emendation, transcriptional reasons do not particularly favour one emendation over another (although the addition of *-que* before *quae* is perhaps marginally easier than the two transpositions). Consequently, we are left with our own stylistic preferences.[304] I tend to agree with Malcovati that the asyndetic *mortuo viverent* is not very well suited to Ciceronian style,[305] but I prefer the vulgate solution to Stangl's *viverentque mortuo*. All the emendations improve on the transmitted reading, which leaves *-que* in manifestly the wrong place.

331. *angit* Mb] *tangit* L. Cf. Ov. *Am.* 2.4.45 *me nova sollicitat, me tangit serior aetas.* Corradus' *angit* (first found in Mb) has not enjoyed much popularity, but Ciceronian usage favours the conjecture. Firstly, Cicero never combines *sollicitare* with *tangere*, whereas there are many examples with *angere*: *Fin.* 1.41 *aut sollicitare possit aut angere, Att.* 1.18.1 *multa sunt enim quae me sollicitant anguntque, QFr.* 3.3.1 *sed me illa cura sollicitat angitque, Sen.* 66, et al. Secondly, there are no examples of the use of *dolor* in conjunction with *tangere*, whereas there are several instances with *angere*: *Att.* 4.18.2 *nullus dolor me angit, Clu.* 13, *Fam.* 4.3.1. (Examples with related

---

[303] Thus, e.g., Martha (1892), Wilkins (1903), Reis (1934).

[304] This is well evidenced by the brief discussions of Badian (1967: 224) and Malcovati (1968: 128). Badian considers the transposition *viverentque mortuo* 'weak on all grounds', but provides no reasons. Malcovati finds the vulgate *mortuoque viverent* 'meno felice' than Stangl's emendation, but she too does not elaborate.

[305] *Mil.* 97 (*gloriam…quae efficeret ut absentes adessemus, mortui viveremus*) would be a close parallel, but in *Brut.* 330 the asyndeton would probably result in too strong a stop before *quae*…. (Cf. also *Amic.* 23 *Quocirca et absentes adsunt et egentes abundant et imbecilli valent et, quod difficilius dictu est, mortui vivunt.*)

230   COMMENTARY

forms of *dol-* and *ang-* include *Fin.* 1.67 *amicorum…pariter dolemus ango-ribus, Marcell.* 2, *Tusc.* 1.30, *Amic.* 59, and *Fam.* 5.14.2.)

Additionally, *angit* is better suited to the context of the sentence. *Dolor* is a stronger word than *cura*, and only *angit* ('pains', 'distresses') conveys the appropriate emotional force. *Tangit* ('touches', 'concerns') is weaker than *sollicitat*. Finally, the concluding paragraphs of *Brut.* contain various echoes of the prologue, and the use of *angere* would secure a verbal connection to the three occurrences of the word in §§5, 7 and (above all) 10 *omnis quae me angebat de re publica cura consederit.*

331. *cura* FΛρ] *me cura* B. In view of the following *et hunc…socium*, most editors accept the reading of B. However, L did not contain this second *me*, and there is insufficient reason to add it. *Mecum* helps to clarify the syntax, and would be redundant if B's conjecture were accepted.[306]

---

[306] Similar is §254 *Graecis* FΛρ] *illis* B, where again B's reading is adopted in most editions. L's *Graecis* is to be preferred: as Peter observed, the contrast with *nobis* is made less emphatic by *illis.*

APPENDIX 1

The Manuscripts and Fifteenth-Century Editions of *Brutus*

Works without a named author are by Cicero. For an alphabetical list of sigla, see Appendix 4. The symbol ∧ denotes that a reproduction of the MS is available online.

1.1 Extant Manuscripts

1. **Barcelona, Biblioteca de Reserva de la Universitat de Barcelona, 12 = Bc∧**
Parchment; Italy; *c*.1450–1470.[1]
Orat., Brut. (f.46ᵛ–107ʳ), *Sen., De remediis fortuitorum* (Ps.-Sen.)
Before 1837, Bc was in the Biblioteca de los Carmelitos Delcalzos (also known as the Convent de Sant Josep) in Barcelona. It must be one of the two manuscripts of *Brut.* mentioned by Haenel (1830: 919) in a brief catalogue of the library. Haenel dated one of these manuscripts to the thirteenth century and the other to the four-teenth. Bc is certainly of the fifteenth century, and so at least one of Haenel's dates is incorrect. The other manuscript, now lost, was surely also a fifteenth-century codex. Manso Rubio (2014: 4–5) attributes two other manuscripts owned by the Universitat de Barcelona, MS 358 and MS 752, both previously in the Biblioteca de los Carmelitos Delcalzos, to the scribe of Bc. Bc's text is a conflation of Vw and δ.

2. **Berlin, Staatsbibliothek zu Berlin, Hamilton 162 = Be**
Parchment; Italy; *s.* xv.[2]
Orat., Brut. (f.42ᵛ–96ᵛ)
Be derives from τ from the beginning of *Brut.* until *c*.§§107–117, and after that from Vm.

3. **Berlin, Staatsbibliothek zu Berlin, Hamilton 164 = Bn**
Parchment; Rome; 1429.
De or., Brut. (f.107ʳ–148ᵛ), *Orat., Paradoxa*
Bn is a palimpsest, but few traces of the undertext remain, and the original con-tents have not been identified.[3] At the end of *Orat.* (f.179ᵛ) is the following

---

[1] Manso Rubio (2014: 4). See further Rubio (1960: 225–239); Mayer (1980: 355–356); Rubio Fernández (1984: 26–27); Garrido i Valls (2003: 163–164). For a complete digital reproduction, see http://bipadi.ub.edu/digital/collection/manuscrits.

[2] Boese (1966: 84).

[3] Boese (1966: 85–86). A few large Gothic initials are still visible, dated by Boese 'wohl 14. Jh.'.

232   APPENDIX 1

subscription: *Johannes frederici de swabenheym scripsit Romae M.CCCC.XXIX.*
Johannes Swabenheym later served as a scribe at the Council of Basel between 1434
and 1439.[4] Elisabetta Caldelli (2006: 52–53) notes that Bn is 'il primo esempio di
codice integralmente umanistico prodotto a Roma, oltre a quelli del Bracciolini'. The
textual link between Bn and Poggio's manuscript, Ff, might help to explain why the
scribe of Bn was writing in humanistic script. Letters of Poggio, the inventor of
the script, reveal that he taught several scribes to write in his new style between 1425
and 1431,[5] and Johannes Swabenheym may have been among the scribes in the
Curia trained by Poggio. Bn derives from Poggio's manuscript, Ff, and is the source
of Fj(Pd)Ve.

**4. Bologna, Archivio Storico della Provincia di Cristo Re dei Frati Minori
dell'Emilia Romagna, 11 = Bo**
Mixed; Emilia-Romagna?; *c.*1430–1450.[6]
Brut. (f.1^r–34^v, §§1–329 *miseriis quae con-*), *Epistula de re familiari* (Ps.-Bernard
of Clairvaux), *Isagogicon* (Bruni), *De militia* (Bruni), *De studiis et litteris* (Bruni),
Geta (Vitalis of Blois), *Liber Faceti* (anon.), *Saturae* (Pers., extr.)
In 1953, Bo was located in the Convent of San Bernardino di Borgonovo Val
Tidone, near Piacenza.[7] It was probably brought to Bologna after the closure of the
convent in 1991. The final page of *Brut.* has been lost. Bo contains all of ρ's chapter
divisions except two: 262.10 *sed ad* and 303.7 *hoc igitur.* Bo derives from θ.

5. Bologna, Biblioteca comunale dell'Archiginnasio, A. 85 = Bl
Paper; 1425–1500.[8]
Brut. (f.1^r–50^v)
Before entering the Archiginnasio collection, Bl was owned by Antonio Magnani
(1743–1811).[9] Bl has a single chapter division at 25.23 *hic ego.* It derives from Mh,
one of the offspring of B.

6. Brescia, Biblioteca Queriniana, E. II. 10 = Br
Parchment; Milan; *s.* xv$^{2/4}$.[10]
De or., Brut. (f.130^r–181^v), *Orat.*
The illumination is of the Lombard school.[11] De la Mare (unpublished) writes that
Br is 'from the ambiente of Pier Candido Decembrio'. Br derives from F via the lost
manuscript ξ.

---

[4] Frenz (2009–) *s.v.* 'Iohannes Swabenheim'.   [5] Ullman (1960: 86–88).
[6] Antonelli and Severi (2015: 63–64) date the MS on the basis of its watermarks and illuminations; they report Stefano Zamponi's opinion that the scribe was from the Po Valley ('in
area padano-veneta'), and Fabrizio Lollini's surmise that the illuminations indicate production
between Bologna and western Emilia-Romagna.
[7] Piana (1953: 12–14).   [8] This date depends on the derivation from Mh.
[9] Mazzatinti et al. (1890–: xxx.48).
[10] De la Mare (unpublished); Detlefsen (1869: 108); Beltrami (1906: 85–86).
[11] According to Simone Signaroli and Ennio Ferraglio in the entry in the online database
Manus (https://manus.iccu.sbn.it).

APPENDIX 1   233

7. **Cambridge, Cambridge University Library, Mm.2.4 = Cm**
Parchment; *s.* xv.[12]
De or., Brut. (f.68^r–96^r), *Orat., Paradoxa, Amic., Sen.*
Cm derives from Cj.

8. **Cambridge, St John's College Library, I.12 = Cj**
Paper; *s.* xv.
De or., Brut. (f.91^r–126^v), *Orat., Paradoxa, Tusc., Amic.*
According to James (1913: 252), Cj is written in a 'quasi-Italian (not Roman) hand'. James also records the following note, which he claims was written at the end of the manuscript: *Cristiernus d. g. dacie norwegie sclavorum gotorumque Rex, comes de oldenborgh et delmenhorst.* This note, suggestive of a Scandinavian provenance, is no longer present. If James' catalogue is correct and Cj did at one time contain this reference to a Danish king (perhaps to be identified as Christian I (1426–1481)), the page on which it was written might have been removed when the manuscript was rebound later in the twentieth century. Cj derives from χ, a descendant of π.

9. **Cremona, Archivio di Stato, Fragm. Com. 81 (ex 295) = C**
Parchment; northern Italy; *s.* ix$^{2/3}$.[13]
Brut. (f.1^r–2^v; §§218 *signa sed* – 227 *sine ulla*, §§265 *quanta severitas* – 274 *ait lucilius*)
C is copied in Caroline minuscule, and a second hand, also of the ninth century, has corrected the text in many places, often erasing the original text and writing letters over the top; most corrections are orthographical. Bernhard Bischoff (1998: 209) and Mirella Ferrari (1998: 183–184) identify the hand of the corrector with that which modernized spellings in Biblioteca Ambrosiana, E. 153 sup. (Quintilian). At the top of f.2^r is written, in a sixteenth-century hand,[14] *Scandolera Ravera et Casteletto di Ponzoni. N° 48.* In the top right-hand corner of the page, the same hand has written, and then crossed out, *N° 10,* and has added the name *Baldesar Frime.* At the bottom of the page, Emilio Giazzi (2005: 495) identified the words *doi giornj* and *Lorenzo,* written by a different, but probably contemporary, hand. He concludes that the fragment was used in the sixteenth century as the cover for a set of documents relating to a census of goods in Scandolara Ravara and Castelponzone, two villages near Cremona. Isabella Pettenazzi brought the fragment to light in 1954.[15] C is a fragment of L.

10. **Dresden, Sächsische Landesbibliothek—Staats- und Universitätsbibliothek, Dc. 108 = D^**
Parchment; Milan?; 1421–1450.[16]
De or., Orat., Brut. (f.147^r–190^v), *Att.* 13.19.4 (extr.)
The insignia of an early owner, together with the letters F. A., are found on f.1^r, 113^v, and 147^r. The titles of *Orat.* and *Brut.* have been added by Georg Fabricius

---

[12] Luard (1861: 125–126).   [13] Bischoff (1998: 209).   [14] Giazzi (2005: 495).
[15] Pettenazzi (1954, 1955–1957); cf. Malcovati (1958: 40–47), with a reproduction of f.1^r between pp. 42 and 43.
[16] De la Mare (unpublished); Schnorr von Carolsfeld and Schmidt (1882: 312–313). For a complete digital reproduction, see https://digital.slub-dresden.de.

234　APPENDIX 1

(1516–1571). D was once owned by the Counts of Werther. Water damage has rendered much of the text illegible. It contains seven of p's chapter divisions. D is a descendant of β and the source of QW.

11. Florence, Biblioteca Medicea Laurenziana (BML), Plut. 50.4 = Fa^
Parchment; Tuscany; Part 1: *c.*1425?;[17] Part 2: *s.* xv[1].
Part 1: *Orat.*, *Brut.* (f.35^r–79^v); Part 2: Asc., *Verr.* (Ps.-Asc.)
Part 1 was copied by the scribe of Laur. 36.23, identified by de la Mare (1977: 98–100) as Bartolomeo di Piero Nerucci of San Gimignano.[18] The headings are apparently by Mattia Lupi.[19] Fa's *Brut.* derives from F via ξ.

12. Florence, BML, Plut. 50.18 = Fb^
Parchment; Florence; 1 October 1423.
Brut. (f.1^r–90^v), *Orat.*
Fb was copied by the Genoese scribe Giacomo Curlo for Cosimo de' Medici.[20] At the end of *Orat.* (f.156^v), Curlo has added the following subscription: *COSMAE. DE. MEDICIS. HOC. OPUS. ABSOLVI. FELICITER. DIE. PRIMA. OCTOBRIS. M.C.C.C. C.X.X.III. EGO. IACOBUS. ANTONII. CURLI. IANUEN. FLORENTIAE.*[21] Fb derives, perhaps directly, from F, and is apparently an ancestor of Vq (and its descendants ElFmFoRoVu) in §§1–158.

13. Florence, BML, Plut. 50.19 = Fc^
Parchment; Florence; *c.*1457–1460.[22]
Orat., *Brut.* (f.44^r–100^v), *Part. or.*, *Top.*
Fc was copied by Leonardo di Giovanni Tolosani da Colle for Giovanni de' Medici. At the end of *Top.* (f.140^v) is written: *LIBER NOBILIS VIRI IOHANNIS COSME DE MEDICIS.* The illumination has been attributed to the Master of the Trivulziana Pharsalia (also known as the 'Fiesole Master'),[23] who was closely associated with Vespasiano da Bisticci. Fc is one of a family of manuscripts deriving from π via a lost ancestor υ.

14. Florence, BML, Plut. 50.22 = Fd^
Parchment; Florence; 27 April 1461.
Orat., *Brut.* (f.38^r–85^v), *Inv. rhet.*, *Part. or.*, *Top.*
Fd has been illuminated by the Master of the Riccardiana Lactantius.[24] This artist was active in Florence between 1450 and 1475, and he may have worked for Vespasiano da Bisticci.[25] The scribe's name has been erased from the subscription,

---

[17] Reeve (2016: 34–35).
[18] Cf. Bandini (1774–1777: ii.503–504). For a complete digital reproduction of this MS, and of nos. 12–20, see http://mss.bmlonline.it.
[19] De la Mare (unpublished).
[20] Ullman (1960: 61–62); de la Mare (1973: 49), (1992: 130), (2000: 74).
[21] Bandini (1774–1777: ii.510).
[22] De la Mare (1985: 435, 509), (1996: 184–185). Cf. Bandini (1774–1777: ii.511).
[23] Ames-Lewis (1984: 174–179).
[24] Ceccanti (1996: 26).
[25] Booton (1993/1996); Galizzi in Bollati (2004: 556–557); cf. Bandini (1774–1777: ii.512–513).

APPENDIX 1   235

which now reads (f.173^v): *HAEC. OPUSCULA. CICERONIS. TRANSCRIPSERAT. V KALENDAS. MAII. ANNO. MCCCCLXI.* Fd is a descendant of F.

15. Florence, BML, Plut. 50.25 = Fe^
Parchment; Italy; *s.* x v^1(?).[26]
Orat., Brut. (f.46^r–109^r)
Fe is a descendant of τ.

16. Florence, BML, Plut. 50.31 = Ff^
Parchment; Rome; June/July 1425?.
De or., Paradoxa, Brut. (f.101^r–138^r), *Orat.*
Ff was copied by Poggio Bracciolini.[27] At the end of *Orat.* (f.166^r) is written: *SCRIPSIT. POGGIUS. MARTIN. PAPAE. V. SECRETAR.* On the basis of Poggio's letters to Niccolò Niccoli, B. L. Ullman (1960: 35–36) dated the manuscript to the second half of 1425. Poggio made a series of requests to Niccoli for the texts of *Orat.* and *Brut.*, the last of them written on 23 June 1425. From the absence of any mention of the rhetorical works in Poggio's next letter to Niccoli, dated to 7 July 1425, Malcovati (1960: 330–331) concludes that Poggio must have received the manuscript he desired and produced his transcription by this point. However, this argument from silence is not probative, and a date of June/July 1425 for the copying of *Brut.* in Ff is likely, but not certain.[28] Ff is a descendant of π and the source of Bn (and its offspring Fj(Pd)Ve), as well as the first part of Vj.

17. Florence, BML, Plut. 50.36 = Fg^
Parchment; Florence; *c.*1460–1470 ('late 1460s?').[29]
Orat., Brut. (f.51^r–118^v), *Part. or., Top.*
Fg was copied by Hubertus W for the Florentine banker Francesco Sassetti.[30] A colophon on f.166^r reads: *FRANCISCUS SASSETTUS THOMAE FILIUS FLOREN-TINUS CIVIS FACIUNDUM CURAVIT.* De la Mare (1976: 181) attributed some notes in the manuscript to Bartolomeo Fonzio; previously, Caroti and Zamponi (1974: 105–106) had judged that the annotations were not by Fonzio himself, but were rather 'di mano di un copista formatosi in ambiente fonziano'. The illuminations are by de la Mare's 'Master of the Pear-Shaped Putti', an illuminator associated with Vespasiano da Bisticci.[31] Fg derives from *v*.

18. Florence, BML, Plut. 50.38 = Fh^
Parchment; Florence; *c.*1450–1456.
De or., Brut. (f.103^r–143^r), *Orat., Part. or., Top.*
Fh was owned by Piero di Cosimo de' Medici. On f.203^v is written: *LIBER PETRI DE MEDICIS COS. FIL.* De la Mare (1985: 435, 510, 545) attributed the headers to Leonardo di Giovanni Tolosani da Colle and the text to the scribe of Laur. 30.12. She

---

[26] Bandini (1774–1777: ii.513–514). M. D. Reeve: 'Decoration suggests *s.* xv^1'.
[27] De la Mare (1973: 62–84). CmCjMd may be contaminated descendants of Ff.
[28] See further Bandini (1774–1777: ii.516–519).
[29] De la Mare (1976: 181).   [30] De la Mare (1976: 164, 194), (1985: 453, 504).
[31] De la Mare (1985: 504), (1996: 180–181). Cf. Bandini (1774–1777: ii.520).

236   APPENDIX 1

hesitantly suggests that this scribe was active between c.1455 and 1470. According to Ames-Lewis (1984: 187–188, 273), the decoration is 'a poor production from the workshop of Francesco d'Antonio del Cherico'. Since Francesco d'Antonio was active from the 1450s, and Fh is among the manuscripts included in an inventory of Piero's library from 1456, the codex can be dated with some confidence to 1450–1456, and was probably produced in the middle of the decade.[32] Fh is a descendant of v.

19. Florence, BML, Plut. 90 sup. 88 = Fi^
Paper; Florence; 1423–c.1455.
Inv. rhet., Rhet. Her. (Ps.-Cic.), *De or., Orat., Brut.* (f.198^v–234^r), *Part. or., Top.*
Fi was copied by the 'Puccini' scribe.[33] Most of the 'Puccini' scribe's manuscripts were written between 1430 and 1450,[34] and Fi was probably copied during this period.[35] It is a descendant of σ and the source of EsVd.

20. Florence, BML, Plut. 91 inf. 8 = Fj^
Parchment; *s.* xv$^{med.}$(?).[36]
De or., Brut. (f.151^r–210^v), *Orat.*
Fj was one of fourteen manuscripts brought to the BML in 1758 from a collection owned by the Frati Riformati di Montepulciano.[37] Fj derives from Bn.

21. Florence, BML, Acquisti e Doni 125 = Fk
Paper; Italy; *s.* xv$^{ex.}$.[38]
Orat., Brut. (f.46^r–100^v), Greek anthology (including Isoc., Socrates, and Solon), *Nat. D.*
Fk was owned by the Florentine humanist Francesco da Castiglione (c.1420–1484)[39] and, according to Lisa Fratini (in Fratini and Zamponi (2004: 31)), part of the manuscript is written in his hand. It was bought by the BML from the bookseller G. B. Paperini in 1815. Fk is a descendant of G, perhaps via a lost ancestor α; it shares an exemplar with Vv.

22. Florence, BML, Ashb. 252 = Fl
Parchment; *s.* xv.
Two letters (Pl. and Dion of Syracuse), *Brut.* (f.4^r–58^v, only §§1–188 *probandum est* and §§195 *etiam filio* – 330 *sin secus*), *De optimo genere oratorum* (fragm.)
At one time, Fl was part of the library of Marchese Paolino Gianfilippi of Verona (1745–1827).[40] A page of *Brut.* (§§188–195) is missing between f.33 and f.34, and the manuscript also lacks the final few paragraphs of the text. Like the other descendants of θ, Bo and Lu, Fl lacks two of ρ's chapter divisions (262.10 *sed ad* and 303.7 *hoc igitur*).

---

[32] Cf. Bandini (1774–1777: ii.521).   [33] Schmidt (1974: 319); Oakley (2016).
[34] Oakley (2016: 354–355).   [35] Cf. Bandini (1774–1777: iii.674).
[36] M. D. Reeve.   [37] Bandini (1774–1777: iv.5), (1990: 94–95).
[38] Rostagno (1898: 130).   [39] Rao (2006: 137).
[40] Paoli et al. (1887–1948: 264).

APPENDIX 1   237

23. **Florence, BML, Edili 207 = Fm**
Parchment; Bologna; 16 October 1437.
Brut. (f.1^r–33^r), *Orat.*, *De or.*, *De optimo genere oratorum*, *Part. or.*, *Top.*
The subscription to *De or.* (f.128^r) reads: *EXPLICIT LAUS DEO AMEN. BONONIE MCCCCXXXVII. XVI. OTTOBR.*[41] Fm derives from Ro, a descendant of Vq.

24. **Florence, BML, Fiesole 186 = Fn**
Parchment; Florence; *c.*1460–1464.
QFr., *Att.*, *Fam.*, *De or.*, *Orat.*, *Brut.* (f.339^r–364^v), *Rhet. Her.* (Ps.-Cic.), *Inv. rhet.*, *Part. or.*, *Top.*
Fn was identified by de la Mare (1985: 560; 1996: 192) as part of a three-volume collection of Cicero's works provided by Vespasiano da Bisticci for the Badia at Fiesole in 1464, on the order of Cosimo de' Medici. Fn was copied by the scribe of BML, Fiesole 49 (Cyprian) and illuminated by the Master of the Trivulziana Pharsalia.[42] Fn derives, perhaps directly, from F.

25. **Florence, Biblioteca Nazionale Centrale, Conv. Soppr. J. I. 14 = F**
Paper; Florence; April–September (April/May?) 1423.
Orat., *Brut.* (f.32^r–74^r)
Vespasiano da Bisticci, in his life of Niccolò Niccoli,[43] records that a manuscript of Cicero's rhetorical works was brought from Milan to Florence by the ambassadors of Filippo Maria Visconti in April 1423 in order to be copied by Niccoli. Ullman (1960: 61–62) established that Niccoli himself was the scribe of F, and F must therefore have been the copy transcribed by Niccoli from this manuscript.[44] F is the source of most of the extant manuscripts of *Brut.* The dating of Fb, one of F's descendants, to 1 October 1423 establishes a *terminus ante quem* for the copying of F.[45] In his will, Niccoli bequeathed F to the Biblioteca di San Marco, in Florence.[46]

26. **Florence, Biblioteca Nazionale Centrale, II. IX. 131 = Fo**
Parchment; Venice?; *c.*1420–1429?.[47]
Brut. (f.1^r–91^v), *Orat.*
According to de la Mare (unpublished), Fo was probably copied by Giovanni Aretino (= ser Giovanni di Cenni d'Arezzo),[48] and the initials may be by the

---

[41] Bandini (1791–1793: i.523–525).
[42] De la Mare (1985: 547–548); Ceccanti (1996). Cf. Bandini (1791–1793: iii.127–128); Hunt (1998: 131–132).
[43] Vespasiano, *Le Vite*, p. 228–229.
[44] Cf. Malcovati (1960: 328–330); de la Mare (1973: 44–61). For a reproduction of part of f.32^r, see Ullman (1960: pl. 29). On the identity of F's exemplar, see pp. 57–58.
[45] Visconti's ambassadors travelled on from Florence and reached Rome in May 1423 (Ricciardi in *Dizionario biografico degli italiani*, xxix.829). If (as seems probable) they took F's exemplar with them, then Niccoli must have finished his copy by May.
[46] Ullman and Stadter (1972: 226). On the front flyleaf is written: *Iste liber est conventus S. Marci de Florentia ordinis predicatorum. de hereditate Nicolai de Nicolis Florentini viri doctissimi.*
[47] De la Mare (unpublished); Mazzatinti et al. (1890–: xii.15).
[48] On Giovanni's sojourn in Venice, and the MSS he copied there, see Regoliosi (1969: 132–133); Davies (1988: 4–5). For further bibliography on Giovanni, see de la Mare (1985: 397 n. 13).

238   APPENDIX 1

Venetian illuminator Cristoforo Cortese. The manuscript was apparently bought for the Biblioteca Magliabechiana in 1805 from the Florentine bookseller Giuseppe Pagano, who had acquired it from the library of Giovanni Giraldi (1712–1753). Fo derives from Vu, a descendant of Vq.

27. Florence, Biblioteca Riccardiana, 557 = Fp
Paper; Florence;[49] 1 July 1479 (*Brut.*).
Orat., Brut. (f.48^r–110^v)
On f.110^v is written: *M. Tullii Ciceronis Brutus finit. Deo Gratias. M.CCCCLXXVIIII Kalendis Iulii. Orat.* was completed on 5 February 1479. Fp has been copied by the same hand as Ricc. 563.[50] From the beginning of *Brut.* until *c.*§§229–264, Fp appears to be a contaminated descendant of La, one of the offspring of *v*. In the second half of the text, Fp derives independently from F.

28. Genoa, Biblioteca Universitaria, E. V. 12 = Ge
Parchment; Florence; 1467.
Orat., Brut. (f.42^r–98^r), *Part. or., Top.*
Ge was copied by Gherardo del Ciriagio, a close associate of Vespasiano da Bisticci.[51] At the end of *Top.* is written: *GHERARDUS CERASIUS FLORENTINUS SCRIPSIT FLORENTIE. M.CCCCLXVII.* Ge derives from π via *v*.

29. Glasgow, University of Glasgow Library, Gen. 334 = Gl
Parchment; France; *s.* xv^2.[52]
Orat., Brut. (f.27^r–32^r, 97^r–102^v, 38^r–48^v, 113^r–118^v, 54^r–62^v), *De or.*
Gl was once owned by Count Karl Heinrich von Hoym (1694–1736). The texts of all three works of Cicero are disordered;[53] the pages of Gl's exemplar must have been disarranged. Gl derives from *ι*, an exemplar shared with StVf.

30. Glasgow, University of Glasgow Library, Hunter 65 (T.3.3) = Gw
Parchment; Florence; *c.*1425.[54]
Brut. (f.1^r–54^v), *Part. or., Top.*
Gw may have been copied by Giovanni Aretino.[55] It derives from Ec via μ, an exemplar shared with Pc.

31. Holkham, Holkham Hall Library, 376 = Ho
Paper; north-east Italy; *s.* xv$^{2/4}$.[56]
Orat., Brut. (f.40^r–98^r)
There is a change of hand at the top of f.61^v (§126 *manus extrema*). The watermarks are similar to Briquet 11662 (Florence, 1432) and Briquet 11663 (Genoa and Florence, 1434–1446).[57] Ho contains most of ρ's chapter divisions in §§1–126, and

---

[49] De Robertis and Miriello (1997: 29).   [50] Ibid.
[51] Ullman (1960: 111–118); de la Mare (1985: 430, 496). Cf. Kristeller (1963–1992: i.242).
[52] Ker (1977: 908–909).   [53] For full details, see Ker (1977: 908–909).
[54] De la Mare (unpublished); Young and Aitken (1908: 75–76).
[55] De la Mare (unpublished).   [56] Reynolds (2015: 284).   [57] Ibid., 284–285.

APPENDIX 1   239

none thereafter. In §§1–126, Ho, the ancestor of Rm, is a contaminated descendant of β, and in the remainder of *Brut.* it is a contaminated descendant of τ.

32. Ithaca, NY, Cornell University Library, 4600 Bd. Ms. 123 + = U
Parchment; Verona;[58] 1428–1450 (*c.*1433?).[59]
De or., Orat., Brut. (179^r–234^v), Veronese inscription
U was copied by Alessio Tedesco,[60] who also copied a manuscript of Justin (British Library (BL), Additional 12012) from an exemplar owned by Guarino in 1433. Arguing from the similarities with the Justin codex, White (1979: 229) proposed that U was probably copied around the same time. Martino Rizzoni, a student of Guarino, added the following subscription on f.234^v:[61] *Ex emendatissimo codice Iohannis Lamole bononiensis viri eruditissimi transcripsit hunc alesius germanus. et ad eundem postea emendatus est.* The citation of an inscription from Verona on f.236^r suggests a Veronese provenance. The manuscript was acquired for A. D. White, President of Cornell University, from the Parisian bookstore Maisonneuve in 1886.[62] U derives from λ, a manuscript copied by Giovanni Lamola in 1428 for Guarino Veronese.

33. London, BL, Additional 10383 = La
Paper; Florence;[63] 1456.
Brut. (f.1^r–66^v), *Orat.*
La was copied by Leonardo di Giovanni Tolosani da Colle.[64] The subscription to *Orat.* (*M. T. C. ORATOR EXPLICIT EX EMENDATISSIMO CODICE LEONARDI ARRETINI EXEMPLATUS. M.CCCC.LVI.* (f.116^r)) reveals that the manuscript's exemplar was a codex once owned by Leonardo Bruni. La was once part of the library of János Zsámboky (= Johannes Sambucus (1531–1584)).[65] It is a descendant of υ and probably the source of the first part of Fp's *Brut.*

34. London, BL, Additional 11922 = Lb
Parchment; November 1422 – October 1423.
De or., Orat., Brut. (f.168^v–219^v)
Copied in an early fifteenth-century semi-Gothic script,[66] Lb was owned by Lorenzo di Marco Benvenuti, who is most famous as the author of an invective against Niccolò Niccoli. Lorenzo died in Florence in October 1423.[67] Lb was subsequently owned by Lorenzo's son Lodovico Benvenuti, by the Florentine Niccolini

---

[58] White (1979: 229).   [59] Calkins (1972: 81).   [60] Stangl (1913: 830).
[61] White (1979: 229, pl. VI–VII (f. 179^r, 234^v)).
[62] Stangl (1913); Sabbadini (1971: 108); White (1979: 224 n. 6). See also Malcovati (1959: 174–180); White (1975).
[63] Watson (1979: i.28; ii, pl. 553 (f.67^r)).   [64] De la Mare (1985: 435, 509).
[65] On Zsámboky's library, see Gerstinger (1926); Kenney (1974: 79–82); Viskolcz (2016).
[66] De la Mare (unpublished).
[67] Grayson in *Dizionario biografico degli italiani*, viii.677. On Benvenuti's library, cf. Field (2017: 262); Poggio, *Lettere* (1984: 72): *Libros Laurentii si in licitationem venient, credo multum extimari. Verumtamen cures, oro, si quid est boni, quod haberi possit equo pretio, ut Poggius tuus aliquid habeat.*

240   APPENDIX 1

family, and by Samuel Butler (1774–1839), Bishop of Lichfield.[68] Lb has ρ's chapter divisions. It appears to derive from O, but with some contamination from δ.

35. London, BL, Harley 2733 = Lc
Parchment; Florence; c.1470–1480.[69]
Orat., Brut. (f.60^r–138^r)
Lc was copied by Nicolaus Sextius of Poppi and illuminated by Mariano del Buono.[70] It was allegedly bought by John Gibson in 1723 from 'a Monastical Library Founded or Endowed by the Guicciardini'.[71] The text is in the same order as Vh. From the beginning of *Brut.* until c.§§280–309, Lc derives from Vh; thereafter, it derives from ψ.

36. London, BL, Harley 2771 = Ld
Parchment; Florence; c.1430–1440.[72]
Orat., Brut. (f.25^r–56^r)
Ld was copied by the scribe of BML, Plut. 54.29, whom de la Mare (unpublished) describes as 'an early Florentine humanistic scribe…probably strongly influenced by Giovanni Aretino, but showing similarities also to Antonio di Mario'. In the fifteenth century, Ld was owned by the brothers Franciscus and Rubertus de Leonibus; a note of ownership is inscribed on f.57^v. Ld derives from κ via ν, an exemplar shared with Vw.

37. London, BL, Harley 4790 = Le
Parchment; Rome?; *s.* x v$^{med.}$.[73]
Orat., Brut. (f.52^r–120^v)
Le is a descendant of Vw.

38. London, BL, Harley 7400 = Lf
Mixed; Florence; 1425–1430.[74]
Brut. (f.1^r–51^r)
The scribe of Lf also copied part of Paris, Bibliothèque de l'Arsenal, 724.[75] The hand of Sozomeno da Pistoia (1387–1458) has been identified in some of the corrections, marginal notes, and folio numbers.[76] Lf was copied in the period when Sozomeno was based in Florence, and consequently Lf may well have been produced

---

[68] Rhodes (1975); British Library, *Explore Archives and Manuscripts*, http://searcharchives.bl.uk.
[69] De la Mare (unpublished); a reproduction of f.1^r may be viewed at http://www.bl.uk/catalogues/illuminatedmanuscripts.
[70] De la Mare (1985: 447–448, 521), (unpublished).
[71] Wright and Wright (1966: 213); Wright (1972: 162–163).
[72] De la Mare (unpublished); a reproduction of f.1^r may be viewed at http://www.bl.uk/catalogues/illuminatedmanuscripts.
[73] De la Mare (unpublished); a reproduction of f.1^r may be viewed at http://www.bl.uk/catalogues/illuminatedmanuscripts.
[74] Ceccherini (2016: 189–192, pl. 55); de la Mare (unpublished).
[75] De la Mare (1973: 97 n. 4).   [76] Wright (1972: 369).

APPENDIX 1   241

there. Sozomeno bequeathed the codex, together with the rest of his library, to the Opera di San Jacopo in Pistoia. At one time, Lf was bound with Harley 4905 (Livy, *Per.*), but Harley 4905 was copied several decades later. Lf is a descendant of τ.

39. Lund, Universitetsbiblioteket, Medeltidshandskrift 42 = Lu^
Parchment; Italy; *s.* xv.[77]
Brut. (f.1^r–85^r), *Part. or.*, *Carmen de morte Ciceronis* (Cornelius Severus)
Lu was previously MS 9153 in the Phillipps collection, and was bought by Lund University Library in 1926.[78] It has ρ's chapter divisions. With the exception of the final few paragraphs (*c.*§§331–333), in which it derives from F, Lu is among the offspring of θ.

40. Madrid, Biblioteca Nacional de España, 10060 = Ma^
Parchment; Florence?; *s.* xv.
Brut. (f.1^r–32^v), *Orat.*
The decoration is Florentine.[79] Ma was once part of the library of Mario Maffei of Volterra (1463–1537).[80] Later, it was owned by the cardinal Francisco Javier de Zelada (1717–1801), and was bequeathed by him to the Cathedral of Toledo, whence it was brought eventually to the Biblioteca Nacional.[81] Together with BrFaMc, Ma derives from F via ξ.

41. Milan, Biblioteca Ambrosiana, A 73 inf. = Mb^
Paper; Milan?; *s.* xv$^{med.}$ (*c.*1460).[82]
De or., Orat., Fam. 6.18 (extr.), *Inst.* 10 (Quint., extr.), *Vita Ciceronis* (anon.),[83]
Brut. (f.105^r–137^v)
The illumination is of the Lombard school.[84] Mb was in the duchy of Milan in the 1400s, since it bears, on f.1^r, a coat of arms identifiable with the Milanese 'de Cavaleriis' of the fifteenth-century Stemmario Trivulziano.[85] The letters *A* and *M* are inscribed on either side of the coat of arms, but the owner of Mb has not yet been identified. In the sixteenth century, the codex was owned by Francesco Ciceri (1521–1596); it was bought by the Ambrosiana from his heirs in 1603. The text of *Brut.* is in the following order: 1.1 – 92.9 *alios quod*, 99.8 *erat alii* – 107.13 *d. brutus*, 92.9 *melius putent* – 99.8 *pueris nobis*, 114.18 *graecis litteris* – 122.19 *gradus persequamur*, 107.13 *m. filius* – 114.18 *vir et*, 122.21 *nobis vero* – 333.19. Mb has ρ's chapter divisions. It derives from Mi, and via it from ϵ.

---

[77] Pellegrin (1954: 30).
[78] For further details, and for a complete digital reproduction, see http://www.alvin-portal.org.
[79] Hernández Aparicio (2000: 317). For a complete digital reproduction, see http://bdh-rd.bne.es.
[80] On Maffei's library, see Ruysschaert (1958).   [81] Hernández Aparicio (2000: 317).
[82] Cipriani (1968: 145). For a complete digital reproduction, see https://ambrosiana.comperio.it.
[83] On this text, see Tilliette (2003); Cook (2009).
[84] Cipriani (1968: 145); cf. Ceruti (1973–1979: i.43).   [85] Maspoli (2000: 127).

242 APPENDIX 1

42. Milan, Biblioteca Ambrosiana, B 125 sup. = Mc
Parchment; northern Italy;[86] 1430–1460?[87]
Orat., Brut. (f.43ᵛ–101ᵛ)
The illumination is of the Lombard school.[88] Mc was bought by the Ambrosiana from the heirs of Cesare Rovida in 1606. It appears to be a contaminated descendant of ξ.

43. Milan, Biblioteca Ambrosiana, C 75 sup. = T^
Parchment; Milan; 1425–*c.*1450 (*c.*1430?).
De or., Orat., Brut. (f.176ʳ–232ᵛ)
T has been copied by several hands and illuminated by the Master of the *Vitae Imperatorum*.[89] In the fifteenth century, the manuscript was owned by Luigi Bossi, and in 1606 it was bought by the Ambrosiana from 'Julianus pictor'. The manuscript is dated by Cipriani (1968: 18) to *c.*1430, and by the Ambrosiana online catalogue to 1451–1500.[90] Cipriani's date seems much more likely, given that Luigi Bossi was active in Milan between 1431 and 1451,[91] and the manuscript's illuminator in the 1430s and 1440s.[92] Sabbadini (1971: 97) claimed that T was probably copied before O (i.e. before 1422), but he must have been mistaken, since part of T's text derives from O. T shares some of Oᵛ's corrections and so cannot have been written before 1425. T contains ρ's chapter divisions; it derives from β in §§1–251, and from O in §§251–333.

44. Milan, Biblioteca Ambrosiana, H 22 inf. = X
Parchment; Milan; 1421–1450.[93]
De or., Orat., Brut. (f.172ʳ–227ʳ), *Vita Zenonis* (Coronatus?, extr., *s.* Ix)
X is the source of θ and its offspring BoFlLu. GX have probably been copied by the same scribe;[94] Massimo Zaggia (*per litteras*) tentatively suggests similarities with the hand of Antonius Crivellus.[95] It was purchased by the Ambrosiana from the bookseller 'Ferandus' in 1603. X contains ρ's chapter divisions. It is a brother of G, both deriving from a common ancestor γ.

---

[86] Jordan and Wool (1984–1989: i.126).
[87] The interval 1430–1460 is given by the Ambrosiana online catalogue (https://ambrosiana. comperio.it); the MS is assigned by Cipriani (1968: 11) to *s.* xvᵐᵉᵈ·, by Jordan and Wool (1984–1989: i.126) to *s.* xv².
[88] Cipriani (1968: 11).   [89] Cipriani (1968: 18).
[90] https://ambrosiana.comperio.it. A complete reproduction of T can be viewed via this website.
[91] Barbero (2016: 151).
[92] Lollini in Bollati (2004: 587–589); cf. Jordan and Wool (1984–1989: ii.105–106); Tremolada (1988: 11); Barbero (2016: 151–155, 162).
[93] Massimo Zaggia (*per litteras*) suggests the location and date primarily on the basis of the style of the illuminated initials. Cf. Cipriani (1968: 244); Ceruti (1973–1979: ii.244). G was copied by the same scribe between 1421 and 1428, and X may well date to the same period.
[94] My own suspicion, shared by Prof. Zaggia.
[95] On Crivellus, see Zaggia (1995: 12–17), (2007: 353–358); Derolez (2018: 143).

APPENDIX 1   243

45. Milan, Biblioteca Ambrosiana, H 197 inf. = Me
Parchment; 1426–1459.[96]
Brut. (f.1^r–36^r), *De falsa relig.* (Lactant., headings)
Me was owned by Nicola Arcimboldi of Parma (1404–1459), an advisor of Filippo
Maria Visconti and Francesco Sforza.[97] It contains ρ's chapter divisions. Me derives
from G via ζ.

46. Milan, Biblioteca Ambrosiana, L 21 sup. = Mf
Parchment; 1423–1450.[98]
Orat., *Brut.* (f.46^r–101^r)
Mf was owned by Bartolomeo Ghisilardi (d. 1505), the Chancellor of Bologna. It
derives from Vm; in the first part of the text, it shares an exemplar with Sd, and from
§215 onwards (and probably from earlier), it apparently derives from Re.

47. Milan, Biblioteca Ambrosiana, L 86 sup. = Mg
Parchment; Parma; 1438 (Cic.).
Somn., *Orat.*, *Brut.* (f.30^v–64^v), *De optimo genere oratorum*, *De or.*, *Cicero novus ex
Plutarcho* (Bruni)
On the first page is written: *hic codex partim Rhegii, partim Parma scriptus, fuit
anno 1438.* At the end of *De or.* (f.151^r) is written: *Scriptus Parma a. d. 1438.* In the
subscription to Bruni's *Cicero novus*, the scribe dates his copying of the text to 1435.
The illumination is of the Emilian school.[99] In the fifteenth century, Mg was owned
by Iohannes Antonius de Baliachis; it was bought by the Ambrosiana from the heirs
of Cesare Rovida in 1606. Malcovati (1959: 181 n. 26) discussed briefly three marginal notes in the manuscript, two of which testify to Gasparino Barzizza's study of
the text of *Brut.* At *Brut.* 172.9 *loqueretur omnium*, a marginal note in Mg reads:
Nescit Gasparinus pergamensis quid hoc loco voluerit Cicero. At 184.25 *laborasse*, a
scribe has added: *testus corruptus est in Veteri. Gasparinus autem dicebat: laboras
quod hoc modo.* It is unclear whether the annotator of Mg obtained these details
from Barzizza's manuscript of *Brut.*, from personal contact with him, or from his
published writings. Mg contains ρ's chapter divisions. It is a contaminated descendant of δ.

48. Milan, Biblioteca Ambrosiana, O 158 sup. = Mi^
Parchment; Lombardy; 1421–1450.[100]
De or., *Orat.*, *Fam.* 6.18 (extr.), *Inst.* 10 (Quint., extr.), *Vita Ciceronis* (anon.),[101]
Brut. (f.65^r–98^v, only §§1–293 *hominem vel*)
Mi has been written by Giovanni da Crema (f.62^r: *EXPLICIT FOELICITER PER
IOHANNEM DE CREMA*), who also copied Escorial L. III. 5 (*De or.* and *Orat.*) and

---

[96] Cipriani (1968: 252); cf. Ceruti (1973–1979: ii.372); Zaggia (1995: 16 n. 75).
[97] On Nicola's library, see Pellegrin (1988: 381).
[98] Biblioteca Ambrosiana online catalogue, https://ambrosiana.comperio.it; cf. Ceruti
(1973–1979: iv.10). The *terminus post quem* depends on the derivation from F.
[99] Cipriani (1968: 86); cf. Ceruti (1973–1979: iv.52).   [100] Cipriani (1968: 98).
[101] Cf. above, p. 241 n. 83.

244   APPENDIX 1

Vat. lat. 442 (August., *De civ. D.*).[102] The illumination is of the Lombard school.[103] Much of *De or.* is now missing, as is the beginning of *Orat.* and the end of *Brut.* The text of *Brut.* is in the same order as in Mb. Mi contains ρ's chapter divisions. It derives from ε, an ancestor shared with Mn, and is the source of Mb.

49. Modena, Biblioteca Estense Universitaria, Lat. 244 = α.O.5.17 = Mo
Parchment; *s.* xv.
Orat., Brut. (f.36ᵛ–86ᵛ)
Mo derives from F via κ; a later hand has corrected the text from another manuscript.

50. Modena, Biblioteca Estense Universitaria, Lat. 257 = α.H.8.4 = Md
Parchment; *s.* xv.
Orat., Brut. (f.26ʳ–61ʳ), *De or.*
Md was once part of the library of Annibale Malvetio, a nobleman in Bologna. It derives from π via χ.

51. Modena, Biblioteca Estense Universitaria, Lat. 261 = α.Q.8.25 = Mh
Parchment; Mantua; 12 September 1425 (*Orat.*).[104]
Brut. (f.1ʳ–35ʳ), transcriptions of epigraphic texts, *Orat.*, poems addressed to Tiberius, Caligula, Julius Caesar, and Augustus (anon.)
The subscription to *Orat.* reads:

Orator ad M. Brutum feliciter explicit transcriptus perfectusque. et ab eo exemplari emendatus. quod a vetusto illo codice primum transcriptum correctumque fuerat. pridie idus septembris 1425. Mantuae.

Although B may have been the exemplar of Mh's *Brut.*, B does not contain *Orat.*, and so Mh's subscription must refer to another manuscript copied from L.[105] Below the subscription the scribe, Francesco Calcagnini, has added his initials.[106] Francesco Calcagnini, a student of Vittorino da Feltre, apparently retained the manuscript, because it was subsequently owned and annotated by his grandson, Celio Calcagnini,[107] while he was in Ferrara. Mh has a single chapter division at 25.23 *hic ego.* Mh derives from B and is an ancestor of BlOd. It also appears to have been the primary source of VenA, the second printed edition of *Brut.*

---

[102] Derolez (2018: 145); cf. Derolez (1984: i.144). For a complete digital reproduction, see https://ambrosiana.comperio.it.
[103] Cipriani (1968: 98); cf. Ceruti (1973–1979: iv.352).
[104] For a more detailed description of Mh, see Ghignoli (2016: 121–123).
[105] Cf. Sabbadini (1971: 102 n. 2).
[106] Stangl (1886: x, xix) doubts whether Francesco Calcagnini was the scribe, but his reservations are unfounded. Ghignoli (2016: 121) confirms that the whole MS is in Francesco's hand. On the scribe, see Ascari in *Dizionario biografico degli italiani*, xvi.498–499.
[107] On the library of Celio Calcagnini, see Ghignoli (2016).

APPENDIX 1   245

52. Montpellier, Bibliothèque Interuniversitaire, Section Médecine, H 214 = M
Parchment; Milan; 1430–1439.[108]
De or., Orat., Brut. (f.174ᵛ–226ᵛ, only §§1–317 *solute et*)
Massimo Zaggia (*per litteras*) considers the hand similar to, but not the same as,
that of Milanus Burrus.[109] In 1721 M was part of the library of Jean Bouhier of Dijon
(1673–1746). It contains most of ρ's chapter divisions. M is a descendant of β and the
ancestor of Y.

53. Munich, Bayerische Staatsbibliothek, Clm 796 = Mu
Parchment; *s.* xv.[110]
Orat., Brut. (f.186ᵛ–201ʳ, only §§1–76 *scripsere in-*, §§91 *igitur inquit* – 99 *filii*
fuerunt, §§178 *suppeditabat oratio* – 207 *fiebant neque*)
This manuscript is incomplete, beginning at f.151ʳ with the start of *Orat.* The text
is in the following order (compare Vh): 1.1 – 59.23 *praeclare tum*; 178.26 *suppedita-*
bat oratio – 207.3 *fiebant neque*; 91.27 *igitur inquit* – 99.4 *filii fuerunt*; 59.24 *illi hom-*
ines – 76.3 *scripsere in-*. Mu derives from Vm via Vh.

54. Munich, Bayerische Staatsbibliothek, Clm 28882 = Mn
Paper; *s.* xv.
De or., Orat., Brut. (f.109ʳ–140ʳ)
At the end of *Brut.* (f.140ᵛ), the scribe has added the following subscription:

Deficiunt pauca, non ultra folia duo ad plus, et ut ego coniecturam facio non
ultra columnam. Plura enim in codice vetustissimo non comperi: ex quo in fine
carte recise iniquitate fortune erant.

Below, the same scribe has written: *Hec ex praeceptore doctissimo Gasparino de*
Barzizis Pergamensi scripta relicta habentur. A later hand has then added: *Scripta per*
[*pro?*] *me Mateum* [final two letters uncertain] *Rhagusio.* A third hand has written
below, *M. T. Ciceronis de oratore liber iste mei* [name deleted] *Bartholomei de puteo*
cremonensis. Johannes Stroux (1930: 286) reported that the 'Seminar für klassische
Philologie, München' had acquired the codex from the antiquarian bookseller
G. Hess.[111] The text of *Brut.* is in the same order as in MbMi, although the scribe has
added a marginal note restoring §§114–122 to their correct place after §§107–114.
Mn contains ρ's chapter divisions. Mn derives from G via ε, an ancestor shared
with Mi.

---

[108] On the authority of Marco Petoletti and Mirella Ferrari, who suggest that the MS was
copied in Lombardy in the 1430s, and Massimo Zaggia, who independently assigns it to
'Milan, 1430–1450' (both views expressed *per litteras*).
[109] On Milanus Burrus and scribal hands similar to his, see Zaggia (1995: 4–12). A few
images of M are available at https://bvmm.irht.cnrs.fr.
[110] Halm and Laubmann (1892: 196).   [111] Cf. Kristeller (1963–1992: iii.626).

246   APPENDIX 1

55. Naples, Biblioteca Nazionale, IV A 40 = Na
Paper; *s. xv.*
Orat., Brut. (f.33^r-79^r), *Part. or.*
The watermarks have been identified with Briquet 11702 (Pisa, 1440).[112] Na was part of the Farnese collection, transferred from Rome to Parma in the middle of the seventeenth century and from Parma to Naples in 1736.[113] Na derives, perhaps directly, from F; later corrections have been made from Ff.

56. Naples, Biblioteca Nazionale, IV A 44 = G
Parchment; Milan; 1421–1428 (probably 1421–1423).[114]
Brut. (f.1^r-57^r)
G has probably been copied by the scribe of X, who may be Antonius Crivellus. At the top of the front flyleaf is written *Guiniforti Barzizii*, and hence the manuscript was once owned by Guiniforte, the son of Gasparino Barzizza. Two notes of possession indicate that G was later owned by Aulo Giano Parrasio (*A. Iani parrhasii et Amicorum Mediolani emptus aureolo*)[115] and then by Antonio Seripando (*Antonii Seripandi ex Iani Parrhasii testamento*). Later, it was owned by the convent of San Giovanni a Carbonara, in Naples, and it almost certainly entered the convent as part of a bequest made, in 1536, by Cardinal Girolamo Seripando, who inherited the library of his brother Antonio in 1531. Sabbadini (1971: 93–94) proposed that G (which he cited with the incorrect shelf-mark IV B 43) was originally part of a manuscript which contained *De or.* and *Orat.* as well as *Brut.*, and that the first part of this manuscript survived as Biblioteca Apostolica Vaticana (BAV), Pal. lat. 1469 (cited by editors of *De or.* and *Orat.* with the siglum P). (Sabbadini further suggested that this manuscript was Gasparino Barzizza's copy of Cosimo Raimondi's transcription of L.)[116] However, as has been independently established by Anna Nunziata (in Gualdo Rosa et al. (1996: 23–24, pl. 4–5)) and Albinia de la Mare,[117] the hand which copied G is plainly different from both hands present in Pal. lat. 1469. The subscription to Pal. lat. 1469 may be in Gasparino Barzizza's hand,[118] and it seems that Sabbadini, having found Guiniforte Barzizza's note of ownership in G, jumped to the conclusion that the two manuscripts must originally have been bound together. Nevertheless, that G and Pal. lat. 1469 probably both originated in the *casa Barzizza* does not prove that they were originally part of the same manuscript or set. Sabbadini's conclusions concerning G should be discarded, as should Scarcia Piacentini's dating of G to 1422 (1983: 126–127), which depended on Sabbadini (1971). G contains ρ's chapter divisions. It derives from β via γ, an exemplar shared with X, and is the source of four manuscript families: α, δ, ϵ, and ζ.

---

[112] Fossier (1982: 110).   [113] Fossier (1982: 7–13).

[114] Nunziata (in Gualdo Rosa et al. (1996: 23–24)) dates G to *s.* xv$^{1/4}$. An absolute *terminus ante quem* is provided by the dating of one of G's offspring, Vn, to 11 February 1428, but the readings shared by Lb and G's descendant δ suggest that G was copied before November 1423.

[115] On Parrasio's library, see Tristano (1988), esp. 23–24, 105–107.

[116] Sabbadini had previously identified G with Raimondi's transcription (Sabbadini 1888: 113–114).

[117] Barbero (2016: 157).   [118] Barbero (2016: 156–158).

APPENDIX 1   247

57. Naples, Biblioteca Nazionale, IV B 36 = Np
Paper; Ferrara; December 1422/early 1423 (*Brut.*).[119]
Ad Brut., *QFr.*, *Att.*, *Epistulae* (Guarino), *Brut.* (f.121^r-154^r), *HN* VII 91 (Plin.),
Latin synonyms, *Ep.* (Plin.), *Hortensius* (fragm.), *Epistulae* (various authors)
Np's *Brut.* was copied by Ugo Mazzolato of Ferrara for his own, and Guarino
Veronese's, use.[120] The pages of *Brut.* have become disordered, and the text is now in
the following order: 1.1 (f.121^r) – 72.25 *natus est* (f.126^v), 135.23 *laus eadem* (f.127^r) –
287.5 *neque possim* (f.142^v), 72.25 *Ennius post* (f.143^r) – 135.23 *locutus quae* (f.148^v),
287.5 *si velim* (f.149^r) – 333.19 (f.154^r). On f.154^v, the following subscription has
been written:

Non erat amplius in exemplari a quo abscisse sunt charte due. Liber iste brutus,
repertus est nuper laude. in quo quidem codice sunt Rhetoricorum ad
Herennium. Rhetorica de oratore. orator ad brutum. et Brutus de oratoribus
claris. M. T. Ciceronis.

Np has ρ's chapter divisions in §§1–130, but none thereafter. Np derives, almost certainly directly, from B.

58. New Haven, Yale University, Beinecke Rare Book and Manuscript Library,
Marston 6 = Y$^\wedge$
Paper; northern Italy; *s.* x v$^{med.\ or\ 3/4}$.[121]
Orationes, *De or.*, *Orat.*, *Brut.* (f.354^r-393^r)
Y is a composite manuscript: the speeches were originally bound separately from
the rhetorical works, and were copied several decades earlier.[122] A watermark on the
pages containing the rhetorical works has been identified as Briquet 15068
(Bordeaux, 1462). Y contains most of ρ's chapter divisions. It derives from M.

59. Oxford, Balliol College Library, 248E = Ob$^\wedge$
Parchment; Florence; 12 November 1445.
Inv. rhet., *Rhet. Her.* (Ps.-Cic.), *De or.*, *Brut.* (f.167^r-198^r), *Orat.*, *Part. or.*, *Top.*,
Synonyma (Ps.-Cic.)
Ob was copied in Florence by the scribe and notary Antonio di Mario; it is part
of a five-volume set of Cicero's works produced by Vespasiano da Bisticci for
William Gray, who would later become Bishop of Ely.[123] On f.241^r is written:
ANTONIUS. MARII. FILIUS. FLORENTINUS. CIVIS ATQUE NOTARIUS

---

[119] Sabbadini (1971: 103–104); cf. Gualdo Rosa in Gualdo Rosa et al. (1996: 28–29).
[120] Sabbadini (1971: 103–104). On f.196^v Mazzolato has copied two letters written by
Guarino, one to Flavio Biondo, thanking him for sending his MS of *Brut.* (B), and the other to
Mazzolato, asking him to make a copy of B (Sabbadini (1915–1919: i.355, 361)).
[121] Shailor (1992: 7–16); cf. Abbamonte (2020: 6–12). For a complete digital reproduction,
see https://collections.library.yale.edu.
[122] De la Mare (unpublished) assigned the speeches to 'northern Italy, *ca.* 1425', and suggested that they might have been copied in Ferrara.
[123] On the scribe, see Ullman (1960: 98–109), de la Mare (1985: 254, 482–484); on the set of
MSS, de la Mare (1996: 177–179); and on William Gray and his library, Mynors (1963: xxiv–xlv).
A complete digital reproduction can be found via http://archives.balliol.ox.ac.uk.

248   APPENDIX 1

TRANSCRIPSIT FLORENTIAE. II. IDUS. NOVEMBRIS. M.CCCC.XLV. VALEAS. Ob derives from Vl, a descendant of τ.

60. Oxford, Bodleian Library, D'Orville 82 = Ox
Parchment; Florence; *s.* x v^med..[124]
Orat., Brut. (f.42^v–97^v)
Ox was once owned by the Florentine notary Nastagio Vespucci.[125] It derives from F via the lost manuscript κ.

61. Oxford, Bodleian Library, Canon. Class. Lat. 214 = Od
Paper; 1425–1500.[126]
Epit. (Just.), *Catonis Uticensis Vita ex Plutarcho* (Bruni), *Somn., Vita Bruti ex Plutarcho* (Jacobus Angelus), *Vita Ciceronis ex Plutarcho* (Jacobus Angelus), *Brut.* (f.131^r–155^v), *Top., Part. or., Commentary on Arist. Ph.* (anon.)
Od has a single chapter division at 25.23 *hic ego*. It derives from Mh, a descendant of B.

62. Paris, Bibliothèque nationale de France (BnF), lat. 7703 = Pa^∧
Parchment; Milan; 24 June 1461 (*Brut.*).
De or., Orat., Brut. (f.122^r–159^r), *Part. or., Top., Inv. rhet., Rhet. Her.* (Ps.-Cic.)
At the end of *Brut.* (f.159^r) is written *Mediolani. VIIII. kl. Iulias 1461. De or.* was completed on 8 May 1461, and *Rhet. Her.* on 14 October 1461. Pa was copied by de la Mare's 'Galeazzo Maria scribe'.[127] It was owned by Galeazzo Maria Sforza, who became Duke of Milan in 1466, and later by Louis XII, King of France (1498–1515) and Duke of Milan (1499–1512).[128] Pa contains ρ's chapter divisions. It appears to be a contaminated descendant of G (perhaps via the lost exemplar α, from which also derive FkVv).

63. Paris, BnF, lat. 7704 = Pb^∧
Parchment; Milan; *s.* x v^2/4 (*c.*1421–1430?).[129]
De or., Orat., Brut. (f.106^v–142^r), *De optimo genere oratorum*
Pb, which contains ρ's chapter divisions, derives from G via δ.

64. Paris, BnF, lat. 7705 = Q^∧
Parchment; *s.* x v^med.(?).[130]
De or., Orat., Brut. (f.161^r–210^v)
Prior to entering the BnF, Q was held by the Bibliothèque Mazarine. It contains the same seven chapter divisions found in D. Q derives from D.

---

[124] Pächt and Alexander (1970: 24); Madan (1897: 58).
[125] On Nastagio and his family, see Schlebusch (2016); Omodeo (2020: 31–33).
[126] Coxe (1854: 203–204). The date depends on the derivation from Mh.
[127] De la Mare (1983: 404 n. 27).
[128] Samaran and Marichal (1962: 425). For a complete digital reproduction of this MS, and of nos. 63–67, see https://gallica.bnf.fr.
[129] According to de la Mare in François Avril's card catalogue of the illuminated MSS of the BnF (accessible via https://archivesetmanuscrits.bnf.fr).
[130] M. D. Reeve.

APPENDIX 1   249

65. Paris, BnF, lat. 7708 = Pc^
Parchment; Florence; *s.* xv$^{2/4}$.[131]
Brut. (f.1^r–52^v), *Orat.*
According to de la Mare (1985: 425, 541), Pc was copied by the scribe of the Barcelona Eusebius (Barcelona Univ. 582), who may be Giovanni Aretino. The illuminator has been identified as Battista di Biagio Sanguigni.[132] The manuscript was transferred to the BnF from the Bibliothèque Colbertine. Pc derives from Ec via the lost exemplar μ.

66. Paris, BnF, lat. 11288 = Pd^
Parchment; Italy; *s.* xv$^{3/4}$.[133]
Brut. (f.1^r–69^v), *Orat.*
Pd was one of a group of 44 manuscripts brought to Paris from the library of Pope Pius VI at the end of the eighteenth century. From the beginning of *Brut.* up to *c.*§§95–97, Pd derives from Bn; thereafter, it derives from F independently of other extant manuscripts.

67. Paris, BnF, lat. 17154 = Pe^
Parchment; Italy; *s.* xv$^{2/4}$?.[134]
Nat. D., Div., Timaeus (fragm.), *Fat., Tusc., Fin., Leg., Acad. pr., Off., Sen., Paradoxa, Amic., Comment. pet.* (Q. Cicero), *Somn., Rhet. Her.* (Ps.-Cic.), *Inv. rhet., Part. or., Orat., Brut.* (f.204^v–218^v), *De or., Orationes, De optimo genere oratorum, Top., Synonyma* (Ps.-Cic.), *Leg. Man., Flac.*
Silvia Rizzo (1983: 113–114) suggests Milan, Bologna, and Rome as possible places of production. This huge volume of Cicero's works was once owned by Achilles Vicecomes, a member of the Visconti family, and later by the Duc de la Vallière.[135] Pe is one of several descendants of Vw.

68. Parma, Biblioteca Palatina, Parm. 895 = Pm
Parchment; *s.* xv^2.[136]
Brut. (f.1^r–49^v), *Orat.*
The coat of arms of the Strozzi family is found on f.1^r. Pm is a descendant of π contaminated with readings from θ.

---

[131] According to an anonymous scholar (probably Albinia de la Mare) in François Avril's card catalogue (see above).
[132] By the same scholar in François Avril's card catalogue. (See notes 129 and 131 above.)
[133] According to François Avril's card catalogue.
[134] De la Mare *ap.* Rizzo (1983: 113–114).
[135] De Bure (1783: 26–28). For a more detailed history of the MS, and for further items of bibliography, see Hunt (1998: 144–146).
[136] According to Silvia Scipioni in the entry in Manus (https://manus.iccu.sbn.it).

250 APPENDIX 1

69. Reims, Bibliothèque municipal, 1109 (N. Fonds) = Re^
Parchment; 1423–1428.[137]
Orat., Brut. (f.88^v–203^r)
Re was copied for the cardinal Guillaume Fillastre (1348–1428), who died in Rome, and who gave many of his manuscripts to the cathedral library in Reims. Re is among the descendants of Vm, and is especially close to Mf and Sd. It may well be the source of Mf from at least §215 onwards.

70. Rome, Biblioteca Angelica, 1768 = Ro
Parchment; 1425–1437?.
Brut. (f.3^r–57^v), *Orat., De or.*
Ro is a descendant of Vq and the ancestor of Fm. The date given here depends on this interpretation of the relationship between FmRoVq: Fm is dated to 1437, and Vq to 1425–1440.[138]

71. Rome, Biblioteca Casanatense, 1912 = Rm
Parchment; *c.*1435?.
De or., Rhet. Her. (Ps.-Cic.), *Inv. rhet., Orat., Brut.* (f.104^r–109^v, only §§1–123 *genus dicendi*)
Rm is made up of four parts (I: *De or.*; II: *Rhet. Her.*; III: *Inv. rhet.*; IV: *Orat., Brut.*), written by various scribes, but it appears to have been produced as a single project. The subscription to *Inv. rhet.* reads (f.91^r):

Explicit liber rethoricorum scriptus per manus Gherardi theoderici de alamagna diocesis traiectensis nec non provincianus hollandiensis. oriundus in oppido dordracensi tempore serenissimi principis ducis guilhelmi bavarie, comitis hollandie, zeelandie, hannonie et domini fresie.

If Valerio Sanzotta (in Busonero et al. (2016: 65–66)) is right that this subscription indicates that *Inv. rhet.* was copied *c.*1435,[139] the rest of the manuscript was probably also copied then. Rm contains most of ρ's chapter divisions. It derives from Ho.

72. San Daniele del Friuli, Biblioteca Guarneriana, 63 = Sd
Parchment; Friuli; *c.*1439.[140]
De or., Orat., Brut. (f.119^r–157^v, only §§1–332 *hospes familiaris*)
Sd was copied by Nicolò da San Vito, and was part of the library of Guarnerio d'Artegna. The codex was one of several stolen from the Guarneriana in 1948. It was later recovered, but it was probably at this time that the final folios, including the end of *Brut.*, were lost. Sd derives from Vm, and is particularly close to Mf and Re; it seems to share an exemplar with Mf in the first part of *Brut.*

---

[137] Re derives from F and so cannot be earlier than 1423; it must have been produced before the death of Guillaume Fillastre. Loriquet (1904: 299) dates the MS to *s.* xv$^{in.}$. For a complete digital reproduction, see https://bvmm.irht.cnrs.fr.
[138] Cf. Mazzatinti et al. (1890–: xxii.183).   [139] Cf. Sanzotta (2015: 137–139, 340, pl. 96).
[140] D'Angelo in Casarsa et al. (1991: i.272; ii, pl. LX–LXI).

APPENDIX 1   251

73. San Daniele del Friuli, Biblioteca Guarneriana, 246 (Fontanini LIX) = Sg
Parchment; s. xv.[141]
De or., *Brut.* (f.110^v–150^v), *Orat.*
Sg derives from τ, and is the source of Vi.

74. San Lorenzo de El Escorial, Real Biblioteca del Monasterio de San Lorenzo de
El Escorial, T. III. 18 = El
Parchment; Milan??; 1423–1450.[142]
Orat., *Brut.* (f.50^r–118^r), *Top.*, *Fat.*, *Acad. post.*, *Rhet. Her.* (Ps.-Cic.)
Terence Hunt (1998: 90–91) proved that El's text of *Acad. post.* derives from the
same manuscript. Its place of production is currently uncertain: Hunt suggests that
it could have been produced in north-west Italy, Spain, or even France, and he
records de la Mare's view that the decoration might be Milanese. *Rhet. Her.* was
originally contained in a separate volume. El is a pure descendant of Vq.

75. San Lorenzo de El Escorial, Real Biblioteca del Monasterio, T. III. 23 = E
Parchment; s. xv (*Brut.*).[143]
Brut. (f.2^r–48^v), *Inv. rhet.*, *Rhet. Her.* (Ps.-Cic.), *De topicis differentiis* (Boethius)
This codex is composed of two parts, one containing *Brut.* (s. xv) and the other
the three remaining texts (s. xiii). The two parts were bound together in the fifteenth
century. E was owned by Diego Hurtado de Mendoza (c.1503–1575). It contains ρ's
chapter divisions. E is an independent descendant of β.

76. San Lorenzo de El Escorial, Real Biblioteca del Monasterio, V. III. 8 = Es
Parchment; s. xv.[144]
Orat., *Brut.* (f.42^r–98^r), *Part. or.*
Es derives from σ via Fi.

77. San Lorenzo de El Escorial, Real Biblioteca del Monasterio, V. III. 17 = Ec
Parchment; 1423–c.1425?.[145]
De or., *Orat.*, *Brut.* (f.199^v–250^r)
Orat. and *Brut.* were originally bound separately from *De or.*[146] Ec derives from κ
until c.§§62–68, and thereafter from τ. Ec's extant descendants are GwPc, which
both derive from an intermediate manuscript, μ.

78. Stockholm, Kungliga Biblioteket, Va 11 = St
Paper; France; s. xv^2.[147]
De or., *Orat.*, *Brut.* (f.63^r–82^v), *Part. or.*, *Cicero novus ex Plutarcho* (Bruni),
Anthologia Latina 603–604

---

[141] Mazzatinti et al. (1890–: iii.149).   [142] Hunt (1998: 89–91); cf. Antolín (1916: 151).
[143] Antolín (1916: 156).   [144] Antolín (1916: 184).
[145] Antolín (1916: 195). This date depends on the derivations of Ec from F and of Gw
from Ec.
[146] Rubio Fernández (1984: 284).
[147] Pellegrin (1954: 13): 'd'une écriture cursive française'.

252   APPENDIX 1

St was once part of the library of Paul Petau (1568–1614). It derives from ι, an exemplar shared with GlVf.

79. Vatican City, Biblioteca Apostolica Vaticana (BAV), Chig. H. V. 148 = Va
Parchment; Italy;[148] 1423–1469.[149]
Orat., Brut. (f.47^v–113^r)
In the fifteenth century, Va was owned by Antonio di Giovanni Rossi; he sold the codex to the cardinal Francesco Tedeschini-Piccolomini in 1469.[150] Va has a single chapter division at 25.23 *hic ego*. From the beginning of *Brut.* until *c.*§§228–265, Va derives from ψ, and after this point it is a pure descendant of Vw.

80. Vatican City, BAV, Ott. lat. 1171 = Vb
Paper; France;[151] *s.* xv^2.[152]
De or., Orat., Brut. (f.198^r–257^v), *Part. or.*
The watermarks are similar to Briquet 8663 (Châlons-en-Champagne, 1479–1480). In the seventeenth century, Vb was owned by Jean Bourdelot, Pierre Michon Bourdelot, and Queen Christina of Sweden. It has one chapter division, at 21.24 *nempe igitur*. Vb derives from Vf, one of the descendants of ι.

81. Vatican City, BAV, Ott. lat. 1449 = Vd
Parchment; Florence; *c.*1442–1450.[153]
Inv. rhet., Rhet. Her. (Ps.-Cic.), *De or., Orat., Brut.* (f.223^r–259^v), *Part. or., Top., De optimo genere oratorum*
Vd was copied by Piero Strozzi for King Alfonso V of Aragon and I of Naples.[154] The illuminations are Florentine. Later, Vd may have been owned by Paul Petau, and was sold by his son Alexandre to Queen Christina of Sweden.[155] It derives from Fi.

82. Vatican City, BAV, Ott. lat. 1592 = B
Paper; Milan; 7–15 October 1422.
Inscription, *De militia* (Bruni), inscription, *Brut.* (f.14^r–58^v), *Epistula ad Flavium Blondum* (Guarino, autograph)[156]
B was copied by Flavio Biondo and sent shortly afterwards to Guarino Veronese. In *Italia Illustrata*, Flavio Biondo reports that his copy of *Brut.* was sent 'first to Guarino in Verona, then to Leonardo Giustiniani in Venice' (*primum Veronam Guarino, post Leonardo Iustiniano Venetias*).[157] Later, the codex was owned by the

---

[148]   Pellegrin et al. (1975–2010: i.307).
[149]   Part of Va derives from F, and so it cannot be earlier than 1423.
[150]   f.117^v: *Nos Franciscus Cardinalis Senensis per manus Montani de Cassia emimus hunc librum ab Antonio Iohannis Rossi die X Martii MCCCCLXVIIII.*
[151]   Pellegrin et al. (1975–2010: i.463).
[152]   This date is contingent on the derivation from Vf, which was copied in the second half of the century.
[153]   Pellegrin et al. (1975–2010: i.567–568); de la Mare (unpublished).
[154]   De la Mare (unpublished). See further De Marinis (1947–1952: i.1–37; ii, pl. 2 (f.79^r, 103^v)); de la Mare (1985: 429).
[155]   Pellegrin et al. (1975–2010: i.568).   [156]   Sabbadini (1915–1919: i.355).
[157]   Biondo, *Italia Illustrata* (2011–2017: iii.152).

APPENDIX 1   253

cardinal Gugliemo Sirleto (1514–1585) and by Giovanni Angelo d'Altemps (1586–1620). On f.19^r, before the chapter division at 49.17 *et graeciae*, Biondo has written the following: *In veteri continuat testus ubique sine capitulo vel testiculo. verum unde hec capitula tu mi Guarine intellegis.* At the top of f.29^r, he has written: *Hic habui exemplar vetus.* Further down the page, next to 130.4 *magnum fuit*, he has added in the left margin: *hic vetus incepi habere exemplar.* At the end of *Brut.* (f.58^v), Biondo has composed the following subscription:

> Non erat amplius in exemplari: q a quo abscisse sunt charte due: quamquam ut mihi videtur nedum charte sed pauca admodum verba deficiunt. Scripsi hunc Brutum Mediolani a nonis ad ydus Octobres 1422. Ad exemplar vetustissimum repertum nuper laude: in quo quidem codice sunt: Rhetoricarum: ad herennium rhetorica: De oratore: Orator ad brutum: et brutus de oratoribus claris: M. T. Ciceronis:

B has most of ρ's chapter divisions up to §130, and none thereafter.[158] From *Brut.* 1.1 to around 130.4 *magnum fuit*, B derives from β, although with corrections from L (marked by the marginal note *in testu* (or *in t.*)); in the remainder of the text, it derives directly from L. B is the source of Mh(BlOd), Np and Vr.

83. Vatican City, BAV, Ott. lat. 1994 = Vf
Parchment; France; 1451–*c.*1472.[159]
De or., Orat., Brut. (f.109^r–144^v), *Part. or., Oratio de laudibus eloquentiae* (Ognibene de' Bonisoli)
Both script and decoration indicate a French origin. Vf was owned and annotated by Guillaume Fichet (1433–*c.*1480),[160] rector of the University of Paris. Fichet apparently brought the codex with him to Rome in 1472, and after his death it was owned by the humanist Giovanni Lorenzi (1440–1501).[161] The work of Ognibene is a later addition by an Italian hand, and José Ruysschaert suggests that it might have been copied by Bartolomeo Sanvito.[162] The codex was subsequently owned by the cardinal Gugliemo Sirleto and by Giovanni Angelo d'Altemps. Like Vb, it has a single chapter division at 21.24 *nempe igitur.* Vf derives from ι, and is the source of Vb.

84. Vatican City, BAV, Ott. lat. 2057 = O^
Parchment; Lombardy; 29 November 1422.
De or., Orat., Brut. (f.93^r–124^r), *De optimo genere oratorum*, Aeschin. *In Ctes.* (tr. Bruni), Dem. *De cor.* (tr. Bruni)

---

[158] Cf. Sabbadini (1971: 103–105); Pellegrin et al. (1975–2010: i.625–626); Malcovati (1970: ix–x). For a reproduction of f.58^v, see Chatelain (1884–1892: pl. XXa).
[159] Pellegrin et al. (1975–2010: i.731–732).
[160] Cf. Beltran (1985: 14).   [161] Gionta (2005: 414–415, 419–420).
[162] Pellegrin et al. (1975–2010: i.732). It is not mentioned, however, in de la Mare and Nuvoloni (2009), and cf. Gionta (2005: 421–422).

254 APPENDIX 1

O, whose script and decoration indicate a Lombard origin,[163] was copied for Francesco Bossi, Bishop of Como. Antonio Cadei (1976: 9–17) attributes the illuminations to Belbello da Pavia.[164] In April 1425, while located in Pavia, O was corrected from L by Antonio and Simone Bossi and by Francesco degli Ardizzi of Vigevano. O contains ρ's chapter divisions. Two subscriptions follow *Brut.* At the very bottom of f.124^r, the scribe who copied the manuscript has written: *MCCCCXXII die penultimo novembris in sero finit.* The second subscription, written by Francesco degli Ardizzi, is four lines below the end of *Brut.*, and reads:

M. Tullii Ciceronis, de Oratore, Orator, Brutus, libri feliciter expliciunt. qui sunt reverendissimi in Christo patris et domini, domini Francisci Bossii, Mediolanensis, Episcopi Cumani ac Comitis, iurisque utrius doctoris, virique gravissimi et pacatissimi, domini Anthonii Bossii, filii ducalis consiliarii et Quęstoris. Qui tres libri oratorii [*corr.* oratorii libri] correcti, auscultati, collecti, emendati, conformati et iustificati fuerunt, cum codice illo vetustissimo et ipsa intuitione religionem quandam mentibus hominum inferente. quem .r. p. et d. d. Gęrardus Landrianus Episcopus Laudensis et Comes in archivio ecclesię suę repperit, litterarum cupidior. per Antonium Iohannis, Simonem Petri, Bossios, et me Franciscum Viglevium de Ardiciis, quanvis cursim MCCCCXXV die XXVI Aprilis. Indictione tercia. in civitate papię, studiorum matre. Non inveni plura in perveteri codice. fortunę quidem iniquitas id totum, si tamen quiddam erat, recidit. Eo tamen urgeor, quod ista dicendi divinitas, multos annos obliviosa, et inculta sic irreligiose prostitit. Ni quidem fuisset dicti pręsulis Laudensis solers bene dicendi studium, vigilantiaque industris, iterum divino careremus hoc munere (Vide quaeso priscorum incuriam) cuius inventione quamplurimum famę et perhennitatis sortitus est. Sed idem Cumanus, aut paris est gloirę, vel non minoris felicitatis. propterea, quod primum veterem et superiorem codicem, non sat a plerisque legibilem, ob antiquarum litterarum effigiem, stilumque incognitum, in latinas et explicatas [*add. sup.:* bene] litteras, studioseque interpunctas, summa diligentia renovavit.

O was copied from ρ and corrected from L; it is the primary source of Lb, and the only source of T in §§251–333.

85. Vatican City, BAV, Pal. lat. 1465 = Vg^
   Parchment; Italy; 1423–1459.[165]
   De or., Orat., Brut. (f.156^r–198^r), *Part. or.* (fragm.)
   Vg was owned by the Florentine humanist Giannozzo Manetti (1396–1459), who added the folio numbers.[166] The codex was subsequently owned by Ulrich Fugger (1526–1584) and by the Bibliotheca Palatina of Heidelberg. The text is in the same order as Vh. Vg derives from Vh.

---

[163] Pellegrin et al. (1975–2010: i.774–776); Barbero (2016: 155–156, 164–165). For a complete digital reproduction of this MS, and of nos. 85, 87, and 89–96, see https://digi.vatlib.it.
[164] Cf. Barbero (2016: 155–156, 164–165).
[165] Vg cannot be earlier than 1423, since it derives from F, and it must have been copied before Manetti's death in 1459.
[166] Pellegrin et al. (1975–2010: ii/2.118). On Manetti's library, see Cagni (1960); de la Mare (1985: 423).

APPENDIX 1   255

86. **Vatican City, BAV, Pal. lat. 1471 = Vh^**
Parchment; Florence; 1423–c.1425.[167]
Orat., Brut. (f.59^r–146^v), *Part. or.*
Vh was owned and annotated by Giannozzo Manetti; Manetti's secretary, Tommaso Tani, added the table of contents. Later, the manuscript was owned by Ulrich Fugger and by the Bibliotheca Palatina of Heidelberg. The pages have become disordered, with the result that the text of *Brut.* is in the following order: 1.1 (f.59^r) – 59.23 *praeclare tum* (f.71^v); 178.26 *suppeditabat oratio* (f.72^r) – 207.3 *fiebant neque* (f.79^v); 91.27 *igitur inquit* (f.80^r) – 99.4 *filii fuerunt* (f.81^v); 59.24 *illi homines* (f.82^r) – 91.26 *interquievissem quid* (f.89^v); 129.23 *-dicus genere* (f.90^r) – 178.26 *publica satis* (f.101^v); 99.4 *quorum c.* (f.102^r) – 129.23 *asper male-* (f.109^v); 207.3 *hoc quod* (f.110^r) – 333.19 (f.146^v). Vh is a descendant of Vm and the source of Mu, Vg, and the second half of Lc.

87. **Vatican City, BAV, Reg. lat. 1841 = Vj^**
Parchment; Italy; *s.* xv.[168]
Inv. rhet., Top., Part. or., Orat., De optimo genere oratorum, Brut. (f.99^r–132^v)
Vj was once owned by the church of San Silvestre al Quirinale, in Rome. Initially, Vj seems to derive from Ff, and then, from *c.*§161 onwards, it apparently derives instead from χ.

88. **Vatican City, BAV, Reg. lat. 2046 = Vk**
Parchment; northern Italy?; 1421–1450.[169]
De or., Orat., Brut. (f.97^r–132^r)
Vk was owned by the church of San Andrea della Valle in Rome. It contains ρ's chapter divisions. Vk derives from ζ, which appears to have been a contaminated descendant of G.

89. **Vatican City, BAV, Urb. lat. 311 = Vl^**
Parchment; Florence; *c.*1425–1430.[170]
De or., Brut. (f.105^r–149^r), *Orat.*
Vl's *Brut.* has been lightly corrected by a second hand. The manuscript was owned in the second half of the fifteenth century by Federico da Montefeltro, Duke of Urbino.[171] It was redecorated for Federico's collection, and the presence of the letters 'F. C.' (rather than 'F. D.') indicates that the new illuminations were added before Federico was appointed Duke, that is, before August 1474.[172] Vl derives from σ via τ, and has produced one copy, Ob.

---

[167] Pellegrin et al. (1975–2010: ii/2.121); de la Mare (unpublished). For a complete digital reproduction, see https://digi.ub.uni-heidelberg.de.
[168] Pellegrin et al. (1975–2010: ii/1.445).
[169] Pellegrin et al. (1975–2010: ii/1.491) suggest the localization on the basis of the decorated initials; they date the MS to *s.* xv$^{in.}$.
[170] De la Mare (1986: 81 n. 2); cf. Pellegrin et al. (1975–2010: ii/2.538–539).
[171] On Federico's library, see de la Mare (1985: 448–451); Hofmann (2008).
[172] Cf. de la Mare (1985: 450).

256 APPENDIX 1

90. Vatican City, BAV, Vat. lat. 1701 = Vm^
Parchment; Italy;[173] 1423–1428.[174]
Orat., Brut. (f.51^v–123^r), *Part. or., Top.*
Vm was acquired by the BAV between 1518 and 1533. To my knowledge, the artist responsible for the decoration sketched at the foot of f.1^r has not yet been identified. Vm derives, perhaps directly, from F, and is the source of Vh (and its descendants (Lc)MuVg), MfReSd, *ι* (and its descendants, GlStVbVf)), and the second part of Be.

91. Vatican City, BAV, Vat. lat. 1702 = Vo^
Parchment; Naples?; 1423–1481.[175]
Orat., Brut. (f.44^v–103^v), *Part. or.*
Vo was in the BAV by 1481. It is a contaminated descendant of Vw.

92. Vatican City, BAV, Vat. lat. 1709 = J^
Paper; Italy; 1428–1500.[176]
Carmen de distinctione orationis (Guarino, extr.), *De or., Div.* (extr.), *Orat., Brut.* (f.116^r–145^r), draft of text (anon.), *Epistula* (Iodocus Zeno to M. Petrus Papaeus)
Pellegrin et al. (1975–2010: iii/1.325) tentatively suggest that the watermark resembles Briquet 8441 (Bologna, 1455). In the fifteenth century, J was bought by a certain Piero da Calabria from some Franciscan friars.[177] The codex was acquired by the BAV in 1549. J derives from λ. A later hand has corrected the text of *Brut.* from ψ (or a descendant).

93. Vatican City, BAV, Vat. lat. 1712 = Vp^
Parchment; Florence; *c.*1450–1473.[178]
De or., Orat., Brut. (f.95^r–122^v), *Rhet. Her.* (Ps.-Cic.), *Inv. rhet., Part. or., Top.*
According to de la Mare (1985: 424, 432, 538, 565), Vp was copied by Sinibaldus C., and the front flyleaf was written by Gherardo del Ciriagio. The manuscript was produced by Vespasiano da Bisticci.[179] Some annotations have been added in the hand of an early owner, the French cardinal Jean Jouffroy (*c.*1412–1473).[180] Vp was acquired by the BAV during the reign of Pope Sixtus IV, and is mentioned in an inventory dated to 1475. Vp contains some of ρ's chapter divisions. It descends from ψ, which appears to have derived from γ, but with contamination from F (or a descendant).

---

[173] Pellegrin et al. (1975–2010: iii/1.318–319).
[174] The outer limits for the date depend on the derivations of Re from Vm and of Vm from F.
[175] Pellegrin et al. (1975–: iii/1.319): 'italienne, peut-être napolitaine d'après l'écriture'.
[176] This date is contingent on the derivation from Lamola's codex. Some of J's corrections in *Orat.* are cited by Yon (1964).
[177] f.I^r: *De miser piero de Calabria conperato dali Fra di San Francescho.*
[178] Pellegrin et al. (1975–2010: iii/1.328–329); de la Mare (1985: 424, 432).
[179] f.I^v: *Vespasianus librarius librum hunc florentie transcribendum curavit*; cf. de la Mare (1985: 565), (1996: 181 n. 51, 206–207).
[180] On the book-collector Jean Jouffroy, see Desachy (2012).

APPENDIX 1   257

94. Vatican City, BAV, Vat. lat. 1720 = Vq^
Parchment; Florence; 1425–1437 (*c*.1425–1429?).[181]
Brut. (f.1^r–38^r), *Orat.* (*integer*), *De or.*, *Orat.* (*mutilus*), *Sen.*, *Amic.*, *Fat.*, *Acad. post.*
In her unpublished notes, de la Mare assigned the illuminations to Battista di Biagio Sanguigni in 1977,[182] but in 2000 she assigned them instead to Bartolomeo Varnucci. De la Mare (unpublished) identified the hand of Guglielmo Tanaglia (1391–1460) in some marginal notes. M. D. Reeve points out that Vq was copied by the same scribe as Vu. From the start of *Brut.* up to *c*.§158, Vq is a contaminated copy of Fb; in §§158–298, Vq appears to derive primarily from another, less faithful, descendant of F; finally, in §§298–333, Vq derives from *v*, one of the offspring of *κ*. Vq is the source of Ro(Fm), El, and Vu(Fo).

95. Vatican City, BAV, Vat. lat. 1721 + Vat. lat. 4533 = Vs^
Paper; Italy; *s.* x v$^{med.}$(?).[183]
Vat. lat. 1721: *Brut.* (f.1^r–84^v, §§1–330 *ipsa loque*-); Vat. lat. 4533: Arist. *Eth. Nic.* (tr. John Argyropoulos), *Brut.* (f.115^r–116^r, §§330 *-rentur mortuo* – 333), *Peri Hermeneias* (Apul.)
The watermarks on the pages containing *Brut.* resemble Briquet 6269 (Venice, 1454) and 6271 (Venice, 1462).[184] At some point in its history, the text was split up: the text of *Brut.* in f.115–116 of Vat. lat. 4533 continues exactly from the end of Vat. lat. 1721, and the two sections are written in the same hand on paper with identical watermarks. Vat. lat. 4533 is a manuscript in two parts: the watermarks and the hand of the second part, containing *Brut.* and Apuleius' *Peri Hermeneias*, are different from those of the first. Rossella Bianchi (2015: 191) has identified notes by Angelo Colocci (1474–1549) on f.119, 121^v, and 137^v of Vat. lat. 4533.[185] Vs is a contaminated descendant of Vw; later corrections have been added from *β* (or a descendant). A later hand has introduced *ρ*'s chapter divisions into Vs. The manuscript has produced one offspring, Vt.

96. Vatican City, BAV, Vat. lat. 3238 = Vu^
Parchment; Florence; 1423–*c*.1429?.[186]
Brut. (f.1^r–44^r), *Orat.* (*integer*), *De or.*, *Orat.* (*mutilus*)
The decoration is by Bartolomeo Varnucci.[187] Vu was annotated in the fifteenth century by Giulio Pomponio Leto,[188] and was owned in the sixteenth century by

---

[181] Hunt (1998: 88–89); Pellegrin et al. (1975–2010: iii/1.335–336); Tichenor (2019: 735–736). Hunt dates the MS to 1425–1440, but since it is an ancestor of Fm, Vq must have been copied before 1437. If Fo, another descendant of Vq, has been dated correctly to the 1420s, Vq must also have been copied before 1430.
[182] Cf. Hunt (1998: 89). For the difficulty of securely attributing illuminations to Battista, see Kanter in Bollati (2004: 67–69).
[183] Pellegrin et al. (1975–2010: iii/1.336, iii/2.423–424); M. D. Reeve.
[184] Pellegrin et al. (1975–2010: iii/1.336).
[185] For the possibility that the second part of Vat. lat. 4533 was owned by Marcello Cervini (1501–1555), see Fossier (1979: 430).
[186] '*s.* xv^{in}' (Pellegrin et al. (1975–2010: iii/2.141–142)), '*s.* xv$^{2/4}$' (Tichenor (2019: 737–738)); de la Mare (unpublished) dates the initials to *c*.1430. Vu must be older than its apograph, Fo, which was apparently copied in the 1420s.
[187] De la Mare (unpublished).   [188] See further Muzzioli (1959).

258 APPENDIX 1

Fulvio Orsini. M. D. Reeve points out that the manuscript was copied by the same scribe as Vq, from which it derives. Vu has one extant descendant, Fo. A second hand has corrected Vu from another of F's offspring, or from F itself. Morris Tichenor (2019: 276) argues that Vu's *mutilus* of *Orat.* also derives from Vq.

97. Vatican City, BAV, Vat. lat. 6871 = Vv
Paper; Italy; *s.* x v.[189]
Brut. (f.1ʳ–98ᵛ), *NA* (Gell., extr.)
The watermarks resemble Briquet 6270 (Venice, 1457).[190] On f.5ᵛ, there is a signed note by the Bolognese humanist Tommaso Sclaricino Gambaro (*c.*1454–1525). According to José Ruysschaert (*ap.* Fanelli 1979: 171 n. 18a), annotations by Angelo Colocci indicate that Vv was once part of his library; but Marco Bernardi (in Motolese et al. (2013: 78)) finds no evidence of Colocci's ownership and rejects the attribution of the annotations to him. Vv is the only descendant of ρ which contains none of its chapter divisions. From the beginning of *Brut.* until *c.*§§310–320, it derives from η, an exemplar shared with Fk. In the final few paragraphs, Vv may derive from the exemplar of Ho, or Vv's exemplar may have been corrected from Ho.

98. Vatican City, BAV, Vat. lat. 11491 = Vw
Parchment; Italy; *s.* x v.[191]
Orat., Brut. (f.25ᵛ–60ʳ)
This manuscript was owned in the sixteenth century by Antonio Constantini and by Marc-Antoine Muret. Later, it was part of the library of the College of Jesuits in Rome. Vw derives from κ via ν, an exemplar shared with Ld; Vw is an ancestor of LePeVoVs(Vt), as well as the final part of Va, and is one of two sources of Bc.

99. Venice, Biblioteca Nazionale Marciana, Lat. Z. 419 (1508) = Ve
Parchment; *s.* x v.[192]
De or., Brut. (f.124ʳ–175ᵛ), *Orat., Paradoxa*
Ve derives from Ff via Bn.

100. Venice, Biblioteca Nazionale Marciana, Lat. Z. 420 (1509) = Vn
Parchment; Parma; 11 February 1428.
De or., Orat., Brut. (f.86ʳ–111ᵛ, only §§1–23, 46–108, 129–191, 209–308, 326–333), *De optimo genere oratorum*
Several folios have been lost, resulting in the following lacunae in the text of *Brut*: 23.8 *dicendi autem* – 46.24 *et paratas*; 108.26 *-lius appi* – 129.22 *sane ut*; 191.27 – *ribus legeret* – 209.20 *ineuntur gratiae*; 308.28 *ego hoc* – 326.11 *crebrarum venustarumque*. Vn was copied by Opizo de Cisiis, a citizen of Parma, for Andrea Valeri of Parma.[193] Opizo also copied Lat. Z. 269 (1757) (in 1428, again for Andrea

---

[189] Pellegrin et al. (1975–2010: iii/2.637–638).
[190] Pellegrin et al. (1975–2010: iii/2.637–638).
[191] Pellegrin et al. (1975–2010: iii/2.833–834). [192] Zorzanello (1980: 11).
[193] f.114ʳ:...*ad instantiam viri nobilis et egregii Andreę de Valeriis de Parma per me Opizonem de Cisiis scriptorem et civem Parmensem anno domini M.cccc.xxviii. die Undecimo Mensis Februarii*; cf. Zorzanello (1980: 11–12). On Andrea Valeri, see Pellegrin et al. (1975–2010: ii/2.77), with ref.; Bertini (2010: 124 n. 48).

APPENDIX 1   259

Valeri) and BAV, Urb. lat. 426 (in 1427).[194] In the eighteenth century, the codex was owned by the Venetian nobleman Giovanni Battista Recanati. Vn contains ρ's chapter divisions. It derives from G via the lost ancestor δ.

101. Venice, Biblioteca Nazionale Marciana, Lat. XI. 67 (3859) = Vc
Parchment; 1423–c.1425.[195]
Brut. (f.1^r–79^r)
Vc was owned, and perhaps copied, by Leon Battista Alberti.[196] In the eighteenth century, it was owned by Giovanni Gentili and then by Antonio Cocchi.[197] Vc derives from κ.

102. Verona, Biblioteca Capitolare, CLV (143) = Vr
Parchment; *s.* xv.[198]
Brut. (f.1^r–58^r, only §§1–320 *certe vivere*)
Vr once belonged to the Biblioteca Muselli. There is a single chapter division at 10.10 *nam cum.* Vr is a slightly contaminated copy of B.

103. Viterbo, Centro diocesano di documentazione – Biblioteca Capitolare, Sezione manoscritti, d 9 = Vt
Parchment; *s.* xv.[199]
Orat., Brut. (f.27^r–63^r), *Part. or.*
In the sixteenth century, Vt was owned by Latino Latini of Viterbo.[200] It derives from Vs.

104. Vienna, Österreichische Nationalbibliothek, Cod. 3090 = S
Paper; *s.* xv.[201]
De or., Orat., Brut. (f.170^r–177^v, only §§1–60 *secundo quaestor*)
The folios have become disarranged, and the text of *Brut.* should be read in the following order: f.170, f.172, f.171, f.174, f.173, f.175–177. S contains ρ's chapter divisions. It derives from β.

105. Vienna, Österreichische Nationalbibliothek, Cod. 3093 = Vi^
Mixed; Florence; *s.* xv^1.[202]
Brut. (f.1^r–38^v), *Orat., De optimo genere oratorum*
De la Mare (unpublished) suggests that Vi might have been copied by Lapo da Castiglionchio the Younger (c.1406–1438). It derives from Sg, one of the descendants of τ.

---

[194] Pellegrin et al. (1975–2010: ii/2.596); Derolez (1984: 154).
[195] Cardini et al. (2005: 404) date Vc to *s.* xv$^{1/4}$, and it cannot be earlier than F, from which it derives.
[196] '[U]n codice che…dà l'impressione, se non la certezza, di essere un prodotto della mano dell'umanisto' (Tristano in Cardini et al. (2005: 46, with pl. 9)).
[197] Cardini et al. (2005: 67, 72); Zorzanello (1980: 502–503).
[198] Spagnolo (1996: 228), with a reproduction of part of f.1^r.
[199] Dorez (1895: 242).
[200] On the library of Latino Latini, see Dorez (1895).
[201] Academia Caesarea Vindobonensis (1868: 194).
[202] Ibid., 195; M. D. Reeve. For a complete digital reproduction, see https://manuscripta.at.

260   APPENDIX 1

106. Wolfenbüttel, Herzog August Bibliothek, 12. 13. Aug. 4° = W^
Parchment; Italy; *s.* x v med. .[203]
De or., Orat., Brut. (f.201^v–262^v)
W was owned by Aubert de Carmonne, an official in Dijon, and by a certain
Nicolaus Recurtius. There is a coat of arms at the foot of f.1^r. W contains the seven
chapter divisions found in D. W is a copy of D.

107. Wolfenbüttel, Herzog August Bibliothek, 38 Gud. Lat. 2° = Wf
Parchment; Italy; *s.* x v.[204]
De or., Orat., Brut. (f.97^r–121^r), *De optimo genere oratorum*
Wf contains ρ's chapter divisions. It derives from G via δ.

Despite reports to the contrary, the following manuscripts do not contain *Brut.*:
Assisi, Biblioteca del Sacro Convento di San Francesco, Assisi Com. 307; Milan,
Biblioteca Ambrosiana, H 21 sup.; Milan, Biblioteca Ambrosiana, L 61 sup.;
Ravenna, Biblioteca Classense, 349.

1.2 Missing Manuscripts

1. Formerly Phillipps 23088[205]
s. x v.
De or., Orat., Brut.
This manuscript, once owned by Thomas Phillipps (1792–1872), was put up for
auction at Maggs Bros. in London in 1938 (catalogue 666, lot 110). I have not been
able to ascertain whether it was sold at the auction.[206]

2. Formerly in the library of John Edmund Severne (1826–1899)
Parchment; Florence?; *s.* x v 2.[207]
Brut., Orat.
This manuscript was owned by Mario Maffei of Volterra (1463–1537). It was later
owned by Anthony Askew (1722–1774), Michael Wodhull (1740–1816), and John
Edmund Severne (1826–1899), and was put up for auction at Christie's, in London, on
8 December 1982 (auction 2553, lot 130). It is not to be identified with Madrid 10060,
another Maffei manuscript, which was already in the Biblioteca Nacional in 1958.[208]

---

[203] Heinemann et al. (1884–1913: vii.168); M. D. Reeve. For a complete digital reproduction, see http://diglib.hab.de/mss/12-13-aug-4f/start.htm.
[204] Heinemann et al. (1884–1913: ix.107).
[205] Schoenberg Database of Manuscripts, 'SDBM_MS_10809', https://sdbm.library.upenn.
edu/manuscripts/10809.
[206] The Maggs Bros. archives are held in the British Library. There are many boxes of correspondence from 1938, and it was unfeasible for me to search through them systematically to try
to identify the buyer of this MS.
[207] Sotheby, Wilkinson, & Hodge (1886: 57); Christie, Manson, & Woods Ltd (1982: 49);
Schoenberg Database of Manuscripts, 'SDBM_MS_790', https://sdbm.library.upenn.edu/
manuscripts/790.
[208] Ruysschaert (1958: 324).

APPENDIX 1   261

3. Formerly Warsaw, Biblioteka Załuskich, 244
Parchment; 1423.
Brut., Orat., Top., Part. or.
According to Janozki (1752: 74), the following subscription was written on the final page of the manuscript: *anno domini MCCCCXXIII. sabbato quatuor temporum Beate Lucie per Petrum de Lamburga.* Peter Wolfram of Lamburga (= Lviv, in modern-day Ukraine) was a notary of the Archbishop of Gniezno at the Council of Constance (1414–1418).[209] In 1428, while serving as Archdeacon of Krakow, he visited Rome on a mission from the newly elected Bishop of Włocławek.[210] The early date makes this manuscript interesting, but it may have been destroyed by the Nazis in October 1944, together with many other books from the Załuski collection.

1.3 Manuscripts with Excerpts

I have conducted only a partial search for MSS containing extracts of *Brut.*, and I record here only those with extracts of more than one sentence.

1. Canterbury, Canterbury Cathedral Library, Additional 129/45^
Paper; 1450–1550.[211]
Brut. (f.1ʳ–1ᵛ, fragments from §§182–186)
This single folio of *Brut.* is very damaged, with much of the page missing. It shares the only significant error of B in the portions extant (185.9 *ita*] om.) and may derive from it.

2. Naples, Biblioteca Nazionale, ex Vienna Lat. 57
Mixed; Padua?; *s.* xv¹.[212]
Various, *Brut.* (§§3–10), various
NOT SEEN. For a detailed description, see Hunt (1998: 168–171).

3. Perugia, Biblioteca Comunale, 309 (E. 57)
Paper; *s.* xv.[213]
Brut. (f.1–20, extr.), various
NOT SEEN.

4. Vatican City, BAV, Vat. lat. 8761^
Paper; Italy; 1451–1483 (f.160–163).[214]
various, *Brut.* (f.163ʳ, §§251 *sed de Caesare* – 253 *existimare debemus*), *HN* (Plin., extr.), *Policraticus* 5.1 (John of Salisbury), various

---

[209] Finke (1928: 358, 360); Fink (1964: 143). A sermon delivered by Peter at the Council is preserved in Vienna, Österreichische Nationalbibliothek, Cod. 4292.
[210] Lisowski (1960: 140).
[211] For a complete digital reproduction, see https://ims.canterbury-cathedral.org.
[212] Hunt (1998: 168).   [213] Mazzatinti et al. (1890–: v.115).
[214] Pellegrin et al. (1975–2010: iii/2.719–721). For a complete digital reproduction, see https://digi.vatlib.it.

262 APPENDIX 1

In the extract of *Brut.*, Vat. lat. 8761 shares all the errors of F (252.26 *exquisitis summoque* Bλρ] *exquisitissumoque* F: *exquisitissimo* Vat. lat. 8761; 253.29 *scripserit* B^{1}λρ] *scripsit* BF Vat. lat. 8761; 253.30 *dixerit* F] *disserit* F^{2mg} Vat. lat. 8761) and may derive from it.

1.4 Fifteenth-Century Printed Editions

Ed. 1. Rome (1469) = Rom^
De or., Orat., Brut.
ISTC ic00643000; *GW* 6754
Rom, the *editio princeps* of *Brut.*, was printed by Conrad Sweynheym and Arnold Pannartz. It contains ρ's chapter divisions.[215]

Ed. 2. Venice (1485) = VenA^
De or., Orat., Top., Part. or., Brut., Comment. pet. (Q. Cicero), *De optimo genere oratorum*, Aeschin. *In Ctes.* (tr. Bruni), Dem. *De cor.* (tr. Bruni)
ISTC ic00662000; *GW* 6750
VenA was produced by the editor Girolamo Squarciafico and printed by Andreas Torresanus de Asula and Bartholomaeus de Blavis.[216]

Ed. 3. Venice (1488) = VenB^
Contents as in VenA
ISTC ic00663000; *GW* 6751
VenB was printed by Thomas de Blavis.[217]

Ed. 4. Venice (1495) = VenC^
Contents as in VenA
ISTC ic00664000; *GW* 6752
VenC was printed by Philippus Pincius.[218]

Ed. 5. Nuremberg (1497) = Nur^
Contents as in VenA
ISTC ic00665000; *GW* 6753
Nur was printed by Anton Koberger.

Ed. 6. Milan (1498) = Mil^
Cicero novus ex Plutarcho (Bruni), *Comment. pet.* (Q. Cicero), *Rhet. Her.* (Ps.-Cic.), *Inv. rhet., De or., Orat., Brut., Top., Part. or., De optimo genere oratorum*, Aeschin. *In Ctes.* (tr. Bruni), Dem. *De cor.* (tr. Bruni), *Commenta in Ciceronis Rhetorica* (Victorinus)

---

[215] For discussion of the Roman printing-house of Sweynheym and Pannartz, and of Rom in particular, see Jury (2018: 142–151).
[216] Ibid., 170–172.   [217] Ibid., 172–174.   [218] Ibid., 174–176.

APPENDIX 1 263

ISTC ic00498000; *GW* 6708
Mil is the first volume of a set of Cicero's works edited by Alexander Minutianus and printed by Guillermus Le Signerre.[219]

1.5 Hypothesized Manuscripts

Below is a list of the Greek sigla that I use to denote hypothesized lost manuscripts, together with their independent descendants.

α: ?Paη?
β: (B)DEMS(TYHo)γ
γ: GXψ
δ: (BcLb)MgPbVnWf
ε: MiMn
ζ: MeVk
η: FkVv
θ: BoFlLu
ι: GlStVf
κ: (Ec)MoOxVcν
λ: JU
μ: GwPc
ν: Ld(Vq)Vw
ξ: BrFaMaMc
π: FfPmσυ
ρ: Oβ
σ: Fiτ
τ: (BeEc)Fe(Ho)LfSgVl
υ: FcFgFhGeLa
φ: F
χ: CjMd(Vj)
ψ: (LcVa)Vp
ω: ?(Mf)Sdι?

---

[219] Ibid., 176–177.

APPENDIX 2

The Descendants of ρ and B

1. The Descendants of O

As I demonstrated in Chapter 2, the final portion of T derives from O. (For a stemma of the descendants of OBXγ, see Figure 7.) The only other manuscript which shares many of O's significant errors is Lb.[1] Lb has various errors not present in O, including:

> 16.14 *quievit*] om.
> 17.21 *petam*] om.
> 265.8 *gravitas...decorabat*] om.
> 268.7 *non ferebat*] om.
> 323.2 *essemus*] om.

As well as sharing ρ's errors and chapter divisions, Lb lacks the significant errors of β, but shares errors with O, including:

> 14.24 *posset esse*] *esse posset*
> 310.12 *loquuntur*] *eloquuntur*
> 311.24 *fecerunt*] *faciunt*
> 324.17 *idem*] *idemque*
> 328.19 *fato suo*] *suo fato*.

Although the text of Lb is most similar to O, Lb appears not to derive exclusively from it. Lb lacks some of O's non-trivial errors (10.13 *itaque*] *atque*, 14.22 *mihi quidem*] *quidem mihi*, 276.28 *totumque*] *totidemque*), and also shares errors with G and with G's descendant δ (discussed further below):

> 20.14 *mihi nuper* Oβ] *nuper mihi* GLbδ
> 21.22 *paulum* OβGLb^c] *paululum* Lbδ
> 21.26 *et* O] *atque* GLbδ
> 23.11 *bene nemo* OβG] *nemo bene* Lbδ
> 215.6 *excellebat autem* OβGLb^c] *autem excellebat* Lbδ.

Since its primary affiliation is to O, but with some errors removed and some errors of δ added, Lb probably derives from O, but with some contamination from δ, or from a descendant of δ. Lb sometimes shares the reading of O^ac and sometimes that of O^v:

---

[1] A group of three MSS (θ) has been contaminated with readings from O: see below, pp. 281–282.

APPENDIX 2   265

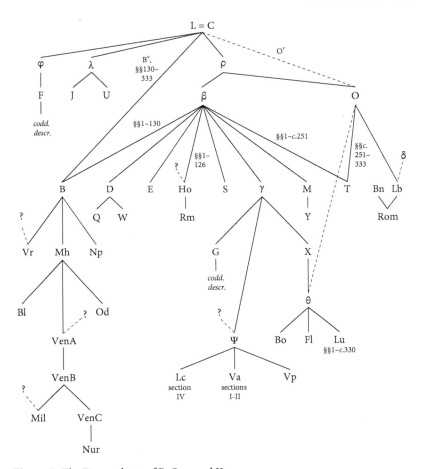

Figure 7: The Descendants of B, O, γ, and X

1.6   *dolebam* O^v] *videbam* O^ac Lb
2.17   *gloriosi* O^vLb] *generosi* O^ac
265.9   *gravitas* O^v] *dignitas* O^ac Lb
268.8   *plena* O^v] *plane* O^ac Lb
317.22   *mihi* O^vLb] *nichil* O^ac
325.25   *dictionis* O^vLb] *orationis* O^ac
328.21   *ominare*] *o mire* O^vLb: *omitte* O^ac.

The readings shared by O^vLb are found in the other descendants of L, and Lb has probably inherited them from δ, since Lb was copied before 1425, the year in which O^v's corrections were added.[2]

---

[2] On Lb's influence on the text of the *editio princeps*, Rom, see below, p. 286.

266 APPENDIX 2

2. The Descendants of B

There are three independent descendants of B (MhNpVr),[3] and two further manuscripts which derive from Mh (BlOd).[4] With two exceptions, to be discussed shortly, these five manuscripts share all the significant errors of B in the sections I have collated, including:

8.27 *ipsis*] om.
25.2 *unam*] om.
31.16 *haec*] om.
32.25 *eam*] *illam*
33.6 *aut...erat*] om.
225.24 *sumus locuti*] *locuti sumus*
266.16 *tuam perpetuam*] *perpetuam tuam*
280.17 *parum a magistris*] *a magistris parum*
320.24 *suum*] om.
321.3 *quod erat*] om.
333.12 *illis*] om.

Additionally, BlMhNpOdVr, like B, share the errors of ρ and β in §§1–130, but not in §§130–333. There can be no doubt that Mh and Np derive from B, because both contain several of B's *vetus*-notes, where the scribe of B has added corrections from L (e.g. 1.8 *inauguratum* B^{v}Mh^{1}Np^1] *mihi auguratum* BMhNp, 5.11 *angimur* BMhNp] *angitur* B^{v}Mh^{1}Np^1, 9.5 *maxume* B^{v}Mh^{1}Np^1] *maxime* BMhNp). The corrections in Mh and Np are in the same format as in B: in each case, the correction has been added in the margin with the note *in testu* or *in t*. Np also includes the beginning of B's initial subscription,[5] the same chapter divisions as B, and a note copied from Biondo's manuscript indicating that L lacked these chapter divisions.[6] Furthermore, in several places the scribe of Np has copied an error from B, apparently without noticing a correction in his exemplar (e.g. 30.6 *dicendi multi* B^c] *multi dicendi* BNp, 266.14 *enim eorum* B^c] *eorum enim* BNp). As a further proof of Mh's derivation from B, there are two places where the scribe of Mh shows awareness of the readings of B^{ac} and B^c (222.19 *diligentiae* B^{c}Mh^1] *digentiae* BMh, 322.20 *dilatare* B^{c}Mh^1] *dilutaret* B: *dilutare* Mh).[7]

---

[3] Mh has been cited in some editions with the siglum M, and Np with the siglum H. Reis (1934: vi–vii) demonstrated that both MSS derive from B, although he still cited them occasionally in his edition. Malcovati (1960: 332–333) showed that Mh and Np are not useful even as sources of conjectures, and she rightly removed them completely from her apparatus.

[4] Four MSS contaminated with readings from B (GlStVbVf) will be discussed among the descendants of F.

[5] See above, pp. 247, 253.

[6] Both B and Np have the following note before 49.17: *In veteri continuat testus ubique sine capitulo vel testiculo. verum unde hec capitula tu mi Guarine intellegis.* Ugo Mazzolato, the scribe of Np, has also copied from B a letter of Guarino Veronese to Flavio Biondo. From the content of two letters of Guarino to Ugo Mazzolato, one of them copied by Mazzolato on f.196^v of Np, it can be deduced that Np was a direct copy of B: see pp. 65–66.

[7] For both Np and Mh, see also 30.9 *fuit* B^{c}Mh] *fueri* B: *fuerit* Np: *fuerunt* Mh^{vl}.

APPENDIX 2   267

Although the scribe of Vr did not copy any of B^v's corrections, he did, like the scribe of Np, miss some of B^c's corrections:

14.22 *optatissimum quidem mihi* B^c] *mihi quidem optatissimum* BVr
20.14 *in tusculano inchoavisti*] *in tusculano incohavisti* B^c: *incohavisti in tusculano* B: *incoavisti in tusculano* Vr
30.6 *dicendi multi* B^c] *multi dicendi* BVr
225.20 *solutus* B^c] *dissolutus* B: *dissollutus* Vr.

Vr shares almost all the significant errors of B. However, there are two exceptions:

266.14 *admodum* Vr] om. BMhNp
268.10 *esse* Vr] om. BMhNp.

Although the second error might conceivably have been corrected by conjecture or by accident, the first could not have been. Therefore, the scribe of Vr cannot have been copying exclusively from B. Since most of B was copied directly from L, one cannot postulate a common ancestor of BVr to explain this situation. Rather, because Vr shares nearly all the significant errors of B in the sections I have collated, Vr must be a descendant of B contaminated with readings from another manuscript. Apart from the two readings cited above, there is no evidence of influence from anywhere except B, and consequently the contamination is probably limited to the correction of a handful of errors.

None of MhNpVr is the source of B, or of any other of the three, since each has significant errors of its own.

Mh: 24.15 *magis*] om.
266.20 *et*[1]] om.
276.31 *esse*] *est*
320.32 *continuatione*] *concinnatione*
324.12 *inter se*] *interesse*.

Np: 14.22 *est*] om.
216.19 *aliud*] *aliquid*
219.20 *stultius*] *subtilius*
223.4 *etiam*] *autem*
276.1 *illa*] om.
326.15 *oratio*] om.
329.28 *ipsius*] *illius*.

Vr: 7.24 *e manibus*] om.
13.14 *inquam esse*] om.
16.9 *nobis*] om.
29.1 *tum fuit*] *fuit tum*
228.26 *aspectum et probatum*] *et probatum et aspectum*
270.20 *numquam in publico*] *in publico nihil*
279.29 *enim*] om.
319.15 *quinquennium fere versatus*] *fere versatus quinquennium*.

268 APPENDIX 2

As mentioned already, Mh has produced two offspring, Bl and Od.[8] These two manuscripts share all the errors of Mh listed above, and they, like Mh, have only one chapter division in *Brut.* (at 25.23 *hic ego*). Bl also has several of Mh's minor errors (e.g. 24.18 *adipisci*] *adpisci*, 25.5 *artium*] *atium*). In one place, Od shares both the text reading and a variant with Mh: 30.9 *fuit* MhOd] *fuerunt* Mh^{vl}Od^{vl}.[9]

Bl and Od share no significant errors, and so they must derive from Mh independently of each other. Bl has errors which prove that neither Mh nor Od descends from it:

> 7.25 *profecto fuit*] *fuit profecto*
> 33.5 *hunc enim*] *enim hunc*
> 224.5 *mentio est*] *est mentio*
> 265.8 *omnia vitae*] *omni virtute*
> 268.7 *si modo orator*] om.

Likewise, Od has errors which prove that neither Mh nor Bl derives from it:

> 16.12 *largitatem*] om.
> 32.4 *quendam*] om.
> 227.12 *ab oratoribus*] om.
> 267.31 *et multa*] om.
> 313.6 *in nobis*] om.

3. The Descendants of G

There are twelve extant descendants of G (see Figure 8). They fall into four families: MgPbVnWf, MbMiMn, MeVk, and FkPaVv.

3.1 The Descendants of δ

MgPbVnWf derive from a common ancestor, δ.[10] The shared errors of MgPbVnWf include:

> 5.7 *frui nobis*] *nobis frui*
> 8.29 *amplissimis*] *amplissimis honoribus*
> 14.20 *mihi*] om.
> 17.19 *ea*] om.

---

[8] The influence of Mh upon VenA will be considered below in my discussion of the printed editions of *Brut.*

[9] Cf. also 25.2 *quadam* Mh^c] *aliquadam* MhOd.

[10] Gabriele Rota tells me that these four MSS form a family in *De optimo genere oratorum* as well.

APPENDIX 2   269

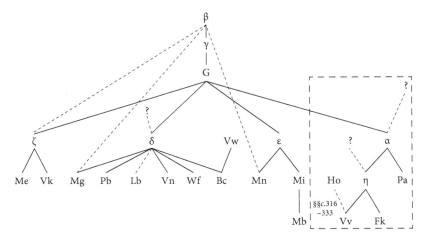

Figure 8: The Descendants of G

19.8   *a te sane*] *sane a te*
216.13 *tardus in cogitando*] *in cogitando tardus*
221.13 *naturalem quandam*] *quandam naturalem*
265.6   *erant*] om.
268.2   *totum*] om.
276.1   *tertia illa*] *illa tertia*
276.5   *et*] *atque*
323.28 *illum*] *istum*.

The provenance and contents of these manuscripts cohere with their derivation from a common exemplar: Mg and Vn were both copied in Parma, and all four contain the same four texts (*De or.*, *Orat.*, *Brut.*, *De optimo genere oratorum*).[11] The texts are in the same order in three of the manuscripts, PbVnWf.[12] δ appears to have been a contaminated descendant of G, since its offspring contain some, but not all, of G's significant errors.[13] The errors of G present in MgPbVnWf include:

2.13   *tempore* G^c] om. GPbVnWf: spat. vac. Mg
12.4   *mihi accidit*] *accidit mihi*
20.14 *mihi nuper*] *nuper mihi*
219.28 *est*] om.
227.9 *quibus*] om.
272.9 *a commentatione*] *commenta* GMgPbWf: *comenta* Vn

---

[11] Mg also has *Somn.* and Bruni's *Cicero novus*.
[12] O is the only other extant MS which has these four works of Cicero in this order.
[13] Pb was cited by various editors (with the siglum D) until Reis (1934: vii–viii) proved that it derives from G.

270   APPENDIX 2

275.25 *agitur autem*] *autem agitur* GpbVnWf: *aut agitur* Mg
316.3 *cnidius*] *ovidius*
325.5 *aeschylus*] *aeschylus aeschines*
326.14 *aut*[1]] om.

The errors of G present in none of MgPbVnWf include:

13.6 *id*] om.
20.13 *id*] om.
46.19 *tyrannis*] *nostra vis* G: *tyrannus* Pb: *tiranmus* Wf
265.11 *oratio*] om.
269.13 *publici*] om.

In general, δ must have been a relatively pure descendant of G, but nevertheless it would have been very difficult for a scribe to have corrected G's corrupt *nostra vis* or to have restored the omitted *oratio* and *publici* without the aid of another manuscript. There was probably a limited amount of contamination involved in the composition of δ, or in an ancestor of δ. The alternative explanation, that Gδ derive from a common exemplar, is improbable, because at 35.20 *quoi*] *quo* FλO: *in quo* βγG^vl: *cui quo* G: *cui in quo* PbWf, the scribe of δ seems to have misinterpreted G's marginal variant *in quo*. (It is possible, but unlikely, that G's exemplar had a similarly ambiguous variant reading.) An additional argument in favour of δ's deriving from G is that δ shares G^ac's omission of *tempore* at 2.13 (see above). In this case, too, G's exemplar might have had the omission and the correction, but it is more probable that the error arose in G.

None of MgPbVnWf derives from any other of the four, since they all have their own significant errors.

Mg: 15.28 *litterarum*] om.
26.13 *se orator*] *orator se*
272.15 *venustus...e*] om.
276.3 *nec...consilio*] om.
317.17 *qui...hortensius*] om.

Pb: 10.16 *novi*] om.
20.16 *nostrum potius*] *potius nostrum*
222.20 *tuum*] om.
268.1 *iniuriarum*] om.
322.10 *exquisitius*] om.

Vn: 12.1 *prosperae res*] *res prospere*
13.11 *salutem*] om.
14.20 *saluti*] om.
20.14 *mihi*] *tibi*
220.9 *effecerit*] om.

Wf: 23.14 *quisquam*] om.
33.9 *quam...observatione*] om.
222.19 *aquili...m.*] om.

APPENDIX 2   271

270.24 *ipsis*] om.
314.20 *nomen*] om.

As well as the errors shared by all four manuscripts, there is a set of errors common to PbVnWf but not present in Mg. Some of these errors are:[14]

5.11 *grato animo*] *animo grato*
25.26 *vero*] *ego*
26.12 *mihi occurrunt*] *occurrunt mihi* PbWf: *mihi occurrit* Mg
28.25 *clarissimus*] *dignissimus*
35.21 *inveniri*] *in currenti*
273.28 *perurbana*] *perturbata*
314.20 *iam*] *iam et.*

On this basis, one might postulate the existence of a common ancestor of PbVnWf, deriving from δ. However, there are also errors of G which are present in PbVnWf but absent from Mg:

25.25 *loco*] om.
217.1 *peroravissem*] *procuravissem* GPbVnWf: *perorassem* Mg
226.31 *causam* Mg^c] om. GMgPbVnWf.

In view of all this evidence, I judge that Mg is a contaminated descendant of δ, and that the contamination has led to the removal of some of the errors of G and δ. Since Mg, like PbVnWf, preserves all the significant errors of β, the contamination in Mg probably comes from another descendant of β, or from β itself. The scribe of Mg cites Gasparino Barzizza twice in marginal annotations to the text of *Brut.*, which suggests that the corrections might have come directly from β (which is probably Barzizza's manuscript).

Another manuscript, Bc, shares some of δ's distinctive readings.[15] Bc is without doubt contaminated, sharing significant errors of F and G.[16] There are two discernible sources of the text of Bc: Vw and δ (or alternatively, their descendants). Vw

---

[14] Vn is mutilated and is absent for some of these readings. Where it is extant, however, it shares the errors of PbWf, including those not in Mg.

[15] Rubio (1960) argued that Bc, to which he gave the siglum b, is a copy of a lost direct copy of L. In attempting to demonstrate the independence of Bc, Rubio cited errors of B and F not shared by Bc, but this evidence proves only that Bc does not derive exclusively from B or F. Rubio then went on to list various places where Bc has a true reading and most, or all, of FOBG have errors (e.g. 25.6 *habeat* G^{c}Bc] *habeant* FJUOBG; 30.7 *abderites* F^{c}Bc] *abderitas* FJUBG: *abderita* O; 91.28 *appareat* Bc] *apparet* FJUOBG), and he suggested that Bc's true readings derive from the archetype. However, all the true readings of Bc noted by Rubio could have been conjectured, and the agreement of Fλρ in these errors proves that Bc's readings do not come from L. Rubio failed to distinguish between significant and trivial errors, and many of the readings cited in his article are orthographical variants with no stemmatic weight. Rubio's arguments are wholly insufficient to prove his claim that Bc is an independent and valuable witness to the text of L.

[16] Errors shared with F include 228.21 *perspici*] *percipi*, 269.13 *acer nimis*] *acerrimus*, and 331.17 *amoris*] *moris.*

272 APPENDIX 2

derives from F and will be discussed further among the descendants of κ. The errors Bc shares with Gδ include:

9.9 *quodam* VnWf] om. G: *quotidiano* BcPb: *quottidiano* Mg
21.26 *et*] *atque*
25.25 *loco*] om.
226.31 *causam*] om.
269.17 *enim*] om.
275.25 *agitur autem*] *autem agitur*
323.3 *sic*] *sic et*
327.22 *et²*] om.

Distinctive readings of δ also present in Bc include:

17.19 *ea*] om.
216.13 *tardus in cogitando*] *in cogitando tardus*
276.5 *et*] *atque*
278.25 *animos* Wf] *animos quod* BcMgPbVn
323.28 *illum*] *istum*
332.6 *pammenes* Mg] *permaenes* PbWf: *parmaenes* Vn: *peramenes* Bc.

In one place (18.26 *tibi* MgVnWf] om. BcPb), Bc shares a significant error with a single descendant of δ. This reading implies that the influence on Bc might come from Pb, rather than from δ, but it is insufficient to prove this inference. I conclude simply that δ, or a descendant of δ, is one of the sources of Bc.

3.2 The Descendants of ε

Another family of manuscripts deriving from G is MbMiMn. These manuscripts agree in the following distinctive errors:

1.8 *iuratus*] *virtus*
4.1 *in civitate*] om.
4.4 *misericordia...quam*] om.
11.19 *eo*] om.
12.5 *meas*] om.
16.7 *sic...obstructus est*] om.
25.5 *quinque*] om.
26.10 *haec est*] *est hec* MbMiMnᶜ: *h est hec* Mn
35.21 *facile*] om.
330.10 *ipsa*] om.

MbMiMn derive from a common ancestor, ε. As well as the shared errors listed above, an additional proof is the fact that MbMiMn have identical textual dislocations, with 99.8 *erat* – 107.13 *brutus* placed before 92.9 *melius*, and with

APPENDIX 2   273

114.18 *graecis* – 122.20 *persequamur* placed before 107.13 *m. filius*. The four sections of text involved in the dislocation (§§92–99, 99–107, 107–114, and 114–122) are of almost exactly the same length, and hence the dislocation must be due to the disordering of pages in a manuscript. Since the dislocations do not correspond to the page divisions in any of MbMiMn, nor to the page divisions in G, from which they derive, the disordering must have occurred in the intermediate manuscript, ε. In Mn, the first hand has added a marginal note restoring §§114–122 to their correct position after §§107–114. Since the scribe of Mn managed to restore the text to exactly the right place, he may well have made the correction from ε itself.

Neither Mb nor Mi derives from Mn, since Mn has significant errors not found in MbMi:

> 5.9 *referre...felicitatem*] om.
> 31.16 *et malis*] om.
> 228.24 *sit satis*] satis sit
> 276.29 *suaviter*] om.
> 326.13 *sic in hoc*] om.

MbMi share many errors against Mn. These errors prove that neither is the source of Mn, and that MbMi are closely related:[17]

> 1.3 *cepi dolorem*] dolorem coepi
> 3.20 *interitum*] mortem
> 7.26 *aut errore hominum*] om.
> 16.11 *diligenter colemus*] colemus diligenter
> 32.2 *docuit alios*] alios docuit
> 222.18 *l. fufius*] om.
> 224.12 *fortunae et vitae*] vitae et fortunae
> 269.18 *mihi*] tamen
> 276.28 *et sanum*] ac suum
> 280.21 *inquit istuc*] istuc inquit.

In fact, Mb derives from Mi. In the collated portions, Mb has all the significant errors of Mi. Mb has very few errors of its own, but it does add the following:[18]

> 216.18 *cn. sicinius*] en sicinius Mi: eu sicinius Mb
> 218.8 *conloquentem*] eloquentem.

---

[17] Both are of Lombard origin; their contents are identical (although some of the pages of Mi have since been lost), and are shared by no other MS.

[18] Mb has many significant errors of its own in the closing section of *Brut.*, including 319.20 *animadvertendum*] admirandum and 325.24 *adulescentiae...senectuti*] om., but the last part of the text is now lacking in Mi, and so these errors cannot help to prove the derivation of Mb from Mi.

274   APPENDIX 2

Both of these errors are relatively minor. Nevertheless, the derivation of Mb from Mi is almost certain, because there are errors introduced by the corrector of Mi which are also present in Mb:[19]

4.3 *mortis opportunitatem*] *oportunitatem mortis* Mi: *oportunitat mortis* Mi^cMb
35.20 *quoi*] *cui quo* GMi: *in quo* G^{vl}Mn: *cui in quo* Mi^cMb
271.25 *amicos nostros*] *equites nostros amicos* Mi: *nostros amicos* Mi^cMb
273.3 *cum*] *enim* Mi: *enim cum* Mi^cMb.

The derivation of ϵ from G is complicated by the fact that Mn is contaminated and does not contain all the errors of G. Nevertheless, MiMb contain almost every significant error of G in the collated portions.[20] These include:

2.13 *tempore* G^c] om. GMiMbMn
9.9 *quodam*] om. GMiMbMn
18.29 *nihil*] *nichi* G: *mihi* MiMbMn
29.28 *theramenes* G^cMn] *therames* G: *theranes* MiMb
227.9 *quibus*] om. GMiMbMn
265.7 *quaedam* Mn] om. GMiMb
275.25 *agitur autem* Mn] *autem agitur* GMiMb
325.5 *aeschylus* Mn] *aeschylus aeschines* GMb.

The only errors of G absent from MiMb in the collated portions which might be considered non-trivial are:

20.14 *mihi nuper* MiMb] *nuper mihi* GMn
279.28 *dubitamus* MiMbMn] *dubitabamus* G.

Since the first of these errors of G is also in Mn, it was almost certainly in ϵ, and then was probably corrected by accident by the scribe of Mi, who was particularly prone to errors of transposition. The second error could have been corrected in ϵ either by conjecture or by accident. Consequently, there is no impediment to the conclusion that ϵ was a pure descendant of G.

In Mn, many of the significant errors of G and its parent γ, but none of those of ρ and β, have been removed. As well as those listed above, the errors not present in Mn include:

217.1 *peroravissem* Mn] *procuravissem* γGMiMb
226.30 *causam* Mn] om. GMiMb

---

[19] In a few other places, Mi has readings which seem more primitive than those of Mb, since they apparently reflect more closely the text which must have been in ϵ: 219.28 *posuisset* Mi^cMbMn^c] *meminisset posuisset* MiMn; 266.14 *utrumque* Mi^cMbMn] *utrum* GMi; 268.8 *plena* Mi^cMbMn] *plene* GMi; 273.29 *accusationes* G^cMi^cMbMn] *accusat*[??]*es* G^{ac}: *accusatones* Mi. Since, as I show below, many of the errors of β, G, and ϵ have been eliminated from Mn by contamination, the absence of some of these errors from Mn does not indicate that they were also absent from ϵ.

[20] MiMb also share one error with G^c: 17.19 *exspectanda*] *expectenda* GMn (and probably β): *expetenda* G^cMiMb.

APPENDIX 2   275

228.16 *doctus...deditus* Mn] om. γGMiMb
265.11 *oratio* Mn] om. GMiMb
269.13 *publici* Mn] om. GMiMb
272.9 *a commentatione* Mn] *commenta* GMiMb
326.14 *aut*[1] Mn] om. GMb.

These errors could not have been corrected by conjecture, and so readings from another manuscript must have been introduced into the text of Mn. Interestingly, in the first section I collated, Mn has all the errors of G and shows no sign of contamination. Upon checking the readings of Mn against a list of G's errors from the whole text, I found that there was no evidence of contamination until 130.1 *fuit* Mn] om. G, but that G's errors were frequently corrected thereafter.

Since almost all the shared errors of MiMbMn are from the first section of text, one might infer that Mn's exemplar was changed at *c.*§130, rather than that contamination was responsible for the removal of many of G's errors. However, two readings confirm that Mn still derives from ε in the latter part of *Brut.*:

219.28 *posuisset* Mi[c]MbMn[c]] *meminisset posuisset* MiMn
330.10 *ipsa*] om. MbMn.

The source of the contamination in Mn is uncertain, because Mn has no particular affiliation to any manuscript except ε. A subscription at the end of Mn, copied in the same hand as the text of *Brut.*, is strikingly similar to the subscription in O, and also reveals knowledge of the number of pages of L missing at the end of *Brut.*[21] This knowledge could not have come from G, which does not include such information. In the subscription itself, the scribe states that the source is the writings of Gasparino Barzizza, and so these words do not indicate that the scribe of Mn had access to L or that he was using the subscription to O as a source of information concerning the *Laudensis*. Rather, it seems that Barzizza had initially written them down as an observation on L's text of *Brut.*, and that after this, Barzizza's observation, having influenced the phrasing of Francesco degli Ardizzi's subscription to O, was copied, perhaps verbatim, by the scribe of Mn in his subscription.[22]

Had O, or any other manuscript independent of β, been the source of the contamination in Mn, one would expect, given the proportion of G's errors that have been removed, that some of β's errors would also have been eliminated. Because this is not the case, the contamination has presumably come from another descendant of β, or from β itself. Indeed, since β was probably Barzizza's manuscript, the scribe of Mn

---

[21] The subscription in Mn reads: *Deficiunt pauca, non ultra folia duo ad plus et ut ego coniecturam facio non ultra columnam. Plura enim in codice vetustissimo non comperi, ex quo in fine carte recise iniquitate fortune erant.* Further down the page is written: *Hec ex praeceptore doctissimo Gasparino de Barzizis Pergamensi scripta relicta habentur.* The subscription in O, copied by one of the later correctors, includes the following: *Non inveni plura in perveteri codice. fortunę quidem iniquitas id totum, si tamen quiddam erat, recidit.*

[22] The scribe of Vat. lat. 2957 (Dictys Cretensis) makes a similar comment on the activity of Gasparino Barzizza; see Oakley (2020: 297–298).

276　APPENDIX 2

might well have copied his subscription directly from β, although the *scripta relicta* of Barzizza could also be a reference to his literary works.

3.3 The Descendants of ζ

Another family deriving from G is MeVk. These two manuscripts share many errors, including:

6.14　*reliquis*] om.
9.4　*fortunate beateque*] *beate fortunateque*
13.8　*litterae*] om.
14.17　*omnem rerum*] *rerum omnium*
29.3　*interdum*] om.
34.15　*necessitate*] om.
266.13　*mentione commotus*] *commotus mentione*
272.10　*tantos processus*] *processus tantos*
309.10　*dies vacuus*] *vacuus dies*
320.24　*illud*] om.
327.20　*adulescens*] *adulescentiis.*

MeVk derive from a common ancestor, ζ. Vk cannot derive from Me, because Me has its own significant errors:

26.13　*primum se*] *se primum*
227.7　*non*] om.
273.22　*qui...fuit*] om.
317.26　*tamen*] om.
320.27　*tantum quasi*] *quasi tantum.*

Likewise, Vk's errors prove that it cannot be the source of Me:

3.20　*erat gloriosius*] *gloriosius erat*
11.22　*cura levatis*] *levatis cura*
35.18　*subtilis*] om.
219.22　*illarum*] om.
220.1　*eius*] om.

MeVk share some, but not all, of G's significant errors. Errors present in GMeVk include:

19.3　*est* G^c] om. GMeVk
46.19　*tyrannis*] *nostra vis*
97.23　*tamen*] om.
157.22　*devenerint*] om.
224.18　*atticorum*] *antiquorum*

APPENDIX 2   277

276.7 *habebat*] *habebat quid inter abesse et deesse referat*
320.29 *existumator*] *exstumator* G^c: *et stumator* GMeVk.

Errors of G absent from MeVk include:

12.4 *mihi accidit*] *accidit mihi*
20.14 *mihi nuper*] *nuper mihi*
25.25 *loco*] om.
226.31 *causam*] om.
265.7 *quaedam*] om.
275.25 *agitur autem*] *autem agitur*.

Although MeVk do not share all the errors of G, there is little doubt that they derive from it. Two further readings help to strengthen the case for the derivation:

95.6 *orator est habitus* G^c] *orator habitus est* G: *habitus orator est* MeVk
121.6 *est* G] om. G^{c}MeVk.

Especially significant is 95.6 *orator est habitus*, because here, the scribe of G, after realizing his mistake, has added the letters *b* and *a* above the line to indicate that *est* and *habitus* should be transposed. However, *b* and *a* are confusingly placed above the final letters of *orator* and *habitus* respectively, which has led the scribe of ζ to make the wrong transposition.

Contamination must have been responsible for the correction of many of G's significant errors. As with Mn, the contamination has not resulted in the elimination of any of β's significant errors, and hence the corrections were probably made from β or a descendant of β.

3.4 Fk, Pa, and Vv

The final family of descendants of G is FkPaVv. These three manuscripts share various distinctive errors, including:

216.11 *una*] om.
217.1 *titinia*] *ticinio*
224.10 *c.*] om.
271.29 *pisaurensem*] *pisauriensem* Fk^{c}PaVv: *pisauriensiem* Fk
312.1 *inde multae*] *multe inde* PaVv: *multae* Fk
318.11 *nimis*] *hic* Pa: *hec* Vv: *haec* Fk.

Some of these errors are minor, but together they constitute quite a strong case that these manuscripts were closely related, perhaps sharing an exemplar (α). Since, as will be shown later, the final part of Vv seems to be contaminated, or to derive from a different exemplar, two additional shared errors of FkPa probably also derive from α:

278 APPENDIX 2

322.13 *bene factorum beneque dictorum*] *bene dictorum beneque factorum* Fk: *benedictorum benefactorumque* Pa: *benefactorum benedictorum* Vv
331.25 *laude iunxisses*] *deiunxisses* ρβγG: *laude devinxisses* FkPa: *laude vinxisses* Vv.

The precise relationship between FkPaVv has been obscured by contamination, but the presence of a clear set of errors shared by FkVv suggests that they derive from a common ancestor, η. Some of the errors of FkVv are:

2.15 *putabant*] om.
3.21 *omnino*] om.
7.19 *consili non ingeni*] *ingenii non conscil(l)ii* Fk(Vv)
8.27 *quamquam*] *quom* Vv: *cum* Fk
14.20 *inquam*] om.
17.19 *inquit brutus*] om.
32.3 *etiam*] om.
274.18 *rerum*] om.
316.15 *habitus*] om.
321.2 *stilo*] om.

Neither Pa nor Vv derives from Fk, since Fk has its own significant errors:

3.21 *adversarium*] *inimicum*
18.28 *tibi molestum*] *molestum tibi*
228.17 *latine loquens*] *loquens latine*
273.4 *voluntate bonorum*] *bonorum voluntate*
332.25 *duplex nos afficit*] om.

Pa's significant errors include:

11.19 *animo ad te*] *ad te animo*
25.25 *hoc*] om.
227.7 *oratio*] om.
273.28 *contiones aliquot*] *aliquot conciones*
316.6 *molonem*] om.

Finally, the significant errors of Vv, a highly corrupt manuscript, include:

15.2 *a doctis*] om.
32.4 *quendam...numerum*] om.
228.20 *maiorem...et*] *in*
311.19 *trium*] om.
327.20 *enim genus illud*] *illud enim genus*.

None of G's distinctive errors are present in all of FkPaVv. However, Pa shares many of G's errors, including:

APPENDIX 2   279

9.9   *quodam*] om.
12.4   *mihi accidit*] *accidit mihi*
13.6   *id* Pa^c] om. GPa
20.14   *mihi nuper*] *nuper mihi*
25.25   *loco*] om.
33.8   *magis tum* G] *magistra* G^{vl}Pa
35.20   *quoi*] *cui quo* GPa: *in quo* βG^{vl}Pa^{vl}
43.28   *praebebat*] *parebat* G: *parabat* G^{c}Pa
275.25   *agitur autem*] *autem agitur*
323.3   *sic*] *sic et*
326.14   *aut^1*] om.

There are also significant errors of G not shared by Pa, such as:

82.29   *rem*] om.
97.23   *tamen*] om.
226.31   *causam*] om.
227.9   *quibus*] om.
265.7   *quaedam*] om.
265.11   *oratio*] om.
269.17   *enim*] om.

One might conclude from these data that Pa shared an exemplar with G, or that Pa was contaminated with readings from G. However, Pa shows no particular affinity to any other branch of the tradition, and because the manuscript also shares some, but not all, of the significant errors of ρ, β, and γ, it is more probable that Pa is a descendant of G, but that contamination and correction have resulted in some errors being removed.

If this conclusion is correct, and if FkVv are closely related to Pa, why do FkVv lack these errors of G? I suspect that η, the shared ancestor of FkVv, was highly contaminated. In the cases discussed earlier in this chapter, the contamination involved was apparently quite limited, but η (or a lost intermediate manuscript between η and α) seems to have been so rigorously corrected from another manuscript that few traces of its original affiliation remained. To support this understanding of the relationship of FkVv to Pa, I present a list of distinctive errors of ρ and β contained in FkVv, which show that they have at least a loose affiliation to this part of the tradition, and one error of FkVv apparently originating from an error of G:

16.14   *quom*] *sępe* βFkVv: *saepe* Pa
22.1   *ecquodnam*] *quodnam* ρFkPaVv
34.14   *et*] om. βFkPaVv
225.23   *revecti*] *reiecti* ρFkPaVv
295.29   *fieri quicquam*] *fieri quicquam fieri* G: *quicquam fieri* FkPaVv
322.18   *iudicum animos*] *animos iudicum* βFkPaVv
328.14   *afuisti*] *affuisses* ρFkPa: *abfuisti* Vv.

280   APPENDIX 2

The stemma I have drawn for FkPaVv (Figure 8) represents one possible relationship between these manuscripts. The principal alternative is that α never actually existed, and that FkVv derive from Pa via a contaminated intermediate manuscript (η). In either case, it remains probable that all of FkPaVv derive primarily from G. What can be said with confidence is that none of the three is of use to an editor of *Brut*.

There is one further complication to consider. In the final part of its text, Vv shares many errors with Ho, including:

316.4 *rhetorum*] *oratorum*
326.18 *mirabantur*] *admirabantur*
327.1 *comprensio*] *reprehensio*
327.6 *concinnitas*] *comitas*
329.28 *ipsius*] *illius*
330.9 *esse oportere*] *oportere esse*
330.11 *salute*] *saluti* L: *saluti essent* HoVv
331.18 *frui virtute*] *virtute frui*
331.20 *erat illud curriculum*] *illud curriculum erat*
332.7 *hospes*] om.
333.11 *unus*] *unus et*.

There are also readings which Ho has inherited from its ancestors, Fσ, which are present in Vv:

333.10 *laudabilis*] *laudibus* σHoVv
333.16 *post*] *p. et* F: *post et* HoVv
333.19 *concursatio*] *a concursatio* F: *accursatio* HoVv.

It is unclear whether the scribe of Vv changed his exemplar in the final part of *Brut*. Ho has errors absent from Vv (e.g. 325.23 *erat*] om., 330.31 *quasi*] om.), and so the final few paragraphs of Vv's *Brut*. are not simply copied from Ho. Vv might perhaps have been copied from Ho's exemplar in this portion of the text, but alternatively Vv's exemplar might have been corrected from Ho (or a relative).

4. The Descendants of X

Three manuscripts, BoFlLu, appear to be contaminated descendants of X. BoFlLu derive from a common exemplar (θ),[23] as can be seen from the numerous errors they share, including:

7.24 *arma posset*] *posset arma*
11.26 *monere te*] *te monere*
16.13 *noster animus*] *animus noster*

---

[23] Pm has been contaminated with readings from θ. See p. 316.

APPENDIX 2   281

24.19 *victoria* Fl^{vl}] *gloria* BoFlLu
216.18 *et cn.* Fl^c] om. BoFlLu
219.22 *iam tempora*] *tempora iam*
277.8 *etiam* Fl^c] *esset* BoFlLu
316.7 *praestantem*] *praestantissimum*
321.3 *augere quantumcumque erat*] *quantumcumque erat augere*
322.26 *unum est oratoris*] *oratoris unum est*
323.6 *illum primo*] *primo illum*
323.6 *mearum gestarum*] *gestarum mearum*
326.17 *cum* Fl^c] *tum* BoFlLu.

BoFlLu share some errors with X, including:

219.27 *quidem*] om.
223.1 *ex*] om.
226.2 *multae ad eum*] *ad eum multae*
272.12 *et*[1] Fl^c] om. XBoFlLu
274.20 *diffluentia*] *deffluentia* X: *defluentia* BoFlLu
280.16 *atque*] *at*
314.12 *et* X^c] om. XBoFlLu
322.17 *esset* Fl^c] *esse* XBoFlLu.

However, BoFlLu do not share all the significant errors of X. Errors present in X but not in BoFlLu include:

5.11 *grato*] om.
22.31 *saepe*] om.
270.22 *sed...dicere*] om.
274.18 *rerum*] om.
322.12 *continetur*] om.
328.18 *dictatore*] om.

The same is true of the errors X has inherited from its ancestors. Although many of the errors of β and γ are in BoFlLu, some are absent, including:

16.14 *quom*] *quam* FΛOBoFlLu: *sępe* βX
48.12 *aliis* BoFlLu] om. βX
111.26 *cum...diceret* BoFlLu] om. βX
228.16 *doctus...deditus* BoFlLu] om. γX
274.8 *prope* BoFlLu] om. βX.

This evidence proves that, while BoFlLu are closely related to X, they cannot derive exclusively from it, or from an exemplar shared with it, since BoFlLu do not contain all the significant errors of X or of its ancestors. In fact, BoFlLu are contaminated descendants of X. The following readings help to demonstrate that θ, the shared exemplar of BoFlLu, apparently contained variants and corrections from O:

282 APPENDIX 2

24.21 *propter* O] *prope* O^{vl}BoFlLu
83.10 *vetustior* O^{c}Bo^{vl}FlLu] *venustior* OBoFl^{vl}
95.32 *gaiusque* O^{v}Fl^c] *gravisque* OβBoFlLu
146.25 *admirandus* Fl^{vl}] *ammirandus* O^v: *admirabilis* βBoFlLu: *ammirabilis* O
278.26 *sanitate* O] *suavitate* O^{vl}BoFlLu
310.12 *loquuntur*] *eloquuntur* OFl^{vl}: *eloquntur* Lu: *eloquimur* BoFl
311.24 *fecerunt* BoFlLu] *faciunt* OFl^{vl}
312.27 *sulla* O^{v}BoFl^{vl}Lu] *silla* OFl
317.17 *tum* O^{v}Fl^{vl}] *tamen* OBoFlLu.

Contamination from O provides a ready explanation for the absence of some errors of X, γ, and β from BoFlLu. Tellingly, there are no significant errors of ρ absent from BoFlLu in the portions I collated.[24] A brief examination of the lists of errors present in BoFlLu and the readings shared with O will reveal that the scribe of Fl has been the most diligent in including these corrections from O, but a sufficient number are present in Bo and Lu for one to be confident that the contamination took place in θ, rather than in Fl.

That none of BoFlLu is the source of the others is proved by the significant errors each has of its own.

Bo: 4.3 *vero*] om.
23.11 *bene nemo potest*] *nemo potest bene*
25.2 *omnium*] om.
227.14 *nemo...aetatis*] om.
277.14 *ipsum etiam*] *etiam ipsum*.

Fl: 3.23 *semper*] om.
7.22 *bene*²] om.
19.5 *id*] om.
50.24 *temporibus illis*] *temporibus* Fl: *illis temporibus* Fl^c
60.8 *unius esset*] *esset unius*.

Lu: 32.22 *domus*] om.
274.8 *potius inter multos*] om.
274.11 *ipsius*] *flexibile*
280.12 *dicere*] om.
326.18 *multitudo movebatur*] om.

Since there is no clear set of errors shared by any two of BoFlLu, all three must be independent copies of θ. All that remains to be discussed is the final portion of the text of Lu, which is palpably different from the rest of Lu's *Brut*. At 331.23, Lu lacks a non-trivial error present in ρOX (*eloquentiae laude iunxisses*] *eloquentia deiunxisses*). At a stretch, one might argue that this error could have been corrected in Lu by emendation. However, two errors shared by Lu with F but not with ρOX (331.17

---

[24] The correction of minor errors of ρ (e.g. 11.22 *praesentem* BoFlLu] *praesente* ρOX) can be attributed to conjecture by the scribe of θ.

APPENDIX 2   283

amoris] *moris* and 333.16 *post*] *p. et*) confirm that the end of Lu's *Brut.* derives from
a different source from the rest of the text. The reason for this apparent change of
exemplar in Lu is not hard to find. Both Bo and Fl lack the last few paragraphs of
Brut., and although their texts finish at slightly different points,[25] θ probably also
lacked some of §§330–333; the final part of *Brut.* has been supplied in Lu from F, or
from a descendant of F. The portion of Lu's text which derives from F is too brief to
allow it to be located more precisely among F's progeny.

5. The Contaminated Descendants of γ

A group of three manuscripts, LcVaVp, derives from a common exemplar, ψ. Vp,
however, is the only manuscript to derive from ψ throughout *Brut.*; Lc only derives
from ψ in section IV of my collations, and Va only in sections I–II.[26] Hence, there
are shared errors of VaVp in §§1–228 and of LcVp from §§309–333. The errors
shared by VaVp include:

4.26 *occidit*] *cecidit*
5.11 *felicitatem*] *facultatem*
8.29 *quo*] om.
10.10 *otiosus domi*] *domi ociosus*
16.15 *efferre fruges*] *fruges efferre* Vp: *fruges afferre* Va
19.5 *id*] *quid*
25.1 *illa*] om.
25.6 *existimari*] *quis existimare*
31.14 *ex*] *ex verborum*
216.14 *et*] om.
221.17 *animos*] *animosus*
224.10 *improbissimus*] om.

The errors shared by LcVp include:

311.24 *quod*] *ut*
313.3 *naevo*] *vacuo*
313.6 *in*] om.
318.5 *interim*] *iterum*
318.10 *maturitatem quandam*] *quamdam maturitatem*
320.29 *existumator*] *et senator*
321.5 *praetor*] *pater*
324.19 *dicendi*] *deinde*
326.14 *interdum utiles*] *utiles interdum*

---

[25] Bo ends at 329.28 *quae con-*, Fl at 330.11 *sin secus*.
[26] Lc is a descendant of Vh in the first part of its text (pp. 293–294); the final portion of Va
derives from Vw (pp. 303–304).

284 APPENDIX 2

326.15 *oratio*] *omnino*
328.15 *declarat*] *delectarat declarat*
329.27 *esse*] om.

The independence of LcVaVp is proved by their singular errors.

Lc: 314.20 *celebratum meum nomen*] *meum nomen celebratum*
317.22 *mihi*] om.
323.3 *duodecim*] om.
329.22 *ut vis inquam*] *inquam ut vis*
333.16 *perfecta nondum*] *nondum perfectum.*

Va: 12.29 *totius*] om.
16.12 *etiam*] om.
19.10 *atque ut possis*] om.
217.22 *erat fasciis*] *fasciis erat*
222.20 *magnum*] om.

Vp: 18.19 *inquit*] om.
217.1 *peroravissem...me*] om.
266.14 *enim eorum*] *eorum enim*
280.21 *distinguis*] *dignius*
323.1 *consul*] om.

A later hand has introduced into J, one of the two extant descendants of λ, some corrections either from Vp or from ψ. This can be seen from such readings as:

4.26 *occidit* J] *cecidit* J²VaVp
4.3 *doleamus* J] *dolemus* J²VaVp
216.18 *e luntre*] *cluntre* J: *cliviter* J²Vp: *eliviter* Va
320.29 *existumator*] *aestumator* J: *et senator* J²LcVp.

Not all J²'s corrections come from Vp, because sometimes J² corrects to a reading different from Vp's (e.g. 309.2 *diodoto* J²] *dioto* J: *diodo* Vp), and so it is perhaps more likely that J²'s corrections have been taken from ψ.[27]

ψ did not derive simply from one part of the tradition, but rather was a conflation of the text of γ (or a descendant) with that of F (or a descendant). The dominant source appears to have been γ, with various distinctive errors of ρ, β, and γ being present in ψ's offspring (e.g. 225.23 *revecti*] *reiecti* ρβγVaVp, 226.29 *iuli illam*] *iulullam* ρβγVp: *iullam* Va, 228.18 *non*] om. βγVaVp, 276.7 *habebat*] *habebat quid inter abesse et deesse referat* γVp, 322.18 *iudicum animos*] *animos iudicum* βγLcVp); however, the majority of the errors of ρβγ have been removed. ψ shares a few of F's errors (e.g. 22.1 *ecquodnam* Oλ] *et quodnam* FVaVp: *quodnam* O^cβ and 333.16 *post*] *p. et* FLcVp), but again most are absent. Interestingly, although ψ, or one of its ancestors, was the product of a careful comparison of two

---

[27] J² may, of course, have made some of these corrections by conjecture.

APPENDIX 2   285

manuscripts, ψ's text was nevertheless very corrupt, as proved by the large number of errors shared by its descendants. It seems that, at some point in the history of the copying of ψ and its ancestors, the diligent attempt to purify the text of *Brut.* by means of correction from another manuscript was undone by a scribe's negligence.

6. A Descendant of Ho

I have already shown that the first part of Ho (§§1–126) derives from β.[28] Ho has produced one offspring, Rm. Where it is extant, Rm shares all the significant errors of Ho, including:[29]

5.7 *non*] om.
9.5 *tum...quibus*] om.
11.23 *vestris*] om.
11.26 *et...visus*] om.
15.26 *temporum*] om.
18.1 *animadverti paulo te*] *animadvertite paulo*
20.13 *est id*] *id est*
20.15 *qui...fuissent*] om.
26.12 *occurrunt*] *occurrerunt*
29.2 *crebri*] om.
31.15 *tum*] om.
34.14 *spiritu*] *scriptu.*

The presence of all the errors of Ho in Rm is sufficient to demonstrate the derivation, but a second proof is that Rm's text of *Brut.* ends exactly at the end of a page, and a quire, of Ho. The scribe of Rm has copied the catchword *dicendi* at the bottom of f.60ᵛ of Ho, but has written nothing further. Since the scribe of Rm did not copy to the end of f.61ʳ, the point where the change of exemplar, and of hand, took place in Ho, I infer that the seventh quire of Ho was detached from the preceding six for a period of time, perhaps while the rest of *Brut.* was being copied onto it.[30]

Ho contains most of ρ's chapter divisions in §§1–126, and Rm's chapter divisions are exactly the same as those in Ho. Rm is an accurate copy of Ho, but it does add a few errors of its own, including:

5.7 *iam*] *non* Rm (del. Rmᶜ)
22.4 *fascisque*] *facesque*

---

[28] pp. 44–45. On the relationship of Ho to Vv, see above, p. 280.
[29] Rm's *Brut.* ends at 123.32 *dicendi*, and so it lacks §§126–333, in which Ho derives from τ (see pp. 318, 321).
[30] If the watermarks are a reliable guide, Ho must have been copied at around the same time as Rm, dated by Sanzotta to *c.*1435.

286 APPENDIX 2

22.6 *obmutuit*] *obmittuit*
68.16 *id*] *ita.*

7 The *Editio Princeps* (Rom)

Four of the six printed editions of *Brut.* from the fifteenth century are based on earlier editions, with only the first two, Rom and VenA, deriving purely from manuscripts. The text of the *editio princeps*, Rom, appears to be a conflation of the texts of at least two manuscripts. Rom shares several of the distinctive errors of Lb, a contaminated descendant of O:

7.26 *pacis*] *civitatis*
225.20 *tam*] *tamen*
271.25 *ne*] *non*
320.28 *quasi*] om.
325.4 *et faceto*] om.[31]

This relatively brief list can be supplemented with some errors inherited by Lb from its two sources, O and γ, and also present in Rom:

1.6 *dolebam* O^v] *videbam* OLbRom
20.14 *mihi nuper*] *nuper mihi* γLbRom
14.24 *posset esse*] *esse posset* OLbRom
265.9 *gravitas* O^v] *dignitas* OLbRom
328.19 *fato suo*] *suo fato* OLbRom.

However, Lb cannot be the only source of Rom, because Rom does not share all the significant errors of Lb.[32] Additionally, the text of Rom displays influence from another part of the tradition. Rom shares various errors with Bn and with its descendants, FjVe.[33] These include:

215.6 *quaedam ex his*] *ex his quaedam*
223.4 *palicanus*] *p. alicanus*
316.10 *supra fluentis*] *super afluentes* Bn: *superaffluentes* Rom
320.30 *cognoscere*] *magnum scelus* L: *cognoscere magnum scelus* BnRom
321.5 *praetor*] *p. r.* BnRom.

Bn derives from F via Ff, the manuscript copied by Poggio Bracciolini; Rom shares some of the distinctive readings Bn has inherited from Ff:

---

[31] Note also 4.27 *lugere*] *lugerer* Lb: *lugeret* Rom, 218.9 *ille sermo* Lb^c] *sermo ille sermo* Lb: *sermo ille* Rom.
[32] Rom shares none of the errors of Lb listed on p. 264.
[33] On Bn(FjVe), see further, pp. 324–326. Bn was copied in Rome, where the *editio princeps* was printed.

APPENDIX 2   287

10.13 *itaque*] *atque*
220.2 *bonitatem*] *vanitatem* F: *varietatem* BnFfRom
280.14 *verisimile*] *verisimiliter* FfRom: *verisimilter* Bn.

As was the case with Lb, there are many significant errors of Bn not present in Rom.[34] I have found no readings of Rom which suggest that other manuscripts were consulted except Bn and Lb, and so I conclude that Rom is a conflation of the texts of Bn and Lb. Malcovati, who occasionally cites Rom in her edition (with the siglum R), was broadly correct when she wrote the following of the manuscript used as its source: 'fuisse videtur aliquis e Florentino (i.e. F) profectus, contaminatus autem atque interpolationibus depravatus' (1965: xiv). Rom does, though, seem to share more readings with Lb, and consequently with O, than with Bn and its ancestor F.

No extant manuscript derives from Rom, since Rom has its own significant errors, including:

218.9 *ille sermo*] *sermo ille*
219.25 *exiens*] *exitus*
220.4 *itaque...censeo*] om.
269.13 *nimis*] om.
275.23 *vocant graeci*] *graeci vocant*.

8. Subsequent Printed Editions

VenA, the second printed edition containing *Brut.*, appeared in 1485, and it seems to have been completely independent of Rom. VenA shares many of the errors of B, including:

32.25 *meo quidem*] *quidem meo*
225.24 *sumus locuti*] *locuti sumus*
266.14 *admodum*] om.
268.9 *terroris*] *horroris*
268.10 *esse*] om.
280.17 *parum a magistris*] *a magistris parum*
320.24 *suum*] om.
321.3 *quod erat*] om.

Among the descendants of B, VenA is especially close to Mh (and to its descendants, Bl and Od); VenA and Mh share the following errors:

30.9 *fuit* B^{c}Mh] *fueri* B: *fuerunt* Mh^{vl}VenA
227.8 *paulum*] *paulo*

---

[34] Of the errors of Bn listed on p. 325, Rom shares only 215.6 *quaedam ex his*] *ex his quaedam*.

288 APPENDIX 2

266.20 *et*[1]] om.
276.31 *esse*] *est*
320.32 *continuatione*] *concinnatione*.

As well as sharing several errors, Mh and VenA both have a single chapter division, at 25.23 *hic ego*. In Mh, the heading *TRACTATUS* is written in red ink before this chapter division, while VenA has the similar *Tractatus Incipit*. The heading is absent from both Bl and Od, and VenA lacks their distinctive errors. Therefore, VenA must derive from Mh independently of BlOd. VenA is not simply a copy of Mh, because some errors present in Mh are not in VenA, including:

8.27 *ipsis*] om.
24.15 *magis*] om.
25.2 *unam*] om.
31.16 *haec*] om.
33.6 *aut...erat*] om.
276.29 *est*[1]] om.
322.20 *propria*] *prova*.

Girolamo Squarciafico, the editor of VenA, must have checked Mh against some other manuscript, or perhaps against Rom,[35] in order to eliminate these errors from his edition. The proportion of errors removed decreases markedly in the later part of *Brut.*, which suggests that Squarciafico became less careful in checking the text of Mh as he continued through the work. VenA cannot be described as a genuinely critical edition, and is much less useful than Rom as a repository of humanist emendations.

VenB, printed in 1488, is a reprint of VenA. This can be seen from the contents and layout, both of which are identical in the two editions, as well as from the fact that VenB shares all of VenA's significant errors and some of its typographical errors. The shared errors include:

5.7 *eo*] *eo non*
14.18 *est*] om.
14.20 *ipsum*] *ipsum quidem*
28.27 *constat fuisse*] *fuisse constat*
220.1 *eius aequalibus*] *aequalibus eius*
224.7 *specie*] *ipse*
280.13 *inquam*] *inquam brute*
309.8 *esse dilatatam*] *dilatam esse*
328.11 *inquit et ista*] *ista inquit*
333.13 *gracchi*] *cracchi*.

---

[35] However, VenA shares none of Rom's distinctive errors in the portions of text I have collated.

APPENDIX 2   289

Because only very minor typographical mistakes are corrected in VenB, it is clear that no manuscript or edition was used to check the text of VenA. The same is true of the third Venice edition, VenC, printed in 1495. VenC is a reprint of VenB. Again, the contents are identical, and there is a dittography of a full line of VenB's text (13.6 *certe...quae te*). VenC has all the significant errors of VenA and VenB, as well as some of their typographical errors. The distinctive errors of VenB present in VenC include:

9.5 *quibus*] om.
10.13 *omnis*] *ominis*
23.7 *istuc*] *instuc*
24.15 *brute*] *bute*
25.24 *expromere*] *exponere*
220.5 *languidiores*] *laguidiores*
317.25 *canuleio*] *manuelio*
325.3 *asia*] *asita*.

The fifth printed edition to contain *Brut*. is Nur, printed in Nuremberg in 1497. Nur is a reprint of VenC. More errors have been removed than by the printers of VenB and VenC, but none which suggest knowledge of any text except that of VenC.[36] The distinctive errors of VenC present in Nur include:

3.18 *nobilis*] *nobilio*
10.10 *xysto*] *yisto*
13.6 *certe...quae*] *certe...quae te certe...quae te*
14.17 *eum*] *est*
224.11 *ridiculus*] *ridiculus ridiculus*
275.26 *consultorum*] *consultarum* VenC: *consulto tam* Nur
322.13 *dictorum*] *ditorrum*
333.14 *et liberiore genere*] *genere et liberiore*.

The final fifteenth-century edition is Mil, printed in Milan in 1498. Mil is not simply a reprint of an earlier edition. Its contents are similar to those of the previous four editions, but not identical. Mil is based on the text of VenB, since it contains some of the distinctive errors of VenA and VenB, but none of those of VenC and Nur. The errors of VenB present in Mil include:

25.24 *expromere*] *exponere* VenB VenC Nur Mil
215.9 *cuiquam*] *cuique* VenB VenC Nur Mil
315.25 *auctum*] *acutum* VenB VenC Nur Mil
320.21 *consulatum* Nur] *consultatum* VenB VenC Mil
325.3 *asia*] *asita* VenB VenC: *a sita* Nur: *asica* Mil.

---

[36] Examples of errors corrected in Nur include 216.15 *commovebat*] *commovebar* and 320.30 *ut in*] *in ut in*.

290   APPENDIX 2

The editor of Mil, Alexander Minutianus, took much more care than those responsible for VenB, VenC, and Nur in trying to remove errors from the text.[37] He eliminated many minor errors, as well as some that are more significant, and their
combined weight indicates that Minutianus probably had recourse to a manuscript,
or perhaps to Rom, in his attempt to improve the text of *Brut*.[38] Some of the errors
present in VenB but not in Mil are:[39]

1.7 *in*[1]] om.
5.11 *summam*] *non summam*
9.5 *quibus*] om.
215.7 *quaedam*] *quaedam ea*
217.24 *gratiam*] *gratias*
317.25 *canuleio*] *manuelio*
322.24 *ad*] om.

The distinctive errors of Mil include:

23.11 *dicere enim*] *enim dicere*
223.4 *etiam*] *autem*
228.22 *cum*] *quin*
271.28 *et*[2]] om.
312.1 *nos*] *non minus*.

Unlike in many textual traditions, there is no sign that any of the fifteenth-century
printed editions has exerted influence upon any extant manuscript. No manuscript
derives from a printed edition, because all the printed editions have significant
errors not present in the manuscripts, and I have found no manuscript that appears
to be contaminated from an incunable.

---

[37]   My findings are in line with Hunt's findings concerning Mil: Hunt (1998: 232–234) argues
that Minutianus' edition of *Acad.* was based on an earlier printed edition (either de Pensis or
Bivilaqua), but that he corrected this edition by comparison with a MS.
[38]   There is, however, no obvious set of shared errors which can point us towards a particular
source of Minutianus' corrections.
[39]   All these errors are in VenC and Nur.

APPENDIX 3

The Descendants of F

F, copied by Niccolò Niccoli in Florence in 1423, had a greater influence on the dissemination of *Brut.* than any other extant manuscript. In fact, more than half of the extant manuscripts of *Brut.* derive either exclusively or primarily from F. In this appendix, I provide evidence for this claim, and I also sketch out the relationships among the descendants of F (see Figure 9).

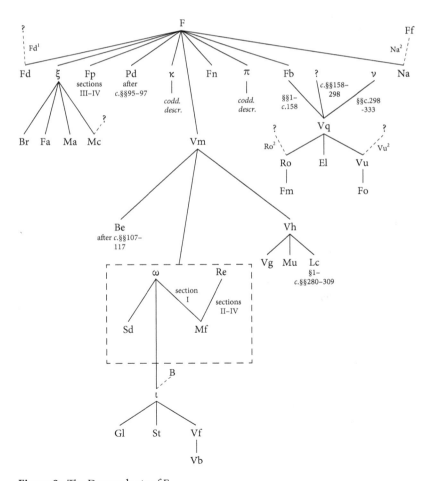

Figure 9: The Descendants of F

292   APPENDIX 3

The most significant errors of F in my collated portions are:

219.20 *stultius*] *sulpicius*
220.2 *bonitatem*] *vanitatem*
222.26 *cn.*] *m.*
269.13 *acer nimis*] *acerrimus*
272.16 *e*] om.
279.5 *redeamus*] *respondeamus*
330.5 *me in vitam*] *me* [spat. vac.] *itam*
331.17 *amoris*] *moris*
333.16 *post*] *p. et.*

Other errors of F which persist in many of its descendants include:

22.1 *ecquodnam*] *et quodnam*
216.19 *oratoris*] *oratori*
225.23 *ad*] *a*
274.12 *aeque*] *eaeque*
274.13 *fuerit*] *fuerunt*
280.21 *quidnam*] *quinam*
333.19 *concursatio*] *a concursatio.*

1 The Descendants of Vm

Vm is a pure descendant of F. This is evident from the fact that Vm shares all the errors of F in both of the above lists, and from an error which Vm shares with F[c]: 223.1 *elegantis*] *eligentis* F: *eligantis* F[c]Vm. Also indicative are errors shared by F[ac]Vm, which include:

16.8 *exaruit* F[c]Vm[c]] *exauruit* FVm
221.15 *et*[2] F[c]] *in* FVm
268.9 *quaereres* F[c]] *quaereres quaereres* FVm
316.7 *scriptoremque* F[c]] *scriptorem* FVm
326.9 *senibus* F[c]] *sensibus* FVm.

Six extant manuscripts derive purely from Vm (MfMuReSdVgVh), as well as a further four contaminated manuscripts (GlStVbVf). Additionally, Be is a pure descendant of Vm in sections II–IV of my collations, and Lc is a pure descendant of Vm in sections I–III. The errors of Vm found in some or all of these manuscripts include:[1]

11.23 *absenti* Re[c]] *absentem* VmLcMfMuReSdVgVh: *absentes* Mf[c]
16.11 *in*] om. VmGlLcMfMuReSdStVbVfVgVh
223.2 *aptissimos*] *aptimos* VmMfReVh: *optimos* BeLcVg

---

[1] Mu contains only §§1–76, 91–99 and 178–207 of *Brut.*

APPENDIX 3   293

226.29 *consulatus*] om. VmBeGlLcMfReSdStVbVfVgVh
227.10 *l.*] om. VmBeLcMfReSdVgVh
268.10 *quod…publica*] om. VmBeLcMfReSdVgVh
278.21 *elicere*] *eligere* VmBeLcMfReVgVh: *elligere* Sd
331.18 *eam*] om. VmBeGlMfReSdStVbVfVgVh.

Additionally, smaller errors of Vm can explain corrupt readings in some of these manuscripts, and these extra readings thus provide further evidence for their derivation from Vm:[2]

2.13 *exstinctus* Re^cVh^c] *extenctus* Vm: *extentus* MuReVh: *exterritus* Vg
7.19 *angor* GlSt^vlVf^vlVh^c] *augor* VmVh: *auguror* MfReSdSt^cVbVf: *auguror al.* *angor* St
34.16 *defici* Re] *defi* Vm: *deficere* GlMfSdStVb: *deici* LcVh^c: *de vi* MuVgVh
227.9 *floruit* Vh^c] *flurit* Vm, Vh (ut vid.): *fl* [spat. vac.] Be.

Since MfMuReSdVgVh have all the significant errors of Vm in the collated portions and add further errors of their own, all six manuscripts must derive from Vm. Likewise, Be contains all the significant errors of Vm in sections II–IV of my collations, and Lc contains all of Vm's significant errors in sections I–III, and consequently Be and Lc must derive these parts of their texts from Vm. In the rest of *Brut.*, Be and Lc are copied from different exemplars, independent of Vm and unrelated to each other.[3]

The relationships among the descendants of Vm can be further defined. Vh is the source of Mu, Vg,[4] and sections I–III of Lc. The following list of Vh's errors provides evidence for this conclusion, and also demonstrates that Vm cannot derive from Vh:

3.24 *communicando*] *in communicando* VhVg: *incommunicando* LcMu
4.27 *lugere*] *legere* VhVg: *ledere* Vh^cMu: *dolere vel lugere* Vh^2: *dolere* Lc
12.2 *res*] *et res* VhLcMuVg
31.20 *a*] *de* VhLcMuVg
34.10 *natura*] om. VhLcMuVg
219.17 *fuisse oblivionem*] *oblivionem fuisse* VhLcVg
226.3 *omnes maxumae*] *maxime omnes* VhLcVg
271.2 *quibus*] om. VhLcVg
271.4 *parata*] om. VhLcVg
272.5 *autem*] om. VhLcVg

---

[2] Cf. also 314.14 *sperata* Vm^cVh^c] *sperata mil* Vm: *sperata mihi* Vh, 327.19 *erat* Vm^cVh^c] *erant* Vm: *eran* Vh.

[3] Initially Be is a descendant of τ (see pp. 318–319); the change of exemplar appears to have occurred between §§107 and 117 (as is evident from such readings as 87.18 *mane* FBe] om. Vm, 89.5 *rutili*] *rutilia* FVm: *rutiliana* τBe, 92.10 *putent* FVm] *putem* τBe, 107.19 *esset* FBe] *est* Vm, 117.12 *augures* Fτ] *augeres* VmBe, 120.5 *academicorumque* Fτ] *academicorum* VmBe, 120.8 *aliquantoque* Fτ] *aliquanto* VmBe). Lc deserts Vm at some point between §§280 and 309, and instead shares an exemplar with Vp (see pp. 283–284). Not having been able to collate any more of Lc, I have been unable to locate the change of exemplar more precisely.

[4] The derivation of Vg from Vh is not a surprise, since both MSS were owned by Giannozzo Manetti.

294 APPENDIX 3

276.5 *natura...quod*] om. VhLcVg
313.8 *non procul*] procul non VhVg
315.25 *et doctore*] om. VhVg
324.12 *vel*] om. VhVg
331.16 *tangit*] om. VhVg.

With the exception of the final section of Lc (and the part of the text lacking in Mu), every significant error of Vh is present in these manuscripts. Consequently, Vh must be the source of LcMuVg. Nevertheless, the following readings constitute further evidence of the derivation:[5]

219.22 *cum...sermone* Vh^{c}Lc^{c}Vg] om. VhLc
223.30 *q.* Vh^c] *q. etiam catulum* Vh: om. Vg (Vh's correction is unclear and has confused the scribe of Vg)
266.19 *istis* Vh^{c}Lc^c] *istis duobus...nec istos* (266.16–17) VhLc: *istis duobus* Vg
329.22 *mea* Vh] *in ea* Vg (Vh has *m/ea* split across two lines).

A final proof is afforded by the disarrangement of the pages of Vh's *Brut.*[6] The same dislocated text is present in LcMuVg. Since the dislocation is clearly a result of the disruption of the order of folios in Vh, all three must derive from Vh.

The singular errors of Lc, Mu, and Vg demonstrate that none of them is the source of any other.

Lc: 13.14 *mihi potuit inquam*] inquam potuit mihi
22.3 *et...cederet*] om.
228.20 *et sulpici*] om.
271.26 *nuper*] om.
279.5 *iam*] om.

Mu: 6.16 *forum*] om.
30.11 *enim*] cum
54.2 *appellatus est*] est appellatus
179.17 *l.*] om.

Vg: 4.5 *et beatissumo*] om. Vg: *et doctissimo* Vg^c
17.20 *attico...fortasse*] om.
219.21 *volebat quae vituperavit*] om.
330.5 *in viam*] om.
333.17 *amplius tantum dico*] om.

Another descendant of Vm is Be. Be only shares Vm's errors for approximately the final two-thirds of *Brut*. Be is independent of Vh, Vh's descendants, and MfReSd, since it does not share their errors. Be has various errors of its own, including:

---

[5] See also 26.12 *qua* Vh^{c}Lc] *quare* VhMuVg, 277.15 *capitis* Vh^c] *captus capitis* VhLc, 324.18 *ante* Vh^c] *et ante* VhVg.
[6] For details of the disarrangement, see the description of Vh in Appendix 1.

APPENDIX 3   295

222.20 *ceperat*] om.
265.8 *elegantia...et*] om.
271.27 *defendi*] om.
279.10 *consecuti*] om.
320.24 *remisit*] om.

The next three descendants of Vm, MfReSd, may share an exemplar. There are a few errors shared by all three manuscripts:

7.19 *angor*] *augor* Vm: *auguror* MfReSd
15.1 *at* Mf^{c}Re^c] *aut* MfReSd
27.16 *fuerunt* Mf^c] *ferunt* MfReSd
27.20 *clisthenem*] *clistenem* Vm: *clistienem* MfReSd
274.16 *lucilius*] *lucidius* MfReSd.

None of these errors is sufficient to prove that MfReSd share an exemplar, but they are suggestive. Far more significant are the errors shared by two of the three. MfSd share the following errors:

16.14 *quom*] *quam* FVm: *quamquam* MfSd
20.16 *nostrum potius*] *potius nostrum*
22.6 *obmutuit*] om.
23.8 *tam*] om.
24.19 *victoria*] om.
26.10 *haec est*] *est hec*
35.19 *perfectum*] *perfectum iam*.

MfRe share many errors, including:

218.13 *misso*] *remisso*
222.26 *populi*] om.
224.8 *quam...homines*] om.
227.5 *tamen*] om.
265.12 *non consideratum*] *inconsideratum*
276.7 *illi*] om.
277.15 *ille*] om.
316.10 *nos*] om.
322.26 *unum est*] *est unum*
327.8 *ille brute*] *brute ille*
329.28 *ipsius*] *illius ipsius*.

It should be noted that the shared errors of MfSd are limited to section I of my collations, and the shared errors of MfRe to sections II–IV. Therefore, whether or not there was a close relationship between all of MfReSd, the lists of errors above make it abundantly clear that in the first part of *Brut.* the scribe of Mf was copying from an exemplar with a text similar to that of Sd, and in the remainder of the text from an

296   APPENDIX 3

exemplar with a text like that of Re. The singular errors of MfReSd may help to clarify the relationship of these manuscripts.

Mf: 14.18 *mihi quidem*] *quidem mihi*
25.25 *propositum...neque*] om.
28.27 *tamen*] *etiam*
219.18 *quidem umquam*] *unquam quidem*
311.18 *recuperanda*] *in recuperanda*
332.4 *est semper*] *semper est.*

Re: 27.17 *aliquem habeat*] *habeat aliquem*
28.24 *etiam eloquentia*] *eloquentia etiam*
28.26 *illum quidem*] *quidem illum.*

Sd: 15.2 *doctis*] *multis doctis*
17.16 *et*] om.
22.4 *iam*] om.
218.12 *inter...esset*] om.
277.13 *in respondendo*] om.
314.21 *profectus...menses cum*] om.

The errors of Mf and Sd prove that no extant manuscript derives from either of them. Hence, on the basis of their shared errors in section I, I infer that MfSd probably derive from a common exemplar, ω, in this part of *Brut.* Re, however, does not have any significant errors of its own in sections II–IV of my collations. The two most substantial errors of Re not present in Mf in sections II–IV are 314.14 *a sperata*] *aspera* and 329.29 *vindicavisse*] *iudicavisse*; these do not prove Mf's independence from Re, because an astute copyist might have been able to correct them. Given that a few of F's errors are absent from Mf (e.g. 223.30 *ordini*] *ordinis,* 279.5 *respondeamus*] *redeamus*), it seems that the scribe of Mf was competent in correcting a Latin text, and so sections II–IV of Mf probably derive from Re.

The final group of manuscripts deriving from Vm is GlStVbVf. These manuscripts share some, but not all, of the significant errors of Vm (see above, pp. 292–293). They also share errors with some or all of MfReSd, including:

7.19 *angor* GlSt^{vl}Vf^{vl}] *augor* Vm: *auguror* MfReSdSt^{c}VbVf: *auguror al. angor* St
13.14 *gratior* Mf^c] *gravior* GlMfSdStVbVf
20.16 *nostrum potius*] *potius nostrum* GlMfSdSt: *potius vestrum* VbVf
22.6 *obmutuit*] om. GlMfSdStVbVf
26.10 *haec est*] *est hec* GlMfSdStVbVf
267.24 *etiam*] *enim* GlSdStVbVf
309.9 *doctori* St] *doctrine* GlSdVbVf.

The precise relationship between GlStVbVf and MfReSd is somewhat unclear, but GlStVbVf might derive from the exemplar of Sd (which is probably also the exemplar of Mf in section I of my collations). The situation is complicated by the fact that GlStVbVf are contaminated. This contamination is evident from the absence of

APPENDIX 3   297

significant errors of Vm, and also from the presence of errors shared with B and its descendants:

22.1 *ecquodnam] et quodnam* FVm: *quodnam* βBStVbVf: *quoddam* Gl
33.9 *casuque] casu quae* FVm: *casu* BGlStVbVf
34.12 *constricta* FVmSt^cVbVf] *circumscripta* BVf^vl: *constricta alias circumscripta* St: *constructa* Gl
35.20 *cui] quo* FVm: *in quo* βBGlStVbVf
268.10 *esse* FVm] om. BGlStVbVf
328.21 *ominare] o mire* FVm: *omitte* BGlStVbVf.

GlStVbVf therefore seem to be descendants of Vm, perhaps via Sd's ancestor (ω), contaminated with readings from B, or a descendant of B. The absence of some of F's errors from GlStVbVf provides additional support for this conclusion:

219.20 *stultius] sulpicius*
220.2 *bonitatem] vanitatem*
279.5 *redeamus] respondeamus*
331.17 *amoris] moris.*

There are a few shared errors of GlStVbVf:

16.10 *seremus* Gl] *feremus* StVbVf
224.13 *esset] esse* StVbVf: *est* Gl
224.17 *atheniensis] atheniensi*
315.30 *lubentibus* VbVf^c] *iubentibus* GlStVf
322.13 *beneque dictorum] benedictorum.*

These errors are all minor, but nevertheless, in view of the fact that GlStVbVf contain almost exactly the same set of errors of B, F, Vm, and Sd(MfRe), they very probably derive from a common ancestor, ι.[7] Geography also tells in favour of this conclusion, because GlStVbVf are the only extant manuscripts of *Brut.* known to have been copied in France. ι presumably contained the variant readings present in both St and Vf (7.19 *angor* St^vlVf^vl] *auguror* St^cVf: *auguror al. angor* St, 34.12 *constricta* St^cVf] *circumscripta* Vf^vl: *constricta alias circumscripta* St). The singular errors of GlStVb prove that no other manuscript derives from them.

Gl: 6.18 *spoliatum atque orbatum] orbatum atque spoliatum*
19.3 *ego...peto]* om.
268.6 *autem]* om.

---

[7] The textual dislocations in Gl suggest that the pages of its exemplar were disordered. StVbVf do not share these dislocations, and so either there was at least one intermediate MS between Gl and ι, or the pages in ι were disarranged after the copying of StVf, but before the copying of Gl.

298   APPENDIX 3

321.8 *ad me*] om.
327.22 *forma*] om.

St: 22.5 *ea*] om.
279.1 *laudibus longe*] *longe laudibus*
327.3 *honores*] *homines*
330.10 *ipsa*] om.
331.22 *et*] om.

Vb: 1.9 *in parentis*] om.
16.5 *nec... est*] om.
24.19 *sed... agamus*] om.
222.22 *etiam... lucullum*] om.
314.17 *dicendi*] om.

All the errors of Vf, though, are shared with Vb, and Vb must therefore derive from Vf. Examples of the shared errors of VfVb are:

1.7 *me*] om.
4.6 *nosmet*] *met*
8.28 *multo magis alia*] *alia multo magis*
30.5 *facta*] om.
219.28 *minime mirum*] *mirum minime*
219.28 *dicenti solitam*] *solitam dicenti*
222.21 *ita*] om.
267.27 *satis studiosus*] *studiosus satis*
316.13 *mutatus*] om.
318.10 *quandam suam*] *suam quandam*
322.27 *impellere*] *impelleret* L: *interpelleret* Vf: *interpellaret* Vb
330.4 *doleo me*] *me doleo*
331.17 *eiusdem*] om.

Additionally, one of Vb's omissions (16.5 *nec... est*) seems to have resulted from a scribe jumping to the line below while copying from Vf. The omission is otherwise hard to explain, and in Vf *nec* is almost directly above *unde*, the word which follows *est*. This omission is not a decisive proof of the derivation, because it does not correspond exactly to a line of Vf's text, but it is indicative. The original contents of VfVb are identical,[8] which accords well with their close relationship within the tradition.

2 The Descendants of κ

κ, a descendant of F, had a significant effect on the later tradition: no fewer than 21 extant manuscripts derive wholly or partially from it (see Figure 10). Those which

---

[8] The work by Ognibene de' Bonisoli is a later addition in Vf.

APPENDIX 3   299

derive independently from κ throughout *Brut.* are LdMoOxVcVw. Additionally, Ec, the ancestor of GwPc, derives from κ in section I of my collations, and Vq, the source of ElFmFoRoVu, derives from κ in section IV. The errors shared by κ's independent descendants include:

4.26   *tum*] *tunc* EcLdMoOxVcVw
16.11   *inculto* Mo²] *occulto* Ld (ut vid.) EcMoOxVcVw
34.12   *constricta*] *constructa* EcLdMoOxVcVw
35.17   *in* EcMo²] om. LdMoOxVcVw
269.17   *enim*] om. LdMoOxVcVw
273.22   *fortuna*] *forma* LdMoOxVcVw
276.4   *altior* Mo²] *alior* LdMoVcVw: *aliorum* Ox
315.1   *atticorum*] *antiquorum* LdMoOxVcVw: *attiquorum* Vq
318.3   *unum* Mo²Vqᶜ] *num* LdMoOxVcVq: *non* Vw
318.4   *nobilis* Vq] *nobis* LdMoOxVcVw
318.11   *ipse* Mo²Vq] om. LdMoOxVcVw
320.25   *omnium*] *omni* LdMoOxVcVqVw.

κ derived from F, since every significant uncorrected error of F from the collated portions is present in all the independent descendants of κ.[9] Additionally, some of the descendants of κ contain errors of Fᵃᶜ, such as:

221.15   *et²* FᶜVcᶜ] *in* FVc: *et in* LdMoVw: om. Ox
268.9   *quaereres* FᶜMoᶜOxVcᶜ] *quaereres quaereres* FLdMoVcVw.

I turn now to consider the relationships between the descendants of κ. Vc, owned by Leon Battista Alberti, is a pure descendant of κ and has no particular affinity to any other manuscript.[10] The errors of Vc not shared with the other independent offspring of κ include:

274.19   *alienum*] *alterum*
309.9   *ita*] *tam*
316.10   *nos*] om.
323.28   *autem*] om.
326.13   *venustae dulcesque sententiae*] om.

---

[9] If one excludes progressive corruptions of F's errors, the only exception is 330.5 *me in vitam*] *me* [spat. vac.] *itam* F, an error which is absent from Fm and which I presume to have been removed by correction or, more probably, by contamination.

[10] Ströbel (1897: 558) argued that Vc, cited by some editors (with the siglum V), derives from F. While accepting this conclusion, Malcovati nevertheless sometimes records Vc's readings; she justified this decision on the basis of Vc's spelling practice, describing it as 'veteris probaeque orthographiae luculentum auctorem' (1965: xiii). However, a *codex descriptus* cannot have authority, whether on orthography or on any other matter, and Vc should only be cited in an apparatus when it contains useful conjectures.

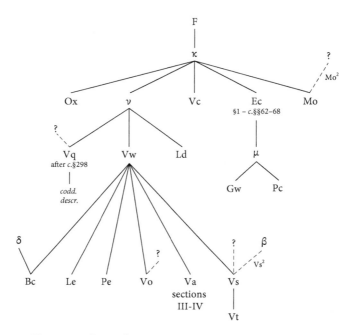

Figure 10: The Descendants of κ

Additionally, while the other independent descendants of κ follow F and L in repeating *in quibus...magis* after *sententiae* at 326.13, this corruption has been removed from Vc; this acts as another proof that none of LdMoOxVqVw derives from Vc.

Another independent and uncontaminated descendant of κ is Ox. The scribe of Ox has occasionally attempted to correct his text (e.g. 219.20 *stultius*] *sulpicius* Fκ: *simplicius* Ox, 225.23 *ad* Ox] *a* Fκ), but the corrections can all be attributed to conjectural emendation. Ox adds many errors of its own, including:

8.28 *lugenda*] *dolenda*
13.12 *tandem*] om.
216.18 *sicinius...cn.*] om.
273.29 *tres eaeque omnes*] om.
326.8 *dicendi...faciebat*] om.

The initial text of Mo derives purely from κ. The only error of κ that I have found to be absent from Mo is 227.11 *probabatur*] *probatur*, where the scribe of Mo has restored the true reading, probably by conjecture. A later hand has added corrections and variants to Mo. Some of these can be seen in the list of κ's errors above. The most significant one, 318.11 *ipse* Mo²] om. LdMoOxVcVw, would have been difficult to correct without recourse to another manuscript. Likewise, most of F's errors have been corrected by Mo² (e.g. 219.20 *stultius* Mo²] *sulpicius* FMo, 220.2

APPENDIX 3   301

bonitatem Mo^2] *vanitatem* FMo, 222.26 *cn.* Mo^2] *m.* FMo), and the difficulty of these emendations, not to mention the high success rate, make it almost certain that Mo^2's corrections derive from another manuscript. Mo's own errors include:

11.26 *brutus*] om.
19.5 *id*] om.
216.19 *in*] om.
276.32 *moveret*] *flecteret*
326.10 *utroque*] *in utroque.*

Ec, another independent descendant of κ, has produced two offspring, Gw and Pc.[11] GwPc share all the significant errors of Ec, including:[12]

5.7 *id*] om.
11.22 *praesentem*] *praesertim*
13.6 *volui*] *volo*
15.2 *eadem mensura*] *eandem mensuram*
28.22 *ex attici*] *exactis* EcGwPc: *exacti* Ec^c
29.28 *suppares*] *scippares*
35.20 *quoi*] om.
218.14 *res*] om.
227.9 *temporibus*] om.
228.19 *interiectusque*] *interitusque*
313.3 *naevo*] *evo*
315.26 *tamen*] om.
328.15 *declarat*] *dederat.*

The presence of corrections by Ec^c in GwPc helps to confirm the derivation:

4.3 *doleamus* Ec] *dolemus* Ec^{c}GwPc
6.16 *quod* Ec] *quo* Ec^{c}GwPc
12.29 *diuturna* Ec] *diurna* Ec^{c}GwPc
24.19 *victoria* EcPc^{vl}] *gloria* Ec^{lvl}GwPc.

That neither Gw nor Pc is the source of each other, or of Ec, is proved by their significant errors.

Gw: 12.2 *multae*] om.
220.7 *habet*] om.

[11] GwPc may both have been copied by Giovanni Aretino.
[12] The only noteworthy exception, found in the first paragraph of *Brut.*, is 1.3 *animo* Pc] om. EcGw. The restoration of *animo* by conjecture is unlikely. However, Pc cannot be a brother of Ec, since, as I demonstrate below, GwPc share errors and must both derive from a descendant of Ec, μ. Perhaps *animo* was added from another MS in the margin of μ. One would expect such small-scale contamination to be more common in the opening paragraphs of a text.

302 APPENDIX 3

221.14 *rebus inveniendis*] *inveniendis rebus*
269.17 *stantes*] om.
323.5 *meus*] om.

Pc: 10.11 *ut consueverat*] om.
216.13 *cum*] om.
273.29 *omnes*] om.
311.23 *adire*] om.
317.20 *sententiam*] om.

The following errors, common to GwPc but absent from Ec, reveal that neither Gw nor Pc was copied directly from Ec, but rather that both manuscripts derive from Ec via a lost exemplar, μ:

2.10 *quod*] *quo*
15.28 *coepissem*] *possem*
30.9 *se*] om.
32.20 *igitur*] om.
219.17 *admirans*] om.
222.19 *ex accusatione*] *excusatione*
225.24 *aliquantum*] *aliquantulum*
313.9 *eoque*] *eo*
319.14 *in²*] *cum*
328.16 *oratio*] *orationis*
330.3 *ab*] om.
331.16 *dolor tangit*] *tangit dolor.*

At some point between §§62 and 68, Ec deserts κ and instead derives from τ, but in §§1–62 Ec and its offspring appear to derive purely from κ.[13] The only error from section I of my collations shared by the other descendants of κ but not by Ec is the omission of *in* at 35.17. The preposition could have been restored before *causis forensibus* by conjecture or by accident, and so this reading does not indicate that Ec was contaminated. Some additional errors of κ from §§35–62 help to confirm Ec's place in this family:[14]

44.4 *romanarum*] *humanarum* EcLdMoOxVc
48.11 *removisse*] *remorasse* EcLdMoᶜVc: *remorassem* Mo: om. Ox
49.20 *memorabilia*] *mirabilia* EcLdMoOxVc
61.19 *ut*] om. EcLdMoOxVc
62.29 *his* MoOx] *his his* LdVc: *his ipsis* Ec.

The next two descendants of κ to be considered, Ld and Vw, derive from a common exemplar, ν, as can be seen from their shared errors:

---

[13] For evidence for the derivation from τ, including readings of τ from shortly after Ec's change of exemplar, see pp. 318–319.

[14] I have not been able to collate Vw in §§35–62.

APPENDIX 3   303

1.8 *quo*] om.
1.10 *debebam*] *solebam*
1.22 *illius a me*] *a me illius*
8.28 *essent multo magis*] *multo magis essent*
16.4 *voluntatem tibi*] *tibi voluntatem*
19.3 *ego*] om.
19.10 *atque ut*] *aut cum*
31.20 *a*] om.
270.19 *ego*] om.
272.19 *nec*] *me.*

In the final portion of *Brut.*, Vq shares most of the errors of *v* and derives from it:[15]

311.23 *et*] om. LdVqVw
317.23 *et* Vq] *de* LdVw
323.2 *honore essemus*] *essemus honoribus* LdVqVw
327.3 *gravius quiddam*] *quiddam gravius* LdVq: *quidam gravius* Vw.

I will discuss Vq and its descendants more fully later, but the absence of an error of *v* (317.23 *et*] *de*) and some of the errors of κ (see above) need not cause concern: the elimination of errors present in its ancestors is characteristic of Vq, which seems to be contaminated.

Ld's singular errors show that it is not the source of any extant manuscript:

228.21 *ipsius*] om.
274.15 *tamquam*] om.
318.5 *interim...hortensius*] om.
319.21 *in hortensio*] om.
332.2 *nec...patronorum*] om.

By contrast, Vw, the brother of Ld, was copied several times. There are two complete and uncontaminated copies, Le and Pe. Additionally, Va is a partial copy, deriving purely from Vw in sections III–IV of my collations.[16] Finally, there are three contaminated manuscripts which share errors of Vw: BcVoVs.[17] The errors of Vw and its descendants include:

1.1 *decedens* BcVoVs] *discedens* VwLePe
9.9 *quodam* BcVoVs] om. VwLePe
11.26 *est* BcVoVs] om. VwLePeVs
217.26 *autem ita* Pe] *ita autem* VwBcLeVoVs
220.1 *vivis* Vs] *unus* VwBcLePeVo

---

[15] The first errors of *v* that I have found in Vq are 298.25 *nec*] *ne* and 300.12 *digressi sumus*] *digressimus*, and so Vq probably derives from *v* from *c.*§298 onwards.
[16] In sections I–II, Va shares an exemplar with the highly contaminated MS Vp (see above, pp. 283–284).
[17] See Appendix 2 for discussion of Bc's relationship to δ.

304   APPENDIX 3

221.12 *tamen* BcVs[2]] om. VwLePeVoVs
272.19 *nec pietate* BcVs[2]] om. VwLePeVaVoVs
276.32 *ut delectaret* BcVs[2]] om. VwLePeVaVoVs
280.18 *ad dicendum* BcVs[2]] om. VwLePeVaVoVs
313.5 *quae* BcVs] om. VwLePeVaVo
315.1 *recte* Bc] om. VwLePeVaVoVs
324.8 *maxume* Vs] *maximis* VwBcLePeVaVo
324.14 *non satis diu* Vs[2vl]] *diu satis non* VwBcLePeVaVoVs.

Le, Pe, and Va (sections III–IV) contain all the significant errors of Vw, as well as many of its minor errors, and, since these manuscripts also have errors of their own, they must derive from Vw. Le's errors include:

10.10 *in*] om.
225.20 *ut*] om.
313.4 *velle*] *videre*
316.10 *iuvenili*] *vivendi*
326.13 *venustae dulcesque sententiae*] om.[18]

That Le derives from Vw is demonstrated not only by the presence of all the significant errors of Vw and the addition of some new ones, but also by Le's repeated *inquit* at 191.29. The scribe of Vw omitted the preceding phrase *et eum... legam*, before supplying it in the margin, but with *inquit* added at the end of the marginal correction. The scribe of Vw must have failed to ascertain the exact portion of text he had omitted, and this led him to add a second *inquit* to the one already in the main text. Le's repeated *inquit* must derive from Vw.

The significant errors of Pe include:

4.27 *rem publicam facilius*] *facilius rem pu.*
15.30 *teque... munere*] om.
35.25 *nihil ornatum*] om.
228.24 *satis*] om.
269.13 *bene*] om.
278.25 *animos*] om.

Another piece of evidence that Pe derives from Vw is the reading 318.12 *et eloquentiam meam*] *et eloquentiam et eloquentiam meam* Vw: *et eloquentiam* Pe. Here, Vw's dittography probably explains the omission of *meam* in Pe. Furthermore, at 216.16 *et* Vw] *id est* Pe, Pe's error has almost certainly been caused by the striking resemblance between Vw's *et* and an abbreviation commonly used in manuscripts for *id est* (.*i.*).

Va, the third manuscript to derive purely from Vw (although only in the final part of its text), has the following errors:

---

[18] Additionally, Le, like Vc, lacks the dittography of *in quibus... magis* at 326.13, and since this corruption is present in VwPeVa, it proves that Le cannot be the source of any of them.

APPENDIX 3   305

266.19 *de istis*] om.
280.21 *inquit istuc*] *istuc inquit*
311.20 *lentulorum*] om.
319.19 *oratoriam*] om.
333.11 *accepimus*] om.

Of the three contaminated descendants of Vw, Vo is by far the purest. In fact, apart from in section I, it contains all the errors of Vw (and of Vw's ancestors κν). Like Le, Vo has inherited the repeated *inquit* from Vw^c at 191.29, and, like Pe, it has corrupted Vw's *et* into *id est* at 216.16. In section I of my collations, however, Vo lacks all the significant errors of Vw. Vo still derives from Vw in this part of the text, though, for two reasons. Firstly, Vo^{ac} has one error in common with Vw^{ac} (34.14 *quasi* Vw^{c}Vo^c] om. VwVo) in the opening portion of the text, and secondly, Vo contains some of the errors of *ν*, the exemplar of LdVw, in this section, including:[19]

1.8   *quo* Vo^c] om. LdVwVo
3.22 *illius a me*] *a me illius*
16.7 *repressus* Vo^c] *impressus* LdVw, Vo (ut vid.)
19.3 *ego*] om.

Therefore, it seems that, at the start of *Brut.*, the scribe of Vo removed many of the errors present in his exemplar. Although conjectural emendation can account for the elimination of some of these errors, only comparison with another manuscript would allow a scribe to correct such errors as 8.28 *essent multo magis*] *multo magis essent*, 9.9 *quodam*] om., and 16.4 *voluntatem tibi*] *tibi voluntatem*. There are no readings of Vo which point to a particular manuscript as the source of the contamination, but the failure to correct any of F's errors indicates that the manuscript was another descendant of F, or perhaps F itself.

Vo's own errors include:

6.14   *civibus*] *viris*
25.4   *magna*] om.
271.3 *dicendi tamen*] *tamen dicendi*
316.6 *romae*] om.
329.22 *vis*] om.

In contrast to Vo, Vs shows evidence of contamination throughout its text.[20] There were, in fact, two waves of contamination. The first wave, which either took place in Vs's exemplar or was carried out by the initial copyist of Vs, resulted in the removal of many errors of κ, *ν*, and Vw. The second wave of contamination involved the later

---

[19] Vo lacks all the other errors of *ν* from section I.
[20] Because Vs^{ac} lacks some of Vw's errors, it remains possible that Vs, rather than deriving from Vw, instead shares an exemplar with it. There is no reason to posit the existence of this lost exemplar, though, and the more economical explanation is that Vs derives from Vw.

306 APPENDIX 3

addition of variants and corrections to Vs, including some distinctive readings of
ρ and β:

16.14 *quom* Vs] *sępe* βVs[2vl]
21.28 *tractum* Vs] *tractatum* ρVs[2vl]
35.20 *quoi*] *quo* FVwVs: *in quo* βVs[2]
227.8 *cum vitio*] *cum vicio* Vs: *cui comvitio* β: *tum convincio* Vs[2vl]: *tum convicio* Vs[vl]
328.14 *afuisti*] *affuisti* Vs: *affuisses* ρVs[2].

There is no sign that the initial scribe of Vs was aware of readings of ρβ, but nevertheless some errors present in FVw are absent from Vs[ac] (e.g. 219.20 *stultius*] *sulpicius* and 220.2 *bonitatem*] *vanitatem*). It seems, then, that the text of Vs[ac] was contaminated from a manuscript independent of F, and that subsequently Vs was checked against β, or an apograph of β, and that Vs[2]'s corrections were added at this time.

Vs has one extant descendant, Vt. Vt shares all the significant errors of Vs in the portions I collated, as well as some of its variants and corrections:[21]

4.3 *necesse*] *necesse est*
7.19 *animo* VsVt] *animi* Vs[c]Vt[c]
13.7 *fructum* VsVt] *voluptatem* Vs[gl]Vt[vl]
30.8 *eleius*] *seleucus*
216.18 *e luntre*] *elucubre* Vs: *celebre* Vs[vl]: *elecebre* Vt
217.22 *fasciis*] *fascies* Vs: *fascis* Vs[c]Vt: *fasceis* Vs[vl]: *fasces* Vt[c]
221.15 *et*[2]] *et in* κVw: *etiam in* VsVt
267.29 *orator* Vs[c]] om. VsVt
272.7 *qui* Vs[vl]] *quam* VsVt
315.29 *cum* Vs[2]] om. VsVt
320.30 *cognoscere*] *magnum scelus* LFVw: *existimare* VsVt (a conjecture peculiar to VsVt).

Vt cannot instead be the origin of Vs, because Vt has its own errors, such as:

4.1 *vixitque... vivere*] om.
10.17 *aut tu*] om.
222.24 *cn.... octavium*] om.
226.2 *multae*] om.
315.24 *numquam*] om.

---

[21] The last two folios of Vs's *Brut.* (§§330–333) have been moved to Vat. lat. 4533. The transfer of the folios probably took place after Vt was copied, because Vt appears to derive from Vs in this section as well.

APPENDIX 3   307

The last descendant of Vw to be discussed is Bc. Bc shares some, but not all, of the errors of Vw, ν, κ, and F.[22] Since, as was shown in Appendix 2, there is discernible influence on Bc's text from δ, Bc must be a contaminated manuscript. I cannot tell which of δ and Vw was the primary source of Bc, since Bc has roughly the same number of distinctive readings of each.

3 The Descendants of ξ

BrFaMa form another family of descendants of F. They share several errors, including:

12.30 *ad aspiciendam*] *ad inspiciendam* BrFa: *adinspiciendam* Ma
18.26 *mehercule*] *me hec hercle*
34.12 *verbis est*] *est verbis*
44.11 *athenae sunt*] *sunt athene*
305.18 *numerabantur*] *nominabantur*
311.22 *censorinus*] *censorinus et*
315.29 *quibuscum* Fa[c]] *quibuscumque* BrFaMa
317.19 *comprendens* Ma[c]] *comprehendes* BrFaMa
323.28 *meo* Fa[c]] *in eo* BrFaMa.

Since each of these manuscripts also has errors of its own, BrFaMa must derive from a common exemplar, ξ. ξ, in turn, must have derived from F, since BrFaMa contain all its significant errors. Some of F's minor errors are not present in BrFaMa (e.g. 24.19 *quo*] *quod* and 280.21 *quidnam*] *quinam*), but these errors could easily have been corrected and do not pose a problem for the derivation of ξ from F.[23]
BrFaMa contain their own singular errors.

Br: 7.19 *non ingeni*] om.
17.17 *pergrata*] *grata*
17.19 *sunt ea*] *ea sunt*
277.17 *tam leniter*] om.
333.17 *sulpicius*] *sulpicius et.*

Fa: 13.11 *ut spero salutem adtulerunt*] *salutem attulerunt ut spero*
273.24 *contra*] om.
279.5 *ad eum*] om.
280.17 *admirabilem ad dicendum*] *ad dicendum admirabilem*
317.22 *actionis genere*] *generis actione.*

---

[22] See the list of Vw's errors above. Bc has one of κ's errors (34.12 *constricta*] *constructa*) and several of ν's (e.g. 1.10 *debebam*] *solebam*, 16.4 *voluntatem tibi*] *tibi voluntatem*, and 323.2 *honore essemus*] *essemus honoribus*).
[23] BrFaMa also share some of the errors of F[ac], including 221.15 *et* F[c]Fa] *in* FFa[c]: *et in* Ma and 326.9 *senibus* F[c]] *sensibus* FBrFaMa.

308   APPENDIX 3

Ma: 42.15 *est attice*] *actice est*
56.18 *aliquid etiam*] *etiam aliquid*
73.11 *fuit aliquanto*] *aliquanto fuit*
314.18 *in asiam proficiscendi*] *proficiendi in asiam*
326.12 *ut*] om.

As well as the errors present in all three manuscripts, there is a set of errors shared by FaMa but not by Br:

6.13 *cetera fortasse*] *fortasse cetera*
13.12 *tam praeclarum litterarum*] *litterarum tam praeclarum*
20.13 *est id*] *id est*
331.21 *non linguam*] *linguam non* Ma: *lingua non* Fa.

These shared errors may derive from a common exemplar of FaMa, but, alternatively, they may be due to variants or corrections in ξ.[24] After collating more of the texts of BrFaMa, I found no further errors shared by FaMa but not by Br, but such negative evidence cannot eliminate the possibility of a common exemplar of FaMa.[25] Two shared errors of BrMa (309.4 *in*] om. and 312.2 *adferebamus*] *efferebamus*) do not help to clarify the situation: even if they were present in ξ and are not simply due to coincidence, they could have been corrected by the scribe of Fa. On balance, however, I think it more likely that BrFaMa derive from a single manuscript ξ, and that the scribes of FaMa failed to notice some corrections in their exemplar.

A fourth manuscript, Mc, shares some of the errors of BrFaMa, including:

311.22 *censorinus*] *censorinus et*
315.29 *quibuscum* Fa[c]] *quibuscumque* BrFaMaMc
317.19 *comprendens* Ma[c]Mc[c]] *comprehendes* BrFaMaMc.

Mc also shares errors with FaMa in places where I have not been able to check the reading of Br (218.9 *omnisque ille sermo*] *ille omnisque sermo* MaMc: *sermo ille omnisque* Fa and 224.10 *improbissimus*] *improbatissimus* FaMaMc), and occasionally shares errors with one of ξ's descendants (16.15 *fruges* Fa[vl]] *fructus* FaMc, 34.12 *constricta* MaMc] *constructa* Ma[c]Mc[c], 35.21 *inveniri* Fa[c]Mc] *invenire* FaMc[vl]). Since Mc shows no particular affiliation to any other extant manuscript, and since it shares some, but not all, of F's significant errors, Mc probably derives from ξ, but with contamination having resulted in the removal of various errors of Fξ. Some of F's errors absent from Mc are:

---

[24] Compare, for example, the descendants of B (pp. 266–267), which have copied some of B[ac]'s transpositions without noticing the corrections by B[c].
[25] FaMa are from Tuscany, whereas Br is Milanese, but this does not increase the probability of a shared exemplar of FaMa, since F was copied in Florence, and so too, we must assume, was ξ.

APPENDIX 3   309

131.11 *de plebe*] om.
156.11 *multo*] *nullo*
161.20 *quidem*] om.
219.20 *stultius*] *sulpicius.*

Mc cannot be the source of any of BrFaMa, since it has its own significant errors:

12.28 *litteris*] om.
19.6 *ut...id inquam*] om.
226.31 *cum ageret*] om.
315.28 *asia tota*] *tota asia*
324.8 *nostrum*] om.

4 The Descendants of Vq

Vq, a contaminated descendant of F, has three independent descendants, ElRoVu.[26]
The shared errors of VqElRoVu include:

1.6 *cogitatione* Vu^2] *cognitione* VqElRoVu
4.26 *tempore* Ro^{2}Vu^2] *turpe* VqElRoVu
8.3 *uterentur* Ro^{2}Vu^2] om. VqElRoVu
15.3 *etiam* Vu^2] om. VqElRoVu
16.12 *impendiis* Ro^{2}Vu^2] *impeditus* VqElRoVu
25.26 *confirmaverim*] *conferam veri* FO^{v}Vu^{2}λ: *confirmaverim veri* VqElRoVu
26.10 *haec est*] *est hec*
216.18 *e luntre* Vu^2] *eluntrix* VqElRoVu
222.19 *fructum* Vu^2] *fratrem* VqElRoVu^{ac}Vu^{3vl}
226.3 *deinde* Ro^2] om. VqElRoVu
269.16 *omnis*] *omnino*
276.30 *quod melius*] *melius quod*
276.31 *efficere*] *efficere denique*
280.15 *crebras quidem certe*] *crebrasque*
313.3 *me*] om.
316.5 *ad*] om.

Since ElRoVu share all the significant errors of Vq and add some of their own, Vq must be their source. The manuscripts' contents help to confirm the relationship. Ro and Vu, like Vq, include *Brut.*, *Orat.*, and *De or.* as the first three works, and, although these texts are frequently found together, the only extant manuscripts to include them in that order are VqRoVu and Ro's offspring Fm. The scribes of Ro and Vu did not copy all the contents of Vq, but Vu does, like Vq, add the mutilated version of

---

[26] Hunt (1998: 89–91) has already demonstrated that El's *Acad. post.* derives from Vq.

310   APPENDIX 3

Orat. after *De or.*[27] El's contents are also similar to those of Vq, since El and Vq are two of only three extant manuscripts to contain *Fat.* and *Acad. post.* as well as *Brut.*[28] In two places, some of ElRoVu share the readings of Vq^ac and Vq^c:

16.6 *ut* Vq^cElRo^cVu^c] *aut* VqRoVu
35.23 *subtiliter* Vq^cRoVu^c] *subtile* VqElRoVu.

In the first section of *Brut.*, Vq shares various errors with Fb, a descendant of F, including:

6.16 *forum* Ro²Vu²] *foro* FbVqElRoVu
7.22 *bene*² Vu²] om. FbVqElRoVu
13.13 *litterarum* Vu²] om. FbVqElRoVu
20.14 *mihi nuper*] *nuper mihi*
20.17 *se velle*] *velle se*
22.5 *ea ipsa* El] *ipsa ea* FbVqEl^cRoVu
23.12 *verae*] *veram.*

Vq's close relationship to Fb ends at *c.*§158; I can find no further shared errors of FbVq thereafter.[29] Even in §§1–158, however, Vq cannot derive exclusively from Fb, because Vq lacks some of Fb's errors, including the omissions of *in ea* at 26.8 and *praestaret... altera* at 155.4. Vq may share an exemplar with Fb in this part of *Brut.*, but I think, for two reasons, that Vq is likely to be a contaminated copy of Fb. Firstly, Fb is probably a direct copy of F. I cannot prove this, but its date and ownership point in this direction: Giacomo Curlo finished copying Fb on 1 October 1423, not long after the arrival of F's exemplar in Florence, and Curlo copied the manuscript for Cosimo de' Medici, with whom Niccolò Niccoli, the scribe and owner of F, was closely associated.

Secondly, though, and more importantly, the scribe of Vq undoubtedly had access to other manuscripts of *Brut.* In §§298–333, Vq shares various errors with *v*,[30] while in §§158–298 I have found no significant errors shared by Vq with either Fb or *v*. A further proof that Vq is contaminated is that it lacks some of the errors present in F and in F's descendants Fb*v*. In §§1–158 and §§298–333, the errors of F absent from Vq (e.g. 24.19 *quo* Vq] *quod* FFb*v*, 59.23 *est* Vq] *etiam* FFb*v*, and 155.5 *tuendum* Vq] *tuendi* FFb*v*) could arguably have been removed by conjecture, but in the middle portion of the text, Vq lacks errors of F which could have been eliminated only through contamination:

161.20 *quidem* Vq] om. FFb*v*
185.5 *horum* Vq] om. FFb*v*.

---

[27] Note also the similar subscriptions of Vq (*nil plus repperi sed tamen parum deficit in fine*) and Ro (*nil plus repperi scio firmiter quod parum deficit*).
[28] The other is Pe, an omnibus volume of Cicero's works.
[29] Errors of FbVq from §§23–158 include 118.21 *disserendo*] *disputando*, 158.4 *est*] *est et*, and 158.5 *perbrevis*] *brevis*.
[30] See above, p. 303.

APPENDIX 3   311

Vq has probably inherited readings not only from Fb and *v*, but also from a manuscript independent of F. The first part of the text derives primarily from Fb and the last part mainly from *v*, but throughout *Brut.* corrections have been imported into an ancestor of Vq from other sources. In the middle part of the text, it is unclear which manuscript was Vq's exemplar. Some of F's errors are present (e.g. 200.24 *quod*] *cum*, 201.3 *hos*] *quos*, and 214.29 *id*] *hic*), but there are no signs of a particular affinity to any other extant manuscript.

As can be seen from the above list of the errors of VqElRoVu, various errors of Vq have been corrected in RoVu. In both manuscripts, the corrections have been made by a later hand. The restoration of omitted words such as *uterentur, etiam,* and *deinde* proves that the corrections made by Ro[2] and Vu[2] are not simply the conjectures of a reader, but rather are the fruit of comparison with another manuscript. In one place, Vu[2] corrects a reading of Vq to an error of F (54.22 *qui* VqVu] *qui me* FVu[2]), which indicates that Vu[2]'s corrections come from F, or from another descendant of F. The source of Ro[2]'s corrections is uncertain: two readings imply that it may have been a manuscript independent of F (149.11 *se tamen sic*] *sed tamen sic se* FVqRo: *se tamen sic se* Ro[2vl] and 201.3 *hos* Ro[2]] *quos* FVqRo), but little more can be said.

Ro has produced one descendant, Fm. The errors shared by RoFm include:

20.12 *quod*] *quid*
228.1 *cedere*] *dicere*
265.8 *et*[1]] om.
272.18 *ita est*] *est ita*
274.22 *dissimulanterque*] *dissimulanteque* Ro: *dissimulateque* Fm
325.21 *floruerit*] *floruit*
325.22 *verissumas*] om.
327.4 *decebat*] *decedebat* Ro: *recedebat* Fm
332.7 *heres*] *here* Ro: *vere* Fm.

The scribe of Fm may have copied the text of Ro before the correcting work of Ro[2], because Fm generally follows the readings of Ro[ac].[31] Examples include:

8.3 *uterentur* Ro[2]] om. VqRoFm
10.13 *me* VqRo[2]] om. RoFm
31.12 *subtilitate* Ro[2]] *sublimitate* VqRoFm
221.12 *sed tamen orator* VqRo[2]] om. RoFm.

Fm adds many errors of its own, including:

14.18 *quidem*] om.
223.30 *equestri*] om.

---

[31] Fm has a few of Ro[2]'s readings, but may have arrived at them by conjecture (e.g. 16.6 *ut* Ro[2]Fm] *aut* Ro, 216.13 *tum* Ro[2]Fm] *tam* Ro).

312   APPENDIX 3

273.28 *contiones*] *actiones*
310.16 *summis*] om.
313.5 *fortasse*] om.

Vu also has one extant descendant, Fo. Fo shares all the significant errors of Vu, including:[32]

24.21 *idem*] *id*
227.11 *etiam*] om.
265.7 *verborum*] *verborum dignitas*
276.5 *natura...quod*] om.
278.23 *minimum*] *nimium*
309.5 *contracta*] *constricta*
310.12 *cum¹*] *enim*
318.10 *maturitatem quandam*] *quandam maturitatem*
323.5 *versati*] *conversati*.

Unlike Fm, Fo was definitely copied after the introduction of the later corrections in its exemplar, since Fo usually follows the reading of Vu²:

13.13 *litterarum* Vu²Fo] om. VqVu
19.2 *quod* Vu²Fo] *quidem* VqVu
216.19 *simile* Vu²Fo] *similiter* VqVu
222.19 *fructum* Vu²Fo] *fratrem* VqVu.

Fo's own errors include:

4.2 *est ita necesse*] *ita necesse est*
218.14 *quas idem caesar*] om.
222.22 *autem*] om.
269.12 *vemens*] om.
324.20 *etiam*] om.

Finally, the errors of El, which demonstrate that it is not the source of any of VqRoFmVuFo, include:

11.19 *atticus*] *amens*
219.20 *inquam brute*] *brute inquam*
219.27 *esset*] om.
274.7 *orator*] om.
318.9 *illud in me*] *in me illud*.

---

[32] See also 16.12 *impendiis* Vu²Foᶜ] *impeditus* VqVuFo.

APPENDIX 3   313

5 The Descendants of π

Thirty manuscripts derive either wholly or in part from a lost ancestor, π (see Figure 11), which appears to have been a descendant of F. Within this large family, there are two major sub-families, σ (BeEcEsFeFiGwHoLfObPcSgVdViVl) and υ (FcFgFhFpGeLa). Ff, copied by Poggio Bracciolini, is the source of a further five of the descendants of π (BnFjPdVe(Vj)).[33] Of the remaining manuscripts, CjCmMd(Vj) derive from a common ancestor (χ) and are loosely associated with Ff, and Pm is a contaminated descendant of π. Some of the errors shared by the descendants of π are:[34]

36.4 *inesset*] *esset*
43.29 *ita*] om.
59.1 *cuius*] *huius*
69.22 *non*] *num* CjFcFfFhFiMdPm: *nun* Fe
95.32 *gaiusque*] *gravisque*
100.21 *numquam sit habitus*] *sit habitus* FeFfFi: *sit habitus non* CjFcFf²FhMdPm
264.2 *aculeone*] *culeone* FcFeFfFhFiMdPm: *culcone* Cj, ut vid.

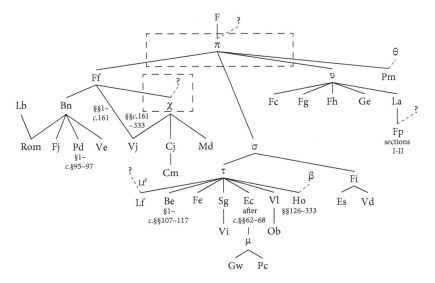

Figure 11: The Descendants of π

---

[33] Ff's relationship to F has been a controversial subject: Heerdegen (1884: xxiii–xxiv) argued for the derivation of Ff from F, but Malcovati (1960: 329–330) objected that Ff (to which she gave the siglum π) does not share all the errors of F. Malcovati does not propose an explanation for the errors shared by FFf.
[34] Unless otherwise stated, these errors are shared by all of CjFcFeFfFhFiMdPm, with FeFi taken as representatives of σ and FcFh of υ.

314   APPENDIX 3

The relationships between the descendants of π are complex and unclear. The most definite pattern is of errors shared by υχFf but not by σ, although even here examples are relatively few:

54.3 *dictatorem* FeFiPm] om. CjFcFfFhMd
64.14 *certos* Fᶜ] *certo* FFeFi: *certe* CjFcFfFhMdPm
167.29 *perargutus* FeFiMdPm] *peracutus* CjFcFfFh
195.23 *formulis* FeFiMd] *formulis qui* FhPm: *formulis quid* CjFf: *formulis quidem* Fc
306.11 *adtentius* FeFiPm] *attentius quod* CjFcFfFhMd.[35]

Sometimes Fi, a descendant of σ, shares errors with υ but not with Ff (e.g. 167.27 *esse* CjFeFfMdPm] om. FcFhFi, 244.5 *notam et aequalem* CjFeFfFiMdPm] *notorum et aequalium* FcFiᶜ: *et aequalium* Fh), and there are also occasional errors shared by CjMd with υ, but not with Ff, even though CjMd are usually more closely associated with Ff (e.g. 253.28 *ad* FeFfFi] *cum ad* CjFcFhMdPm). Various other contradictory pieces of evidence could be adduced in addition to these, but the essential problem is clear. The sub-families deriving from π cannot be put into a simple stemma. The reason for this is not hard to find: Ff shows clear evidence of scribal emendation throughout *Brut.*, and υ must have been similarly corrected, since its descendants share numerous conjectures. Contamination can be detected in Pm, as will be shown below, but it may also be present in other descendants of π. The twin forces of contamination and conjectural emendation have meant that, even with full collations of the text of *Brut.* in some of π's descendants, I have not been able to determine with confidence the relationships between σ, υ, Ff, χ, and Pm. They may be five independent copies of π, but the situation may be more complex.

The relationship between π and F is of greater importance. Malcovati sometimes cites Fc and Ff in her apparatus (with the sigla γ and π respectively), but she appears to have been uncertain how they relate to F.[36] The descendants of π share many of F's distinctive errors, including:[37]

149.11 *se tamen sic*] *sed tamen sic se*
200.24 *quod*] *cum*
201.3 *hos* Cj] *quos* FFcFeFfFhFiMdPm
211.31 *c.*] om.
212.12 *ti.*] om.
214.29 *id*] *hic* FCjFcFeFfFhMdPm: *hoc* Fi
256.29 *l.*] om.

---

[35] There are also emendations present in υχFf but not in σ, such as 123.3 *me numera inquit*] *enumera inquit* FλρFeFiPm: *enumera inquit me* CjFcFfMd: *et munera inquit me* Fh, and 203.17 *maxume* FeFi] *maxime omnium* CjFcFfFhMdPm.

[36] Malcovati (1960: 329–332).

[37] In this list, and in the two lists which follow, CjFcFeFfFhFiMdPm are again taken as representatives of the different families which derive from π.

APPENDIX 3   315

331.17 *amoris*] *moris*
333.16 *post*] *p. et* FCjFcFeFfFhMdPm: *p.* Fi.

Additionally, the descendants of π share some errors with F[c]:

214.2 *clauderet* F] *claudicaret* F[c]CjFcFeFfFhMdPm: *claudiret* Fi, ut vid.
292.26 *ipsum* F[ac], ut vid.] *ipsam* F[c]π
298.28 *facultate* FFePm[c]] *facultatem* F[c]CjFcFfFhMd[c]Pm: *voluntatem facultatem* Md.

However, π cannot have derived exclusively from F, because it lacked significant errors of F, including:

131.11 *de plebe*] om.
156.11 *multo*] *nullo*
161.20 *quidem*] om.
185.5 *horum*] om.
219.20 *stultius*] *sulpicius*
242.17 *homines*] *honores*.

A further piece of evidence that π was not simply a copy of F is that several of π's descendants, including FcFgFhFiLaPm[ac], have the reading *pavilo* for *paulo* at 129.23. This reading is shared with λO[v]G[c]T (G[ac] has *pavilio*), and it must therefore have been present in L.[38] Since F has *paulo*, and since the reading *pavilo* is hardly likely to have arisen in π or its descendants by coincidence, it must either have been inherited from L via F's exemplar, φ, or introduced by contamination. If the former is true, then π descended from F's exemplar independently of F. This might seem prima facie the more probable of the two explanations, because it would be odd for a scribe to choose the nonsensical *pavilo* over the perfectly normal *paulo*. However, this argument is not decisive, because scribes do sometimes make strange choices, and also because we cannot be sure that the scribe of π did make a conscious choice; he may have been copying from an exemplar with the variants *paulo* and *pavilo*, and may have chosen *pavilo* unthinkingly, perhaps without even noticing the other reading. Alternatively, he may have somehow come to know that *pavilo* was, or was likely to be, the reading of L.

Aside from this reading, the evidence tells in favour of π's having been a contaminated descendant of F. In all the other places where F has corrected an error of L, π's descendants share F's reading, not L's, and so 129.23 *paulo*] *pavilo* is an isolated instance. The nature of the errors which F does, and does not, share with π suggests contamination. Contamination generally results in the removal of some of the most obvious errors (omissions, nonsensical readings, etc.), but readings which are not so plainly corrupt will often be left intact. This is exactly the situation with F and π. Omissions and glaring errors like 219.20 *stultius*] *sulpicius* are absent from π,

---

[38] L's *pavilo* was presumably a corruption of an earlier *paullo*.

316   APPENDIX 3

whereas readings such as 149.11 *se tamen sic*] *sed tamen sic se*, 201.3 *hos*] *quos*, and 331.17 *amoris*] *moris* are present in π as well as in F. On the basis of this consideration, as well as the evidence of the errors shared by F$^c\pi$, I conclude that π was probably a contaminated descendant of F.[39] Even if one were to judge that π's descendants are independent of F, a reconstructed text of π would be of little use to an editor of *Brut*. Several of π's offspring are useful sources of conjectures, but it is highly unlikely that the labour of collating in full all the independent descendants of π would enable us to refine our knowledge of the text of L. The consistent citation of these manuscripts in an apparatus would be unhelpful to readers.

Before turning to the various sub-families deriving from π, I will consider briefly Pm, the only descendant of π which does not fall into one of these groups. Pm, copied in the second half of the fifteenth century, shares π's errors. However, Pm also shares some of the errors of θ, the source of BoFlLu, including, in addition to several minor errors:

> 13.10   *inquam*] *inquit*
> 24.19   *victoria* Fl^{vl}] *gloria* BoFlLuPm
> 265.4   *dixisses* Fl^c] *non dixisses* BoFlLuPm
> 275.27 *esset* Fl^c] *etiam* BoFlLuPm
> 316.7   *praestantem*] *praestantissimum.*

Hence, Pm apparently derives from π, but with a little contamination from θ, or one of its descendants. Examples of Pm's own errors are:

> 218.15 *caesar*] *sermo*
> 268.3   *naturae*] om.
> 277.8   *cum*] *quod*
> 314.14 *potius periculum mihi*] *periculum mihi potius*
> 315.1   *in illis numerari*] *numerari in illis.*

5.1 The Descendants of σ

The first sub-family, deriving from π via a lost intermediary σ, is made up of fourteen manuscripts (BeEcEsFeFiGwHoLfObPcSgVdViVl). Of these, five (FeFiLfSgVl) derive from σ independently of other extant manuscripts throughout *Brut*. Be

---

[39] Unfortunately, our ignorance of what happened to F's exemplar after Niccoli completed his copy means that the historical evidence cannot add much force to the textual argument for the derivation of π from F. (The exemplar may well have been owned by Giovanni Corvini, who came to Florence in April 1423 as one of the ambassadors of Filippo Maria Visconti, and he may have taken it with him: Corvini travelled on to Rome, where he acted as an ambassador to the pope in May–June 1423 (Ricciardi in *Dizionario biografico degli italiani*, xxix.829).) The Florentine origin of many of π's descendants is certainly coherent with π's having been copied from F, a MS whose owner, Niccolò Niccoli, is known to have lent his books out frequently for use as exemplars in Florence (Vespasiano, *Le Vite*, p. 231). On F's exemplar, see further pp. 57–58.

APPENDIX 3   317

derives independently from σ in section I of my collations, and EcHo are independent descendants of σ in sections II–IV. The six remaining manuscripts (EsGwObPcVdVi) are *codices descripti* of other members of the family. The errors shared by the independent descendants of σ include:

25.4   *earum*] *earum rerum* BeFeFiLfSgVl
27.15   *scripta* Lf^c] om. BeFeFiLfSgVl
222.22   *patremque*] *patriumque* FeFiHoSgVl: *primumque* EcLf
224.5   *facta mentio*] *mentio facta* EcFeFiHoLfSgVl
272.12   *et*[1]] om. EcFeFiHoLfSgVl
273.1   *contentione*] *contione* EcFeFiLfSgVl: *contemptione* Ho
273.2   *quae*] *quam* EcFeFiHoLfSgVl
279.2   *quocumque* Ho] *quaecumque* EcFeFiLfSgVl
326.13   *venustae dulcesque sententiae*] om. EcFeFiHoLfSgVl
333.10   *laudabilis*] *laudibus* EcFeFiHoLfSgVl.

Fi has produced two extant copies, Es and Vd.[40] FiEsVd share many errors, including:[41]

12.28   *litteris*] *litteris et*
23.9   *exercitatioque*] *excusatioque*
26.11   *intueor*] *intuerer*
32.1   *is*] om.
266.16   *tuam*] *etiam*
268.2   *totum*] *tantum*
269.18   *videare*] *viderere*
274.16   *structum…insolens*] om.
309.7   *brute*] om.
311.25   *potuissemus*] *potuimus*
314.15   *dicendi*] om.

Since EsVd include all of Fi's significant errors, they must derive from it. The presence of Fi^c's corrections and errors in EsVd provides further proof of the derivation:

1.7   *cooptatum* FiEsVd] *coaptatum* Fi^cVd^c
10.14   *consederit* Vd] *consederat* Fi: *consideret* Fi^cEs
31.18   *ab* Fi^cEs^cVd^c] *ad* FiEsVd
273.26   *quam eius* FiEsVd] *cuius* Fi^cVd^c
278.22   *nulla perturbatio animi* Fi^cVd^c] om. FiEsVd.

---

[40] M. D. Reeve (in Reynolds (1983: 102 n. 12)) has already observed that Vd's *De optimo genere oratorum* derives from Fi. The production of offspring is characteristic of the MSS copied by the 'Puccini' scribe (Oakley (2016: 346)).

[41] Additionally, FiEs have the subscription *parum deest* at the end of *Brut.*, while Vd has *deest parum*. No other extant MS uses this wording to indicate the incomplete state of the text. Note also the common Florentine origin and identical contents of FiVd.

318 APPENDIX 3

Es and Vd both have their own significant errors, and hence they must have derived from Fi independently of one another.[42]

Es: 25.4 *ipsa*] om.
227.12 *quaedam*] om.
278.24 *nostros animos*] *animos nostros*
280.15 *certe*] om.
324.16 *causas*] *omnes.*

Vd: 217.21 *curioque multa dixisset*] om.
219.27 *ne*] om.
317.21 *iam*] om.
319.16 *veni*] om.
327.22 *certe*] om.

All the descendants of σ except FiEsVd derive from a common exemplar, τ. The independent descendants of τ, FeLfSgVl, together with Be (section I) and EcHo (sections II–IV), share the following errors:

3.18 *memoriae*] om.
20.15 *fuissent*] om.
266.14 *eorum*] om.
272.8 *umquam*] om.
274.19 *non*] *nunc* EcFeLfSgVl: *nec* Ho
277.8 *in* Ho] om. EcFeLfSgVl
316.5 *ad* Ho] om. EcFeLfSgVl.

There are a few errors shared by some of BeEcFeHoLfSgVl, but they do not form a clear pattern, and should probably be attributed to coincidence or to variants and corrections in τ:

10.11 *m. ad me brutus* Fe] *m. brutus ad me* BeLfSgVl
323.6 *primo leviter*] *primo leniter* EcFeHo: *leniter primo* LfSgVl^c: *leniter primum* Vl
332.28 *tuis* EcHoVl] om. FeLfSg.

Be derives from τ from the beginning of *Brut.* to c.§§107–117, from which point it derives from Vm.[43] Its singular errors from the opening portion of text include:

3.19 *poetarum*] om.
12.31 *illam*] om.

---

[42] I have found one non-trivial error absent from Fi but shared by EsVd (215.6 *excellebat autem*] *autem excellebat*). This shared error is probably due to coincidence: it would have been tempting to take *Antonius* with *excellebat...actione*, rather than with *reperiebat...comprehendebat*, and this mistake would lead naturally to the transposition of *excellebat* and *autem*.

[43] See above, pp. 292–295.

APPENDIX 3   319

31.18 *quod*] om.
32.24 *magister*] om.

Fe derives from τ throughout *Brut*. Its errors include:

11.19 *ad te*] om.
13.16 *quasi*] om.
14.20 *ipsum*] om.
271.26 *mortui sunt*] *sunt mortui*
272.6 *ne*] om.

Likewise, Lf derives from τ throughout the text.[44] Its errors include:

30.8 *hippias*] *lippius*
222.28 *et in praesidiis*] om.
272.10 *aut a cogitando*] om.
309.10 *tamen*] om.
325.2 *frequentatum*] om.

Ec, an ancestor of μ and its offspring GwPc, initially derives from κ,[45] but at some point between §§62 and 68, a change of exemplar took place and for the rest of the text Ec derives from τ. Two of τ's errors from soon after the change of exemplar are:

70.3 *sed*] om. BeEcFeGwLfPcSgVl
71.21 *latina*] om. BeEcFeGwLfPcSgVl.

The next descendant of τ, Sg, has one offspring, Vi. That Vi derives from Sg is clear from the following readings:

2.17 *amiseram* SgVi] *ammissem* Sg^vl: *amissem* Vi^vl
16.9 *in*] om. SgVi
18.23 *ego*] *vero* Sg: *ego vero* Sg^cVi
34.14 *spiritu*] *in spiritu* SgVi
34.15 *terminatur* Sg^c] *termnatur* Sg: *termiatur* Vi (Sg^c's correction misunderstood)
221.17 *pugnans*] *pugnatis* SgVi
224.7 *specie*] *in specie* SgVi
227.12 *erat*] om. SgVi
315.1 *recte potest* Sg^c] *potest recte* SgVi
320.26 *putabat*] *putat* SgVi

[44] A few corrections have been introduced into Lf by a later hand, identified by Ceccherini (2016: 191) as that of Sozomeno da Pistoia; some of these (e.g. 27.15 *scripta* Lf^2] om. σLf) should probably be attributed to contamination, rather than to scribal emendation.
[45] See above, pp. 299, 301–302, where I also provide evidence of the derivation of GwPc from Ec.

320 APPENDIX 3

326.15 *et erat*] *eerat* Sg: *erat* Vi
333.19 *oportunorum*] *oportunorum et omni* SgVi^c: *oportumorum et omni* Vi.[46]

Proof that Vi derives from Sg can be found in Vi's omission of *multa...quae* at 15.25 (with *cum* then deleted by Vi^c). In Sg, *est...quidem*, which immediately precedes *multa*, was initially omitted, before being added at the bottom of the page. The scribe of Vi, however, has misunderstood this correction, mistakenly thinking that *est...quidem* was intended to replace the rest of the text up to the end of the page in Sg, that is, *multa...quae cum*, and has therefore excised this section of text. Additionally, at 315.1 Sg's *numerari*, split across two lines as *nu/merari*, is probably responsible for Vi's corruption *mirari*.

Vi's significant errors include:

22.32 *crebro*] om.
28.22 *annis*] om.
224.13 *licere*] om.
279.1 *laudibus*] om.
326.10 *adulescens*] om.

Vl has also produced one copy, Ob. With the exception of a few trivial errors, Ob shares all the corruptions of Vl, including:

26.12 *occurrunt*] *incurrunt*
33.9 *casuque*] *causa quae*
221.17 *lateribus*] *laboribus*
226.31 *ageret*] *agerit* Vl: *egerit* Ob
271.1 *cluentio*] *cluentino*
317.19 *verbis*] om.
319.15 *patronis* Vl^c] *patronisque* VlOb
319.18 *omnis*] om.
320.27 *tantum*] *tantum tantum*
331.13 *in te*] *in te in te*
332.26 *tamen*] *autem.*

Ob adds various errors of its own. Some of these are:

14.22 *mihi*] om.
16.10 *aliquid*] om.
266.21 *omittamus*] *expectamus*
268.9 *terroris oratio*] *terrore*
326.17 *et stomachantem*] om.

---

[46] Sg's addition of *et omni* at the end of *Brut.* was of sufficient interest to Malcovati for her to include it in her apparatus, but the words do not help with the sense and, since there is no other indication that Sg has independent authority in the reconstruction of the archetype, this reading can safely be ignored (cf. Malcovati (1960: 333–334)).

APPENDIX 3   321

Ho is only a partial descendant of τ. I have already shown that Ho is a contaminated descendant of β in §§1–126.[47] The change of scribe at 126.25 *manus* coincides with a change of exemplar. Before §126, Ho shows no particular affinity to F, π, σ, or τ, but after this point Ho contains various errors of F (e.g. 149.11 *se tamen sic*] *sed tamen sic se*, 169.8 *et*] om., 200.24 *quod*] *cum*), together with most of those of σ and τ.[48] However, the absence of a few errors of $\sigma\tau$ suggests the possibility of contamination, and this is confirmed by the significant errors shared by Ho with $\rho\beta$, including:

164.26 *in*²] om. ρHo
167.22 *temporis*] *temporibus* βHo
255.15 *non*] *non solum* βHo
261.20 *emendat*] *emendabat* ρHo.

In §§126–333, then, Ho derives predominantly from τ, but contamination has resulted in the removal of a few of τ's errors and the addition of a few errors of $\rho\beta$. Ho's singular errors prove that it is not the source of any other manuscript in this part of the text:

217.1 *cottae*] om.
266.13 *torquati et triari*] *triarii et torquati*
280.11 *te inquit brutus*] om.
313.5 *fortasse*] om.
313.8 *a vitae periculo*] om.

5.2 The Descendants of v

v is the source of another family deriving from π. v has five independent descendants, FcFgFhGeLa. These manuscripts share the following errors:

15.1 *grato tamen*] *tamen grato*
33.9 *casuque*] *casu quam* FcFgGeLa: *casu* Fh
47.2 *conscripsisset*] *scripsisset*
54.7 *incitatam*] *concitatam*
128.14 *quaestio*] *quaestione*
128.15 *c.*] *p.*
146.23 *edisserendi*] *et disserendi* FcFgGeLa: *disserendi* Fh
268.3 *naturae*] *naturae ei*
269.11 *vero*] *verum.*

---

[47] See above, pp. 44–45.
[48] A further proof of the change of exemplar is that the chapter divisions Ho has inherited from ρ cease after 122.19 *nunc reliquorum.*

322 APPENDIX 3

FcFgFhGeLa derive independently from v, since they all have their own errors.

Fc: 23.12 *quare*] *qua*
56.24 *omnino*] *animo*
265.7 *et*] om.
280.14 *verisimile*] *verisimiliter*
332.8 *maioris*] om.

Fg: 7.27 *timore*] *tremore*
19.10 *cum*] *ut*
269.18 *videare*] om.
279.7 *etiam*] om.
279.10 *eloquentiae laudem*] *laudem eloquentiae.*

Fh: 2.16 *mearum*] om.
32.22 *domus... officina*] om.
221.15 *expeditus... verbis*] om.
275.24 *insignibus*] om.
332.8 *similes*] om.

Ge: 14.22 *mihi quidem*] *quidem mihi*
27.9 *annis*] om.
217.24 *gratiam*] *gratias*
223.31 *dissedisset*] *discessisset*
331.14 *quasi*] om.

La: 17.20 *attico*] om.
32.21 *ante*] om.
216.13 *dissipatus*] *cogitatus*
267.25 *bibulus*] om.
274.12 *aeque*] om.

A sixth manuscript, Fp, is related to this family. It has all the errors of v in the list above except the final two. Additionally, Fp shares errors with La, including:

3.23 *adiutus*] *auditus*
4.1 *tam*] om.
6.15 *sustineret*] *sustinere* La: *sostinere* Fp
6.16 *quod*] om.
16.7 *exustusque*] *exutusque*
26.7 *sit*] om.
26.14 *mandari*] om.
223.3 *in*[2]] om.
223.3 *perturbem*] *perturbemus*
224.5 *generis*] om.
224.7 *specie*] *spede* La: *pede* Fp
224.14 *plebem*] *plebeus.*

APPENDIX 3   323

Fp cannot derive exclusively from La, since it does not share La's significant errors listed above. Neither can Fp be the source of La, because Fp was copied 23 years later, and also because Fp has various errors of its own, including:

15.29 *salutaris*] om.
24.19 *neminem video*] *video neminem*
227.12 *erat*] om.
269.18 *m. servilium*] om.
310.14 *sed...latine*] om.

Significantly, Fp lacks all the non-trivial errors of π, υ, and La in sections III–IV of my collations. Additionally, in sections III–IV Fp contains various errors of F not present in FcFgFhGeLa, including:

271.5 *argumenta*] *argumento*
274.12 *aeque*] *eaeque*
279.5 *redeamus*] *respondeamus*
315.1 *atticorum* FcFcFgFhGeLa] *attiquorum* F: *apti quorum* Fp
316.12 *diffluentis*] *diffluenti*.

These data indicate that the exemplar of Fp was changed between sections II and III, and that Fp derives from F independently of π after the change of exemplar. Since Fp shares all the significant errors of F in the section copied from this second exemplar, while showing no particular affinity to any of F's descendants, this part of Fp's *Brut.* derives from F independently of any extant manuscript.

In the first part of *Brut.*, however, Fp seems to be a slightly contaminated copy of La. Fp lacks a few of La's errors: some could have been removed by conjecture (e.g. 2.14 *prudentiae* Fp] *prudentis* La), but two more significant errors (17.20 *attico* Fp] om. La, 32.21 *ante* Fp] om. La) demonstrate that Fp cannot derive exclusively from La. One could therefore postulate a common exemplar of FpLa, but there are two reasons why Fp is more likely to be a contaminated descendant of La. Firstly, in addition to a few of La's errors, Fp lacks some errors present in the other descendants of υ and in some or all of the other manuscripts which derive from π (59.1 *cuius*] *huius*, 64.14 *certos*] *certe*, 72.4 *tarento*] *tarentum*, 78.19 *in*] om., 95.32 *gaiusque*] *gravisque* π: *c.* Fp, 101.25 *cooptatus*] *coactus*).

Secondly, the scribe of La, Leonardo di Giovanni Tolosani da Colle, tells us in the subscription to *Orat.* that he was copying from a highly corrected text. The subscription reads: *M. T. C. ORATOR EXPLICIT EX EMENDATISSIMO CODICE LEONARDI ARRETINI* (i.e. Leonardo Bruni) *EXEMPLATUS. M.CCCC.LVI.* It is possible that Leonardo di Giovanni Tolosani only copied *Orat.* from Bruni's codex, but La's subscription would fit well with the following evidence for scribal emendation in υ's *Brut.*:[49]

---

[49] FcFgFhFpGeLa all contain both *Orat.* and *Brut.*, and we can assume that υ did too.

324 APPENDIX 3

253.1 *cogitata praeclare eloqui ut*] *cogitata praeclare eloqui* BFλρFp: *ut cogitata praeclare eloqui* FcFgFhGeLa
262.8 *volent*] *volunt* FλρFp: *velint* FcFgFhGe: *vellent* La
273.26 *quam eius* BFλρFp] *cuius* FcFgFhGeLa
277.11 *deferre* FcFgGeLa] *differre* BFλρFhFp
322.22 *traducere* FcFgFhGeLa] *traduceret* BFλρFp
325.26 *quam* FcFgFhGeLa] *numquam* BFλρFp
331.16 *me* BFcFgFhGeLa] om. FλρFp.[50]

By contrast, I have found only one error of L corrected in FpLa but preserved by FcFgFhGe: 7.26 *aut errore* Fp^cLa^c] *aut terrore* FFpLaλρ. Likewise, there are no errors of F absent from FpLa and yet present in the other descendants of *v*. If Bruni's manuscript had been a descendant of *v* and the shared ancestor of FpLa, then, in keeping with Leonardo di Giovanni Tolosani's description of Bruni's codex as *emendatissimus*, there ought to have been various emendations present in FpLa, but not in *v*. Since there is only one such example, it is much more likely that Bruni's manuscript was *v* itself, and that La was copied directly from *v*.[51]

Circumstantial evidence also points to the conclusion that La is a direct copy of *v*. La's scribe, Leonardo di Giovanni Tolosani, was involved in the composition of two other descendants of *v*, writing the text of Fc and the headers in Fh. The dating of the production of FcFhLa to a 10-year period between 1450 and 1460 adds to the likelihood that all were copied from the same exemplar. If La was indeed a direct copy of *v*, then a shared exemplar of FpLa cannot provide the explanation for their shared errors. Rather, Fp is probably a descendant of La contaminated with readings from some other manuscript, perhaps the one used as Fp's exemplar in the second half of the text.

5.3 The Descendants of Ff

Bn is the only manuscript which derives from Poggio's copy, Ff,[52] independently of other manuscripts throughout *Brut*. Bn was copied in Rome in 1429, when Poggio was resident in the city, and contains the same set of works as Ff (albeit in a different order). The proof of the derivation, however, is that Bn shares all the significant errors of Ff, including:

10.13 *me*] om.
14.22 *mihi quidem*] *quidem mihi*
80.7 *dicendo*] om.
92.10 *se*] om.

---

[50] Malcovati cites various readings of Fc in her apparatus (with the siglum γ), and many of these emendations are also present in the other descendants of *v*.

[51] For another family of MSS deriving from a codex owned by Leonardo Bruni, see Reeve (2016: 51–70).

[52] See below for discussion of the corrections introduced into Na from Ff.

APPENDIX 3   325

217.23 *artuum*] om.
221.16 *oratorem*] *auctorem*
269.17 *aliquando sunt*] *sunt aliquando*
324.20 *nostris*] om.
328.21 *quaeso*] *inquit* Ff: om. Ff*Bn.[53]

Bn is in turn the source of a further three manuscripts. FjVe derive from Bn throughout the text, while Pd derives from Bn from the start of *Brut.* up to *c.*§§95–97.[54] Fj(Pd)Ve share all the significant errors of Bn, including:

7.19 *angor*] om. BnFjPdVe
9.8 *nostris*] om. BnFjPdVe
20.17 *hic audire se velle*] *se velle audire* BnFjPdVe
34.14 *quid inane sit*] *sit quod inane* BnFjPdVe
215.5 *ea*] om. BnFjVe
215.6 *quaedam ex his*] *ex his quaedam* BnFjVe
270.22 *illud*] om. BnFjVe
273.2 *non*] om. BnFjVe
315.31 *disertissimus*] *peritissimus* BnFjVe
320.22 *videret*] om. BnFjVe
322.16 *quando*] om. BnFjVe
323.4 *ille*] om. BnFjVe
325.25 *dictionis*] *actionis* BnFjVe
330.30 *clarissimi*] *clarissimi viri* BnFjVe.

In two places, the corrections in Bn serve as a further proof that some of FjPdVe derive from it:[55]

3.18 *poetas nobilis*] *poetis nobilis* BnPdVe: *poetam nobilem* Bn^cVe^c: *poetam nobilis* Fj
24.18 *se non aut* Bn^cVe] *se aut non* Bn: *aut se non* Pd: *se non* Fj. (Pd's reading is due to a misunderstanding of Bn's correction; the same may be true of Fj's error.)

FjPdVe have no shared errors which are absent from Bn. Since all three manuscripts have errors of their own, they must derive from Bn independently of each other.

Fj: 18.2 *paulo te*] *te paulo*
29.1 *ipse*] *non*

---

[53] See also 82.3 *laeli* Ff^c] *l.* FfBn, where Bn has an error which may have originated in Ff.
[54] Pd's change of exemplar probably occurred between 95.32 *gaiusque*] *gravisque* πFfBnPd and 97.24 *nimis* Pd] *minus* FfBnPd; after this point, Pd's scribe copied from another descendant of F, or perhaps from F itself.
[55] The shared errors of Bn^acFjPdVe (25.23 *igitur eloquentiam* Bn^cPdVe] *eloquentiam igitur* BnFj, 32.25 *aluit* Bn^c] *aliud* BnFjPdVe, 217.2 *ille contra* Bn^cVe] *contra ille* BnFj, 273.23 *plebis fuit* Bn^cVe] *fuit plebis* BnFj, 313.10 *eram* Bn^c] *etiam* BnFjVe) may well have originated in Bn.

326   APPENDIX 3

222.19 *tamen*] om.
228.24 *latinis litteris*] om.
327.4 *nec decebat idem*] om.

Ve: 26.13 *primum...extulit*] om.
29.1 *maxume*] *magis*
32.4 *quendam...numerum*] om.
215.7 *quaedam*] om.
329.22 *inquam*] om.

Pd (§§1–95): 11.25 *inquit*] om.
12.1 *proelio populus se romanus*] *populus se romanus proelio*
16.10 *patuit*] om.
26.12 *attice*] om.
28.22 *potest perspici*] *perspici potest.*

Vj seems to be a partial descendant of Ff. In the first half of the text, Vj shares all the significant errors of Ff that I have found in my collations, but after *c*.§161, only a few.[56]

5.4 The Descendants of χ

Three further descendants of π are CjCmMd. Some uncertainties remain about how these manuscripts relate to Ff and π, but it is clear that Cm derives from Cj. These two manuscripts, both now located in Cambridge, have very similar contents, and also share many errors, including:

2.15 *putabant...mearum*] om.
21.25 *causam*] om.
23.8 *fructus*] *fructus quam*
24.15 *dicis*] om.
216.14 *meminisse*] *meminisci* Cj: *meministi* Cm
228.19 *duas*] om.
269.16 *diu*] om.
272.8 *illi umquam*] *umquam illi*
278.25 *loco...pro*] om.
312.29 *sex.*] om.
313.3 *non*] om.
322.14 *ad*] *ad id.*

The only non-trivial error present in Cj but not in Cm is 35.20 *perfectum*] *prope perfectum*, but *prope* could have been omitted by the scribe of Cm, either

---

[56] In the second half of the text, Vj instead seems to be more closely related to CjCmMd, a group of MSS discussed below.

APPENDIX 3   327

accidentally or as a deliberate correction. There is no doubt that Cm derives from Cj, since Cm omits a line of Cj's text (11.24 *recreatus... inquit*).[57] Cm adds many errors of its own, including:

> 22.4 *aetas*] om.
> 23.9 *delectat... bene*] om.
> 218.10 *actum... esset*] om.
> 271.4 *quaedam... autem*] om.
> 325.1 *laudabiles... genere*] om.

Cj(Cm) share various significant errors with Md, and, in the second half of the text, also with Vj:

> 2.11 *civium bonorumque* Vj] *civiumque bonorum* CjCmMd
> 16.15 *fruges* Vj] *fructus* CjCmMd
> 25.25 *nobis est* Vj] *est nobis* CjMd: *nobis* Cm
> 35.20 *perfectum* CmVj] *prope perfectum* CjMd
> 216.16 *et*] om. CjCmMdVj
> 221.16 *quem*] om. CjCmMdVj
> 222.27 *m.*[2]] *m.que* CjCmMdVj
> 267.26 *appius*] *et ap.* CjCmMdVj
> 272.10 *processus*] *progressus* CjCmMdVj[c]: *progressos* Vj
> 317.19 *solute et facile sententiam*] *facile et solute sententiam* MdVj: *facile et sententiam solute* CjCm
> 331.24 *eloquentiae laude*] *laude eloquentiae* CjCmMdVj
> 332.8 *similes maioris partis oratorum*] *maioris partis oratorum similes* CjCmMdVj.

Because of these shared errors, and also because the manuscripts all add errors of their own, Cj(Cm)Md and the second half of Vj must derive from a common ancestor, χ. Some of Cj's errors have been listed above. Md's errors, which prove that neither Cj nor Vj derives from it, include:

> 47.2 *conscripsisset*] *scripsisset*
> 218.15 *administravisset*] *ministravisset*
> 318.13 *meam perspicias*] *perspicias meam*
> 330.8 *forti animo*] *animo forti*.

Vj's errors include:

> 10.10 *cum*] om.
> 20.14 *mihi nuper*] *nuper mihi*
> 221.10 *igitur*] *genere*

---

[57] See also 221.15 *expeditus... abiectus* Cj] om. Cm and 279.5 *sit... restat* Cj] om. Cm; in both cases Cm's scribe, while copying a line of Cj's text, has jumped to the line below.

328 APPENDIX 3

271.26 *spoletinum…cornelium*] om.
309.6 *putanda…eloquentiam*] om.

Among the descendants of π, χ seems to have been especially close to Ff. The contents of CjCm suggest an affinity to Ff, since the combination of the first four works in CjCm (*De or., Brut., Orat., Paradoxa*) is shared only with Pe, a large manuscript containing many of Cicero's works, and with Ff and its descendants. More significantly, χ's descendants share some of the errors of Ff and Ff^c:

4.5 *et beatissumo viro* Md] *viro et beatissimo* FfCj
217.3 *cantionibus* Ff] *cantationibus* Ff^{c}CjMdVj
222.18 *multum* Ff^{c}MdVj] *multus* FfCj
222.27 *m. catonem patrem* Ff^c] *m. catonem q. patrem* Ff: *m.que catonem patrem* MdVj: *m.que catonem q. patrem* Cj
277.13 *me*] *memini me* FfCjMdVj.

Taken together, these readings suggest that Ff had some link to χ, and perhaps especially to Cj. χ may, for example, have been a contaminated copy of Ff, or a copy of π corrected from Ff. However, the evidence is rather thin, and I suspend judgement as to the exact relationship between χ and Ff. Nevertheless, Sandys' classification of the text of *Orat.* in CjCm as 'connected' (1885: lxxxvii) with Poggio's manuscript does seem to hold for *Brut.* as well.

6 Other Descendants of F

Three extant manuscripts, FdFnNa, derive from F but cannot be grouped into any of the above families. A fourth manuscript, Fb, has been discussed briefly as the probable source of Vq and its descendants in *Brut.* 1–158;[58] throughout the text Fb derives from F independently of other manuscripts. A fifth, Pd, derives from Bn from the beginning of *Brut.* up to *c.*§§95–97, but is another independent descendant of F thereafter. FbFdFnNa(Pd) share every significant error of F.[59] The following readings strengthen the case for the derivation of FbFdFnNaPd from F:

15.3 *cumulatiore* F^{c}Na^c] *cumulatiores ipsos* F: *cumulatiores* FnNa
16.8 *exaruit* F^{c}Na^c] *exauruit* F, Na (ut vid.)
223.1 *elegantis* Na] *eligentis* FFn: *eligantis* F^{c}FbNa^c
268.9 *quaereres* F^{c}Na^c] *quaereres quaereres* FFbNa
277.10 *chirographa* F^c] *chirographum* FFn^c: *chirographam* Fn

---

[58] See p. 310.
[59] The only possible exception is 156.11 *multo* Fd] *nullo* F; but here F's error produces nonsense, and Fd has probably arrived at the truth by conjecture.

APPENDIX 3   329

320.30 *cognoscere*] *magnum scelus* BFλρFbNa: *cognoscere magnum scelus*
FᶜFdFnPd
326.9 *senibus* FᶜNaᶜ] *sensibus* FNa.

Fn's omission of a complete line of F's text (333.12 *cato...fuerunt*] *erunt* Fn) is decisive proof that Fn derives from F. Not as cogent, but still significant, is Fb's omission of *et...effeceras* at 332.28, since *ut*, the next word after *effeceras*, is almost directly beneath *et* in F. However, there can be little doubt that F is the source of all five manuscripts, since they contain all its significant errors and add some of their own.

Fb: 26.8 *in ea*] om.
216.11 *magis oratorem commendari*] *oratorem magis commendari*
219.18 *quidem*] om.
318.9 *illud in me*] *in me illud*
332.28 *et... effeceras*] om.

Fd: 29.2 *compressione*] *compositione*
224.10 *improbissimus*] om.
227.14 *nemo*] om.
278.25 *isto loco vix*] *vix isto loco*
329.29 *morte*] om.

Fn: 12.31 *marcelli*] om.
225.20 *in gestu*] om.
311.19 *scaevolae carbonis antisti*] om.
317.2 *et canorum*] om.
333.12 *cato...fuerunt*] *erunt*.

Na: 24.18 *non aut*] *aut non*
271.3 *ut*] om.
316.9 *id*] om.
324.8 *perspecta*] *perfecta*
333.19 *concursatio*] om.

Pd (§§95–333): 220.6 *et quasi alere*] om.
224.6 *saturninus*] om.
267.24 *etiam ex iis*] *ex his etiam*
314.16 *vocis*] om.
332.26 *careas... te*] om.

The corrections in FdFnNa merit a brief discussion. In Fn, a later hand has made a few emendations to the text, but all are apparently conjectures (e.g. 220.2 *bonitatem*] *vanitatem* FFn: *volubilitatem* Fn², 274.18 *rerum*] *verum* Fn: *solum* Fn²). The corrections in Fd and Na, however, suggest contamination. The initial scribe of Fd has added a few corrections in the margin, of which the most significant is 131.11 *de plebe* Fd¹] om. FFd. This correction, and perhaps some others, have been introduced after comparison of Fd with another manuscript. In Na, the source of the

330 APPENDIX 3

contamination can be identified more exactly. A later hand in Na has made extensive corrections, removing most of Na's errors, as well as some of F's. Many, and perhaps all, of Na²'s corrections have come from Ff, because Na² has added various errors and conjectures present in Ff and its descendants. These include:

6.15 *aut*¹ FfNa²] *et* FλρNa
26.11 *quam* Na] *qua* FfNa²
33.9 *quam* FfNa²] om. FλρNa
221.16 *oratorem* Na] *auctorem* FfNa²
228.20 *maiorem* FfᶜNa²] *maioris* BFλρFfNa
274.14 *adhaeresceret* Na] *ardesceret* FfNa²
277.13 *me* Na] *memini me* FfNa²
280.14 *verisimile* Na] *verisimiliter* FfNa².

APPENDIX 4

Alphabetical List of Sigla

B = Vatican City, BAV, Ott. lat. 1592
C = Cremona, Archivio di Stato, Fragm. Com. 81 (ex 295)
D = Dresden, Sächsische Landesbibliothek—Staats- und
    Universitätsbibliothek, Dc. 108
E = San Lorenzo de El Escorial, Real Biblioteca del Monasterio, T. III. 23
F = Florence, Biblioteca Nazionale Centrale, Conv. Soppr. J. I. 14
G = Naples, Biblioteca Nazionale, IV A 44
J = Vatican City, BAV, Vat. lat. 1709
L = *Codex Laudensis*
M = Montpellier, Bibliothèque Interuniversitaire, Section Médecine, H 214
O = Vatican City, BAV, Ott. lat. 2057
Q = Paris, BnF, lat. 7705
S = Vienna, Österreichische Nationalbibliothek, Cod. 3090
T = Milan, Biblioteca Ambrosiana, C 75 sup.
U = Ithaca, NY, Cornell University Library, 4600 Bd. Ms. 123 +
W = Wolfenbüttel, Herzog August Bibliothek, 12. 13. Aug. 4°
X = Milan, Biblioteca Ambrosiana, H 22 inf.
Y = New Haven, Yale University, Beinecke Rare Book and Manuscript Library,
    Marston 6
Bc = Barcelona, Biblioteca de Reserva de la Universitat de Barcelona, 12
Be = Berlin, Staatsbibliothek zu Berlin, Hamilton 162
Bl = Bologna, Biblioteca comunale dell'Archiginnasio, A. 85
Bn = Berlin, Staatsbibliothek zu Berlin, Hamilton 164
Bo = Bologna, Archivio Storico della Provincia di Cristo Re dei Frati Minori
    dell'Emilia Romagna, 11
Br = Brescia, Biblioteca Queriniana, E. II. 10
Cj = Cambridge, St John's College Library, I.12
Cm = Cambridge, Cambridge University Library, Mm.2.4
Ec = San Lorenzo de El Escorial, Real Biblioteca del Monasterio, V. III. 17
El = San Lorenzo de El Escorial, Real Biblioteca del Monasterio de San Lorenzo de
    El Escorial, T. III. 18
Es = San Lorenzo de El Escorial, Real Biblioteca del Monasterio, V. III. 8
Fa = Florence, BML, Plut. 50.4
Fb = Florence, BML, Plut. 50.18
Fc = Florence, BML, Plut. 50.19
Fd = Florence, BML, Plut. 50.22
Fe = Florence, BML, Plut. 50.25
Ff = Florence, BML, Plut. 50.31
Fg = Florence, BML, Plut. 50.36

332 APPENDIX 4

Fh = Florence, BML, Plut. 50.38
Fi = Florence, BML, Plut. 90 sup. 88
Fj = Florence, BML, Plut. 91 inf. 8
Fk = Florence, BML, Acquisti e Doni 125
Fl = Florence, BML, Ashb. 252
Fm = Florence, BML, Edili 207
Fn = Florence, BML, Fiesole 186
Fo = Florence, Biblioteca Nazionale Centrale, II. IX. 131
Fp = Florence, Biblioteca Riccardiana, 557
Ge = Genoa, Biblioteca Universitaria, E. V. 12
Gl = Glasgow, University of Glasgow Library, Gen. 334
Gw = Glasgow, University of Glasgow Library, Hunter 65 (T.3.3)
Ho = Holkham, Holkham Hall Library, 376
La = London, BL, Additional 10383
Lb = London, BL, Additional 11922
Lc = London, BL, Harley 2733
Ld = London, BL, Harley 2771
Le = London, BL, Harley 4790
Lf = London, BL, Harley 7400
Lu = Lund, Universitetsbiblioteket, Medeltidshandskrift 42
Ma = Madrid, Biblioteca Nacional de España, 10060
Mb = Milan, Biblioteca Ambrosiana, A 73 inf.
Mc = Milan, Biblioteca Ambrosiana, B 125 sup.
Md = Modena, Biblioteca Estense Universitaria, Lat. 257 = α.H.8.4
Me = Milan, Biblioteca Ambrosiana, H 197 inf.
Mf = Milan, Biblioteca Ambrosiana, L 21 sup.
Mg = Milan, Biblioteca Ambrosiana, L 86 sup.
Mh = Modena, Biblioteca Estense Universitaria, Lat. 261 = α.Q.8.25
Mi = Milan, Biblioteca Ambrosiana, O 158 sup.
Mn = Munich, Bayerische Staatsbibliothek, Clm 28882
Mo = Modena, Biblioteca Estense Universitaria, Lat. 244 = α.O.5.17
Mu = Munich, Bayerische Staatsbibliothek, Clm 796
Na = Naples, Biblioteca Nazionale, IV A 40
Np = Naples, Biblioteca Nazionale, IV B 36
Ob = Oxford, Balliol College Library, 248E
Od = Oxford, Bodleian Library, Canon. Class. Lat. 214
Ox = Oxford, Bodleian Library, D'Orville 82
Pa = Paris, BnF, lat. 7703
Pb = Paris, BnF, lat. 7704
Pc = Paris, BnF, lat. 7708
Pd = Paris, BnF, lat. 11288
Pe = Paris, BnF, lat. 17154
Pm = Parma, Biblioteca Palatina, Parm. 895
Re = Reims, Bibliothèque municipal, 1109 (N. Fonds)
Rm = Rome, Biblioteca Casanatense, 1912
Ro = Rome, Biblioteca Angelica, 1768

APPENDIX 4   333

Sd = San Daniele del Friuli, Biblioteca Guarneriana, 63
Sg = San Daniele del Friuli, Biblioteca Guarneriana, 246 (Fontanini LIX)
St = Stockholm, Kungliga Biblioteket, Va 11
Va = Vatican City, BAV, Chig. H. V. 148
Vb = Vatican City, BAV, Ott. lat. 1171
Vc = Venice, Biblioteca Nazionale Marciana, Lat. XI. 67 (3859)
Vd = Vatican City, BAV, Ott. lat. 1449
Ve = Venice, Biblioteca Nazionale Marciana, Lat. Z. 419 (1508)
Vf = Vatican City, BAV, Ott. lat. 1994
Vg = Vatican City, BAV, Pal. lat. 1465
Vh = Vatican City, BAV, Pal. lat. 1471
Vi = Vienna, Österreichische Nationalbibliothek, Cod. 3093
Vj = Vatican City, BAV, Reg. lat. 1841
Vk = Vatican City, BAV, Reg. lat. 2046
Vl = Vatican City, BAV, Urb. lat. 311
Vm = Vatican City, BAV, Vat. lat. 1701
Vn = Venice, Biblioteca Nazionale Marciana, Lat. Z. 420 (1509)
Vo = Vatican City, BAV, Vat. lat. 1702
Vp = Vatican City, BAV, Vat. lat. 1712
Vq = Vatican City, BAV, Vat. lat. 1720
Vr = Verona, Biblioteca Capitolare, CLV (143)
Vs = Vatican City, BAV, Vat. lat. 1721 + Vat. lat. 4533
Vt = Viterbo, Centro diocesano di documentazione—Biblioteca Capitolare, Sezione manoscritti, d 9
Vu = Vatican City, BAV, Vat. lat. 3238
Vv = Vatican City, BAV, Vat. lat. 6871
Vw = Vatican City, BAV, Vat. lat. 11491
Wf = Wolfenbüttel, Herzog August Bibliothek, 38 Gud. Lat. 2°

Bibliography

Journal titles are abbreviated according to the norms of *L'Année philologique*.

Brutus: Editions, Translations, and Commentaries

Baiter, J. G., and C. L. Kayser (eds). 1860. *M. Tullii Ciceronis opera quae supersunt omnia*, vol. 2 (Leipzig: Tauchnitz).

Corradus, S. 1552. *Commentarius, in quo M. T. Ciceronis De claris oratoribus liber, qui dicitur Brutus, et loci pene innumerabiles quum aliorum scriptorum, tum Ciceronis ipsius explicantur* (Florence: Officina Laurentii Torrentini Ducalis typographi).

Douglas, A. E. (ed.). 1966. *M. Tulli Ciceronis Brutus* (Oxford: Clarendon Press).

Ellendt, F. (ed.). 1844. *M. Tullii Ciceronis De claris oratoribus liber qui dicitur Brutus*, 2nd edn (Kaliningrad: Borntraeger).

Ernesti, I. A. (ed.). 1783. *M. Tullii Ciceronis Liber de claris oratoribus, Ad Marcum Brutum Orator, Ad Trebatium Topica, De partitione oratoria dialogus* (Halle: Impensis Orphanotrophei).

Friedrich, W. (ed.). 1902. *M. Tulli Ciceronis scripta quae manserunt omnia. Pars 1: Opera rhetorica*, vol. 2 (Leipzig: Teubner).

Hendrickson, G. L. (ed. and tr.). 1962. *Cicero: Brutus*, with *Orator*, ed. and tr. by H. M. Hubbell, Loeb Classical Library 342, rev. edn (Cambridge, MA: Harvard University Press).

Jahn, O. (ed.). 1849. *Ciceros Brutus de claris oratoribus* (Leipzig: Weidmann).

Jahn, O. (ed.). 1865. *Ciceros Brutus de claris oratoribus* 3rd edn (Berlin: Weidmann).

Jahn, O., and A. Eberhard (eds). 1877. *Ciceros Brutus de claris oratoribus* (Berlin: Weidmann).

Jahn, O., and W. Kroll (eds). 1908. *Cicero: Brutus* (Berlin: Weidmann).

Jahn, O., W. Kroll, and B. Kytzler (eds). 1962. *Cicero: Brutus* (Berlin: Weidmann).

Kaster, R. A. (tr.). 2020. *Cicero: Brutus and Orator* (Oxford: Oxford University Press).

Lambinus, D. (ed.). 1566. *Marci Tullii Ciceronis opera omnia quae exstant*, vol. 1 (Paris: Jacques du Puys).

Lambinus, D. (ed.). 1584. *M. Tullii Ciceronis opera omnia quae exstant*, vol. 1 (Geneva: Jérémie des Planches).

Malcovati, H. (ed.). 1970. *M. Tulli Ciceronis scripta quae manserunt omnia. Fasc. 4: Brutus*, 2nd edn (Leipzig: Teubner); 1st edn = Malcovati (1965).

Manutius, A. (ed.). 1514. *In hoc volumine haec continentur: Rhetoricorum ad C. Herennium lib. IIII, M. T. Ciceronis De inventione lib. II, ...* (Venice: Manutius).

Marchese, R. R. (ed. and tr.). 2011. *Cicerone, Bruto* (Rome: Carocci).

Martha, J. (ed.). 1892. *Oeuvres de Cicéron: Brutus* (Paris: Hachette).

Meyer, H. (ed.). 1838. *M. Tullii Ciceronis Brutus* (Halle: Sumptibus Orphanotrophei).

336 BIBLIOGRAPHY

Orelli, I. C. (ed.). 1830. *M. Tullii Ciceronis Orator, Brutus, Topica, De optimo genere oratorum* (Zurich: Typis Orellii, Füsslini et sociorum).
Peter, C. (ed.). 1839. *M. Tullii Ciceronis De claris oratoribus liber qui dicitur Brutus* (Leipzig: Vogel).
Piderit, K. W. (ed.). 1875. *Cicero: Brutus de claris oratoribus*, 2nd edn (Leipzig: Teubner).
Piderit, K. W., and W. Friedrich (eds). 1889. *Ciceros Brutus* (Leipzig: Teubner).
Reis, P. (ed.). 1934. *Brutus* (Leipzig: Teubner).
Schütz, C. G. (ed.). 1815. *M. Tullii Ciceronis opera quae supersunt omnia ac deperdita torum fragmenta*, vol. 3 (Leipzig: Fleischer).
Stangl, T. (ed.). 1886. *M. Tulli Ciceronis Brutus de claris oratoribus* (Leipzig: Freytag).
Wetzel, J. C. F. (ed.). 1795. *Cicero's Brutus* (Braunschweig: Königliche Real-schule zu Berlin).
Wilkins, A. S. (ed.). 1903. *M. Tullii Ciceronis Rhetorica*, vol. 2 (Oxford: Oxford University Press).

General Bibliography

Abbamonte, G. 2020. 'Problemi di *recensio* ed ecdotica relativi al testo del *Brutus* ciceroniano', in *Omne tulit punctum qui miscuit utile dulci: Studi in onore di Arturo De Vivo*, ed. by G. Polara, Filologia e tradizione classica 11 (Naples: Satura Editrice), pp. 1–13.
Academia Caesarea Vindobonensis. 1868. *Tabulae codicum manu scriptorum praeter Graecos et orientales in bibliotheca palatina Vindobonensi asservatorum*, vol. 2 (Vienna: Caroli Geroldi filius).
Adams, J. N. 1978. 'Conventions of Naming in Cicero', *CQ*, 28: 145–166.
Adams, J. N. 2003. *Bilingualism and the Latin Language* (Cambridge: Cambridge University Press).
Adams, J. N. 2007. *The Regional Diversification of Latin 200 BC – AD 600* (Cambridge: Cambridge University Press).
Adams, J. N. 2016. 'Infinitives with Verbs of Motion from Latin to Romance', in *Early and Late Latin: Continuity or Change?*, ed. by J. N Adams and N. Vincent (Cambridge: Cambridge University Press), pp. 265–293.
Adams, J. N. 2021. *Asyndeton and its Interpretation in Latin Literature: History, Patterns, Textual Criticism* (Cambridge: Cambridge University Press).
Ames-Lewis, F. 1984. *The Library and Manuscripts of Piero di Cosimo de' Medici* (New York: Garland).
Amundsen, L. 1939. 'Notes to the *Brutus* of Cicero', *SO*, 19: 124–128.
Antolín, G. 1916. *Catálogo de los codices latinos de la Real biblioteca del Escorial*, vol. 4 (Madrid: Imprenta helénica).
Antonelli, A., and A. Severi. 2015. 'Per una ritrovata miscellanea medioevale e umanistica (contenente il *Brutus*, l'*Epistola Bernardi de re familiari*, opere del Bruni, il *Geta*, il *Liber faceti* e le *Satirae* di Persio)', *Medioevo e Rinascimento*, n.s., 26: 61–91.
Badian, E. 1964. *Studies in Greek and Roman History* (Oxford: Blackwell).
Badian, E. 1967. Review of Malcovati (1965) and Douglas (1966), *JRS*, 57: 223–230.
Bandini, A. M. 1774–1777. *Catalogus codicum latinorum Bibliothecae Mediceae Laurentianae*, 4 vols (Florence: Biblioteca Medicea Laurenziana).

BIBLIOGRAPHY 337

Bandini, A. M. 1791–1793. *Bibliotheca Leopoldina Laurentiana*, 3 vols (Florence: Biblioteca Medicea Laurenziana).

Bandini, A. M. 1990. *Dei princìpi e progressi della real Biblioteca Mediceo Laurenziana (Ms. Laur. Acquisti e Doni 142)*, ed. by R. Pintaudi, M. Tesi, and A. R. Fantoni, Documenti inediti di cultura toscana: Nuova serie 3 (Florence: Gonnelli).

Barbero, G. 2016. 'Manoscritti e scrittura in Lombardia nel secondo quarto del secolo XV', in Black et al. (2016), pp. 149–168.

Beltrami, A. 1906. 'Index codicum classicorum latinorum qui in Bybliotheca Quiriniana Brixiensi adservantur', *SIFC*, 14: 17–96.

Beltran, E. 1985. 'Les sources de la *Rhétorique* de Fichet', *BiblH&R*, 47: 7–25.

Bertini, G. 2010. 'Center and Periphery: Art Patronage in Renaissance Piacenza and Parma', in *The Court Cities of Northern Italy: Milan, Parma, Piacenza, Mantua, Ferrara, Bologna, Urbino, Pesaro, and Rimini*, ed. by C. M. Rosenberg (Cambridge: Cambridge University Press), pp. 71–137.

Bianchi, R. 2015. 'Nella biblioteca di Angelo Colocci: Libri già noti e nuove identificazioni', *SMU*, 13: 157–196.

Biedl, A. 1930. 'De Memmiorum familia', *WS*, 48: 98–107.

Biondo, F. 2005. *Italy Illuminated*, ed. and tr. by J. A. White, I Tatti Renaissance Library 20, vol. 1 (Cambridge, MA: Harvard University Press).

Biondo, F. 2011–2017. *Italia Illustrata*, ed. by P. Pontari, Edizione delle Opere di Biondo Flavio 4, 3 vols (Rome: Istituto storico italiano per il Medio Evo).

Birkenmajer, A. 1922. *Bibljoteka Ryszarda de Fournival, poety i uczonego francuskiego z początku XIII-go wieku i jej późniejsze losy* (Krakow: Polska Akademja Umiejętności).

Birkenmajer, A. 1970. 'La bibliothèque de Richard de Fournival, poète et érudit français du début du XIIIe siècle et son sort ultérieur', in *Études d'histoire des sciences et de la philosophie du Moyen Âge*, ed. by A. M. Birkenmajer and J. B. Korolec, tr. by T. Chłapowska et al. (Wrocław: Zakład Narodowy im. Ossolińskich), pp. 117–249.

Bischoff, B. 1998. *Katalog der festländischen Handschriften des neunten Jahrhunderts (mit Ausnahme der wisigotischen)*, vol. 1 (Wiesbaden: Harrassowitz).

Black, R., J. Kraye, and L. Nuvoloni. 2016. *Palaeography, Manuscript Illumination and Humanism in Renaissance Italy: Studies in Memory of A. C. de la Mare, Warburg Institute Colloquia 28* (London: Warburg Institute).

Boese, H. 1966. *Die lateinischen Handschriften der Sammlung Hamilton zu Berlin* (Wiesbaden: Harrassowitz).

Bollati, M. (ed.). 2004. *Dizionario biografico dei miniatori italiani: Secoli IX–XVI* (Milan: Bonnard).

Booton, D. E. 1993/1996. 'The Master of the Riccardiana Lactantius: Folios from a Florentine Choir Book', *Miniatura*, 5/6, 61–66.

Brightbill, M. A. 1932. 'The Text of Cicero's *De oratore* in Codex D (Cornell University MSS B 2)' (unpublished doctoral dissertation, Cornell University).

Briscoe, J. (ed.). 1998. *Valeri Maximi Facta et dicta memorabilia*, vol. 2 (Stuttgart: Teubner).

Briscoe, J. (ed.). 2019. *Valerius Maximus, Facta et dicta memorabilia, Book 8: Text, Introduction and Commentary*, Untersuchungen zur antiken Literatur und Geschichte 141 (Berlin: De Gruyter).

338 BIBLIOGRAPHY

Busche, K. 1919. 'Zu Ciceros *Brutus*', *Wochenschrift für klassische Philologie*, 36: 310–312.

Busonero, P., et al. 2016. *I manoscritti datati delle biblioteche Casanatense e Vallicelliana di Roma*, Manoscritti datati d'Italia 25 (Florence: SISMEL—Edizioni del Galluzzo).

Büttner, R. 1893. *Porcius Licinus und der litterarische Kreis des Q. Lutatius Catulus* (Leipzig: Teubner).

Cadei, A. 1976. *Belbello, miniatore lombardo: Artisti del libro alla corte dei Visconti*, Studi di storia dell'arte 6 (Roma: Bulzoni).

Cagni, G. M. 1960. 'I codici Vaticani Palatino-Latini appartenuti alla biblioteca di Giannozzo Manetti', *La Bibliofilía*, 62: 1–43.

Caldelli, E. 2006. *Copisti a Roma nel Quattrocento*, Scritture e libri del medioevo 4 (Rome: Viella).

Calkins, R. G. 1972. *Medieval and Renaissance Illuminated Manuscripts in the Cornell University Library*, The Cornell Library Journal 13 (Ithaca, NY: Cornell University Library).

Campe, J. F. C. 1860. 'Beiträge zur Kritik des Cicero. I', in *Friedrich-Wilhelms-Gymnasium zu Greiffenberg in Pommern VIII* (Greiffenberg in Pommern: Kraut), pp. 3–26.

Carcopino, J. 1929. 'Correction au *Brutus* XXVIII, 109', *RPh*, 3: 5–12.

Cardini, R., L. Bertolini, and M. Regoliosi. 2005. *Leon Battista Alberti: La biblioteca di un umanista* (Florence: Mandragora).

Caroti, S., and S. Zamponi. 1974. *Lo scrittoio di Bartolomeo Fonzio umanista fiorentino*, Documenti sulle arti del libro 10 (Milan: Il polifilo).

Casarsa, L., M. d'Angelo, and C. Scalon. 1991. *La libreria di Guarnerio d'Artegna*, 2 vols (Udine: Casamassima).

Castiglioni, L. 1935. Review of P. Reis, *Orator* (1932) and *Brutus* (1934), *Athenaeum*, n.s., 13: 348–353.

Cavarzere, A. 2012. 'Cic. *Brut.* 92: un "passaggio (troppo) nascosto"?', *SIFC*, 4th ser., 10: 100–104.

Ceccanti, M. 1996. 'I miniatori nei codici quattrocenteschi della Badia Fiesolana' (unpublished master's thesis, Università degli studi di Firenze).

Ceccherini, I. 2016. *Sozomeno da Pistoia (1387–1458): Scrittura e libri di un umanista*, Biblioteca dell'*Archivum Romanicum*, Serie 1: Storia, Letteratura, Paleografia 431 (Florence: Olschki).

Ceruti, A. 1973–1979. *Inventario Ceruti dei manoscritti della Biblioteca Ambrosiana*, 5 vols (Trezzano sul Naviglio: Etimar).

Chatelain, É. 1884–1892. *Paléographie des classiques latins*, vol. 1 (Paris: Hachette).

Chiron, P. (ed. and tr.). 2002. *Pseudo-Aristote: Rhétorique à Alexandre* (Paris: Les Belles Lettres).

Christie, Manson, & Woods Ltd. 1982. *Valuable Early Printed Books and Manuscripts: The Property of the Earl of Shelburne Sir William Gladstone, Bt., the Trustees of the Major N. D. Martin Books Settlement, and from various sources* (London: Christie, Manson, & Woods Ltd).

Cipriani, R. 1968. *Codici miniati dell'Ambrosiana* (Milan: Neri Pozza).

Clark, A. C. (ed.). 1905. *M. Tulli Ciceronis Orationes*, vol. 1 (Oxford: Clarendon Press).

BIBLIOGRAPHY   339

Cole, T. 1991. 'Who Was Corax?', *ICS*, 16: 65–84.

Cook, B. L. 2009. 'Tully's Late Medieval Life: The Roots of the Renaissance in Cicero's Biography', *C&M*, 60: 347–370.

Courtney, E. (ed.). 1993. *The Fragmentary Latin Poets* (Oxford: Clarendon Press).

Coxe, H. O. 1854. *Catalogus codicum manuscriptorum Bibliothecae Bodleianae*, vol. 3 (Oxford: Typographeum Academicum).

Crawford, M. H. (ed.). 1996. *Roman Statutes*, Bulletin of the Institute of Classical Studies Supplement 64, 2 vols (London: Institute of Classical Studies).

Crook, J. A. 1984. 'Lex Aquilia', *Athenaeum*, n.s., 62: 67–77.

D'Alessandro, P. (ed.). 2004. *Rufini Antiochensis Commentaria in metra Terentiana et De compositione et de numeris oratorum* (Hildesheim: Olms).

Davies, M. C. 1988. 'An Enigma and a Phantom: Giovanni Aretino and Giacomo Languschi', *HumLov*, 37: 1–29.

De Bure, G. 1783. *Catalogue des livres de la bibliothèque de feu M. le duc de la Vallière*, vol. 2 (Paris: De Bure).

De la Mare, A. C. 1973. *The Handwriting of Italian Humanists*, vol. 1 (Oxford: Association internationale de bibliophilie).

De la Mare, A. C. 1976. 'The Library of Francesco Sassetti (1421–90)', in *Cultural Aspects of the Italian Renaissance: Essays in Honour of Paul Oskar Kristeller*, ed. by C. H. Clough (Manchester: Manchester University Press; New York: Zambelli), pp. 160–201.

De la Mare, A. C. 1977. 'Humanistic Script: The First Ten Years', in *Das Verhältnis der Humanisten zum Buch*, ed. by F. Krafft and D. Wuttke, Kommission für Humanismusforschung Mitteilung 4 (Boppard: Boldt), pp. 89–110.

De la Mare, A. C. 1983. 'Script and Manuscripts in Milan under the Sforzas', in *Milano nell'età di Ludovico il Moro*, no named editor, vol. 2 (Milan: Archivio Storico Civico and Biblioteca Trivulziana), pp. 399–408.

De la Mare, A. C. 1985. 'New Research on Humanistic Scribes in Florence', in *Miniatura fiorentina del Rinascimento 1440–1525: Un primo censimento*, ed. by A. Garzelli, vol. 1, Inventari e cataloghi toscani 18 (Florence: Giunta regionale toscana and La nuova Italia), pp. 393–600.

De la Mare, A. C. 1986. 'Vespasiano da Bisticci e i copisti Fiorentini di Federico', in *Federico di Montefeltro: Lo stato, le arti, la cultura*, ed. by G. C. Baiardi, G. Chittolini, and P. Floriani, vol. 3 (Rome: Bulzoni), pp. 81–96.

De la Mare, A. C. 1992. 'Cosimo and His Books', in *Cosimo 'il Vecchio' de' Medici, 1389–1464: Essays in Commemoration of the 600th Anniversary of Cosimo de' Medici's Birth*, ed. by F. Ames-Lewis (Oxford: Clarendon Press), pp. 115–156.

De la Mare, A. C. 1996. 'Vespasiano da Bisticci as Producer of Classical Manuscripts in Fifteenth-Century Florence', in *Medieval Manuscripts of the Latin Classics: Production and Use*, ed. by C. A. Chavannes-Mazel and M. M. Smith (Los Altos Hills: Anderson-Lovelace; London: Red Gull Press), pp. 167–208.

De la Mare, A. C. 2000. 'A Livy Copied by Giacomo Curlo Dismembered by Otto Ege', in *Interpreting and Collecting Fragments of Medieval Books*, ed. by L. L. Brownrigg and M. M. Smith (Los Altos Hills: Anderson-Lovelace; London: Red Gull Press), pp. 57–88.

De la Mare, A. C. unpublished. Archive A. C. de la Mare, Bodleian Library.

340 BIBLIOGRAPHY

De la Mare, A. C., and L. Nuvoloni. 2009. *Bartolomeo Sanvito: The Life & Work of a Renaissance Scribe*, ed. by A. Hobson and C. de Hamel (Paris: Association internationale de bibliophilie).

De Ligt, L. 2001. 'Studies in Legal and Agrarian History III: Appian and the *lex Thoria*', *Athenaeum*, n.s., 89: 121–144.

Delisle, L. 1874. *Le cabinet des manuscrits de la Bibliothèque nationale*, vol. 2 (Paris: Imprimerie nationale).

Della Corte, F. 1971. Review of Malcovati (1970), *Maia*, 23: 377.

De Marinis, T. 1947–1952. *La biblioteca napoletana dei re d'Aragona*, 4 vols (Milan: Hoepli).

De Melo, W. D. C. 2007. *The Early Latin Verb System: Archaic Forms in Plautus, Terence, and Beyond* (Oxford: Oxford University Press).

De Meo, C. 2005. *Lingue tecniche del latino*, 3rd edn (Bologna: Pàtron).

Demoen, K. 1997. 'A Paradigm for the Analysis of Paradigms: The Rhetorical *Exemplum* in Ancient and Imperial Greek Theory', *Rhetorica*, 15: 125–158.

Den Boeft, J. 2015. 'Ammianus Ciceronianus?', in *Culture and Literature in Latin Late Antiquity: Continuities and Discontinuities*, ed. by P. F. Moretti, R. Ricci, and C. Torre (Turnhout: Brepols), pp. 221–232.

De Robertis, T., and R. Miriello. 1997. *I manoscritti datati della Biblioteca Riccardiana di Firenze*, vol. 1, Manoscritti datati d'Italia 2 (Florence: SISMEL—Edizioni del Galluzzo).

Derolez, A. 1984. *Codicologie des manuscrits en écriture humanistique sur parchemin*, vol. 1, Bibliologia: Elementa ad librorum studia pertinentia 5 (Turnhout: Brepols).

Derolez, A. 2018. *Archaeology of the Manuscript Book of the Italian Renaissance* (Rome: Arbor Sapientiae Editore).

Desachy, M. 2012. *Deux bibliophiles humanistiques: Bibliothèques et manuscrits de Jean Jouffroy et d'Hélion Jouffroy* (Paris: Centre national de la recherche scientifique).

Detlefsen, S. D. F. 1869. 'Über die mittelalterlichen Bibliotheken Nord-Italiens', *Verhandlungen der 27. Versammlung Deutscher Philologen und Schulmänner in Kiel* (Leipzig: Teubner), pp. 87–109.

Devine, A. M., and L. D. Stephens. 2006. *Latin Word Order: Structured Meaning and Information* (Oxford: Oxford University Press).

De Vleeschauwer, H. J. 1965. *La Biblionomia de Richard de Fournival du manuscrit 636 de la Bibliothèque de la Sorbonne, Mousaion 62* (Pretoria: Unisa).

Dickey, E., and A. Chahoud (eds). 2010. *Colloquial and Literary Latin* (Cambridge: Cambridge University Press).

Dizionario biografico degli italiani, 100 vols (Rome: Istituto dell'Enciclopedia italiana, 1960–2020).

Dorez, L. 1895. 'Latino Latini et la Bibliothèque Capitulaire de Viterbe', *Revue des Bibliothèques*, 5: 237–255.

Ellendt, F. 1836. Review of K. L. Roth, L. Cornelii Sisennae historici Romani vita (1834), *Neue Jahrbücher für Philologie und Paedagogik*, 18: 259–262.

Fanelli, V. 1979. *Ricerche su Angelo Colocci e sulla Roma cinquecentesca* (Vatican City: Biblioteca Apostolica Vaticana).

BIBLIOGRAPHY   341

Fantham, E. (ed.). 2013. *Cicero's Pro L. Murena Oratio* (New York: Oxford University Press).

Feeney, D. 2002. '*Una cum scriptore meo*: Poetry, Principate and the Traditions of Literary History in the Epistle to Augustus', in *Traditions and Contexts in the Poetry of Horace*, ed. by T. Woodman and D. Feeney (Cambridge: Cambridge University Press), pp. 172–187.

Ferrari, M. 1984. 'Fra i 'latini scriptores' di Pier Candido Decembrio e biblioteche umanistiche milanesi: Codici di Vitruvio e Quintiliano', in *Vestigia: Studi in onore di Giuseppe Billanovich*, ed. by R. Avesani et al., vol. 1, Storia e letteratura: Raccolta di studi e testi 162 (Rome: Storia e letteratura), pp. 247–296.

Ferrari, M. 1998. 'Frammenti di classici: Quintiliano e Virgilio nella biblioteca dell'Università del S. Cuore a Milano', *Aevum*, 72: 183–191.

Field, A. 2017. *The Intellectual Struggle for Florence: Humanists and the Beginnings of the Medici Regime, 1420–1440* (Oxford: Oxford University Press).

Fink, K. A. 1964. 'Die Wahl Martins V', in *Das Konzil von Konstanz: Beiträge zu seiner Geschichte und Theologie*, ed. by A. Franzen and W. Müller (Freiburg: Herder), pp. 138–151.

Finke, H. (ed.). 1928. *Acta Concilii constanciensis*, vol. 4 (Münster: Regensbergsche Buchhandlung).

Fleckeisen, A. 1883. 'Zu Ciceros Brutus', *Neue Jahrbücher für Philologie und Paedagogik*, 127: 208–210.

Fossier, F. 1979. 'Premières recherches sur les manuscrits latins du cardinal Marcello Cervini (1501–1555)', *MEFRM*, 91: 381–456.

Fossier, F. 1982. *La bibliothèque Farnèse: Étude des manuscrits latins et en langue vernaculaire, Le Palais Farnèse 3:2* (Rome: École française de Rome).

Fratini, L., and S. Zamponi. 2004. *I manoscritti datati del fondo acquisti e doni e dei fondi minori della Biblioteca Medicea Laurenziana di Firenze, Manoscritti datati d'Italia 12* (Florence: SISMEL—Edizioni del Galluzzo).

Frenz, T. 2009–. 'Conspectus generalis personarum alphabeticus', *Repertorium Officiorum Romane Curie (RORC)*, https://www.phil.uni-passau.de/histhw/ forschung/ rorc [accessed 29 January 2021].

Friedrich, W. 1873. 'Zu Ciceros Brutus', *Neue Jahrbücher für Philologie und Paedagogik*, 107: 845–851.

Friedrich, W. 1880. 'Zu Ciceros *Brutus* und *Orator*', *Neue Jahrbücher für Philologie und Paedagogik*, 121: 137–147.

Fuchs, H. 1956. 'Nachträge in Ciceros Brutus', in *Navicula Chiloniensis: Studia philologa Felici Jacoby professori Chiloniensi emerito octogenario oblata*, no named editor (Leiden: Brill), pp. 123–143.

Furietttus, J. A. (ed.). 1723. *Gasparini Barzizii Bergomatis et Guiniforti filii opera* (Rome: J. M. Salvioni).

Garcea, A. (ed.). 2012. *Caesar's De analogia: Edition, Translation and Commentary* (Oxford: Oxford University Press).

Garrido i Valls, J.-D. 2003. 'L'escriptura humanística al Principat de Catalunya', *Faventia* 25: 139–169.

Gerstinger, H. 1926. 'Johannes Sambucus als Handschriftensammler', in *Festschrift der Nationalbibliothek in Wien herausgegeben zur Feier des 200jährigen Bestehens*

342 BIBLIOGRAPHY

des Gebäudes, ed. by the Österreichische Nationalbibliothek (Vienna: Österreichische Staatsdruckerei), pp. 251–400.

Ghignoli, A. 2016. '*Chartacea supellex*': *L'inventario dei libri di Celio Calcagnini* (Rome: Istituto storico italiano per il Medio Evo).

Giazzi, E. 2005. 'Spigolature cremonesi: frammenti di classici nell'Archivio di Stato', *Aevum*, 79: 491–512.

Giomini, R. (ed.). 1996. *M. Tulli Ciceronis Partitiones oratoriae* (Rome: Herder).

Gionta, D. 2005. 'Un manoscritto ciceroniano di Guillaume Fichet', *SMU*, 3: 412–423.

Glucker, J. 1997. 'Socrates in the Academic Books and Other Ciceronian Works', in *Assent and Argument: Studies in Cicero's Academic Books*, ed. by B. Inwood and J. Mansfeld (Leiden: Brill), pp. 58–88.

Goh, I. 2018. 'An Asianist Sensation: Horace on Lucilius as Hortensius', *AJPh*, 139: 641–674.

Gonzalez, J. M. 2011. *The Epic Rhapsode and His Craft: Homeric Performance in a Diachronic Perspective*, Hellenic Studies Series 47 (Washington, DC: Center for Hellenic Studies).

Gowers, E. 2019. 'Knight's Moves: The Son-in-law in Cicero and Tacitus', *ClAnt*, 38: 2–35.

Gowing, A. 2000. 'Memory and Silence in Cicero's *Brutus*', *Eranos*, 98: 39–64.

Grenfell, B. P., and A. S. Hunt (eds). 1903. *The Oxyrhynchus Papyri*, vol. 3 (London: Egypt Exploration Fund).

Gruen, E. S. 1965. 'The *lex Varia*', *JRS*, 55: 59–73.

Gruen, E. S. 1968. *Roman Politics and the Criminal Courts, 149–78 B.C.* (Cambridge, MA: Harvard University Press).

Gualdo Rosa, L., S. Ingegno, and A. Nunziata. 1996. '*Molto più preziosi dell'oro*': *Codici di casa Barzizza alla Biblioteca nazionale di Napoli* (Naples: Luciano).

Gudeman, A. 1915. 'Ciceros *Brutus* und die antike Buchpublikation', *Berliner Philologische Wochenschrift*, 35: 574–576.

Haenel, G. 1830. *Catalogi librorum manuscriptorum qui in bibliothecis Galliae, Helvetiae, Belgii, Britanniae M., Hispaniae, Lusitaniae asservantur* (Leipzig: J. C. Hinrichs).

Hagendahl, H. 1958. *Latin Fathers and the Classics: A Study on the Apologists, Jerome and Other Christian Writers* (Gothenburg: Elanders Boktryckeri).

Hall, J. 2013. 'Saviour of the Republic and Father of the Fatherland: Cicero and Political Crisis', in *The Cambridge Companion to Cicero*, ed. by C. Steel (Cambridge: Cambridge University Press), pp. 215–229.

Halm, K., and G. Laubmann. 1892. *Catalogus codicum latinorum bibliothecae regiae Monacensis*, 2nd edn, vol. 1 (Munich: Bibliotheca Regia).

Hamilton, J. R. 1968. 'Cicero, *Brutus* 304–5', *CQ*, 18: 412–413.

Hand, F. 1829. *Tursellinus, seu de particulis latinis commentarii*, vol. 1 (Leipzig: Weidmann).

Haupt, M. 1876. *Opuscula*, vol. 2 (Leipzig: Salomon Hirzel).

Haye, T. 2010. 'Canon ou catalogue? Perspectives historico-littéraires dans la *Biblionomia* de Richard de Fournival', *Romania*, 128: 213–233.

Heerdegen, F. (ed.). 1884. *M. Tulli Ciceronis Ad M. Brutum Orator* (Leipzig: Teubner).

BIBLIOGRAPHY 343

Heinemann, O. von, et al. 1884-1913. *Die Handschriften der herzoglichen Bibliothek zu Wolfenbüttel*, 9 vols (Wolfenbüttel: Julius Zwissler).

Heraeus, W. 1934. 'Furius Pilus u. a', *Rhm*, 83: 53–65.

Hernández Aparicio, P. 2000. *Inventario general de manuscritos de la Biblioteca Nacional*, vol. 14 (Madrid: Biblioteca Nacional).

Heumann, H. G., and E. Seckel. 1907. *Heumanns Handlexikon zu den Quellen des römischen Rechts*, 9th edn (Jena: Fischer).

Hinks, D. A. G. 1940. 'Tisias and Corax and the Invention of Rhetoric', *CQ*, 34: 61–69.

Hinton, T. 2016. 'Conceptualizing Medieval Book Collections', *French Studies*, 70: 171–186.

Hoffmann, E. 1876. 'Zu Ciceros Brutus', *Neue Jahrbücher für Philologie und Paedagogik*, 113: 243–244.

Hofmann, H. 2008. 'Literary Culture at the Court of Urbino during the Reign of Federico da Montefeltro', *HumLov*, 57: 1–59.

Hunt, T. J. 1998. *A Textual History of Cicero's Academici Libri*, Mnemosyne Suppl. 181 (Leiden: Brill).

Hutchinson, G. O. 1995. 'Rhythm, Style, and Meaning in Cicero's Prose', *CQ*, 45: 485–499.

James, M. R. 1913. *A Descriptive Catalogue of the Manuscripts in the Library of St John's College, Cambridge* (Cambridge: Cambridge University Press).

Janozki, J. D. A. 1752. *Specimen catalogi codicum manuscriptorum bibliothecae Zaluscianae* (Dresden: [n. pub.]).

Jażdżewska, K. 2018. 'Indications of Speakers in Ancient Dialogue: A Reappraisal', *JHS*, 138: 249–260.

Johannsen, K. 1971. *Die lex agraria des Jahres 111 v. Chr.: Text und Kommentar* (Munich: s. n.).

Jordan, L., and S. Wool. 1984-1989. *Inventory of Western Manuscripts in the Biblioteca Ambrosiana, from the Medieval Institute of the University of Notre Dame, the Frank M. Folson Microfilm Collection*, 3 vols (Notre Dame: University of Notre Dame Press).

Jury, J. 2018. 'Cicero's De oratore from Antiquity to the Advent of Print' (unpublished doctoral dissertation, Georgia State University).

Kelly, G. 2008. *Ammianus Marcellinus: The Allusive Historian* (Cambridge: Cambridge University Press).

Kennedy, G. A. 1963. *History of Rhetoric*, vol. 1 (Princeton: Princeton University Press).

Kennedy, S. M. 2010. 'A Commentary on Cicero, *Tusculan Disputations* Book 1' (unpublished doctoral dissertation, University of Exeter).

Kenney, E. J. 1974. *The Classical Text: Aspects of Editing in the Age of the Printed Book* (Berkeley and Los Angeles: University of California Press).

Ker, N. R. 1977. *Medieval Manuscripts in British Libraries*, vol. 2 (Oxford: Clarendon Press).

Koch, H. A. 1861. 'Zu Ciceros rhetorischen Schriften', *Rhm*, 16: 482–486.

Kovacs, D. 1989. 'Notes on Latin Prose Authors', *AJPh*, 110: 233–236.

Kristeller, P. O. 1963-1992. *Iter Italicum: A Finding List of Uncatalogued or Incompletely Catalogued Humanistic Manuscripts of the Renaissance in Italian and Other Libraries*, 6 vols (London: Warburg Institute; Leiden: Brill).

344 BIBLIOGRAPHY

Kroon, C. 1989. 'Rarum dictu: The Latin Second Supine Construction', *Glotta*, 67: 198–228.

Krostenko, B. A. 2001. *Cicero, Catullus, and the Language of Social Performance* (Chicago: University of Chicago Press).

Kühner, R. 1877–1878. *Ausführliche Grammatik der lateinischen Sprache*, 2 vols (Hanover: Hahn).

Kumaniecki, K. F. 1965. 'Ad Ciceronis libros De oratore adnotationes criticae', in *Miscellanea critica: Aus Anlaß des 150jährigen Bestehens der Verlagsgesellschaft und des graphischen Betriebes B. G. Teubner, Leipzig*, ed. by J. Irmscher et al., vol. 2 (Leipzig: Teubner), pp. 197–205.

Kumaniecki, K. F. (ed.). 1969. *M. Tulli Ciceronis scripta quae manserunt omnia. Fasc. 3: De oratore* (Leipzig: Teubner).

Laughton, E. 1964. *The Participle in Cicero* (London: Oxford University Press).

Laurand, L. 1908. Review of Jahn-Kroll (1908), *Bulletin critique*, 29: 447–450.

Lausberg, H. 1998. *Handbook of Literary Rhetoric: A Foundation for Literary Study*, ed. by D. E. Orton and R. D. Anderson (Leiden: Brill).

Leeman, A. D. 1969. Review of Douglas (1966), *Mnemosyne*, 4th ser., 22: 93–96.

Leeman, A. D., et al. 1981–2008. *De oratore libri III: Kommentar*, 5 vols (Heidelberg: Winter).

Lintott, A. 1992. *Judicial Reform and Land Reform in the Roman Republic: A New Edition, with Translation and Commentary, of the Laws from Urbino* (Cambridge: Cambridge University Press).

Lintott, A. 2008. *Cicero as Evidence: A Historian's Companion* (Oxford: Oxford University Press).

Lisowski, I. (ed.). 1960. *Polonica ex libris 'Obligationum et solutionum' Camerae Apostolicae ab a. 1373*, Elementa ad Fontium Editiones 1 (Rome: Institutum Historicum Polonicum Romae).

Loriquet, H. 1904. *Catalogue général des manuscrits des bibliothèques publiques des départements*, vol. 39 (Paris: Plon).

Luard, H. R. (ed.). 1861. *A Catalogue of the Manuscripts Preserved in the Library of the University of Cambridge*, vol. 4 (Cambridge: Cambridge University Press).

Lucarini, C. M. 2015. 'I due stili asiani (Cic. *Br.* 325; *P. Artemid.*) e l'origine dell'Atticismo letterario', *ZPE*, 193: 11–24.

Maas, P. 1958. *Textual Criticism*, tr. by Barbara Flower (Oxford: Clarendon Press).

Madan, F. 1897. *A Summary Catalogue of Western Manuscripts in the Bodleian Library at Oxford*, vol. 4 (Oxford: Clarendon Press).

Madvig, I. N. 1884. *Adversaria critica ad scriptores graecos et latinos*, vol. 3 (Copenhagen: Libraria Gyldendaliana).

Malcovati, E. 1958. 'La tradizione del *Brutus* e il nuovo frammento cremonese', *Athenaeum*, n.s., 36: 30–47.

Malcovati, E. 1959. 'Ancora sulla tradizione del *Brutus*', *Athenaeum*, n.s., 37: 174–183.

Malcovati, E. 1960. 'Per una nuova edizione del *Brutus*', *Athenaeum*, n.s., 38: 328–340.

Malcovati, E. 1968. 'Sulle ultime edizioni del *Brutus*', *Athenaeum*, n.s., 46: 122–130.

Malcovati, E. 1971. 'Sulle opere retoriche di Cicerone', *Athenaeum*, n.s., 49: 398–400.

BIBLIOGRAPHY   345

Malcovati, E. 1975. 'Rileggendo il *Brutus*', in *Ciceroniana: Hommages à Kazimierz Kumaniecki*, ed. by A. Michel and R. Verdière, Roma Aeterna 9 (Leiden: Brill), pp. 160–166.

Manso Rubio, M. 2014. '*M. T.* Ciceronis, *Orator ad Brutum, Brutus* i *De senectute ad Athicum* [*sic*]; L. Annei [*sic*] Senecae, *ad Gallionem De remediis fortuitorum*: Estudi codicològic del Ms. 12 de la Biblioteca Universitària de Barcelona' (unpublished master's thesis, Universitat de Barcelona).

Marggraff, E. 1855. 'Observationes criticae in Ottonis Jahnii editionem Bruti Ciceroniani', in *Programme d'invitation à l'examen public du Collège Royal Français fixé au 2 Octobre 1855* (Berlin: Starcke), pp. 1–26.

Marinone, N. 1997. *Cronologia ciceroniana* (Rome: Centro di studi ciceroniani).

Martellotti, G. 1983. *Dante e Boccaccio e altri scrittori dall'umanesimo al romanticismo* (Florence: Olschki).

Maspoli, C. 2000. *Stemmario trivulziano* (Milan: Niccolò Orsini de Marzo).

Mayer, M. 1980. 'Manuscrits de biblioteques renaixentistes il·lustres a la Biblioteca Universitària de Barcelona', in *Estudis de llengua i literatura catalanes oferts a R. Aramon i Serra en el seu setantè aniversari*, ed. by M. Jorba, vol. 2 (Barcelona: Curial), pp. 335–358.

Mayer, R. G. 2005. 'The Impracticability of Latin "Kunstprosa"', in *Aspects of the Language of Latin Prose*, ed. by T. Reinhardt, M. Lapidge, and J. N. Adams, Proceedings of the British Academy 129 (Oxford: Oxford University Press), pp. 195–210.

Mazzatinti, G., et al. 1890–. *Inventari dei manoscritti delle biblioteche d'Italia* (Forlì: Bordandini; Florence: Olschki).

McLaughlin, M. 2009. 'Alberti and the Classical Canon', in *Italy and the Classical Tradition: Language, Thought and Poetry 1300–1600*, ed. by C. Caruso and A. Laird (London: Duckworth), pp. 73–100.

Mercer, R. G. G. 1979. *The Teaching of Gasparino Barzizza, with Special Reference to His Place in Paduan Humanism* (London: Modern Humanities Research Association).

Meyenberg, R. 1990. 'Un nouveau manuscrit autographe de Guillaume Fichet', *BiblH&R*, 52: 77–87.

Michael, H. 1874. *De Ammiani Marcellini studiis Ciceronianis* (Wrocław: Korn).

Moles, J. L. 2017. *A Commentary on Plutarch's* Brutus, Histos Supplement 7 (Newcastle: Histos).

Mommsen, T. 1899. *Römisches Strafrecht* (Leipzig: Duncker & Humblot).

Morstein-Marx, R. 2004. *Mass Oratory and Political Power in the Late Roman Republic* (Cambridge: Cambridge University Press).

Motolese, M., P. Procaccioli, and E. Russo (eds). 2013. *Autografi dei letterati italiani: Il Cinquecento*, vol. 2 (Rome: Salerno).

Münzer, F. 1905. 'Atticus als Geschichtschreiber', *Hermes*, 40: 50–100.

Murgia, C. E. 1981. Review of H. C. Gotoff, *Cicero's Elegant Style: An Analysis of the* Pro Archia (1979), *CPh*, 76: 301–313.

Murgia, C. E. 2002. 'Critica varia', in *Vertis in usum: Studies in Honor of Edward Courtney*, ed. by J. F. Miller, C. Damon, and K. Sara Myers, Beiträge zur Altertumskunde 161 (Munich: Saur), pp. 67–75.

346 BIBLIOGRAPHY

Muzzioli, G. 1959. 'Due nuovi codici autografi di Pomponio Leto', *IMU*, 2: 337–351.

Mynors, R. A. B. 1963. *Catalogue of the Manuscripts of Balliol College, Oxford* (Oxford: Clarendon Press).

Neue, F., and C. Wagener. 1902. *Formenlehre der lateinischen Sprache*, 3rd edn, vol. 1 (Leipzig: Reisland).

Nicolet, C. 1960. '*Consul togatus*: Remarques sur le vocabulaire politique de Cicéron et de Tite-Live', *REL*, 38: 236–263.

Norden, E. 1913. 'Aus Ciceros Werkstatt', *Sitzungsberichte der königlich preussischen Akademie der Wissenschaften*, [no vol. no.]: 2–32.

Oakley, S. P. 2005. *A Commentary on Livy, Books VI–X*, vol. 3 (Oxford: Clarendon Press).

Oakley, S. P. 2016. 'The "Puccini Scribe" and the Transmission of Latin Texts in Fifteenth-Century Florence', in Black et al. (2016), pp. 345–364.

Oakley, S. P. 2020. *Studies in the Transmission of Latin Texts*, vol. 1 (Oxford: Oxford University Press).

Omodeo, P. 2020. *Amerigo Vespucci: The Historical Context of His Explorations and Scientific Contribution*, ed. by P. D. Omodeo, Knowledge Hegemonies in the Early Modern World 1 (Venice: Ca' Foscari).

Otto, A. 1890. *Die Sprichwörter und sprichwörtlichen Redensarten der Römer* (Leipzig: Teubner).

Pächt, O., and J. J. G. Alexander. 1970. *Illuminated Manuscripts in the Bodleian Library, Oxford*, vol. 2 (Oxford: Clarendon Press).

Paoli, C., E. Rostagno, and T. Lodi. 1887–1948. *I codici ashburnhamiani della R. Biblioteca Medicea-Laurenziana di Firenze*, vol. 1 (Rome: La libreria dello stato).

Papke, R. 1988. '*Caesars De analogia*' (unpublished doctoral dissertation, Katholische Universität Eichstätt-Ingolstadt).

Parker, W. 1904. Review of Wilkins (1903), *Hermathena*, 13: 247–253.

Paschalidis, P. 2008. 'What Did *iniuria* in the *lex Aquilia* Actually Mean?', *RIDA*, 55: 321–363.

Pasquali, G. 1932. 'Recentiores, non deteriores: Collazioni umanistiche ed editiones principes', *Annali della R. Scuola Normale Superiore di Pisa: Lettere, Storia e Filosofia*, 2nd ser., 1: 53–84.

Pellegrin, É. 1954. 'Manuscrits d'auteurs latins de l'époque classique conservés dans les bibliothèques publiques de Suède', *Bulletin d'information de l'Institut de Recherche et d'Histoire des Textes*, 3: 7–32.

Pellegrin, É. 1988. *Bibliothèques retrouvées: Manuscrits, bibliothèques et bibliophiles du Moyen Âge et de la Renaissance* (Paris: Centre national de la recherche scientifique).

Pellegrin, É., et al. 1975–2010. *Les manuscrits classiques latins de la bibliothèque Vaticane*, 3 vols (Paris: Centre national de la recherche scientifique).

Pettenazzi, I. 1954. 'A proposito del ritrovamento di frammenti di codici nell'Archivio Storico Comunale', *Bollettino storico cremonese*, 19: 170–172.

Pettenazzi, I. 1955–1957. 'Di un frammento del *Brutus* del sec. IX', *Bollettino storico cremonese*, 20: 83–97.

Philippson, R. 1936. Review of P. Reis, *Orator* (1932) and *Brutus* (1934), *Philologische Wochenschrift*, 56: 1333–1343.

BIBLIOGRAPHY   347

Piana, C. 1953. 'I codici della Biblioteca del Convento di San Bernardino di Borgonovo Val Tidone', *Bollettino storico piacentino*, 48: 10–16.

Piderit, K. W. 1860. 'Zur Kritik und Exegese von Ciceros *Brutus*', in *Kurfürstliches Gymnasium zu Hanau: Programm* (Hanau: Waisenhausbuchdruckerei), pp. 2–20.

Pigman III, G. W. 1981. 'Barzizza's Studies of Cicero', *Rinascimento*, 21: 123–163.

Pina Polo, F., and A. Díaz Fernández. 2019. *The Quaestorship in the Roman Republic*, Klio Beihefte n.s. 31 (Berlin: De Gruyter).

Pinkster, H. 1970. 'Ad Cic. *Brut.* 31', *Mnemosyne*, 4th ser., 23: 306.

Pinkster, H. 2015. *The Oxford Latin Syntax*, vol. 1 (Oxford: Oxford University Press).

Poggio Bracciolini, G. F. 1984. *Lettere*, ed. by H. Harth, vol. 1 (Florence: Olschki).

Powell, J. G. F. (ed.). 2006. *M. Tulli Ciceronis De re publica, De legibus, Cato Maior de senectute, Laelius de amicitia* (Oxford: Oxford University Press).

Powell, J. G. F. 2010. 'Hyperbaton and Register in Cicero', in Dickey and Chahoud (2010), pp. 163–185.

Rackham, H. (ed. and tr.). 1942. *On the Orator: Book 3. On Fate. Stoic Paradoxes. Divisions of Oratory*, Loeb Classical Library 349 (Cambridge, MA: Harvard University Press).

Radermacher, L. 1951. *Artium scriptores: Reste der voraristotelischen Rhetorik* (Vienna: Rohrer).

Rao, I. G. 2006. 'Per la biblioteca di Francesco da Castiglione', in *Il capitolo di San Lorenzo nel Quattrocento: Convegno di studi, Firenze, 28–29 marzo 2003*, ed. by P. Viti, Biblioteca dell'*Archivum romanicum*: Serie 1, Storia, letteratura, paleografia 325 (Florence: Olschki), pp. 131–144.

Reeve, M. D. 2011. *Manuscripts and Methods: Essays on Editing and Transmission*, Storia e letteratura: Raccolta di studi e testi 270 (Rome: Storia e letteratura).

Reeve, M. D. 2016. 'The Medieval Tradition of Cicero's *Verrines*', *ExClass*, 20: 19–90.

Regoliosi, M. 1969. 'Nuove ricerche intorno a Giovanni Tortelli', *IMU*, 12: 129–196.

Reid, J. S. 1905. 'Notes on Cicero *Ad Atticum* II', *Hermathena*, 13: 354–392.

Reynolds, L. D. (ed.). 1983. *Texts and Transmission: A Survey of the Latin Classics* (Oxford: Clarendon Press).

Reynolds, S. 2015. *A Catalogue of the Manuscripts in the Library at Holkham Hall*, vol. 1 (Turnhout: Brepols).

Rhodes, D. E. 1975. 'Note 389. More Light on the Niccolini Library', *Book Collector*, 24: 603–606.

Rizzo, S. 1983. *Catalogo dei codici della* Pro Cluentio *ciceroniana* (Genoa: Istituto di filologia classica e medievale).

Rizzo, S. 1995. 'Per una tipologia delle tradizioni manoscritte di classici latini in età umanistica', in *Formative Stages of Classical Traditions: Latin Texts from Antiquity to the Renaissance*, ed. by O. Pecere and M. D. Reeve, Biblioteca del Centro per il collegamento degli studi medievali e umanistici in Umbria 15 (Spoleto: Centro italiano di studi sull'alto Medievo), pp. 371–407.

Roberts, W. R. 1904. 'The New Rhetorical Fragment (Oxyrhynchus Papyri, Part III., pp. 27–30) in Relation to the Sicilian Rhetoric of Corax and Tisias', *CR*, 18: 18–21.

Robinson, E. A. 1951. 'The Date of Cicero's *Brutus*', *HSPh*, 60: 137–146.

Rodger, A. 2006. 'What Did *damnum iniuria* Actually Mean?', in *Mapping the Law: Essays in Memory of Peter Birks*, ed. by A. Burrows and A. Rodger (Oxford: Oxford University Press), pp. 421–438.

348 BIBLIOGRAPHY

Ronconi, A. 1958. 'Quaeque notando (III serie)', *PP*, 13: 143–148.

Roselaar, S. T. 2010. *Public Land in the Roman Republic: A Social and Economic History of ager publicus in Italy, 396–89 BC* (Oxford: Oxford University Press).

Rostagno, H. 1898. 'Indicis codicum graecorum Bybliothecae Laurentianae supplementum', *SIFC*, 6: 129–166.

Rouse, R. H. 1967. 'The Early Library of the Sorbonne', *Scriptorium*, 21: 42–71, 227–251.

Rouse, R. H. 1974. 'Manuscripts Belonging to Richard de Fournival', *RHT*, 3: 253–269.

Rouse, R. H. 1979. 'Florilegia and Latin Classical Authors in Twelfth- and Thirteenth-Century Orléans', *Viator*, 10: 131–160.

Rubio, L. 1960. 'Un importante códice de Cicerón en la Biblioteca Universitaria de Barcelona', *Emerita*, 28: 225–239.

Rubio Fernández, L. 1984. *Catálogo de los manuscritos clásicos latinos existentes en España* (Madrid: Editorial de la Universidad Complutense).

Russell, D. A. (ed. and tr.). 2002. *Quintilian: The Orator's Education, Books 9–10*, Loeb Classical Library 127 (Cambridge, MA: Harvard University Press).

Ruysschaert, J. 1958. 'Recherche des deux bibliothèques romaines Maffei des XVᵉ et XVIᵉ siècles', *La Bibliofilía*, 60: 306–355.

Sabbadini, R. 1888. 'I codici delle opere rettoriche di Cicerone', *RFIC*, 16: 97–120.

Sabbadini, R. 1890. 'Cronologia documentata della vita di Giovanni Lamola', *Il Propugnatore*, n.s., 3: 417–436.

Sabbadini, R. (ed.). 1915–1919. *Epistolario di Guarino Veronese*, 3 vols (Venice: A spese della Società).

Sabbadini, R. (ed.). 1931. *Carteggio di Giovanni Aurispa* (Rome: Tipografia del Senato).

Sabbadini, R. 1971. *Storia e critica di testi latini*, 2nd edn (Padua: Antenore).

Sacchi, O. 2006. *Regime della terra e imposizione fondiaria nell'età dei Gracchi: Testo e commento storico-giuridico della legge agraria del 111 a.C.* (Naples: Jovene).

Samaran, C., and R. Marichal. 1962. *Catalogue des manuscrits en écriture latine portant des indications de date, de lieu ou de copiste*, vol. 2 (Paris: Centre national de la recherche scientifique).

Sandys, J. E. (ed.). 1885. *M. Tulli Ciceronis Ad M. Brutum Orator* (Cambridge: Cambridge University Press).

Santangelo, F. 2012. 'Authoritative Forgeries: Late Republican History Re-told in Pseudo-Sallust', *Histos*, 6: 27–51.

Santini, P. 1979. 'Due note critico-testuali a Cicerone retore', *A&R*, n.s., 24: 50–56.

Sanzotta, V. 2015. *I manoscritti classici latini della Biblioteca Casanatense di Roma*, Indici e Cataloghi n.s. 22 (Rome: Istituto poligrafico e Zecca dello Stato).

Sarpe, G. 1819. *Quaestiones philologicae* (Rostock: Adler).

Scarcia Piacentini, P. 1983. 'La tradizione laudense di Cicerone ed un inesplorato manoscritto della Biblioteca Vaticana (Vat. Lat. 3237)', *RHT*, 11: 123–146.

Scheid, J. (ed. and tr.). 2007. *Res gestae divi Augusti* (Paris: Les Belles Lettres).

Schiefsky, M. J. 2005. *Hippocrates, On Ancient Medicine: Translated with an Introduction and Commentary*, Studies in Ancient Medicine 28 (Leiden: Brill).

Schlebusch, K. 2016. 'Giorgio Antonio Vespucci: 1434–1514', in Black et al. (2016), pp. 215–229.

BIBLIOGRAPHY 349

Schmidt, P. L. 1974. *Die Überlieferung von Ciceros Schrift De legibus in Mittelalter und Renaissance* (Munich: Fink).

Schnorr von Carolsfeld, F., and L. Schmidt. 1882. *Katalog der Handschriften der königlichen öffentlichen Bibliothek zu Dresden*, vol. 1 (Leipzig: Teubner).

Schöpsdau, K. 1994. 'Das Nachleben der *Technon Synagoge* bei Cicero, Quintilian und in den griechischen Prolegomena zur Rhetorik', in *Peripatetic Rhetoric after Aristotle*, ed. by W. W. Fortenbaugh and D. C. Mirhady, Rutgers University Studies in Classical Humanities 5 (New Brunswick, NJ: Transaction Publishers), pp. 192–216.

Schröder, B.-J. 1999. *Titel und Text: Zur Entwicklung lateinischer Gedichtüberschriften. Mit Untersuchungen zu lateinischen Buchtiteln, Inhaltsverzeichnissen und anderen Gliederungsmitteln* (Berlin: De Gruyter).

Schulze, W. 1904. *Zur Geschichte lateinischer Eigennamen* (Berlin: Weidmann).

Seager, R. 1967. 'Cicero, *Brutus* 136', *CR*, n.s., 17: 12–13.

Shackleton Bailey, D. R. 1960. 'The Roman Nobility in the Second Civil War', *CQ*, 10: 253–267.

Shackleton Bailey, D. R. 1976. *Two Studies in Roman Nomenclature*, American Classical Studies 3 (New York: Interbook).

Shackleton Bailey, D. R. (ed. and tr.). 2000. *Valerius Maximus: Memorable Doings and Sayings, Books 6–9*, Loeb Classical Library 493 (Cambridge, MA: Harvard University Press).

Shailor, B. A. 1992. *Catalogue of Medieval and Renaissance Manuscripts in the Beinecke Rare Book and Manuscript Library, Yale University*, vol. 3, Medieval and Renaissance Texts and Studies 100 (Binghamton: Center for Medieval and Early Renaissance Studies, State University of New York).

Simchen, G. 1953. 'Heilung zweier Stellen in Ciceros *Brutus*', *WS*, 66: 167–168.

Simon, J. 1887. *Kritische Bemerkungen zu Ciceros Brutus: Programm der K. bayer. Studienanstalt Kaiserslautern für das Schuljahr 1886/87* (Kaiserslautern: Königlich bayerische Studienanstalt).

Sisani, S. 2015. *L'ager publicus in età graccana (133–11 a.C.): Una rilettura testuale, storica e giuridica della lex agraria epigrafica* (Rome: Quasar).

Skutsch, O. 1968. *Studia Enniana* (London: Athlone Press).

Solodow, J. B. 1978. *The Latin Particle* quidem, American Classical Studies 4 (Boulder, CO: Johnson).

Sotheby, Wilkinson, & Hodge. 1886. *Catalogue of the Extensive and Valuable Library Collected at the End of the Last and Beginning of the Present Century by Michael Wodhull, Esq., Translator of Euripides, etc., the Property of J. E. Severne, Esq. M. P., of Thenford House, Banbury, Northamptonshire* (London: Dryden).

Spagnolo, A. 1996. *I manoscritti della Biblioteca Capitolare di Verona*, ed. by S. Marchi (Verona: Mazziana).

Stangl, T. 1913. 'Cicerofund Charles L. Durhams', *Berliner Philologische Wochenschrift*, 33: 829–832, 860–864.

Stockton, D. 1979. *The Gracchi* (Oxford: Clarendon Press).

Ströbel, E. 1897. 'Zu Ciceros Brutus', *Blätter für das bayerische Gymnasialschulwesen*, 33: 556–561.

Stroux, J. 1921. *Handschriftliche Studien zu Cicero De oratore: Die Rekonstruktion der Handschrift von Lodi* (Leipzig: Teubner).

350 BIBLIOGRAPHY

Stroux, J. 1930. Review of J. Rosenthal, *Beiträge zur Forschung*, vol. 2 (1929), *Gnomon*, 6: 283–286.

Sumner, G. V. 1971. 'The *lex annalis* under Caesar', *Phoenix*, 25: 246–271, 357–371.

Sumner, G. V. 1973. *The Orators in Cicero's Brutus: Prosopography and Chronology*, Phoenix Supplementary Volume 11 (Toronto: University of Toronto Press).

Sumner, G. V. 1978. Review of Shackleton Bailey (1976), *CPh*, 73: 159–164.

Sydow, R. 1932. 'Kritische Beiträge zu Ciceros rhetorischen Schriften', *RhM*, 81: 232–242.

Syme, R. 1958. 'Pseudo-Sallust', *MH*, 15: 46–55.

Syme, R. 1962. 'The Damaging Names in Pseudo-Sallust', *MH*, 19: 177–179.

Taylor, P. R. 1993. '*Codices integri* and the Transmission of the *Ad Herennium* in Late Antiquity', *RHT*, 23: 113–142.

Taylor-Briggs, R. 2006. 'Reading Between the Lines: The Textual History and Manuscript Transmission of Cicero's Rhetorical Works', in *The Rhetoric of Cicero in its Medieval and Early Renaissance Commentary Tradition*, ed. by V. Cox and J. O. Ward (Leiden: Brill), pp. 77–108.

Thomson, I. 1969. 'Studies in the Life, Scholarship, and Educational Achievement of Guarino da Verona (1374–1460)' (unpublished doctoral dissertation, University of St Andrews).

Tichenor, M. B. 2019. 'Cicero's Incomplete *Orator*: The Transmission and Reception of the *Mutilus* Text' (unpublished doctoral dissertation, University of Toronto).

Tilliette, J.-Y. 2003. 'Une biographie inédite de Cicéron, composée au début du XIVᵉ siècle', *CRAI*, 147: 1049–1077.

Timpanaro, S. 2005. *The Genesis of Lachmann's Method*, tr. by G. W. Most (Chicago: University of Chicago Press).

Tremolada, M. P. 1988. 'I manoscritti di Gasparino Barzizza conservati nelle biblioteche milanesi', *Libri & documenti*, 14: 1–36.

Tristano, C. 1988. *La biblioteca di un umanista calabrese: Aulo Giano Parrasio* (Rome: Vecchiarelli).

Trovato, P. 2017. *Everything You Always Wanted to Know about Lachmann's Method: A Non-Standard Handbook of Genealogical Textual Criticism in the Age of Post-Structuralism, Cladistics, and Copy-Text*, tr. by F. Poole, 2nd edn (Padua: Libreriauniversitaria.it edizioni).

Ullman, B. L. 1960. *The Origin and Development of Humanistic Script*, Storia e letteratura: Raccolta di studi e testi 79 (Rome: Storia e letteratura).

Ullman, B. L., and P. A. Stadter. 1972. *The Public Library of Renaissance Florence: Niccolò Niccoli, Cosimo de' Medici and the Library of San Marco*, Medioevo e Umanesimo 10 (Padua: Antenore).

Van den Bruwaene, M. 1967. Review of Douglas (1966), *Latomus*, 26: 820–822.

Vespasiano da Bisticci. 1976. *Le Vite*, ed. by A. Greco, vol. 2 (Florence: Istituto nazionale di studi sul Rinascimento).

Viskolcz, N. 2016. 'The Fate of Johannes Sambucus' Library', *Hungarian Studies*, 30: 155–166.

Walldén, S. 1943. 'Lat. *levis* und *lenis*: Eine wortgeschichtliche Untersuchung', *Philologus*, 95: 142–160.

Walz, C. (ed.). 1832–1836. *Rhetores Graeci*, 9 vols (Stuttgart: Cotta; London: Black, Young, and Young; Paris: Firmin Didot).

BIBLIOGRAPHY 351

Watson, A. G. 1979. *Catalogue of Dated and Datable Manuscripts, c. 700–1600, in the Department of Manuscripts, the British Library*, 2 vols (London: British Library).

Watt, W. S. 1983. 'Tulliana', *CPh*, 78: 226–231.

Watt, W. S. 1996. 'Tulliana', *Sileno*, 22: 373–383.

Watt, W. S. (ed.). 1998. *Vellei Paterculi historiarum ad M. Vinicium consulem libri duo*, 2nd edn (Stuttgart: Teubner).

Weidner, A. 1879. 'Zur kritik der rhetorischen und philosophischen schriften Cicero's', *Philologus*, 38: 63–90.

White, J. A. 1975. 'A Collation and an Historical and Codicological Study of Cicero's *Brutus* in the Cornell University Library MS. U' (unpublished doctoral dissertation, The State University of New York at Buffalo).

White, J. A. 1979. '*Fata habent libelli manuscripti*: Some Notes on a Justin Codex', *Latomus* 38: 223–230.

Willcock, J. S. M. 1982. 'The *lex Thoria* and Cicero, *Brutus* 136', *CQ*, 32: 474–475.

Willi, A. 2010. 'Campaigning for *utilitas*: Style, Grammar and Philosophy in C. Iulius Caesar', in Dickey and Chahoud (2010), pp. 229–242.

Winterbottom, M. 1967. Review of Douglas (1966), *CR*, n.s., 17: 301–303.

Wiseman, T. P. 1967. 'Lucius Memmius and His Family', *CQ*, 17: 164–167.

Wiseman, T. P. 1971. *New Men in the Roman Senate, 139 B.C. – A.D. 14* (London: Oxford University Press).

Woodman, A. J. (ed.). 1983. *Velleius Paterculus: The Caesarian and Augustan Narrative (2.41–93)*, Cambridge Classical Texts and Commentaries 25 (Cambridge: Cambridge University Press).

Wright, C. E. 1972. *Fontes Harleiani: A Study of the Sources of the Harleian Collection of Manuscripts Preserved in the Department of Manuscripts in the British Museum* (London: British Museum).

Wright, C. E., and R. C. Wright. 1966. *The Diary of Humfrey Wanley: 1715–1726*, vol. 2 (London: Bibliographical Society).

Yon, A. (ed. and tr.). 1964. *Cicéron: L'orateur; Du meilleur genre d'orateurs* (Paris: Les Belles Lettres).

Young, J., and P. H. Aitken. 1908. *A Catalogue of the Manuscripts in the Library of the Hunterian Museum in the University of Glasgow* (Glasgow: MacLehose).

Zaggia, M. 1995. 'Copisti e committenti di codici a Milano nella prima metà del Quattrocento', *Libri & documenti*, 21: 1–45.

Zaggia, M. 2007. 'Codici milanesi del Quattrocento all'Ambrosiana: per il periodo dal 1450 al 1476', in *Nuove ricerche su codici in scrittura latina dell'Ambrosiana: Atti del Convegno, Milano, 6–7 ottobre 2005*, ed. by M. Ferrari and M. Navoni (Milan: Vita e Pensiero), pp. 331–384.

Zorzanello, P. 1980. *Catalogo dei codici latini della Biblioteca nazionale marciana di Venezia non compresi nel catalogo di G. Valentinelli*, vol. 1 (Trezzano sul Naviglio: Etimar).

Index

Tables and figures are indicated by an italic *t* and *f* following the page number.

Academic scepticism, *see under* Cicero,
  Marcus Tullius
actio, as rhetorical term 208–9, 217–19
adornatus, use of comparative
  adjective 174–5
Alberti, Leon Battista 70, 174 n.82, 259
alius, word order in repeated *ali– ali–* structures
  175–6, 220
an, repetition of 177
ango 229–30
Antonio di Mario (scribe) 69, 247–8
Ardizzi, Francesco degli (scribe) 34, 59, 254
  vetus corrections in O 23, 33–4, 45–7, 254
Aretino, Giovanni (i.e. ser Giovanni di Cenni
  d'Arezzo, scribe) 69, 237, 238, 249
asyndeton bimembre 185–6, 202
Atticus, Titus Pomponius 163–4, 222
  Liber annalis 157–8, 160–1, 162–3
ausim 160

barbaria 213
Barzizza, Gasparino:
  annotations on *Brut.* 243, 275–6
  chapter divisions 31, 32*t*, 38, 63
  manuscript of *Brut.* 43, 55–6, 62–4, 246
  manuscript of *De or.* and *Orat.* 62 n.4, 246
  ownership of L 19, 24, 52, 54–7, 58–9, 61
Benvenuti, Lorenzo di Marco 64, 239
Biblionomia, see Fournival, Richard de
Billienus, Gaius (jurist) 194–5
Biondo, Flavio (scribe):
  Italia Illustrata 16, 51–2, 53–4, 56,
    67, 252
  marginal annotations in B 17, 22,
    23, 35, 253
  transcription of B 34–6, 53–4, 64,
    65–6, 252–3
  vetus corrections in B 36
Bossi, Francesco 34, 37, 62 n.53, 254
Bruni, Leonardo 69, 71, 218 n.252,
  239, 323–4

Brutus:
  ancient readers 48
  date of composition 48
  prevalence of textual corruption 8–9
Brutus, Marcus Junius (pr. 44):
  date of birth 226

Caelius, Marcus (pr. 48) 218–19
Caesar, Gaius Julius:
  De analogia 211
Calcagnini, Francesco (scribe) 66, 244
caleo, as rhetorical term 208–9
Calvus, Gaius Licinius 219–20
Cicero, Marcus Tullius:
  Brut., see *Brutus*
  De or. 2.236: 226
  Mur. 54–57, 69: 216–17
  Orat. 120: 158, 161 n.22, 162
  Tull. 9, 10–12, 38–43: 185–6
  Academic scepticism 163–4
  colloquialisms 164–5, 190
  prose rhythm 163, 164, 173, 220, 222, 229
Ciriagio, Gherardo del (scribe) 69, 238, 256
contamination:
  instances in the transmission of
    Brut. 44–45, 265*f*, 269*f*, 291*f*, 300*f*, 313*f*
  theoretical discussion 7
Corax and Tisias 167–70
Corvini, Giovanni (Renaissance
  humanist) 58, 67, 316 n.39
Cotta, Lucius Aurelius (pr. *c.*95) 214–15
Cremona fragment:
  corrections 18, 22–3, 25–8, 49, 233
  discovery 5, 15, 61–2
  identification with L 5–6, 15, 17–19, 21–4
  images 20*f*, 21*f*, 22*f*, 24*f*
  orthography 20–1, 22–3, 25–8, 49
  provenance 15, 18, 23 n.29, 24, 25, 49,
    61–2, 233
  word division 19–20
Crivellus, Antonius (scribe) 242, 246

354 INDEX

Curio, Gaius Scribonius (cos. 76) 205–6
Curlo, Giacomo (scribe) 67, 234, 310

defensiuncula, as rhetorical term 190–1
devoro 219–20
disquisitio, as rhetorical term 176–7

enumeratio, as rhetorical term 225
esse, omission of finite forms in periphrastic
tenses 205, 210

facetus, as rhetorical term 181, 227
Fournival, Richard de 49–51

Gracchus, Gaius Sempronius (tr. pl. 123)
179–81
Guarino Veronese 52, 58 n.36, 60, 65–6,
71–2, 239, 247, 252

Hirtilius, Gaius 215

iaceo, 'to have a poor reputation' 207
indico, absolute use 173
instruo, as rhetorical term 204

Lamola, Giovanni (scribe) 16, 17–18, 57
n.31, 59–61, 71–2, 239
Landriani, Gerardo 16, 19, 51–3, 54–6, 62,
63 n.60, 254
Laudensis, Codex:
contents 15, 53–4
date of production 16, 18, 19, 48
disappearance 61
discovery 1, 16, 51–4
legibility 16, 18–19
transcriptions 29–30, 31, 34–6, 54–61
see also Cremona fragment
lenis, see *levis*
Leonardo di Giovanni Tolosani da Colle
(scribe) 69, 234, 235, 239, 323–4
levis, confusion with *lenis* 201, 213–14
lex Aquilia 184–6
lex Thoria 186–8
lex Varia 223
Lysias (oratorical style) 221–2

Maffei, Mario (of Volterra) 241, 260
Manetti, Giannozzo (Renaissance
humanist) 70, 254, 255

Master of the Trivulziana Pharsalia
(illuminator) 69, 234, 237
Mazzolato, Ugo (scribe) 65–6, 247, 266 n.6
Medici, Cosimo de' 67, 234, 237, 310
memoria 157–8, 160–1, 194
Minutianus, Alexander (early editor of *Brut.*)
263, 290
Molo of Rhodes 224–5

Nepos, Cornelius:
Att. 18.2: 160–1
Niccoli, Niccolò 20–1, 58, 67–8, 71, 235, 237,
316 n.39

Philippus, Lucius Marcius (cos. 91) 223–4
Philus, Lucius Furius (cos. 136) 212–13
Poggio Bracciolini 68, 232, 235, 324
conjectures 2, 10, 157, 174, 193, 202, 213
politus, as rhetorical term 166, 221–2, 227
Pompeius Rufus, Quintus (cos. 88) 201–2, 223
Pomponius, Gnaeus (tr. pl. 90) 206–7
Postumius, Titus 215–17
P.Oxy.III 410: 169–70
prope, with superlative 196
'Puccini' scribe 68–9, 218 n.252, 236,
317 n.40

Quintilian 214
Inst. 1.5.12: 193–4
Inst. 2.8.11: 201
Inst. 10.1.78: 222
Inst. 11.1.51: 218
Inst. 11.3.129: 205
Inst. 12.10.31: 193

Raimondi, Cosimo (scribe) 24, 52, 55–7,
61, 62–4
ratio 220–1
retinnio 193
Rhetorica ad Alexandrum 1444a18–25: 168

Squarciafico, Girolamo (early editor of
Brut.) 262, 288
Sallust, Pseudo–:
Ad Caes. sen. 2.9.4: 216–17
Scaurus, Marcus Aemilius (cos. 115) 181–2
scripts, orators' use of 167–70
sitis 159
Socratic irony 163–4

INDEX   355

Sopater:
 Commentary on Hermogenes, Walz
  5.6.20–24: 169
studiosus, with genitive 161–2
Swabenheym, Johannes (scribe) 68, 231–2

Tacitus, Publius Cornelius:
 Dial. 21.4: 218

tectus, 'guarded' 181
Tisias, *see* Corax and Tisias

unctus, as rhetorical term 173–4

Varius, Quintus (tr. pl. 90) 206–7
Vespasiano da Bisticci 52–3, 58, 69, 71, 237,
 247, 256